THE DIVINE COMEDY

OF

DANTE ALIGHIERI

DANTE ALIGHIERI

The Divine Comedy

TEXT WITH TRANSLATION
in the metre of the original by
GEOFFREY L. BICKERSTETH
COMMENDATORE DELL' ORDINE AL MERITO
DELLA REPUBBLICA ITALIANA

BASIL BLACKWELL

First published for the Shakespeare Head Press in 1965
New edition 1972 Revised
Paperback edition (with corrections) 1981
Reprinted 1985, 1986

Basil Blackwell Ltd
108 Cowley Road, Oxford OX4 1JF, UK

Basil Blackwell Inc.
432 Park Avenue South, Suite 1503,
New York, NY 10016, USA

ISBN 0 631 12926 X

Printed in Great Britain by
Whitstable Litho, Whitstable, Kent

FOREWORD

In the field of Anglo-Italian studies Geoffrey L. Bickersteth was unique. Born in 1884, he went as a scholar to Charterhouse where, inspired by a gifted master, Thomas Ethelbert Page, he acquired a love of the Classics and of modern literature. He went on to read Greats at Christ Church, Oxford, where he studied under J. A. Stewart, whose work on Plato and the use of imagery in poetry remained a life-long influence. Such rigorous training in the Classics and wide reading in European literature, especially English, combined with a household familiarity with theology (his father, the Rev. Samuel Bickersteth, Canon of Canterbury, was a Doctor of Divinity) provided a preparation for the study of Dante which no contemporary specialist in Italian in the British academic world could equal.

In 1909, after travelling in Germany and Italy, Bickersteth was appointed Assistant Master at Marlborough College, where he taught Latin, Greek, German, French and English. One of his pupils was Charles Sorley, the War poet, killed in 1915, whose sister he later married. While at Marlborough he tried his hand at verse translation from French, German, Italian, Latin and Greek. He became interested in the poetry of Giosuè Carducci and in 1913, while still under thirty, published his remarkable edition and verse translation of close on seventy poems of this major Italian poet, then virtually unknown in England.[1]

This impressive early work presents features which anticipate his translation of Dante. First and foremost is his expert understanding of versification. The third of his Introductory Essays, on Carducci's experiment in applying the rules of Latin prosody to Italian, is a model of clarity

[1] *Carducci. A Selection of his Poems, with Verse Translations, and Three Introductory Essays* (Longmans, Green and Co., 1913).

and remains the best discourse in English or Italian on this difficult and complex subject.

Between 1913 and 1914 Bickersteth studied at the Universities of Munich and Heidelberg. His thesis on the influence of Italian chivalric romances on the poetry of Byron was interrupted by the outbreak of war. Having served in Naval Intelligence with the honorary rank of Captain, he was appointed in 1919 to a post as Senior Lecturer in English at Glasgow University.

His pioneering work on Carducci was followed in 1923 by his even more remarkable edition and verse translation of the *Canti* of Giacomo Leopardi.[1] The Introduction, consisting of three long sections: 'The Poet's Life', 'The Poet's Art' and 'The Poet's Thought', is a major contribution to Leopardi criticism. The Notes, more abundant and informative than in any other English edition of the *Canti*, and rich in comparisons with Greek, Latin, Italian and English poetry, are in themselves a liberal education. Both the Carducci and the Leopardi volumes have long been out of print in England.[2] This is a loss to readers in general and a deprivation in particular to students of Italian literature. There has been no adequate replacement in respect of either poet.

Such was the prelude and for some time the accompaniment to Geoffrey L. Bickersteth's fifty years of work on Dante. From the outset his preference was to provide a dual text. He offered his translation not as an equivalent of the original but as an interpretation. By interpretation he meant a communication of form as well as of content. Agreeing with Shelley that it was 'an essential justice to an author to render him in the same form', he held that verse translation could be practised 'as one of the *useful* arts by those who lay no claim to be themselves poets. It constitutes indeed a very valuable addition to the equipment of the

---

[1] *The Poems of Leopardi. Edited with Introduction and Notes and a Verse Translation in the Metres of the Original* (Cambridge University Press, 1923).

[2] A reprint of the Leopardi was published in the U.S.A. by Russell and Russell in 1973.

critic, besides being a fascinating occupation in itself.'[1]
His skill in this useful and exacting art is brilliantly
illustrated in his rendering of Carducci's rigorous poems.
His translations of Leopardi's *Canti*, faithful in many more
senses than the merely literal, are poetry in their own right.

In 1932 Bickersteth brought out his translation of
Dante's *Paradiso*.[2] Like the Carducci and the Leopardi
volumes, this was a dual text. In 1955, by then Professor
of English at the University of Aberdeen, he published his
translation of the entire *Commedia*.[3] To his regret, for
reasons of expense, this did not contain the original
Italian. The defect, as he regarded it, was remedied in
1965, the seventh centenary of the birth of Dante, when
Blackwells of Oxford issued an elegant single volume
printed on India paper containing both the original (in
Porena's edition) and Bickersteth's revised translation. It
is this which is now published in paperback.

In the Introductions to his Dante volumes, Bickersteth
develops his views on the translation of poetry, especially
of the *Commedia*.[4] He is convinced (and his exceptional
knowledge of prosody lends authority to his views) that
Dante's poem must be rendered in the form in which it was
written, namely *terza rima*. Nothing else will do: not prose,
not blank verse, not any of the English traditional narrative
stanzas. Rhyme is essential and it must be used as Dante
used it. What a poet says and the metrical form in which he
says it cannot be divided without doing violence to content
as well as to structure:

> The *Faerie Queene* could not be rebuilt in blank verse or
> in a stanza of other rhyme-scheme without complete
> destruction of its character. No more can the *Divine
> Comedy*.[5]

[1] *Carducci*, ed. cit., p. viii.
[2] *The Paradiso of Dante Alighieri. With a Translation into English
Triple Rhyme* (Cambridge University Press, 1932).
[3] *The Divine Comedy of Dante Alighieri. Translated from the
Italian into English Triple Rhyme* (Aberdeen: The University Press,
1955).
[4] See also his Herford Memorial Lecture to the Manchester
Dante Society, 'On Translating Dante', 1934.
[5] *Paradiso*, ed. cit., p. xxiv.

This view is a striking challenge to the facile and wide-spread assumption that *terza rima* makes such irreconcilable demands that the translator does well to avoid it. Bickersteth freely owns that there are formidable difficulties in translating Dante but he turns the admission to strengthen the case for using *terza rima:*

> . . . the translator, in seeking to reproduce [the features of Dante's style] in English, will be immensely aided by using Dante's own metre.[1]

He confirmed this opinion eleven years later in his Introduction to the dual edition, reinforcing it as follows:

> . . . Only thus [*i.e.* by using *terza rima*] will [the translator] be able to deal at all adequately with certain problems of expression with which the poet's love of words and word-play frequently confronts him. Only thus, too – which is far more important – can he hope to inform and thereby unify his own poem (in so far as his translation succeeds in meriting that title) with the same concept of poetry as that which inspired Dante to compose his masterpiece.[2]

Even more striking are Bickersteth's views on Dante's own use of *terza rima*. It is distinct, he considers, from *terza rima* as used by any Italian poets subsequent to Dante. It is also quite different from English triple rhyme as written, for instance, by Shelley, who imposed on it the rhythms of blank verse. The translator of Dante must learn to write *terza rima* in English in such a way that it follows the rules which Dante himself evolved while writing the *Commedia*, for which he invented the metre, which shaped the poem and was in turn shaped by it as he progressed. Starting from this entirely original perception, Bickersteth set himself to write *terza rima* 'not in the English but after the Italian manner', to create, in a sense, a new poetic mode.

According to Bickersteth, what distinguishes Dante's *terza rima* is his characteristic use of rhyme. First, it

[1] *ibid.* p. xxx.
[2] See p. xlvii of the present edition.

serves to link the stanzas with subtle simplicity, achieving
a compromise between the continuous form of blank verse
and the discontinuous form of stanzaic measures. This is
essential to the structure. Secondly, Dante uses rhyme to
point the sense and to guide the meaning. In the Italian
hendecasyllabic line, since the tenth syllable is always
stressed, the end is specially emphatic, and rhyme rein-
forces the emphasis. Dante so constructs his *terzine* that
at least one of the three rhymes is a key-word of the
argument, with the result that the drift of a whole passage
can be followed by glancing at the rhymes. Finally, the
rhyme influences the cadences, the third in a sequence
being often especially beautiful, and aids the mind to
appreciate the music no less than the logic of the thought.

Original also is Bickersteth's opinion that the category
to which the *Commedia* belongs is satire – not in the
narrow but in the wide sense of the term which admits
within its scope the modes of epic, drama and lyric. He
stresses to an unusual degree the role of poetry and poet-
seers throughout the work. Dante is lost in the dark wood
because he is in danger of losing his power of vision as a
poet. He is rescued by the poet-seer, Virgil, 'the first of a
series of rescuers who, as has too little been noticed by
commentators, are all poet-seers likewise, and not philoso-
phers or theologians (say an Aristotle or an Aquinas) as
might have been expected, had Dante-personaggio been
intended by Dante-poeta to be imagined as an intel-
lectualist.'[1]

Bickersteth is unusual, further, in the view he takes of
the allegory, attaching greater importance than most
commentators to the literal meaning. There is no need, he
maintains, to allegorise the poem except in those few
places where Dante makes it clear that he intends the
reader to do so. But the literal meaning for Bickersteth
was not restricted to the story; for him the literal and the
spiritual meaning were one. In other words, he took
literally the spiritual meaning of the last line of the poem:

L'Amor che move 'l sole e l'altre stelle.

[1] See p. liv of the present edition.

For him the *Commedia*, particularly the third *cantica*, was the supreme expression (apart from the Bible) of the Christian faith. Ideally speaking, the effect of reading it should be to induce a state of mind and soul in which 'the joy that pulses and blazes throughout the *Paradiso*'[1] can be experienced spiritually (not merely apprehended) and, despite all the contrary indications in the sinful world, God's love can be seen, felt and known. This is not a fashionable approach to Dante, nor does it find much currency in academic circles. It may, however, prove the most enduring.[2]

For Bickersteth the *Commedia* was not only a supreme expression of the Christian faith, a faith which he shared. It was also a supreme achievement of the poet's art. While admitting that no translation, however good, can ever be the equivalent of the original, he disagreed with Dante's famous saying that poetry cannot be translated without being destroyed.[3] On the contrary:

> ... poetry, far from being destroyed by translation, only escapes destruction because it *is* translatable and, in fact, always in course of being translated.[4]

His aim was to produce a 'faithful and genuinely English rendering'. By a faithful rendering he meant one which says in English neither more nor less than what Dante says in Italian and says it in the same way. By a genuinely English rendering he meant one which read like an original English poem. The late Dr. Gilbert F. Cunningham, whose knowledge of English translations of the *Commedia* was unsurpassed,[5] considered that Bickersteth went a long way towards achieving a 'faithful rendering' and also towards writing *terza rima* in the same fashion as Dante. About the achievement of a genuinely English rendering

---

[1] From a letter to the present writer.

[2] Among modern interpreters, two exceptions come to mind: Dr. Kenelm Foster, O.P. and the late Dorothy L. Sayers, both of whom take Dante's spiritual message seriously.

[3] *Il Convivio* I vii.

[4] *The Divine Comedy*, ed. cit., p. xi.

[5] See *The Divine Comedy in English*, Vol. I, 1965, Vol. II, 1966 (Oliver and Boyd).

he was not so sure. And indeed, between the desire to write *terza rima* not in the English but the Dantesque manner and the desire to produce a translation which reads like an original English poem there is a conflict which appears irreconcilable. Bickersteth himself seems to admit this when he says that the translator must endeavour to make his own style Dantesque and, without making it an italianized or 'translatese' English, must 'enrich his own language and literature by adding new words to its vocabulary, greater flexibility to its syntax, fresh variety to its rhythms, and to its music a melody perhaps never heard before.'[1]

No translator of Dante ever set himself so creative and exacting a task. The very criteria by which he desires his translation to be judged are in themselves a contribution to Dante criticism. It is not surprising if he occasionally fails to achieve his highest aims. The remarkable thing is how often he succeeds.

CAMBRIDGE   BARBARA REYNOLDS
July 1981

[1] See p. xxxi of the present edition.

PREFACE

THE text of the *Divine Comedy* adopted for this transla-
tion is, with a few variants, that edited by the eminent
Italian Dantist, the late Professor Manfredi Porena, in his
frequently reprinted three-volume commentary on the
poem, published by Nicola Zanichelli, Bologna (my copy
of which is dated 1956). For permission to reproduce it
here I am indebted to the courtesy of Porena's family and
his publisher, for which I am all the more grateful because
he intended his text and commentary for the same kind
of public as Dante himself had in mind, when he chose to
write the *Comedy* not in Latin (the language of scholars)
but in Italian; and as I too have had, while translating it.
He intended it, that is, not for professional philologists,
theologians and philosophers, but for ordinary well-
educated men and women with a taste for poetry and the
will to read a very long poem right through continuously
from start to finish.

In its readings Porena's text keeps, for the most part,
to that prepared for the Italian Dante Society (referred to,
in brief, as the 'Dantesca') by G. Vandelli, first published
by Bemporad and Son, Florence, in 1921 and again, only
very slightly revised, in the Scartazzini-Vandelli commen-
tary on the poem, published by U. Hoepli, Milan, in 1932.

Owing to Vandelli's admitted, and at that time un-
rivalled, first-hand knowledge of all the MSS., and to the
fact that his text was given a certain official status because
it had received the imprimatur of a committee of distin-
guished men of letters, it claimed, not, of course, to be
definitive (no possible text of the *Comedy* can be that),
but more 'authoritative' than Witte's or Edward Moore's.
(It was published, however, and so far as I know still
remains, without an apparatus criticus—surely an un-
pardonable defect.) But, as A. E. Housman (in the fifth
volume of his Manilius), with reference to textual criticism,

insisted: 'The merits essential to a correction are those without which it cannot be true and *closeness to the MSS. is not one of them*: the indispensable things are fitness to the context and propriety to the genius of the author. . . . Judging an emendation requires in some measure the same qualities as the emendation itself, and the requirement is formidable. To read attentively, think correctly, and repress self-will, are not ordinary accomplishments; yet an emendator needs much besides: just literary perception, congenial intimacy with the author, experience which must have been won by study, and mother wit which he must have brought from his mother's womb.'

If it be asked whether Vandelli possessed all these qualities, the answer of one great Italian Dantist after another—to mention, besides Porena, only Casini-Barbi, Torraca and Momigliano—who have published or reprinted their commentaries on the *Comedy* since 1921, has been, with reference to many of the readings, the punctuation and word-formations (spelling) of the Dantesca, to echo, each in his own way, Momigliano's regretful cry 'ho pensato che quell' edizione andrebbe riveduta da un uomo *di più sicuro buon gusto*'; and they have not reprinted Vandelli's text. Even Sapegno, who does, finds much to criticize in it (beginning with *Inf.* 3, 31). As for Vandelli's *trecento* spelling of the words, it is enough to say, with S. A. Barbi, that 'it is not at all certain that the forms given by the Dantesca are in every case those used by Dante'. Indeed, if Dante resembled Leopardi, he may well have spelt the same word differently, even on the same page, according as in each context his ear demanded.

To his task as editor and annotator of the *Comedy*, Porena brought a refreshingly independent judgment, critical acumen, great learning, 'just literary perception and mother wit'. With regard to the *grafia*, by distinguishing on a definite and easily intelligible system between archaic and modern forms, he provides a text which, to the eye, accords far better than Vandelli's with that to which, in general, Italians and foreigners have for generations been accustomed, and therefore makes it much simpler for

Preface

them to read. 'Le forme a cui non ho potuto rassegnarmi e a cui non mi rassegnerei se non vedendole in un sicuro autografo di Dante, sono *etterno*, *puose* e *rispuose*.' I would merely add that, for the benefit of those students who use the Dantesca (which is indispensable to the scholar), I have included in the notes, and translated, not all, but the most important of its readings which Porena questions or definitely rejects.

As for the translation, the purpose of which is explained in the Introduction, it has, off and on, occupied much of my leisure time, and been subject to constant revision, since I first began it, now over fifty years ago; a period during which I have had the advantage of knowing personally, and (either by word of mouth or by correspondence) discussing Dante with such distinguished English Dantists as J. A. Stewart, Edward Moore, W. P. Ker, Bishop W. Boyd-Carpenter, Edmund Gardner, and, more recently, Mr. Colin Hardie; and, among translators of the poet, J. D. Sinclair, Laurence Binyon, Dorothy Sayers, Dr. Barbara Reynolds and Mr. H. S. Vere-Hodge. Nor can I omit to mention my lifelong friend, the late Cesare Foligno, to whom Italian studies in this country have owed so much and who was ever ready to help me with mine.

My version of the *Paradiso* (now out of print) facing Vandelli's text, was published by the Cambridge University Press in 1932; and that (still in print) of the whole poem but without the Italian text, by the Aberdeen University Press in 1954. For the appearance of the present book I have to thank Sir Basil Blackwell, who, besides consenting to publish translation and original *in a single volume*, has taken the greatest personal interest in its production, and has done his utmost—for which I cannot be too grateful—to make it as worthy a tribute as possible from this country to the *altissimo poeta* on the seven hundredth anniversary of his birth.

As on an earlier occasion, I am under a great obligation to my friend Dr. G. F. Cunningham, who possesses an exhaustive knowledge of *all* the English translations of the *Comedy*, and is himself an accomplished verse-translator

of poems in Italian as well as in many other foreign
languages, for having found time to read the proofs of
this translation and of the Italian text, and for helping me
with many valuable criticisms and suggestions.

It is to my daughter Ursula, however, that I am more
indebted than to anyone else, not only for typing and
constantly retyping the manuscript and for careful reading
of the proofs, but also for aiding me time and time again
with her taste in deciding between alternative versions of
this or that passage of the original. Arrived as I now have

> in quella parte
> di mia etade ove ciascun dovrebbe
> calar le vele e raccoglier le sarte,

I should never have ventured on this latest of my many
long voyages over the great ocean of the *Divine Comedy*
without knowing that I could count on her never-failing
encouragement, sympathy and help.   G.L.B.

PREFACE TO THE SECOND EDITION

NEITHER G. Petrocchi's four-volume critical, nor G.
Giacalone's three-volume variorum, edition of the *Comedy*
was published till after my first edition; in revising which
I have been able to make use of both. The latter has the
further interest of applying throughout E. Auerbach's
'figural' interpretation of the poem, now much in favour
with Italian Dantists.

I have slightly rewritten and lengthened the introduction,
added a few more notes, and altered many words, single
lines, and terzine of the translation to bring it into closer
relation with both the content and form of the original.

Once again I should like to thank my daughter and my
publisher for their continued help, and to express my
gratitude to the staff of the University Press, Oxford, for
the skill with which they have accomplished their part in
the production of this book.   G.L.B.

PREFACE TO THE THIRD EDITION

M<small>Y FATHER</small>, who died in his 90th year in 1974, continued to revise his translation after the publication of the second edition in 1972. The English text of this third edition includes his revisions. I am most grateful to Dr. Barbara Reynolds for writing the foreword, and to Sir Basil Blackwell and all his staff for their interest and care in producing this volume.

July 1981   U<small>RSULA</small> B<small>ICKERSTETH</small>

CONTENTS

*

'*Visionary power
attends the motions of the viewless winds
embodied in the mystery of words:
there, darkness makes abode, and all the host
of shadowy things work endless changes,—there,
as in a mansion like their proper home,
even forms and substances are circumfused
by that transparent veil with light divine,
and, through the turnings intricate of verse,
present themselves as objects recognized,
in flashes, and with glory not their own.*'

*

'*A spirit and a vision are not, as the modern philosophy
supposes, a cloudy vapour or nothing; they are organized
and minutely articulated beyond all that the mortal and
perishing nature can produce. He who does not imagine in
stronger and better lineaments, and in stronger and better
light, than his perishing and mortal eye can see, does not
imagine at all.*'

*

INTRODUCTION

Non vide me' di me chi vide il vero

Dante Gabriel Rossetti, the preraphaelite translator of Dante's lyrical poems in the metres of the original, a poet moreover in his own right, with the further advantage of being bi-lingual, declared 'the lifeblood of a rhythmical translation' to be this commandment—that 'a good poem should not be turned into a bad one.'[1] This commandment, however, is of no practical value to would-be translators of *The Divine Comedy*, or of any other 'good' poem, unless he had gone on to state (which he failed to do) what, in his own opinion, are the qualities that distinguish good poetry from bad (or, in Crocean terms, 'poetry' from 'non-poetry').

I say 'in his own opinion' because it has so far defeated the wit of man to formulate a definition of poetry which has met with universal acceptance. There exists therefore no absolute standard by which to test the relative degree to which any given poem, or translation of it, achieves or fails to achieve perfection. A poem, considered in one age (for whatever reason) to be good, will in another age be considered (for whatever reason) to be bad: a fact which no one knew better than Dante himself, who goes out of his way to draw attention to it.[2] Even within the same age the same poem will be praised by one school of critics and vilified by another, each of the two being equally cocksure that it alone is possessed of, or correctly uses, the right principles for arriving at a valid judgment. Moreover, the same critic may hold different, often diametrically opposed, opinions about the goodness or badness of the same poem,

[1] D. G. Rossetti: Preface to the first edition of his *Early Italian Poets* (1861).
[2] Cp. *Purg.* 26, 110–26 (noting especially line 113 with its qualifying clause 'quanto durerà l'uso moderno'). Cp. also *Purg.* 24, 49–62, referring to the 'sweet *new* style': and *Purg.* 11, 96–9.

even of a so-called 'classic' at different periods of his own life. *The Divine Comedy* itself, since it was published six and a half centuries ago has passed through 'gravi tempi'[1] of misprision, 'fin che l'ha vinto il ver con più persone'[2]; and *Paradise Lost* is only now emerging from one in this country, it being the hallmark of a 'classic' that it always does so emerge.

For this reason, therefore, namely the great variety of opinion concerning the name, nature and proper function of poetry, and in the hope—probably vain—of not having applied to the verse-translation, here printed facing its original, criteria quite foreign to its purpose, I should like to emphasize that my principal aim in composing it was to draw the reader's attention to *The Divine Comedy* in its *specific quality of poetry*, but to do this in the sense, and only in the sense, which that abstract term bore for Dante himself, and which it is clear that he intended his poem to illustrate in the concrete, simply as it stands—that is, without need of any extraneous explanation—not only by its structure (in verse, not prose, whether colloquial or rhythmical) and by its effect (the state of mind it induces) but also by the leading role he assigned to poets (himself *qua* poet among them as protagonist) in the action or plot of the story which it tells.

In other words, though I have tried to obey Rossetti's injunction not to turn a good poem into a bad one, I have deliberately *not* made it my aim—as, quite legitimately of course, other translators obeying (in their own way) that injunction have made it theirs—to annex the *Comedy* to English literature by finding some native English form and manner corresponding to those of the medieval Italian original, because they consider the latter too outlandish or difficult or indeed impossible to be reproduced in the English medium. Thus to take a typical example of this type of translation (which Goethe called 'parodistic') Cary, for his blank verse rendering of the *Comedy* (which has in

---

[1] Cp. *Par.* 32, 127, where the phrase is used in reference to the persecution of the Church foretold by the author of the Apocalypse.
[2] Cp. *Purg.* 26, 126.

fact become a part of English poetic literature) chose eighteenth-century Miltonic, with a judicious admixture of Shakespearean vocabulary, as that which he considered the best substitute for Dante's style. It is this substitute which, in translations of this kind, slips in between the original and the reader, who is presented not with Dante, but with a 'parody' of him—Dante converted into a Milton, a Spenser or a Marvell[1] or into the translator himself; indeed, not so much a parody as a travesty, if the latter's conception of poetry be that which became prevalent in this country during the period between the two world wars, and resulted in poems (or what claim to be poems) composed in a style about as far removed from Dante's as it is possible to imagine.

To fulfil the aim, as just stated, of my own translation, what, to state that aim positively, I have tried to do—so far as the difference between the two languages permits—is to give a faithful and genuinely English rendering of the Italian original in the metre in which this is written. That there be no misunderstanding of my purpose as thus summarily expressed, I will explain it rather more fully. By a 'faithful' rendering I mean one which says in English neither more nor less than what Dante says in Italian, and which says it in the same way. By 'genuinely' English I mean a translation which, by reason of its sentence structure (grammar, syntax and word-order), reads like an original English poem, and would in these respects be taken for such by one born and bred an Englishman ignorant that it was in fact a translation. By the 'metre' in which it is written I mean the intricately rhymed and strictly metrical verse-form called *terza rima* (triple rhyme). But by this verse-form I do not mean *terza rima* as it is abstractly defined in Italian, still less in English, text-books on prosody; nor *terza rima* as it has at times been composed

---

[1] By Spenser I refer to G. Musgrave's translation of the *Inferno* into Spenserian stanzas, and by Marvell to C. L. Shadwell's of the *Purgatorio* and *Paradiso* into the stanza of Marvell's *Ode to Cromwell*; both of them in their own way beautiful English poems, but quite as unlike Dante's in shape and movement as is Cary's blank verse.

when employed by great English poets (e.g. Shelley)[1] or even by great Italian poets (e.g. Petrarch and Ariosto) subsequent to Dante, who according to Bembo invented it. I mean *terza rima* only when it is so written in English as to obey the rules (involving, when obeyed, the technical procedure) which careful study of the *Comedy*[2] shows to be those that, consciously or unconsciously, to Dante himself, determined the general character and account for the peculiar features of his versification, and his ways of varying it in correspondence with changes in his subject matter and his emotional reaction to them, while he was in the act of composing *this particular poem*.

No translation of *The Divine Comedy*, even though written in triple rhyme, deserves in my opinion to be called a translation of it in the full and proper sense of that term, unless it aims at fulfilling, and does to some degree in fact fulfil, all the conditions just mentioned. For, in no other very long[3] narrative poem in European literature from Homer to the present day, are form and content so closely integrated, that failure anywhere to give a rendering of the one inevitably involves failure to give a rendering of the other. The translator, like Dante himself, must learn to think in *terzine*, and in *terzine* which are specifically Dantean in their quality. This takes time. It took Dante himself a long time to master his medium, and to discover

[1] In the *Triumph of Life*: Petrarch in his *Trionfi*; Ariosto in his *Satiri*.

[2] There being no other source of information concerning them. Had Dante completed the *De Vulgari Eloquentia* he would probably have dealt with the 'comic' (i.e. 'vulgar') style, there contrasted with the 'tragic' (i.e. 'elevated'), in the fourth book of that treatise—composed, it is thought, between 1304 and 1306. But his mind did not stay still; and by the time, many years later when he began the *Comedy*, his views on the 'comic' style and on poems in the 'lowly' and 'middle' vernacular would probably have changed; as in fact we can watch them changing in the course of his composition of the *Comedy* itself: which, so entitled in the *Inferno* (16, 128 and 21, 2) has become *lo sacrato poema* in the *Paradiso* (23, 62) and *il poema sacro* (ib. 25, 1) to which Heaven as well as Earth has set its hand.

[3] The *Comedy* contains 14,233 lines: viz. 4,720 in the *Inferno*, 4,755 in the *Purgatorio* and 4,758 in the *Paradiso*. *Paradise Lost* contains 10,565 lines, and the *Aeneid* 9,896.

and make use of all the resources of his chosen verse-form. No artist is impeccable, and it was not until he began writing the *Paradiso* that, doubtless inspired by his subject, his by then consummate craftsmanship proved adequate to all the tremendous demands he made upon it, and in the poem's final canto enabled him, with a hand that did *not* tremble, to achieve 'what, in its colossal context, represents perhaps the highest flight to which human speech has ever attained'.[1]

Of the three levels which Goethe (in a passage already referred to) distinguishes in the translation of poetry, my aim here has been to reach the third and highest level, the lowest and first being a literal bald word-for-word prose translation, which, 'though it kills outright all that gives life to the original, namely its poetry, brings us into immediate contact with what is foreign in it and thereby "mitten in unserer nationellen Häuslichkeit", surprises us and, without our knowing how it happens, by heightening our state of mind, edifies us, as, e.g. does Luther's translation of the Bible'. The second and higher level of translation, which Goethe calls 'parodistic', aims indeed, he says, 'at entering into the foreigner's frame of mind, his way of thinking and expressing himself, but is really concerned to assimilate this to his own, and to make the latter serve as its substitute'. The third and highest level of translation is defined by Goethe as that 'at which we should like *to make the translation identical with the original*, so that it may here have the value not of a substitute for the original, but of the original itself'. He added that 'this kind of translation meets at first with great resistance: for the translator, who sticks closely to his original, more or less surrenders the originality of his own nation, and thus a third thing is born to which the public has to educate itself'.[2] By 'identical with the original' Goethe does not of course mean that the perfect translation *is* the original (which it manifestly is not and never can be: even in the same language to alter, however

[1] C. R. Buxton: *Prophets of Heaven and Hell*, p. 35.
[2] *Noten und Abhandlungen zum Westöstlichen Divan (Übersetzungen)*.

slightly, the way of saying a thing is to alter the thing
said); but that it can, *in value*, take the place of the original,
the one doing for us intellectually, morally, spiritually,
aesthetically and for all practical purposes precisely what
the other does; so that, as of St. Francis and St. Dominic

d'amendue
si dice l'un pregiando, quale uom prende.[1]

To merit this praise the translator of the *Comedy* does not
substitute for the style of the original some already existing
English style (probably that fashionable at the moment,
and, quite likely, soon to become out of date) which he
deems the most closely corresponding to it, or a style ex-
pressive of his own immediate emotional reaction to the
original—the 'feel' of it to him personally: he endeavours
to make his own style Dantesque. But as he knows, none
better, that he cannot become a Dante, he asks Dante to
become him,[2] hoping, however much against hope, that his
petition will, at any rate occasionally, be granted; or that,
failing this, his translation in general may be such that in
striving to identify itself with the original, it leads or rather
forces the reader back to the *Grundtext* and thereby is not
only of real help to him in understanding the content of the
poem, but also serves him, if in nothing else, as a con-
densed commentary upon its *form* as a work of art.

Translation of the *Comedy* at Goethe's third level is
admittedly of extreme difficulty, and not least because,
though the style is to be Dante's, the translator must
nevertheless write genuine, not an italianized or 'translatese'
English. He must exhaust the capabilities of his material,
the English language, as it has been written at *all* periods,
in order to shape it to his purpose, and yet at the same time
refrain from doing that which the nature of his material
forbids. He must be intolerant, not like Browning (in the
case of a no less 'immensely famous original') tolerant, of
clumsiness in trying to furnish the reader with 'the very

[1] *Par.* 11, 40–1.
[2] Like Shelley invoking the West Wind: 'Make me thy lyre! Be
thou, Spirit fierce, my spirit! Be thou me, impetuous one!'

turn of each phrase' in as Dantesque a fashion as the English tongue, without ceasing to be (in syntax, grammar and word-order) unquestionably English, will bear; and yet, through his very fidelity to the form of the original, must enrich his own language and literature by adding new words to its vocabulary, greater flexibility to its syntax, fresh variety to its rhythms, and to its music a melody perhaps never heard before. The translator of this type certainly requires to understand Dante's meaning down to its finest shades, but what he requires even more is to hear it. For the meaning of poetry though contained in its component sentences and, strictly speaking, solely in the poem *as a whole*, only *speaks* through their music, while their rhythm is its very soul.

The study of Dante's poetic technique in the *Comedy*, of the verse-form, of the reason for it, and of the laws which govern it, has been almost entirely neglected by English Dantists and until recently by Italian Dantists too.[1] The first point to be grasped, or Dante's main artistic purpose will be entirely missed, is that in pattern his verse is neither epic nor dramatic, and still less is it lyrical. It was chosen because it admitted all these modes, but its norm is none of them: it is satiric, as the term was understood by our great classical satirists, in whom, as W. P. Ker (echoing Swinburne) very happily put it, 'the narrow sound of satire opens out to a large sea. The beauty of his (Pope's) satiric poetry is its reflection of the whole world, not steadily, or as the great masters render it in Epic or Tragedy, but with all the lights of the greater modes represented here and there—so that anywhere you may be caught away, for a moment, to different regions.' In just the same way it may be said that the narrow sound of the Italian *sirventese* opens out into the large sea of Dante's *Divine Comedy*. For the

---

[1] Cp. Mario Fubini: *Metrica e Poesia dal duecento al Petrarca*, p. 13 (1962). 'Dobbiamo constatare che, mentre gli studi di metrica sono abbastanza sviluppati nelle altre nazioni, in Italia essi sono più che altro riservati all'origine dei metri (fondamentali sempre gli studi del D'Ovidio raccolti nel volume *Versificazione italiana e Arte poetica medioevale*), quando non si tratti di manuali che offrano nozioni di carattere puramente tecnico.'

sirventese, as an established poetic *genre* passed on its characteristic features to the *Comedy* both in content and form. Taken over from Provençal literature, the Italians made it predominantly narrative, sententious, didactic and (as we know from a *sirventese* written by Dante himself on the sixty most beautiful women in Florence[1]) also laudatory. In subject it dealt with passing events, that is actual events, and not with a romantic, ideal or sentimentalized world of the poet's own invention.[2] So, too, the *Comedy* is in form a waking vision of the really existent—not like the *Pilgrim's Progress* a dream—described by an eye-witness who, as such, is mainly concerned to give an accurate report, and at the same time sound reason for the truth of everything, however unprecedented, that in imagination he had actually beheld.

To achieve this purpose Dante aimed, as Dryden did in such a poem as *The Hind and the Panther*, at a style which would equally admit of the 'majestic turns of heroic poesie'; deal 'plainly' with subjects that were 'matters of dispute'; possess, when required, the 'freedom and familiarity of domestic conversation', and be no less at home with 'the commonplaces of satire'[3]—all of them objects which the great English satirist achieved, or aimed at achieving, within the strict limits of the heroic couplet, and Dante within the far stricter ones of *terza rima*.

Metrically as well as for its variety of style, the *Comedy* may be considered as related to, if not derived from, the *sirventese*, which—to give one example of it—was composed of linked stanzas of two or three hendecasyllables each, mono-rhymed, with a *quinario*, a verse of five

[1] Cp. *Vita Nuova*, VI. This *sirventese* has not survived, but is alluded to in the famous early sonnet (*Guido, vorrei che tu e Lapo ed io*) which Dante addressed to his friend Guido Cavalcanti, the poet, to whom he dedicated the *Vita nuova*. Detached from its context Sordello's speech in *Purg.* 7, 88–136 is a *sirventese*.

[2] Such as the dream-world imagined by Bunyan in the *Pilgrim's Progress* (see its opening sentence). Dante's Purgatory had its own accurately defined latitude and longitude on the map, where no one would think of looking for Bunyan's Hill Difficulty (or the island in Shakespeare's *Tempest*).

[3] *The Hind and the Panther*: Preface, last two paragraphs.

syllables, as a *coda* or tail which supplied a rhyme for the next stanza, thus:

AAAb, BBBc, etc.

Dante's own stanza, of three hendecasyllables in triple rhyme, which repeats itself continuously from start to finish of the canto, is linked by the rhymes thus:

ABA, BCB, C . . . YX, YZY, Z

(closing not with a quatrain, but in a single verse) and was a development rather than a variant of the other. For it is not found in any extant *sirventese* and was presumably invented by Dante himself as suiting the symbolism of numbers (with special reference to the Trinity and Unity of the Godhead) by which the whole structure of the *Comedy* is determined.[1]

If technically, then, the *Divine Comedy* must not be classified as epic or drama or lyric, but is properly speaking a great complex of narrative, personal, religious, moral, satirical, laudatory or didactic *sirventesi*, each canto consisting of some forty or fifty rhyme-linked three-verse stanzas, and all reduced to one organic whole by an imagination freely accepting and working within the strict limits which the chosen form prescribes, certain obvious consequences follow for any translator who regards form and matter as indissoluble in poetry, and desires to achieve a faithful rendering of both. Neither blank verse (supposing he could write it) nor any of the great traditional narrative stanzas, employed by English poets—e.g. the rhyme-royal, the Spenserian or the octave—and still less any lyric or elegiac stanza, will serve his purpose. On the contrary their associations are such that they would

---

[1] I say 'presumably' because, so far as I am aware, there is no evidence that Dante had the doctrine of the Trinity in mind when he chose to write his poem in *terza rima*. But it seems probable; for though he wrote the *Divine Comedy* in exaltation of Beatrice, he regarded himself as inspired to write it by God, who, symbolized by the Sun, occurs so frequently throughout the poem (for which reason, I suppose, Porena in his text prints the word, where thus symbolic, with an initial capital, in which I have generally followed him).

inevitably defeat it. And since rhyme he must have, and a stanza in which the rhythms do not, or only very rarely, overrun the stanza ending, he is left with only two possible metres: either the heroic couplet as handled by Dryden and Pope, or Dante's own *terza rima*, composed—an important qualification—in the same manner as Dante himself composed it. And surely—since, as Shelley said, in specific reference to translation of the *Divine Comedy*, 'it is an essential justice to an author to render him in the same form'[1]—the latter must be deemed preferable unless there are insuperable objections.

Such objections have been held to exist: and they may be briefly stated as follows beginning with the weightiest. It has been argued that English thought-forms do not naturally fit themselves to the *terza rima* measure. If they did, why should Shelley, the only major English poet who ever composed a long poem in triple rhyme, have imposed upon it the rhythms of blank verse? Again, does not the fact that English poets do not construct their sonnets, though originally imitated from the Italian, on *terza rima* cadences, prove that they find it difficult to bring the triple rhyme melody to a close? And, further, is not this difficulty obviously connected with the scarcity of rhyming words in English as contrasted with their abundance in Italian? And, finally, even suppose the rhymes to be found without resort to bad rhymes,[2] misplaced emphasis, mistranslations, mere padding, and ugly inversions[3] (all of them used in order to obtain the third rhyme) is not the frequency of the rhyme, at any rate in a poem so long as the *Comedy*, displeasing to the English ear?

[1] Thomas Medwin: Life of P. B. Shelley, Vol. II, pp. 15 ff., à propos of Shelley's triple rhyme translation of *Purg.* 28, 1–51.

[2] By this I mean, in English verse, identical rhymes, cockney rhymes, and eye-rhymes; assonances; accented, rhyming with un accented, final syllables etc.

[3] Some, generally all, of these defects, characterize such English triple-rhyme renderings of the poem with which I am myself acquainted. Their authors invariably excuse themselves on the ground that it is impossible to write an English triple-rhyme version without them, with the implication that what they themselves cannot do cannot be done at all: in answer to which, to quote Dante himself, cp. *Par.* 28, 58–60.

The one convincing answer to these objections would be an actually existing example of a triple rhyme translation of the *Comedy*, to which, though written in English, none of them was by qualified judges[1] felt to apply. And such, as I have already said, is the answer that has been attempted (for the first time, so far as I know) in the present translation of the poem. However far it falls short (as of course it does fall short) of its aim—and from this, as from all other points of view, it must be its own excuse; for, if it cannot justify itself, none else can perform this office for it, least of all its author—it can, I hope justly, claim to be at any rate a genuine and consistent *attempt* to write English triple rhyme in Dante's own form and manner. These, of course, require to be understood (and loved) before they can be imitated; and a full inquiry into the particular characteristics of his craftmanship as *fabbro del parlar materno*, which he passionately loved,[2] would involve consideration not only of his management of rhythm and of rhyme, but also of the part played by such things as length and shortness of syllables, words and sentences, vowel and consonantal music, intonation, alliteration,[3] assonance, syntax, inversions (frequently violent), repetition, archaisms, dialect, latinisms, neologisms (of which there are scores), word-play (which pleased him), puns, slang, proper names, proverbial expressions (often concluding a *terzina*), figures of speech,[4] the grouping of *terzine* and *canti* and so on. But though the translator ought to have made a minute study of all these and be everywhere ready with a practical solution of the nice problems they are perpetually raising

---

[1] By whom I mean critics who by their familiarity with the great classics of English poetic literature know just how far their authors' employment of, say, eye-rhymes and inversions, justify a sparing use of them by the translator on linguistic grounds or for a definite artistic purpose.

[2] Cp. *Convivio* I, 10–13.

[3] Often used for emphasis or, as in Virgil's last words to Dante (*Purg*. 27, 141), to 'solemnise the style' (G. Giacalone) *fallo-fora-fare* (fault-forth-fiat).

[4] One of Dante's favourites among these is chiasmus. Cp. *Par*. 14, 28–30, the double chiasmus, one within the other, which exactly reflect the meaning.

for him, it is with the rhythm, the rhyme and the diction that he must chiefly concern himself, if he is to produce the general effect of Dante's versification in simple and credible English, and avoid 'translatese'. These, therefore, I will now very briefly consider, before pointing out, more briefly still, how his technique results inevitably from his conception of the art of poetry[1]—its nature, function and practical purpose as illustrated in the *Divine Comedy*.

First, then, what determined rhythm in Dante's verse, as in English verse, is the relation of word-values accentually to one another, not the absolute time as m asured by the metre. For the latter is a pure abstraction, with which the movement of the verse, though for ever suggesting it, hardly ever in fact exactly coincides. Nor, indeed when once the translator has satisfied himself, by reading both aloud with their natural speech accents, that the English ten-syllable or five-stress line (blank verse) is the nearest metrical equivalent of the Italian hendecasyllable (*verso sciolto*) need he think of metre again. Whichever

---

[1] By 'art' Dante as a philosopher (though not as a poet) meant the activity of the practical (as distinguished from the purely speculative) intellect, i.e. the mind as its operates, according as it has knowledge, for the sake of *doing*, or for the sake of *knowing* simply as an end in itself. The practical order itself he divided into two entirely distinct spheres, which the ancients termed (i) Action (*agibile*, πρακτόν) i.e. that of morality or of human conduct as good, the sphere of Ethics and (ii) Making (*factibile*, ποιητόν). The latter, defined as 'productive' action, is what it ought to be, i.e. is 'technically' good, if it conforms to the rules and ends peculiar to the work produced, in the present case, the *Divine Comedy*. The sphere of Making is the sphere of Art (technique) which is the activity of the practical intellect in impressing an idea on a matter, *materia*, which in the art of poetry is human language; to each species of art its own chosen material. 'Art therefore remains outside of the line of human conduct, with an end, rules and values which are not those of man, but of the work to be produced. That work is everything for art, — one law only governs it — the exigencies and the good of the work.' (J. Maritain: *Art and Scholasticism*, p. 6 f., English translation, 1932). It is to the end, rules and values that are those of the *Comedy* that a faithful English translation of it should conform, so that when the two are compared the same law will be found to govern both. Dante made no distinction between fine art and useful art (i.e. between artist and artisan). The product of each was equally an artifact, though, spiritually, the former possesses value which the latter lacks.

method of scansion be adopted,[1] Italian or English, the ear recognizes that it is confronted in both verses with essentially the same rhythmical movement of the line as a whole.

---

[1] Tozer in his chapter on 'The metre of the *Divina Commedia*' appended to Moore's *Textual Criticism* applies the English method of scanning blank verse to Dante's hendecasyllable, and scans the first verse of the *Divine Comedy*:

nel mézz | o dél | cammín | di nós | tra ví | ta,

which Ewart (in *Centenary Essays on Dante*, p. 85, Oxford, 1965) rightly calls little short of fantastic. For the usual English method is to scan an English verse on the classical (Latin) analogy by the number of its feet and metrical stresses—in blank verse five—with the speech-accents counterpointed upon them. The number of its syllables varies. These are normally ten, with a rising rhythm, increased to any number which the metre can carry without collapsing; or, allowing for a pause or pauses, they may be less than ten.

But the Italian prosodist knows nothing of feet. He measures and classifies an Italian verse as long or short by the number of syllables, allowing for elision and crasis, which it contains. In the hendecasyllable (the longest verse) these, as its name denotes, are normally eleven, in which case the verse is called *piano* (e.g. *Inf.* 1, 1); though it may also (though rarely and for a special effect) have its last syllable cut off, when it is called *tronco* (e.g. *Inf.* 31, 145); or an unaccented one added at the end, when it is called *sdrucciolo* (e.g. *Inf.* 15, 1). Of 'primary' accents the metre requires that it should contain two and no more; one falling always on the tenth (i.e. the penultimate) syllable, the other on either the fourth or the sixth, so that, metrically, at one or other of these points, the verse divides itself into two uneven sections. 'Secondary' accents occur within each of these. But though of course they affect the rhythm of the verse as a whole, they are metrically invalid, since they vary from verse to verse in number and incidence, whereas the 'primary' accents are in both these respects fixed.

There are about forty anomalous verses in the poem. These, to make them scan, require that an accent should be placed on a syllable which, in the natural syntactic accentuation, it does not bear. Otherwise, all the verses can be made to obey the rules above stated, except *Inf.* 31, 67 (which in any case is intended to be unintelligible, and even so can be made to scan, if *amech* be pronounced as trisyllabic, *amécche*, for the reason Porena suggests in his commentary ad loc.).

The forty irregular verses can be reduced in number (1) by supposing the accented syllable to be justified rhetorically, e.g. by italicizing *ben* in *Par.* 5, 103; (2) by treating adverbs ending in *-mente* as the two words which by etymology they are, and thus giving each of them an accent, e.g. in *Inf.* 6, 14 by pronouncing *caninaménte* as if it were *canina-ménte*; (3) by restoring to a word, which by itself is naturally accented, the accent it had lost in the syntactical context of the verse, e.g. in *Inf.* 10, 125 by reading *séi* for *sei*.

There remain eight really anomalous verses, those namely ending with the so-called *rima composta*, a rhyme composed of two or more words involving a misplaced accent, of which the strangest is that in *Inf.* 30, 87 *non ci ha*, which, to rhyme with *oncia* and *sconcia*, must

The translator, therefore, who *come a buon cantor buon citarista*,[1] would fain make his own verse keep time with Dante's, rather than breaking up the latter into abstract metrical units, should aim at distinguishing its real rhythmical phrases; and to these he must chiefly guide himself by the sense and natural grouping of the words, by the necessary pauses (not always marked by punctuation) and by a sensitive discrimination between the primary and secondary stresses. For it is the phrasal rhythms—controlled, doubtless, in delivery by a conscious or subconscious feeling for the metre into which they are theoretically divisible—that enable him to appreciate the melody to which the poet is writing, and under the influence of which alone, though by means that defy exact analysis, the thought-form and the rhythmical come into simultaneous existence.

But even if he attends as he must to the phrasing, the translator will entirely fail to reproduce the characteristic form and movement of the Dantesque *terzina* unless he makes his rhythms exactly coincident with this. For the real rhythmical unit is not the verse but the stanza, as the linking of its phrases over and over again makes clear. This fact in itself would make a line-for-line translation, even if in verse it were possible (as it is in prose), not only needless, but actually mistranslation; for it ignores Dante's own practice. Within the *terzina*—and I give examples from the *Paradiso*, where his versification has achieved its utmost perfection—he readily, when his ear so demands, separates by the line-ending the adjective from its noun (13, 19), and ends a verse with a conjunction (18, 97), or with the first

be pronounced *nóncia* instead of *noncià* (as if a modern Italian were to rhyme *libertà* with *apérta*). I have translated one such rhyme correspondingly, to enable the reader to judge what it sounds like in English (*Inf.* 28, 123). Most of these anomalous verses were probably due to Dante's admiration of Provençal poets, notably Arnaut Daniel (cp. *Purg.* 26, 116–17), and he makes less and less use of them as the poem proceeds. Cp. also *Par.* 24, 16, where the adverb is divided between two verses, which I have imitated by dividing a compound adjective in a similar way (as Milton does in *Paradise Lost* 10, 581). It should be noted that a verse of this kind is, like many others in the poem, without a caesura.

[1] *Par.* 20, 142.

half of a compound one (14, 16; 18, 31), or with the copulative (8, 44), or the relative pronoun (2, 11; 9, 94), or the definite article (11, 13), or even with part of a word (24, 16); whereas between the end of one *terzina* and the beginning of the next, as the punctuation indicates, he allows no synaphea. At that point rhythmically as well as syntactically there is either a pause or a full stop, and the two *terzine* are connected by rhyme alone.[1]

A whole rhythmical period, however—as, for the translator, it is extremely important to notice—by no means always coincides with one *terzina*; in fact it rarely ever does, except in the first *canti* of the poem. It extends to two or more *terzine*, as the context may demand—on occasion to as many as eight (*Par.* 13, 1–24), though always on condition that the unit (the *terzina*) be preserved rhythmically intact. To preserve this condition, as the translator also must, would have been impossible even for Dante had he written in long complex sentences, clause within clause, as Milton did. But he does not. His purpose—plain description, syllogistic argument—suits with sentence-structure mostly paratactic, or, if otherwise, having the simple relationship of short propositions connected by precisely placed conjunctions like 'as' and 'so', or 'so' and 'that'. Thus in one case the simile, in the other the premises and conclusion, fall easily into three verses apiece, although, as already remarked, many more than a single *terzina* may be required before the whole rhythmical period, infinitely varied in detail, comes with the final cadence to a full stop.

Now it is undoubtedly true that the English translator, unless he has trained his ear and mind to adjust his thought-forms almost unconsciously to successive units of three verses exactly, will find his own rhythms tending by nature to overrun the limit. From the time of Shakespeare and more especially of Milton, their free rhythms have not only

[1] There are exceptions, but not many (and mostly in the first *cantica*), where the *terzina* continues without a break of any sort into the next one, so that structurally the two form a single stanza; or the *terzina* completes itself before its last word which syntactically and rhythmically becomes part of the next *terzina* (notably *Inf.* 26, 90). For the rest cp. *Inf.* 2, 3; 3, 72; 13, 18.

set the norm for English blank verse, but have imposed themselves on the heroic verse-couplet as well. Shelley's triple rhyme is for this reason not *terza rima* at all, but as it were rhymed blank verse, as utterly different from Dante's as his Spenserian stanza in *Adonais* is in rhythm and tempo different from Spenser's in the *Faerie Queene*. Yet there is no reason in theory why, if English poetry can adjust its rhythms to the closed couplet, it should not equally well adjust them to the closed *terzina*. It does in fact do so, sometimes for several triplets together, in satires of Dryden and Pope, who, though writing in closed couplets, often needed an extra verse, and that not always an alexandrine, to complete the rhythm of their thought.[1] We need not suppose that any technical obstacles would have prevented them from composing a poem as long as a canto of the *Comedy* in *terzine*, had they so desired. Couplets, however, happened to be the new fashion; so they preferred them.

We are driven to conclude, therefore, that the supposed difficulty—by so many verse-translators asserted to be the impossibility—of writing of English *terza rima* in Dante's manner must lie, not in the stanza itself, but in the rhyme-scheme: a difficulty greatly increased under the conditions imposed by translation, where the writer is bound by his original. But here it is necessary to distinguish. No one, surely, can seriously maintain that a language is deficient in words of a like-sounding termination, which boasts of the *Faerie Queene* and *Don Juan*. For in these immensely long poems the stanza of the one requires four, and of the other three, verses to be written on the same rhyme. It is certainly true that Italian contains a vastly greater number[2]

---

[1] e.g. when, in *The Hind and the Panther* Dryden writes the end-stopped couplet:

> Can I believe the eternal God could lye
> Disguised in mortal mould and infancy?

but feels impelled to complete the rhythm by adding the superb verse

> That the great Maker of the world could die?

he has thereby converted the couplet into a *terzina* such as Dante would feel proud to have written had he been English.

[2] Which, owing to the fluid state in his time of the language (which he was engaged in creating) Dante enormously increased, by using dialectal and archaic words and verbal inflections, now obsolete, and by spelling practically as he liked.

of rhyming words than English does, and further allows of identical or 'rich' rhymes (i.e. where the identity of sound is extended to the consonant immediately preceding the final stressed vowel),[1] which English by custom does not. But, even so, the Spenserian stanza is proof positive that English possesses enough rhymes for the purposes of *terza rima*. Their relative scarcity, while no excuse for using bad English rhymes, will, however, justify the translator of Dante in departing from the latter's practice in one respect, and one only. He may permit himself to do what Dante very rarely does, and that is to repeat the same set of rhymes in the same canto, so long of course as they are not consecutive. With regard to the rhymes themselves he may allow himself the judicious use of eye-rhymes,[2] and rhymes of open with close vowel syllables, and of breathed with unbreathed consonants, or of vowels with diphthongs of which one element is the vowel concerned:[3] and that without apology for two reasons: first, because he has the authority of all the greatest English poets for so doing; and, second, because to employ these kinds of rhyme from time to time serves to dispose of the objection, referred to above, that the frequency of rhyme, if always phonetically a true one, would prove trying to the English ear. The sole respect in which his own language will fail him in writing Dantesque *terza rima* is its deficiency in *rime aspre*, of which, for artistic reasons, Dante uses so many in the

[1] But Dante makes it a rule which he rarely breaks that where he rhymes two identical words, they should differ in meaning. The three most notable exceptions are *Cristo*, out of reverence, in *Par.* 14, 104; *ammenda*, in irony, in *Purg.* 20, 67; and *vidi*, for extreme emphasis, in *Par.* 30, 95.

[2] Often, originally, true rhymes, and still such in dialect (e.g. 'love' pronounced to rhyme with 'move' in the Yorkshire dialect); and serviceable to the translator as are the Latin, archaic and dialect forms freely employed by Dante for the sake of easier rhyming; and sometimes by myself too, for the same reason, both at the end of a line (e.g. archaic 'owes' for 'owns' *Inf.* 11, 35), and as he also does, where convenient metrically, within the line.

[3] I never rhyme '-ents' with '-ence' or 'ense', or (though the r is not pronounced in southern England) 'dawn' with 'worn', and still less 'loss' with 'course'.

Inferno[1] and in which the Italian language abounds. Of cacophonous rhymes in English the translator may well find two to supply his need, or even think of three, but the third will rarely, if ever, suit the context.[2] He may, however, make up for this deficiency through being able to produce the desired effect by suitable words within, instead of at the end of, the verse, and must certainly do so if he can.

The real difficulty of writing Dantesque *terza rima* in English is, however, not to find the rhymes, but to imitate Dante in his artistic use of them. He employs rhyme in this respect for three clearly distinguishable purposes. By linking the stanzas, it is no less essential to the structure of the poem, than are the quadruple rhyme and alexandrine to the structure of the Spenserian stanza. And over and over again the central verse of a *terzina*, but especially its last word, which prepares the ear for the words rhyming with it in the following *terzina*, is the bud out of which the latter's meaning also flowers. The rhymes therefore not only link the *terzine* structurally, and weld the whole poem into one indissoluble whole, but they also—and this is their second important role—serve to point the sense and guide the meaning. The rhyme-word is the outstanding key-word of the argument. So true is this, that in whole passages together you may follow the drift of the thought by a mere glance at the rhymes; a fact which any reader may note for himself on almost any page where he opens the poem.[3]

---

[1] Cp. *Inf.* 32, 1–12 (Necessità di asprezza — « *quanto al suono de lo dittato che a tanta materia non conviene essere leno* », *Convivio* IV, 2, 13 — che mai sente nel Purgatorio e nel Paradiso, ove naturalmente l'aspirazione è volta a rime dolci e piane. Aldo Vallone: *Studi sulla Div. Com.* p. 58). Cp. also *De Vulgari Eloquentia* II, 4 and 7.

[2] For examples of Dante's use of *rime aspre e chiocce* the reader should refer to those two *canti* of the *Inferno* (16 and 21) where the poet's reference to his poem by the title Comedia indicates that he is about to make free use of this type of rhyme and of vulgar diction. But they occur wherever his subject-matter warrants them, even in the *Paradiso*.

[3] e.g. the rhyme-words—*vita, oscura, smarrita, dura, forte, paura*—of the opening six lines of the poem at once subtly induce the frame of mind appropriate to the journey through Hell that follows. It is impossible to over-emphasize the importance of the rhyme (whether *difficile* or *dolce*) and Dante's extreme skill in his use and choice of it

It would be foolish to insist that the translator must always so manipulate his rendering of what the words mean as to emphasize by rhyme the very same idea that Dante's rhyme-word does. For translation of poetry is art, not mechanism; and the translator must conceal his art (though Dante from time to time cannot refrain from drawing the reader's attention to his own superb artistry, and, after some *tour de force* of versification congratulating himself upon it with unconcealed complacency)[1] and must make his rhymes occur as easily and as inevitably as (with few exceptions)[2] they occur in the original. This they can only do, if, while adopting, so far as may be, Dante's principle of linking the important idea with the rhyme, he remains free to emphasize by this means whatever word the logic of his own rendering of Dante's argument raises to special importance. Yet there are countless passages where unless he can contrive *without awkwardness* to place at the end of the line the same word as Dante does, he will not in the strict sense be translating him. Where a new topic of conversation is introduced on the rhyme, or where the key-word of the sentence is reserved for the final cadence, or where this comes as a climax, he can hardly forsake his author without committing a translator's gravest error—an outstanding misplacement or neglect of what is intended to be, and is in the Italian, emphasized in the strongest way possible. It is everywhere an error I have done my best to avoid, both within and at the end of a verse.

The third way in which Dante exploits rhyme must be

in this and in other respects throughout the poem. He may even have chosen *terza rima* itself in which to compose it, not only for mnemonic convenience (which certainly weighed with him; cp. my note on *Inf*. 34, 79), but also, as Tatlock pointed out, to make an interpolation virtually impossible by others or a later insertion by himself without extensive re-casting (cp. Ewert, op. cit., p. 82) of at least two *terzine*, one before and one after it.

[1] Cp. *Inf*. 25, 94–102; *Purg*. 9, 70–2.

[2] The author of the *Ottimo Commento* (in his note on *Inf*. 10, 85) says he himself had heard Dante say that 'never had a rhyme made him say other than he would.' But this is not strictly true. For there are verses, though not many, where he has obviously had to bow to the tyranny of rhyme; which is the translator's best excuse for having to do so sometimes himself also.

studied in connection with the sound of his verse, which he varies as he varies his rhythms, to accord with the changes in his emotional reaction to the object of his vision. In the *Inferno* it is often deliberately harsh; in the *Purgatorio* it takes on an elegiac tone; in the *Paradiso* it is consistently euphonious. The rhyme plays its part in emphasizing the cadences, especially the third rhyme of the last of a series of *terzine*, where it brings a long drawn-out melody to a full close. The tones of Francesca's voice are those we associate with the *dolce stil nuovo*, as are those of Guido Guinicelli (who originated that style).[1] The voice of Beatrice, when she visits Virgil in Limbo, resembles in its modulations the voices of the angels in Heaven. In passages of sustained philosophical argument the rhymes provide an indispensable accompaniment to it by pointing and thus clarifying the logic of the thought. If anyone doubts this, let him test the matter by turning such a discourse as *Par.* 2, or *Par.* 13, 37–111 into prose and try to estimate what it loses in meaning, or shades of meaning, by being deprived of the rhymes.

Nor may the translator excuse himself for failure in his duties here by either of the two pleas, often advanced, but equally false, that the English language is inherently less musical than the Italian, and that about philosophical speculation there is something unavoidably prosaic. With regard to the first it is doubtless true that Italian is much richer in pure vowels than modern English, and that over and over again in the *Comedy* lines like *quasi obliando d'ire a farsi belle* or *quale nei plenilunii sereni* defy translation into their musical equivalent; not because English is incapable of producing the same quality of sound (for it can),[2] but because the thought here has to be rendered as well as the melody, and consequently the right-sounding words may not be available. On the other hand, English possesses many more vowels than Italian does, and has the further advantage over that language in its mixture of Teutonic

---

[1] *Purg.* 26, 97–9 and 109–14.
[2] e.g. Herrick's 'melting melodious notes on lutes of amber' or Keats's 'tall oaks, branched-charmèd by the earnest stars'.

and Latin vocabulary, and above all in its abundance of monosyllabic words with their long (or short) vowels and vibrating terminal consonants.[1] The English translator of Dante who thinks of Italian as musical and of his own language as, relatively speaking, harsh, either possesses no ear or is little acquainted with English poetry.[2]

As for the commonly expressed opinion that the poetry of the *Comedy*, and more particularly of the *Paradiso*, is impaired, or interrupted, by the intrusion of dry disquisitions on obsolete philosophical theories, it is enough by way of reply to point to the widespread revival of Thomism in our own day; and to remind ourselves that the philosophy of St. Thomas has now for long been the official philosophy of the Roman Catholic Church with its over five hundred million adherents; and, on the relation of poetry to philosophy, to observe with the poet-philosopher Santayana that 'the life of theory is not less human or less emotional than the life of sense; it is more typically human and more keenly emotional . . . To object to theory in poetry would be like objecting to words there; for words, too, are symbols without the sensuous character of the things they stand for; and yet it is only by the net of new connections which words throw over things, in recalling them, that poetry arises at all.'[3]

---

[1] Of both these advantages, Hamlet's last words to Horatio may serve as a typical example:

> If thou didst ever hold me in thy heart
> absent thee from felicity awhile
> and in this harsh world draw thy breath in pain
> to tell my story.

[2] By 'musical' I refer of course to the sound of words in themselves as the material medium of poetry, not to their incidental suitability for being converted to its own ends by the kindred but quite distinct art of music. In the sense of 'more easily *sung*' Italian may well be more musical than English. But in either language 'numerous verse', if truly poetry, is and always has been, of its very nature

> more tunable than needed lute or harp
> to add more sweetness.

[3] G. Santayana: *Three Philosophical Poets* (1910), p. 124. It should not be forgotten, as it was by Croce (and often, under his influence, by such an otherwise sensitive critic as Momigliano), that unlike a philosophical or theological treatise which is intended to be taken in abstraction from the mind that thinks it, such discourses (numerous in the *Paradiso* and already frequent in the *Purgatorio*)

Of Dante's vocabulary it is characteristic that no word, learned or vulgar (in both sense of the term) can be too expressive or too clear. All his five senses and all his personal and exceptionally wide knowledge of the practical and fine arts (architecture, painting—he himself painted—sculpture, music, dancing, etc., as well as his own art, poetry) are summoned to illustrate his thought; and it has been aptly remarked that in no other poem comparable in length with the *Comedy* does the individual word seem, each one, to be so much an individual creation, so clearly a unique, fully developed, definite, living picture. He uses words—and consequently so should his translator—with the greatest precision. Each *cantica* has its own distinctive vocabulary. In the *Paradiso*, where he makes such constant use of light,[1] sound and movement, his numerous terms for these are as nicely distinguished as his theological, philosophical and scientific terminology is technically correct. He never uses an adjective when he can do without one, or two adjectives let alone three, when a single one will serve his purpose; nor must his translator. His illustrations never, as Coleridge complained that his own often did, 'swallow up his thesis'. Metaphors are vivid, sometimes far-fetched ('metaphysical') perhaps out of need for a rhyme; occasionally, *we* may think, quaint, but always primarily means to an end: the clearer presentation of the things described or the more lucid exposition of the thought.

are, in the *Comedy*, all 'in character', i.e. dramatic and, as such, present, where they occur, because structurally required for the smooth continuation of the action, of which therefore they form an essential part, e.g. the Aquinas-in-the-poem when he philosophizes to the Dante-in-the-poem does so because he is intellectually in love (*amor*, cp. *Par*. 13, 36) with the truth, and wishes to instruct him as a master instructs his pupil. But his motive in doing so is his love (carità, ἀγάπη) of the man Dante, his whole personality, not his embodied intellect only.

[1] Dante observed light in all its gradations (and consequently colours too, cp. *Purg*. 32, 58 f.) with the closest attention, and finds words to discriminate between all its varieties and degrees, down to its absence, with the greatest accuracy. There is one distinction, that the translator must be particularly careful not to confuse, namely that between *luce*, the source of light, *lume* the radiance it emits, and *splendore* the radiance when reflected by the object it illuminates (*Convivio* III, 14, 6).

If a speaker asks a question the reply is always—or almost always—rigidly restricted to answering what has been asked, and that with the utmost economy of phrase. The frequent simile is so constructed as to illustrate the one or two points of likeness observed between the objects compared, and no more. Nothing in the simile is superfluous,[1] and nothing, if properly understood, inappropriate.[2]

These are all features of Dante's style which the reader of the *Comedy*, without glancing at the original Italian, should be able to gather from a competent translation of it, or indeed of any one of its *terzine*: for in style each *terzina* is the whole poem in miniature. Nor can there be any question but that the translator, in seeking to reproduce them in English, will be immensely aided by using Dante's own verse-form and technique. In fact only thus will he be able to deal at all adequately with certain problems of expression with which the poet's love of words and word-play frequently confronts him. Only thus, too—which is far more important—can he hope to inform and thereby unify his own poem (in so far as his translation succeeds in meriting that title) with the same concept of poetry as that which inspired Dante to compose his masterpiece.

By his word-play I mean those exhibitions of verbal dexterity and invention which Dante, like his masters the

[1] There are occasional exceptions: e.g. the long simile, extending to five *terzine*, at the beginning of *Inf.* 24 is by most Italian commentators considered to be in part irrelevant, and at the same time too highly stylized for its context. But see the concluding sentence of Sapegno's long introductory note to this *canto*.

[2] I say 'if properly understood' because there are similes in the *Comedy* notably one of the most beautiful in its perhaps most beautiful canto, richer in similes than any other, namely *Par.* 23, 25–7. Here there is a striking lack of equilibrium between the two terms (moonlight and sunlight) compared; its function being 'neither scientific nor descriptively, sensorially realistic; *it is purely emotional* (my italics) and as such not only successful but the most convincing in the poem. Indeed, that ecstatic vision of nocturnal beatitude passes from our eyes and ears into our hearts, and we feel that moonlit heaven within us.' (Aldo Scaglione: *Imagery in Paradiso 23* printed in *From Time to Eternity, Essays on Dante's D.C.*, p. 163: Ed. T. S. Bergin, Yale U.P. 1967.) The image contained in the simile creates the atmosphere of, and imparts its tone to, the whole *canto*, and should be so translated as to come as near doing this as possible in English also.

Provençal troubadours, delighted for artistic reasons at times to indulge in, and which his translator should certainly imitate if by any means possible. Thus Dante will sometimes begin a number of successive stanzas, or a series of double *terzine*, with the same word (e.g. *Inf.* 5, 100–8; 13, 1–9; *Purg.* 12, 25–63; *Par.* 19, 115–47; 20, 40–70). As remarkable, and as necessary to imitate in English, are those intricately yet neatly constructed verses in which changes are rung, as in a peal of bells, by stress and rhyme alike, on a single repeated word (e.g. *Par.* 20, 96–9; 21, 49–50; 33, 5–6). Instead of the noun he constantly, for vividness, prefers to use the verb-noun infinitive. For the same reason the descending rhythms of the famous opening four lines of the last *canto* of the poem, *Vérgine, úmile, términe tú se' colei*, should be noted and reproduced. So should mere sound jingles and alliteration, e.g. *Purg.* 25, 42 *le vene vane*—pervades the veins, and puns e.g. *Inf.* 2, 20–1 *impero . . . Empireo*—empire he, Empyréan, and *Par.* 3, 57 *vóti o vòti*—vowed were void. There are two acrostics, if they were really intended as such, in *Purg.* 12 and *Par.* 19, which I have translated into their English equivalents, 'man' and 'rot'.[1] The philosophical and theological technical terms must be rendered with scrupulous accuracy, or the translator may inadvertently (or in ignorance) make Dante talk heresy. More difficult are Dante's numerous neologisms, for the most part verbs compounded of the preposition 'in' with a noun, adjective, adverb or pronoun, like *imparadisare* from which Milton coined 'imparadise'. On the analogy of 'inform' in its scholastic sense, I have translated *invogliare* 'inwill', and have ventured on rendering *immiarsi, intuarsi, inluiarsi* and *riprofondavan se* literally but have shied at 'inalways itself' for *insemprarsi* and at a literal translation of most verbs compounded of 'in' with an adverb or adjective.[2] Some Latin words and phrases I have

---

[1] On the analogy of 'there's something *rotten* in the state of Denmark'. Dante is describing bad rulers, who are a *lue* (pest) to their subjects. The other acrostic is *uom* (man) whose root sin is pride.

[2] Dante's reason, or one of his reasons, for employing so many neologisms may well have been that which induced Coleridge to

left untranslated or, as Dante himself did, only partially so. The passage he composed in Provençal (*Purg.* 26, 140–7) has been turned into middle English.

As for the conception of Poetry and its function, the *concetto fulcro*,[1] as Umberto Cosmo called it, which gave birth to the *Comedy*, welds it together and gives it organic unity (the question which since Croce has been more discussed by Italian Dantists than any other, but which I am concerned with here only as it affects the translator), I agree with him in finding it in the conception of 'Order' (in the moral sphere 'Justice'), which is the 'form' of the Universe[2] rather than with those who, accepting the authenticity of the Epistle to Can Grande,[3] take the traditional view that the 'soul' of the poem—that is, in scholastic phrase, the 'form' of its body—is the Allegory. Before writing the Comedy, Dante had made his reputation as an allegorizer in verse (the *Vita Nuova* and *canzoni* like the *Tre Donne*) and as a popularizing philosopher in prose (the *Convivio*); and in the Divine Comedy too there is much precise allegorical meaning, though not nearly so much, I venture to think, as his commentators have discovered, and continue, with ever greater elaboration and ever subtler distinctions,

coin the verb 'intensify' (now in common use) which he defended in the footnote on p. 87 of his *Biog. Lit.* Vol. 2 (Clarendon Press, 1907) as follows; 'I am aware that this word occurs neither in Johnson's Dictionary or in any classical writer. But the word "to intend" which Newton and others before him employ in this sense is now so completely appropriated to another meaning, that I could not use it without ambiguity: while to paraphrase the sense, as by "render intense" would often break up the sentence and destroy that *harmony of position of the words with the logical position of the thoughts which is a beauty in all composition, and more especially desirable in a close philosophical investigation.* I have therefore hazarded the word intensify; though I confess it sounds uncouth to my own ear.' (My italics.)

[1] U. Cosmo: *L'ultima Ascesa*, chap. 2.
[2] *Par.* 1, 103–5.
[3] I am myself disposed to agree with those who regard it as spurious. But in my opinion the problem does not admit of a convincing conclusion, and I cannot discuss it here. Among English Dantists Moore argued that the epistle is Dante's, and Mr. Colin Hardie argues the contrary, as also among Italian Dantists D'Ovidio, Porena and Nardi.

to discover there. But as J. A. Stewart observed,[1] it counts for little that really matters. Following the fashion of his time, he uses it as a literary trope; but it is always—even where this trope is in evidence—the narrative, whether true or fictitious, with its persons and places, that is his first concern. The *Comedy contains* much philosophy and theology, but, as against the majority of present-day commentators who (in violent reaction against 19th century Romanticism in general and de Sanctis in particular) seem to regard Dante as pre-eminently a thinker, and the *Comedy* as his contribution to contemporary speculation, it is important to emphasize that it is not a philosophical or theological treatise, but a Poem—a Greek word, ποίημα which means 'thing made' or 'created'. As such, it may rightly be called, fundamentally, a religious poem—apart from the Fourth Gospel, the greatest Christian poem extant—in which God as an idea or metaphysical concept, when the poem requires mention of Him as such (which it often does) can only be represented by a material symbol —the sun or an Euclidean point of intense light; that is, allegorically. But it is the God of Christianity regarded as the *Creator*, and in that sense the supreme and ultimately the sole perfect Poet (ποιητής),[2] with whom, naturally enough, the *poet* Dante, as distinguished from the theologian, is primarily concerned. As thus imagined, the Trinity, though still represented within the poem as three persons—Power, Wisdom, and Love, who in the theological sense of the concept 'person' (*hypostasis*, latinised *substantia* and later *essentia*) are the joint agent of creation[3]—becomes

---

[1] *The Myths of Plato* of this great English Dantist is the best introduction to the poetry of the Divine Comedy known to me. I quote him from a paper on *Myth and Allegory* read to the Oxford Dante Society over forty years ago and subsequently published in *Theology*, an off-print of which he sent me.

[2] The Bible begins with God regarded as Creator or Poet, as (the word being Greek) is seen clearest in the Septuagint version of *Gen.* 1, 1, if rendered into English thus: ἐν ἀρχῇ (in the beginning) ἐποίησεν (there was a Poet) ὁ θεός (who was God) τὸν οὐρανὸν καὶ τὴν γῆν (and the universe was his poem).

[3] Cp. St. Thomas: S.T. Pt. I. Q. 45, Art. 6, where we are told that the divine nature, though common to the three Persons, yet belongs to them as creative in a 'kind of order'. 'Ita etiam et *virtus creandi*

1

instead the One sole eternal divine Being (*Par.* 24, 130 f.), 'personal' in the sense of that term in which we employ it with reference to ourselves as individual *human* beings. As such He needs no allegorizing. But Dante does not commit Milton's artistic error in *Paradise Lost* of introducing Him anthropomorphically into the *Comedy* as a *dramatis persona*.[1] He substitutes for Him poetically (not, of course, theologically, which would be the grossest heresy) the Virgin Mary, no personified abstraction, but a real person true to history, who was God-bearer (as Christians believe) to Mankind, and Beatrice, an equally real person historically, who was God-bearer (as Dante believed) to himself. Apart from the special affection which he tells us that Beatrice, as he himself,[2] had for the Virgin, Dante in the *Comedy* always closely relates the two women to one another, as well as each of them (in due degree) to God.

Where God is concerned then, Dante, when allegorizing the Deity, may be considered a Thomist (though no slavish one) in love (an *amor intellectualis*) with God as *the* Truth; a truth only fully 'revealed' to him by Scripture, but conceptually up to a certain point capable of being arrived at by reasoning. On the other hand, Dante (who, as a student of philosophy and theology, was nothing if not eclectic) when he imagines and refers to God as Creator or Poet must be regarded as a Bonaventurist—St. Francis was

---

licet sit communis tribus personis, *ordine* tamen *quodam* eis convenit.' And compare this with the first two *terzine* of *Par.* 10 especially line 5, where God, all three Persons, is referred to as Creator or Poet and the universe as His poem. For Dante, as for Aquinas, the mystery of the Trinity seems to have had a special fascination; for he devotes a number of carefully phrased and theologically scrupulously orthodox *terzine* to it, in its various aspects, concluding with the verbal masterpiece (*Par.* 33, 124–6), which is the most remarkable of them all.

[1] The Jesus of the Synoptic Gospels nowhere appears personally in the *Comedy*, though every important event in his life from the Nativity to the Ascension is referred to. His Mother represents Him spiritually, morally and physically (cp. *Par.* 32, 85 'La faccia che a Cristo più si somiglia').

[2] Cp. respectively, *Vita Nuova* XXIX and *Par.* 23, 88 f.

Dante's favourite saint, and St. Bonaventura was a Franciscan not a Dominican as was St. Thomas—in love (a love of the heart not head) with the Deity as Love itself, or rather Lover, who creates a deiform Universe[1] and man in His own image out of no motive but love, and in order that both may return that love, each in due degree, to Himself,[2] for Whom he had implanted in Adam an innate desire;[3] a truth arrived at not by process of reasoning, but 'seen' intuitively by a God-given spiritual vision experiencing directly the Divine.[4] The *Comedy* therefore, though it *contains* allegory, was not conceived as an allegorical poem, It is not a mere fable invented to popularize the author's theological speculations, but the imagined vision of a prophet-seer, who as he himself believed is by the special grace of God endowed by the Holy Spirit[5] with insight into

[1] *Inf.* 1. 38–40: 70–5.
[2] Cp. *Par.* 7, 64–6, and *Par.* 29, 13–18.
[3] Cp. *Par.* 7, 142–8.
[4] In contrast with the Aristotelianism of St. Thomas, the neo-Platonism of St. Bonaventura unites theology with mysticism. Without faith the human reason is incapable of arriving at a knowledge of God. Following St. Augustine's doctrine of divine illumination and that of the Victorine mystics, he held that all human wisdom is folly when compared with the *supernatural* enlightenment which God sheds on Christians as a reward of their faith; and this essentially mystical theory of knowledge he expounded in his short treatise *Itinerarium mentis in Deum* (written at La Verna, under the influence of St. Francis who received the stigmata there), which might well serve as a sub-title for the *Divine Comedy*. The beatitude of the saints in Heaven, the Franciscans held, did not, as the Dominicans taught, consist formally in the intellectual vision of God, but in the act of loving Him. To know God at all we must first love Him, not *vice versa*. Dante admired and for his poetic purposes used both great saints and reconciled the one with the other in the *Comedy* when he imagines himself being addressed by each in turn in the heaven of the Sun, and there hears them praising one another. (*Par.* 12, 34–6, 142–4).
[5] That is, Divine Love. Cp. the famous *terzina* which has given rise to a vast literature concerning Dante's theory and practice of poetry: *Purg.* 24, 52–4.

> Io mi son un che quando
> Amor mi spira, noto, ed a quel modo
> ch'ei ditta dentro vo significando,

where the word *Amor* links the love which inspired the *modo* (the *dolce stil nuovo*) of the love-lyrics, which had made Dante famous, with the Love which informs the *Divine Comedy*—*L'Amor che move il Sole e l'altre stelle*—and by inspiring him, enabled him to write it.

the 'life of things' (that is, the very things themselves, not merely with the correct thought about them) and is simultaneously however mysteriously supplied with the verbal means, his poem, to communicate that 'life' to others. By means of his *alta fantasia* he 'makes' (to speak with Plato)[1] a great cosmic myth (μῦθος); a story, that is, so composed as to induce in us an amplitude of mind, *magnanimità*, in which, as we read on, there comes to us with cumulative effect a vision symbolic of human life and destiny, sombre to begin with, but not so sombre as to kill hope (a hope which grows, to be at the end gloriously realized) and which is felt immediately and without question to be the guarantee of its own truth and, though necessarily transient was, while it lasted, a real experience of the mind. It is a story 'not imagined', as Michele Barbi rightly observed, 'so that Dante might spin out gossamers of subtle ideas, but that he might announce what God wanted him to see and hear, in his fateful journey, for the purpose of saving misguided humanity. Hence the importance of the literal meaning of the poem and *the great role that pure poetry plays in its doctrines and practical ends.*'[2]

It is moreover primarily in the character not of an intellectualist (though he *is* that also) but of a poet-seer (*vates*), like Isaiah or the author of the Apocalypse, that

---

[1] On the quality of Dante's Platonism, the 'personal' Platonism of poets (as exemplified in the myths of Plato himself) which is vital in all great poetry and defined as 'love of the unseen and eternal cherished by one who rejoices in the seen and the temporal', the reader should acquaint himself with the paper entitled *Platonism in English poetry*, contributed by J. A. Stewart to the volume of essays collected by G. S. Gordon entitled *English literature aud the Classics* (1912), especially the following p. 31: 'As poet, Dante is one who cannot take his eyes off the things of this visible world; and, as he looks intently at them, or vividly recalls them in solitary reflection, they charm him into dreaming them; he sees them with the eye, not of wayward fancy, but, since he is a born Platonist, with the eye of steady imagination—sees them altered, on a sudden, into their own eternal meaning (I crave pardon for this hard saying)— sees them become vehicles of the unseen and eternal world which is substantially present in them behind the veil of their sensible attributes.'

[2] Barbi: *Life of Dante* (trans. P. G. Ruggiers, 1964, p. 87). (My italics.)

Dante imagines himself as the protagonist of the story[1]; a fact which in the latter capacity he often mentions to those whom he meets,[2] is reminded of by Beatrice[3] and as poet emphasizes at the very outset of his poem. He is a poet-seer, however, who, through his own aberration has indeed not lost but so dimmed or obscured his power of vision that he is in danger of losing it altogether.[4] Made aware of this danger by the grace of God symbolized by the rays of the Sun, *che mena dritto altrui per ogni calle* (*Inf.* 1, 18), which reveal to him the *dilettoso monte, ch'è principio e cagion di tutta gioia* (Ib. 77–8), he is prevented from climbing the mountain by the three wild-beasts. These turn him back to the *selva oscura* from which he was trying to escape, and, unable to save himself, he is saved by the poet-seer Virgil ('Poeta fui' Ib. 73), the first of a

[1] Cp. *Inf.* 1, 85–7. We are not told who the protagonist of the story (the Dante within the poem) is, until nearly two-thirds of the way through it (*Purg.* 30, 55), but in this *terzina* of the *Inferno* we are told at the very outset, *what* he is, namely a student of poetry and a poet himself; one who a little later is acknowledged by the first souls he meets and talks with in Hell, the five greatest poets known to him, to rank in genius with themselves. (*Inf.* 4, 102).

[2] Cp. *Inf.* 32, 91–3; which incidentally makes it very difficult, indeed impossible, always to make a sharp distinction between Dante–poeta, the historical Dante, and Dante–personaggio, the Dante in the poem, as it has long been fashionable to do in many Italian and American commentaries: both are the same poet (maker) of the Comedy, the former after writing it and the latter taking notes for its future composition.

[3] Cp. *Purg.* 33, 52–7; where Beatrice instructs Dante as author or future author of the Comedy what to put in it, and throughout the poem there are occasions when Dante–personaggio tells other characters that he is taking notes in preparation to immortalize them in its pages (e.g. *Inf.* 32, 93).

[4] The word *smarrita* in *Inf.* 1, 3 is invariably mistranslated by English Dantists as 'lost' whereas it means 'confused' or 'perplexed' (cp. Landino's note ad loc.). Dante does not imagine himself as one who has lost the straight way, but as one who could not see it clearly, because it lay 'through the perplexed paths of this drear wood' (Milton, *Comus*, 37). Of these paths, *intellectually*, Averroism may have been one; *morally*, his difficulty of reconciling his love of Beatrice with his love of philosophy, or of other women after her death (referred to by her in *Purg.* 30, 125–32 and 31, 58–60 respectively) may have been another; and *politically* his initial uncertainty about the true relationship between the Pope and Emperor as world-rulers may have been a third (if, as is now thought by some commentators, he changed his mind on this question between writing the *Monarchia* and the *Divine Comedy*).

series of rescuers who, as has too little been noticed by commentators, are all poet-seers likewise, and not philosophers or theologians (say an Aristotle or an Aquinas) as might have been expected, had Dante–personaggio been intended by Dante–poeta to be imagined as primarily an intellectualist. They occur, as we proceed through the poem, in the following order in time. The authoress of the Magnificat, the earliest and greatest of all essentially Christian poems, seeing his plight in the mind of God, the supreme Poet, 'who sees all', sends Lucy, the patron saint of those with weak sight to Beatrice, who loves Dante (*Inf.* 2, 72) and was like Milton's Urania his heavenly Muse; for she it was who, by making him a Christian, had at the same time made *him* a poet, and in that sense, *her* own poem. Beatrice in turn descends to Hell and summons the poet-seer Virgil to rescue him by beginning to clarify his vision, so far as the author of *Aeneid* 6 could do so.[1] Just as Nessus at Chiron's, the only good Centaur's, command (*Inf.* 12, 98), and by Virgil's consent, temporarily takes the latter's place in the first ring of the seventh circle of Hell (*Inf.* 12, 114), so, also at his request (*Purg.* 7, 62), does Sordello, temporarily, in Ante-Purgatory, as a guide to the Valley of the Princes; and both Chiron by tradition and Sordello in fact were poets. Virgil's limited vision is supplemented in turn by the poet Statius, who, being once like Virgil a pagan poet, was set on the way to Christianity by reading the Fourth Eclogue (*Purg.* 22, 73: *per te poeta fui, per te cristiano*) and thereby gained a deeper insight than Virgil's into the way in which God as Poet sees things (*Purg.* 25, 31–3); and the two together leave Dante to Beatrice in the Earthly Paradise, having by their talk to one another (the talk of poets about poetry) so far clarified his mind as to give it *a poetar intelletto*, insight into the art of composing poetry, that is, of expressing verbally things as a

[1] Cp. *Aen.* 6, 724 ff. which state a Stoic conception of the one impersonal Spirit (*Mens*) that informs the Whole; true so far as it goes, for the personal God of Christianity as well as transcending, is also immanent in, the Universe, but for which fact it would instantly cease to exist.

poet sees them. Beatrice whose poetic insight, now that she is beatified, has been perfected by her love of God, and who out of her love for Dante and concern for his spiritual welfare has descended from Heaven, meets him in the Earthly Paradise, and conducts him thence through the nine heavens, in succession, to the extreme limits of the material universe, where she ushers him into the Empyrean, with his mortal vision now clarified, but not yet sufficiently so that he can see God, as he essentially is, face to face. The Empyrean is outside space and time, a fact represented in the poem by Dante's falling into a trance.[1] In this trance, the poet, by the special grace of God, procured for him by the Virgin Mary, to whom God refuses nothing, invoked thereto by the mystic St. Bernard, enters on the mystic way; which culminates (or, rather, which he 'believes' culminated) in the actual experience, instantaneous or timeless (hence unimaginable, therefore incommunicable) of having his spiritual vision made one with the Divine, so that up to his capacity while still retaining his individuality, he sees the world as God sees it—one perfectly ordered whole (κόσμος) wherein consists its beauty— and the Godhead as It sees, and, seeing, loves and smiles upon Itself—three Persons in one sole God and two Natures in one Person,

l'*Amor* che move il Sol e l'altre stelle.

That, in sum, is the literal meaning of the *Divine Comedy*, and the great role that poetry plays dramatically in its doctrines and practical ends. And there is no need to allegorize it except at those places, always clearly indicated, where the poet himself tells the reader that he intends him to do so. Nor except in those incidents, relatively few in number, where the narrative makes it obvious that this *must* be done (notably *Purg*. 29, where the pageant in the Earthly Paradise is part of the action, at a crucial point in it, like the play within the play in *Hamlet*) is there need to allegorize the characters in the story more than in any poetry its metaphorical language suggests, allegory itself being only

---

[1] It is thus that I understand the *assonna* of *Par*. 32, 139.

an extended metaphor. For the *dramatis personae* are all of them real persons, in the double sense of being true to history and, as such, highly complex human beings, and not mere personifications of a single virtue or vice. It is true that, as an orthodox theologian, Dante puts sinners unrepentant at death into Hell; or rather sees them eagerly putting themselves there[1] (for God never sends much less predestinates anyone to Hell, but on the contrary became incarnate and died to save them from going there). But, as a poet he pities them and makes the reader too pity them—even an Ugolino.[2] For great poets, if great dramatists like Dante, see each individual as a complex whole of virtues and vices (which in fact every human being is, even the saintliest) and, to be true to their vision must make him such in their poems.[3] For the same reason, whenever

[1] Cp. *Inf.* 3, 124–6.

[2] If any reader disagrees, let him honestly compare his emotional reaction to the horrible picture of Ugolino's bestial repast in *Inf.* 32, 127–9 with his reaction to exactly the same picture of it repeated in Ib. 33, 76, *after* Ugolino has told Dante (*personaggio*) how he and his children were starved to death; and let him ask himself if that story has not considerably modified the feelings with which he read the former *terzina*, and if so in what way. If it has done so, as it surely must, by way of creating some sympathy with Ugolino, then Dante the poet and no one else is responsible. We have an instance of a virtue, paternal love, still being exercised and without misuse of it, in Hell as it had been in Ugolino's lifetime; for he would gladly have died to save his children from death; and we have the highest authority for saying that no father can have greater love for his son than this. Dante the poet makes as little of Ugolino's treachery as he makes much of his paternal love; or rather by setting them equally in conflict with one another creates in him a figure of tragedy, as he does in Virgil himself, and in Farinata, Ulysses and Brunetto Latini, each in his own way.

[3] 'If the allegoric personage [in an allegory] be strongly individualized, so as to interest us, we cease to think of it as an allegory; and, if it does not interest us, it had better be away'. (S. T. Coleridge, *3rd lecture of the 1818 series on Gothic art and architecture*.)

The Dante whom the author of the *Comedy* imagines as walking through Hell is imagined to be a man still alive in the flesh (*Inf.* 28, 46)—a Christian now in grace, and as such bound by his creed never to confound the sinner with his sin, but to love (i.e. will the good of) the sinner while hating the sin; which is exactly what he does, except where, in the lowest depths of Hell the sin being punished is to Dante *poeta* so abominable that he makes Dante *personaggio* hate the sinner, Fra Alberigo, and thus confound him with his sin. He might in excuse have instanced Virgil *poeta*, who for the same reason makes Aeneas, who would have spared Lausus,

Dante's imagination and his theology are at odds, it is always the latter that gives way to the former, just as his science does also. Like all his contemporaries he took for granted that a poet, to deserve the name, must be 'doctus'; but throughout his life, from his earliest poem to his latest (the *Divine Comedy*) he was primarily a love-poet and, in flat contradiction of St. Thomas, ranked poets and their intuitive insight above philosophers and their conceptual knowledge; just as God, when he created the angels, *amori* as they all are, placed the Seraphim, the pre-eminently 'loving' spirits, higher and hence nearer to Himself than the Cherubim, the pre-eminently 'knowing' spirits; for the Seraphs partake more of His essence, which is Love not Reason. To know God man must first love Him. Nor is it surprising that the God-inspired *vates* such as Dante imagines himself to be, when writing the *Comedy*, should be in this matter ahead of his time. Though contemporary with the Cahorsine money-loving Pope John the 22nd— only less his *bête noire* than was Boniface the 8th—he sometimes seems to forecast the late Pope John the 23rd, and might even, if alive now, have recognized in that supremely Christian pope the *Veltro*, whom he longed for and confidently expected would in due time arrive.[1] That is why Dante strikes us as more 'up to date' than the medieval Catholic, or in one word, more charitable. For what the modern world needs, to cure its ills, is not more science, of which it has plenty, but more love, in the Fourth Gospel's sense of that word.

Now, to see the sum-total of things as God sees it was,

forget his *pietas* and slaughter his prisoners at Pallas's funeral in revenge for the latter's death, though they were quite innocent of it. The allegorizing theologian, by personifying the sin, identifies it with the sinner and thus hates both, since they are one and the same thing. For the *poet* Dante, such beings are unimaginable, even in Hell, till he reaches Lucifer who is purely allegorical—Death personified—and for that reason never, as Milton's Satan does, comes alive. All the characters in the *Comedy* are imagined as being true (or what Dante believes to be true) to history, and as such cannot be simultaneously allegorical. Nor in fact, while reading and under the spell of the poem, do we think of them as such, however much Dante the theologian may have intended us to do so.

[1] Cp. *Inf.* 1, 100–11.

for Dante, to see it as God, its Maker, its Poet, had seen it in idea; and, so seeing, had simultaneously created it as an 'ordered' whole, in which every single one of its countless constituents, from the most ingodded Seraph down to the minutest speck of material dust, was playing its predestined and proper part,[1] and all its values were in the right hierarchical relation to one another; and such an ordered universe Dante, when making nothing less than this the object of his own creative imagination, aimed at making his poem also; a poor poem doubtless—even infinitely so— when compared with God's, but nevertheless worthwhile making, if thereby he could even in the slightest degree induce mankind to see their moral and spiritual dis-orderliness. And just as God's poem was the object of Dante's imagination, so, *not God's* but Dante's poem should be in turn the object of the translator's imagination, when he tries to turn it into English, and must be similar in its effect. It must, so far as is possible, reproduce its original in the exact 'order' which is the original's form—the form that makes the Universe like unto God—if it is to deserve to be called a translation at all. Apart from the fact that the translator lacks Dante's penetrating intellect and soar-ing imagination, his translation will, even at its best, be but a pale reflection of a reflection, which, in comparison with its own original is, as its author is never tired of telling us, itself the palest of the pale. But the translator must at least strive to preserve his original's form, its 'order', and so to exercise his art of translation that if Nature's art is as it were the child, and Dante's the grandchild (cp. *Inf.* 11, 99–105) his own art can justly claim to be the great-grandchild of God's art. The one important exception is that, of the four arts thus related, God's art is unique in that He creates *ex nihilo* whereas the other three make their artefacts out of pre-existent material (cp. *Par.* 3, 86–7); God supplies His creation as her material to Nature,

[1] Including the evil, which, in creating the world, He foresaw would corrupt it, after the Fall, but which He would make subservient to its ultimate good by His Incarnation (the supreme proof of His love for erring mankind—cp. *Par.* 7, 30–3), which would never have taken place, had there been no Fall (cp. *Purg.* 3, 38).

Nature her artefact as his material to the poet, and the poet his poem as material to the translator, whose art, though ultimately derived from God's, is thus three times removed from it.

The effect of its original, the *Divine Comedy* itself, psychologically, upon the reader who may be conscious that his own visionary power is defective or perhaps sick unto death—a common state of mind in the present world—ought, if he reads the poem aright, to be that described by a poet (acutely aware that he had, spiritually, gone all to pieces) after he had heard Wordsworth recite a poem 'on the growth of an individual mind'. That poet was Coleridge and the poem which Wordsworth read to him was the as yet unpublished *Prelude*.

Coleridge's poem begins thus—and let the reader imagine that it is not Coleridge but he himself who is addressing not Wordsworth but Dante, after hearing the Divine Comedy read by him aloud from start to finish.

Friend of the wise! and teacher of the Good!
into my heart have I received that Lay
more than historic, that prophetic Lay
wherein (high theme by thee first sung aright)
of the foundation and the building up
of a human spirit thou hast dared to tell
what may be told, to *the understanding mind*
revealable; and what within the mind
by vital breathings secret as the soul
of vernal growth, oft quickens *in the heart*
thoughts all too deep for words!—Theme hard as high!

and ends thus:

And when . . .
that long sustainéd song finally closed, . . .
scarce conscious, and yet conscious of its close
I sat, my being blended in one thought
(thought was it? or aspiration? or resolve?)
absorbed, yet hanging still upon the sound—
and when I rose, *I found myself in prayer.*

Such, ideally speaking, should also be the effect of reading, to its close, a translation of the *Comedy*, if it can be truly described as being so faithful to its original as to be comparable with it *poetically* in value. This effect it can only achieve if like its original, though more faintly, it leaves one convinced that 'it is God's love—to be seen, felt, known, realized everywhere and always in human life—which is Dante's message to mankind. . . . That very love may call you to disappointments, batter you with undeserved blows, fling you aside rejected, yes, plunge you into hell, or bid you climb the bitter steep of Purgatory; but it will not leave you or forsake you; it will bring you out into the sweet table-land of peace; it will show you at length that life is always under the rule of that eternal love by which the sun, the stars and all creation move.'[1]

[1] Bishop W. Boyd Carpenter, concluding words of *The Spiritual Message of Dante* (London, 1914).

HELL

*

'As no man apprehends what vice is as he who is truly virtuous, no man knows Hell like him who converses in Heaven.'

*

'It is a heaven upon earth, when a man's mind rests on Providence, moves in Charity, and turns upon the poles of Truth.'

*

INFERNO

CANTO 1

Nᴇʟ mezzo del cammin di nostra vita
　mi ritrovai per una selva oscura,
　che la diritta via era smarrita. 　　　　　3
Ah quanto a dir qual era è cosa dura
　esta selva selvaggia e aspra e forte,
　che nel pensier rinnova la paura! 　　　　6
Tanto è amara che poco è più morte;
　ma per trattar del ben ch'io vi trovai
　dirò de l'altre cose ch'io v'ho scorte. 　　9
Io non so ben ridir com'io v'entrai,
　tant'era pieno di sonno a quel punto
　che la verace via abbandonai. 　　　　　12
Ma poi ch'io fui al piè d'un colle giunto,
　là dove terminava quella valle
　che m'avea di paura il cor compunto, 　　15
guardai in alto e vidi le sue spalle
　vestite già dei raggi del pianeta
　che mena dritto altrui per ogni calle. 　　18
Allor fu la paura un poco queta
　che nel lago del cor m'era durata
　la notte ch'io passai con tanta pieta. 　　21
E come quei che con lena affannata
　uscito fuor del pelago alla riva,
　si volge a l'acqua perigliosa, e guata, 　24
così l'animo mio, che ancor fuggiva,
　si volse a dietro a rimirar lo passo
　che non lasciò giammai persona viva. 　　27
Poi ch'ei posato un poco il corpo lasso,
　ripresi via per la piaggia deserta,
　sì che il piè fermo sempre era il più basso. 　30

HELL

CANTO 1

At midpoint of the journey of our life
　　I woke to find me astray in a dark wood,
　　perplexed by paths with the straight way at strife.
Ah, had I words, if such there be, that could
　　describe this forest wild and rough and dour,
　　by which, in thought, my terror is renew'd!
So bitter it is that death is scarcely more;
　　but of the good I found there I will treat
　　by saying what else there I'd discerned before.
I cannot well recall how I entered it,
　　so drowsy at that moment did I feel
　　when first from the true way I turned my feet.
But after I had reached the base of a hill
　　where to an end that valley came which had
　　so pierced my heart with fear and pierced it still,
I looked on high and saw its shoulders clad
　　already with the planet's beams whose light
　　leadeth men straight, through all paths good or bad.
Then did the fear a little lose its might,
　　which in my heart's lake had persisted there
　　through the long hours of such a piteous night.
And as a man who, gasping still for air,
　　'scaped from deep sea to shore and scarce alive,
　　turns to the perilous wave, his eyes a-stare,
so did my spirit, still a fugitive,
　　turn back to view the pass whose deadly power
　　ne'er let a body held in it survive.
My tired limbs somewhat rested, I once more
　　pursued my way across the lone hillside,
　　so that the firm foot was always the lower.

3

Ed ecco, quasi al cominciar de l'erta,
  una lonza leggiera e presta molto
  che di pel maculato era coperta;   33
e non mi si partìa dinanzi al volto
  anzi impediva tanto il mio cammino
  ch'io fui per ritornar più volte volto.   36
Tempo era dal principio del mattino,
  e il Sol montava in sù con quelle stelle
  ch'eran con lui quando l'amor divino   39
mosse da prima quelle cose belle,
  sì che a bene sperar m'era cagione
  di quella fera alla gaietta pelle   42
l'ora del tempo e la dolce stagione;
  ma non sì, che paura non mi desse
  la vista che m'apparve d'un leone.   45
Questi parea che contra me venesse
  con la test'alta e con rabbiosa fame,
  sì che parea che l'aere ne temesse.   48
E d'una lupa, che di tutte brame
  sembiava carca ne la sua magrezza,
  e molte genti fe' già viver grame.   51
Questa mi porse tanto di gravezza
  con la paura che uscìa di sua vista,
  ch'io perdei la speranza de l'altezza.   54
E qual è quei che volontieri acquista
  e giugne il tempo che perder lo face,
  che in tutti i suoi pensier piange e s'attrista,   57
tal me fece la bestia senza pace,
  che, venendomi incontro, a poco a poco
  mi ripigneva là dove il Sol tace.   60
Mentre ch'io rovinava in basso loco,
  dinanzi a gli occhi mi si fu offerto
  chi per lungo silenzio parea fioco.   63
Quando vidi costui nel gran diserto
  « Miserere di me » gridai a lui,
  « qual che tu sii, od ombra od uomo certo ».   66
Risposemi: « Non uomo, uomo già fui,
  e li parenti miei furon lombardi
  e mantovani per patria ambedui.   69

And lo, just ere the steep began, there hied
  a leopard, light and nimble in the extreme,
  covered with hair by spots diversified;
nor did it shun me, rather did it seem
  so much to block my road of set design,
  that, to retreat, my feet were oft in trim.
The hour was that when dawn begins to shine:
  the Sun was mounting with the stars whose ways
  marched with his own, when first by Love divine
were set in motion those fair presences;
  thus the sweet season and the time of day
  alike conspired within my heart to raise
good hope of that wild beast with skin so gay;
  yet not such as to leave me undismay'd
  when there appeared a lion in the way;
which appeared coming against me, with his head
  held high and with a raging hunger, so
  that even the air appeared thereof afraid;
and a she-wolf, that looked as lean as though
  still burdened with all ravenings—yea, her might
  ere this had made much people live in woe;
which, for the fear that issued from the sight
  of her, o'erwhelmed me with a lassitude
  so heavy, that I lost hope of the height.
And even as he who joys in gaining, should
  the time arrive which makes him lose, will suit
  whate'er he thinks of to his saddened mood;
such was I rendered by the unresting brute,
  which, coming against me, pushed me pace by pace
  back to the region where the Sun is mute.
While I was ruining to that low place,
  before my eyes presented himself one
  who seemed enfeebled through long silentness.
To him, in that great waste where else was none,
  '*Miserere mei*,' I cried, 'whatso thou be,
  whether a shade or real man!' Whereon
'Not man—man once I *was*,' he answered me:
  'my parents, members of the Lombard State,
  were Mantuans by birth, both he and she.

Nacqui, sub Iulio, ancor che fosse tardi,
 e vissi a Roma sotto il buono Augusto,
 al tempo de li dei falsi e bugiardi.   72
Poeta fui, e cantai di quel giusto
 figliuol d'Anchise che venne da Troia
 poi che il superbo Ilion fu combusto.   75
Ma tu perchè ritorni a tanta noia?
 Perchè non sali il dilettoso monte
 ch'è principio e cagion di tutta gioia?»   78
« Or sei tu quel Virgilio e quella fonte
 che spandi di parlar sì largo fiume?»
 risposi io lui con vergognosa fronte.   81
« O de gli altri poeti onore e lume,
 vagliami il lungo studio e il grande amore
 che m'ha fatto cercar lo tuo volume.   84
Tu sei lo mio maestro e 'l mio autore;
 tu sei solo colui da cui io tolsi
 lo bello stile che m'ha fatto onore.   87
Vedi la bestia per cui io mi volsi:
 aiutami da lei, famoso saggio,
 ch'ella mi fa tremar le vene e i polsi».   90
« A te convien tenere altro viaggio»
 rispose poi che lagrimar mi vide,
 « se vuoi campar d'esto loco selvaggio;   93
chè quella bestia per la qual tu gride,
 non lascia altrui passar per la sua via,
 ma tanto l'impedisce che l'uccide;   96
e ha natura sì malvagia e ria,
 che mai non empie la bramosa voglia,
 e dopo il pasto ha più fame che pria.   99
Molti son gli animali a cui s'ammoglia,
 e più saranno ancora, in fin che il Veltro
 verrà, che la farà morir con doglia.   102
Questi non ciberà terra nè peltro,
 ma sapienza, amore e virtute,
 e sua nazion sarà tra Feltro e Feltro.   105
Di quell'umile Italia fia salute
 per cui morì la vergine Camilla,
 Eurialo e Turno e Niso, di ferute.   108

Sub Julio was I born, albeit 'twas late,
  and lived at Rome when the good Augustus reign'd,
  what time false gods that lied were worshipped yet.
Poet I *was*, and sang of virtue's friend,
  that just Anchìsiades who came from Troy,
  when flames had brought proud Ilion to an end.
But thou, to misery so fearful why
  turn'st back? Why climb'st thou not the blissful mount?'
  which is the cause and principle of all joy?'
'And art thou, then, that Vìrgil, thou that fount
  whence pours a stream of speech so broad and bright?'
  thus I replied to him with bashful front.
'O of all other poets honour and light,
  may the great love that long hath made me pore
  over thy volume stead me in this plight.
Thou art my master and my author; nor
  from any save from thee came I to take
  the style whose beauty I've been honoured for.
Behold the beast which turned me backward: make
  me safe from her, renownéd sage, for she
  causes each vein and pulse in me to quake.'
'Another course must needs be held by thee'
  he answered, when he marked my sobbing breath,
  'wilt thou from out this savage place win free:
for yonder beast which now occasioneth
  thy cries, lets no one pass along her way,
  but so impedes him as to cause his death;
and is so evil, so malign, no prey
  can ever glut her greedy appetite,
  which feeding does but aggravate, not stay.
Many are the animals she's paired with: quite
  as many more there will be, till the Hound
  comes, who with painful death shall quell her might.
Not lands nor pelf he'll feed on—nought beyond
  wisdom and love and valour; and between
  Feltro and Feltro his birthplace shall be found.
Safety for that poor Italy he'll win
  which Turnus, Nisus and Euryalus bled
  and died for, and Camilla the virgin.

7

Questi la caccerà per ogni villa
  fin che l'avrà rimessa ne l'inferno,
  là onde invidia prima dipartilla.   111
Ond'io per lo tuo me' penso e discerno
  che tu mi segui; ed io sarò tua guida
  e trarrotti di qui per loco eterno,   114
ove udirai le disperate strida,
  vedrai gli antichi spiriti dolenti
  che la seconda morte ciascun grida;   117
e vederai color che son contenti
  nel foco, perchè speran di venire,
  quando che sia, a le beate genti.   120
A le qua' poi se tu vorrai salire,
  anima fia a ciò più di me degna:
  con lei ti lascerò nel mio partire;   123
chè quello imperador che lassù regna,
  perch'io fui ribellante a la sua legge,
  non vuol che in sua città per me si vegna.   126
In tutte parti impera e quivi regge;
  quivi è la sua città e l'alto seggio:
  o felice colui cui ivi elegge!»   129
E io a lui: « Poeta, io ti richieggio
  per quello Dio che tu non conoscesti,
  a ciò ch'io fugga questo male e peggio,   132
che tu mi meni là dov'or dicesti,
  sì ch'io veggia la porta di san Pietro
  e color cui tu fai cotanto mesti».   135
Allor si mosse, ed io li tenni retro.

CANTO 2

Lo giorno se n'andava, e l'aere bruno
  toglieva gli animai che sono in Terra
  da le fatiche loro, ed io sol uno   3
m'apparecchiava a sostener la guerra
  sì del cammino e sì de la pietate,
  che ritrarrà la mente che non erra.   6

'Tis he will hunt the wolf from stead to stead,
   till back in hell he puts her by duress,
   e'en there whence first by envy she was sped.
Therefore I judge this fittest for thy case—
   to follow me, and I will be thy guide
   and draw thee hence through an eternal place,
where thou shalt hear them crying whose hope hath died,
   shalt see the olden spirits in pain who attest
   by shrieks the second death wherein they abide;
and thou shalt see those who contented rest
   within the fire, as hoping in the end,
   come when it may, to arrive among the Blest.
To whom thereafter wouldst thou fain ascend,
   there'll be, for that, a worthier soul than I;
   she, when I leave thee, will thy steps befriend:
for that imperial Ruler, there on high,
   since I was alien to his ordering,
   will have none to his court through me draw nigh.
In all parts he is emperor, there he's king;
   there is his city and his lofty seat:
   oh blest whom thither he elects to bring!'
And I made answer: 'Poet, I entreat
   thee by that God thou knewest not, that so
   I may escape this evil and worse than it,
to bring me thither where thou saidst but now
   I may behold Saint Peter's gate and find
   those thou describest as so full of woe.'
Then he moved on, and I kept close behind.

CANTO 2

Day was departing, and the air, embrown'd,
   was taking all alive on Earth away
   from their sore labours; me alone it found
arming myself to undergo the fray
   alike with pity and with the road ahead,
   which my unerring memory shall portray.

O Muse, o alto ingegno, or m'aiutate;
  o mente, che scrivesti ciò ch'io vidi,
  qui si parrà la tua nobilitate.   9

Io cominciai: « Poeta che mi guidi,
  guarda la mia virtù s'ella è possente,
  prima che a l'alto passo tu mi fidi.   12

Tu dici che di Silvio lo parente,
  corruttibile ancora, ad immortale
  secolo andò; e fu sensibilmente.   15

Però se l'avversario d'ogni male
  cortese i fu, pensando l'alto effetto
  che uscir dovea di lui, e il chi, e il quale, 18

non pare indegno ad uomo d'intelletto:
  chè ei fu dell'alma Roma e di suo impero
  ne l'Empireo ciel per padre eletto.   21

La quale e il quale, a voler dir lo vero,
  fu stabilita per lo loco santo
  u' siede il successor del maggior Piero. 24

Per quest'andata onde li dài tu vanto,
  intese cose che furon cagione
  di sua vittoria e del papale ammanto. 27

Andovvi poi lo Vas d'elezione
  per recarne conforto a quella fede
  ch'è principio a la via di salvazione. 30

Ma io perchè venirvi? o chi il concede?
  Io non Enea, io non Paolo sono:
  me degno a ciò nè io nè altri crede.   33

Per che, se del venire io m'abbandono,
  temo che la venuta non sia folle:
  sei savio, e intendi me' ch'io non ragiono ». 36

E qual è quei che disvuol ciò che volle
  e per novi pensier cangia proposta,
  sì che dal cominciar tutto si tolle,   39

tal mi fec'io in quell'oscura costa,
  perchè pensando consumai l'impresa
  che fu nel cominciar cotanto tosta.   42

« Se io ho ben la tua parola intesa »
  rispose del magnanimo quell'ombra,
  « l'anima tua è da viltade offesa;   45

O Muses, o high Wit, be now my aid;
 O Mind, that wrotest that which I descried,
 here shall be shown how nobly thou art bred.

I began: 'Poet, thou that art my guide,
 look to my strength, if it suffices, ere
 to the hard pass thou trust me all untried.

The father of Silvius—so thy words declare—
 still mortal, to a world where death is not,
 once went, thereof being sensibly aware.

But if the Foe of every evil wrought
 courteously with him, weighing the high effect—
 his destined issue, who it was and what,

this seems not undeserved, when we reflect
 how of genial Rome and of her empire he
 in the empyréan was sealed as sire-elect:

both which (to speak plain truth) divine decree
 established as the sanctuary where
 reigns the successor to great Peter's see.

This journey, of which thou art the blazoner,
 instructed him in things from which there grew
 his victory and the papal mantle: there

went afterward the Chosen Vessel too,
 to bring thence confirmation of that faith
 which opens out salvation to man's view.

But I, why thither come? Who is it saith
 I may? I'm not Aeneas, Paul I'm not:
 me none deems fit—I least—to tread their path.

To come, then, would I fear be folly, if brought
 I *were* to coming: thou art wise—more skilled
 to understand, than I to speak, my thought.'

And as doth he who un-wills what he willed
 and through new thoughts changes his first intent,
 fain now to leave it wholly unfulfilled,

did I, by too much thinking o'er the event,
 consume on that dim slope the enterprise
 at first embarked on so incontinent.

'If rightly what thou meanest I surmise,'
 that shade of the magnanimous replied,
 'thy soul by cowardice now crippled lies,

11

la qual spesse fiate l'uomo ingombra
  sì, che d'onrata impresa lo rivolve,
  come falso veder bestia quand'ombra.   48
Da questa tema acciò che tu ti solve
  dirotti perch'io venni e quel che intesi
  nel primo punto che di te mi dolve.   51
Io era tra color che son sospesi,
  e donna mi chiamò beata e bella,
  tal che di comandare io la richiesi.   54
Lucevan gli occhi suoi più che la stella;
  e cominciommi a dir soave e piana,
  con angelica voce, in sua favella: 57
— O anima cortese mantovana,
  di cui la fama ancor nel mondo dura
  e durerà quanto il mondo lontana: 60
l'amico mio, e non de la ventura,
  ne la diserta piaggia è impedito
  sì nel cammin, che volto è per paura;   63
e temo che non sia già sì smarrito,
  ch'io mi sia tardi al soccorso levata
  per quel che ho di lui in cielo udito.   66
Or movi, e con la tua parola ornata
  e con ciò ch'è mestieri al suo campare
  l'aiuta sì ch'io ne sia consolata.   69
Io son Beatrice, che ti faccio andare;
  vegno di loco ove tornar desio;
  amor mi mosse, che mi fa parlare.   72
Quando sarò dinanzi al Signor mio
  di te mi loderò sovente a Lui —.
  Tacette allora; e poi cominciai io: 75
— O donna di virtù sola per cui
  l'umana spezie eccede ogni contento
  da quel ciel ch'ha minor li cerchi sui,   78
tanto m'aggrada il tuo comandamento,
  che l'ubbidir, se già fosse, m'è tardi:
  più non t'è uopo aprirmi il tuo talento.   81
Ma dimmi la cagion che non ti guardi
  de lo scender quaggiuso in questo centro
  da l'ampio loco ove tornar tu ardi —.   84

by which a man is oft so clogged and tied,
   that from a noble quest he backs away,
   as shies a beast at objects ill-descried.
But, that thou rid thyself of this dismay,
   I'll tell thee why I came, the words—and whence—
   which made me first such ruth for thee display.
I was among those biding in suspense,
   when hailed me a dame, so blesséd and so fair,
   I begged her to command my obedience.
Her eyes were beaming—brighter shines no star:
   and thus, in low clear tones she spoke to me
   with a voice sweet as angels' voices are:
"O Mantuan spirit, soul of courtesy,
   whose fame yet lasteth in the world and shall
   unfading last, as long as world there be,
there's one who is my friend—I cannot call
   him Fortune's—on the lone hillside waylaid,
   so let, that terror makes him backward fall.
Indeed, I fear from things about him said
   in Heav'n, he may already so far err,
   that I have risen too late to bring him aid.
Armed with thine ornate speech and with whate'er
   is needful for his rescue, move, then, quick
   to help him and be thus my comforter.
I'm Beatrice, I that bid thee go; to seek
   the place I come from thou behold'st me fain:
   love moved me, and 'tis love that makes me speak.
When once I stand before my Lord again,
   to Him oft-times I'll praise thy graciousness."
   Here she fell silent, and I answered then:
"O lady of the sole virtue able to place
   mankind above all else contained within
   that heav'n which wheels the most confined in space,
so much thy bidding pleases me that, e'en
   were it already done, I'd seem too slow;
   thy will of me need'st say no more to win.
But say why to this centre here below
   thou reck'st not of descending from the wide
   room back to which thou art on fire to go."

13

— Dacchè tu vuoi saper cotanto addentro,
    dirotti brevemente — mi rispose
    — perch'io non temo di venir qua entro.   87

Temer si dee di sole quelle cose
    ch'hanno potenza di fare altrui male:
    de l'altre no, chè non son paurose.   90

Io son fatta da Dio, sua mercè, tale
    che la vostra miseria non mi tange
    nè fiamma d'esto incendio non m'assale.   93

Donna è gentil nel ciel, che si compiange
    di questo impedimento ov'io ti mando,
    sì che duro giudicio lassù frange.   96

Questa chiese Lucia in suo dimando,
    e disse: 'Or ha bisogno il tuo fedele
    di te, e io a te lo raccomando'.   99

Lucia, nimica di ciascun crudele,
    si mosse, e venne al loco dov'io era,
    che mi sedea con l'antica Rachele.   102

Disse: 'Beatrice, loda di Dio vera,
    chè non soccorri quel che t'amò tanto
    che uscì per te de la volgare schiera?   105

Non odi tu la pieta del suo pianto?
    non vedi tu la morte che il combatte
    su la fiumana ove il mar non ha vanto?'   108

Al mondo non fur mai persone ratte
    a far lor pro o a fuggir lor danno
    com'io, dopo cotai parole fatte,   111

venni quaggiù dal mio beato scanno,
    fidandomi nel tuo parlare onesto
    che onora te e quei che udito l'hanno —.   114

Poscia che m'ebbe ragionato questo,
    gli occhi lucenti lagrimando volse;
    per che mi fece del venir più presto.   117

E venni a te così com'ella volse;
    dinanzi a quella fiera ti levai
    che del bel monte il corto andar ti tolse.   120

Dunque che è? perchè, perchè ristai?
    perchè tanta viltà nel cuore allette?
    perchè ardire e franchezza non hai   123

14

"Since thou wouldst penetrate so far inside
   this matter, I will briefly tell thee why
   I fear not entering hither," she replied.
"Those things alone are rightly feared whereby
   one can be injured: but not so the rest,
   for, of them, none hath power to terrify.
I am so framed by God (his grace be blest)
   that me your misery touches not, nor me
   doth yonder burning with its flame molest.
There dwells in Heaven a noble Lady; she,
   pitying this let wherewith I'd have thee deal,
   makes the stern Judge up there yield to her plea.
She called to Lucy, wording her appeal
   thuswise: 'Thy liegeman stands in urgent need
   of thee, and I entrust to thee his weal.'
Hied Lucy, hating as she ever did
   aught cruel, and, where *I* sat neighbour to
   the ancient Rachel, thither came with speed.
She said: 'Why dost not, Beatrice, thou true
   praise of God, succour him who loved thee so
   that for thy sake he left the vulgar crew
Dost thou not hear his piteous cry of woe?
   not see the death which grapples him on the flood
   whose rage not even the sea's can overcrow?'
None on earth ever with such promptitude
   sought his own triumph or shunned his own defeat,
   as I, when she had made these words conclude,
descended hither from my blesséd seat,
   confiding in thy gracious rhetoric,
   which honours thee and those who've harkened it."
As soon as she had left off thus to speak,
   she turned away her shining eyes and wept,
   which to come hither made me still more quick.
I came to thee as she desired; I stepp'd
   between thee and that beast by which from going
   straight up the sunlit mountain thou wert kept.
What ails thee, then? Why, why hold back, allowing
   such craven fear to harbour in thy breast?
   why art thou not a bold free spirit showing,

poscia che tai tre donne benedette
　curan di te ne la corte del cielo,
　e il mio parlar tanto ben t'impromette?»　　126
Quali i fioretti dal notturno gelo
　chinati e chiusi, poi che il Sol li imbianca
　si drizzan tutti aperti in loro stelo,　　129
tal mi fec'io di mia virtute stanca;
　e tanto buono ardire al cor mi corse,
　ch'io cominciai come persona franca:　　132
« Oh pietosa colei che mi soccorse!
　e tu cortese, che ubbidisti tosto
　a le vere parole che ti porse.　　135
Tu m'hai con desiderio il cor disposto
　sì al venir con le parole tue,
　ch'io son tornato nel primo proposto.　　138
Or va, chè un sol volere è d'ambedue:
　tu duca, tu signore e tu maestro».
　Così li dissi; e poi che mosso fue　　141
entrai per lo cammino alto e silvestro.

CANTO 3

« Per me si va ne la città dolente,
　per me si va ne l'eterno dolore,
　per me si va tra la perduta gente.　　3
Giustizia mosse il mio alto fattore;
　fecemi la divina potestate,
　la somma sapienza e il primo amore.　　6
Dinanzi a me non fur cose create
　se non eterne, e io eterno duro.
　Lasciate ogni speranza voi ch'entrate».　　9
Queste parole di colore oscuro
　vid'io scritte al sommo d'una porta;
　per ch'io: « Maestro, il senso lor m'è duro».　　12

when three such ladies, so supremely blest,
   work for thy welfare in the court on high,
   and I stand so much pledged to thy interest?'
As little flowers, all closed and wilted by
   the night-frost, soon as brightens them the Sun,
   straight'ning their stems, stand up with opened eye,
so with my drooping powers by me was done;
   and I replied like to a man set free,
   into my heart did so much courage run:
'To aid me thus, oh, full of pity she!
   and courteous thou, to obey with quick consent
   the words of truth which she set forth to thee.
Thou hast my heart with so much ardour bent
   on coming, by thy words, that now in troth
   I have returned unto my first intent.
Now on, for one sole will is in us both;
   thou guide, thou lord, thou master.' In this mode
   I spake: and when he set forth, nothing loth
I entered on the wild, deep-sunken road.

CANTO 3

'*THROUGH me ye pass into the city of woe,*
   through me ye pass eternal pain to prove,
   through me ye pass among the lost below.
Justice did my sublime creator move:
   I was created by the Power divine,
   the sovereign Wisdom and the primal Love.
Save things eternal, ere this being of mine
   nought was, and I eternally endure.
   Abandon every hope, you that come in.'
These words in colour of a tint obscure
   I saw inscribed above a gate and said:
   'Master, of what they mean I feel unsure.'

Ed egli a me come persona accorta:
« Qui si convien lasciare ogni sospetto;
ogni viltà convien che qui sia morta.   15
Noi siam venuti al loco ov'io t'ho detto
che tu vedrai le genti dolorose
ch'hanno perduto il ben de l'intelletto ».   18
E poi che la sua mano a la mia pose
con lieto volto, ond'io mi confortai,
mi mise dentro a le segrete cose.   21
Quivi sospiri, pianti ed alti guai
risonavan per l'aere sanza stelle,
per ch'io al cominciar ne lacrimai.   24
Diverse lingue, orribili favelle,
parole di dolore, accenti d'ira,
voci alte e fioche, e suon di man con elle,   27
facevano un tumulto il qual s'aggira
sempre in quell'aura sanza tempo tinta,
come la rena quando a turbo spira.   30
E io, che avea d'orror la testa cinta,
dissi: « Maestro, che è quel ch'i' odo?
e che gente è che par nel duol sì vinta? »   33
Ed egli a me: « Questo misero modo
tengon l'anime triste di coloro
che visser sanza infamia e sanza lodo.   36
Mischiate sono a quel cattivo coro
de gli angeli che non furon ribelli
nè fur fedeli a Dio, ma per sè foro.   39
Cacciarli i ciel per non esser men belli,
nè lo profondo inferno li riceve,
chè alcuna gloria i rei avrebber d'elli ».   42
E io: « Maestro, che è tanto greve
a lor, che lamentar li fa si forte? »
Rispose: « Dicerolti molto breve.   45
Questi non hanno speranza di morte,
e la lor cieca vita è tanto bassa,
che invidiosi son d'ogni altra sorte.   48
Fama di loro il mondo esser non lassa;
misericordia e giustizia li sdegna:
non ragioniam di lor, ma guarda e passa ».   51

And he to me, like one experiencéd:
   'Here needs must all misgiving straight be check'd;
   all craven scruples needs must here be dead.
We've reached the place I told thee to expect,
   where thou shalt see the folk to sorrow bann'd
   through having lost the good of the intellect.'
Having said this, he laid on mine his hand
   with cheerful mien and put me, thus consoled,
   among the things of that secluded land.
There sighs, sobs and loud lamentations rolled
   resounding 'neath the starless firmament,
   so that at first my tears ran uncontrolled.
Uncouth tongues, horrible utterances were blent
   with words of woe, accents of anger, sound
   of hands that joined with voices loud and faint
to make thereof a tumult, swirling round
   without cease, in that air forever dyed,
   as sand does, when the whirlwind is unbound.
And I, whose head was girt with horror, cried:
   'Master, whence comes this din? What people crazed
   as though by torture in this place abide?'
And he to me: 'This dismal strain is raised
   by those disbodied wretches who were loth,
   when living, to be either blamed or praised.
They're mixed with that bad choir of angels, both
   unfaithful and unwilling to rebel
   against God, who but with themselves kept troth.
Fear to lose beauty caused the heavens to expel
   these caitiffs; nor, lest to the damned they then
   gave cause to boast, receives them the deep hell.'
And I: 'But, Master, what so grievous pain
   afflicts them, that they raise this vehement cry?'
   He answered: 'I will tell thee in briefest vein.
These have no hope that they will ever die,
   and their blind life is here so spat upon,
   they look on all lots else with envious eye.
The world allows no mention of them, none;
   mercy and justice visit them with scorn:
   of them let's talk not: just look, then pass on.'

E io che riguardai, vidi un'insegna
    che girando correva tanto ratta
    che d'ogni posa mi pareva indegna;   54
e dietro le venia sì lunga tratta
    di gente, ch'io non averei creduto
    che morte tanta n'avesse disfatta.   57
Poscia ch'io v'ebbi alcun riconosciuto,
    vidi e conobbi l'ombra di colui
    che fece per viltà il gran rifiuto.   60
Incontanente intesi e certo fui
    che questa era la setta de' cattivi
    a Dio spiacenti ed ai nemici sui.   63
Questi sciaurati, che mai non fur vivi,
    erano ignudi e stimolati molto
    da mosconi e da vespe ch'eran ivi.   66
Elle rigavan lor di sangue il volto,
    che, mischiato di lacrime, ai lor piedi
    da fastidiosi vermi era ricolto.   69
E poi che a riguardare oltre mi diedi,
    vidi gente a la riva d'un gran fiume;
    per ch'io dissi: « Maestro, or mi concedi   72
ch'io sappia quali sono e qual costume
    le fa di trapassar parer sì pronte,
    com'io discerno per lo fioco lume ».   75
Ed egli a me: « Le cose ti fien conte
    quando noi fermerem li nostri passi
    su la trista riviera d'Acheronte ».   78
Allor, con gli occhi vergognosi e bassi,
    temendo no 'l mio dir li fosse grave,
    infino al fiume di parlar mi trassi.   81
Ed ecco verso noi venir per nave
    un vecchio bianco per antico pelo,
    gridando: « Guai a voi, anime prave!   84
Non isperate mai veder lo cielo:
    io vegno per menarvi a l'altra riva,
    ne le tenebre eterne, in caldo e in gelo.   87
E tu che sei costì, anima viva,
    partiti da cotesti che son morti ».
    Ma poi che vide ch'io non mi partiva,   90

And, as I gazed, I saw a banner borne
  whirling along so fast, it seemed a thing,
  as having earned no rest, thereof forlorn.
Behind it followed in an endless string
  a train so long, I scarce could deem it true
  death had undone such hosts past numbering,
When some there I had recognized, there too
  the shade of him who made through cowardice
  the great refusal I both saw and knew.
Straightway I understood that surely this
  could be no other than the abandoned race
  odious to God and to his enemies.
These recreants who had ne'er possessed the grace
  really to live, were naked and sore stung
  by wasps and gadflies that infest this place.
These streaked with blood their cheeks, and from them wrung
  tears, mingled with the blood, that down below
  was licked up by foul worms they trod among.
Then, as I searched what else the place might show,
  I saw folk on the bank of a great stream;
  so I said: 'Master, grant me now to know
who those are, and what instinct makes them seem
  thus eager to pass over and be gone,
  so far as I discern by this faint gleam.'
And he to me: 'Thou'lt be informed thereon
  when halt we at the spot where now we aim,
  upon the dismal shore of Acheron.'
Then, with my eyes cast down and full of shame,
  fearing my words offensive to his ear,
  I forbore speech till to the stream we came.
And lo, to us-ward on shipboard drew near
  one, white with hoary locks, exceeding old,
  exclaiming, 'Woe to you, spirits sinister!
Nevermore hope to see the heavens unfold:
  I come to waft you to the farther shore,
  to eternal darkness, into heat and cold.
But thou there, soul alive, shalt not pass o'er:
  part thyself from among these who are dead.'
  Then, seeing me yet stand where I stood before,

disse: « Per altre vie, per altri porti
 verrai a piaggia, non qui; per passare
 più lieve legno convien che ti porti ».   93
E il duca a lui: « Caron, non ti crucciare:
 vuolsi così colà dove si puote
 ciò che si vuole; e più non dimandare ». 96
Quinci fur quete le lanose gote
 al nocchier de la livida palude,
 che intorno a gli occhi avea di fiamme rote. 99
Ma quell'anime, ch'eran lasse e nude,
 cangiar colore e dibattero i denti
 ratto che inteser le parole crude. 102
Bestemmiavano Dio e i lor parenti,
 l'umana spezie, e il loco, e il tempo, e il seme
 di lor semenza e di lor nascimenti. 105
Poi si raccolser tutte quante insieme,
 forte piangendo, a la riva malvagia
 che attende ciascun uom che Dio non teme. 108
Caron dimonio, con occhi di bragia,
 loro accennando tutte le raccoglie;
 batte col remo qualunque s'adagia. 111
Come d'autunno si levan le foglie
 l'una appresso de l'altra, fin che il ramo
 vede a la terra tutte le sue spoglie, 114
similemente il mal seme d'Adamo:
 gittansi di quel lito ad una ad una
 per cenni, come augel per suo richiamo. 117
Così sen vanno su per l'onda bruna,
 ed avanti che sian di là discese
 anche di qua nova schiera s'aduna. 120
« Figliuol mio » disse il maestro cortese,
 « quelli che muoion ne l'ira di Dio
 tutti convegnon qui d'ogni paese. 123
E pronti sono a trapassar lo rio
 chè la divina giustizia li sprona
 sì, che la tema si volge in disio. 126
Quinci non passa mai anima buona;
 e però, se Caron di te si lagna,
 ben puoi sapere omai che il suo dir suona ». 129

'By other ways, by other ports,' he said,
  'not here, thou'lt reach the coast of thy desire:
  a lighter craft than this must serve thy stead.'
To him my leader: 'Charon, quell thine ire:
  'tis so willed there, where there is power to do
  that which is willed, and more forbear to enquire.'
Quiet thenceforth the fleecy jawbones grew
  of him, the pilot of the livid fen,
  tho' flame still round his eyes red circles drew.
But they, those weary naked wraiths of men,
  grew pale and gnashed their teeth, when once the worth
  of the harsh words he spoke had pierced their ken.
God they blasphemed, their parents, man on earth
  created, and the place, the time, the seed
  of their engendering and of their birth.
Then, all together, weeping loudly, did
  they congregate unto that evil shore
  awaiting those who pay to God no heed.
With eyes of glowing coal that demon hoar,
  Charon, makes signs to and collects them all:
  any that linger smites he with his oar.
Like as in autumn leaves drop off and fall,
  one, and then one, till all its finery
  the bough sees strewn on the earth beyond recall;
so on the marge wait Adam's progeny
  ill-born, and one by one fling themselves thence,
  at signals, as to its lure a hawk will fly.
Thus o'er the murky wave depart they hence,
  and ere they land upon the farther side,
  a fresh troop is on this one growing dense.
'Know thou, dear son,' explained the courteous guide,
  'that, drawn from every land, assemble here
  all those who in the wrath of God have died.
And they thus eager are to cross the mere,
  for divine justice goads them, so that they
  now desire that which once aroused their fear.
No soul that's good doth ever pass this way:
  therefore, if Charon of thyself complain,
  know now what meaning in his utterance lay.'

23

Finito questo, la buia campagna
 tremò si forte, che de lo spavento
 la mente di sudore ancor mi bagna.   132
La terra lagrimosa diede vento
 che balenò una luce vermiglia
 la qual mi vinse ciascun sentimento; 135
e caddi come l'uom cui sonno piglia.

CANTO 4

Rᴜᴘᴘᴇᴍɪ l'alto sonno ne la testa
 un greve tuono, sì ch'io mi riscossi
 come persona ch'è per forza desta; 3
e l'occhio riposato intorno mossi
 dritto levato, e fiso riguardai
 per conoscer lo loco dov'io fossi. 6
Vero è che in su la proda mi trovai
 de la valle d'abisso dolorosa
 che tuono accoglie d'infiniti guai. 9
Oscura e profonda era e nebulosa,
 tanto che, per ficcar lo viso al fondo,
 io non vi discerneva alcuna cosa. 12
« Or discendiam qua giù nel cieco mondo »
 cominciò il poeta tutto smorto:
 « io sarò primo e tu sarai secondo ». 15
E io, che del color mi fui accorto,
 dissi: « Come verrò, se tu paventi,
 che suoli al mio dubbiare esser conforto? » 18
Ed egli a me: « L'angoscia de le genti
 che son qua giù, nel viso mi dipigne
 quella pietà che tu per tema senti. 21
Andiam, chè la via lunga ne sospigne ».
 Così si mise e così mi fe' intrare
 nel primo cerchio che l'abisso cigne. 24

Scarce had he ended, when the dark terrayne
  shook so tremendously, that still my mind
  for terror bathes me in sweat as it did then.
The tear-drenched ground let forth a blast of wind
  out of which flashed a light, vermilion-hued,
  that instantly struck all my senses blind:
and I fell, like to one by sleep subdued.

CANTO 4

Rattle of thunder broke the stubborn drowse
  which numbed my brain, so that I started as
  a man would whom a violent blow doth rouse;
and, risen, I gazed intently around, because,
  my eyes now rested, I desired to know
  the nature of the place in which I was.
I found myself, in fact, where sheer below
  yawned the abyss, its doleful valley loud
  with one roar, blent of myriad cries of woe.
Gloomy it was, and deep and full of cloud
  so dense, that in its depths I could nohow
  distinguish aught at all, peer as I would.
'Down there, to the blind world, descend we now'
  began the poet, turning deadly pale:
  and then: 'I will go first, and second thou.'
I, who his change of hue had noted well,
  said: 'How shall *I* come, if *thou* art afraid
  who art wont to comfort me when doubts assail?'
'The anguish of the folk down there' he said
  'paints that compassion, on my face express'd,
  which thou as fear hast misinterpreted.
Let's go, for the long journey bids us haste.'
  So he advanced, and me too did he bring
  to the first circle round the abysm traced.

Quivi, secondo che per ascoltare,
    non avea pianto ma' che di sospiri
    che l'aura eterna facevan tremare.   27
Ciò avvenia di duol sanza martiri
    che avean le turbe, ch'eran molto grandi,
    d'infanti e di femmine e di viri.   30
Lo buon maestro a me: « Tu non dimandi
    che spiriti son questi che tu vedi:
    or vo' che sappi, innanzi che più andi,   33
ch'ei non peccaro; e s'elli hanno mercedi,
    non basta, perchè non ebber battesmo,
    che è porta de la fede che tu credi;   36
e se furon dinanzi al cristianesmo
    non adorar debitamente Dio;
    e di questi cotai son io medesmo.   39
Per tai difetti, non per altro rio,
    semo perduti, e sol di tanto offesi
    che sanza speme vivemo in disio ».   42
Gran duol mi prese al cor quando lo intesi,
    però che gente di molto valore
    conobbi che in quel Limbo eran sospesi.   45
« Dimmi, maestro mio, dimmi, signore,»
    comincià' io per voler esser certo
    di quella fede che vince ogni errore;   48
« uscicci mai alcuno, o per suo merto
    o per altrui, che poi fosse beato? »
    E quei, che intese il mio parlar coperto,   51
rispose: « Io era novo in questo stato
    quando ci vidi venire un possente,
    con segno di vittoria coronato,   54
Trasseci l'ombra del primo parente,
    d'Abel suo figlio e quella di Noè,
    di Moisè, legista e obbediente;   57
Abraam patriarca e David re,
    Isràel con lo padre e co' suoi nati
    e con Rachele per cui tanto fe';   60
e altri molti, e feceli beati;
    e vo' che sappi che dinanzi ad essi
    spiriti umani non eran salvati ».   63

Here, if one only judged by listening,
　　there was no lamentation except sighs,
　　which kept the eternal air still quivering;
the cause whereof in grief, not torment lies,
　　by infants felt, by women and by men
　　in vast crowds and of all varieties.
'Thou askest not' said the good master then
　　'what spirits are these thou seest: now be it not hid
　　from thee ere going farther that these, when
on earth, sinned not: but any good they did
　　falls short, because they had not baptism,
　　the portal of the faith which is thy creed.
And, lived they ere the Christian gospel came,
　　they failed to worship God in the right way:
　　and I myself am counted one of them.
For such defects, though guiltless else, are they—
　　and I too—lost: in nought save this offended,
　　we live without hope in desire for aye.'
Sore grieved my heart, when I had apprehended
　　his words, for people of much worth I knew,
　　who in that Borderland were held suspended.
'Tell me, my master, tell me, sir, pray do,'
　　began I, eager to be certified
　　of that faith which doth every doubt subdue,
'did ever any, issuing hence, upbuoyed
　　by his own merit or another's, get
　　to Heav'n?' Divining what my words implied,
he answered: 'I was newly in this state
　　when I saw hither come, his brows array'd
　　with victory's sign, a mighty Potentate.
He drew from hence our primal parent's shade,
　　Abel his son, and Noah, nor forgot
　　Moses who gave the laws himself obey'd;
patriarch Abraham and king David, not
　　neglecting Israel, with his sire and sons
　　and Rachel, for whose sake so much he wrought,
and many more, and made them blessèd ones;
　　and I would have thee know 'tis vain to seek
　　men's spirits saved ere these, for saved was none's.'

27

Non lasciavam l'andar perch'ei dicessi,
  ma passavam la selva tuttavia,
  la selva, dico, di spiriti spessi.   66
Non era lunga ancor la nostra via
  di qua dal sonno, quando vidi un foco
  ch'emisperio di tenebre vincìa.   69
Di lunga n'eravamo ancora un poco,
  ma non sì, ch'io non discernessi in parte
  che orrevol gente possedea quel loco.   72
« O tu che onori e scienza ed arte,
  questi chi son, che hanno cotanta orranza
  che dal modo degli altri li diparte? »   75
E quelli a me: « L'onrata nominanza
  che di lor suona su ne la tua vita,
  grazia acquista nel ciel, che sì li avanza ».   78
Intanto voce fu per me udita:
  « Onorate l'altissimo poeta:
  l'ombra sua torna, ch'era dipartita ».   81
Poi che la voce fu restata e queta,
  vidi quattro grand'ombre a noi venire:
  sembianza aveano nè trista nè lieta.   84
Lo buon maestro cominciò a dire:
  « Mira colui con quella spada in mano,
  che vien dinanzi ai tre sì come sire.   87
Quelli è Omero, poeta sovrano;
  l'altro è Orazio satiro, che viene;
  Ovidio è il terzo, e l'ultimo è Lucano.   90
Però che ciascun meco si conviene
  nel nome che sonò la voce sola,
  fannomi onore, e di ciò fanno bene ».   93
Cosi vidi adunar la bella scuola
  di quel signor de l'altissimo canto,
  che sovra gli altri com'aquila vola.   96
Da ch'ebber ragionato insieme alquanto,
  volsersi a me con salutevol cenno;
  e il mio maestro sorrise di tanto.   99
E più d'onore ancor assai mi fenno,
  ch'essi mi fecer de la loro schiera,
  sì ch'io fui sesto tra cotanto senno.   102

We ceased not going for that he thus did speak,
  but all the while were passing through the wood,
  the wood, I mean, of spirits crowded thick.
Not much this side my sleep had we pursued
  our path, when I perceived a fire, whereby
  a hemisphere of darkness was subdued.
That place, though somewhat farther on, could I
  yet in some measure see had been possess'd
  by personages who stood in honour high.
'O thou who art and science honourest,
  what folk are these to whom such honour's shown
  as parts them from the manner of the rest?'
And he to me: 'The honourable renown
  that of them echoes in thy life above
  wins grace in heav'n, which thus their worth doth own.'
Meanwhile I heard a voice, the cry whereof
  was: 'Honour ye the loftiest poet: his shade
  returns, which had departed.' Tow'rds us move,
when the voice paused and nothing more was said,
  I beheld four majestic shades: and they
  in mien were neither sorrowful nor glad.
And the good master straight began to say:
  'Give heed to him with that sword in his hand,
  who, lord-like, leads the other three this way.
That's Homer, prince of poets: understand
  'tis Horace comes next, for satire notable;
  Ovid's the third: Lucan completes the band.
Since each of them like me 'tis right to hail
  by that name which the sole voice made to ring,
  they do me honour, and in that do well.'
Thus saw I the fair school, associating,
  of that lord of the song that's loftiest styled,
  who o'er the rest soars with an eagle's wing.
They turned, when they in mutual talk had whiled
  some time away, and to myself made sign
  of welcome; seeing which, my master smiled.
To honour me still more did they combine:
  for, in that of their guild they made me one,
  mid so much wisdom the sixth place was mine.

Così n'andammo infino a la lumiera,
  parlando cose che il tacere è bello,
  sì com'era il parlar colà dov'era.   105
Giugnemmo al piè d'un nobile castello
  sette volte cerchiato d'alte mura,
  difeso intorno d'un bel fiumicello.   108
Questo passammo come terra dura;
  per sette porte intrai con questi savi,
  venimmo in prato di fresca verdura.   111
Genti v'eran con occhi tardi e gravi,
  di grande autorità ne' lor sembianti;
  parlavan rado, con voci soavi.   114
Traemmoci così da l'un dei canti,
  in luogo aperto, luminoso e alto,
  sì che veder si potean tutti quanti.   117
Colà diritto, sovra il verde smalto
  mi fur mostrati li spiriti magni
  che del vedere in me stesso m'esalto.   120
Io vidi Elettra con molti compagni
  tra' quai conobbi Ettore ed Enea,
  Cesare armato con gli occhi grifagni.   123
Vidi Camilla e la Pentesilea
  da l'altra parte, e vidi il re Latino
  che con Lavinia sua figlia sedea.   126
Vidi quel Bruto che cacciò Tarquino,
  Lucrezia, Iulia, Marzia e Corniglia,
  e solo, in parte, vidi il Saladino.   129
Poi ch'innalzai un poco più le ciglia,
  vidi il maestro di color che sanno
  seder tra filosofica famiglia.   132
Tutti lo miran, tutti onor li fanno:
  quivi vid' io Socrate e Platone,
  che innanzi a gli altri più presso li stanno;   135
Democrito che il mondo a caso pone,
  Diogenès, Anassagora e Tale,
  Empedoclès, Eraclito e Zenone.   138
E vidi il buono accoglitor del quale,
  Dioscoride dico; e vidi Orfeo,
  Tullio e Lino e Seneca morale;   141

Thus we advanced to where the brightness shone,
   in talk, of which I do well to say nought,
   as to talk thus in that place was well done.

Then came we to a noble castle's foot,
   seven times by lofty ramparts circled round;
   a limpid streamlet served it as a moat.

This we passed over as on solid ground:
   through seven gates with these sages did I go:
   and, come to a meadow of fresh grass, we found

folk there whose eyes were grave and glances slow,
   of eminent authority in mien:
   they spoke but seldom and in voices low.

So, drawing aside, we stationed ourselves in
   an open space, well lighted and raised high,
   whence, one and all, they could be clearly seen.

There, on the green enamel, eye to eye
   were shown me the great spirits, whom I pride
   myself to have seen, and inwardly feel joy.

I saw Electra, and many by her side,
   among them Hector and Aeneas, who
   had with them Caesar, armed and falcon-eyed.

I saw Camilla, Penthesilea too,
   on the other side: then king Latinus, seen
   beside his child Lavinia, met my view.

I saw the Brutus who expelled Tarquin,
   Cornelia, Marcia, Julia, Lucrece; and,
   by himself, aloof, I saw the Saladin.

Raising my eyes a little, mid souls then scann'd,
   I saw the master-spirit of those who know,
   seated among a philosophic band.

All gaze on him, all do him honour show:
   there saw I Socrates and Plato: stance
   near him have they; the rest are ranged below.

Democritus, who ascribes the world to chance,
   Thales, Diogenes, Empedocles,
   Zeno and Anaxagoras met my glance.

I saw Heraclítus, Dioscorides,
   skilled herb-collector, Orpheus and Tully, then
   Linus and moral Seneca; with these

Euclide geometra e Tolomeo,
  Ippocrate, Avicenna e Galieno,
  Averroìs che il gran comento feo.   144
Io non posso ritrar di tutti a pieno,
  però che sì mi caccia il lungo tema,
  che molte volte al fatto il dir vien meno.   147
La sesta compagnia in due si scema:
  per altra via mi mena il savio duca
  fuor de la queta ne l'aura che trema;   150
e vegno in parte ove non è che luca.

CANTO 5

Così discesi del cerchio primaio
  giù nel secondo, che men loco cinghia
  e tanto più dolor, che pugne a guaio.   3
Stavvi Minòs orribilmente, e ringhia;
  esamina le colpe ne l'entrata,
  giudica e manda secondo che avvinghia.   6
Dico che quando l'anima malnata
  li vien dinanzi, tutta si confessa;
  e quel conoscitor de le peccata   9
vede qual luogo d'Inferno è da essa;
  cignesi con la coda tante volte
  quantunque gradi vuol che giù sia messa.   12
Sempre dinanzi a lui ne stanno molte;
  vanno a vicenda ciascuna al giudizio,
  dicono e odono e poi son giù volte.   15
« O tu che vieni al doloroso ospizio »,
  disse Minòs a me quando mi vide,
  lasciando l'atto di cotanto offizio,   18
« guarda com'entri e di cui tu ti fide:
  non t'inganni l'ampiezza de l'entrare! »
  E il duca mio a lui: « Perchè pur gride?   21

Galen, Hippocrates and Avicen,
  Euclid the geometrician, Ptolemy
  and—the great Comment owe we to his pen—
Averroes: nor sketch them all can I
  in full: so drives me on my lengthy theme,
  words oft fall short of the reality.
Our six now drops to two: I come with him,
  my guide, whose wisdom by another way
  brings me from out the calm into the dim
and trembling air to a part where shines no ray.

CANTO 5

So from the circle that comes first I went
  down to the second, which engirds less space,
  but more pain, such as goads to loud lament.
There presides Minos, grisly sight to face,
  snarling; inspects the faults as they come in,
  dooms and, by how he girds him, allots their place.
I say, each ill-born spirit, once within
  his presence, leaveth nothing unconfess'd;
  and he, that grand appraiser of all sin,
sees with what place in Hell it tallies best;
  as many grades as down he'd have it go,
  so often with his tail he belts his waist.
Passing before him in an endless row,
  they go in turn each to the judgment; then
  they speak, they hear, and straight are hurled below.
'O thou that comest to the abode of pain,'
  to me, when he beheld me, Minos cried,
  letting his great charge unperformed remain,
'ere entering, look in whom thy hopes confide;
  beware lest the entry's breadth should prove a liar!'
  'Why keep on clamouring?' answered him my guide.

non impedir lo suo fatale andare:
  vuolsi così colà dove si puote
  ciò che si vuole, e più non dimandare ».   24
Ora incomincian le dolenti note
  a farmisi sentire; or son venuto
  là dove molto pianto mi percuote.   27
Io venni in luogo d'ogni luce muto
  che mugghia come mar fa per tempesta
  se da contrari venti è combattuto.   30
La bufera infernal, che mai non resta,
  mena li spirti con la sua rapina;
  voltando e percotendo li molesta.   33
Quando giungon davanti a la ruina,
  quivi le strida, il compianto, il lamento,
  bestemmian quivi la virtù divina.   36
Intesi che a così fatto tormento
  enno dannati i peccator carnali
  che la ragion sommettono al talento.   39
E come li stornei ne portan l'ali,
  nel freddo tempo, a schiera larga e piena,
  così quel fiato li spiriti mali: 42
di qua, di là, di sù, di giù li mena;
  nulla speranza li conforta mai
  non che di posa, ma di minor pena.   45
E come i gru van cantando lor lai,
  facendo in aere di sè lunga riga,
  così vidi venir, traendo guai,   48
ombre portate da la detta briga;
  per ch'io dissi: « Maestro, chi son quelle
  genti che l'aura nera sì gastiga? »   51
« La prima di color di cui novelle
  tu vuoi saper » mi disse quegli allotta,
  « fu imperadrice di molte favelle.   54
A vizio di lussuria fu sì rotta,
  che libito fe' licito in sua legge,
  per torre il biasmo in che era condotta.   57
Ell'è Semiramìs, di cui si legge
  che succedette a Nino e fu sua sposa;
  tenne la terra che il Soldan corregge.   60

'His going is fated and brooks no denier:
  'tis so willed there, where there is power to do
  that which is willed, and more forbear to enquire.'
Now begin moans that, as they louder grow,
  force themselves on my ear: now I am come
  thither where many wailings strike me thro'.
I came to a place, of light completely dumb,
  which bellows like the sea when a storm rages,
  if cross-winds battle therewith for masterdom.
The blast of hell, which nothing e'er assuages,
  seizes and, as it sweeps the spirits along,
  a whirling, buffeting war upon them wages.
When they arrive at the brink o' the landslip, strong
  is the outcry there, wailing and lamentation;
  there they revile God's power with blasphemous tongue.
Condemned to be tormented in this fashion
  are, I was told, the carnal sinners, they
  who submit reason to the sway of passion.
And as their wings, come winter, bear away
  the starlings in a dense flock, far outspread,
  so does that blast the evil spirits for aye:
now here, now there, now up, now down, they are sped;
  and by no hope, not only of repose
  but of less pain, are ever comforted.
And as of cranes a long succession goes
  strung out upon the air, chanting their dirge,
  so saw I approach us, crying aloud their woes,
shades borne upon the aforesaid gusty surge:
  hence 'Master, who may yonder people be,'
  I asked him, 'whom the black air so doth scourge?'
'The foremost of those,' then he said to me,
  'concerning whom thou askest to have word,
  held over many tongues the empery.
Lascivious vice so broke her that she dared
  to make, by law, lust licit in her days,
  to annul the scandal which she had incurr'd.
She is Semiramis who, legend says,
  succeeded Ninus and his wife had been:
  hers was the land which now the Soldan sways.

35

L'altra è colei che s'ancise amorosa
  e ruppe fede al cener di Sicheo;
  poi è Cleopatràs lussuriosa.   63
Elena vedi, per cui tanto reo
  tempo si volse, e vedi il grande Achille,
  che con amore al fine combatteo.   66
Vedi Parìs, Tristano»; e più di mille
  ombre mostrommi, e nominolle, a dito,
  che amor di nostra vita dipartille.   69
Poscia ch'io ebbi il mio dottore udito
  nomar le donne antiche e i cavalieri,
  pietà mi giunse, e fui quasi smarrito.   72
Io cominciai: «Poeta, volentieri
  parlerei a que' due che insieme vanno
  e paion sì al vento esser leggieri».   75
Ed egli a me: «Vedrai quando saranno
  più presso a noi; e tu allor li prega
  per quell'amor che i mena, e quei verranno».   78
Sì tosto come il vento a noi li piega,
  mossi la voce: «O anime affannate,
  venite a noi parlar, s'altri nol niega!»   81
Quali colombe, dal disio chiamate
  con l'ali aperte e ferme al dolce nido
  vengon per l'aere, dal voler portate,   84
cotali uscir de la schiera ov'è Dido
  a noi venendo per l'aere maligno,
  sì forte fu l'affettuoso grido.   87
«O animal grazioso e benigno
  che visitando vai per l'aer perso
  noi che tignemmo il mondo di sanguigno,   90
se fosse amico il re de l'universo
  noi pregheremmo lui per la tua pace,
  poi ch'hai pietà del nostro mal perverso.   93
Di quel che udire e che parlar vi piace
  noi udiremo e parleremo a vui,
  mentre che il vento, come fa, ci tace.   96
Siede la terra dove nata fui
  su la marina dove il Po discende
  per aver pace coi seguaci sui.   99

Then the self-slayer comes, that love-lorn queen
  who to Sichaeus' ashes broke her faith;
  and next, lascivious Cleopatra, seen
with Helen, look! for whom, while she drew breath,
  such ills were done and suffered: see the great
  Achilles, who in war with love met death.
See Paris, Tristan,' and a thousand yet,
  and still more, were the shades he pointed to,
  and named, whom love from life did separate.
After I'd heard my teacher thus run through
  so many knights and dames of yore, my mind,
  was well nigh wildered, overcome by rue.
I began: 'Poet, much do I feel inclined
  to address yon two, together going by,
  who seem to float so lightly on the wind.'
And he to me: 'Watch till they come more nigh;
  and then by that same love which they obey,
  do thou entreat them, and they will comply.'
So when the wind had drifted them our way,
  I lifted up my voice: 'O souls toil-worn,
  come, speak with us, saith not Another nay.'
As doves, when longing summons them, return
  with open steady wings to their sweet nest,
  cleaving the air, by their volition borne;
so they, from out the troop where Dido's placed,
  at once through the malign air tow'rds us sped,
  such power had my compassionate request.
'O kind and gracious being, unafraid
  to venture through the perse air visiting
  us who in dying tinged the world blood-red,
had we for friend the universe's King.
  we would petition him to give thee peace
  who pitiest so our perverse suffering.
All that thou fain wouldst hear and speak of, this
  we will both hear, and speak with you thereo'er,
  while the wind, lulled as now, for us doth cease.
Throned is my native city on the shore
  where, to have peace, the Po comes flowing down
  together with the streams that swell his power.

Amor, che a cor gentil ratto s'apprende,
 prese costui de la bella persona
 che mi fu tolta; e il modo ancor m'offende. 102
Amor, che a nullo amato amar perdona,
 mi prese del costui piacer sì forte
 che, come vedi, ancor non m'abbandona. 105
Amor condusse noi ad una morte:
 Caino attende chi vita ci spense».
 Queste parole da lor ci fur porte. 108
Quand'io intesi quell'anime offense
 chinai 'l viso, e tanto il tenni basso
 fin che il poeta mi disse: « Che pense? » 111
Quando risposi, cominciai: « Oh lasso!
 Quanti dolci pensier, quanto disio
 menò costoro al doloroso passo! » 114
Poi mi rivolsi a loro e parla' io,
 e cominciai: « Francesca, i tuoi martiri
 a lacrimar mi fanno tristo e pio. 117
Ma dimmi: al tempo dei dolci sospiri,
 a che e come concedette Amore
 che conosceste i dubbiosi desiri? » 120
E quella a me: « Nessun maggior dolore
 che ricordarsi del tempo felice
 ne la miseria; e ciò sa il tuo dottore. 123
Ma se a conoscer la prima radice
 del nostro amor tu hai cotanto affetto,
 farò come colui che piange e dice. 126
Noi leggevamo un giorno per diletto
 di Lancilotto, come amor lo strinse:
 soli eravamo e sanza alcun sospetto. 129
Per più fiate gli occhi ci sospinse
 quella lettura, e scolorocci il viso;
 ma solo un punto fu quel che ci vinse. 132
Quando leggemmo il disiato riso
 esser baciato da cotanto amante,
 questi, che mai da me non fia diviso, 135
la bocca mi baciò tutto tremante.
 Galeotto fu il libro e chi lo scrisse.
 Quel giorno più non vi leggemmo avante ». 138

Love, that of noble heart takes hold full soon,
   took *him* for the fair body, from me removed;
   and still I'm sore-bested by the way 'twas done.
Love, that from loving lets off none beloved,
   took *me* for the beauty of him so strongly, that
   it still hath, as thou seëst, my master proved.
Love led us to one death: predestinate
   to Cain is he by whom our blood was shed.'
   These words were borne to us from them; whereat,
when I had heard those souls, thus sore-bested,
   I bowed my face, and held it down so long,
   that 'On what musest thou?' the poet said.
'Ah me, sweet thoughts how many, and what strong
   desire brought these unto the woeful pass!'
   When first I spoke, these words from me were wrung.
Then, turning back to them, now I it was
   who spoke: 'Francesca,' I said, 'thine agonies
   move me to weep, such pity and grief they cause.
But tell me: in the season of sweet sighs
   what sign made Love that led you to confess
   your vague desires? How opened he your eyes?'
And she to me: 'Nought brings one more distress,
   as well thy teacher knows, than to recall
   in time of misery former happiness.
But if to know the primal root of all
   our love thou hast so great a longing, I
   will do as one that weeps, yet tells withal.
Reading we were one day, entranced thereby,
   of Lancelot, how by love he was fast held:
   we were alone and deemed no danger nigh.
That reading oft and oft our eyes impell'd
   to meet, and blanched our faces' hue: but o'er
   us one point, and one point alone, prevail'd.
When read we of the smile, so thirsted for,
   being kissed by such a lover, he that may
   now from myself be parted nevermore,
all trembling, kissed my mouth: destined to play
   our Gallehault was the book and he, as well,
   who wrote it: further read we not that day.'

Mentre che l'uno spirto questo disse
  l'altro piangeva sì, che di pietade
  io venni men così com'io morisse;   141
e caddi come corpo morto cade.

CANTO 6

AL tornar de la mente, che si chiuse
  dinanzi a la pietà de' due cognati,
  che di tristizia tutto mi confuse,   3
novi tormenti e novi tormentati
  mi veggio intorno come ch'io mi mova
  e ch'io mi volga e come ch'io mi guati.   6
Io sono al terzo cerchio, de la piova
  eterna, maledetta, fredda e greve:
  regola e qualità mai non l'è nova.   9
Grandine grossa, e acqua tinta, e neve
  per l'aere tenebroso si riversa:
  pute la terra che questo riceve.   12
Cerbero, fiera crudele e diversa,
  con tre gole caninamente latra
  sopra la gente che quivi è sommersa.   15
Gli occhi ha vermigli, la barba unta ed atra,
  e il ventre largo, e unghiate le mani,
  graffia li spiriti, scuoia ed isquatra.   18
Urlar li fa la pioggia come cani;
  de l'un dei lati fanno a l'altro schermo:
  volgonsi spesso i miseri profani.   21
Quando ci scorse Cerbero, il gran vermo,
  le bocche aperse e mostrocci le sanne:
  non avea membro che tenesse fermo.   24
Lo duca mio distese le sue spanne,
  prese la terra, e con piene le pugna
  la gittò dentro a le bramose canne.   27
Qual è quel cane che abbaiando agugna,
  e si racqueta poi che il pasto morde,
  che solo a divorarlo intende e pugna,   30

While the one spirit said this, throughout the tale
  so piteous were the tears the other shed,
   I swooned, as though in death: and down I fell
as a man's body drops, when dropping dead.

CANTO 6

Upon my mind's revival from the stroke
  of grief which closed it wholly, when I fainted
  away through pity for the two kinsfolk,
new torments and new hosts of the tormented,
  where'er I turn, where'er move, where'er strain
  my searching gaze, are to my eyes presented.
I'm now in the third circle—that of rain
  eternal, curséd, cold and charged with woe:
  its mode and measure aye unchanged remain.
Big hailstones and foul sleet, and therewith snow,
  are poured down through the murky air: the ground
  stinks that receives this as it falls below.
Cerberus, fell beast, whose like was never found,
  with thrée gullets in dog-like fashion howls
  over the people lying there half-drown'd.
His eyes red, greasy and black his bearded jowls,
  his belly huge, and his hands armed with claws,
  he rips and flays and quarters-up the souls.
Howl, as of hounds, the deluge from them draws:
  to screen the one flank with the other squirm
  they and twist oft-times, the miserable outlaws.
When he perceived us, Cerberus, the great worm,
  opened his mouths, with all the fangs laid bare;
  not a limb held he for one moment firm.
My leader, palms spread wide, was quick to tear
  some soil up and, with fists full, hurled it down
  the three voracious gullets then and there.
As with the dog that, baying for hunger, soon
  falls dumb again when once he mouths his food,
  bolting it fiercely, bent on this alone;

cotai si fecer quelle facce lorde
  de lo demonio Cerbero, che introna
  l'anime sì, ch'esser vorrebber sorde.   33
Noi passavam su per l'ombre che adona
  la greve pioggia, e ponevam le piante
  sopra lor vanità che par persona.   36
Elle giacean per terra tutte quante,
  fuor ch'una, che a seder si levò, ratto
  ch'ella ci vide passarsi davante.   39
« O tu che sei per quest'inferno tratto »
  mi disse, « riconoscimi, se sai:
  tu fosti prima ch'io disfatto, fatto ».   42
E io a lei: « L'angoscia che tu hai
  forse ti tira fuor de la mia mente,
  sì che non par ch'io ti vedessi mai.   45
Ma dimmi chi tu sei che in sì dolente
  loco sei messa, ed a sì fatta pena,
  che s'altra è maggio, nulla è sì spiacente ».   48
Ed egli a me: « La tua città, ch'è piena
  d'invidia sì che già trabocca il sacco,
  seco mi tenne in la vita serena.   51
Voi cittadini mi chiamaste Ciacco.
  Per la dannosa colpa de la gola,
  come tu vedi a la pioggia mi fiacco.   54
E io anima trista non son sola,
  chè tutte queste a simil pena stanno
  per simil colpa ». E più non fe' parola.   57
Io li risposi: « Ciacco, il tuo affanno
  mi pesa sì, che a lagrimar m'invita;
  ma dimmi, se tu sai, a che verranno   60
li cittadin de la città partita,
  se alcun v'è giusto, e dimmi la cagione
  per che l'ha tanta discordia assalita ».   63
Ed egli a me: « Dopo lunga tenzone
  verranno al sangue, e la parte selvaggia
  caccerà l'altra con molta offensione.   66
Poi appresso convien che questa caggia
  infra tre soli, e che l'altra sormonti
  con la forza di tal che testè piaggia.   69

so happed it with those faces filth-imbrued
  of Cerberus, fiend who at the souls so storms
  that they would fain be deaf, if but they could.
We, passing o'er the shades laid flat in swarms
  by the rain's heavy pelt, kept treading on
  their emptiness, which seems corporeal forms.
They, each and all, were lying outstretched upon
  the ground, save one, who quickly raised his head
  and sat up, when he saw us past him gone.
'Ho, thou who through this hell art being led,
  recognize me, an thou canst,' he said to me:
  'for thou wast ere my own unmaking made.'
And I to him; 'Thy present agony
  perhaps withdraws thy features from my mind,
  so 'tis as if I'd ne'er set eyes on thee.
But tell me who thou art, down here assign'd
  a place so grim and penalty so devised,
  that none, if worse, is of so foul a kind.'
And he to me: 'Thy city, in which comprised
  is so much envy that the sack spills o'er,
  was mine in the life by sunshine tranquillized.
You citizens nicknamed me Ciacco: for
  the soul-destroying fault of gluttony
  I languish, as thou seest, in this downpour.
Nor, in my dismal state, alone am I,
  for these are likewise punished, one and all,
  for a like fault.' Here halted his reply.
I answered: 'Ciacco, thy afflictions call
  on me to weep, so much they weigh me down:
  but tell me, if thou knowest, what shall befall
the townsmen of the faction-ridden town:
  if any, there, be just; and what the root
  from which the discord rending it has grown.'
And he: 'Befall them after long dispute
  shall bloodshed, and the rustic party ·most
  injuriously shall drive the other out.
For less than three suns will it rule the roast,
  and then shall fall, the other o'er it rise
  by aid of one who just now hugs the coast.

Alte terrà lungo tempo le fronti,
  tenendo l'altra sotto gravi pesi,
  come che di ciò pianga e che n'adonti.   72
Giusti son due, ma non vi sono intesi.
  Superbia, invidia ed avarizia sono
  le tre faville ch'hanno i cori accesi».   75
Qui pose fine al lacrimabil suono.
  Ed io a lui: «Ancor vuo' che m'insegni
  e che di più parlar mi facci dono: 78
Farinata e'l Tegghiaio che fur sì degni,
  Iacopo Rusticucci, Arrigo, e il Mosca,
  e gli altri che a ben far poser l'ingegni,   81
dimmi ove sono e fa ch'io li conosca,
  chè gran disio mi stringe di sapere
  se il ciel li addolcia o l'inferno li attosca».   84
E quegli: «Ei son tra l'anime più nere;
  diversa colpa giù li grava al fondo:
  se tanto scendi li potrai vedere.   87
Ma quando tu sarai nel dolce mondo,
  priegoti che a la mente altrui mi rechi:
  più non ti dico e più non ti rispondo».   90
Li diritti occhi torse allora in biechi,
  guardommi un poco, poi chinò la testa,
  cadde con essa a par de gli altri ciechi.   93
E il duca disse a me: «Più non si desta
  di qua dal suon de l'angelica tromba,
  quando verrà la nimica podesta: 96
ciascun ritroverà la trista tomba,
  ripiglierà sua carne e sua figura,
  udirà quel che in eterno rimbomba».   99
Sì trapassammo per sozza mistura
  de l'ombre e de la pioggia, a passi lenti,
  toccando un poco la vita futura.   102
Per ch'io dissi: «Maestro, esti tormenti
  cresceranno ei dopo la gran sentenza,
  o fien minori, o saran sì cocenti?»   105
Ed egli a me: «Ritorna a tua scienza
  che vuol quanto la cosa è più perfetta
  più senta il bene, e così la doglienza.   108

44

With head held high it long will grasp its prise,
   keeping with heavy weights the other low,
   for all its shame and lamentable cries.
Two men are just, but there unheeded go:
   pride, envy, avarice—these three alone
   the sparks are, which have set men's hearts aglow.'
Here put he an ending to his grievous moan.
   And I to him: 'Oh, still instruct me, please,
   and of more speaking grant me, I pray, the boon.
Tegghiaio and Farinata—great men, these—
   James Rusticucci, Harry, Mosca, as well
   as others, set on doing what righteous is,
tell me about them, and where now they dwell;
   for a keen longing urges me to learn
   if sweets of heav'n they taste or poison of hell.'
And he: 'Their's is the blacker spirits' bourne,
   the pit tow'rds which they 're sunk by divers sin:
   descend'st thou as far, thou'lt see them each in turn.
But prithee, when thy way back thou shalt win
   to the sweet world, bring me to others' mind;
   No more I'll tell thee, and no more speech begin.'
Next, wrenched he his forthright gaze askew, inclined
   it tow'rds me awhile and then, bowing his head,
   dropped with it flat beside the other blind.
'He rouses up no more' my leader said,
   'this side the Last Trump, when the advent looms
   of One, supreme in power, the foe they dread.
Then all will find again their dismal tombs,
   will take again their fleshly shapes, will hear
   that which to all eternity re-booms.'
Thus, treading with slow steps that filthy layer
   of souls and slush, we, on the life to come
   touching a little, onward passed from there.
So I said: 'Master, will more burdensome,
   or less, these torments grow, or will their pain
   burn just like this, after the final doom?'
And he to me: 'Turn to thy science again,
   which holds that, as the thing's more perfect, more
   it feels the good and so, likewise, the bane.

D   45

Tutto che questa gente maledetta
  in vera perfezion già mai non vada,
  di là più che di qua essere aspetta ».   111

Noi aggirammo a tondo quella strada,
  parlando più assai ch'io non ridico;
  venimmo al punto dove si digrada: 114
quivi trovammo Pluto, il gran nimico.

CANTO 7

« Papè Satàn, pape Satàn aleppe »
  cominciò Pluto con la voce chioccia;
  e quel savio gentil, che tutto seppe,   3
disse per confortarmi: « Non ti noccia
  la tua paura, chè, poter ch'egli abbia,
  non ci torrà lo scender questa roccia ».   6

Poi si rivolse a quella enfiata labbia
  e disse: « Taci, maledetto lupo:
  consuma dentro te con la tua rabbia.   9

Non è sanza cagion l'andare al cupo:
  vuolsi ne l'alto là dove Michele
  fe' la vendetta del superbo strupo ».   12

Quali dal vento le gonfiate vele
  caggion avvolte poi che l'alber fiacca,
  tal cadde a terra la fiera crudele.   15

Così, scendemmo ne la quarta lacca,
  pigliando più de la dolente ripa
  che il mal de l'universo tutto insacca.   18

Ahi giustizia di Dio! tante chi stipa
  nove travaglie e pene quant'io viddi,
  e perchè nostra colpa sì ne scipa?   21

Come fa l'onda là sovra Cariddi,
  che si frange con quella in cui s'intoppa,
  così convien che qui la gente riddi.   24

Qui vidi gente più che altrove troppa,
  e d'una parte e d'altra, con grand'urli,
  voltando pesi per forza di poppa.   27

Though true perfection never lies in store
  for these damned souls, they look to attain thereto
  more nearly, after judgment than before.'
That curving road we ceased not to pursue,
  with much more talk than I repeat, till we
  came to the point where one descends anew:
there found we Pluto, the great enemy.

CANTO 7

'PAPÈ Satàn, papè Satàn, aléppe'
  thus Pluto's voice clucked: and with heartening mien
  that noble sage, who knew all, said: 'No step he
can take will do thee mischief, were he e'en
  more powerful than he is: so fear not lest
  he stay thee from descending this ravine.'
Thereupon, turning round, he thus address'd
  that bloated lip: 'Peace, cursèd wolf; consume
  thee inwardly with thy rage: and there digest
this too, that not without cause to the gloom
  we go: 'tis willed on high, where Michael took
  revenge, and the proud rebel met his doom.'
As puffed sails in more wind than they can brook
  fall in a heap, when the mast snaps, o'erstrain'd,
  so fell to earth that fierce and cruel spook.
So, into the fourth trough did we descend,
  still gaining on the doleful slope, that sack
  wherein the whole world's evil is contain'd.
Justice of God! Ah, who piles up a stack
  of such strange toils and dooms as met my glance?
  Why does our guilt so squander us, alack?
As, there, upon Charybdis waves advance,
  breaking their strength on others no less strong,
  so needs must here the people counterdance.
Here saw I crowds, more dense than elsewhere, throng
  this side and that, who, with loud howls, by sway
  and heave of chest were rolling weights along.

47

Percotevansi incontro, e poscia pur lì
 si rivolgea ciascun voltando a retro,
 gridando: « Perchè tieni? » e « Perchè burli? »   30
Così tornavan per lo cerchio tetro
 da ogni mano a l'opposito punto,
 gridandosi anche lor ontoso metro;   33
poi si volgea ciascun, quand'era giunto
 per lo suo mezzo cerchio a l'altra giostra.
 E io, che avea lo cor quasi compunto,   36
dissi: « Maestro mio, or mi dimostra
 che gente è questa e se tutti fur cherci
 questi chercuti a la sinistra nostra ».   39
Ed egli a me: « Tutti quanti fur guerci
 sì de la mente in la vita primaia,
 che con misura nullo spendio ferci.   42
Assai la voce lor chiaro l'abbaia
 quando vengono ai due punti del cerchio
 dove colpa contraria li dispaia.   45
Questi fur cherci, che non han coperchio
 piloso al capo, e papi, e cardinali,
 in cui usa avarizia il suo soperchio ».   48
E io: « Maestro, tra questi cotali
 dovre' io ben riconoscere alcuni
 che furo immondi di cotesti mali »,   51
Ed egli a me: « Vano pensiero aduni:
 la sconoscente vita che i fe' sozzi
 ad ogni conoscenza or li fa bruni,   54
In eterno verranno a li due cozzi:
 questi risurgeranno dal sepulcro
 col pugno chiuso, e questi coi crin mozzi.   57
Mal dare e mal tener lo mondo pulcro
 ha tolto loro e posti a questa zuffa:
 qual ella sia, parole non ci appulcro.   60
Or puoi veder, figliuol, la corta buffa
 dei ben che son commessi a la Fortuna,
 per che l'umana gente si rabbuffa: 63
chè tutto l'oro ch'è sotto la Luna
 e che già fu di quest'anime stanche,
 non poterebbe farne posar una. »   66

They met with a shock: then, just there making stay,
  each, facing round, went rolling back again,
  bawling: 'Why hoardest?' and 'Why fling'st away?'
Thus turned they through the circle dark in grain
  on both hands to the counterpoint, there too
  all shouting their opprobrious refrain.
Then each wheeled round, when he was come right through
  his demi-volt to the other tiltyard. And
  I, who at heart was well-nigh sick with rue,
said: 'Now, my master, make me to understand
  what folk this is, and if all clerks they were,
  these with the tonsured scalps on our left hand.'
'All of them, when alive in the upper air,'
  said he, 'in mental vision squinted so,
  that they spent nothing in due measure there.
This, by their baying it forth, they clearly show
  each time they reach the two points of the round
  whence back, dis-paired by a contrary fault, they go.
These on whose heads no hairy thatch is found
  were each a clerk, a pope or cardinal,
  among whom avarice tops its utmost bound.'
And I said: 'Master, surely among them all
  there must be some I ought to recognize
  who to these filthy evils lived in thrall.'
And he to me: 'Thine is a vain surmise:
  the witless life that made them foul now blocks
  their recognition by the keenest eyes.
Forever will they come to the two shocks:
  these from the sepulchre will rise again
  with the fist clenched, and these with shorn-off locks.
Ill-giving and ill-keeping have from them ta'en
  the bright world and consigned them to this pother:
  of what sort, I dress up no words to explain.
The goods in Fortune's gift I need not bother
  now, son, to prove a farce—played out how soon!
  though for their sake men buffet one another;
for all the gold that is beneath the Moon,
  or ever was, of rest to not so much
  as one of these tired souls could grant the boon.'

« Maestro » diss'io lui « or mi dì anche:
   questa Fortuna di che tu mi tocche,
   che è, che i ben del mondo ha sì tra branche? »   69
Ed egli a me: « Oh creature sciocche,
   quanta ignoranza è quella che v'offende!
   Or vo' che tu mia sentenza ne imbocche.   72
Colui lo cui saver tutto trascende
   fece li cieli e diè lor chi conduce
   sì che ogni parte ad ogni parte splende,   75
distribuendo igualmente la luce.
   Similemente a li splendor mondani
   ordinò general ministra e duce   78
che permutasse a tempo li ben vani
   di gente in gente e d'uno in altro sangue
   oltre la difension de' senni umani;   81
per che una gente impera ed altra langue
   seguendo lo giudicio di costei,
   che è occulto come in erba l'angue.   84
Vostro saver non ha contrasto a lei:
   questa provede, giudica e persegue
   suo regno come il loro gli altri dei.   87
Le sue permutazion non hanno tregue;
   necessità la fa esser veloce;
   sì spesso vien chi vicenda consegue.   90
Questa è colei ch'è tanto posta in croce
   pur da color che le dovrien dar lode,
   dandole biasmo a torto e mala voce.   93
Ma ella s'è beata e ciò non ode:
   con l'altre prime creature lieta
   volve sua spera, e beata si gode.   96
Or discendiamo omai a maggior pieta:
   già ogni stella cadde che saliva
   quand'io mi mossi, e il troppo star si vieta ».   99
Noi ricidemmo il cerchio a l'altra riva
   sovra una fonte che bolle e riversa
   per un fossato che da lei deriva.   102
L'acqua era buia assai più che persa,
   e noi, in compagnia de l'onde bige,
   entrammo giù per una via diversa.   105

'This Fortune, sir, on which thy words but touch,
   what *is* she?' I said: 'that also tell me now—
   she who has worldly goods so in her clutch.'
And he to me: 'O foolish creatures, how
   great is the ignorance which makes you trip!
   My view of her is this, imbibe it thou.
Wisdom supreme, which caused the heav'ns to leap
   into existence and gave *them* their guide
   so that they share, in equal partnership,
each raying on each, the light to each supplied,
   likewise ordained a general leader who,
   as steward, o'er *earthly* splendours might preside
and shift from folk to folk, in season due,
   the vain goods, and from blood to blood, in ways
   past all that human wits oppose thereto.
Thus, one folk rules, another languishes,
   pursuant to her judgment which, as 'twere
   a snake in grass, is hidden from man's gaze.
Your wisdom has no means of countering her;
   she foresees, judges, and pursues her reign,
   no less god, than the gods who reign elsewhere.
Her permutations have no respite: main
   necessity compels her to be swift,
   so fast they come who must their turn obtain.
Yea, this is she whom men so freely lift
   upon the cross and whom they blame amiss,
   and curse when they should rather praise her gift.
But she is blessèd and hears nought of this:
   with the other primal creatures, blithe as they,
   she turns her sphere, rejoicing in her bliss.
Now to worse woes let us descend straightway;
   sinking is now each star that rose when I
   set forth, and we're forbidden too long a stay.'
We crossed the cirque to its other edge, hard by
   a spring that boils up, whence a gully draws
   the tumbling brook which never leaves it dry.
Darker by far than perse the water was:
   by its dim ripple accompanied, down the screes—
   weird pathway—went we on without a pause.

Una palude fa che ha nome Stige
  questo triste ruscel quando è disceso
  a piè de le maligne piagge grige.   108
Ed io, che di mirare stava inteso,
  vidi genti fangose in quel pantano,
  ignude tutte, con sembiante offeso.   111
Queste si percotean non pur con mano,
  ma con la testa e col petto e coi piedi,
  troncandosi coi denti a brano a brano.   114
Lo buon maestro disse: « Figlio, or vedi
  l'anime di color cui vinse l'ira;
  e anche vo' che tu per certo credi   117
che sotto l'acqua ha gente che sospira,
  e fanno pullular quest'acqua al summo,
  come l'occhio ti dice u' che s'aggira.   120
Fitti nel limo dicon: 'tristi fummo
  ne l'aere dolce che dal Sol s allegra,
  portando dentro accidioso fummo: 123
or ci attristiam ne la belletta negra'.
  Quest'inno si gorgoglian ne la strozza,
  chè dir nol posson con parola integra ».   126
Così girammo de la lorda pozza
  grand'arco tra la ripa secca e il mézzo,
  con gli occhi volti a chi del fango ingozza;   129
venimmo al piè d'una torre al dassezzo.

CANTO 8

Io dico, seguitando, che assai prima
  che noi fossimo al piè de l'alta torre,
  gli occhi nostri n'andar suso alla cima   3
per due fiammette che i vedemmo porre,
  ed un'altra da lungi render cenno
  tanto che appena il potea l'occhio tòrre.   6
E io mi volsi al mar di tutto il senno;
  dissi: « Questo che dice? e che risponde
  quell'altro foco? e chi son quei che il fenno? »   9

This dismal streamlet forms the bog which is
   called Styx, when it has ended its descent
   of the malignant grey declivities.
And I, on gazing and nought else intent,
   saw, muddied in that slough, folk, all of them
   naked, and such as hurt makes violent.
For, fighting, not with hands alone they came
   to blows, but with the head and breast and feet:
   with teeth, too, did piece-meal each other maim.
'Son,' the good master said, 'thine eyes now meet
   the souls of those whom wrath subdued: and I
   would have thee also sure of this, to wit,
that 'neath the water there are folk who sigh
   and make its surface bubble, as, where'er
   it turns, thy roving glance can certify.
Stuck in the slime they moan: "In the sweet air
   made cheerful by the sun sullen were we
   and did a sluggish smoke within us bear;
now in the black ooze sullen shall we be
   for aye": this hymn they gurgle in the throat,
   for they can speak no word intelligibly.'
So round a great arc of the filthy moat,
   between the dry bank and the swamp, we pass'd,
   of those who gulped the mire still taking note;
we reached the foot of a high tower at last.

CANTO 8

I SAY, continuing, that long before
   we reached its foot, our eyes had onward sped
   up to the summit of the lofty tower,
because we saw two beacons it display'd
   and—from so far, 'twas well nigh past discerning—
   another, which gave back the sign they made.
And I, turn'd tow'rds the deep sea of all learning,
   said: 'What does this one say? And what replies
   that other fire? And who have set it burning?'

Ed egli a me: « Su per le sucide onde
    già scorgere puoi quello che s'aspetta,
    se il fummo del pantan nol ti nasconde ».   12
Corda non pinse mai da sè saetta
    che sì corresse via per l'aere snella
    com'io vidi una nave piccioletta   15
venir per l'acqua verso noi in quella,
    sotto il governo d'un sol galeoto
    che gridava: « Or se' giunta, anima fella! »   18
« Flegiàs, Flegiàs, tu gridi a voto »
    disse lo mio signore, « a questa volta
    più non ci avrai che sol passando il loto ».   21
Qual è colui che grande inganno ascolta
    che li sia fatto, e poi se ne rammarca,
    fecesi Flegiàs ne l'ira accolta.   24
Lo duca mio discese ne la barca
    e poi mi fece intrare appresso lui,
    e sol quand'io fui dentro parve carca.   27
Tosto che il duca e io nel legno fui,
    segando se ne va l'antica prora
    de l'acqua più che non suol con altrui.   30
Mentre noi correvam la morta gora,
    dinanzi mi si fece un pien di fango,
    e disse: « Chi sei tu che vieni anzi ora? »   33
E io a lui: « S'io vengo, non rimango;
    ma tu chi sei, che sì se' fatto brutto? »
    Rispose: « Vedi che son un che piango ».   36
E io a lui: « Con piangere e con lutto,
    spirito maledetto, ti rimani,
    ch'io ti conosco, ancor sie lordo tutto ».   39
Allora stese al legno ambo le mani;
    per che 'l maestro accorto lo sospinse
    dicendo: « Via, costà, con gli altri cani! »   42
Lo collo poi con le braccia mi cinse,
    baciommi il volto e disse: « Alma sdegnosa,
    benedetta colei che in te s'incinse!   45
Quei fu al mondo persona orgogliosa;
    bontà non è che sua memoria fregi:
    così s'è l'ombra sua qui furiosa.   48

'Over the slimy waves,' he said, 'there nighs
  what's waited for, already clear in view,
  unless the marsh-fog hides it from thine eyes.'
Ne'er from itself did string drive shaft that flew
  away thro' the air with such a rapid flight
  as I saw a tiny skiff which meanwhile through
the bog in our direction hove in sight
  under the guidance of a single rower,
  who cried: 'I've got thee now, thou wicked sprite!'
'Phlegias, Phlegias,' bade my lord, 'give o'er!
  this time thy clamour is but wasted breath:
  the slough once passed, we shall evade thy power.'
As he who hears of some great fraud that hath
  been practised on him and becomes irate,
  such became Phlegias in his gathered wrath.
My guide stepped down into the boat, then set
  me too beside him there; and only when
  I was in, seemed it burdened with a freight.
The ancient prow, having embarked the twain—
  me and my guide—went ploughing the water more
  deeply than e'er with others up till then.
While through the stagnant channel on we bore,
  one, caked with mud, placed himself in my way,
  and said: 'Who 'rt thou, that comest ere thine hour?'
And I to him: 'Though come, I do not stay:
  but thou, who 'rt thou, that art befouléd so?'
  'Thou seëst I'm one in woe,' did he then say.
And I to him: 'In anguish, as in woe,
  acccurséd spirit, stay thou here: for thee,
  all filthy as thou art, well do I know.'
Then clutched he the boat with both hands furiously:
  but the ware master thrust him off and cried:
  'Away to thy fellow-curs in this doggery!'
Next, throwing his arms about my neck, with pride
  he kissed me and said: 'Breather of righteous scorn,
  blesséd is she who bore thee 'neath her side.
Arrogant was this man in life; to adorn
  his memory left he nothing good: and hence
  his shade is here by furious passions torn.

Quanti si tengon or là sù gran regi,
  che qui staranno come porci in brago,
  di sè lasciando orribili dispregi!»   51
E io: «Maestro, molto sarei vago
  di vederlo attuffare in questa broda
  prima che noi uscissimo del lago».   54
Ed egli a me: «Avante che la proda
  ti si lasci veder, tu sarai sazio:
  di tal disio converrà che tu goda».   57
Dopo ciò poco vid'io quello strazio
  far di costui a le fangose genti,
  che Dio ancor ne lodo e ne ringrazio.   60
Tutti gridavano: «A Filippo Argenti!»;
  e il fiorentino spirito bizzarro
  in sè medesimo si volgea coi denti.   63
Quivi il lasciammo, chè più non ne narro.
  Ma ne l'orecchio mi percosse un duolo,
  per ch'io avante l'occhio intento sbarro.   66
Lo buon maestro disse: «Omai, figliuolo,
  s'appressa la città che ha nome Dite,
  coi gravi cittadin, col grande stuolo».   69
E io: «Maestro, già le sue meschite
  là entro certe ne la valle cerno,
  vermiglie come se di foco uscite   72
fossero». Ed ei mi disse: «Il foco eterno
  ch'entro le affoca le dimostra rosse
  come tu vedi, in questo basso Inferno».   75
Noi pur giugnemmo dentro a l'alte fosse
  che vallan quella terra sconsolata;
  le mura mi parea che ferro fosse.   78
Non sanza prima far grande aggirata,
  venimmo in parte dove il nocchier, forte
  «Uscite» ci gridò «qui è l'entrata».   81
Io vidi più di mille in su le porte
  da ciel piovuti, che stizzosamente
  dicean: «Chi è costui che sanza morte   84
va per lo regno de la morta gente?»
  E il savio mio maestro fece segno
  di voler lor parlar segretamente.   87

How many up there on earth now make pretence
  of kingship, who'll grout here like pigs in mud,
  bequeathing horrible tales of their violence!'
And I: 'There's nothing, Master, that I should
  like more, than to behold him in this stew
  well soused, before we quit the lake for good.'
And he to me: 'Ere the shore comes in view,
  thou shalt be satisfied: for it is meet
  that thou shouldst see this wish of thine come true.'
Not long thereafter I beheld them beat
  and tear him so, the muddy folk, that I
  to God still render praise and thanks for it.
'At him, at Philip Argenti!' was their cry:
  and on himself turned that fierce spirit, bred
  in Florence, with his own teeth savagely.
There left we him—of whom no more be said:
  but to my ears a wailing pierced its way,
  so I unbar my eyes and look ahead.
'Son, from now on,' did the good master say,
  'draws near the city that is named of Dis,
  with its stern burghers, with its vast array.'
'Master,' I said, 'its mosques had I ere this,
  there in the valley's depth, discerned right well,
  scarlet, as if just risen from an abyss
of fire.' And he: 'The fire unquenchable,
  which fires them inwardly, shows them red-hot,
  e'en as thou seëst, in this nether Hell.'
Now right into the deep moats were we got
  which fortify that city of despair;
  its walls, meseemed, were out of iron wrought.
Not till we'd made a lengthy circuit were
  we come to a place at which the bos'n, loud
  cried to us: 'Out with you; look, the entry's there!'
I saw at the gates more than a thousand crowd
  of those rained down from heav'n, who fiercely **broke**
  out with: 'Who's this that, still by death unbow'd,
goes traversing the realm of the dead folk?'
  And sign did my sage master make that fain
  would he engage them privily in talk.

Allor chiusero un poco il gran disdegno
 e disser: «Vien tu solo, e quei sen vada,
 che sì ardito entrò per questo regno.   90
Sol si ritorni per la folle strada:
 provi, se sa; chè tu qui rimarrai
 che gli hai scorta sì buia contrada».   93
Pensa, lettor, se io mi sconfortai
 nel suon de le parole maledette,
 che non credetti ritornarci mai.   96
«O caro duca mio, che più di sette
 volte m'hai sicurtà renduta, e tratto
 d'alto periglio che incontra mi stette,   99
non mi lasciar» diss'io «così disfatto,
 e se il passar più oltre ci è negato,
 ritroviam l'orme nostre insieme ratto».   102
E quel signor che lì m'avea menato
 mi disse: «Non temer, che il nostro passo
 non ci può tòrre alcun: da tal n'è dato.   105
Ma qui m'attendi, e lo spirito lasso
 conforta e ciba di speranza buona,
 ch'io non ti lascerò nel mondo basso».   108
Così sen va, e quivi m'abbandona
 lo dolce padre, e io rimango in forse,
 che no e sì nel capo mi tenzona.   111
Udir non potei quello che a lor porse;
 ma ei non stette là con essi guari,
 che ciascun dentro a prova si ricorse.   114
Chiuser le porte quei nostri avversari
 nel petto al mio signor, che fuor rimase
 e rivolsesi a me con passi rari.   117
Gli occhi a la terra, e le ciglia avea rase
 d'ogni baldanza, e dicea ne' sospiri:
 «Chi m'ha negate le dolenti case!»   120
E a me disse: «Tu, per ch'io m'adiri,
 non sbigottir, ch'io vincerò la prova
 qual che a la difension dentro s'aggiri.   123
Questa lor tracotanza non è nova,
 chè già la usaro a men secreta porta,
 la qual sanza serrame ancor si trova.   126

Then did they curb a little their great disdain
   and said: 'Come thou alone, let *him* begone
   who intrudes so rashly hither where we reign.
Let him retrace his madcap road alone,
   try if he can; for thou down here shalt stay
   who through so dark a country hast led him down.'
Judge, Reader, if I did not feel dismay,
   when by these devilish words my ears were riven,
   deeming myself barred from return for aye.
'O my dear leader, who hast more than seven
   times re-assured and from deep peril drawn
   me safe, when vainly against it I had striven,
leave me not' I implored him 'thus undone;
   if further progress be to us denied,
   let us go back together, nay, let's run.'
And he, my lord who had brought me there, replied:
   'Fear not, by Such 'tis granted us, that no
   foes could prevent our passage, though they tried.
Wait for me here: comfort and nourish thou
   thy flagging spirit with good hope, for I
   will not desert thee in the world below.'
Thus goes his way, abandoning me, my
   sweet father, and I'm left in doubt, for in
   my head fight 'yes' and 'no' for victory.
I could not hear what plea he urged to win
   them over, but he had not stayed there long
   when, each with each vying, all rushed back within.
They slammed and barred the gates, that hostile throng,
   in my lord's face: outside did he remain,
   and turned back to myself with steps that hung,
and eyes cast down to earth, and brows that then
   were shorn of confidence, and saying with sighs,
   'Who has denied me the abodes of pain?'
To me 'For all my wrath be thou nowise
   alarmed,' he said; 'this contest I'll win through,
   no matter who, in there, to impede us tries.
This truculence of theirs is nothing new:
   they showed it once at a less secret gate,
   yet that was then unbarred, and still is too.

Sopr'essa vedestù la scritta morta;
  e già di qua da lei discende l'erta,
  passando per li cerchi sanza scorta,   129
tal che per lui ne fia la terra aperta».

CANTO 9

Quel color che viltà di fuor mi pinse
  veggendo il duca mio tornare in volta,
  più tosto dentro il suo novo ristrinse.   3
Attento si fermò com'uom che ascolta:
  chè l'occhio nol potea menare a lunga
  per l'aer nero e per la nebbia folta.   6
« Pur a noi converrà vincer la punga»
  cominciò ei, «se non.... Tal ne s'offerse...
  Oh quanto tarda a me ch'altri qui giunga!»   9
Io vidi ben sì com'ei ricoperse
  lo cominciar con l'altro che poi venne,
  che fur parole a le prime diverse;   12
ma nondimen paura il suo dir dienne,
  perch'io traeva la parola tronca
  forse a peggior sentenza che non tenne.   15
« In questo fondo de la trista conca
  discende mai alcun del primo grado
  che sol per pena ha la speranza cionca?»   18
Questa question fec'io; e quei: « Di rado
  incontra» mi rispose «che di nui
  faccia il cammino alcun pel qual io vado.   21
Vero è ch'altra fiata qua giù fui,
  congiurato da quella Eritòn cruda
  che richiamava l'ombre ai corpi sui.   24
Di poco era di me la carne nuda,
  ch'ella mi fece intrar dentro a quel muro
  per trarne un spirto del cerchio di Giuda.   27
Quello è il più basso loco e il più oscuro
  e il più lontan dal ciel che tutto gira:
  ben so il cammin, però ti fa sicuro.   30

O'er it thou saw'st the dead inscription set:
  e'en now, this side thereof, descends the steep,
  zone by zone, unescorted, One who yet
will open unto us this donjon-keep.'

CANTO 9

THE hue which cowardice had outwardly
  limned on me, seeing my guide turn back, repress'd
  his own new colour the more speedily.
He stopped attentive, like a man address'd
  to listening; for not far had eyes the might
  to lead him through the black air and thick mist.
'Yet it must needs be we shall win the fight,'
  began he, 'or else—Such was the proffered aid:
  oh, when, when will that Other come in sight!'
I noted well how he had overlaid
  his opening words with those that later came,
  which differed so from what he first had said;
with fear his utterance filled me, all the same,
  since haply I drew the word which broken fell
  to a worse purport than had been his aim.
'Down unto *this* depth of the dismal shell
  comes ever any from the first degree,
  whose only doom is without hope to dwell?'
So questioned I; and 'Seldom' answered he
  'comes it to pass that any of us the way
  e'er treads which now is being trodden by me.
Yet, once before, Erechtho (truth to say)
  conjured me down here—that fell witch, I mean,
  who used to call the shades back to their clay.
Bare of me but short while my flesh had been,
  when, spelled by her, I passed within yon wall
  to draw a soul thence guilty of Judas' sin.
His is the lowest, darkest place of all,
  and farthest from the heav'n that wheels the skies;
  but fear nought, for the road I well recall.

Questa palude che il gran puzzo spira
 cinge d'intorno la città dolente
 u' non potemo intrare omai sanz'ira...». 33
E altro disse, ma non l'ho a mente;
 però che l'occhio m'avea tutto tratto
 ver l'alta torre a la cima rovente, 36
dove in un punto furon dritte ratto
 tre Furie infernal di sangue tinte,
 che membra femminine aveano ed atto, 39
e con idre verdissime eran cinte;
 serpentelli e ceraste avean per crine,
 onde le fiere tempie erano avvinte. 42
E quei, che ben conobbe le meschine
 de la regina de l'eterno pianto,
 « Guarda » mi disse « le feroci Erine. 45
Questa è Megera, dal sinistro canto;
 quella che piange dal destro è Aletto;
 Tesifone è nel mezzo ». E tacque a tanto. 48
Con l'unghie si fendea ciascuna il petto,
 batteansi a palme, e gridavan sì alto
 ch'io mi strinsi al poeta per sospetto. 51
« Venga Medusa: sì il farem di smalto »
 dicevan tutte riguardando in giuso,
 « mal non vengiammo in Teseo l'assalto! » 54
«Volgiti indietro e tien lo viso chiuso;
 chè se il Gorgon si mostra e tu il vedessi,
 nulla sarebbe del tornar mai suso ». 57
Così disse il maestro; ed elli stessi
 mi volse, e non si tenne alle mie mani,
 che con le sue ancor non mi chiudessi. 60
O voi che avete gl'intelletti sani,
 mirate la dottrina che s'asconde
 sotto il velame de li versi strani. 63
E già venia su per le torbid'onde
 un fracasso d'un suon pien di spavento,
 per che tremavano ambedue le sponde, 66
non altrimenti fatto che d'un vento
 impetuoso per gli avversi ardori,
 che fier la selva, e sanz'alcun rattento 69

This fen, exhaling the vast fetor, lies
  all round the city of woe, by which now faced,
  we can, without wrath, enter it nowise.'
He said more, but my mind stores not the rest;
  for by my eyes I had been wholly drawn
  up tow'rd the high tower with the glowing crest,
where all at once were risen erect thereon
  three Furies out of hell, with blood stained red;
  a woman's limbs and carriage had they, each one.
With bright green hydras were they girt; instead
  of hair they had small serpents: and, with these,
  horned aspics did their savage temples braid.
And he, who well knew which of them each is,
  that serve the queen of timeless dule and dree,
  'Look' exclaimed, 'Look! the fierce Erinnyes!
This is Megaera on the left coign: she
  on the right, wailing, is Alecto: placed
  midmost, the third one is Tisiphone.'
He ceased. Each with her nails was clawing her breast;
  self-smitten with their palms, they screamed so shrill,
  that I, for dread, close to the poet press'd.
'Summon Medusa hither: so we will
  turn him to stone' all, looking downward, cried:
  'we avenged on Theseus his assault but ill.'
'Turn thee about: thine eyes, quick, hide them, hide;
  for, if the Gorgon's face by thee were seen,
  no return upward hence could e'er betide.'
Thus spake the master; and with anxious mien
  turned me himself, not trusting to my hands,
  but with his own, too, made for me a screen.
O ye of a sane mind that understands,
  note the strange verses well, and ponder o'er
  the doctrine veiled 'neath their close-woven strands.
And tow'rds us now the turbid waters bore
  a crash of deafening sound, full of affright,
  at which a shudder ran through either shore;
a sound as of a wind, roused to the height
  of fury against the heats 'tis countered by,
  which smites the wood and with resistless might

li rami schianta, abbatte e porta fuori;
  dinanzi polveroso va superbo,
  e fa fuggir le fiere e li pastori.   72
Gli occhi mi sciolse e disse: «Or drizza il nerbo
  del viso su per quella schiuma antica
  per indi ove quel fummo è più acerbo».   75
Come le rane innanzi a la nimica
  biscia per l'acqua si dileguan tutte
  finch'a la terra ciascuna s'abbica,   78
vid'io più di mille anime distrutte
  fuggir così dinanzi ad un, che al passo
  passava Stige con le piante asciutte.   81
Dal volto rimovea quell'aere grasso
  menando la sinistra innanzi spesso,
  e sol di quell'angoscia parea lasso.   84
Ben m'accorsi ch'egli era da ciel messo,
  e volsimi al maestro; e quei fe' segno
  che stessi queto ed inchinassi ad esso.   87
Ahi quanto mi parea pien di disdegno!
  Venne alla porta, e con una verghetta
  l'aperse che non v'ebbe alcun ritegno.   90
«O cacciati del ciel, gente dispetta»
  cominciò egli in su l'orribil soglia,
  «onde esta oìtracotanza in voi s'alletta?   93
Perchè recalcitrate a quella voglia
  a cui non puote il fin mai esser mozzo
  e che più volte v'ha cresciuta doglia?   96
Che giova ne le fata dar di cozzo?
  Cerbero vostro, se ben vi ricorda,
  ne porta ancor pelato il mento e il gozzo». 99
Poi si rivolse per la strada lorda
  e non fe' motto a noi; ma fe' sembiante
  d'uomo cui altra cura stringa e morda   102
che quella di colui che gli è davante.
  E noi movemmo i piedi inver la terra,
  sicuri appresso le parole sante.   105
Dentro vi entrammo sanz'alcuna guerra;
  e io che avea di riguardar disio
  la condizion che tal fortezza serra,   108

shivers the boughs, beats down and hurls them high;
   dust-clad in front, it sweeps superbly on,
   while from its onset beasts and shepherds fly.
He freed my eyes: 'Thy visual nerve upon
   that age-old scum' he said, 'direct thou now
   there, where the sourest fume lies thick thereon.'
As frogs before the snake, their hated foe,
   all vanish through the water, till they get
   each to the bottom, and, heaped there, lie low
beheld I more than a thousand desperate
   spirits flee thus from One, who at the ferry
   was passing over Styx with soles unwet.
Oft to his face his left hand did he carry
   to fan away before him that gross air;
   and only of that toil did he seem weary.
Him well I knew for Heaven's messenger
   and, turning to my guide, a signal got
   to bow low in that Presence, nor elsewise stir.
Ah, with what high disdain his mien was fraught!
   He reached the gate, and with a slender rod
   opened it wide, and it resisted not.
'O chased from heav'n, ye despicable brood.'
   began he, halting on the dreadful sill,
   'whence call ye up this overweening mood?
For what cause do ye kick against that Will
   whose end can ne'er be lopped, and which has made,
   time and again, your sufferings greater still?
What boots it 'gainst the fates to butt your head,
   Your Cerberus, if ye well remember, show'd
   for this—and still does—chin and gullet flay'd.'
Then he turned back along the miry road,
   and said no word to us, but had the look
   of one some other care doth urge and goad
than his who stands before him. So we took
   our way on tow'rds the city, feeling quite
   secure after the holy words he spoke.
We entered in there without any fight;
   I, keen to see the state of those inside
   a stronghold of such formidable might,

com'io fui dentro, l'occhio intorno invio;
   e veggio ad ogni man grande campagna
   piena di duolo e di tormento rio.   111
Sì come ad Arli, ove Rodano stagna,
   sì come a Pola presso del Carnaro,
   che Italia chiude e suoi termini bagna,   114
fanno i sepolcri tutto il loco varo,
   così facevan quivi d'ogni parte,
   salvo che il modo v'era piu amaro;   117
chè tra gli avelli fiamme erano sparte,
   per le quali eran sì del tutto accesi
   che ferro più non chiede verun'arte.   120
Tutti li lor coperchi eran sospesi
   e fuor n'usicvan sì duri lamenti,
   che ben parean di miseri e d'offesi.   123
E io: « Maestro, quai son quelle genti
   che, seppellite dentro da quell'arche,
   si fan sentir con li sospir dolenti? »   126
Ed egli a me: « Qui son gli eresiarche
   coi lor seguaci, d'ogni setta, e molto
   più che non credi son le tombe carche.   129
Simile qui con simile è sepolto,
   e i monimenti son più e men caldi ».
   E poi che a la man destra si fu volto,   132
entrammo tra i martìri e gli alti spaldi.

CANTO 10

Ora sen va per un secreto calle
   tra il muro de la terra e li martìri
   lo mio maestro, e io dopo le spalle.   3
« O virtù somma che per gli empi giri
   mi volvi » cominciai « come a te piace,
   parlami e sodisfammi a' miei disiri.   6
La gente che per li sepolcri giace
   potrebbesi veder? Già son levati
   tutti i coperchi, e nessun guardia face ».   9

when I was in, look round me far and wide;
   and see on either hand a vast champaign
   teeming with torments dire, woe multiplied.
Just as at Arles, where the Rhone's swamps begin,
   just as at Pola near Quarnaro's sound,
   which bathes her confines and shuts Italy in,
sepulchres make uneven all the ground,
   so did they here in every quarter, save
   that here a fashion of harsher sort is found;
for flames were scattered between grave and grave,
   whose heat so throughly sets them all aglow,
   that more from iron no handicraft would crave.
The lids of all were raised, and from below
   issued such dire laments as well were seen
   to come from tortured souls in bitter woe.
'Master,' I asked, 'what sort of folk within
   these chests are laid, who make one's ear detect
   their presence by the sighs that speak their teen?'
'Here with their followers of every sect
   lie the arch-heretics,' he said: 'and far
   more crowded are the tombs than thou'dst expect.
Here like with like is buried; and they are,
   these monuments, some more and some less hot.'
   Then on, when he'd turned rightward, did we bear
between the torments and the high redoubt.

CANTO 10

Now by a strait, secluded path that lay
   between the ramparts and the torturing fires
   my guide, with me behind him, goes his way.
'O power supreme, who through these impious gyres
   wheel'st me at will,' I said, 'if nothing let,
   speak to me, and content thou my desires.
The people whom these tombs incarcerate,
   might they be seen? The lids have all been thrown
   open already, and no watch is set.'

Ed egli a me: « Tutti saran serrati
   quando di Iosafàt qui torneranno
   coi corpi che lassù hanno lasciati.   12
Suo cimitero da questa parte hanno
   con Epicuro tutti i suoi seguaci,
   che l'anima col corpo morta fanno.   15
Però a la dimanda che mi faci
   quinc'entro sodisfatto sarai tosto,
   e al disio ancor che tu mi taci ».   18
E io: « Buon duca, non tegno riposto
   a te mio cor se non per dicer poco,
   e tu m'hai non pur mo' a ciò disposto ».   21
« O Tosco, che per la città del foco
   vivo ten vai così parlando onesto,
   piacciati di restare in questo loco.   24
La tua loquela ti fa manifesto
   di quella nobil patria natio
   a la qual forse fui troppo molesto ».   27
Subitamente questo suono uscío
   d'una de l'arche, però m'accostai,
   temendo, un poco più al duca mio.   30
Ed ei mi disse: « Volgiti, che fai?
   vedi là Farinata che s'è dritto:
   da la cintola in sù tutto il vedrai ».   33
Io avea già il mio viso nel suo fitto;
   ed ei s'ergea col petto e con la fronte,
   come avesse l'inferno in gran dispitto.   36
E le animose man del duca e pronte
   mi pinser tra le sepolture a lui,
   dicendo: « Le parole tue sien conte ».   39
Com'io al piè de la sua tomba fui
   guardommi un poco, e poi, quasi sdegnoso,
   mi dimandò : « Chi fur li maggior tui? »   42
Io, ch'era d'ubbidir desideroso,
   non gliel celai, ma tutto gliel apersi;
   ond'ei levò le ciglia un poco in soso,   45
poi disse: « Fieramente furo avversi
   a me, ed a miei primi, ed a mia parte:
   sì che per due fiate li dispersi ».   48

And he to me: 'All will be fast shut down,
  when back here from Jehoshaphat they hie,
  each with the body once, up there, his own.
On this side of the cemetery lie
  with Epicurus all his train, who assume
  that man's soul, when his body does, will die.
Therefore to what thou askest me shall come
  quick answer. here within, and to that too,
  thy other wish, whereof to me thou art dumb.'
And I: 'Good leader, that my words be few
  I hide my heart from thee, not of desire;
  thyself, but now, warned me of this anew.'
'O Tuscan, walking through the city of fire
  alive, and speaking in such seemly wise,
  be pleased to halt awhile and to stand nigher.
Thy way of speech proves thee, beyond disguise,
  a native of that noble ɪatherland,
  which, maybe, I used o'er much to victimize.'
This sound from out a coffer close at hand
  came of a sudden: therefore by my guide,
  for dread, I somewhat closer took my stand.
'Nay, but turn round: what ails thee, then?' he cried.
  'See there, that's Farinata, risen upright:
  all of him, up from the waist, can be descried.'
I had already fixed on him my sight;
  and he, uplifting breast and forehead, made
  as were he holding hell in great despite.
My guide, with bold quick hands upon me laid,
  to him, where mid the vaults we saw him show,
  urged me on, saying: 'Be thy words well weigh'd.'
When I at his tomb's foot was standing now,
  he eyed me awhile: then, almost with disdain,
  he asked me: 'Of what lineage are *thou*?'
I, eager to obey, spoke out quite plain:
  I hid not, but detailed my kindred all;
  at which he slightly raised his eyebrows, then
thus answered: 'They were fiercely inimical
  to me, my forbears and my party, so
  that twice by scattering them I wrought their fall.'

« S'ei fur cacciati, ei tornar d'ogni parte »
 risposi lui « l'una e l'altra fiata;
 ma i vostri non appreser ben quell'arte ». 51

Allor surse a la vista scoperchiata
 un'ombra lungo questa infino al mento:
 credo che s'era in ginocchio levata. 54

Dintorno mi guardò, come talento
 avesse di veder s'altri era meco;
 e poi che il sospecciar fu tutto spento 57

piangendo disse: « Se per questo cieco
 carcere vai per altezza d'ingegno,
 mio figlio ov'è? e perchè non è teco? » 60

E io a lui: « Da me stesso non vegno:
 colui che attende là, per qui mi mena
 forse cui Guido vostro ebbe a disdegno ». 63

Le sue parole e il modo de la pena
 m'avevan di costui già letto il nome;
 però fu la risposta così piena. 66

Di subito drizzato gridò: « Come
 dicesti? egli *ebbe*? non vive egli ancora?
 non fiere gli occhi suoi lo dolce lome? » 69

Quando s'accorse d'alcuna dimora
 ch'io faceva davanti a la risposta,
 supin ricadde, e più non parve fora. 72

Ma quell'altro magnanimo a cui posta
 restato m'era, non mutò aspetto,
 nè mosse collo, nè piegò sua costa; 75

e sè continuando al primo detto
 « S'elli han quell'arte » disse « male appresa,
 ciò mi tormenta più che questo letto. 78

Ma non cinquanta volte fia raccesa
 la faccia de la donna che qui regge,
 che tu saprai quanto quell'arte pesa. 81

E se tu mai nel dolce mondo regge,
 dimmi; perchè quel popolo è sì empio
 incontro a' miei in ciascuna sua legge? » 84

Ond'io a lui: « Lo strazio e il grande scempio
 che fece l'Arbia colorata in rosso
 tali orazion fa far nel nostro tempio ». 87

'They from all quarters and both times, although
  chased forth, returned,' I answered him, 'which is
  an art that *yours* have ill learned hitherto.'
Then clear to sight, in the same tomb as his,
  rose from his side a shade, high as the chin:
  I think that it had risen upon its knees.
It peered all round, as had its impulse been
  to see if someone else was there with me;
  but vain the hope and, this once clearly seen,
weeping it said: 'If lofty genius be
  thy passport through this prison, of light forlorn,
  where is my son? Why is he not with thee?'
And I to him: 'I come not here self-borne:
  he, who waits there, p'r'aps brings me by this road
  to her, to be brought to whom your Guy thought scorn.'
By now his words, together with the mode
  of punishment, had read for me aright
  that spirit's name, as my full answer show'd.
'What' cried he, suddenly risen to his full height,
  'saidest thou "thought"? Lives he no longer, then?
  Strikes not upon his eyes the sweet daylight?'
Ere answering I made some delay: and when
  aware of this, he straight, without more said,
  fell backward, nor appeared outside again.
But he, that other, the great soul who'd bade
  me halt, changed not his aspect, nor so much
  as sideways bent, nor even turned his head.
'And if'—pursuing our previous talk—'with such
  ill-success they have learned that art,' said he,
  ' 'tis *that* torments me more than does this couch.
But not re-kindled fifty times shall be
  the lady's face who rules here, ere how great
  that art's dead weight is shalt be felt by thee.
Now tell me—so the sweet world mayst thou yet
  re-visit—why that people against mine
  in all its laws is so infuriate?'
'The slaughterous rout that made incarnadine
  the Arbia' I replied to him 'is why
  such prayers are uttered in our temple-shrine.'

71

Poi ch'ebbe sospirato e il capo scosso
« A ciò non fui io sol » disse « nè certo
senza cagion con gli altri sarei mosso. 90
Ma fui io solo, là dove sofferto
fu per ciascun di tòrre via Fiorenza,
colui che la difesi a viso aperto », 93
« Deh, se riposi mai vostra semenza »,
pregai io lui « solvetemi quel nodo
che qui ha inviluppata mia sentenza. 96
Ei par che voi veggiate, se ben odo,
dinanzi quel che il tempo seco adduce,
e nel presente tenete altro modo ». 99
« Noi veggiam come quei che ha mala luce
le cose » disse « che ne son lontano;
cotanto ancor ne splende il sommo duce. 102
Quando s'appressano o son, tutto è vano
nostro intelletto, e s'altri non ci apporta,
nulla sapem di vostro stato umano. 105
Però comprender puoi che tutta morta
fia nostra conoscenza da quel punto
che del futuro fia chiusa la porta ». 108
Allor, come di mia colpa compunto,
dissi: « Or direte dunque a quel caduto
che il suo nato è coi vivi ancor congiunto; 111
e s'io fui, dianzi, a la riposta muto,
fat'ei saper che il fei perchè pensava
già ne l'error che m'avete soluto ». 114
E già il maestro mio mi richiamava;
perch'io pregai lo spirito più avaccio
che mi dicesse chi con lui si stava. 117
Dissemi: « Qui con più di mille giaccio:
qua dentro è il secondo Federico,
e il Cardinale; e de gli altri mi taccio ». 120
Indi s'ascose; ed io inver l'antico
poeta volsi i passi, ripensando
a quel parlar che mi parea nemico. 123
Elli si mosse; e poi, così andando,
mi disse: « Perchè sei tu sì smarrito? »
E io li sodisfeci al suo dimando. 126

Shaking his head, he answered with a sigh:
  'There I was not alone nor, sooth, had e'er
  marched with the others save with warranty.

But it was I alone, in the place where
  all voted Florence should be swept away,
  yes, I alone, who boldly championed her.'

'Pray you, so may your seed repose for aye,'
  thus I implored him, 'loose for me the knot
  which here deprives my judgment of free play.

You seem, if I hear rightly, to have got
  clear sight of that which time will with it bring,
  but in the present other is your lot.'

'We see, like one with faulty vision, a thing'
  said he 'which is at distance from us set;
  so much light still vouchsafes to us heav'n's king.

When it draws nigh, or is, our minds are met
  by vacancy; and, save another bear
  us word, we know nought of your human state.

Hence, as from this 'tis easy to infer,
  the future's door once closed, from that point on
  we shall possess no knowledge whatsoe'er.'

Then said I—for my conscience had begun
  to prick me—: 'Pray tell him who sank below,
  that yet joined with the living is his son.

And if, before, I spoke not, let him know
  that even then my thoughts were occupied
  by the doubt which you freed me from just now.'

Recalling me already was my guide:
  wherefore I urged the spirit with greater haste
  to tell me who was with him; he replied:

'With more than a thousand souls I lie here: placed
  in here the second Frederick lies, in here
  the Cardinal; I'll say nought of the rest.'

With that he hid himself; and I drew near
  the ancient poet, pondering what to me
  seemed hostile in that speech and far from clear.

He moved on; and 'Why so bewildered?' he
  then asked, the while we ceased not to proceed:
  and I replied to his question readily.

« La mente tua conservi quel che udito
   hai contra te» mi comandò quel saggio;
« e ora attendi qui» e drizzò il dito: 129
« quando sarai dinanzi al dolce raggio
   di quella il cui bell'occhio tutto vede,
   da lei saprai di tua vita il viaggio.»   132
Appresso volse a man sinistra il piede;
   lasciammo il muro, e gimmo in ver lo mezzo
   per un sentier che ad una valle fiede   135
che infin là sù facea spiacer suo lezzo.

CANTO 11

In su l'estremità d'un' alta ripa
   che facevan gran pietre rotte in cerchio,
   venimmo sopra più crudele stipa;   3
e quivi per l'orribile soperchio
   del puzzo che il profondo abisso gitta,
   ci raccostammo dietro ad un coperchio   6
d'un grande avello, ov'io vidi una scritta
   che diceva *Anastasio papa guardo*
   lo qual trasse Fotin da la via dritta.   9
« Lo nostro scender convien esser tardo,
   sì che s'aùsi prima un poco il senso
   al tristo fiato; e poi non fia riguardo».   12
Così il maestro; e io: « Alcun compenso »
   dissi lui « trova, che il tempo non passi
   perduto». Ed elli: « Vedi che a ciò penso».   15
« Figliuol mio, dentro da cotesti sassi»
   cominciò poi a dir « son tre cerchietti
   di grado in grado, come quei che lassi.   18
Tutti son pien di spirti maledetti,
   ma perchè poi ti basti pur la vista,
   intendi come e perchè son costretti.   21
D'ogni malizia ch'odio in cielo acquista
   ingiuria è il fine, ed ogni fin cotale
   o con forza o con frode altrui contrista.   24

'What thou has heard against thyself' so bid
   the sage 'store up within thy mind, but now'—
   he raised his finger—'give thou *here* good heed.
When thou art basking in the radiant glow
   of her whose peerless eye sees all complete,
   from her thou'lt learn the way thy life will go.'
Whereon to the left hand he turned his feet:
   we took a transverse path that serves to link
   the wall we quitted with the central pit,
which even up there sickened us with its stink.

CANTO 11

From the edge of a high bank formed, circle-wise,
   of immense broken rocks a stowage yet
   more cruel, which lay below us, met our eyes:
and there by reason of the inordinate
   stench, which the deep abyss throws up, we took
   refuge behind the cover of a great
monument, where I saw inscribed what spoke
   thuswise: 'I hold pope Anastasius who,
   drawn by Photinus, the right way forsook.'
'Tis well we pause before descending, so
   that thus the sense may first grow a bit resign'd
   to the vile reek, then pay no heed thereto.'
Thus spake the master; and I answered: 'Find
   some offset, that the time may not pass by
   unused;' and he: 'Look, that was in my mind.'
'My son,' he then continued to reply,
   'ringed by these rocks and graded like the rounds
   which thou art leaving, three small circles lie.
Damned spirits fill them all: but, that good grounds
   thou have henceforth to know them at mere sight,
   understand how and why they are in bonds.
All kinds of malice that in heav'n excite
   abhorrence aim to hurt: which aim doth or
   by force or fraud on others wreak its spite.

Ma perchè frode è de l'uom proprio male
   più spiace a Dio, e però stan di sutto
   li frodolenti e più dolor li assale.   27
Dei violenti il primo cerchio è tutto;
   ma perchè si fa forza a tre persone,
   in tre gironi è distinto e costrutto.   30
A Dio, a sè, al prossimo si puone
   far forza: dico in loro ed in lor cose,
   come udirai con aperta ragione.   33
Morte per forza e ferute dogliose
   nel prossimo si dànno, e nel suo avere
   ruine, incendi e tollette dannose;   36
onde omicide e ciascun che mal fiere,
   guastatori e predon, tutti tormenta
   lo giron primo per diverse schiere.   39
Puote omo avere in sè man violenta
   e ne' suoi beni; e però nel secondo
   giron convien che sanza pro si penta   42
qualunque priva sè del vostro mondo,
   biscazza e fonde la sua facultade,
   e piange là dov'esser dee giocondo.   45
Puossi far forza ne la deitade,
   col cuor negando e bestemmiando quella
   e spregiando natura e sua bontade;   48
e però lo minor giron suggella
   del segno suo e Sodoma e Caorsa
   e chi, spregiando Dio col cor, favella.   51
La frode, onde ogni coscienza è morsa,
   può l'uomo usare in colui che si fida
   ed in quei che fidanza non imborsa.   54
Questo modo di retro par che uccida
   pur lo vincol d'amor che fa Natura;
   onde nel cerchio secondo s'annida   57
ipocrisia, lusinghe e chi affattura,
   falsità, ladroneccio, simonia,
   ruffian, baratti, e simile lordura.   60
Per l'altro modo quell'amor s'oblia
   che fa Natura, e quel ch'è poi aggiunto,
   di che la fede spezial si cria;   63

But fraud, as man's peculiar vice, before
  all else displeases God; hence lowest are set
  the fraudulent, and pain afflicts them more.
The violent fill the whole first circle; yet,
  since persons on whom force is wrought are three,
  it is in three rings built, each separate.
God, man's self, and his neighbour—each may be
  rough-handled: each, I say, and what is his,
  as thou shalt hear me prove convincingly.
By force are death and painful injuries
  wrought on one's neighbour: and, on what he owes,
  destruction, fires and ruinous levies.
Hence homicides and whoso deals foul blows,
  spoilers and plunderers, all in divers bands
  the first ring persecutes with divers woes.
A man may on himself lay violent hands,
  and on his goods; hence in the second ring
  with justice, bootlessly repenting, stands
whoe'er doth strip himself of your world, fling
  his goods away on the hazard of a die,
  and there weeps, where for gladness he should sing.
Force can be wrought upon the Deity
  by at heart denying and by blaspheming it,
  and scorning Nature and her benignity;
therefore the smallest ring stamps, as is meet,
  with its mark Sodom and Cahors, and those
  who speak the scorn of God their hearts secrete.
The fraud whose gnawing every conscience knows
  a man may use tow'rds one who trusts him and
  tow'rds one whose purse doth no such trust enclose.
The latter mode destroys, thou'lt understand,
  only the bond of love which Nature makes:
  hence in the second circle, thither bann'd,
nest hypocrites, and flatterers, whoso takes
  to witchcraft, forging, theft and simony,
  procurers, barrators and suchlike jakes.
By the other mode both loves are made to die,
  the natural and what supervenes thereon,
  source of the trust which forms a special tie.

onde nel cerchio minore, ov'è il punto
 de l'universo in su che Dite siede,
 qualunque trade in eterno è consunto».   66
E io: «Maestro, assai chiara procede
 la tua ragione, ed assai ben distingue
 questo baratro e il popol che il possiede.   69
Ma dimmi: quei de la palude pingue,
 che mena il vento, e che batte la pioggia,
 e che s'incontran con sì aspre lingue,   72
perchè non dentro da la città roggia
 son ei puniti se Dio li ha in ira,
 e se non li ha, perchè sono a tal foggia?»   75
Ed egli a me: «Perchè tanto delira»
 disse «lo ingegno tuo da quel che suole,
 o ver la mente tua altrove mira?   78
Non ti rimembra di quelle parole
 con le quai la tua Etica pertratta
 le tre disposizion che il ciel non vuole: 81
incontinenza, malizia e la matta
 bestialitade, e come incontinenza
 men Dio offende e men biasimo accatta?   84
Se tu riguardi ben questa sentenza,
 e rechiti a la mente chi son quelli
 che su di fuor sostengon penitenza,   87
tu vedrai ben perchè da questi felli
 sien dipartiti, e perchè men crucciata
 la divina vendetta li martelli».   90
«O sol che sani ogni vista turbata,
 tu mi contenti sì quando tu solvi,
 che, non men che saper, dubbiar m'aggrata.   93
Ancora un poco indietro ti rivolvi»
 diss'io «là dove di' che usura offende
 la divina bontade, e il groppo solvi».   96
«Filosofia» mi disse «a chi la intende,
 nota non pure in una sola parte
 come Natura lo suo corso prende   99
da divino intelletto e da su' arte;
 e se tu ben la tua Fisica note
 tu troverai, non dopo molte carte,   102

78

Hence in the smallest circle, and the one
  wherein the whole world centres and Dis reigns,
  all traitors are eternally undone.'
'Master,' I said, 'thy discourse well explains
  and well indeed distinguishes what rules
  control this gulf and all its denizens.
But tell me: those, stuck in the slimy pools,
  whom the wind drives, and whom the raindrops smite,
  and who, when clashing, vent such bitter howls,
if worthy of his anger in God's sight,
  why aren't they punished in the city of flame?
  And if not, why are *they* in such a plight?'
'Why go thy wits so far astray?' thus came
  his answer: 'thou art wont to show more skill;
  or is thy mind pursuing some other aim?
Hast thou not in thy recollection still
  those words with which thy *Ethics* treats the three
  main dispositions adverse to heav'n's will—
incontinence, malice, bestiality
  run mad? and how incontinence earns less
  blame, as offending God in less degree?
If thou mark well this dictum, and their case
  recall, and what they are, whose sins provoke
  chastisement up above, outside this place,
thou'lt well see why they're set from this vile folk
  apart, and why upon them with less wrath
  the divine vengeance plies its hammer-stroke.'
'O sun that show'st to all dim eyes the path,
  thou so content'st me, when thou solvest aught,
  that doubt hath charms not less than knowledge hath.
Once more,' said I, 'go somewhat back in thought
  to where thou saidst that usury offends
  the divine goodness, and untie that knot.'
'Philosophy,' he said, 'for whoso bends
  his mind to her, notes, nor in one sole part,
  how Nature, in the course she takes, descends
from divine intellect and from its art;
  and, if thou notest well thy *Physics*, there
  thou'lt find, not many pages from the start,

che l'arte vostra quella quanto puote
  segue, come il maestro fa il discente;
  sì che vostr'arte a Dio quasi è nipote.   105
Da queste due, se tu ti rechi a mente
  lo Genesì dal principio, conviene
  prender sua vita ed avanzar la gente;   108
e perchè l'usuriere altra via tiene,
  per sè Natura e per la sua seguace
  dispregia, poi ch'in altro pon la spene.   111
Ma seguimi oramai, chè il gir mi piace;
  chè i Pesci guizzan su per l'orizzonta,
  e il Carro tutto sovra il Coro giace,   114
e il balzo via là oltre si dismonta ».

CANTO 12

Era lo loco ove a scender la riva
  venimmo, alpestro, e per quel ch'ivi era, anco
  tal che ogni vista ne sarebbe schiva.   3
Qual è quella ruina che nel fianco
  di qua da Trento l'Adice percosse,
  o per tremoto o per sostegno manco,   6
che da cima del monte, onde si mosse,
  al piano è sì la roccia discoscesa
  che alcuna via darebbe a chi su fosse;   9
cotal di quel burrato era la scesa;
  e in su la punta de la rotta lacca
  l'infamia di Creti era distesa   12
che fu concetta ne la falsa vacca.
  E quando vide noi se stesso morse
  sì come quei cui l'ira dentro fiacca.   15
Lo savio mio inver lui gridò: « Forse
  tu credi che qui sia 'l duca d'Atene
  che su nel mondo la morte ti porse?   18

that your art does its best to follow her,
   e'en as the pupil does his master, so
   that your art is God's grandchild, as it were.
From these two, if thou recollectest how
   Genesis opens, it behoveth men
   to get the means by which they live and grow;
but usurers another way have ta'en:
   and, since they set their hope elsewhere, despise
   Nature, both in herself and in her train.
But follow me now, since to proceed were wise:
   the Fishes glint above the horizon, all
   the Wain by this time over Caurus lies,
and one descends, far on, the steep rock-wall.'

CANTO 12

THE place we reached to clamber down the cliff
   was alpine and, for what was there as well,
   such as all eyes would turn from with relief.
As is the landslip this side Trent, which fell
   on the Ádige in flank, through lack of prop
   it may be, or through earthquake (who can tell?);
where from the mountain-head which let them drop,
   down to the plain the shattered rocks so lie
   as to afford some passage from the top;
such was the steep scaur we descended by:
   and on the broken chasm's very brow
   there lay outstretched the Cretan infamy
which was conceived in the pretended cow;
   who, when he saw us, bit himself, like one
   inwardly rent by anger. 'Haply thou
deemst that the duke of Athens, by whom done
   to death wast thou in the upper world, draws near'
   my sage, turn'd tow'rds him, cried and then went on:

Pàrtiti, bestia, chè questi non viene
  ammaestrato da la tua sorella,
  ma vassi per veder le vostre pene ».   21
Qual è quel toro che si slaccia in quella
  che ha ricevuto già 'l colpo mortale,
  che gir non sa, ma qua e là saltella,   24
vid'io lo Minotauro far cotale;
  e quello accorto gridò: « Corri al varco:
  mentre che infuria è buon che tu ti cale ».   27
Così prendemmo via giù per lo scarco
  di quelle pietre, che spesso moviensi
  sotto i miei piedi per lo novo carco.   30
Io già pensando; e quei disse: « Tu pensi
  forse in questa ruina ch'è guardata
  da quell'ira bestial ch'i' ora spensi.   33
Or vo' che sappi che l'altra fiata
  ch'io discesi qua giù nel basso inferno,
  questa roccia non era ancor cascata.   36
Ma certo poco pria, se ben discerno,
  che venisse colui che la gran preda
  levò a Dite del cerchio superno,   39
da tutte parti l'alta valle feda,
  tremò sì, ch'io pensai che l'universo
  sentisse amor, per lo qual è chi creda   42
più volte il mondo in caos converso;
  ed in quel punto questa vecchia roccia
  qui ed altrove fece tal riverso.   45
Ma ficca gli occhi a valle, chè s'approccia
  la riviera del sangue, in la qual bolle
  qual che per violenza in altrui noccia ».   48
Oh cieca cupidigia, o ira folle,
  che sì ci sproni ne la vita corta
  e ne l'eterna poi sì mal c'immolle!   51
Io vidi un'ampia fossa in arco torta,
  come quella che tutto il piano abbraccia,
  secondo che avea detto la mia scorta;   54
e tra il piè de la ripa ed essa, in traccia
  correan centauri armati di saette,
  come solean nel mondo andare a caccia.   57

'Off with thee, beast: for this man comes not here
   schooled by thy sister, but to contemplate
   the punishments whereof thou'rt overseer.'
As is the bull that breaks its halter at
   the moment it receives the deathstroke, tries
   to advance, yet can but plunge this way and that,
I saw the Minotaur behave likewise;
   and 'Run to the pass' my wary leader cried:
   'best to descend while he thus raging lies.'
So down by that discharge of stones we hied,
   and oft, by reason of the unwonted load,
   under my feet the scree would slip and slide.
I went bemused; and he: 'Perchance some food
   for thought this ruin gives thee, where on guard
   is set that bestial wrath I've just subdued.
Know, therefore, that the other time I fared
   down here to lower hell, this precipice,
   not tumbled yet, still stood with face unscarr'd.
But of a truth, discern I not amiss,
   shortly ere His descent, who the great spoil
   of the upmost circle carried off from Dis,
the gulf to its depth, through all its loathsome coil,
   so trembled that the universe, methought,
   felt love, which more than once in vast turmoil,
as some deem, hath the world to chaos brought:
   and at that moment, both elsewhere and here,
   on this old cliff the ruin thou seest was wrought.
But fix thine eyes below; for, there, draws near
   the river of blood, boiling in which thou'lt see
   all who thro' violence spread fell havoc and fear.'
Oh foolish rage and blind cupidity,
   which in the short life goads us so, and then,
   in the eternal, steeps us so illy!
I saw a broad dike, bent to a bow, and when
   I farther looked, could see its curve embracing,
   just as my guide had said, the entire plain.
Between it and the escarpment's foot were racing,
   on the trail, Centaurs armed with arrows, like
   as they were wont on earth to go a-chasing.

Veggendoci calar ciascun ristette,
  e da la schiera tre si dipartiro
  con archi ed asticciuole prima elette.   60
E l'un gridò da lungi: «A qual martiro
  venite voi che scendete la costa?
  Ditel costinci, se non l'arco tiro».   63
Lo mio maestro disse: «La riposta
  farem noi a Chiron, costà di presso:
  mal fu la voglia tua sempre sì tosta!»   66
Poi mi tentò e disse: «Quegli è Nesso
  che morì per la bella Deianira
  e fe' di sè la vendetta elli stesso.   69
E quel di mezzo, che al petto si mira,
  è il gran Chirone, il qual nutrì Achille;
  quell'altro è Folo, che fu sì pien d'ira.   72
Dintorno al fosso vanno a mille a mille,
  saettando qual anima si svelle
  dal sangue più che sua colpa sortille».   75
Noi ci appressammo a quelle fere snelle.
  Chiron prese uno strale, e con la cocca
  fece la barba indietro, alle mascelle.   78
Quando s'ebbe scoperta la gran bocca
  disse ai compagni: «Siete voi accorti
  che quel di retro move ciò ch'ei tocca?   81
Così non soglion fare i piè dei morti».
  E il mio buon duca, che già gli era al petto
  dove le due nature son consorti,   84
rispose: «Ben è vivo, e sì soletto
  mostrarli mi convien la valle buia:
  necessità 'l c'induce, e non diletto.   87
Tal si partì da cantare alleluia
  che mi commise quest'ufficio novo;
  non è ladron, nè io anima fuia.   90
Ma per quella virtù per cui io movo
  li passi miei per sì selvaggia strada,
  danne un de' tuoi a cui noi siamo a provo,   93
e che ne mostri là dove si guada
  e che porti costui in su la groppa,
  chè non è spirto che per l'aere vada».   96

All, when they saw us dropping tow'rds the dike,
   stopped short, and from the squadron three moved out
   with bows, and shafts they'd chosen, aimed to strike.
'You on the slope there, what are you about?
   Bound for which torment come ye?' one, while still
   far off, cried: 'speak from there, or else I shoot.'
Whereat my master said: 'The answer will
   we make to Chiron there beside thee: thou
   wert ever thus in haste, to thine own ill!'
Then, nudging me, he said: 'That's Nessus, who,
   slain for fair Deianeira, made his own
   self his avenger and his slayer slew.
The midmost, at his own breast looking down,
   is the great Chiron, nurse to Peleus' son;
   the third is Pholus, for his rage well known.
Around the dike they in their thousands run,
   shooting at whoso from the blood withdraws
   more of himself than his crime lets be done.'
We neared those swift beasts. Chiron then it was
   who, drawing forth an arrow, with the notch
   pushed back the shaggy beard, upon his jaws:
and, having freed his great mouth, said thus much
   to his companions: 'Have ye noticed how
   the one behind there moves what he doth touch?
Thus are not wont a dead man's feet to do.'
   And my good leader, by now at his breast,
   where join the natures which in him are two,
answered: 'Yes, he's alive: on his lone quest
   'tis mine to show him all this dark abode,
   not fain, but at necessity's behest.
On me did one, who left the place that's loud
   with alleluias, lay this novel charge:
   no robber he, nor I a spirit of fraud.
But through that power by which I move at large
   my steps o'er this wild road do thou supply
   us now with one of thine, by the stream's marge
to guide us, and show where the ford doth lie,
   and carry this man o'er it on his croup,
   for he's no spirit who through the air can fly.'

Chiron si volse in su la destra poppa,
  e disse a Nesso: « Torna e sì li guida,
  e fa cansar s'altra schiera v'intoppa ».   99
Or ci movemmo con la scorta fida
  lungo la proda del bollor vermiglio,
  dove i bolliti facean alte strida.   102
Io vidi gente sotto infino al ciglio,
  e il gran centauro disse: « Ei son tiranni,
  che dier nel sangue e ne l'aver di piglio.   105
Quivi si piangon li spietati danni;
  quivi è Alessandro, e Dionisio fero
  che fe' Cicilia aver dolorosi anni.   108
E quella fronte che ha il pel così nero
  è Azzolino; e quell'altro ch'è biondo
  è Obizzo da Esti, il qual per vero   111
fu spento dal figliastro sù nel mondo ».
  Allor mi volsi al poeta, e quei disse:
  « Questi ti sia or primo e io secondo ».   114
Poco più oltre il centauro s'affisse
  sovra una gente che infino alla gola
  parea che di quel bulicame uscisse.   117
Mostrocci un'ombra da l'un canto sola
  dicendo: « Colui fesse in grembo a Dio
  lo cor che in sul Tamigi ancor si cola ».   120
Poi vidi gente che di fuor del rio
  tenea la testa ed ancor tutto il casso;
  e di costoro assai riconobb'io.   123
Così a più a più si facea basso
  quel sangue sì che cocea pur li piedi;
  e quindi fu del fosso il nostro passo.   126
« Sì come tu da questa parte vedi
  lo bulicame che sempre si scema »
  disse il centauro « voglio che tu credi   129
che da quest'altra a più a più giù prema
  lo fondo suo, infin ch'ei si raggiunge
  ove la tirannia convien che gema.   132
La divina giustizia di qua punge
  quell'Attila che fu flagello in Terra,
  e Pirro, e Sesto; ed in eterno munge   135

Chiron, wheeling on his right breast, called up
   Nessus and said: 'Turn and so guide them: make
   it give way, if ye meet another troop.'
Now with that trusty escort did we take
   our way beside the boiling crimson flood,
   whence from the boiled ones loud laments outbrake.
I saw folk in it—steeped to the brow they stood:
   and the great Centaur said: 'These that one nears
   were tyrants, set on plunder and on blood.
Here they bewail their ruthless rapine: here's
   with Alexander fell Dionysius, who
   made Sicily endure such dolorous years.
Yon forehead with the hair so black in hue
   is Ezzelin: that other, who is fair,
   Obizzo of Este, whom, if truth be true,
his stepson robbed of life in the world up there.'
   I turned round to the poet then, who said:
   'Deem *him* thy guide now, me his follower.'
His steps, a short way on, the Centaur stay'd
   above some who as far as the throat appeared
   to issue from the boiling: there a shade
he pointed to—a shade whom no one neared—
   saying: ' 'Twas he, who clove in the lap of God
   the heart which on the Thames is still revered.'
Next, I saw folk who raised from out the flood
   the head, nay more, the whole chest, and of these
   I could myself name many, if I would.
Thus became ever shallower by degrees
   that blood, until it scalded but the feet:
   and thence it was we crossed the dike with ease.
'The boiling brook, e'en as thou seest that it
   on this side ever loses depth,' then said
   the Centaur, 'so, I'd have thee now to wit
keeps lowering on this other side its bed
   more and more, till its circuit thither brings
   it back where tyranny her tears must shed.
The righteousness of God on this side stings
   that Attila called 'scourge' on Earth: likewise
   Pyrrhus and Sextus; and forever wrings

le lacrime che col bollor disserra
   a Rinier da Corneto, a Rinier Pazzo
   che fecero a le strade tanta guerra ».   138
Poi si rivolse e ripassossi il guazzo.

CANTO 13

Non era ancor di là Nesso arrivato
   quando noi ci mettemmo per un bosco
   che da nessun sentiero era segnato.   3
Non fronde verdi, ma di color fosco;
   non rami schietti, ma nodosi e involti;
   non pomi v'eran ma stecchi con tosco.   6
Non han sì aspri sterpi nè si folti
   quelle fere selvagge che in odio hanno
   tra Cecina e Corneto i luoghi colti.   9
Quivi le brutte Arpie lor nidi fanno,
   che cacciar de le Strofade i Troiani
   con tristo annunzio di futuro danno.   12
Ali hanno late, e colli e visi umani,
   piè con artigli, e pennuto il gran ventre;
   fanno lamenti in su gli alberi, strani.   15
E il buon maestro: « Prima che più entre
   sappi che sei nel secondo girone »
   mi cominciò a dire « e sarai mentre   18
che tu verrai ne l'orribil sabbione:
   però riguarda bene, e sì vedrai
   cose che torrien fede al mio sermone ».   21
Io sentia d'ogni parte trarre guai,
   e non vedea persona che il facesse;
   per ch'io tutto smarrito m'arrestai.   24
Io credo ch'ei credette ch'io credesse
   che tante voci uscisser tra quei bronchi
   da gente che per noi si nascondesse.   27
Però disse il maestro: « Se tu tronchi
   qualche fraschetta d'una d'este piante,
   li pensier ch'hai si faran tutti monchi ».   30

the tears, which with the boiling it unties,
   from both Corneto's and Pazzo's Riniér,
   whose war on travellers caused such bitter cries.'
Then turned he and recrossed the sump just there.

CANTO 13

Not yet had Nessus as he waded back
   reached shore, when we for our part pushed on through
   a wood unmarked by any beaten track.
Not green the leaves, but of a dusky hue;
   not smooth the boughs, but gnarled and interwound;
   not fruit-trees there, but poisonous brambles grew.
Not rougher brakes or thicker could be found,
   to lurk in, by those wild beasts that fight shy,
   'twixt Cécina and Corneto, of tilled ground.
Hither, to roost, the loathsome Harpies fly,
   who chased the Trojans from the Strophades
   with dismal presage of mischief drawing nigh.
Broad-wing'd, a human face and neck have these,
   great feathered paunch, and claws for toe and heel;
   they croak, high on the boughs, weird threnodies.
Then the good master thus began: 'I will
   thou shouldst, ere entering farther, understand
   thou'rt now in the second ring, and shalt be, till
thou comest to the waste of horrible sand.
   Look well, then, and thus things that would my tale
   discredit, thou shalt here see close at hand.'
I heard now all around me one long wail,
   and saw no person whence it could proceed:
   wherefore I stopped, deeming my wits to fail.
I think that *he* thought that *I* thought that mid
   the tree-trunks all those voices made their way
   from people who, whence *we* then stood, were hid.
And so my master said: 'Break off a spray
   from aught that's planted here, and thou'lt soon know
   how far the thoughts thou hast are gone astray.'

Allor porsi la mano un poco avante
  e colsi un ramicel da un gran pruno;
  e il tronco suo gridò: « Perchè mi schiante? »   33
Da che fatto fu poi di sangue bruno
  ricominciò a dir: « Perchè mi scerpi?
  Non hai tu spirto di pietate alcuno?   36
Uomini fummo, ed or siam fatti sterpi;
  ben dovrebb'esser la tua man più pia
  se stati fossimo anime di serpi ».   39
Come d'un stizzo verde ch'arso sia
  da l'un dei capi, che da l'altro geme
  e cigola per vento che va via,   42
sì de la scheggia rotta usciva insieme
  parole e sangue, ond'io lasciai la cima
  cadere, e stetti come l'uom che teme.   45
« S'egli avesse potuto creder prima »
  rispose il savio mio, « anima lesa,
  ciò che ha veduto pur con la mia rima,   48
non averebbe in te la man distesa;
  ma la cosa incredibile mi fece
  indurlo ad opra che a me stesso pesa.   51
Ma dilli chi tu fosti, sì che, in vece
  d'alcun'ammenda, tua fama rinfreschi
  nel mondo sù, dove tornar li lece ».   54
E il tronco: « Sì col dolce dir m'adeschi
  ch'io non posso tacere, e voi non gravi
  perch'io un poco a ragionar m'inveschi.   57
Io son colui che tenni ambo le chiavi
  del cor di Federico, e che le volsi,
  serrando e disserrando, sì soavi   60
che dal secreto suo quasi ogn'uom tolsi.
  Fede portai al glorioso offizio
  tanto ch'io ne perdei li sonni e i polsi.   63
La meretrice che mai da l'ospizio
  di Cesare non torse gli occhi putti,
  morte comune e de le corti vizio,   66
infiammò contra me gli animi tutti
  e gl'infiammati infiammar sì Augusto
  che i lieti onor tornaro in tristi lutti.   69

Then, putting out my hand, from a great sloe
  I plucked a tiny twig, and therewithal
  its trunk cried out: 'Why dost thou rend me so?'
I saw 't grow dark with blood, then heard it call
  out once again: 'Why maim'st thou me? Awakes
  my cruel lot no pity in thee at all?
Each of us, once of human shape, here takes
  a stock's: thy hand ought surely to have shown
  more mercy, had our souls been those of snakes.'
As from a green log which, one end alone
  on fire, at the other oozes from the wood
  and hisses by reason of the wind thence blown,
so from the broken splinter words and blood
  came forth together: whence I, like one un-nerved,
  thereupon let the tip fall where I stood.
'If what my verse alone till now has served
  to show him he'd been able to believe
  beforehand, poor hurt soul,' my sage observed,
'thee had he ne'er stretched forth his hand to reave;
  but 'twas the thing's being past belief that made
  me prompt his deed, for which I too now grieve.
But tell him who thou wast, that so, instead
  of some amends, he may revive thy fame
  on earth, to return whereto he is licenséd.'
'So sweet thy words are, that, enticed by them,
  I cannot be mute,' the trunk said: 'and do ye,
  if talk belimes me a little, forgive the same.
'Twas I that held the one and the other key
  of Frederick's heart, which I grew so adept
  at locking and unlocking silently,
that from its secrets nigh all men I kept:
  so faithful was I to my glorious charge,
  that I for it lost strength, nay, scarcely slept.
The drab against whose strumpet eyes no targe
  is proof in Caesar's household—she that is
  the vice of courts and death to men at large—
set against me all minds aflame, and these,
  inflamed, in turn inflamed Augustus, so
  that gracious honours turned to obloquies.

L'animo mio, per disdegnoso gusto
  credendo col morir fuggir disdegno,
  ingiusto fece me contra me giusto.   72
Per le nuove radici d'esto legno
  vi giuro che già mai non ruppi fede
  al mio signor, che fu d'onor sì degno.   75
E se di voi alcun nel mondo riede,
  conforti la memoria mia, che giace
  ancor del colpo che invidia le diede ».   78
Un poco attese, e poi: « Da ch'ei si tace »
  disse il poeta a me, « non perder l'ora;
  ma parla, e chiedi a lui, se più ti piace ».   81
Ond'io a lui: « Domanda tu ancora
  di quel che credi che a me satisfaccia,
  ch'io non potrei, tanta pietà m'accora ».   84
Però ricominciò: « Se l'uom ti faccia
  liberamente ciò che il tuo dir priega,
  spirito incarcerato, ancor ti piaccia   87
di dirne come l'anima si lega
  in questi nocchi; e dinne, se tu puoi,
  se alcuna mai di tai membra si spiega ».   90
Allor soffiò lo tronco forte, e poi
  si convertì quel vento in cotal voce:
  « Brevemente sarà risposto a voi.   93
Quando si parte l'anima feroce
  dal corpo ond'ella stessa s'è disvelta,
  Minos la manda a la settima foce.   96
Cade in la selva e non l'è parte scelta;
  ma là dove fortuna la balestra,
  quivi germoglia come gran di spelta.   99
Surge in vermena ed in pianta silvestra;
  le Arpie pascendo poi de le sue foglie
  fanno dolore ed al dolor finestra.   102
Come l'altre verrem per nostre spoglie,
  ma non però che alcuna sen rivesta,
  chè non è giusto aver ciò ch'uom si toglie.   105
Qui le strascineremo, e per la mesta
  selva saranno i nostri corpi appesi,
  ciascuno al prun de l'ombra sua molesta ».   108

My mind that, with contemptuous relish, now
  by dying thought to escape contempt, to my
  own righteous self dealt an unrighteous blow.

But by the strange roots of this tree do I
  swear that I never with my lord broke faith,
  whom all so justly held in honour high.

If one of you to the world re-journeyeth,
  let him restore my memory, 'neath the stroke
  still prostrate whereby envy sought its death.'

Waiting awhile, the poet to me then spoke:
  'Since he is silent, lose not the hour, but if
  thou would'st know more, speak and his word invoke.'

Whence I to him: 'Aught that in thy belief
  would satisfy me, ask him further thou;
  I could not, so o'erwhelm me pity and grief.'

Hence 'So may this man do for thee' he now
  began again 'without stint all thy prayer,
  imprisoned sprite—please tell us further how

the soul is bound within these gnarls, nor spare
  to tell us, an thou canst, if it be true
  that any ever doffs the limbs ye wear.'

Mightily thereupon the tree-trunk blew;
  the wind was then converted to this speech:
  'Your question shall be answered and in few.

When quits its body the violent spirit which
  is torn therefrom by action of its own,
  Minos consigns it to the seventh ditch.

It falls into the wood and there, where thrown
  by chance (no place is chosen for it), then
  sprouts, as a grain of spelt does, where it's sown.

To a sapling's height, and tree's, doth it attain:
  next, on its leaves for food the harpies pounce,
  and cause pain, and a loophole for the pain.

Like the others we shall come for what we once
  stripped off, but not again to don it; for
  men justly lose what they themselves renounce.

Here we shall drag it and, the sad wood o'er,
  each on the thorn-tree of its hostile shade,
  our bodies will be hung for evermore.'

Noi eravamo ancora al tronco attesi,
  credendo ch'altro ne volesse dire,
  quando noi fummo d'un romor sorpresi   111
similemente a colui che venire
  sente il porco e la caccia a la sua posta,
  ch'ode le bestie e le frasche stormire.   114
Ed ecco due da la sinistra costa
  nudi e graffiati, fuggendo sì forte
  che de la selva rompieno ogni rosta.   117
Quel dinanzi: « or accorri, accorri, morte! »
  E l'altro, cui pareva tardar troppo,
  gridava: « Lano, non sì furo accorte   120
le gambe tue a le giostre del Toppo! »
  E poi che forse li fallia la lena,
  di sè e d'un cespuglio fece un groppo.   123
Di retro a loro era la selva piena
  di nere cagne, bramose e correnti
  come veltri che uscisser di catena.   126
In quel che s'appiattò miser li denti,
  e quel dilaceraro a brano a brano;
  poi sen portar quelle membra dolenti.   129
Présemi allor la mia scorta per mano,
  e menommi al cespuglio che piangea
  per le rotture sanguinenti, invano.   132
« O Giacomo » dicea « da Sant'Andrea,
  che t'è giovato di me fare schermo?
  Che colpa ho io de la tua vita rea? »   135
Quando il maestro fu sovr'esso fermo,
  disse: « Chi fosti, che per tante punte
  soffii col sangue doloroso sermo? »   138
Ed egli a noi: « O anime che giunte
  siete a veder lo strazio disonesto
  ch'ha le mie fronde sì da me disgiunte,   141
raccoglietele al piè del tristo cesto.
  Io fui de la città che nel Battista
  mutò il primo padrone; ond'ei per questo   144
sempre con l'arte sua la farà trista;
  e se non fosse che in sul passo d'Arno
  rimane ancor di lui alcuna vista,   147

Deeming its say had not yet all been said,
  we were still paying attention to the tree,
  when such an uproar startled us as made
us like to him who marks the approach where he
  is stationed of the wild boar and the chase,
  and hears the beasts and the boughs crash: and, see!
two spirits upon our left at headlong pace
  naked and scratched, come fleeing so fast that they
  forced every switch in the wood to yield them place.
He in front: 'Death, come now, come quick!' and 'Hey!
  Lano,' the other, who seemed to himself o'erslow,
  was crying: 'thy legs were not so spry that day
when by the Toppo thou didst a-tilting go!'
  and, breathless maybe, he crouched close in beside
  a bush, and, grown one group with it, lay low.
Behind them the wood was swarming far and wide
  with great black bitches, ravenous, running as were
  they greyhounds slipped from the thong that holds
On him that squatted I saw them leap and tear   [them tied.
  him savagely with their teeth piecemeal, and then
  carry those suffering members off elsewhere.
Taking my hand when all was still again,
  my escort led me to the bush which bled
  and wept through all its fractures, but in vain.
'O James o' St. Andrew's Chapel,' so it said,
  'how has it helped thee to make *me* thy screen?
  For thy bad life why must *my* blood be shed?'
Halting above it: 'Who mayst *thou* have been,'
  the master said, 'who through so many a stub
  blowest forth with blood a speech that vents thy spleen?'
And he to us: 'O souls that through this scrub
  are come to see the unseemly havoc wrought
  by severance of its leaves on my poor shrub,
gather them, pray, again about its foot.
  I hailed from the city which for the Baptist changed
  her first patron; wherefore he'll always plot,
by plaguing her with his art, to be revenged;
  and, did there not, where Arno's crossed, remain
  some semblance still of him she thus estranged,

quei cittadin che poi la rifondarno
  sovra il cener che d'Attila rimase,
  avrebber fatto lavorare indarno.   150
Io fei giubbetto a me de le mie case».

CANTO 14

Poi che la carità del natìo loco
  mi strinse, raunai le fronde sparte,
  e rendeile a colui ch'era già fioco.   3
Indi venimmo al fine ove si parte
  lo secondo giron dal terzo, e dove
  si vede di giustizia orribil arte.   6
A ben manifestar le cose nove,
  dico che arrivammo ad una landa
  che dal suo letto ogni pianta rimove.   9
La dolorosa selva l'è ghirlanda
  intorno, come il fosso tristo ad essa:
  quivi fermammo i passi a randa a randa.   12
Lo spazzo era una rena arida e spessa,
  non d'altra foggia fatta che colei
  che fu dai piè di Caton già soppressa.   15
O vendetta di Dio, quanto tu dei
  esser temuta da ciascun che legge
  ciò che fu manifesto a gli occhi miei!   18
D'anime nude vidi molte gregge
  che piangean tutte assai miseramente,
  e parea posta lor diversa legge: 21
supin giaceva in terra alcuna gente,
  alcuna si sedea tutta raccolta,
  ed altra andava continuamente.   24
Quella che giva intorno era più molta,
  e quella men che giaceva al tormento
  ma più al duolo avea la lingua sciolta.   27
Sopra tutto il sabbion d'un cader lento
  piovean di foco dilatate falde
  come di neve in alpe sanza vento.   30

those citizens who founded her again
   on the ashes left by Attila would be
   as had they spent their labour all in vain.
I made me a gibbet of my own roof-tree.'

CANTO 14

CONSTRAINED by affection for my native place
   I gathered and gave back the scattered leaves
   to him, whose strength of voice had now grown less.
Then came we to the boundary where gives
   the second ring room to the third and where
   one now of justice a horrible mode perceives.
To make the new things patent I declare
   that we had reached a plain which from its bed
   rejects all vegetation whatsoe'er.
By the grim wood it is engarlanded
   all round, as that is by the dismal dike:
   here at the very edge our steps were stay'd.
Of dry, deep sand, the ground was not unlike
   in fashion to that parched and arid waste
   across which Cato's feet once had to strike.
Vengeance of God, oh, how shouldst thou be faced
   with fear by whosoever haps to read
   what to my own eyes was made manifest!
Of naked souls I saw great herds amid
   the sand, who all wept very miserably,
   but diverse lots seemed unto them decreed.
Flat on the ground face-upward did I see
   some, and some sitting all hunched up: again
   others were on the move continually.
The latter far outnumbered, it was plain,
   those who were lying in the torment, though
   these had their tongues more loosened by the pain.
O'er the whole sandy desert, falling slow,
   dilated flakes of fire were being rain'd,
   as on a windless alp descendeth snow.

Quali Alessandro in quelle parti calde
    d'India vide sopra lo suo stuolo
    fiamme cadere infino a terra salde,   33
perch'ei provvide a scalpitar lo suolo
    con le sue schiere, acciò che lo vapore
    me' si stingueva mentre ch'era solo,   36
tale scendeva l'eternale ardore,
    onde la rena s'accendea com'esca
    sotto focile, a doppiar lo dolore.   39
Sanza riposo mai era la tresca
    de le misere mani, or quindi or quinci
    iscotendo da sè l'arsura fresca.   42
Io cominciai: « Maestro, tu che vinci
    tutte le cose, fuor che i dimon duri
    che a l'entrar de la porta incontro uscinci,   45
chi è quel grande che non par che curi
    l'incendio, e giace dispettoso e torto,
    sì che la pioggia non par che il maturi? »   48
E quel medesmo, che si fu accorto
    ch'io domandava il mio duca di lui,
    gridò: « Qual io fui vivo, tal son morto.   51
Se Giove stanchi il suo fabbro, da cui
    crucciato prese la folgore acuta
    onde l'ultimo dì percosso fui;   54
o s'elli stanchi gli altri a muta a muta
    in Mongibello a la fucina negra
    chiamando: 'Buon Vulcano, aiuta, aiuta!'   57
sì com'ei fece alla pugna di Flegra,
    e me saetti di tutta sua forza,
    non ne potrebbe aver vendetta allegra ».   60
Allora il duca mio parlò di forza
    tanto, ch'io non l'avea sì forte udito:
    « O Capaneo, in ciò che non s'ammorza   63
la tua superbia, sei tu più punito:
    nullo martiro fuor che la tua rabbia
    sarebbe al tuo furor dolor compito ».   66
Poi si rivolse a me con miglior labbia
    dicendo: « Quei fu l'un dei sette regi
    che assiser Tebe, ed ebbe, e par ch'egli abbia   69

Such flames as Alexander, when he attain'd
    to those hot parts of Ind, upon his host
    saw, even to the ground unbrok'n, descend;
wherefore he bade his troops, ere time were lost,
    stamp on the soil, because the ignited air
    was easiest quenched, where isolated most.
Just so the eternal heat kept falling there,
    Whereby, to increase the pain twofold, the sand,
    like tinder under steel, was set aflare.
Each hand in counterdance with tortured hand,
    this side and that, sought ever without rest
    to fend off the fresh burning ere it should land.
I began: 'Master, thou that conquerest
    all things, except the fiends who, when we fain
    had entered, barred the gate with stubborn gest,
who is that big one who of the burning pain
    seems heedless, and in scorn writhes on his bed,
    so that he seems unmellowed by the rain?'
And he himself, catching what I had said
    unto my leader touching him, straightway
    cried: 'As I was in life, such am I dead.
Jove, let him wear his smith out as he may,
    from whom he took the pointed levin to burn
    and blast me in his wrath on my last day—
or let him wear the rest out turn by turn
    at the black forge in Mongibello and cry
    "Help, help, good Vulcan," and the like concern
show as at Phlegra's battle to let fly
    at me his arrows with his utmost might—
    yet from his vengeance shall derive no joy.'
Then spoke my guide, his voice raised to a height
    of vehemence I had never heard before:
    'O Cápaneus, in that thine arrogant spite
burns unextinguished, thou art punished the more:
    no torment short of thy own rage were pain
    enough to pay thy fury its full score.'
He turned round and in milder accents then
    to me said: 'One of those seven kings was he
    who besieged Thebes; he held God in disdain,

Dio in disdegno, e poco par che il pregi;
  ma, com'io dissi lui, li suoi dispetti
  sono al suo petto assai debiti fregi.   72
Or mi vien dietro, e guarda che non metti
  ancor li piedi ne la rena arsiccia,
  ma sempre al bosco tienili ristretti ».   75
Tacendo divenimmo là 've spiccia
  fuor de la selva un picciol fiumicello,
  lo cui rossore ancor mi raccapriccia.   78
Quale del Bulicame esce ruscello
  che parton poi tra lor le peccatrici,
  tal per la rena giù sen giva quello.   81
Lo fondo suo ed ambo le pendici
  fatt'era in pietra e i margini da lato;
  perch'io m'accorsi che il passo era lici.   84
« Tra tutto l'altro che t'ho dimostrato
  poscia che noi entrammo per la porta
  lo cui sogliare a nessuno è negato,   87
cosa non fu da gli occhi tuoi scorta
  notabil come lo presente rio
  che sopra sè tutte fiammelle ammorta ».   90
Queste parole fur del duca mio;
  per ch'io 'l pregai che mi largisse il pasto
  di cui largito m'aveva il disio.   93
« In medio mar siede un paese guasto »
  diss'egli allora « che s'appella Creta,
  sotto il cui rege fu già il mondo casto.   96
Una montagna v'è che già fu lieta
  d'acqua e di fronde, che si chiamò Ida;
  ora è diserta, come cosa vieta.   99
Rea la scelse già per cuna fida
  del suo figliuolo, e per celarlo meglio,
  quando piangea vi facea far le grida.   102
Dentro dal monte sta dritto un gran veglio
  che tien volte le spalle inver Damiata
  e Roma guarda sì come suo speglio.   105
La sua testa è di fin oro formata,
  e puro argento son le braccia e il petto,
  poi è di rame infino a la forcata.   108

recked of him little, and still does, seemingly;
  but, as I told him, to adorn his breast
  nought suits so well as his own blasphemy.
Come now behind me, and be careful lest
  thou set thy feet on the scorched sand: to keep
  them still well back within the wood were best.'
Silent we came to where spurts forth from deep
  within the woodland a small rivulet,
  whose blood-red colour makes my flesh still creep.
As from the Bulicame finds outlet
  the brook which prostitutes then 'mongst them share,
  so down the sand its course did that one set.
Its bed was made of stone, as also were
  both banks, the margins too on either side:
  whence I perceived the passage must be there.
'Of all that I have shown thee as thy guide
  from when our entrance through the gate was made
  of which the threshold is to none denied,
nothing before thine eyes hath been display'd
  so worth thy notice as this present stream,
  which renders all fire-flakes above it dead.'
My leader thus; hence I entreated him
  to give me of the food whereof to taste
  he'd given me now a craving so extreme.
'In mid-sea there is set a land, all waste,'
  he then went on, 'the name of which is Crete,
  under whose king the world, one time, was chaste.
A mountain 's there, called Ida, happy seat
  of fountains once and foliage: now it lies
  deserted, as if time had mouldered it.
Rhea once chose it to guard, cradle-wise,
  her babe and caused it, that he better pass
  unnoticed when he wailed, to ring with cries.
An Ancient, caverned huge in the mountain's mass,
  his back turn'd tow'rds Damietta, stands upright,
  gazing on Rome, as on his looking-glass.
His head is fashioned of fine gold, and bright
  with purest silver are his arms and breast,
  next he's of brass till the fork comes in sight.

Da indi in giuso è tutto ferro eletto,
    salvo che il destro piede è terra cotta,
    e sta in su quel più che in su l'altro eretto.   111
Ciascuna parte, fuor che l'oro, è rotta
    d'una fessura che lagrime goccia,
    le quali, accolte, foran quella grotta.   114
Lor corso in questa valle si diroccia:
    fanno Acheronte, Stige e Flegetonta;
    poi sen van giù per questa stretta doccia   117
infin là ove più non si dismonta:
    fanno Cocito; e qual sia quello stagno
    tu lo vedrai, però qui non si conta ».   120
Ed io a lui: « Se il presente rigagno
    si deriva così dal nostro mondo,
    perchè ci appar pure a questo vivagno? »   123
Ed egli a me: « Tu sai che il luogo è tondo,
    e tutto che tu sie venuto molto
    pur a sinistra giù calando al fondo,   126
non sei ancor per tutto il cerchio volto;
    per che se cosa n'apparisce nova,
    non dee addur maraviglia al tuo volto ».   129
E io ancor: « Maestro, ove si trova
    Flegetonta e Letè? chè de l'un taci
    e l'altro di' che si fa d'esta piova? »   132
« In tutte tue question certo mi piaci »
    rispose « ma il bollor de l'acqua rossa
    dovea ben solver l'una che tu faci.   135
Letè vedrai, ma fuor di questa fossa,
    là dove vanno l'anime a lavarsi
    quando la colpa pentuta è rimossa ».   138
Poi disse: « Omai è tempo da scostarsi
    dal bosco; fa che di retro a me vegne:
    li margini fan via, che non son arsi,   141
e sopra loro ogni vapor si spegne ».

Thence downward of choice iron is all the rest,
 save the right foot of potter's clay, whereon
 rather than on the left his stance is based.
Throughout each part except the gold doth run
 a fissure, dripping tears, which accumulate,
 then pierce that cavern's floor and, plunging down
from rock to rock into this gulf, create
 Acheron, Styx, and Phlegethon, then bend
 their course down through this narrow sluice, and get
at last to where one can no more descend:
 they form Cocytus; and what kind of mere
 that is, thou'lt see: so at this point I'll end.'
And I to him: 'If the rill, present here,
 derives in this way from our world beyond,
 why but at *this* verge do we see it appear?'
And he to me: 'Thou knowest the place is round;
 and great as is the arc thou hast travelled through,
 constantly leftward, down tow'rd hell's profound,
yet of the circuit much remains to do;
 it should not to thy face bring wonder, then,
 if we at times encounter something new.'
'Master, where's Phlegethon?' thus I again:
 'and Lethe? For the one thou dost not name,
 and the other's made thou sayest, by this rain.'
'Doubt not that all thy questions please me,' came
 his answer; 'but the boiling of the red
 water might well have solved the first of them.
Lethe thou'lt see, but there—beyond this dread
 abyss—where the souls go to wash them clean,
 when they've repented, and their guilt is shed.'
Then said he: 'Let us no more keep within
 the wood; see thou behind me come; a route
 the margins furnish, where no fire is seen,
since over them all vapours are put out.'

CANTO 15

Ora cen porta l'un dei duri margini,
   e il fummo del ruscel di sopra aduggia,
   sì che dal foco salva l'acqua e gli argini.   3
Quale i Fiamminghi tra Guizzante e Bruggia,
   temendo il fiotto che inver lor s'avventa,
   fanno lo schermo perchè il mar si fuggia;   6
e quale i Padovan lungo la Brenta,
   per difender lor ville e lor castelli
   anzi che Chiarentana il caldo senta;   9
a tale immagine eran fatti quelli,
   tutto che nè sì alti nè sì grossi,
   qual che si fosse, lo maestro felli.   12
Già eravam da la selva rimossi
   tanto, ch'io non avrei visto dov'era
   perch'io indietro rivolto mi fossi,   15
quando incontrammo d'anime una schiera
   che venian lungo l'argine, e ciascuna
   ci riguardava come suol da sera   18
guardar l'un l'altro sotto nuova luna,
   e sì ver noi aguzzavan le ciglia
   come vecchio sartor fa ne la cruna.   21
Così adocchiato da cotal famiglia,
   fui conosciuto da un, che mi prese
   per lo lembo e gridò: « Qual maraviglia! »   24
E io, quando il suo braccio a me distese,
   ficcai gli occhi per lo cotto aspetto
   sì, che il viso abbruciato non difese   27
la conoscenza sua al mio intelletto;
   e chinando la mia a la sua faccia
   risposi: « Siete voi qui, Ser Brunetto! »   30
E quelli: « O figliuol mio, non ti dispiaccia
   se Brunetto Latini un poco teco
   ritorna indietro e lascia andar la traccia ».   33
Io dissi lui: « Quanto posso ven preco!
   e se volete che con voi m'asseggia,
   faròl, se piace a costui, che vo seco ».   36

CANTO 15

Now one of the hard margins bears us on,
  steam from the brook so shadowing overhead,
  that of the fire water and banks get none.
As Flemings 'twixt Wissánt and Bruges, in dread
  of the spring tide when it is blown their way,
  build dikes, that the sea's inrush may be stay'd;
and as along the Brenta, so that they
  may guard their towns and castles, Paduans rear
  dams, ere Carinthia feels the warmth of May;
not otherwise were the embankments here,
  save that he'd built them not so high and wide,
  whoe'er he was, that master-engineer.
Already from the woodland we had hied
  so far that, had I turned to look, it could
  no longer, where I was, have been descried,
when we met souls approaching in a crowd
  beside the embankment who, as each passed by,
  eyed us, as one man, comes the evening, would
another, when the new moon's in the sky;
  puckering at us their eyebrows in such wise
  as does the old tailor at his needle's eye.
Submitted thus to such a family's
  inspection, I was known of one, who caught
  my skirt, and cried: 'Can I believe my eyes!'
I, when to me he stretched his arm out, brought
  my gaze to rest so squarely on his baked
  appearance, that his scorched face stayed me not
from recognizing him with my intellect;
  and '*You* here, Ser Brunetto!' stooping down
  my face to his, I said: and my heart ached.
And he: 'May't not displease thee, my dear son,
  if Brunetto Latini turn with thee
  a short way back, and let the file pass on.'
'With all my heart I beg you to; and be
  it your wish,' I said, 'that I sit with you, I will,
  if he there, whom I'm going with, agree.'

« O figliuol » disse « qual di questa greggia
   s'arresta punto, giace poi cent'anni
   sanz'arrostarsi quando 'l foco il feggia.   39
Però va oltre: io ti verrò ai panni,
   e poi rigiugnerò la mia masnada,
   che va piangendo i suoi eterni danni ».   42
Io non osava scender de la strada
   per andar par di lui, ma il capo chino
   tenea, com'uom che reverente vada.   45
Ei cominciò: « Qual fortuna o destino
   anzi l'ultimo dì qua giù ti mena,
   e chi è questi che mostra il cammino? »   48
« Là su di sopra, in la vita serena »
   rispos'io lui « mi smarrii 'n una valle
   avanti che l'età mia fosse piena.   51
Pur ier mattina le volsi le spalle;
   questi m'apparve tornand'io in quella,
   e reducemi a ca' per questo calle ».   54
Ed egli a me: « Se tu segui tua stella,
   non puoi fallire a glorioso porto,
   se ben m'accorsi ne la vita bella: 57
e s'io non fossi sì per tempo morto,
   veggendo il cielo a te così benigno,
   dato t'avrei a l'opera conforto.   60
Ma quell'ingrato popolo maligno
   che discese di Fiesole ab antico,
   e tiene ancor del monte e del macigno,   63
ti si farà, per tuo ben far, nimico:
   ed è ragion, chè tra li lazzi sorbi
   si disconvien fruttare il dolce fico.   66
Vecchia fama nel mondo li chiama orbi:
   gente avara, invidiosa e superba!
   dai lor costumi fa che tu ti forbi.   69
La tua fortuna tanto onor ti serba,
   che l'una parte e l'altra avranno fame
   di te: ma lungi fia dal becco l'erba.   72
Faccian le bestie fiesolane strame
   di lor medesme, e non tocchin la pianta,
   se alcuna sorge ancora in lor letame,   75

'O son,' he said, 'who of this herd stands still
  one instant, lies ten decades then supine
  and powerless to brush off the fiery ill.

Move forward, then: I at these skirts of thine
  will follow, then rejoin my company,
  who, as they go, for aye lament and pine.'

I dared not step down from the path to be
  on the same level with him, but kept my head
  bent low, like to one walking reverently.

And he began: 'What chance or fate has led
  thee ere thy last day down into this pit?
  And who is this, whose guidance lends thee aid?'

'Up there,' I answered him, 'in the life lit
  by sunshine, in a valley I went astray,
  ere half my sum of days was yet complete.

From it I turned at dawn but yesterday:
  as to it I re-turned did he appear
  and leads me home now by this narrow way.'

And he to me: 'An thou pursue thy star,
  thou canst not fail to reach the glorious port,
  if I judged well in the glad life up there;

and had my days not been o'ersoon cut short,
  seeing heav'n thus kind to thee I would have lent
  thy work my aid and been thy strong support.

But that ungrateful commons, on evil bent,
  who down from Fiésole came long ago,
  and still of rock and mountain keep some taint,

will, for thy good deeds, make themselves thy foe;
  and with good reason, for sweet figs are seen
  to fruit but ill where bitter sorb-trees grow.

Long deemed by the world purblind, they've ever been
  a greedy envious folk, whose pride doth pass
  all limits: from their ways see thou keep clean.

Thy fortune holds for thee such honour as
  that either side will long to make a meal
  of thee: but far from goat shall be the grass.

Let the brute-beasts of Fiésole have still
  themselves for fodder and not touch the tree
  (if any yet grows up in their dung-hill)

in cui riviva la sementa santa
di quei Roman che vi rimaser quando
fu fatto il nido di malizia tanta ».   78
« Se fosse tutto pieno il mio dimando »
risposi lui « voi non sareste ancora
de l'umana natura posto in bando;   81
chè in la mente m'è fitta, ed or m'accora,
la cara e buona immagine paterna
di voi, quando nel mondo, ad ora ad ora,   84
m'insegnavate come l'uom s'eterna;
e quanto io l'abbia in grado, mentr'io vivo
convien che ne la mia lingua si scerna.   87
Ciò che narrate di mio corso, scrivo
e serbolo a chiosar, con altro testo,
a donna che saprà, se a lei arrivo.   90
Tanto vogl'io che vi sia manifesto,
pur che mia coscienza non mi garra,
che a la Fortuna, come vuol, son presto.   93
Non è nuova a gli orecchi miei tale arra:
però giri Fortuna la sua rota
come le piace, e il villan la sua marra ».   96
Lo mio maestro allora in su la gota
destra si volse in dietro e riguardommi;
poi disse: « Ben ascolta chi la nota! »   99
Nè, per tanto, di men parlando vommi
con ser Brunetto, e dimando chi sono
li suoi compagni più noti e più sommi.   102
Ed egli a me: « Saper d'alcuno è buono;
de gli altri fia laudabile tacerci,
chè il tempo saria corto a tanto suono.   105
In somma, sappi che tutti fur cherci
e litterati grandi e di gran fama,
d'un peccato medesmo al mondo lerci.   108
Priscian sen va con quella turba grama
e Francesco d'Accorso; anche vedervi,
s'avessi avuto di tal tigna brama,   111
colui potei che dal servo dei servi
fu trasmutato d'Arno in Bacchiglione,
dove lasciò li mal protesi nervi.   114

sprung from the holy seed left anciently
  by those few Romans who remained there when
  'twas made the nest of such malignity.'
'Had I been able' I replied 'to attain
  to my desire in full, you had not yet
  been banished from the natural state of men;
for on my mind is stamped your affectionate
  and kind paternal look—heart-breaking now—
  when in the world you taught me early and late
the art by which man grows eternal: how
  deep is my gratitude, so long as e'er
  I live, 'tis meet my tongue should clearly show.
What you narrate of how my steps shall fare
  I write, and keep with other texts to gloze
  by a wise lady, if I attain to her.
Yet this much I would fain to you disclose:
  so conscience chide me not, I'm unafraid
  of Fortune—well prepared for all her blows.
Unto my ears have arles like this been paid
  before now; so let Fortune whirl her sphere
  e'en as she pleases, and the churl his spade.'
On that, my master rightward to his rear
  turned his cheek round, then, eyeing me for a spell,
  said: 'Well they listen, who profit by what they hear.'
None the less I beg Ser Brunetto tell
  me further who of all his company
  are highest in rank and the most notable.
' 'Tis well to know of some,' he said to me;
  'the rest, since time for so much speech is short,
  had better be passed over silently.
Know briefly that, by one and the same sort
  of sin defiled on earth, they all of them
  were clerks, great scholars and of wide report.
With that sad crowd goes Priscian: 'mongst the same
  is Francis of Accorso; and wert thou keen
  to see such scum, he too a glance might claim,
who, having by the servants' servant been
  from Arno's moved to Bacchiglione's strand,
  there left the nerves he'd strained to indulge his sin.

Di più direi, ma il venire e il sermone
  più lungo esser non può, però ch'io veggio
  là surger novo fummo dal sabbione.   117
Gente vien con la quale esser non deggio;
  sieti raccomandato il mio Tesoro
  nel qual io vivo ancora; e più non cheggio».   120
Poi si rivolse, e parve di coloro
  che corrono a Verona il drappo verde
  per la campagna; e parve di costoro   123
quelli che vince, non quelli che perde.

CANTO 16

Già era in loco onde s'udia il rimbombo
  de l'acqua che cadea ne l'altro giro,
  simile a quel che l'arnie fanno rombo,   3
quando tre ombre insieme si partiro
  correndo, d'una torma che passava
  sotto la pioggia de l'aspro martiro.   6
Venian ver noi, e ciascuna gridava:
  « Sostati tu che a l'abito ne sembri
  esser alcun di nostra terra prava».   9
Ahimè, che piaghe vidi nei loro membri,
  recenti e vecchie, da le fiamme incese!
  Ancor men duol pur ch'io me ne rimembri.   12
A le lor grida il mio dottor s'attese;
  volse il viso ver me e disse: « Aspetta;
  a costor si vuol essere cortese.   15
E se non fosse il foco che saetta
  la natura del loco, io dicerei
  che meglio stesse a te che a lor la fretta».   18
Ricominciar, come noi restammo, ei
  l'antico verso; e quando a noi fur giunti
  fenno una rota di sè tutti e trei,   21
qual sogliono i campion far nudi e unti,
  avvisando lor presa e lor vantaggio,
  prima che sien tra lor battuti e punti.   24

I would say more: but farther coming and
   discoursing is forbidden, for I see
   new smoke arising yonder from the sand.
People approach with whom I must not be:
   take good care of my *Treasure*, for in that
   I still live, and no more I ask of thee.'
Then he turned round and seemed of those who at
   Verona run cross-country for the green
   cloth-mantle; and, of those who aim thereat,
seemed not a loser, but the one who'll win.

CANTO 16

I'd reached a place now whence the rumble, coming
   from where the water plunged to the next ring,
   was heard, as 'twere the drone of beehives humming,
when three shades, forth together issuing
   from others in a troop then passing by
   beneath the rain that scorched them with its sting,
ran tow'rds ourselves, the while each raised the cry:
   'Thou there, a native, if thy garb speaks true,
   of our bad city, stop till we come nigh.'
Ah me, upon their limbs what scars both new
   and old I saw burnt in them by the flame!
   Mere thought thereof still fills my heart with rue.
My teacher, when he heard them thus exclaim,
   paid heed and, facing tow'rds me, said: 'Now wait;
   one would be courteous unto souls like them.
And, were it not this region's natural state
   to dart forth fire, I'd e'en say that to thee
   more than to them would haste be appropriate.'
They recommenced their former stave, as we
   stood still; and when close up to us they drew,
   they formed themselves into a wheel, all three,
as champions, stript and oiled, are wont to do,
   watching to seize their grip and vantage ere,
   closing, with thrusts and punches they set to;

E si rotando, ciascuno il visaggio
  drizzava a me, sì che in contrario il collo
  faceva ai piè continuo viaggio.   27
E « Se miseria d'esto loco sollo
  rende in dispetto noi e i nostri prieghi »
  cominciò l'uno « e il tristo aspetto e brollo,   30
la fama nostra l'animo tuo pieghi
  a dirne chi tu sei, che i vivi piedi
  così sicuro per l'Inferno freghi.   33
Questi, l'orme di cui pestar mi vedi,
  tutto che nudo e dipelato vada,
  fu di grado maggior che tu non credi.   36
Nepote fu de la buona Gualdrada;
  Guido Guerra ebbe nome, ed in sua vita
  fece col senno assai e con la spada.   39
L'altro, che appresso a me la rena trita,
  è Tegghiaio Aldobrandi, la cui voce
  nel mondo sù dovria esser gradita.   42
E io, che posto son con loro in croce,
  Iacopo Rusticucci fui; e certo
  la fiera moglie più ch'altro mi nuoce ».   45
S'io fossi stato dal foco coperto,
  gittato mi sarei tra lor di sotto,
  e credo che il dottor l'avria sofferto;   48
ma perch'io mi sarei bruciato e cotto,
  vinse paura la mia buona voglia
  che di loro abbracciar mi facea ghiotto.   51
Poi cominciai: « Non dispetto, ma doglia
  la vostra condizion dentro mi fisse,
  tanta che tardi tutta si dispoglia,   54
tosto che questo mio signor mi disse
  parole per le quali io mi pensai
  che qual voi siete, tal gente venisse.   57
Di vostra terra sono, e sempre mai
  l'opra di voi e gli onorati nomi
  con affezion ritrassi ed ascoltai.   60
Lascio lo fele e vo pei dolci pomi
  promessi a me per lo verace duca;
  ma infino al centro pria convien ch'io tomi ».   63

and each, in wheeling round, so brought to bear
  his visage upon me, that counterwise
  still to his feet he made his neck to fare.
And 'If this loose sand and its miseries,'
  began one 'and our blackened, hairless fell
  bring scorn upon us and our pleading cries,
let our renown incline thy mind to tell
  us who thou art that, undiscomfited,
  shufflest along thy living feet through Hell.
He in whose footprints thou behold'st me tread
  stood higher than thou deemest in degree,
  for all that he go peeled now and unclad.
A grandson of the good Gualdrada, he
  was named Guy Guerra and, while life was his,
  by his wits and sword won many a victory.
The other, who pounds the sand behind me, is
  Tegghiaio Aldobrandi, whose name up there
  men ought to cherish in their memories.
I was James Rusticucci: and that I share
  with them this cross is due, I would submit,
  to my fierce wife, or most of all to her.'
Had I been sheltered from the fire one whit,
  I should have thrown me down among them, and
  I think my tutor would have suffered it;
but fear lest, if I did, the flames would brand
  and bake me overcame the right good will
  which made me long to embrace them out of hand.
And I began: 'Not scorn did I then feel
  for your condition but grief so sore that I
  long hence shall find it fixed within me still,
when this my lord said words to me whereby
  my mind was made to entertain the thought
  that men of your sort might be drawing nigh.
Your city's mine, and never have I not
  heard with affection and recounted all
  your honoured names and the great deeds ye wrought.
I'm one who's seeking, quit now of the gall,
  the sweet fruits promised me by my true guide,
  but to the centre first I needs must fall.'

« Se lungamente l'anima conduca
  le membra tue » rispose quegli allora
  « e se la fama tua dopo te luca,   66
cortesia e valor di' se dimora
  ne la nostra città, sì come suole,
  o se del tutto se n'è gita fora;   69
chè Guglielmo Borsiere, il qual si duole
  con noi per poco, e va là coi compagni,
  assai ne cruccia con le sue parole ».   72
« La gente nova e i sùbiti guadagni
  orgoglio e dismisura han generata,
  Fiorenza, in te, sì che tu già ten piagni »   75
Così gridai con la faccia levata;
  e i tre, che ciò inteser per risposta,
  guatar l'un l'altro come al ver si guata.   78
« Se l'altre volte sì poco ti costa »
  risposer tutti « il satisfare altrui,
  felice te che sì parli a tua posta!   81
Però se campi d'esti lochi bui
  e torni a riveder le belle stelle,
  quando ti gioverà dicer 'Io fui'   84
fa che di noi a la gente favelle ».
  Indi rupper la rota, ed a fuggirsi
  ali sembiar le gambe loro snelle.   87
Un amen non saria potuto dirsi
  tosto così com'ei furo spariti;
  per che al maestro parve di partirsi.   90
Io lo seguiva, e poco eravam iti
  che il suon de l'acqua n'era sì vicino,
  che per parlar saremmo a pena uditi.   93
Come quel fiume che ha proprio cammino
  primo da monte Veso inver levante,
  da la sinistra costa d'Appennino,   96
che si chiama Acquacheta suso, avante
  che si divalli giù nel basso letto,
  ed a Forlì di quel nome è vacante,   99
rimbomba là sovra San Benedetto
  de l'Alpe, per cadere ad una scesa
  dove dovria per mille esser ricetto;   102

'So may thy soul for long yet' he replied
   'conduct thy limbs, and so too may thy fame
   continue shining after thou hast died—
tell us if courtesy and valour, the same
   as ever, dwell within our city, or
   whether she now has wholly banished them;
for William Borsiér, who not long before
   this joined us in our pain and yonder goes
   with his companions, says what grieves us sore.'
'Florence, in thee new men and sudden inflows
   of wealth have bred pride and excess which brook
   no curb, so that e'en now they swell thy woes.'
Thus, with face raised, I cried; and the three took
   my words, when heard, for answer, and each one
   looked at the others, as at truth men look.
'Canst thou so briefly at other times,' thereon
   all answered 'satisfy another's ear,
   happy art thou, whose words so freely run!
Therefore, if thou escape this gloomy lair
   and win to see the lovely stars again,
   when thou'lt rejoice to say "I once was where . . ."
see that thou speak of us to living men.'
   Thereat they broke their wheel and, as they fled,
   their nimble legs seemed wings upon the plain.
They ran so fast that, ere one could have said
   Amen, they had completely disappear'd;
   wherefore, so willing, on the master led.
I followed him, and soon, that now we near'd
   the water where it fell, its sound gave sign,
   for, had we spoken, we had scarce been heard.
Just as that stream—the first which, on a line
   all its own, down from Monte Viso flows
   eastward on the left flank of Apennine—
which, up above called Acquacheta, goes
   thus named until it drops to its low bed,
   and at Forlì doth then that title lose,
booms, as in one leap from the mountainhead
   it falls—above Saint Bennet's convent ground—
   where it might well a thousand leaps have made;

così giù d'una ripa discoscesa
    trovammo risonar quell'acqua tinta,
    sì che in poc'ora avria l'orecchia offesa.   105
Io aveva una corda intorno cinta;
    e con essa pensai alcuna volta
    prender la lonza a la pelle dipinta.   108
Poscia che l'ebbi tutta da me sciolta,
    sì come il duca m'avea comandato,
    porsila a lui aggroppata e ravvolta.   111
Ond'ei si volse inver lo destro lato,
    ed alquanto di lunge da la sponda
    la gittò giuso in quell'alto burrato.   114
« E pur convien che novità risponda »
    dicea tra me medesmo « al novo cenno
    che il maestro con l'occhio sì seconda ».   117
Ahi quanto cauti gli uomini esser denno
    presso a color che non veggion pur l'opra,
    ma per entro i pensier miran col senno!   120
Ei disse a me: « Tosto verrà di sopra
    ciò ch'io attendo e che il tuo pensier sogna:
    tosto convien che al tuo viso si scopra ».   123
Sempre a quel ver che ha faccia di menzogna
    dee l'uom chiuder le labbra fin ch'ei puote,
    però che sanza colpa fa vergogna.   126
Ma qui tacer nol posso; e per le note
    di questa comedìa, lettor, ti giuro
    s'elle non sien di lunga grazia vote,   129
ch'io vidi per quell'aere grosso e scuro
    venir notando una figura in suso,
    maravigliosa ad ogni cor sicuro,   132
sì come torna colui che va giuso
    talora a solver àncora, che aggrappa
    o scoglio o altro che nel mare è chiuso,   135
che in sù si stende e da piè si rattrappa.

so down from a sheer precipice we found
   that tinted water falling with a din,
   such that the ear had soon thereby been stunn'd.
I had a cord girt round me and had been
   at one time thinking that with it I might
   capture the leopard with the spotted skin.
I loosened this and, after I had quite
   removed it, as commanded by my guide,
   handed it to him coiled and rolled up tight.
Whereon he turned himself to his right side
   and out some distance from the edge then threw
   it plumb down into that unfathomed void.
'Surely there'll come in answer something new.'
   I said within myself 'to this new sign
   which with his eye my lord doth so pursue.'
Ah, how to caution should one's mind incline,
   when near those seeing not alone the act,
   but the inward thoughts, which their keen wits divine!
He said to me: 'Yes, soon will rise in fact
   what I await, and soon upon thine eye
   shall what thy mind is dreaming make impact.'
Still not to speak that truth which seems a lie
   if spoken, men should take the utmost pains,
   because, though blameless, they are shamed thereby;
but speak it here I must; and by the strains
   of this my Comedy, Reader, I swear—
   so may't long keep what favour it obtains—
that I saw through that gross and murky air
   come swimming up a shape, appalling to
   anyone's heart, however stout it were,
as comes back he who, whiles, goes diving through
   the sea, to work an anchor loose, when it
   is fouled by a rock or other snag, and who
strains himself upward and draws in his feet.

CANTO 17

« Ecco la fiera con la coda aguzza
  che passa i monti e rompe i muri e l'armi;
  ecco colei che tutto il mondo appuzza ».   3
Sì cominciò lo mio duca a parlarmi;
  ed accennolle che venisse a proda,
  vicino al fin dei passeggiati marmi.   6
E quella sozza immagine di froda
  sen venne, ed arrivò la testa e il busto,
  ma in su la ripa non trasse la coda.   9
La faccia sua era faccia d'uom giusto,
  tanto benigna avea di fuor la pelle,
  e d'un serpente tutto l'altro fusto.   12
Due branche avea, pilose infin l'ascelle;
  lo dosso e il petto ed ambedue le coste
  dipinti avea di nodi e di rotelle.   15
Con più color, sommesse e soprapposte
  non fer mai drappi Tartari nè Turchi,
  nè fur tai tele per Aragne imposte.   18
Come talvolta stanno a riva i burchi
  che parte sono in acqua e parte in terra,
  e come là tra li Tedeschi lurchi   21
lo bevero s'assetta a far sua guerra,
  così la fiera pessima si stava
  su l'orlo che, di pietra, il sabbion serra.   24
Nel vano tutta sua coda guizzava,
  torcendo in sù la venenosa forca
  che a guisa di scorpion la punta armava.   27
Lo duca disse: « Or convien che si torca
  la nostra via un poco insino a quella
  bestia malvagia che colà si corca ».   30
Però scendemmo a la destra mammella,
  e dieci passi femmo in su lo stremo
  per ben cessar la rena e la fiammella.   33
E quando noi a lei venuti semo,
  poco più oltre veggio in su la rena
  gente seder propinqua al loco scemo.   36

CANTO 17

'Lo, the fierce monster with the pointed tail,
  who crosses mountains, storms the strongest fort,
  lo, that which makes the whole world stink of hell!'
My guide it was who spoke after this sort
  to me, then beckoned it to land close by,
  near where the marble causeway broke off short.
Whereupon that foul shape of fraud drew nigh
  and brought its head and chest ashore, but not
  its tail, which off the bank it still let lie.
Its face was the face an honest man hath got,
  so benign looked it outwardly, but its
  remaining parts were a serpent's, all the lot.
It had two paws, hairy to the armpits;
  its back and breast and both sides of its spine
  had, painted on them, knots and annulets:
with dyes more numerous, groundwork and design,
  never were cloths by Turk or Tartar made,
  ne'er did Arachne lay-on webs so fine.
As sometimes barges on the beach are stay'd,
  each lying part in water, part on land,
  or as, o'er there where Germans guzzle, to aid
him wage his war the beaver takes his stand,
  so stationed was that worst of beasts upon
  the edge which, made of stone, confines the sand.
Its tail twitched in the void—for of that none
  had grounded—twisting up the venomed fork
  which armed the point, as in a scorpion.
My guide said: 'We must round a little work
  our way now, would we reach, as is my aim,
  yon noxious beast that lies there in the murk.'
Therefore, descending to the right, we came
  ten steps along the brink of the precipice,
  to keep well clear of the sand and flakes of flame.
When we had reached its lair, not far past this
  I saw folk squatting on the sand, their seat
  being close to where beneath them yawned the abyss.

Quivi il maestro: « Acciò che tutta piena
   esperienza d'esto giron porti »
   mi disse « va e vedi la lor mena.   39
Li tuoi ragionamenti sien là corti:
   mentre che torni, parlerò con questa
   che ne conceda i suoi omeri forti ».   42
Così ancor su per la strema testa
   di quel settimo cerchio, tutto solo
   andai dove sedea la gente mesta.   45
Per gli occhi fora scoppiava lor duolo;
   di qua, di là, soccorrien con le mani
   quando ai vapori e quando al caldo suolo. 48
Non altrimenti fan di state i cani,
   or col ceffo, or col piè, quando son morsi
   o da pulci o da mosche o da tafani.   51
Poi che nel viso a certi gli occhi porsi
   nei quali il doloroso foco casca,
   non ne conobbi alcun, ma io m'accorsi   54
che dal collo a ciascun pendea una tasca
   che avea certo colore e certo segno,
   e quindi par che il loro occhio si pasca. 57
E com'io riguardando tra lor vegno,
   in una borsa gialla vidi azzurro
   che d'un leone avea faccia e contegno. 60
Poi, procedendo di mio sguardo il curro,
   vidine un'altra come sangue rossa
   mostrare un'oca più bianca che burro.   63
E un che d'una scrofa azzurra e grossa
   segnato avea lo suo sacchetto bianco,
   mi disse: «Che fai tu in questa fossa? 66
Or te ne va, e perchè sei vivo anco
   sappi che il mio vicin Vitaliano
   sederà qui dal mio sinistro fianco.   69
Con questi fiorentin son padovano;
   spesse fiate m'intronan gli orecchi
   gridando: 'Vegna il cavalier sovrano   72
che recherà la tasca coi tre becchi!' ».
   Qui distorse la bocca, e di fuor trasse
   la lingua come bue che naso lecchi.   75

Here my lord said to me: 'That quite complete
  be thy experience of this circle, go
  and see the state they are in, and ponder it.
But let thy converse there be brief: till thou
  returnest I will parley with this Thing
  for the use of its strong shoulders here and now.'
So, still along the extreme verge bordering
  that seventh circle, all alone for a while
  I went to where the folk sat sorrowing.
Their grief burst from their eyes; in ceaseless toil
  they used their hands as shields, this side and that,
  now from the vapours, now from the hot soil.
Not otherwise do dogs when summer's at
  its zenith use their paws or else their snout,
  if they are bitten by flea or breese or gnat.
Hard as I tried to make the features out
  of some on whom the dolorous fire was shed,
  I recognized not one; but slung about
the neck of each I marked a wallet, made
  with charge and tincture clearly blazoned thereon,
  and therewith seems it that their eye is fed.
And, as I came among them gazing, one
  purse I observed charged azure upon or,
  on which a lion's face and outline shone.
Then, looking on, I saw another bore
  a charge that showed whiter than curd, to wit,
  a goose, argent, on gules the tint of gore.
And one, whose satchel had impressed on it
  a sow in farrow, azure on argent, met
  my glance with: 'What dost *thou* here in this pit?
Begone: but since thou'rt still alive, I'll let
  thee know my townsman, Vitalián, will here
  on my left side soon find his haunches set.
Florentines these, a Paduan I: my ear
  is oft-times deafened by their shout which goes
  thundering: "Let come the sovereign cavalier,
whose purse is famed for the three goats it shows." '
  Hereat he writhed his mouth and thrust therefrom
  his tongue out like an ox that licks its nose.

E io, temendo no 'l più star crucciasse
  lui che di poco star m'avea ammonito,
  tornaimi indietro da l'anime lasse. 78
Trovai lo duca mio ch'era salito
  già su la groppa del fiero animale;
  e disse a me: « Or sii forte ed ardito. 81
Omai si scende per siffatte scale.
  Monta dinanzi, ch'io voglio esser mezzo,
  sì che la coda non possa far male ». 84
Qual è colui che si presso ha il riprezzo
  de la quartana, che ha già l'unghie smorte
  e trema tutto pur guardando il rezzo, 87
tal divenn'io a le parole porte;
  ma vergogna mi fè le sue minacce,
  che innanzi a buon signor fa servo forte. 90
Io m'assettai in su quelle spallacce.
  Sì volli dir, ma la voce non venne
  com'io credetti: « Fa che tu m'abbracce ». 93
Ma esso, che altra volta mi sovvenne
  ad altro forse, tosto ch' io montai
  con le braccia m'avvinse e mi sostenne. 96
E disse: « Gerion, moviti omai:
  le rote larghe e lo scender sia poco:
  pensa la nova soma che tu hai ». 99
Come la navicella esce di loco
  in dietro in dietro, sì quindi si tolse,
  e poi che al tutto si sentì a gioco 102
là 'v'era il petto la coda rivolse,
  e quella, tesa, come anguilla mosse,
  e con le branche l'aere a sè raccolse. 105
Maggior paura non credo che fosse
  quando Feton abbandonò li freni,
  per che'l ciel, come pare ancor, si cosse, 108
nè quando Icaro misero le reni
  sentì spennar per la scaldata cera,
  gridando il padre a lui: « Mala via tieni! » 111
che fu la mia, quando vidi ch'io era
  ne l'aere d'ogni parte, e vidi spenta
  ogni veduta fuor che de la fera. 114

And I, afraid of vexing him by whom
  I had been warned to tarry there not long,
  turned back and left the tired souls to their doom.
I found my leader had already sprung
  up on the monster's croup and, seated there,
  he said to me: 'Now be thou bold and strong.
Henceforth by stairs like this we downward fare:
  mount thou in front, I'll sit between the tail
  and thee, lest it should sting thee unaware.'
Like one who by a shivering fit knows well
  the ague's on him, nails already blue,
  and who, should he but glimpse the shade, doth quail,
so at these words I shuddered and changed hue;
  but soon for very shame took heart of grace,
  as, seeing his master brave, the man is too.
I on those monstrous shoulders took my place:
  true, I wished to say, but the words I intended failed
  to come: 'Do hold me tight in thine embrace.'
But he, who another time, when there assail'd
  me another doubt, had saved me, round me cast
  his arms, when I was mounted and kept me upheld:
and said: 'Now, Geryon, set forth: nor too fast
  be thy descent, but wide thy wheelings: bear
  in mind the unwonted burden that thou hast.'
As a small vessel from its berth with care
  backs slowly out, so did the beast begin
  withdrawing; and when it felt itself quite clear,
it turned its tail to where its breast had been
  and moved it, stretched out eel-like, with its paws
  to itself ever gathering the air in.
Intenser fear I do not think there was
  when Phaëthon had let the reins go slack,
  whereby the sky was scorched (the mark still shows);
or when mis'rable Icarus felt his back
  unfeathering by the melted wax, while cried
  his father to him: 'Ill thou keep'st the track!'
than mine was, when I saw on every side
  air only, and saw all visible objects gone
  except the beast on which I sat astride.

Ella sen va notando lenta lenta;
  rota e discende, ma non me n'accorgo
  se non che al viso e di sotto mi venta.   117
Io sentìa già da la man destra il gorgo
  far sotto noi un orribile scroscio,
  per che con gli occhi in giù la testa sporgo.   120
Allor fu' io più timido a lo scoscio,
  però ch'io vidi fuochi e sentii pianti,
  ond'io tremando tutto mi raccoscio.   123
E vidi poi, chè nol vedea davanti,
  lo scendere e il girar, per li gran mali
  che s'appressavan da diversi canti.   126
Come il falcon ch'è stato assai su l'ali
  che senza veder logoro od uccello
  fa dire al falconiere: « Omè, tu cali »   129
discende lasso onde si mosse snello
  per cento rote, e da lunge si pone
  dal suo maestro disdegnoso e fello,   132
così ne pose al fondo Gerione
  al piè al piè de la stagliata rocca;
  e discarcate le nostre persone,   135
si dileguò come da corda cocca.

CANTO 18

Luogo è in Inferno detto Malebolge,
  tutto di pietra di color ferrigno
  come la cerchia che dintorno il volge.   3
Nel dritto mezzo del campo maligno
  vaneggia un pozzo assai largo e profondo,
  di cui suo loco dicerò l'ordigno.   6
Quel cinghio che rimane, adunque, è tondo,
  tra il pozzo e il piè de l'alta ripa dura,
  e ha distinto in dieci valli il fondo.   9
Quale, dove per guardia de le mura
  più e più fossi cingon li castelli,
  la parte dove son rende figura,   12

It goes its way, still slowly swimming on,
   wheels, sinks, but I aware of this nowise
   save by the head-wind from beneath me blown.

Already I heard on my right hand arise
   from the whirlpool below us a horrible roar:
   wherefore I crane my head with down-turned eyes.

Then was I of falling off afraid still more,
   because I saw fires and heard wails, whereat,
   trembling, I cleave to my seat with all my power.

And then I saw, unseen by me ere that,
   our downward-wheeling by the drawing nigh,
   all round, of the great ills I am gazing at.

As falcon, that hath long been poised on high
   without seeing bird or lure with which to close,
   till 'Ah, thou stoopest' is the falconer's cry,

descending tired whence swift it started, goes
   thro' a hundred wheels, nor by its master but
   far off alights, disdainful and morose;

so Geryon placed us, at the very foot
   of the precipitous cliff, in the next ring,
   and, lightened of our persons, upward shot

and vanished, like bolt-notch from the bow-string.

CANTO 18

There is a place in Hell's remoter deeps
   called Evilpouches, all of stone the hue
   of iron, like the cliff that round it sweeps.

And sunk in this malignant field right through
   its centre yawns a wide deep pit: how all is
   arranged therein *suo loco* I'll review.

Between the pit and the high rocky wall is
   the intervening region, therefore, round:
   and has its floor split up into ten valleys.

As where, to guard the walls, one trench beyond
   another girds a castle, so that where
   they curve they trace a pattern on the ground;

tale immagine quivi facean quelli;
 e come a tai fortezze dai lor sogli
 a la ripa di fuor son ponticelli,   15
così da imo de la roccia scogli
 movien che recidean gli argini e i fossi,
 infino al pozzo che i tronca e raccogli. 18
In questo loco, de la schiena scossi
 di Gerion, trovammoci; e il poeta
 tenne a sinistra, ed io dietro mi mossi. 21
A la man destra vidi nova pieta:
 novo tormento e novi frustatori
 di che la prima bolgia era repleta.   24
Nel fondo erano ignudi i peccatori;
 dal mezzo in qua ci venien verso il volto,
 di là con noi, ma con passi maggiori: 27
come i Roman, per l'esercito molto
 l'anno del Giubileo su per lo ponte
 hanno a passar la gente modo colto,   30
che da l'un lato tutti hanno la fronte
 verso il Castello, e vanno a Santo Pietro,
 da l'altra sponda vanno verso il monte. 33
Di qua, di là, su per lo sasso tetro
 vidi demon cornuti con gran ferze,
 che li battean crudelmente di retro.   36
Ahi come facean lor levar le berze
 a le prime percosse! già nessuno
 le seconde aspettava nè le terze.   39
Mentr'io andava, gli occhi miei in uno
 furo scontrati; ed io sì tosto dissi:
 « Già di veder costui non son digiuno ». 42
Però a figurarlo i piedi affissi:
 e il dolce duca meco si ristette,
 ed assentio che alquanto indietro gissi. 45
E quel frustato celarsi credette
 bassando il viso; ma poco li valse,
 ch'io dissi: « O tu che l'occhio a terra gette, 48
se le fazion che porti non son false,
 Venedico sei tu Caccianimico.
 Ma che ti mena a sì pungenti salse? » 51

e'en such was the design which those made there;
   and as such strongholds have slim bridges thrown
   from their gate-sills to the outmost barrier,
so, springing from the cliff's foot, ribs of stone
   crossed banks and trenches till they reached the pit,
   which cuts them short and joins them all in one.
In this place, shaken off, as he alit,
   from Geryon's back, we found ourselves: and to
   the left the poet, I following, turned his feet.
On the right hand new anguish met my view,
   new torments and new torturers who plied
   the lash, which filled the first pouch through and through.
Down in it, naked, were the sinners: this side
   the middle they came on facing us, beyond
   it with us went, but with a longer stride:
as was the expedient which the Romans found
   to pass folk o'er the bridge, when, in the year
   of Jubilee, vast crowds beset the ground:
that on the one side go all those that are
   facing the Castle to St. Peter's; those
   bound for the Mount on the other rim must fare.
Horned demons stood, where the rock, glooming, rose,
   this side and that, huge whips in hand, prepared
   to flog them from behind with cruel blows.
Ah, how they made them skip, that wretched herd,
   as fell the first strokes! and thereafter none
   stayed for the second, let alone the third.
My glance, as I proceeded, was on one
   arrested; and so 'Him' I promptly said
   ' 'tis not the first time I've set eyes upon.'
Therefore, to shape him out, my feet I stay'd:
   and the kind leader halted with me, and by
   his leave my way I somewhat backward made.
And the flogged scoundrel lowered his face to try
   and hide it, but small good thereby he got:
   for I said: 'Thou there, with the downcast eye,
Venédico, thou'rt Caccianemíco: if not
   thy features speak untruth; but to so tart
   a pickle as this by what hast *thou* been brought?'

Ed egli a me: « Mal volentier lo dico;
  ma sforzami la tua chiara favella
  che mi fa sovvenir del mondo antico.   54
Io fui colui che la Ghisolabella
  condussi a far la voglia del Marchese,
  come che suoni la sconcia novella.   57
E non pur io qui piango bolognese;
  anzi n'è questo loco tanto pieno,
  che tante lingue non son ora apprese   60
a dicer *sipa* tra Savena e il Reno;
  e se di ciò vuoi fede o testimonio,
  recati a mente il nostro avaro seno ».   63
Così parlando, il percosse un demonio
  de la sua scuriada e disse: « Via,
  ruffian! qui non son femmine da conio! »   66
Io mi raggiunsi con la scorta mia;
  poscia con pochi passi divenimmo
  là 've uno scoglio de la ripa uscia.   69
Assai leggeramente quel salimmo,
  e volti a destra, su per la sua scheggia
  da quelle cerchie eterne ci partimmo.   72
Quando noi fummo là dov'ei vaneggia
  di sotto per dar passo a li sferzati,
  lo duca disse: « Attienti, e fa che feggia   75
lo viso in te di quest'altri malnati
  ai quali ancor non vedesti la faccia
  però che son con noi insieme andati ».   78
Dal vecchio ponte guardavam la traccia
  che venia verso noi da l'altra banda,
  e che la ferza similmente caccia.   81
E il buon maestro, sanza mia dimanda,
  mi disse: « Guarda quel grande che viene
  e per dolor non par lagrima spanda.   84
Quanto aspetto reale ancor ritiene!
  Quegli è Giason, che per cuore e per senno
  li Colchi del monton privati fene.   87
Elli passò per l'isola di Lenno
  poi che l'ardite femmine spietate
  tutti li maschi loro a morte dienno.   90

And he to me: ' 'Tis that I'm loth to impart;
  but thy plain speech, which brings to memory
  old days, constrains me to speak out my heart.
To do the Marquis' will it was by me
  that the fair Ghísola was led, howe'er
  on earth the unseemly tale may bruited be.
Nor hath Bologna sent but me to share
  this weeping, nay, of us it here hath placed
  such numbers that, 'twixt Sáven' and Rheno, there
are fewer, now, taught to lip *sipa*: lest
  thou doubt this, lacking proof, call thou to mind
  as evidence our money-loving breast.'
While he thus spoke, a demon from behind
  cut at him with his scourge and said: 'Begone
  thou pimp! here are no women to be coin'd.'
Then I rejoined my escort; and anon
  we reached the spot (to which our steps were few)
  where from the bank a crag was outward thrown.
We mounted that (which was not hard to do)
  and turning rightward up by its ridge to fare,
  from those eternal circles we withdrew.
When we had reached that point upon it where
  it yawns beneath, to yield the scourged a way,
  my guide said: 'Pause, and bring thy sight to bear
upon these others born in an ill day,
  whom thou as yet hast had no chance of facing,
  since the way we've been going so have they.'
From the ancient bridge we watched, towards us racing
  the file that travelled on the other rim,
  and whom the lash was in like manner chasing.
My kindly lord without my asking him
  said, 'Mark that great one drawing near, who deigns
  not even, it seems, to weep for pain so grim.
How royal the aspect which he still retains!
  That's Jason—he, who from the Colchians bore
  the ram off by his prowess and by his brains.
He passed by the isle of Lemnos where, before,
  its womenkind, as ruthless as bold-witted,
  had all their males to death delivered o'er.

Ivi con segni e con parole ornate
  Isifile ingannò la giovinetta
  che prima avea tutte l'altre ingannate.   93
Lasciolla quivi gravida e soletta:
  tal colpa a tal martirio lui condanna;
  e anche di Medea si fa vendetta.   96
Con lui sen va chi da tal parte inganna.
  E questo basti de la prima valle
  sapere, e di color che in sè assanna ».   99
Già eravam là 've lo stretto calle
  con l'argine secondo s'incrocicchia,
  e fa di quello ad un altr'arco spalle.   102
Quindi sentimmo gente che si nicchia
  ne l'altra bolgia, e che col muso sbuffa
  e se medesma con le palme picchia.   105
Le ripe eran grommate d'una muffa,
  per l'alito di giù che vi s'appasta,
  che con gli occhi e col naso facea zuffa.   108
Lo fondo è cupo sì che non ci basta
  l'occhio a veder sanza montare al dosso
  de l'arco ove lo scoglio più sovrasta.   111
Quivi venimmo; e quindi giù nel fosso
  vidi gente attuffata in uno sterco
  che da gli uman privati parea mosso.   114
E mentre ch'io là giù con l'occhio cerco
  vidi un col capo sì di merda lordo
  che non parea s'era laico o chierco.   117
Quei mi sgridò: « Perchè sei tu sì ingordo
  di riguardar più me che gli altri brutti? »
  Ed io a lui: « Perchè, se ben ricordo,   120
già t'ho veduto coi capelli asciutti;
  e sei Alessio Interminei da Lucca:
  però t'adocchio più che gli altri tutti ».   123
Ed egli allor battendosi la zucca:
  « Qua giù m'hanno sommerso le lusinghe
  ond'io non ebbi mai la lingua stucca ».   126
Appresso ciò lo duca: « Fa che pinghe »
  mi disse « il viso un poco più avante,
  sì che la faccia ben con l'occhio attinghe   129

There he with tokens and words well-conceited
  cheated Hypsipyle, scarce woman grown,
  who first had all the other women cheated.
He left her there with child and all alone:
  such guilt condemns him to such torment meet;
  and for Medea too is vengeance done.
With him go whosoe'er in such wise cheat;
  let this which of the first vale hath been said
  suffice, and of those gripped in the fangs of it.'
We were now where the narrow pathway led
  across the second embankment, whereof thus
  the shoulders for another arch are made.
There, from the next pouch hubbub dolorous
  of folk that grunt, snort with their muzzles, smack
  themselves with the palm of the hand, came up to us.
Each bank with mould was coated, in their track
  left sticking there by effluvia from below,
  against which eyes and nose alike fought back.
The bottom is so dark and deep that no
  place is there whence to see it save one spot,
  where the rock highest o'erhangs, on the arch's brow.
Thither we came; and thence, down in the moat,
  I beheld people plunged in excrement,
  such that from human privies it seemed brought.
And as my searching gaze I downward bent,
  I saw the head of one, but whether lay
  or clerk appeared not, 'twas so shit-besprent.
He shouted at me: 'Why such greed display
  to pick out me from all this filth?' And I
  to him: 'Because if memory does not play
me false, I've seen thee once with thy hair dry:
  Alessio Interminei of Lucca art thou:
  so if I eye thee more than them, that's why.'
And he then, smiting his own pumpkin-pow:
  'they've sunk me down to this, the flatteries
  of which my tongue could never have enow.'
Anon my leader said: 'Try in such wise
  to thrust thy face a little farther out,
  that thou quite reach the visage with thine eyes

di quella sozza e scapigliata fante
　che là si graffia con l'unghie merdose
　e or s'accoscia, e ora è in piede stante.　　　132
Taide è, la puttana che rispose
　al drudo suo quando disse: 'Ho io grazie
　grandi appo te?' — 'Anzi maravigliose!'　　　135
E quinci sien le nostre viste sazie ».

CANTO 19

O Simon mago, o miseri seguaci,
　che le cose di Dio, che di bontate
　deon essere spose, voi, rapaci,　　　　　　3
per oro e per argento adulterate,
　or convien che per voi suoni la tromba
　però che ne la terza bolgia state.　　　　　6
Già eravamo a la seguente tomba
　montati de lo scoglio in quella parte
　che a punto sovra mezzo il fosso piomba.　　9
O somma sapienza, quanta è l'arte
　che mostri in Cielo, in Terra e nel mal mondo,
　e quanto giusto tua virtù comparte!　　　　12
Io vidi per le coste e per lo fondo
　piena la pietra livida di fori
　d'un largo tutti e ciascuno era tondo.　　　15
Non mi parean men ampi nè maggiori
　che quei che son nel mio bel San Giovanni
　fatti per luogo dei battezzatori,　　　　　18
l'un de li quali, ancor non è molt'anni,
　rupp'io per un che dentro v'annegava:
　e questo sia suggel che ogn'uomo sganni.　21
Fuor de la bocca a ciascun soperchiava
　d'un peccator li piedi e de le gambe
　infino al grosso, e l'altro dentro stava.　　24
Le piante erano a tutti accese intrambe,
　per che sì forte guizzavan le giunte
　che spezzate averien ritorte e strambe.　　27

of yonder filthy and dishevelled slut
   scratching herself there with her nails dung-dyed,
   who squats and stands up, turn and turn about.
That is the harlot, Thais, who, when cried
   her leman to her "Am I, then, in great
   favour with thee?", "Nay, marvellous!" replied.
And herewith let our eyes be satiate.'

CANTO 19

O SIMON MAGUS, O his miscreant breed,
   for that, whereas the things God owneth should
   be brides of righteousness, you, in your greed,
for gold and silver prostitute them; loud
   must now the trumpet sound for all and each
   of you, since the third pouch is your abode.
We were now at the next tomb, over which
   we'd scaled the crag up to that eminence
   which hangs plumb o'er the middle of the ditch.
What wondrous skill thou showest, O Sapience
   supreme, in Heav'n, in Earth, in Hell's profound:
   yea, and how justly doth thy power dispense!
I saw the gully's sides and the whole ground
   between them full of holes, all of one size,
   drilled through the livid stone, and each was round.
They seemed not more nor less wide to my eyes
   than those my beautiful St. John's can show
   as stations made for them who there baptize;
one of which I, not many years ago,
   broke, to save one stuck suffocating therein;
   which, hereby sealed, for fact let all men know.
Protruding from the mouth of each were seen
   a sinner's feet and legs so much as came
   up to the calf: the rest remained within.
All had the soles of both their feet aflame:
   whereby their joints jerked in such violent throes
   that ropes and withes would have been snapped by them.

Qual suole il fiammeggiar de le cose unte
   muoversi pur su per l'estrema buccia,
   tal era lì dai calcagni a le punte.   30
« Chi è colui, maestro, che si cruccia
   guizzando più che gli altri suoi consorti »
   diss'io « e cui più roggia fiamma succia? »   33
Ed egli a me: « Se tu vuoi ch'io ti porti
   là giù per quella ripa che più giace,
   da lui saprai di sè e de' suoi torti ».   36
E io: « Tanto m'è bel quanto a te piace:
   tu sei signore, e sai ch'io non mi parte
   dal tuo volere, e sai quel che si tace ».   39
Allor venimmo in su l'argine quarto,
   volgemmo e discendemmo a mano stanca
   là giù nel fondo foracchiato ed arto.   42
Lo buon maestro ancor de la su' anca
   non mi dipose, sì mi giunse al rotto
   di quel che sì piangeva con la zanca.   45
« O qual che sei che il di sù tien di sotto,
   anima trista come pal commessa »
   comincia' io a dir « se puoi fa motto ».   48
Io stava come il frate che confessa
   lo perfido assassin, che poi ch'è fitto
   richiama lui, per che la morte cessa.   51
Ed ei gridò: « Sei tu già costì ritto?
   sei tu già costì ritto, Bonifazio?
   Di parecchi anni mi mentì lo scritto.   54
Sei tu sì tosto di quell'aver sazio
   per lo qual non temesti torre a inganno
   la bella donna, e poi di farne strazio? »   57
Tal mi fec'io quai son color che stanno,
   per non intender ciò ch'è lor risposto,
   quasi scornati, e risponder non sanno.   60
Allor Virgilio disse: « Dilli tosto:
   'Non son colui, non son colui che credi' ».
   E io risposi come a me fu imposto.   63
Per che lo spirto tutti storse i piedi;
   poi sospirando e con voce di pianto
   mi disse: « Dunque che a me richiedi?   66

As flame on objects that are oily flows
  o'er the outer surface only, with like flux
  it there did too, gliding from heel to toes.
'Master, who's he, that by his jerking looks
  more tortured than the rest, his consorts there,'
  said I, 'and whom a ruddier flamelet sucks?'
And he to me: 'If thou wilt have me bear
  thee down by yonder bank that lower lies,
  he'll tell thee himself, and what his misdeeds were.'
And I: 'What pleases thee doth me likewise:
  thou'rt lord, and knowest that I depart not from
  thy will, and knowest thoughts that unspoken rise.'
Then to the fourth embankment did we come;
  and, turning, went on leftward down the bank
  into the pitted bottom's narrow room.
The kindly master did not from his flank
  set me down, till he'd brought me to the break
  of him lamenting so with either shank.
'O whosoe'er thou art, set like a stake,
  thou wretched soul, with top end underneath,
  give utterance, if thou canst:' 'twas thus I spake,
like to the friar confessing one that hath
  done treacherous murder, who, when fixed inside
  the pit, recalls him and thus puts off death.
'Art thou already standing there?' he cried:
  'art standing there already, Boniface?
  By several years, then, has the record lied.
Art so soon cloyed with that, which to possess,
  thou didst not fear to ravish by deceit
  the fair Dame, then add outrage to disgrace?'
Like those who without understanding it
  receive an answer, felt I then as though
  bemocked, nor how to answer knew one whit.
Then Virgil said: 'Say to him quick "No, no—
  I am not he, not he thou imaginest":'
  and I made answer, as enjoined, just so.
At that with vehemence did the spirit twist
  his feet, then sighing and in a plaintive tone
  say to me: 'What, then, dost thou of me request?

Se di saper chi i' sia ti cal cotanto
   che tu abbi però la ripa corsa,
   sappi ch'io fui vestito del gran manto.   69
E veramente fui figliuol de l'orsa,
   cupido sì per avanzar gli orsatti
   che sù l'avere e me qui misi in borsa.   72
Di sotto al capo mio son gli altri tratti
   che procedetter me simoneggiando
   per la fessura de la pietra piatti.   75
Là giù cascherò io altresì quando
   verrà colui ch'io credea che tu fossi
   allor ch'io feci il subito dimando.   78
Ma più è il tempo già che i piè mi cossi
   e ch'io son stato così sottosopra
   ch'ei non starà piantato coi piè rossi.   81
Chè dopo lui verrà di più laid'opra
   di ver ponente un pastor sanza legge,
   tal che convien che lui e me ricopra.   84
Novo Iason sarà, di cui si legge
   ne' Maccabei, e come a quel fu molle
   suo re, così fia a lui chi Francia regge».   87
Io non so s'io mi fui qui troppo folle,
   ch'io pur risposi lui a questo metro:
   « Deh or mi di' : quanto tesoro volle   90
Nostro Signore in prima da San Pietro
   ch'ei ponesse le chiavi in sua balìa?
   Certo non chiese se non: Viemmi retro.   93
Nè Pier nè gli altri tolsero a Mattia
   oro od argento, quando fu sortito
   al luogo che perdè l'anima ria.   96
Però ti sta, chè tu sei ben punito;
   e guarda ben la mal tolta moneta
   ch'esser ti fece contra Carlo ardito!   99
E se non fosse che ancor lo mi vieta
   la reverenza de le somme chiavi
   che tu tenesti ne la vita lieta,   102
i' userei parole ancor più gravi;
   chè la vostra avarizia il mundo attrista,
   calcando i buoni e sollevando i pravi.   105

If mere concern to know my name hath down
    the bank thus sped thee, know of me thus much—
    I once wore the great mantle; and true son
of the she-bear was I: my lust was such
    to advance the ursine cubs that I up there
    put wealth, but here myself, into the pouch.
Below my head are the others drawn who were
    simoniacs before me, more and more
    squeezed through the fissures of our rocky lair.
Therein shall I in my turn sink yet lower,
    when he comes hither—he whom, when I made
    my sudden question, I mistook thee for.
But more's the time already I've roast-ed
    my feet and stood thus upside down, than he
    shall stand here planted with his feet baked red.
For after him shall come, of villainy
    more foul, a lawless shepherd from the west,
    one meet to cover up both him and me.
He'll be a new Jason, like to him thou may'st
    read of in *Maccabees*, to whom his king
    bowed, as the French king shall to this one's hest.'
I know not if I here was venturing
    too far, when I but answered in this strain:
    'Come tell me now, what money or costly thing
was from Saint Peter by our Sovëreign
    craved, ere He gave the keys to his control?
    Surely no more than "Come thou in my train."
Piers and the ten took from Matthias no toll
    of silver or gold, when he was chosen by lot
    to fill the place lost by the guilty soul.
Therefore, since thou art justly punished, stir not
    from here; and guard thou well the ill-raised coin
    which made thine ardour to brave Charles so hot.
And if some impulse did not still enjoin
    my tongue to venerate the supreme keys
    which thou didst hold when the glad life was thine,
I should use words still graver; for it is
    your greed which saddens the world, to affluence brings
    the wicked, and beats good men to their knees.

Di voi pastor s'accorse il Vangelista
   quando colei che siede sopra l'acque
   puttaneggiar coi regi a lui fu vista: 108
quella che con le sette teste nacque,
   e da le dieci corna ebbe argomento
   fin che virtute al suo marito piacque.   111
Fatto v'avete Dio d'oro e d'argento:
   e che altro è da voi a l'idolatre
   se non ch'egli uno e voi ne orate cento?   114
Ahi Costantin, di quanto mal fu matre,
   non la tua conversion, ma quella dote
   che da te prese il primo ricco patre!»   117
E mentr'io li cantava cotai note,
   o ira o conscienza che il mordesse,
   forte spingava con ambo le piote.   120
Io credo ben che al mio duca piacesse,
   con sì contenta labbia sempre attese
   lo suon de le parole vere espresse.   123
Però con ambo le braccia mi prese,
   e poi che tutto sù mi s'ebbe al petto,
   rimontò per la via onde discese.   126
Nè si stancò d'avermi a sè distretto,
   sì men portò sovra il colmo de l'arco
   che dal quarto al quinto argine è tragetto.   129
Quivi soavemente spose il carco,
   soave per lo scoglio sconcio ed erto
   che sarebbe a le capre duro varco.   132
Indi un altro vallon mi fu scoperto.

CANTO 20

Di nova pena mi convien far versi
   e dar materia al ventesimo canto
   de la prima canzon, ch'è dei sommersi.   3
Io era già disposto tutto quanto
   a riguardar ne lo scoperto fondo,
   che si bagnava d'angoscioso pianto;   6

The Evangelist perceived your shepherdings,
   ay yours, when she that sits upon the flood
   was seen by him a-whoring with the kings;
she that was born with the seven heads, and could
   call the ten horns in proof, so long as he
   that was her husband joyed in doing good.
Ye've made of silver and gold your deity:
   and differ idolaters from you in aught,
   save that they worship one, and hundreds ye?
Ah, Constantine, with how much ill was fraught,
   not thy conversion, but the dowry, ta'en
   from thee, which the first wealthy father got!'
And while I chanted to him in this strain,
   he kicked out hard with both feet, whether spurr'd
   by conscience or that rage increased his pain.
I'm sure my guide was pleased with what he heard,
   he listened all the time with so content
   a mien as I pronounced each truthful word.
Therefore he took me in both his arms and went
   on up, when he'd quite got me on his breast,
   the same way back by which he'd made descent.
Nor did he tire of clasping me, but press'd
   right on, until he'd reached that arch's crown
   which joins the fourth to the fifth embankment's crest.
And here he gently set his burden down—
   gently, because the crag was steep and rough,
   where even for goats a passage scarce had shown:
thence was disclosed to me another trough.

CANTO 20

For a new punishment must rhymes be found
   and matter furnished for the twentieth fytte
   of the first lay, which treats of the deep-drown'd.
I was now well placed, as regards the pit,
   its bottom being disclosed right under me,
   to observe the tears of anguish drenching it;

e vidi gente per lo vallon tondo
   venir, tacendo e lagrimando, al passo
   che fanno le letane in questo mondo.   9
Come il viso mi scese in lor più basso,
   mirabilmente apparve esser travolto
   ciascun tra il mento e il principio del casso;   12
chè da le reni era tornato il volto,
   ed in dietro venir li convenia,
   perchè il veder dinanzi era lor tolto.   15
Forse per forza già di parlasia
   si travolse così alcun del tutto;
   ma io nol vidi nè credo che sia.   18
Se Dio ti lasci, lettor, prender frutto
   di tua lezione, or pensa per te stesso
   com'io potea tener lo viso asciutto,   21
quando la nostra immagine da presso
   vidi sì torta, che il pianto de gli occhi
   le natiche bagnava per lo fesso.   24
Certo io piangea, poggiato a l'un dei rocchi
   del duro scoglio, sì che la mia scorta
   mi disse: « Ancor se' tu de gli altri sciocchi?   27
Qui vive la pietà quand'è ben morta.
   Chi è più scellerato di colui
   che al giudicio divin passion comporta?   30
Drizza la testa, drizza, e vedi a cui
   s'aperse a gli occhi dei Teban la terra;
   per ch'ei gridavan tutti: 'Dove rui,   33
Anfiarao? perchè lasci la guerra?'
   E non restò di ruinare a valle
   fino a Minòs che ciascheduno afferra.   36
Mira che ha fatto petto de le spalle:
   perchè volle veder troppo davante
   diretro guarda, e fa retroso calle.   39
Vedi Tiresia che mutò sembiante
   quando di maschio femmina divenne,
   cangiandosi le membra tutte quante;   42
e prima poi ribatter li convenne
   li duo serpenti avvolti, con la verga,
   che riavesse le maschili penne.   45

and round the great trench people did I see
   come, mute and weeping, at the pace men go
   in this world as they chant the litany.
When I had lowered my gaze, I noticed how
   grotesquely each seemed twisted round between
   the chin and where the chest begins to show;
for they must needs, because the face had been
   turn'd tow'rds the loins, walk backwards, inasmuch
   as to look forwards was denied their een.
Possibly ere now some, when in the clutch
   of palsy, have been thus quite wrenched awry;
   I doubt it, though, and never witnessed such.
Reader—so from thy reading mayst thou by
   God's graciousness pluck fruit—ask thy own mind
   whether I long could keep my visage dry,
when, close at hand, the image of our kind
   I saw so twisted round, that plaint from the eyes
   watered the buttocks through the cleft behind.
Propped 'gainst a jut of that hard crag, disguise
   my tears I could not, whence my escort said:
   'If the rest play the fool, must thou likewise?
Here pity lives when it is wholly dead:
   who's wickeder than he that would subdue
   God's judgment to his own, by passion sway'd?
Lift, lift thy head and see him yonder who,
   when Earth gaped, vanished from the Thebans' sight,
   so that all cried: "Where art thou hurtling to,
Amphiaraüs? Why leav'st thou the fight?"
   And yet his headlong plunge could none arrest,
   till Minos did, who seizes every wight.
Look how of shoulders he has made a breast:
   because his glance too far before him ranged,
   he casts it back now and goes rearward-faced.
Behold Teiresias, whose semblance changed
   when he from male into a woman grew,
   in every limb from his old self estranged;
who, later, had to smite again the two
   twined serpents with his rod, ere he could show
   his members with male plumage imped anew.

Aronta è quel che al ventre li s'atterga,
   che nei monti di Luni, dove ronca
   lo Carrarese che di sotto alberga,   48
ebbe tra i bianchi marmi la spelonca
   per sua dimora; onde a veder le stelle
   e il mar non gli era la veduta tronca.   51
E quella che ricopre le mammelle,
   che tu non vedi, con le trecce sciolte,
   ed ha di là ogni pilosa pelle,   54
Manto fu, che cercò per terre molte,
   poscia si pose là dove nacqu'io;
   onde un poco mi piace che m'ascolte.   57
Poscia che il padre suo di vita uscìo
   e venne serva la città di Baco,
   questa gran tempo per lo mondo gìo.   60
Suso in Italia bella giace un laco
   a piè de l'Alpe che serra Lamagna
   sovra Tiralli, ed ha nome Benaco.   63
Per mille fonti, credo, e più, si bagna
   tra Garda e Val Camonica Pennino
   de l'acqua che nel detto laco stagna.   66
Luogo è nel mezzo là dove il trentino
   pastore, e quel di Brescia, e il veronese
   segnar porìa, se fesse quel cammino.   69
Siede Peschiera, bello e forte arnese
   da fronteggiar Bresciani e Bergamaschi,
   ove la riva intorno più discese.   72
Ivi convien che tutto quanto caschi
   ciò che in grembo a Benaco star non può,
   e fassi fiume giù per verdi paschi.   75
Tosto che l'acqua a correr mette co
   non più Benaco, ma Mincio si chiama
   fino a Governo, dove cade in Po.   78
Non molto ha corso che trova una lama
   ne la qual si distende, e la impaluda,
   e suol di state talora esser grama.   81
Quindi passando, la vergine cruda
   vide terra nel mezzo del pantano
   sanza coltura e d'abitanti nuda.   84

Backing tow'rd this one's paunch see Aruns go,
  who upon Luna's mountain-slopes, where hoes
  the Carrarese who is inned below,
midst the white marbles for his dwelling chose
  a cavern, whence his viewing far and wide
  star-shine and seascape there was nought to oppose.
And she that doth with her loose tresses hide
  her breasts, which standing here thou seëst not,
  and all whose hairy skin is on that side,
was Manto, who through many countries sought
  asylum, till she settled in my own
  birthplace; whereon please let me enlarge somewhat.
After her father's death, when Bacchus' town
  had been reduced to servitude, did she
  long through the world go wandering up and down.
There lies a lake up in fair Italy
  by name Benaco, at the mountain's base
  which o'er the Tyrol locks-in Germany.
The Pennine's bathed by a thousand springs, I guess,
  or more, 'twixt Garda and Val Camónica,
  with water whereof that lake's the resting-place.
Midway's a spot where the three pastors—they
  of Trent and Brescia and Verona—might
  bestow their blessing, if they went that way.
Peschiera, fortress fair and strong to affright
  the Bergamese and men of Brescia, stands
  where the surrounding shore is least in height.
All that within its bosom's restricting bands
  Benaco holds not, there must downward go,
  forming a river, through green pasture-lands.
As soon as on its course it starts to flow,
  no more Benaco, but 'tis Mincio named,
  down to Governo, where it joins the Po.
Nor has it run far ere its current is tamed
  by a flat, where spreading out it makes a fen,
  at times in summer for its air ill-famed.
Passing from there the savage virgin then
  saw firm ground in the midst of the morass,
  untilled and bare of any denizen.

Lì, per fuggire ogni consorzio umano,
  ristette con suoi servi a far sue arti,
  e visse, e vi lasciò suo corpo vano.   87

Gli uomini poi che intorno erano sparti
  s'accolsero a quel loco, ch'era forte
  per lo pantan che avea da tutte parti.   90

Fer la città sovra quell'ossa morte,
  e per colei che il luogo prima elesse,
  Mantova l'appellar sanz'altra sorte.   93

Già fur le genti sue dentro più spesse
  prima che la mattia di Casalodi
  da Pinamonte inganno ricevesse.   96

Però t'assenno che se tu mai odi
  originar la mia terra altrimenti,
  la verità nulla menzogna frodi».   99

E io: «Maestro, i tuoi ragionamenti
  mi son sì certi e prendon sì mia fede,
  che gli altri mi sarien carboni spenti.   102

Ma dimmi de la gente che procede,
  se tu ne vedi alcun degno di nota;
  chè solo a ciò la mia mente rifiede».   105

Allor mi disse: « Quei che da la gota
  porge la barba in su le spalle brune,
  fu, quando Grecia fu di maschi vota   108

sì che a pena rimaser per le cune,
  augure, e diede il punto con Calcanta
  in Aulide a tagliar la prima fune.   111

Euripilo ebbe nome, e così il canta
  l'alta mia tragedìa in alcun loco:
  ben lo sai tu che la sai tutta quanta.»   114

Quell'altro che nei fianchi è così poco
  Michele Scotto fu, che veramente
  de le magiche frodi seppe il gioco.   117

Vedi Guido Bonatti, vedi Asdente
  che avere inteso al cuoio ed a lo spago
  ora vorrebbe, ma tardi si pente.   120

Vedi le triste che lasciaron l'ago,
  la spola e il fuso, e fecersi indovine;
  fecer malie con erbe e con imago.   123

There, to shun every human tie and pass
   her days in witchcraft with her serfs, she stay'd:
   there left her body when it lifeless was.
The widely-scattered country-folk were led
   in time to draw together to that spot,
   strong as it was with swamps all round it spread.
Built over those dead bones, their city got
   for her sake who first made the site her choice
   the name of Mantua, nor drew further lot.
In streets more crowded did it once rejoice,
   ere Casalodi's folly was cheated by
   Pinamonte's unscrupulous device.
I do thee this to wit, so that if my
   birthplace thou ever hear had otherwise
   its source, the truth be cozened by no lie.'
'Master,' I said, 'thy words such certainties
   convey, and so hold my belief, that like
   spent embers will all else be in my eyes.
But tell me, of the folk who tread this dike,
   if thou seest any worthy of notice; for
   back to this only does my mind now strike.'
Then said he: 'Yonder soul whose beard doth o'er
   his swarthy shoulders from his cheek flow down,
   was, when of males Greece had such scanty store
that in the cradles there remained scarce one,
   an augur, and with Calchas timed the blow
   which severed the first cable in Aulis town.
Eurypylus was the name he had, and so
   sings him my lofty tragedy somewhere:
   well know'st it thou, who knowest the poem all thro'.`
That other one, about the loins so spare,
   was Michael Scot, who in good sooth well knew
   all juggling tricks and was their cunning player.
See Guy Bonatti, see Asdente, who
   would now wish that to thread and leather he
   had paid attention, but too late doth rue.
See the vile hags who forsook huswifry,
   shuttle and distaff for divining, fain
   to charm with herbs and with an effigy.

Ma vienne omai, chè già tiene il confine
  d'amendue gli emisperi e tocca l'onda
  sotto Sibilia Caino e le spine.   126
E già iernotte fu la luna tonda;
  ben ten dee ricordar, chè non ti nocque
  alcuna volta per la selva fonda».   129
Sì mi parlava, ed andavamo introcque.

CANTO 21

Così di ponte in ponte, altro parlando
  che la mia comedìa cantar non cura,
  venimmo, e tenevamo il colmo, quando   3
restammo per veder l'altra fessura
  di Malebolge e gli altri pianti vani;
  e vidila mirabilmente oscura.   6
Quale ne l'arzanà dei Viniziani
  bolle l'inverno la tenace pece
  a rimpalmare i legni lor non sani,   9
chè navigar non ponno, e in quella vece
  chi fa suo legno novo e chi ristoppa
  le coste a quel che più viaggi fece;   12
chi ribatte da proda e chi da poppa,
  altri fa remi ed altri volge sarte,
  chi terzeruolo ed artimon rintoppa;   15
tal, non per foco ma per divin'arte,
  bollia laggiuso una pegola spessa
  che inviscava la ripa d'ogni parte.   18
Io vedea lei, ma non vedeva in essa
  ma' che le bolle che il bollor levava,
  e gonfiar tutta, e riseder compressa.   21
Mentr'io laggiù fisamente mirava,
  lo duca mio dicendo: «Guarda, guarda»
  mi trasse a sè del loco dov'io stava.   24
Allor mi volsi come l'uom cui tarda
  di veder quel che li convien fuggire,
  e cui paura subita sgagliarda,   27

But come, for with his thorns already Cain
  holds the confine of either hemisphere
  and touches 'neath Seville the wide sea-main;
last night, too, already the moon was full: quite clear
  should this be in thy memory, for her ray
  in the deep wood, at no time hurt thee there.'
So spake he, and meanwhile we went our way.

CANTO 21

From bridge to bridge thus came we, talking then
  of things my Comedy deems off the mark
  to sing now, and had reached the summit, when
we stopped to see in the next fissured arc
  of Evilpouches the next wailings, all
  quite futile; and I saw it strangely dark.
As boils in the Venetians' arsenal,
  when winter comes, the viscous pitch to aid
  them caulk their ships that need an overhaul,
for none can sail, and one constructs instead
  his new boat, and one plugs, with like concern,
  the ribs of that which many a voyage hath made;
one hammers at the prow, one at the stern;
  some patch the mainsail, some the jib; to twine
  cordage and to make oars do others turn—
so, not by fire, rather by art divine,
  was boiling down below there a thick tar,
  which smeared the bank along the entire incline.
I saw this, but saw naught within it, bar
  the bubbles the boiling raised, and the whole mass
  heave and, compress'd, subsiding near and far.
I still was gazing intently down, whenas
  my leader said: 'Look out, look out ' and me
  drew close to him from the place in which I was.
Then I turned round, like one in haste to see
  what he must flee from, whom the sudden shock
  of fear yet so completely unmans that he

che, per veder, non indugia il partire;
  e vidi dietro a noi un diavol nero
  correndo su per lo scoglio venire.   30
Ahi quanto egli era ne l'aspetto fero!
  e quanto mi parea ne l'atto acerbo,
  con l'ali aperte, e sovra i piè leggiero!   33
L'omero suo, ch'era acuto e superbo,
  carcava un peccator con ambo l'anche,
  e quei tenea dei piè ghermito il nerbo.   36
Dal nostro ponte disse: « O Malebranche,
  ecco un de gli anzian di Santa Zita.
  Mettetel sotto, ch'io torno per anche   39
a quella terra che n'è ben fornita:
  ogni uom v'è barattier, fuorchè Bonturo;
  del *no* per lo danar vi si fa *ita* ».   42
Là giù li buttò; e per lo scoglio duro
  si volse; e mai non fu mastino sciolto
  con tanta fretta a seguitar lo furo.   45
Quel s'attuffò, e tornò sù convolto;
  ma i demon che del ponte avean coperchio
  gridar: « Qui non ha loco il Santo Volto: 48
qui si nuota altrimenti che nel Serchio!
  Però se tu non vuoi de' nostri graffi,
  non far sopra la pegola soperchio ».   51
Poi l'addentar con più di cento raffi
  disser: « Coverto convien che qui balli,
  sì che, se puoi, nascosamente accaffi ».   54
Non altrimenti i cuochi ai loro vassalli
  fanno attuffare in mezzo la caldaia
  la carne con gli uncin, perchè non galli.   57
Lo buon maestro: « A ciò che non si paia
  che tu ci sia » mi disse « giù t'acquatta
  dopo uno scheggio, che alcun schermo t'aia;   60
e per nulla offension che mi sia fatta
  non temer tu, ch'io ho le cose conte,
  e altra volta fui a tal baratta ».   63
Poscia passò di là dal co del ponte;
  e come giunse in su la ripa sesta
  mestier li fu d'aver sicura fronte.   66

stays not his going to take one moment's stock
   of what he sees; and I beheld a black
   devil come running behind us up the rock.
Ah, how fierce he looked! how set to attack
   he seemed to me in his gest and cruel eye,
   with wings spread wide and feet that skimmed the track!
For freight his shoulder, which was sharp and high,
   bore the two haunches of a sinner: 'twas
   the sinews of the feet he gripped him by.
He shouted from our bridge: 'Ho, Evilclaws,
   here's one of St. Zita's elders! Thrust him under:
   I'm off to his city again for more, because
it's amply stocked with many a such-like bounder:
   except Bonturo, all are jobbers there,
   where "no"'s exchanged for "yep" to grab more plunder.
He hurled him down and turned back o'er the bare
   hard crag, and never did unleashed mastiff strain
   its utmost so, to track a thief to his lair.
The wretch plunged and, besmeared, bobbed up again;
   but the fiends, under the bridge, began to jeer:
   'Here for the Holy Face one seeks in vain:
It's not like swimming in the Serchio here!
   so unless thou want'st our grapples at thee catching,
   let nought of thee above the pitch show clear.'
With countless prongs pricking him then and scratching
   they cried: 'Dance here, submerged, so that remote
   from sight thou, if thou canst, may'st do thy snatching.'
Not otherwise cooks bid their scullions note
   where meat seethes in the pot and thrust it deep
   down with their flesh-hooks, that it may not float.
My kind lord said to me: 'That thou mayst slip
   their notice, find some splinter which somewhat
   will screen thee, squat down, and behind it keep.
Nor, what rebuff soe'er to me be wrought,
   fear thou, for these are things to me well known:
   I've faced this traffic before and mind it not.'
Then past the bridgehead on he went alone,
   and need there was, when on the sixth bank he
   had set foot, that a bold front should be shown.

Con quel furore e con quella tempesta
   ch'escono i cani addosso al poverello,
   che di subito chiede ove s'arresta,   69
usciron quei di sotto al ponticello
   e porser verso lui tutti i roncigli;
   ma ei gridò: « Nessun di voi sia fello.   72
Innanzi che l'uncin vostro mi pigli,
   traggasi avante l'un di voi che m'oda,
   e poi d'arroncigliarmi si consigli ».   75
Tutti gridaron: « Vada Malacoda! »
   per ch'un si mosse, e gli altri stetter fermi;
   e venne a lui dicendo: « Che gli approda? »   78
«Credi tu, Malacoda, qui vedermi
   esser venuto » disse il mio maestro
   « sicuro già da tutti i vostri schermi,   81
sanza voler divino e fato destro?
   Lasciane andar, chè nel cielo è voluto
   ch'io mostri altrui questo cammin silvestro ». 84
Allor li fu l'orgoglio sì caduto
   che si lasciò cascar l'uncino ai piedi,
   e disse a gli altri: « Omai non sia feruto ».   87
E il duca mio a me: « O tu che siedi
   tra li scheggion del ponte quatto quatto,
   sicuramente omai a me ti riedi ».   90
Per ch'io mi mossi, ed a lui venni ratto;
   e i diavoli si fecer tutti avanti,
   sì ch'io temetti ch'ei tenesser patto.   93
E così vid'io già temer li fanti
   che uscivan patteggiati di Caprona,
   veggendo sè tra nemici cotanti.   96
Io m'accostai con tutta la persona
   lungo il mio duca, e non torceva gli occhi
   da la sembianza lor ch'era non buona.   99
E chinavan li raffi, e « Vuoi che il tocchi »
   diceva l'un con l'altro « in sul groppone? »
   E rispondea: « Sì, fa che gliele accocchi! » 102
Ma quel demonio che tenea sermone
   col duca mio, si volse tutto presto,
   e disse, « Posa, posa, Scarmiglione! »   105

For with the fierce tempestuous savagery
  of dogs that rush out at some poor man, who
  suddenly, where he stops, prefers his plea.
out from beneath the little bridge they flew
  and turned against him all their gaffs; but straight
  cried he: 'No mischief, now, from any of you!
Before those hooks of yours in me be set,
  one of you first step forth to hear me: an so
  ye then will, then on gaffing me debate.'
They all exclaimed: 'Let Malacoda go!';
  so one moved—the rest halting—and came near
  him growling out: 'What good will it do him, though?'
'Thinkest thou, Malacoda, that thou here'
  my lord said 'seest me come thus far uncow'd
  by all your hindrances, unless it were
by Will divine and Fate that bodes me good?
  Let me pass on, for 'tis in Heaven will'd
  that I show to another this wild road.'
Then how crestfallen he, of late so fill'd
  with pride! He let the hook drop at his feet
  and to the rest said: 'Strike not, we must yield.'
My leader then to me: 'Thou that dost sit
  squat on the bridge there where the rock is crack'd,
  come down now: thou mayst safely venture it.'
Therefore I moved and came to him—swift to act;
  for all the fiends advanced, and the fear rose
  within me that they might not keep the pact.
And once I saw the footmen in like throes
  of fear, when issuing under treaty from
  Caprona, at seeing themselves so girt with foes.
With my whole frame, as close I could come,
  I drew up to my guide, while well in view
  keeping their looks, which were not humoursome.
They lowered their prongs and 'Wouldst thou like me to,
  I'll tickle him on the rump' was saying one,
  the rest replying: 'Ay, nick it for him, do!'
But he, that demon who had just begun
  to parley with my leader, turned sharp round
  and said: 'Be quiet, be quiet, Scarmiglión.'

Poi disse a noi: « Più oltre andar per questo
   iscoglio non si può, però che giace
   tutto spezzato, al fondo, l'arco sesto.   108
E se l'andare avante pur vi piace,
   andatevene sù per questa grotta:
   presso è un altro scoglio che via face.   111
Ier, più oltre cinqu'ore che quest'otta,
   mille dugento con sessantasei
   anni compier che qui la via fu rotta.   114
Io mando verso là di questi miei
   a riguardar se alcun se ne sciorina:
   gite con lor, che non saranno rei.   117
Tratti avante, Alichino e Calcabrina »
   cominciò egli a dire « e tu Cagnazzo;
   e Barbariccia guidi la decina.   120
Libicocco vegna oltre e Draghignazzo,
   Ciriatto sannuto e Graffiacane
   e Farfarello e Rubicante pazzo.   123
Cercate intorno le boglienti pane;
   costor sien salvi infino a l'altro scheggio
   che tutto intero va sopra le tane ».   126
« Omè, maestro, che è quel ch'io veggio? »
   diss'io. « Deh, sanza scorta andiamci soli,
   se tu sai ir, ch'io per me non la cheggio. 129
Se tu sei sì accorto come suoli,
   non vedi tu ch'ei digrignan li denti,
   e con le ciglia ne minaccian duoli? » 132
Ed egli a me: « Non vuo' che tu paventi:
   lasciali digrignar pure a lor senno,
   ch'ei fanno ciò per li lessi dolenti ».   135
Per l'argine sinistro volta dienno;
   ma prima avea ciascun la lingua stretta
   coi denti verso lor duca, per cenno;   138
ed egli avea del cul fatto trombetta.

And then to us: 'By this crag will be found
  no means of progress, for the sixth arch lies
  in the pit's depth, all shattered to the ground.

But if it still seems pleasing in your eyes
  to go on, take this bank, and soon there'll show
  another crag, o'er which a pathway hies.

Yesterday, five hours later than 'tis now,
  twelve hundred sixty and six years had gone by
  exactly since this bridge's overthrow.

I'm sending that way scouts of mine, to spy
  on any venturing out to take the air:
  go with them, they'll not treat you spitefully.'

'Alichin, Cálcabrin, step forward there!'
  he went on: 'and Cagnazzo, thou as well:
  let Barbariccia lead the ten, d'ye hear?

Next, Libicocco and Draghignazzo, fell
  Ciriatt' o' the tusks and Graffiacane: then
  mad Rubicante, back of Farfarél.

Scout round the boiling bird-lime; give these twain
  safe conduct to the next rock-rib that on,
  unbroken, goes o'er each successive den.'

'Ah me, sir, what a sight!' said I: 'alone,
  without an escort, pray, if thou know'st how,
  let's travel; for on my part I want none.

If thou'rt as wary as thou art wont, dost thou
  not see the way they gnash their teeth, the way
  they threaten us mischief with their lowering brow?'

And he: 'I would not have thee feel dismay:
  let them go gnashing on, if so they like;
  'tis at the boiled ones that they bristle and bay.'

To the left hand they wheeled along the dike;
  but first, as signal tow'rd their captain, each
  had bitten tongue with teeth; and he to strike
a bugle's note, had utilized his breech.

CANTO 22

Io vidi già cavalier mover campo,
  e cominciare stormo e far lor mostra,
  e talvolta partir per loro scampo;   3
corridor vidi per la terra vostra,
  o Aretini, e vidi gir gualdane,
  ferir torneamenti e correr giostra;   6
quando con trombe e quando con campane,
  con tamburi e con cenni di castella,
  e con cose nostrali e con istrane;   9
nè già con sì diversa cennamella
  cavalier vidi mover, nè pedoni,
  nè nave a segno di terra o di stella.   12
Noi andavam con li dieci demoni:
  ahi fiera compagnia! Ma ne la chiesa
  coi santi ed in taverna coi ghiottoni!   15
Pure a la pegola era la mia intesa,
  per veder de la bolgia ogni contegno
  e de la gente ch'entro v'era incesa.   18
Come i delfini quando fanno segno
  ai marinar, con l'arco de la schiena,
  che s'argomentin di campar lor legno,   21
talor così, ad alleggiar la pena,
  mostrava alcun dei peccatori il dosso
  e il nascondeva, in men che non balena.   24
E come a l'orlo de l'acqua d'un fosso
  stanno i ranocchi pur col muso fuori,
  sì che celano i piedi e l'altro grosso,   27
sì stavan d'ogni parte i peccatori;
  ma come s'appressava Barbariccia,
  così si ritraean sotto i bollori.   30
Io vidi, ed anco il cor me n'accapriccia,
  uno aspettar così com'egli incontra
  che una rana rimane ed altra spiccia.   33
E Graffiacan, che gli era più di contra,
  gli arroncigliò le impegolate chiome,
  e trassel sù che mi parve una lontra.   36

CANTO 22

I'VE seen before now cavalry strike camp,
  and open the attack, and make their muster,
  and sometimes, in retreat, their horses' ramp;
seen scouts about your land, ye folk that cluster
  around Arezzo, seen the forayer's raid,
  the clash of tournaments, and charge of jouster;
with clang of bells, with blare by trumpets bray'd,
  with drums, with castle-signals and what are
  all 'larums else, our own and foreign-made;
but to a flageolet so singular
  I never yet saw move or horse or foot,
  or ship by mark of landfall or of star.
With the ten demons we pursued our route:
  ah, fierce companions! But 'with saints at church,
  with guzzlers at the tavern,' as may suit.
Only the pitch was I intent to search,
  viewing the pouch all over, fain to note
  what souls it smothered in the scald and smirch.
Like dolphins, when they sign to men afloat
  by the arching of their backs, the sailors then
  adopting measures which will save their boat;
at times, thuswise, to alleviate the pain,
  some wretched sinner here and there would hitch
  his back up, and like lightning dip it again.
And, as at the edge of water in a ditch
  frogs set themselves, with just the snout outside,
  their feet and bulk else hidd'n; on either beach
so did the sinners squat: but if they spied,
  however, Barbariccia drawing nigh,
  straightway they drew back 'neath the boiling tide.
Thus—and my heart still shudders at it—I
  saw one wait, as mayhap of frogs one squatter,
  when all the rest jump in, stays high and dry;
and Graffiacán, who on his scent was hotter
  than the others, hooked him by his tarry pow
  and hauled him up as one might do an otter.

Io sapea già di tutti quanti il nome,
  sì li notai quando furono eletti,
  e poi che si chiamaro, attesi come.   39

« O Rubicante, fa che tu li metti
  gli unghioni addosso sì che tu lo scuoi »
  gridavan tutti insieme i maledetti.   42

E io: « Maestro mio, fa, se tu puoi,
  che tu sappi chi è lo sciagurato
  venuto a man de gli avversari suoi ».   45

Lo duca mio li s'accostò a lato;
  domandollo ond'ei fosse, ed ei rispose:
  « Io fui del regno di Navarra nato.   48

Mia madre a servo d'un signor mi pose,
  chè m'avea generato d'un ribaldo
  distruggitor di sè e di sue cose.   51

Poi fui famiglio del buon re Tebaldo:
  quivi mi misi a far baratteria,
  di che rendo ragione in questo caldo ».   54

E Ciriatto, a cui di bocca uscìa
  d'ogni parte une sanna come a porco,
  li fe' sentir come l'una sdrucìa.   57

Tra male gatte era venuto il sorco;
  ma Barbariccia il chiuse con le braccia,
  e disse: « State in là mentr'io l'inforco ».   60

Ed al maestro mio volse la faccia:
  « Domanda » disse « ancor, se più disii
  saper da lui, prima ch'altri il disfaccia ».   63

Lo duca dunque: « Or dì: de gli altri rii
  conosci tu alcun che sia latino
  sotto la pece? »   E quegli: « Io mi partii   66

poco è, da un che fu di là vicino:
  così foss'io ancor con lui coperto,
  ch'io non temerei unghia nè uncino! »   69

E Libicocco: « Troppo avem sofferto »
  disse; e preseli il braccio col ronciglio,
  sì che, stracciando, ne portò un lacerto.   72

Draghignazzo anche i volle dar di piglio
  giuso a le gambe; onde il decurio loro
  si volse intorno intorno con mal piglio.   75

I knew them all, and what their names, by now:
  so well I'd marked them while being singled out,
  and, when they hailed each other, listened how.
With one voice, 'Go for him, Rubicante: put
  thy claws to his back so as to flay him' those
  accurséd creatures all began to shout.
'Do, master, if thou canst, make him disclose
  his name,' said I, '—this wretch whose evil star
  has lodged him in the fell clutch of his foes.'
My leader neared him, close beside the tar,
  asked whence he was and he replied: 'My place
  of birth was in the kingdom of Navarre.
My mother hired to one of the noblesse
  my service, for the rogue she'd borne me to
  destroyed himself and left her penniless,
Then, placed in good king Tibbald's household, grew
  I skilled there in the jobbery wherefor
  I render payment in this scalding glue.'
And Ciriatto, who had, like a wild boar,
  a tusk that each side from his mouth stuck out,
  gave him to feel how one of these could score.
By evil cats the mouse was ringed about;
  but Barbariccia, clasping him, exclaimed:
  'Back! while he's in my clutch, ye devil's rout.'
Then, turning, at my guide a glance he aimed;
  'Ask on,' he said, 'if thou desire to know
  more from him, ere by others he be maimed.'
My guide then: 'Of the other rogues dost thou
  know any, tell us, of the Latian stock
  under the pitch?' And he: 'It was but now
I quitted one who neighboured such: and mock—
  yes, so I still were with him in yon stuff
  well hid—I'd mock alike at claw and hook.'
Then Libicocco said: 'We've stood enough
  of this'; and gaffed his arm, and with one rip
  tore thence a sinew out and bore it off.
Next, Draghignazzo had a mind to grip
  his legs low down; whence he that led the ten
  turned round and round and curled a threatening lip.

Quand'elli un poco rappaciati foro,
  a lui, che ancor mirava sua ferita,
  domandò il duca mio sanza dimoro: 78
« Chi fu colui da cui mala partita
  di' che facesti per venire a proda? »
  Ed ei rispose: « Fu frate Gomita,   81
quel di Gallura, vasel d'ogni froda,
  ch'ebbe i nemici di suo donno in mano,
  e fe' lor sì che ciascun se ne loda.   84
Danar si tolse e lasciolli di piano,
  sì com'ei dice; e ne gli altri offici anche
  barattier fu non picciol ma sovrano.   87
Usa con esso donno Michel Zanche
  di Logodoro, e a dir di Sardigna
  le lingue lor non si sentono stanche.   90
Omè, vedete l'altro che digrigna:
  io direi anche, ma io temo ch'ello
  non s'apparecchi a grattarmi la tigna ».   93
E il gran proposto, volto a Farfarello
  che stralunava gli occhi per ferire,
  disse: « Fatti in costà, malvagio uccello! »   96
« Se voi volete veder o udire »,
  ricominciò lo spaurato appresso
  « Toschi o Lombardi, io ne farò venire;   99
ma stieno i Malebranche un poco in cesso,
  sì ch'ei non teman de le lor vendette;
  e io, seggendo in questo loco stesso,   102
per un ch'io son ne farò venir sette,
  quand'io sufolerò, com'è nostr'uso
  di fare allor che fuori alcun si mette ».   105
Cagnazzo a cotal motto levò il muso
  crollando il capo, e disse: « Odi malizia
  ch'egli ha pensata per gettarsi giuso! »   108
Ond'ei, che avea lacciuoli a gran divizia,
  rispose: « Malizioso son io troppo,
  quand'io procuro a' miei maggior tristizia! »   111
Alichin non si tenne, e, di rintoppo
  a gli altri, disse a lui: « Se tu ti cali,
  io non ti verrò dietro di galoppo,   114

When they were somewhat quieted again,
  of him, who still was gazing at his wound,
  my guide without delay enquired then:
'Who was the soul that, in an hour ill-found,
  thou didst, thou sayest, quit to come ashore?'
  ' 'Twas Fra Gomito,' he replied, 'renown'd
throughout Gallura for his endless store
  of frauds, who held his master's foes in fee
  and dealt with them in a way all praise him for.
He took a bribe and "quietly" set them free,
  so he says; and in other matters too
  no petty cheat, but prince of jobbers he!
With him consorts don Michael Zanche who
  ruled Logodor'; Sardinia's still the theme
  their tireless tongues incessantly pursue.
Ah me, behold that other devil, him
  who grinds his teeth: I've more to tell, but fear
  he'll scratch my scurf for me, he looks so grim.'
Their great chief turned, saw Farfarello leer
  and roll his eyes in the act of striking home,
  and said: 'Accurséd kite, be off from here!'
'If ye desire to see or listen to some
  from Tuscany or Lombardy,' his address
  the scared one then resumed, 'I'll make them come.
But let the Evilclaws withdraw a space,
  that none who comes may fear their vengeance; and
  I, ceasing not to sit in this same place,
for my sole self will summon seven to land
  by whistling, as our custom is, when out
  gets any soul belonging to our band.'
Cagnazzo, at these words, turned up his snout
  and shook his head, exclaiming: 'Hear the trick
  he's hatched, for diving in again, no doubt.'
Whereat he, rich in stratagems, said quick:
  'O'ertricky indeed am I, when thus to lure
  my mates to greater woe is what I seek.'
No more of this could Alichin endure:
  despite the rest, he warned him: 'Div'st thou, then
  not at a gallop shall I be on thy spoor,

ma batterò sopra la pece l'ali!
　　Lascisi il collo, e sia la ripa scudo
　　a veder se tu sol più di noi vali ».   117
O tu che leggi, udirai novo ludo.
　　Ciascun da l'altra costa gli occhi volse,
　　quei prima che a ciò fare era più crudo.   120
Lo Navarrese ben suo tempo colse:
　　fermò le piante a terra, ed in un punto
　　saltò e dal proposto lor si sciolse.   123
Di che ciascun di colpa fu compunto,
　　ma quei più che cagion fu del difetto;
　　però si mosse e gridò: « Tu se' giunto! »   126
Ma poco i valse, chè l'ali al sospetto
　　non potero avanzar; quegli andò sotto
　　e quei drizzò, volando, suso il petto: 129
non altrimenti l'anitra, di botto,
　　quando il falcon s'appressa, giù s'attuffa,
　　ed ei ritorna sù crucciato e rotto.   132
Irato Calcabrina de la buffa,
　　volando dietro li tenne, invaghito
　　che quei campasse per aver la zuffa;   135
e come il barattier fu disparito,
　　così volse li artigli al suo compagno,
　　e fu con lui sopra il fosso ghermito.   138
Ma l'altro fu bene sparvier grifagno
　　ad artiglar ben lui, ed amendue
　　cadder nel mezzo del bogliente stagno.   141
Lo caldo sghermitor subito fue;
　　ma però del levarsi era niente,
　　sì avieno inviscate l'ali sue.   144
Barbariccia, con gli altri suoi dolente,
　　quattro ne fe' volar da l'altra costa
　　con tutti i raffi, ed assai prestamente   147
di qua di là discesero a la posta;
　　porser gli uncini verso gl'impaniati
　　ch'eran già cotti dentro da la crosta;   150
e noi lasciammo lor così impacciati.

but skim with beating wings the tarry plane;
  make we the bank our screen, quitting its brow,
  to see if, single, thou canst beat our ten.'
To novel sport, my Reader, hearken now;
  all tow'rds the other slope their glances bent,
  he first, who that had been least fain to allow.
The Navarrese, his time well chosen, leant
  forward, dug in his toes, and, quick as thought,
  leapt, and broke loose thus from their provost's restraint.
Compunction stung them all, but most it wrought
  to fury him who'd caused the blunder; so
  he started in pursuit and yelled: 'Thou'rt caught!'
But of small use was that, for there are no
  wings that can outstrip fear: the one dived in,
  the other raised his breast while skimming low:
so, in a trice, the duck, when she has seen
  the falcon near her, dives: and he, his rape
  thus foiled, soars up again, full of chagrin.
Calcabrin, mad with anger at the jape,
  flew after him and, spoiling for a fight,
  was eager that the quarry should escape;
and, as the barrator passed out of sight,
  that moment 'gainst his fellow turned his claws,
  closed with him o'er the trench and clutched him tight.
But, sooth, to claw him well the other was
  a full-grown sparrow-hawk, and down the two
  dropped, both at once, into the boiling brose.
The heat unclutched them instantly; but do
  what either might, to rise was past their power,
  their wings were so encrusted by the glue.
Then Barbariccia, with his comrades, sore
  perturbed, bade a quaternion fly in haste
  to the other bank, with gaffs and all: the four,
this side and that, soon lighted and, thus placed,
  stretched out their hooks to the beliméd pair,
  who now were cooked right through beneath the paste:
and, seeing them in this broil, we left them there.

CANTO 23

Taciti, soli, sanza compagnia
   n'andavam, l'un dinanzi e l'altro dopo
   come i frati minor vanno per via.   3
Volto era in su la favola d'Isopo
   lo mio pensier, per la presente rissa,
   dov'ei parlò de la rana e del topo;   6
chè più non si pareggia *mo* ed *issa*
   che l'un con l'altro fa, se ben s'accoppia
   principio e fine con la mente fissa.   9
E come l'un pensier de l'altro scoppia,
   così nacque di quello un altro poi
   che la prima paura mi fe' doppia.   12
Io pensava così: « Questi per noi
   sono scherniti con danno e con beffa
   sì fatta, che assai credo che lor nòi.   15
Se l'ira sovra il malvoler s'aggueffa,
   ei ne verranno dietro più crudeli
   che il cane a quella lievre ch'egli acceffa ».   18
Già mi sentia tutti arricciar li peli
   de la paura, e stava indietro intento,
   quand'io dissi: « Maestro, se non celi   21
te e me tostamente, i' ho pavento
   dei Malebranche: noi li avem già dietro:
   io l'imagino sì, che già li sento! »   24
E quei: « S'io fossi di piombato vetro,
   l'imagine di fuor tua non trarrei
   più tosto a me, che quella d'entro impetro.   27
Pur mo venieno i tuoi pensier fra i miei
   con simil atto e con simile faccia,
   sì che d'entrambi un sol consiglio fei.   30
S'egli è che sì la destra costa giaccia
   che noi possiam ne l'altra bolgia scendere,
   noi fuggirem l'imaginata caccia ».   33
Già non compiè di tal consiglio rendere,
   ch'io li vidi venir con l'ali tese,
   non molto lungi, per volerne prendere.   36

CANTO 23

SILENT, alone and unescorted, he
　　first and then I, as Friars minor jog
　　along a road in file, so on trudged we.
Turned were my thoughts to Aesop's apologue
　　by the just witnessed fray—I mean the one
　　in which he spoke about the mouse and frog;
for more alike are not 'soon' and 'anon'
　　than this case is to that, if rightly paired
　　be start and finish by a mind fixed thereon.
And as from one thought bursts another, spurred
　　by that another then grew active, thus
　　making me by the first fear doubly scared.
I argued in this way: 'They have through us
　　been so befooled, hurt, mocked at, all at once,
　　as must have made their tempers venomous.
If rage be reeled round malice, then to trounce
　　us they will come more cruelly on our heel
　　than hounds after the hare on which they pounce.'
Backwards intent, I could already feel
　　my hair all bristling with the fear which made
　　me say: 'Master, unless thou canst conceal
thyself and me right quickly, I'm afraid
　　of the Evilclaws: e'en now they're close behind:
　　I imagine that e'en now I hear their tread!'
And he: 'Were I of glass that's leaden-lined,
　　I should not sooner to myself draw thine
　　exterior, than I get what's in thy mind.
Even now thy thoughts have entered among mine
　　with similar features and with similar gest,
　　so that of both I've formed one sole design.
If to our right the bank lie so depress'd,
　　that to the next pouch we can make descent,
　　we shall escape the chase thou imaginest.'
He'd not yet finished broaching this intent
　　when I beheld them coming, with wings spread,
　　not very far off, on our seizure bent.

Lo duca mio di subito mi prese,
   come la madre che al romore è desta
   e vede presso a sè le fiamme accese,   39
che prende il figlio, e fugge, e non s'arresta,
   avendo più di lui che di sè cura,
   tanto che solo una camicia vesta;   42
e giù dal collo de la ripa dura
   supin si diede a la pendente roccia
   che l'un dei lati a l'altra bolgia tura.   45
Non corse mai sì tosto acqua per doccia
   a volger rota di molin terragno,
   quand'ella più verso le pale approccia,   48
come il maestro mio per quel vivagno,
   portandosene me sovra il suo petto,
   come suo figlio, non come compagno.   51
A pena foro i piè suoi giunti al letto
   del fondo giù, ch'ei furono in sul colle
   sovr'esso noi, ma non gli era sospetto;   54
chè l'alta providenza, che lor volle
   porre ministri de la fossa quinta,
   poder di partirs'indi a tutti tolle.   57
Là giù trovammo una gente dipinta
   che giva intorno assai con lenti passi
   piangendo, e nel sembiante stanca e vinta.   60
Elli avean cappe con cappucci bassi
   dinanzi a gli occhi, fatte de la taglia
   che in Clugnì per li monaci fassi.   63
Di fuor dorate son, sì ch'elli abbaglia;
   ma dentro tutte piombo, e gravi tanto
   che Federico le mettea di paglia.   66
Oh in eterno faticoso manto!
   Noi ci volgemmo ancor pure a man manca
   con loro insieme, intenti al tristo pianto.   69
Ma per lo peso quella gente stanca
   venìa sì pian, che noi eravam nuovi
   di compagnia ad ogni mover d'anca.   72
Per ch'io al duca mio: « Fa che tu trovi
   alcun che al fatto o al nome si conosca,
   e gli occhi, sì andando, intorno movi ».   75

My leader straightway seized me—as from bed
   roused by the roar and seeing the flames alight
   near her the mother, who, by nothing stay'd,
seizes her son and instantly takes flight,
   donning not even a shift, so much is he
   more than herself of value in her sight—
and slid supine down the declivity
   of rock which walls one side of the next pit,
   quitting the ridge o' that bank of flinty scree.
Never did water faster through a leat
   to turn the wheel of a mill on the bankside run,
   when the blades are on the point of receiving it,
than sped my master down that slope right on
   and over the rim, bearing me on his breast,
   not as a comrade, but as his own son.
Scarce were his feet on touching bottom based
   firm on its bed when lo, they were on the hill
   right over us; but now his fears could rest;
for that exalted Providence, whose will
   placed them to serve the fifth trench, also took
   from all of them the power to cross its sill.
Down there below we found a painted folk,
   who moved-on round with steps exceeding slow,
   weeping and with a weary, vanquished look.
They had on cloaks with cowls that were drawn low
   over the eyes, and shaped like those that in
   Cluný are for the monks still fashioned so.
Gilded without, they are of dazzling sheen,
   but heavy (such that Frederick's by compare
   would seem of straw) for all are lead within.
Oh toilsome mantle for eternal wear!
   We turned again and still to leftward kept
   along with them, their plaints our only care.
But, through the weight, those weary people crept
   so slowly on, that we had ever new
   associates at every pace we stepp'd
I, therefore, to my guide: 'Discover, do,
   some one of known name or, for deeds, renown'd;
   and, as we go, glance round with that in view.'

Ed un che intese la parola tosca,
 di retro a noi gridò: « Tenete i piedi,
 voi che correte sì per l'aura fosca.   78
Forse che avrai da me quel che tu chiedi ».
 Onde il duca si volse e disse: « Aspetta,
 e poi secondo il suo passo procedi ».   81
Ristetti, e vidi due mostrar gran fretta
 de l'animo, col viso, d'esser meco;
 ma tardavali il carco e la via stretta.   84
Quando fur giunti, assai con l'occhio bieco
 mi rimiraron sanza far parola;
 poi si volsero in sè, e dicean seco: 87
« Costui par vivo a l'atto de la gola;
 e se son morti, per qual privilegio
 vanno scoperti de la grave stola? »   90
Poi disser me: « O tosco, che al collegio
 de l'ipocriti tristi sei venuto,
 dir chi tu sei non avere in dispregio ». 93
Ed io a loro: « Io fui nato e cresciuto
 sovra il bel fiume d'Arno, a la gran villa,
 e son col corpo ch'io ho sempre avuto. 96
Ma voi chi siete, a cui tanto distilla
 quant'io veggio dolor giù per le guance?
 e che pena è in voi, che sì sfavilla? » 99
E l'un rispose a me: « Le cappe rance
 son di piombo, e sì grosse che li pesi
 fan così cigolar le lor bilance.   102
Frati Godenti fummo, e bolognesi;
 io Catalano, e questi Loderingo
 nomati, e da tua terra insieme presi, 105
come suol esser tolto un uom solingo,
 per conservar sua pace; e fummo tali
 che ancor si pare intorno dal Gardingo ». 108
Io cominciai: « O frati, i vostri mali... »
 ma più non dissi, chè all'occhio mi corse
 un, crucifisso in terra con tre pali. 111
Quando mi vide, tutto si distorse
 soffiando ne la barba con sospiri;
 e il frate Catalan, che a ciò s'accorse, 114

And one behind us, when he caught the sound
  of Tuscan speech, cried out: 'Walk slower, ye
  that through the dark air so devour the ground:
perhaps thou wilt obtain thy wish from me.'
  Whereat my leader turned, exclaiming: 'Stay,
  and then proceed at the same pace as he.'
I stopped and by their looks saw two betray
  much haste of mind to join me, though delay'd
  by their great burden and the crowded way.
When they'd toiled up, with sidelong glance each shade
  eyed me awhile in silence, then 'This soul,'
  turn'd tow'rd the other, each to the other said,
'seems living, for beneath his breath's control
  his throat works; and by what immunity
  go they, if dead, without the ponderous stole?
O Tuscan, brought to the college'—this to me—
  'of the hypocrites, who go thus sorrily clad,
  scorn not to tell us what thy name may be.'
'Born was I in the great town, and from lad
  to man grew up, on the fair stream men know
  as Arno, and am with the body I've always had.'
Thus I, and then: 'But you, whose bitter woe
  distils thus down your cheeks, say who are you?
  what penalty is it that on you glitters so?'
And one replied: 'The cloaks of orange hue
  cause by their weight—so thick they are with lead—
  the scales to emit the creak thou art listening to.
Jovial Friars were we, Bologna-bred:
  I Catalán, Loderingo he, by name—
  the joint officials whom thy city instead
of the usual single one chose, each the same,
  to keep its peace, and what we were it takes
  still but Gardingo's purlieus to proclaim.'
I began: 'Friars, your evil . . .' but here breaks
  my speech off short, for to mine eyes there sped
  one to the ground pinned crosswise by three stakes;
who, when he saw me, writhed from foot to head
  and blew into his beard a storm of sighs;
  which Friar Catalán observing to me said:

mi disse: « Quel confitto che tu miri
  consigliò i Farisei che conveniva
  porre un uom per lo popolo ai martiri. 117
Attraversato è, nudo, ne la via,
  come tu vedi, ed è mestier ch'ei senta
  qualunque passa come pesa, pria. 120
E a tal modo il suocero si stenta
  in questa fossa, e gli altri del concilio
  che fu per li Giudei mala sementa ». 123
Allor vid'io maravigliar Virgilio
  sovra colui ch'era disteso in croce
  tanto vilmente ne l'eterno esilio. 126
Poscia drizzò al frate cotal voce:
  « Non vi dispiaccia, se vi lece, dirci
  se a la man destra giace alcuna foce, 129
onde noi amendue possiamo uscirci,
  sanza costringer de gli angeli neri
  che vengan d'esto fondo a dipartirci ». 132
Rispose adunque: « Più che tu non speri
  s'appressa un sasso che da la gran cerchia
  si move, e varca tutti i vallon feri, 135
salvo che in questo è rotto e nol coperchia.
  Montar potrete su per la ruina,
  che giace in costa e nel fondo soverchia ». 138
Lo duca stette un poco a testa china;
  poi disse: « Mal contava la bisogna
  colui che i peccator di là uncina! » 141
E il frate: « Io udii già dire a Bologna
  del diavol vizi assai; tra i quali udi'
  ch'elli è bugiardo e padre di menzogna ». 144
Appresso il duca a gran passi sen gì,
  turbato un poco d'ira nel sembiante;
  ond'io da gl'incarcati mi parti' 147
dietro a le poste de le care piante.

'That impaled wretch for whom thou art all eyes,
  counselled the Pharisees 'twas well to let
  one man for the people die in agonies.
He's stretched out, naked, as thou seëst, straight
  along the pathway and, no matter who's
  going by, has first to feel his ponderous weight.
His father-in-law within this gully rues
  his sin, thus racked, and the others too who lent
  counsel which proved an ill seed for the Jews.'
Then I saw Virgil stand in wonderment
  o'er him spread-eagled there to form a cross
  so vilely in the eternal banishment.
Afterwards he addressed the friar thus:
  'May't not displease ye, if none forbids, to say
  if any passage lies to the right of us
by which we two can issue and so may
  avoid constraining any of the black
  angels to get us from this gulf away.'
'Nearer than thou dost hope,' he answered back,
  'a crag lies, which from the great Ring juts out,
  bridging in turn each rugged valley-track
save this, where, being broken, it spans it not:
  mount could ye by the ruin which strews the bare
  incline and rises piled up from its foot.'
My leader stood awhile with bowed head, ere
  he said: 'An ill account did he devise
  of this, that hooker of sinners over there.'
And the friar: 'At Bologna I've heard the wise
  tell ere now of the Devil faults enough,
  'mongst which, that he's a liar and father of lies.'
At this my leader with great strides stalked off,
  his looks disturbed a little and showing some heat;
  so I left those burdened souls and down the trough
followed the prints of the belovéd feet.

CANTO 24

IN quella parte del giovanetto anno
   che il Sole i crin sotto l'Aquario tempra
   e già le notti al mezzo dì sen vanno,   3
quando la brina in su la terra assempra
   l'imagine di sua sorella bianca,
   ma poco dura a la sua penna tempra;   6
lo villanello a cui la roba manca
   si leva, e guarda, e vede la campagna
   biancheggiar tutta, ond'ei si batte l'anca;   9
ritorna in casa, e qua e là si lagna,
   come il tapin che non sa che si faccia;
   poi riede, e la speranza ringavagna   12
veggendo il mondo aver cangiata faccia
   in poco d'ora, e prende suo vincastro
   e fuor le pecorelle a pascer caccia.   15
Così mi fece sbigottir lo mastro
   quand'io li vidi sì turbar la fronte,
   e così tosto al mal giunse l'impiastro;   18
chè, come noi venimmo al guasto ponte,
   lo duca a me si volse con quel piglio
   dolce ch'io vidi prima a piè del monte: 21
le braccia aperse, dopo alcun consiglio
   eletto seco, riguardando prima
   ben la ruina, e diedemi di piglio;   24
e come quei che adopera ed estima,
   che sempre par che innanzi si proveggia,
   così, levando me sù ver la cima   27
d'un ronchione, avvisava un'altra scheggia,
   dicendo: « Sovra quella poi t'aggrappa,
   ma tenta pria s'è tal ch'ella ti reggia ».   30
Non era via da vestiti di cappa,
   chè noi appena, ei lieve ed io sospinto,
   potevam sù montar di chiappa in chiappa.   33
E se non fosse che da quel precinto
   più che da l'altro era la costa corta,
   non so di lui, ma io sarei ben vinto.   36

CANTO 24

WHAT time the year's still young, and day by day
   the sun beneath Aquarius warms his hair
   and nights already southward pass away;
when the rime copies on the ground her fair
   white sister's image, but her pen runs dry
   too soon to let the likeness linger there;
the hind, whose fodder is in short supply,
   gets up, and looks, and sees all round him spread
   a sheet of white; at which he slaps his thigh,
goes in, and, grumbling, up and down doth tread,
   like a poor wretch who knows not what to do;
   then comes back with his hope re-basketed,
beholding how the world has changed its hue
   in a brief while, and catches up his crook,
   and forth to pasture drives his sheep anew;
so did my master by his troubled look
   depress me, and just so the salve applied
   to heal the sore no longer in coming took;
for, as we reached the shattered bridge, my guide,
   turned himself tow'rds me with the same sweet smile
   I'd seen before, beneath the lone hillside.
He opened his arms, first with himself awhile
   consulting, then laid hold of me, but not
   till he had well surveyed the tumbled pile.
And as is he who while at work takes thought
   and every next step seems to calculate;
   so, with his mind—even before he'd got
me a-top of one big stone—already set
   on the next jag he'd say: 'Of that catch hold
   now, but try first if it will bear thy weight.'
That was no pathway for the leaden-stoled,
   for to ascend from ledge to ledge, he light,
   I pushed up, found we of difficulty untold.
And if the slope had not been less in height
   on that rim than on the other, I won't say he,
   but I for my part had been vanquished quite.

Ma perchè Malebolge in ver la porta
  del bassissimo pozzo tutto pende,
  lo sito di ciascuna valle porta   39
che l'una costa surge e l'altra scende:
  noi pur venimmo alfine in su la punta
  onde l'ultima pietra si scoscende.   42
La lena m'era dal polmon sì munta
  quand'io fui sù, ch'io non potea più oltre;
  anzi, m'assisi ne la prima giunta.   45
« Omai convien che tu così ti spoltre »
  disse il maestro « chè seggendo in piuma
  in fama non si vien nè sotto coltre;   48
sanza la qual chi sua vita consuma
  cotal vestigio in Terra di sè lascia
  qual fummo in aere od in acqua la schiuma.   51
E però leva sù: vinci l'ambascia
  con l'animo che vince ogni battaglia,
  se col suo grave corpo non s'accascia.   54
Più lunga scala convien che si saglia;
  non basta da costoro esser partito:
  se tu m'intendi, or fa sì che ti vaglia ».   57
Levaimi allor, mostrandomi fornito
  meglio di lena ch'io non mi sentia,
  e dissi: « Va, ch'io son forte ed ardito ».   60
Su per lo scoglio prendemmo la via,
  ch'era ronchioso, stretto, e malagevole,
  ed erto più assai che quel di pria.   63
Parlando andava per non parer fievole;
  onde una voce uscì de l'altro fosso,
  a parole formar disconvenevole.   66
Non so che disse, ancor che sovra il dosso
  fossi de l'arco già che varca quivi;
  ma chi parlava ad ire parea mosso.   69
Io era volto in giù ma gli occhi vivi
  non poteano ire al fondo per lo scuro;
  per ch'io: « Maestro, fa che tu arrivi   72
da l'altro cinghio e dismontiam lo muro;
  chè, com'io odo quinci e non intendo,
  così giù veggio e niente affiguro ».   75

But seeing that Evilpouches steadily
  slopes tow'rds the central pit, it must befall
  that, of its valleys, each successively
should have the outer higher than the inner wall:
  we did, however, reach the point in the end
  whence broken off is the last stone of all.
When I was up, my lungs were so much drain'd
  of breath that I could go no farther; nay,
  rather I sat me down, the top once gain'd.
'Henceforth thou thus must shake off sloth; for they
  who sit on down or lie 'neath quilts will ne'er
  to fame,' the master said, 'find out the way;
without which men but waste their lives up there
  on Earth, and of themselves leave no more trace
  than foam on water or than smoke in the air.
Rise, therefore: with the spirit which, unless
  crushed by its body's weight, is conqueror
  in every fight, conquer thy weariness.
A longer stair must needs be mounted: nor
  is it enough to have left yon dismal throng:
  if learnt, now see thou profit by this lore.'
I rose then, showing myself, though still a long
  way off from feeling, better stored with breath,
  and said: 'Go on, for I am bold and strong.'
Up the rock-bridge we climbed, which was, i' faith,
  narrow and rough and hard to tread upon,
  far steeper than the last—an arduous path.
I went on talking, not to seem fordone;
  whereat a voice rose from the next ditch, though
  aptness to fashion language it had none.
I know not what it said, albeit I now
  was on the crown of the arch which crosses there;
  but who was speaking seemed to be on the go.
I had bent downward, but no eyes that e'er
  lived could reach bottom through the dark's thick pall;
  so I said: 'Master, see thou get to where
lies the next ring, and let's descend the wall;
  for, as from hence I hear, nor understand,
  so I look down, and nought discern at all.'

« Altra risposta » disse « non ti rendo
   se non lo far; chè la dimanda onesta
   si dee seguir con l'opera tacendo ».   78
Noi discendemmo il ponte da la testa
   dove s'aggiugne con l'ottava ripa;
   e poi mi fu la bolgia manifesta.   81
E vidivi entro terribile stipa
   di serpenti, e di sì diversa mena
   che la memoria il sangue ancor mi scipa.   84
Più non si vanti Libia con sua rena
   chè se chelidri, iaculi e faree
   produce, e cencri con anfisibena,   87
nè tante pestilenzie nè sì ree
   mostrò giammai con tutta l'Etiopia,
   nè con ciò che disopra il Mar Rosso èe.   90
Tra questa cruda e tristissima copia
   correvan genti nude e spaventate,
   sanza sperar pertugio od elitropia;   93
con serpi le man dietro avean legate;
   quelle ficcavan per le ren la coda
   e il capo, ed eran dinanzi aggroppate.   96
Ed ecco, ad un ch'era da nostra proda
   s'avventò un serpente che il trafisse
   là dove il collo a le spalle s'annoda.   99
Nè *o* sì tosto mai nè *i* si scrisse
   com'ei s'accese e arse e cener tutto
   convenne che cascando divenisse;   102
e poi che fu a terra sì distrutto,
   la polver si raccolse per se stessa
   e in quel medesmo ritornò di butto.   105
Così per li gran savi si confessa
   che la fenice muore e poi rinasce
   quando al cinquecentesim'anno appressa.   108
Erba nè biada in sua vita non pasce,
   ma sol d'incenso lacrime e d'amomo,
   e nardo e mirra son l'ultime fasce.   111
E qual è quei che cade e non sa como,
   per forza di demon che a terra il tira
   o d'altra oppilazion che lega l'uomo,   114

'Other response' he said 'to thy demand
  I make not than to do it: a fair request
  action should follow, and all words be bann'd.'
We went on down the bridge that side its crest
  where't joins the eighth bank; and, when once I stood
  at that point, then the pouch was manifest;
and serpents there, a gruesome multitude,
  of kinds so various saw I packed within,
  that still the recollection thins my blood.
No more let Libya vaunt her sands; for e'en
  if she produces hydras, jaculi,
  pharéas, cenchres and the amphisbene,
yet never plagues so many and dire did she
  display, nor all the land of the Ethiope,
  nor that which lies alongside the Red Sea.
Mid these dread, loathly swarms ran, without hope
  of rescue, people stripped and terrified—
  no hole to hide in and no heliotrope.
They had their hands, which were behind them, tied
  with serpents: through their loins these thrust the tail
  and head, and twisted up on their front side.
And lo, on one, of a sudden, a serpent fell
  and stung him just where neck and shoulder meet—
  as he was near our bank, I saw it well.
Never was *O* or *I* so quickly writ,
  as he took fire and burned and needs must be
  reduced in ruin to ashes, every whit:
then as, destroyed, thus on the ground lay he,
  the dust, collecting of its own accord,
  into that same man turned back instantly:
thus dies the phoenix and is then restor'd
  to life (at least great sages so aver)
  when close on her five hundredth year is scor'd.
Herb, while she lives, nor grain is food for her,
  only amomum and the tears that flow
  from incense; and her shroud's of nard and myrrh.
And as is he who falls and knows not how,
  whether an oppilation (which oft ties
  a man up) or a demon lays him low—

175

quando si leva, che intorno si mira
    tutto smarrito de la grande angoscia
    ch'egli ha sofferta, e guardando sospira;   117
tal era il peccator levato poscia.
    Oh potenza di Dio, quant'è severa,
    che cotai colpi per vendetta croscia!   120
Lo duca il domandò poi chi egli era;
    per ch'ei rispose: « Io piovvi di Toscana,
    poco tempo è, in questa gola fera.   123
Vita bestial mi piacque e non umana,
    sì come a mul ch'io fui; son Vanni Fucci
    bestia, e Pistoia mi fu degna tana ».   126
E io al duca: « Dilli che non mucci,
    e domanda che colpa quaggiù il pinse;
    ch'io il vidi uomo di sangue e di crucci ».   129
E il peccator, che intese, non s'infinse,
    ma drizzò verso me l'animo e il volto,
    e di trista vergogna si dipinse.   132
Poi disse: « Più mi duol che tu m'hai colto
    ne la miseria dove tu mi vedi,
    che quando fui de l'altra vita tolto.   135
Io non posso negar quel che tu chiedi:
    in giù son messo tanto, perch'io fui
    ladro a la sagrestia de' belli arredi;   138
e falsamente già fu apposto altrui.
    Ma perchè di tal vista tu non godi
    se mai sarai di fuor da' luoghi bui,   141
apri gli orecchi al mio annunzio, e odi:
    Pistoia in pria de' Neri si dimagra;
    poi Fiorenza rinnova genti e modi.   144
Tragge Marte vapor di Val di Magra
    ch'è di torbidi nuvoli involuto;
    e con tempesta impetuosa ed agra   147
sovra Campo Picen fia combattuto;
    ond'ei repente spezzerà la nebbia,
    sì ch'ogni Bianco ne sarà feruto.   150
E detto l'ho perchè doler ti debbia ».

who, when he rises, casts about his eyes,
   dazed and bewildered by the mighty throes
   of anguish he's endured and, staring, sighs;
such had the sinner risen, in look and pose.
   Oh, awful power of God, how stern it is,
   which showers down, for punishment, such blows!
My guide then asked him who he was, and his
   reply was: 'Down from Tuscany did I rain
   into this savage maw not long ere this.
A beast's life pleased me, and not that of men,
   mule that I was: I'm Vanni Fucci, sheer
   beast, and Pistoia was my fitting den.'
'Let him not slip away,' I begged the seer:
   'I knew him as a man of wrath and blood,
   so ask him for what fault he's thrust down here.'
The sinner heard, dissembled not, but glued
   his mind and countenance on me, and then,
   painting himself with dismal shame, pursued:
'That thou hast caught me undergoing the pain
   wherein thou seest me, gives me greater grief
   than when I from the other life was ta'en.
Yet answer thee I must: know, then, in brief,
   I'm put so low, since at the Sacristy
   of the Fair Ornaments I was a thief,
a crime to another's charge laid wrongfully.
   But lest at such a sight, if e'er thou win
   forth from the dark abodes, thou vent thy glee,
open thy ears and take my announcement in:
   Pistoia first denudes herself of Blacks,
   next, in Florence, new men and ways are seen.
Mars draws from Val di Magra a mist, that packs
   around it turbid clouds and piles them high;
   and o'er Piceno's field a storm shall wax
of combat fierce and bitter battle-cry:
   whence with such force he'll rend the cloud apart,
   that not a White but shall be smitten thereby:
and this I've said, to stab thee to the heart.'

CANTO 25

Aᴌ fine de le sue parole il ladro
le mani alzò con ambedue le fiche
gridando: « Togli, Dio, che a te le squadro! »   3
Da indi in qua mi fur le serpi amiche,
perch'una li s'avvolse allora al collo,
come dicesse: 'Non vo' che più diche'   6
ed un'altra a le braccia, e rilegollo
ribadendo se stessa sì dinanzi
che non potea con esse dare un crollo.   9
Ahi Pistoia, Pistoia, chè non stanzi
d'incenerarti sì che più non duri,
poi che in mal far lo seme tuo avanzi?   12
Per tutti i cerchi de l'Inferno oscuri
non vidi spirto in Dio tanto superbo;
non quel che cadde a Tebe giù dai muri.   15
Ei si fuggì, che non parlò più verbo.
Ed io vidi un centauro pien di rabbia,
venir chiamando: « Ov'è, ov'è l'acerbo? »   18
Maremma non cred'io che tante n'abbia
quante bisce egli avea su per la groppa
infin ove comincia nostra labbia.   21
Sovra le spalle, dietro de la coppa,
con l'ali aperte li giaceva un draco,
e quello affuoca qualunque s'intoppa.   24
Lo mio maestro disse: « Questi è Caco,
che sotto il sasso di monte Aventino
di sangue fece spesse volte laco.   27
Non va co' suoi fratei per un cammino
per lo furar che frodolento fece
del grande armento ch'egli ebbe a vicino,   30
onde cessar le sue opere biece
sotto la mazza d'Ercole, che forse
li ne diè cento e non sentì le diece ».   33
Mentre che sì parlava ed ei trascorse,
e tre spiriti venner sotto noi,
de' quai nè io nè il duca mio s'accorse,   36

CANTO 25

CONCLUDING thus, the robber instantly
   flung up his hands with both the figs and yell'd:
   'Take that, God, for I level them at thee!'
As friends of mine from that time forth I held
   the snakes: for one then twisted itself round
   his neck, as did it say: 'Too long thou hast rail'd';
and round his arms another, and re-bound
   him, clinching itself in front, so that nohow
   not e'en by a single jerk, could he respond.
Pistoia, ah, Pistoia, why not now
   cease being, and burn thyself down to the sod,
   in that thy crimes thy own seed's far outgo?
Through all the gloomy circles that I trod
   of Hell I saw no spirit—not him that fell
   from Thebes's walls—so arrogant tow'rds God.
Silenced, he fled; but hard upon his trail
   I saw a Centaur full of fury race,
   and 'Where's the ribald, where?' I heard him yell.
Over his hindparts, up to where our face
   begins, swarmed snakes so many, that I'd say
   e'en the Maremma's would amount to less.
Behind the nape, upon his shoulders lay
   a dragon with open wings: the kind that would
   set any wretch on fire who crossed its way.
'That's Cacus,' said my master, 'who abode
   beneath the rock of the Aventine and made
   times out of number there a lake of blood.
Not his the pathway that his brethren tread,
   because o' the trick by which he dragged to his den
   and stole the mighty herd that near it fed:
whereby his crooked dealings ceased, for then
   Hercules with his club rained on him nigh
   a hundred blows, tho' he felt not even ten.'
While he spoke thus, the Centaur had rushed by,
   and 'neath us spirits were come, in number three,
   of whom nor was my leader ware, nor I,

se non quando gridar: « Chi siete voi? »
  per che nostra novella si ristette
  ed intendemmo pur ad essi poi.   39

Io non li conoscea, ma ei seguette,
  come suol seguitar per alcun caso,
  che l'un nomar un altro convenette   42

dicendo: « Cianfa dove fia rimaso? »
  per ch'io, a ciò che il duca stesse attento,
  mi posi il dito sù dal mento al naso.   45

Se tu sei or, lettore, a creder lento
  ciò ch'io dirò, non sarà meraviglia,
  chè io che il vidi, appena il mi consento.   48

Com'io tenea levate in lor le ciglia,
  ed un serpente con sei piè si lancia
  dinanzi a l'uno, e tutto a lui s'appiglia.   51

Coi piè di mezzo gli avvinse la pancia
  e con gli anterior le braccia prese;
  poi gli addentò e l'una e l'altra guancia.   54

Li deretani a le cosce distese,
  e miseli la coda tra ambedue
  e dietro per le ren sù la ritese.   57

Ellera abbarbicata mai non fue
  ad alber sì, come l'orribil fiera
  per l'altrui membra avviticchiò le sue.   60

Poi s'appiccar come di calda cera
  fossero stati, e mischiar lor colore:
  nè l'un nè l'altro già parea quel ch'era,   63

come procede innanzi da l'ardore
  per lo papiro in suso un color bruno
  che non è nero ancora e il bianco more.   66

Gli altri due riguardavano, e ciascuno
  gridava: « Omè, Agnel, come ti muti!
  vedi che già non sei nè due nè uno ».   69

Già eran li due capi un divenuti
  quando n'apparver due figure miste
  in una faccia ov'eran due perduti.   72

Fersi le braccia due di quattro liste;
  le cosce con le gambe e il ventre e il casso
  divenner membra che non fur mai viste.   75

until we heard them shouting 'Who are ye?':
   at which our tale broke off, and from then on
   we gave our minds to them exclusively.
I did not know them; but it happed anon,
   as hap it will if luck should so dispose,
   that one of them by saying 'Where's Cianfa gone?'
could not but thus another's name disclose;
   I, therefore, that my leader might attend,
   pointed my finger up from chin to nose.
If credence, Reader, thou art slow to lend
   to things I'm going to say, no wonder; for
   myself, who saw them, well might deem them feign'd.
While I was eyeing them with all my power,
   lo, a six-footed serpent darted out
   in front of one and clung to him all o'er.
With its midfeet it clasped his paunch, and got
   with those in front firm hold of the arms likewise;
   then fanging both cheeks, sank therein its snout.
Its hindfeet it extended to his thighs
   and thrust its tail between these and behind—
   over the loins—stretched upward made it rise.
Never did ivy round a tree so wind
   and root itself, as that dread beast between
   and o'er the other's limbs its own entwined.
Then like hot wax they stuck, each melting in
   to the other's shape, and mixed their hue: which **made**
   neither to seem now that which it had been,
as upward over paper creeps ahead
   of where it burns a colour that is brown,
   not black yet, though the white begins to fade.
The other two, who'd watched this being done,
   both cried: 'O me, how thou art changed, Agnél!
   See how thou now art neither two nor one.'
The two heads, one now and inseparable,
   showed us two countenances in one face,
   so fused that which was which we could not tell.
The arms, no more four strips, became a brace;
   into limbs, such as ne'er were seen, the chest
   and belly turned, the thighs and legs no less.

Ogni primaio aspetto ivi era casso:
  due e nessun l'immagine perversa
  pareva, e tal sen gìa con lento passo.   78
Come il ramarro sotto la gran fersa
  dei dì canicolar, cangiando siepe
  folgore par se la via attraversa,   81
sì pareva, venendo verso l'epe
  de gli altri due, un serpentello acceso,
  livido e nero come gran di pepe.   84
E quella parte donde prima è preso
  nostro alimento, a un di lor trafisse;
  poi cadde giuso innanzi lui disteso.   87
Lo trafitto il mirò, ma nulla disse,
  anzi, coi piè fermati, sbadigliava
  pur come sonno o febbre l'assalisse.   90
Egli il serpente e quel lui riguardava;
  l'un per la piaga e l'altro per la bocca
  fumavan forte e il fumo si scontrava.   93
Taccia Lucano omai là dove tocca
  del misero Sabello e di Nassidio,
  ed attenda a udir quel ch'or si scocca.   96
Taccia di Cadmo e d'Aretusa Ovidio,
  chè se quello in serpente e quella in fonte
  converte poetando, io non l'invidio;   99
chè due nature mai a fronte a fronte
  non trasmutò sì ch'ambedue le forme
  a cambiar lor materia fosser pronte.   102
Insieme si risposero a tai norme,
  che il serpente la coda in forca fesse,
  e il feruto ristrinse insieme l'orme.   105
Le gambe con le cosce seco stesse
  s'appiccar sì che in poco la giuntura
  non facea segno alcun che si paresse.   108
Togliea la coda fessa la figura
  che si perdeva là, e la sua pelle
  si facea molle, e quella di là dura.   111
Io vidi entrar le braccia per l'ascelle,
  e i due piè de la fiera, ch'eran corti,
  tanto allungar quanto accorciavan quelle.   114

All former features were by now effaced:
  two and yet none the monstrous image show'd,
  and, thus transformed, away it slowly paced.
As the green lizard, 'neath the mighty goad
  of the dog-days, seems lightning if, to gain
  another hedge, it streaks across the road;
so seemed, as tow'rd the guts of the other twain
  it darted, a small serpent, all aflame,
  livid and black as any pepper-grain.
And it transfixed that part in one of them
  whence to begin with we derive our food;
  then dropped, and lay outstretched before the same.
The pierced one gazed at it, but spoke not—stood,
  rather, quite still and yawned, as though by a fit
  of fever or by drowsiness subdued.
The serpent stared at him, and he at it:
  one from the mouth, one whence he felt the sting,
  smoked fiercely, and I saw the smoke-jets meet.
Silent henceforth be Lucan, would he sing
  of poor Sabellus and Nasidius: let
  him wait and hear the word that now takes wing.
Of Cadmus and of Arethusa's fate
  silent be Ovid: him into a snake,
  her let his muse into a spring translate,
for all I care, since never did he make
  two natures, front to front, interchange so
  that both forms could each other's matter take.
They mutually responded—this is how:
  the serpent caused its tail to split fork-wise,
  the stung one pressed his feet together below.
So closely, of themselves, the legs and thighs
  clave each to each, that soon, where they had joined,
  no mark remained apparent to the eyes.
The split tail took the shape that had defined
  the limbs being elsewhere lost; and e'en as its
  skin softened, so grew hard the other's rind,
I saw his arms draw in through the armpits
  and, in proportion as they thus withdrew,
  the beast's two short feet lengthen out by bits.

Poscia li piè di retro, insieme attorti,
   diventaron lo membro che l'uom cela,
   e il misero del suo n'avea due porti.   117
Mentre che il fumo l'uno e l'altro vela
   di color novo, e genera il pel suso
   per l'una parte e da l'altra il dipela,   120
l'un si levò e l'altro cadde giuso,
   non torcendo però le lucerne empie
   sotto le quai ciascun cambiava muso.   123
Quel ch'era dritto il trasse ver le tempie,
   e di troppa materia che in là venne
   uscir gli orecchi de le gote scempie;   126
ciò che non corse indietro e si ritenne
   di quel soverchio, fe' naso a la faccia
   e le labbra ingrossò quanto convenne.   129
Quel che giaceva il muso innanzi caccia
   e gli orecchi ritira per la testa
   come face le corna la lumaccia;   132
e la lingua, che aveva unita e presta
   prima a parlar, si fende, e la forcuta
   ne l'altro si richiude, e il fumo resta.   135
L'anima ch'era fera divenuta
   sufolando si fugge per la valle,
   e l'altro dietro a lui parlando sputa.   138
Poscia li volse le novelle spalle
   e disse a l'altro: « Io vo' che Buoso corra,
   com'ho fatt'io, carpon per questo calle ».   141
Così, vid'io la settima zavorra
   mutar e trasmutare, e qui mi scusi
   la novità se fior la penna abborra.   144
E avvegna che gli occhi miei confusi
   fossero alquanto e l'animo smagato,
   non poter quei fuggirsi tanto chiusi   147
ch'io non scorgessi ben Puccio Sciancato;
   ed era quel che sol, de' tre compagni
   che venner prima, non era mutato;   150
l'altro era quel che tu, Gaville, piagni.

Next, the hindfeet by intertwining grew
  into man's privy member, and from his
  the wretch of such-like feet had put forth two.

While the smoke with unwonted colour is
  investing both, and causing hair to sprout
  over that part and stripping it from this,

the one stood up, t'other fell down, without
  turning, howe'er, the baleful lamps aside,
  under which each assumed the other's snout.

His the erect one tow'rds his temples plied,
  and from the smooth cheeks ears then issued, made
  out of the excess of stuff which thither hied.

That which did *not* run to the back, but stay'd,
  out of that surplus formed for the face a nose
  and thickened the lips so much as need for it bade.

He that was lying prostrate, forward throws
  his snout, and into his head draws back his ears,
  as a snail might its horns, if so it chose:

his tongue, once whole and apt for speech, appears
  now cleft, and in the other's which was split,
  the fork now closes up, and the smoke clears.

The soul, turned brute, the process once complete
  that made it such, fled hissing down the valley,
  and the other, sputtering words out, followed it;

and, turning to it his new back, did but dally
  to say to the one left: 'I'd have Buoso run,
  as I did, on all fours along this alley.'

Thus did I see the seventh ballast go on
  to and fro changing; and if here my pen
  at all errs, be my excuse the strange things done.

And though it happened that my eyes were then
  a bit blurred, and my mind confused, yet not
  so privily could those souls escape my ken,

but that I well marked Puccio, the hip-shot:
  in him alone, of the triple fellowship
  that came first, had no change at all been wrought:

the other was he whom thou, Gavíll', dost weep.

CANTO 26

Godi, Fiorenza, poi che sei sì grande
  che per mare e per terra batti l'ali,
  e per l'Inferno tuo nome si spande!   3
Tra li ladron trovai cinque cotali
  tuoi cittadini onde mi vien vergogna,
  e tu in grande orranza non ne sali.   6
Ma se presso al mattin del ver si sogna,
  tu sentirai di qua da picciol tempo
  di quel che Prato, non ch'altri, t'agogna.   9
E se già fosse, non saria per tempo.
  Così foss'ei, da che pur esser dee,
  chè più mi graverà com più m'attempo.   12
Noi ci partimmo, e sù per le scalee
  che n'avean fatte i borni a scender pria
  rimontò il duca mio e trasse mee;   15
e proseguendo la solinga via
  tra le schegge e tra i rocchi de lo scoglio,
  lo piè sanza la man non si spedia.   18
Allor mi dolsi, ed ora mi ridoglio
  quando drizzo la mente a ciò ch'io vidi,
  e più l'ingegno affreno ch'io non soglio,   21
perchè non corra che virtù nol guidi,
  sì che, se stella buona o miglior cosa
  m'ha dato il bene, io stesso nol m'invidi. 24
Quante il villan che al poggio si riposa
  nel tempo che colui che il mondo schiara
  la faccia sua a noi tien meno ascosa,   27
come la mosca cede a la zanzara
  vede lucciole giù per la vallea,
  forse colà dove vendemmia e ara;   30
di tante fiamme tutta risplendea
  l'ottava bolgia, sì com'io m'accorsi
  tosto che fui là 've il fondo parea.   33
E qual colui che si vengiò con gli orsi
  vide il carro d'Elia al dipartire,
  quando i cavalli al cielo erti levorsi,   36

CANTO 26

Joy, Florence, joy, for thou hast thriven so well
    that thou dost beat thy wings o'er land and sea,
    joy, for thy name is spread abroad through Hell!
Five of thy townsmen, all of high degree,
    I found among the thieves, which shames me, and sooth!
    no mighty honour thence accrues to thee.
But if, near morning, dreams reveal the truth,
    thou wilt before long feel what Prato's rage,
    to name none else, craves for thee without ruth.
Were it come now—not at some later stage—
    since come it must, 'twere not too soon; for it
    will weigh the more on me, the more I age.
We parted thence, re-mounting bit by bit
    (my master first, he dragging me) the stair
    of slabs down which we'd erewhile neared the pit.
Thus midst the crag's rough boulders and the bare
    split rocks our lonely way did we pursue,
    foot needing hand to speed us upward there.
I sorrowed then, and sorrow now anew,
    when I remember what I saw, and bring
    my wit to heel more than I'm wont to do,
for fear it slip from Virtue's leading-string;
    lest, if a kind star, or aught better still,
    have given it me, I grudge me that good thing.
As many as to the peasant—who on the hill
    is resting at the time of year when that
    which lights the world doth least its face conceal,
at the hour the fly surrenders to the gnat—
    appear the fireflies, haunting the vale below,
    chance where he ploughs or treads his grapes for the vat;
with e'en so many flames was all aglow
    the eighth pouch, as I then perceived, when I
    came where its bottom first began to show.
And as he, whom the bears avenged by and by,
    beheld Elijah's chariot start to rise,
    what time its horses reared and climbed the sky;

che nol potea sì con gli occhi seguire
   ch'ei vedesse altro che la fiamma sola
   sì come nuvoletta in sù salire;   39
tal si movea ciascuna per la gola
   del fosso, chè nessuna mostra il furto,
   ed ogni fiamma un peccatore invola.   42
Io stava sovra il ponte a veder surto
   sì che s'io non avessi un ronchion preso
   caduto sarei giù sanz'esser urto.   45
E il duca, che me vide tanto atteso,
   disse: « Dentro dai fuochi son li spirti:
   ciascun si fascia di quel ch'egli è inceso ». 48
« Maestro mio » risposi « per udirti
   son io più certo, ma già m'era avviso
   che così fosse, e già voleva dirti: 51
chi è in quel foco che vien sì diviso
   di sopra, che par sorger da la pira
   dove Eteòcle col fratel fu miso? »   54
Risposemi : « Là entro si martira
   Ulisse e Diomede, e così insieme
   a la vendetta vanno, come a l'ira.   57
E dentro da la fiamma lor si geme
   l'agguato del caval che fe' la porta
   onde uscì dei Romani il gentil seme.   60
Piangevisi entro l'arte per che, morta,
   Deidamìa ancor si duol d'Achille,
   e del Palladio pena vi si porta ».   63
« S'ei posson dentro da quelle faville
   parlar » diss'io « maestro, assai ten priego
   e ripriego, che il priego vaglia mille, 66
che non mi facci de l'attender niego
   fin che la fiamma cornuta qua vegna :
   vedi che del disio ver lei mi piego! » 69
Ed egli a me: « La tua preghiera è degna
   di molta lode, e io però l'accetto;
   ma fa che la tua lingua si sostegna; 72
lascia parlare a me, ch'io ho concetto
   ciò che tu vuoi; ch'ei sarebbero schivi,
   perch'ei fur greci, forse del tuo detto ». 75

who could not so pursue it with his eyes
   as to see more than just the flame alone,
   mounting, like to a small cloud; in such wise
each of those flames moved through the gorge, for none
   shows what it steals, yet every flame's a thief,
   filching away a sinner unbeknown.
I craned so o'er the bridge to look that, if
   I had not firmly clutched a rock, I might
   without being pushed have fallen down the cliff.
'Within the fires,' observing me thus quite
   absorbed, my guide said, 'are the spirits: and know,
   they are swathed in that which sets them each alight.'
'Sir, I'd already deemed that this was so,'
   I answered him, 'though hearing thee has made
   me surer, and I wished to ask thee who
is in that fire which, where it comes to a head,
   is cleft so, that it seems to rise from the pyre
   where, with his brother, Eteocles was laid?'
'Ulysses' he replied, 'within that fire
   is burned with Diömed: they thus proceed
   joined in their punishment as in their ire.
And therewithin bemoaned is what lay hid
   inside the horse by which the gate was made
   from which went forth the Romans' noble seed.
Bewept in 't is the trick whereby, though dead,
   Deïdamia mourns Achilles still,
   and for the Palladium, there, the price is paid.'
'If souls within those sparkles can and will
   speak,' I said, 'master, much I pray thee, and pray
   again, that a thousandfold my prayer may skill
to make thee not refuse me time to stay
   awhile here, till the hornéd flame draw nigh:
   thou seest how longingly I lean that way.'
'Thy prayer deserves much praise' was his reply;
   'therefore I grant what thou dost so beseech:
   but on thy own tongue see thou place a tie.
Leave me to talk (I know the question which
   thy heart is big with) for it in them lies,
   since they were Greeks, maybe to shun thy speech.'

Poi che la fiamma fu venuta quivi,
  come parve al mio duca tempo e loco
  in questa forma lui parlare audivi: 78
« O voi che siete due dentro ad un foco,
  s'io meritai di voi mentre ch'io vissi,
  s'io meritai di voi assai o poco   81
quando nel mondo gli alti versi scrissi,
  non vi movete, ma l'un di voi dica
  dove per lui perduto a morir gissi ».   84
Lo maggior corno de la fiamma antica
  cominciò a crollarsi, mormorando
  pur come quella cui vento affatica;   87
indi la cima qua e là menando
  come fosse la lingua che parlasse,
  gittò voce di fuori e disse: « Quando   90
mi dipartii da Circe, che sottrasse
  mi più d'un anno là presso a Gaeta,
  prima che sì Enea la nomasse,   93
nè dolcezza di figlio, nè la pieta
  del vecchio padre, nè il debito amore
  lo qual dovea Penelope far lieta,   96
vincer poter dentro da me l'ardore
  ch'io ebbi a divenir del mondo esperto,
  e de li vizi umani e del valore;   99
ma misi me per l'alto mare aperto,
  sol con un legno e con quella compagna
  picciola da la qual non fui diserto.   102
L'un lito e l'altro vidi, infin la Spagna,
  fin nel Morrocco, e l'isola dei Sardi,
  e l'altre che quel mare intorno bagna.   105
Io e i compagni eravam vecchi e tardi
  quando venimmo a quella foce stretta
  dov'Ercole segnò li suoi riguardi   108
a ciò che l'uom più oltre non si metta.
  Da la man destra mi lasciai Sibilia,
  da l'altra già m'avea lasciata Setta.   111
'O frati — dissi — che per cento milia
  perigli siete giunti a l'occidente,
  a questa tanto picciola vigilia   114

After the flame was come where in the eyes
  of my conductor, time and place seemed such
  as was required, I heard him speak thuswise:
'O ye who are two in a single fire's fell clutch,
  if I deserved of you while I drew breath,
  if I deserved of you or little or much,
when in the world what my great poem saith
  I indited, stand, and one of you declare
  whither, when lost, he went to meet his death.'
Of the ancient flame the larger of its pair
  of horns began to shake and murmur then,
  e'en as a flame wearied by gusty air.
Next, waving to and fro its tip, as fain
  to emulate a tongue that talks, it cast
  a voice abroad and spake as follows: 'When
I quitted Circe who had held me fast
  for more than twelve months near Gaëta, ere
  Aeneas had so named it, at long last
no fondness for my son, nor filial care
  of my old father, nor the love I owed
  Penelope which should have gladdened her,
could quench the ardour which within me glowed
  to gain experience of all lands that be,
  and of man's nature whether bad or good;
but I set forth o'er the high, open sea
  with one ship only, and with that small band
  of comrades who had not deserted me.
I saw both coasts, far as Morocco's strand
  and far as Spain, and the Sardinians' isle
  and, of that sea, each other wave-girt land.
I and my comrades had grown old the while,
  and slow, ere we approached the narrows where
  Hercules set his landmarks up to foil
the aim of whoso would beyond them dare:
  I left Seville to starboard, Ceuta I'd
  already seen to larboard disappear.
"O brothers, who have reached the west," I cried,
  "thro' a hundred thousand perils, do not let
  our senses' last brief vigil be denied

dei nostri sensi ch'è del rimanente,
  non vogliate negar l'esperienza,
  diretro al Sol, del mondo sanza gente.   117
Considerate la vostra semenza:
  fatti non foste a viver come bruti,
  ma per seguir virtute e conoscenza'.   120
Li miei compagni fec'io sì acuti,
  con questa orazion picciola, al cammino,
  che a pena poscia li avrei ritenuti.   123
E volta nostra poppa nel mattino,
  dei remi facemmo ali al folle volo,
  sempre acquistando dal lato mancino.   126
Tutte le stelle già de l'altro polo
  vedea la notte, e il nostro tanto basso
  che non surgeva fuor del marin suolo.   129
Cinque volte racceso e tante casso
  lo lume era di sotto de la luna
  poi che intrati eravam ne l'alto passo,   132
quando ne apparve una montagna, bruna
  per la distanza, e parvemi alta tanto
  quanto veduta non aveva alcuna.   135
Noi ci allegrammo; e tosto tornò in pianto,
  chè de la nova terra un turbo nacque
  e percosse del legno il primo canto.   138
Tre volte il fe' girar con tutte l'acque;
  a la quarta levar la poppa in suso
  e la prora ire in giù, com'altrui piacque,   141
infin che il mar fu sopra noi richiuso ».

CANTO 27

GIA era dritta in sù la fiamma e queta
  per non dir più, e già da noi sen gìa
  con la licenza del dolce poeta,   3
quando un'altra, che dietro a lei venia,
  ne fece volger gli occhi a la sua cima
  per un confuso suon che fuor n'uscia.   6

the chance which now is offered them to get
  experience of the world undenizen'd,
  by following the Sun e'en farther yet.
Think of your breed: nature did not intend
  mankind to live as brutes, but to pursue
  virtue and knowledge to the very end."
So keen-set for the voyage I made my crew
  with this short speech, that I should scarce have kept
  them back thereafter, had I wanted to.
And so, our poop turn'd tow'rd the morning, shaped
  we our course, with oars made wings for the mad flight,
  and gaining still to larboard, on we swept.
Nightly I now saw all the stars that light
  the other pole, and ours had sunk so low
  it rose not from the ocean-floor to sight.
Five times re-lit, as many quenched, had now
  the light been 'neath the moon, since first to run
  across the vast deep we had turned our prow,
when, by its distance dimm'd, there loomed upon
  our view a mountain, so immensely high,
  as of its size, meseemed, I had seen none.
We cheered, but soon it turned to a woeful cry
  for from the new land rose a whirlwind, found
  the ship and smote its forepart violently.
Three times it caused her to whirl round and round
  with all the waters: at the fourth—for thus
  Another willed—it raised the poop and downed
the prow, until the sea closed over us.'

CANTO 27

Erect and still now, having said its say,
  the flame, already of our presence quit
  with the sweet poet's leave, was going its way,
when lo, another, coming after it,
  compelled our eyes to travel tow'rds its crest
  through a vague sound which this began to emit.

Come il bue cicilian che mugghiò prima
   col pianto di colui, e ciò fu dritto,
   che l'avea temperato con sua lima,   9
mugghiava con la voce de l'afflitto,
   sì che, con tutto che fosse di rame,
   pur ei pareva dal dolor trafitto;   12
così, per non aver via nè forame,
   dal principio, nel foco, in suo linguaggio
   si convertivan le parole grame.   15
Ma poscia ch'ebber colto lor viaggio
   su per la punta dandole quel guizzo
   che dato avea la lingua in lor passaggio,   18
udimmo dire: « O tu a cui io drizzo
   la voce e che parlavi mo lombardo
   dicendo *istra ten va, più non t'adizzo*,   21
perch'io sia giunto forse alquanto tardo
   non t'incresca restare a parlar meco:
   vedi che non incresce a me, e ardo!   24
Se tu pur mo in questo mondo cieco
   caduto sei di quella dolce terra
   latina ond'io mia colpa tutta reco,   27
dimmi se i Romagnoli han pace o guerra;
   ch'io fui de' monti là intra Urbino
   e il giogo di che Tever si disserra ».   30
Io era in giuso ancora attento e chino,
   quando il mio duca mi tentò di costa
   dicendo: « Parla tu; questi è latino ».   33
Ed io che avea già pronta la risposta
   sanza indugio a parlare incominciai:
   « O anima che sei là giù nascosta,   36
Romagna tua non è e non fu mai
   sanza guerra nei cor de' suoi tiranni,
   ma palese nessuna or ven lasciai.   39
Ravenna sta come è stata molti anni:
   l'aquila da Polenta la si cova
   sì, che Cervia ricopre co' suoi vanni.   42
La terra che fe' già la lunga prova
   e di Franceschi sanguinoso mucchio,
   sotto le branche verdi si ritrova.   45

As the Sicilian bull—whose earliest
  bellow was but the moan (and justly so)
  of him who with his file had shaped the beast—
roared with its victim's voice, so that, altho'
  it was in fact entirely made of brass,
  yet it seemed pierced with anguish thro' and thro';
so, lacking way or vent through which to pass,
  the woeful words at first were forced to ape
  the speech o' the fire in which their speaker was.
But later, when they'd found a way to escape
  up through the point, giving to this the same
  flicker the tongue had giv'n, as they took shape,
we heard it say: 'O thou at whom I aim
  my voice, who in Lombard speech "Now gang thy ways,
  nae mair I urge thee" didst but now exclaim:
be irked not, though my coming late delays
  thee a little perhaps, to pause and speak with me:
  thou seest it irks not me, tho' I am ablaze.
If thou into this world where none can see,
  hast dropped but now from that sweet Latin land
  whence I bring all my guilt, may I hear from thee—
for mine were the mountains 'twixt Urbino and
  the yoke whence Tiber is unlocked—if now
  the Romagnóls have peace, or wars on hand?'
I was still listening with a down-bent brow,
  when he, my leader, touched me on the side,
  saying: 'A Latian this, so answer thou.'
And I delayed not, but at once replied,
  having already weighed my words with care:
  'O soul below there whom a flame doth hide,
thy own Romagna is not, nor was e'er,
  without war in her tyrants' hearts, but none
  raged openly of late when I was there.
Ravenna bides as she for years hath done:
  Polenta's eagle broods her so, that o'er
  Cervia too he spreads his pinïon.
The city, of which long trial was made before
  it raised a gory pile of Frenchmen, 'neath
  the talons *vert* now finds itself once more.

Il mastin vecchio e il novo da Verrucchio,
  che fecer di Montagna il mal governo,
  là dove soglion fan dei denti succhio.   48
Le città di Lamone e di Santerno
  conduce il leoncel dal nido bianco
  che muta parte de la state al verno.   51
E quella cui il Savio bagna il fianco,
  così com'ella sie' tra il piano e il monte,
  tra tirannia si vive e stato franco.   54
Ora chi sei ti prego che ne conte:
  non esser duro più ch'altri sia stato,
  se il nome tuo nel mondo tegna fronte».   57
Poscia che il foco alquanto ebbe rugghiato
  al modo suo, l'acuta punta mosse
  di qua, di là, e poi diè cotal fiato: 60
« S'io credessi che mia risposta fosse
  a persona che mai tornasse al mondo,
  questa fiamma staria sanza più scosse;   63
ma però che giammai di questo fondo
  non tornò vivo alcun, s'io odo il vero,
  sanza tema d'infamia ti rispondo.   66
Io fui uom d'arme, e poi fui cordigliero,
  credendomi sì cinto fare ammenda;
  e certo il creder mio veniva intero   69
se non fosse il gran prete — a cui mal prenda! —
  che mi rimise ne le prime colpe;
  e come e *quare*, voglio che m'intenda.   72
Mentre ch'io forma fui d'ossa e di polpe
  che la madre mi diè, l'opere mie
  non furon leonine, ma di volpe.   75
Gli accorgimenti e le coperte vie
  io seppi tutti, e sì menai lor arte
  che al fine de la Terra il suono uscìe.   78
Quando mi vidi giunto in quella parte
  di mia etade ove ciascun dovrebbe
  calar le vele e raccoglier le sarte,   81
ciò che pria mi piaceva allor m'increbbe,
  e, pentuto e confesso, mi rendei;
  ahi miser lasso! e giovato sarebbe.   84

The old mastiff of Verruchio and therewith
   the young one who misruled Montagna, make
   where they are wont, a wimble of their teeth
Lamone's and Santerno's cities take
   their hue from the lion-cub in the *argent* den,
   who changes sides in summer's and winter's wake.
And she whose flank the Savio laves, 'twixt plain
   and mountain lying, lives the way she lies,
   nor thrall nor free, but poised betwixt the twain.
But us now, prithee, of who thou art apprise,
   that in the world thy name may hold its front:
   others have shown compliance, do thou likewise.'
The fire, when it had roared after its wont
   a little while, moved itself to and fro,
   then breathed this utterance forth from its sharp point:
'If to a person who should ever go
   back to the world I thought that my reply
   were made, this flame would flicker nevermoe.
But seeing that from this gulf none e'er, if I
   hear truth, returned alive, I have no fear
   that, answering, I shall smirch my fame thereby.
I was a man of arms, turn'd cordelier,
   thinking, so girt, to make amends: and true
   that thought had surely come, to this I swear,
but for the high priest—ill befall him—who
   replunged me in my former sins; I would
   thou hear how this befell, and wherefore too.
While I informed the bones and pulp I owed
   to her who bore me, all my doings smacked
   not of the lion's but of the vulpine brood.
Shrewd wiles and covert ways, of these I lacked
   none, and so deftly practised them, I made
   their sound go forth to Earth's remotest tract.
Come to that stage of life when men are led,
   if they are wise, to haul their tackle in
   and lower their sails, it irked me then, instead
of pleasing me (as once), to live in sin;
   repentant and confessed, I took the vows,
   ah me! and my salvation it would have been.

Il principe dei novi Farisei,
   avendo guerra presso a Laterano
   (e non con Saracin nè con Giudei,   87
chè ciascun suo nemico era cristiano,
   e nessuno era stato a vincer Acri,
   nè mercatante in terra di Soldano),   90
nè sommo officio nè ordini sacri
   guardò in sè, nè in me quel capestro
   che solea fare i suoi cinti più macri;   93
ma come Costantin chiese Silvestro
   dentro Siratti a guarir de la lebbre,
   così mi chiese questi per maestro   96
a guarir de la sua superba febbre:
   domandommi consiglio, ed io tacetti
   perchè le sue parole parver ebbre.   99
E poi mi disse: 'Tuo cor non sospetti:
   finor t'assolvo, e tu m'insegna fare
   sì come Penestrino in terra getti.   102
Lo ciel poss'io serrare e disserrare,
   come tu sai; però son due le chiavi
   che il mio antecessor non ebbe care'.   105
Allor mi pinser gli argomenti gravi
   là 've il tacer mi fu avviso il peggio;
   e dissi: 'Padre, da che tu mi lavi   108
di quel peccato ov'io mo cader deggio,
   lunga promessa con l'attender corte
   ti farà trionfar ne l'alto seggio'.   111
Francesco venne poi, com'io fui morto,
   per me; ma l'un dei neri cherubini
   li disse: 'Nol portar, non mi far torto! 114
Venir sen deve giù tra i miei meschini,
   perchè diede il consiglio frodolente
   dal quale in qua stato li sono ai crini, 117
chè assolver non si può chi non si pente,
   nè pentère e volere insieme puossi,
   per la contradizion che nol consente'. 120
Omè dolente! come mi riscossi
   quando mi prese dicendomi: 'Forse
   tu non pensavi ch'io loico fossi!'   123

The prince of modern Pharisees—who chose
    to wage a war hard by the Lateran
    and not with Saracens and not with Jews;
for all his foes were Christians to a man,
    and none had joined in conquering Acre, and none
    in trading where the Soldan's fiat ran—
heeded not in himself his supreme throne
    or holy orders or that cord in me,
    which used to emaciate those who girt it on.
As Constantine, to cure his leprosy,
    summoned Sylvester from Soracte's side,
    so call me in as master-leech did he,
to heal him of the fever of his pride:
    he asked me for advice—I deemed him just
    a drunkard blethering, and no word replied.
Then spoke he again: "Let not thy heart mistrust;
    I, from now on, absolve thee: and teach me thou
    how to lay Palestrina in the dust.
Heaven I have the power, as thou dost know,
    to lock and unlock: hence two are the keys
    whose worth my predecessor rated low."
Then, pushed by weighty arguments like these
    to a point where speech seemed, more than silence, fit,
    "Father, since thus to cleanse me thou dost please
from that sin I'm about now to commit,
    large promise with scant keeping—this," I said,
    "will make thee triumph in thy lofty seat."
Francis came afterwards, when I was dead,
    for me; but a black cherub cried: "Forbear
    to take him: let no trick on me be play'd.
Down among my familiars must he fare,
    because the advice he gave was fraudulent,
    from which time forth I've had him by the hair.
For none can be absolved save he repent,
    nor both repent and will the sin's commission:
    the contradiction won't thereto consent."
Ah, wretched me, how conscious of perdition
    was I, when seizing me he said: "May be
    thou didst not think that I was a logician!"

A Minòs mi portò; e quegli attorse
  otto volte la coda al dosso duro,
  e poi che per gran rabbia la si morse,   126
disse: 'Questi è de' rei del foco furo'.
  Per ch'io là dove vedi son perduto,
  e sì vestito andando, mi rancuro».   129
Quand'egli ebbe il suo dir così compiuto,
  la fiamma dolorando si partìo
  torcendo e dibattendo il corno acuto.   132
Noi passamm'oltre, io e il duca mio,
  su per lo scoglio, infino in su l'altr'arco
  che copre il fosso in che si paga il fio   135
da quei che scommettendo acquistan carco.

CANTO 28

Chi poria mai pur con parole sciolte
  dicer del sangue e de le piaghe a pieno
  ch'io ora vidi, per narrar più volte?   3
Ogni lingua per certo verria meno,
  per lo nostro sermone e per la mente
  ch'hanno a tanto comprender poco seno.   6
Se s'adunasse ancor tutta la gente
  che già in su la fortunata terra
  di Puglia fu del suo sangue dolente   9
per li Trojani e per la lunga guerra
  che de l'anella fe' sì alte spoglie,
  come Livio scrive, che non erra;   12
con quella che sentì di colpi doglie
  per contrastare a Roberto Guiscardo;
  e l'altra il cui ossame ancor s'accoglie   15
a Ceperan, là dove fu bugiardo
  ciascun Pugliese, e là da Tagliacozzo,
  dove sanz'arme vinse il vecchio Alardo;   18
e qual forato suo membro e qual mozzo
  mostrasse, da equar sarebbe nulla
  il modo de la nona bolgia sozzo.   21

He bore me off to Minos: eight times he
  wound his tail round his hard back, in fierce ire
  gnawed it awhile, and then pronounced on me:
"This is a sinner for the thievish fire";
  so, where thou seest, I'm lost, forever borne
  along, lamenting, clad in this attire.'
Its story told, and ceasing not to mourn,
  the flame departed, and, while going, sway'd
  this side and that, and tossed, its pointed horn.
And, passing on, I and my leader made
  our way up the crag as far as the arch which rode
  the fosse wherein their fee by those is paid
who by dissevering acquire their load.

CANTO 28

Who could e'er, e'en with words that were set free
  from bonds, describe in full the wounds and blood
  I saw now, though he tried repeatedly?
Truly all tongues would fail, since to include
  so wide a field our speech—nay, add thereto
  our memory—lacks sufficient amplitude.
Were all the people re-assembled who
  throughout Apulia's fateful land of yore
  bewailed their blood—both those the Trojans slew
and those who fell in that protracted war
  which (as writes Livy, who goes not astray)
  made such a high-heaped spoil of rings; and, more,
those who in barring Robert Guiscard's way
  felt blows that smarted, and the other folk
  whose bones are heaped up even to this day
at Ceperán, where each Apulian broke
  his word, and there, by Tagliacozzo, where
  old Erard conquered, though he struck no stroke;
and some should show their stabbed, and others their
  dissevered limbs, 'twould equal not one whit
  the ghastly scene which the ninth pouch laid bare.

Già veggia, per mezzul perdere o lulla,
  com'io vidi un, così non si pertugia,
  rotto dal mento infin dove si trulla.   24
Tra le gambe pendevan le minugia,
  la corata pareva e il tristo sacco
  che merda fa di quel che si trangugia.   27
Mentre che tutto in lui veder m'attacco,
  guardommi, e con le man s'aperse il petto
  dicendo: « Or vedi com'io mi dilacco!   30
Vedi come storpiato è Maometto!
  Dinanzi a me sen va piangendo Alì,
  fesso nel volto dal mento al ciuffetto.   33
E tutti quelli che tu vedi qui
  seminator di scandalo e di scisma
  fur vivi, e però son fessi così.   36
Un diavolo è qua dietro che n'accisma
  sì crudelmente, al taglio de la spada
  rimettendo ciascun di questa risma   39
quando avem volta la dolente strada;
  però che le ferite son richiuse
  prima ch'altri dinanzi li rivada.   42
Ma tu chi sei che in su lo scoglio muse,
  forse per indugiar d'ire a la pena
  ch'è giudicata in su le tue accuse? »   45
« Nè morte il giunse ancor nè colpa il mena »
  rispose il mio maestro « a tormentarlo;
  ma per dar lui esperienza piena,   48
a me, che morto son, convien menarlo
  per l'Inferno qua giù di giro in giro;
  e questo è ver così com'io ti parlo ».   51
Più fur di cento che, quando l'udiro,
  s'arrestaron nel fosso a riguardarmi,
  per maraviglia obliando il martiro.   54
« Or dì a fra Dolcin dunque che s'armi,
  tu che forse vedrai lo Sole in breve,
  s'ello non vuol qui tosto seguitarmi,   57
sì di vivanda, che stretta di neve
  non rechi la vittoria al Novarese,
  che altrimenti acquistar non saria leve ».   60

Even a cask yawns not so wide, when it
    has lost a cant or stave, as one among
    those souls I saw from chin to fart-hole split.
Dangling between his legs the entrails hung:
    the pluck appeared, and the foul sack thereunder,
    which turns whate'er is swallowed into dung.
He eyed me, as I stared at him in wonder,
    and with his hands opened his breast and groan'd:
    'Behold now how I tear myself asunder!
Behold how mutilated is Mahoúnd!
    Cleft in the face from chin to forelock hies
    Alì before me, and bewails his wound.
And all the rest whom here thine eye descries
    were sowers of scandal and of schism, while yet
    alive, and that is why they are cleft thuswise.
A devil, who behind there lies in wait,
    trims us thus cruelly, putting anew
    to the sword's edge each member of this set
when we have passed the whole grim circle through;
    because our wounds close up again, ere we
    come, any of us, again within his view.
But who art thou, bemused on the crag, may be
    to put off going to the punishment
    which, self-accused, thou'st had adjudged to thee?'
'Death has not reached him yet, nor to torment
    him does Guilt bring him' said my guide: 'but so
    that he be given full experience, sent
was I, who am dead, to bring him here below
    through Hell from circle to circle: and this is
    as true as that I'm speaking to thee now.'
More than a hundred were they who at these
    last words stopped in the ditch to stare at me,
    for wonder, oblivious of their agonies.
'Do thou, then, who perhaps ere long wilt see
    the Sun, tell Fra Dolcín', unless he fain
    would follow me down hither speedily,
to arm him so with victuals that the strain
    imposed by snow give not Novara's folk
    a victory else not easy to obtain.'

Poi che l'un piè per girsene sospese
   Maometto mi disse esta parola;
   indi a partirsi in terra lo ritese.   63
E un altro, che forata avea la gola
   e tronco il naso fin sotto le ciglia,
   e non avea ma' che un'orecchia sola,   66
ristato a riguardar per maraviglia
   con gli altri, innanzi a gli altri aprì la canna,
   ch'era di fuor d'ogni parte vermiglia,   69
e disse: « O tu cui colpa non condanna,
   e cui io vidi sù 'n terra latina,
   se troppa somiglianza non m'inganna,   72
rimembriti di Pier da Medicina,
   se mai torni a veder lo dolce piano
   che da Vercelli a Marcabò dichina.   75
E fa sapere ai due miglior di Fano,
   a messer Guido, ed anco ad Angiolello,
   che se l'antiveder qui non è vano   78
gittati saran fuor di lor vasello
   e mazzerati presso a la Cattolica,
   per tradimento d'un tiranno fello.   81
Tra l'isola di Cipri e la Maiolica
   non vide mai sì gran fallo Nettuno,
   non da pirati, non da gente argolica.   84
Quel traditor che vede pur con l'uno,
   e tien la terra che tale è qui meco
   vorrebbe di vedere esser digiuno,   87
farà venirli a parlamento seco;
   poi farà sì che al vento di Focara
   non sarà lor mestier voto nè preco ».   90
E io a lui: « Dimostrami e dichiara,
   se vuoi ch'io porti sù di te novella,
   chi è colui da la veduta amara ».   93
Allor pose la mano a la mascella
   d'un suo compagno, e la bocca gli aperse,
   gridando: « Questi è desso, e non favella.   96
Questi, scacciato, il dubitar sommerse
   in Cesare, affermando che il fornito
   sempre con danno l'attender sofferse ».   99

After he'd raised one foot to go on, spoke
  Mahomet to me thus, then laid it out
  flat on the ground and his departure took.
Another, with a hole pierced through his throat,
  and nose sliced off right up to the eyebrows,
  and only one ear left, who'd turned about
with the others and stood staring, now ere those
  others had time to, cleared his windpipe, which
  was outwardly all crimson, and thus chose
to speak: 'O guiltless comer to this ditch,
  thou whom I saw, be close resemblance no
  deceiver, up where men use Latin speech,
bethink thee of Pier da Medicina, so
  thou e'er return to see the lovely plain
  which from Vercelli slopes to Marcabò.
And make it known to Fano's two best men,
  Ser Guido and Agnolél, that they shall be
  (if our pre-vision here is not all vain)
cast forth out of their ship, and in the sea
  be sunk near la Cattólica: for this
  is planned by a fell tyrant's treachery.
'Twixt Cyprus and Majorca ne'er, I wis,
  has Neptune seen so foul an outrage done
  by pirates nor by men of the Argolis.
That traitor, who of his eyes sees but with one,
  and rules the city, which there's someone nigh
  me here would wish he'd ne'er set eyes upon,
will lure them to a parley; and by and by
  so manage that against Focara's wind
  they'll have no need of prayer or votive cry.'
And I to him: 'Wouldst have me well inclined
  to carry up news of thee, point out and say
  who it is, whose seeing was of that bitter kind.'
Then on the jaw of one there did he lay
  his hand, and open the mouth of him, and shout:
  'This is he! Look, he's speechless now for aye!
'Twas he who, exiled, put the saw about,
  "Delaying always harms the well-prepared",
  and thus in Caesar's mind suppressed the doubt.'

Oh quanto mi pareva sbigottito,
  con la lingua tagliata ne la strozza,
  Curio, che a dicer fu così ardito!   102
E un che avea l'una e l'altra man mozza,
  levando i moncherin per l'aura fosca
  sì che il sangue facea la faccia sozza,   105
gridò: « Ricordera' ti anche del Mosca,
  che dissi, lasso, *Capo ha cosa fatta*,
  che fu il mal seme per la gente tosca ».   108
E io gli aggiunsi: « E morte di tua schiatta ».
  Per ch'egli, accumulando duol con duolo,
  sen giò come persona trista e matta.   111
Ma io rimasi a riguardar lo stuolo,
  e vidi cosa ch'io avrei paura
  sanza più prova di contarla solo;   114
se non che coscienza m'assicura:
  la buona compagnia che l'uom francheggia
  sotto l'usbergo del sentirsi pura.   117
Io vidi certo, ed ancor par che il veggia,
  un busto sanza capo andar sì come
  andavan gli altri de la trista greggia;   120
e il capo tronco tenea per le chiome,
  pesol con mano a guisa di lanterna,
  e quel mirava noi e dicea *Oh me!*   123
Di sè faceva a se stesso lucerna,
  ed eran due in uno ed uno in due:
  com'esser può, quei sa che sì governa.   126
Quando diritto al piè del ponte fue,
  levò il braccio alto con tutta la testa
  per appressarne le parole sue,   129
che furo: « Or vedi la pena molesta,
  tu che spirando vai veggendo i morti;
  vedi se alcuna è grande come questa.   132
E perchè tu di me novella porti,
  sappi ch'io son Bertram del Bormio, quelli
  che diedi al Re Giovane i mai conforti.   135
Io feci il padre e il figlio in sè ribelli;
  Achitofèl non fe' più d'Absalone
  e di Davìd coi malvagi pungelli.   138

Oh how dejected Curio now appeared,
   with tongue slit in his gorge, who, when 'twas whole,
   had in his use of it so greatly dared!
With both his hands lopped off another soul,
   blood dripping from the stumps he lifted through
   the gloom, and making all his visage foul,
cried out: 'Bethink thee also of Mosca who,
   by saying, alas, "Thing done is ended" had
   cast among Tuscan folk the seed of woe.'
'And death to thy own stock' did I here add;
   whereat, accumulating pain on pain,
   he went off like to one by grief driv'n mad.
But I remained to watch the troop and then
   saw something I, without more proof, should fear
   to tell, as counting my sole witness vain,
did not my conscience reassure me here,
   man's good companion, which emboldens him
   under the mail of feeling itself clear.
I saw, for sure, a headless trunk and seem
   to see it still, proceeding there below me
   just like the others of that dismal team.
It held in its hand by the hair and to and fro' me
   let the dissevered head swing lantern-wise;
   and that was watching us and saying: 'Oh me!'
To lamp itself its own self it employs,
   which selves were two in one and one in two:
   but how, He knows, whose judgments thus chastise.
Arrived below the bridge and full in view,
   it raised its arm up high with the whole head,
   thus to bring near to us the words it threw.
'Now see my grievous punishment' it said,
   'see if with this there's aught that can compare,
   thou who, still breathing, com'st to see the dead.
And know, to the end that news of me thou bear,
   that I'm Bertrán de Born, the man who gave
   counsels to the young king that evil were.
I goaded son and father each to outbrave
   the other: into David and Absalom
   Achitophel no spurs more spiteful drave.

Perch'io partii così giunte persone,
  partito porto il mio cerebro, lasso!
  dal suo principio ch'è in questo troncone;   141
così s'osserva in me lo contrapasso».

CANTO 29

La molta gente e le diverse piaghe
  avean le luci mie sì inebriate
  che de lo stare a piangere eran vaghe.   3
Ma Virgilio mi disse: «Che pur guate?
  perchè la vista tua pur si soffolge
  là giù tra l'ombre triste smozzicate?   6
Tu non hai fatto sì a l'altre bolge;
  pensa, se tu annoverar le credi,
  che miglia ventidue la valle volge.   9
E già la Luna è sotto i nostri piedi:
  lo tempo è poco omai che n'è concesso,
  e altro è da veder che tu non vedi».   12
«Se tu avessi» rispos'io appresso
  «atteso a la cagion per ch'io guardava,
  forse m'avresti ancor lo star dimesso».   15
Parte sen giva, e io retro gli andava,
  lo duca, già facendo la risposta
  e soggiugnendo: «Dentro a quella cava   18
dov'io tenea or gli occhi sì a posta,
  credo che un spirto del mio sangue pianga
  la colpa che là giù cotanto costa».   21
Allor disse il maestro: «Non si franga
  lo tuo pensier da qui innanzi sovr'ello:
  attendi ad altro, ed ei là si rimanga;   24
ch'io vidi lui a piè del ponticello
  mostrarti e minacciar forte col ditto,
  ed udiil nominar Geri del Bello.   27
Tu eri allor sì del tutto impedito
  sovra colui che già tenne Altaforte,
  che non guardasti in là, sì fu partito».   30

Because I parted those so joined, my doom
  is that I parted bear my brain, alack!
  from that which in this trunk it issued from;
and thus with like for like I am paid back.'

CANTO 29

THE many people and the divers wounds
  had made mine eyes so maudlin they were now
  filled with a wish to weep that knew no bounds.
But Virgil said to me: 'On what art thou
  still gazing? why still dwells thy sight upon
  the mutilated shades down there in woe?
Not thus at the other pouches hast thou done:
  wouldst number the vale's inmates, think that it
  for two and twenty miles goes winding on.
The moon, too, is by now beneath our feet:
  more's to be seen than thou seest here, and needed
  is all our licensed time, now short, to see 't.'
'Hadst thou' was my immediate answer 'heeded
  what caused me thus to stand and stare, maybe
  thou wouldst my staying yet longer have conceded.'
Meanwhile my leader had gone on, with me
  behind him, making this reply: which made,
  I then subjoined: 'Within that cavity
on which my eyes just now were riveted,
  I think a spirit, one of my blood, may weep
  the crime for which down there so much is paid.'
'On something else,' then said the master, 'keep
  thy thought engaged: henceforward vex it not
  with him, but let him bide there in the deep.
I saw him at the bridgefoot point thee out
  with fiercely threatening finger: Geri, son
  of Bello, so I heard them name the lout.
Thine eyes just then were wholly intent upon
  him who once held Hautefórt, nor turned aside
  to look that way at all, till he was gone.'

« O duca mio, la violenta morte
  che non gli è vendicata ancor » diss'io
  « per alcun che de l'onta sia consorte,   33
fece lui disdegnoso, ond'ei sen gìo
  sanza parlarmi, sì com'io estimo:
  ed in ciò m'ha ei fatto a sè più pio ».   36
Così parlammo infino al luogo primo
  che da lo scoglio l'altra valle mostra,
  se più lume vi fosse, tutto ad imo.   39
Quando noi fummo su l'ultima chiostra
  di Malebolge, sì che i suoi conversi
  potean parere a la veduta nostra,   42
lamenti saettaron me diversi
  che di pietà ferrati avean li strali;
  ond'io gli orecchi con le man copersi.   45
Qual dolor fora se de li spedali
  di Valdichiana, tra il luglio e il settembre,
  e di Maremma e di Sardigna i mali   48
fossero in una fossa tutti insembre,
  tal era quivi, e tal puzzo n'usciva
  qual suol venir de le marcite membre.   51
Noi discendemmo in su l'ultima riva
  dal lungo scoglio, pur da man sinistra;
  ed allor fu la mia vista più viva   54
giù ver lo fondo, là 've la ministra
  de l'alto sire infallibil giustizia
  punisce i falsator, che qui registra.   57
Non credo che a veder maggior tristizia
  fosse in Egina il popol tutto infermo,
  (quando fu l'aer sì pien di malizia,   60
che gli animali infino al picciol vermo
  cascaron tutti, e poi le genti antiche,
  secondo che i poeti hanno per fermo,   63
si ristorar di seme di formiche),
  ch'era a veder per quell'oscura valle
  languir li spirti per diverse biche.   66
Qual sopra il ventre e qual sopra le spalle
  l'un de l'altro giaceva, e qual carpone
  si trasmutava per lo tristo calle.   69

'O good my lord, the violent death he died,
   still unavenged by anyone' said I
   'who shares in the disgrace, hath touched his pride
and makes him furious; that, I think, is why
   he went off without speaking to me; which
   makes me for him still more inclined to sigh.'
Thus talking did we mount the crag and reach
   the first point whence, with stronger light, we could
   have seen, right to its bottom, the next ditch.
When we above the final cloister stood
   of Evilpouches, and could thus command
   a clearer view of its lay-brotherhood,
manifold wailings, more than I could stand,
   their arrows barbed with pity, pierced me through;
   so that to both my ears I clapped a hand.
If in one fosse lay all the sick that stew
   in Valdichiana's spitals, and in those
   of the Maremma and Sardinia too,
from July to September, such the woes
   here, and thence issued such a stench as from
   their gangrened limbs is wont to smite the nose.
Descending, still to leftward, did we come
   to the last rampart from the long rock-spur,
   and then my sight pierced quicker through the gloom
down tow'rd the depth, where she who cannot err,
   Justice, the high Lord's handmaid, punisheth
   the falsifiers she here doth register.
Not with more grief, methinks, did men draw breath
   to see in Aegina its whole people ail,
   (when so infected was the air with death,
that, e'en to the little worm, all creatures fell
   down dead, and the oldtime inhabitants,
   as bards assure us who record the tale,
were restored later from the seed of ants),
   than I, to see, as divers-heaped they lay
   languishing, that dark valley's occupants.
Prone on the belly some, and some would stay
   them, one on the other's shoulders; some would crawl,
   to shift their place, along the dismal way.

Passo passo andavam sanza sermone,
　guardando ed ascoltando gli ammalati,
　che non potean levar le lor persone.　　　　　72
Io vidi due sedere a sè poggiati
　come a scaldar si poggia tegghia a tegghia,
　dal capo al piè di schianze maculati.　　　　75
E non vidi già mai menare stregghia
　a ragazzo aspettato dal signorso
　nè a colui che mal volentier vegghia,　　　　78
come ciascun menava spesso il morso
　de l'unghie sopra sè, per la gran rabbia
　del pizzicor che non ha più soccorso;　　　　81
e si traevan giù l'unghie la scabbia
　come cortel di scardova le scaglie
　o d'altro pesce che più larghe l'abbia.　　　84
« O tu che con le dita ti dismaglie »
　cominciò il duca mio a l'un di loro.
　« e che fai d'esse talvolta tanaglie,　　　　87
dinne se alcun latino è tra costoro
　che son quinc'entro, se l'unghia ti basti
　eternalmente a cotesto lavoro ».　　　　　90
« Latin siam noi che tu vedi sì guasti
　qui ambedue » rispose l'un piangendo;
　« ma tu chi sei che di noi dimandasti? »　　93
E il duca disse: « Io son un che discendo
　con questo vivo giù di balzo in balzo,
　e di mostrar l'Inferno a lui intendo ».　　96
Allor si ruppe lo comun rincalzo,
　e tremando ciascuno a me si volse
　con altri che l'udiron di rimbalzo.　　　　99
Lo buon maestro a me tutto s'accolse
　dicendo: « Dì a lor ciò che tu vuoli ».
　E io incominciai, poscia ch'ei volse:　　　102
« Se la vostra memoria non s'imboli
　nel primo mondo da l'umane menti,
　ma s'ella viva sotto molti soli,　　　　　105
ditemi chi voi siete e di che genti:
　la vostra sconcia e fastidiosa pena
　di palesarvi a me non vi spaventi ».　　　108

So step by step we went, not letting fall
   one word, but eyeing and listening to the sick,
   who could not raise their persons up at all.
Sitting propped on each other, as men stick
   up pan 'gainst pan to warm, I noticed two,
   with scabs from head to foot bespotted thick.
Ne'er saw I horse-comb plied by a lad that knew
   he kept his master waiting, or by one
   whose time for going to bed was overdue;
as each, to scratch, was plying up and down
   over himself his nails, so maddened him
   the itching which, save this relief, has none;
and like a whittle as it scrapes a bream,
   or fish with scales yet larger overlaid,
   such did the nails, peeling the scurf off, seem.
'O thou,' to one of them my leader said,
   'stripping thy mail off with thy fingers, yea
   and, whiles, as pincers using them instead;
among the souls confined here, tell us, pray,
   if any is Latian—so may to that task
   thy nail suffice, for ever and for aye.'
'We whom thou seest in this disfiguring mask,
   were Latians both: but who art thou?' replied
   one of them, weeping, 'and why dost thou ask?'
And 'I am one descending' said my guide
   'with this live man, downward from round to round,
   to show him Hell, nor purpose aught beside.'
Then broke their mutual propping; and, astound,
   to me they both turned trembling, with the rest
   by whom his words were caught on the rebound.
Close up beside me the good master press'd:
   then 'Say to them what'er thou wilt' he said;
   and I began, since such was his behest:
'So may the memory left of you not fade
   in the first world from human minds, but there
   live on while many suns their radiance shed—
tell me your names and of what folk ye were:
   let not your vile and loathsome penalty
   of making this disclosure give you fear.'

« Io fui d'Arezzo, e Albero da Siena »
  rispose l'un « mi fe' mettere al foco;
  ma quel per ch'io morii qui non mi mena.   111
Vero è ch'io dissi lui, parlando a gioco,
  ch'io mi saprei levar per l'aere a volo.
    E quei, ch'avea vaghezza e senno poco,   114
volle ch'io li mostrassi l'arte, e solo
  perch'io nol feci Dedalo, mi fece
  ardere a tal che l'avea per figliuolo.   117
Ma ne l'ultima bolgia de le diece
  me per l'alchimia che nel mondo usai
  dannò Minòs, a cui fallar non lece ».   120
E io dissi al poeta: « Or fu già mai
  gente sì vana come la sanese?
  Certo non la francesca sì d'assai ».   123
Onde l'altro lebbroso, che m'intese,
  rispose al detto mio: « Trammene Stricca
  che seppe far le temperate spese: 126
e Niccolò che la costuma ricca
  del garofano prima discoperse
  ne l'orto dove tal seme s'appicca;   129
e tranne la brigata in che disperse
  Caccia d'Ascian la vigna e la gran fronda,
  e l'Abbagliato suo senno proferse.   132
Ma perchè sappi chi sì ti seconda
  contra i Sanesi, aguzza ver me l'occhio
  sì che la faccia mia ben ti risponda;   135
sì vedrai ch'io son l'ombra di Capocchio
  che falsai li metalli con alchimia;
  e ti dee ricordar, se ben t'adocchio,   138
com'io fui di natura buona scimia ».

CANTO 30

NEL tempo che Giunone era crucciata
  per Semelè contro il sangue tebano,
  come mostrò una ed altra fiata,   3

'I was an Aretine, and Albert—he
  of Siena—had me burned,' so one confess'd;
  'but not for that which brings me where you see.
'Tis true I said to him, though but in jest,
  "I can take wings and fly": and how 'twas done,
  he, being curious and a fool at best,
wished me to show him and, for that alone
  I made him not a Daedalus, had me then
  sent to the stake by one who called him son.
But Minos, the unerring, at my arraign
  doomed me to this, the tenth and lowest pouch,
  for the alchemy I practised among men.'
And I to the poet said: 'Now was there such
  a hare-brained folk as Siena's ever yet?
  In very sooth, not so the French by much.'
Whence the other leper, who had heard them, met
  my words with these: 'Except me Stricca, who
  knew how to make his outlays moderate;
and Nicholas, who first found out and grew
  the clove, for gourmets, in the garden where
  such seed takes ready root: except me, too,
the club in which Caccia d'Ascián whilere
  squandered his wealth of vineyards and great trees,
  and where his wit was aired by the Blunderer.
But that thou know who thus thy backer is
  'gainst Siena's folk, sharpen thine eye tow'rds me,
  to get my face clear; so thou'lt see that 'tis
Capocchio's shade, who once by alchemy
  falsified metals: nor should it escape
  thy memory, if errs not my own of thee,
how I was Nature's most accomplished ape.'

CANTO 30

WHAT time relentless Juno wreaked upon
  the Theban blood because of Semele
  her fury, as she did more times than one,

Atamante divenne tanto insano,
  che veggendo la moglie con due figli
  andar carcata da ciascuna mano,   6
gridò: «Tendiam le reti sì ch'io pigli
  la leonessa e i leoncini al varco»;
  e poi distese i dispietati artigli,   9
prendendo l'un che avea nome Learco,
  e rotollo e percosselo ad un sasso;
  e quella s'annegò con l'altro carco.   12
E quando la fortuna volse in basso
  l'altezza dei Trojan che tutto ardiva,
  sì che insieme col regno il re fu casso,   15
Ecuba trista, misera e cattiva,
  poscia che vide Polissena morta,
  e del suo Polidoro in su la riva   18
del mar si fu, la dolorosa!, accorta,
  forsennata latrò sì come cane,
  tanto il dolor le fe' la mente torta.   21
Ma nè di Tebe furie nè troiane
  si vider mai in alcun tanto crude,
  non punger bestie non che membra umane,   24
quant'io vidi due ombre smorte e nude
  che mordendo correvan, di quel modo
  che il porco quando del porcil si schiude.   27
L'una giunse a Capocchio, ed in sul nodo
  del collo l'assannò, sì che, tirando,
  grattar li fece il ventre al fondo sodo.   30
E l'Aretin, che rimase tremando,
  mi disse: «Quel folletto è Gianni Schicchi,
  e va rabbioso altrui così conciando».   33
«Oh» diss'io lui «se l'altro non ti ficchi
  li denti addosso, non ti sia fatica
  a dir chi è pria che di qui si spicchi».   36
Ed egli a me: «Quella è l'anima antica
  di Mirra scellerata, che divenne
  al padre fuor del dritto amore amica.   39
Questa a peccar con esso così venne,
  falsificando sè in altrui forma,
  come l'altro che là sen va sostenne,   42

Athamas turned so wildly insane that he
  seeing his wife go burdened with two sons,
  one on each arm, cried out in savage glee:
'Spread we the toils that, as she past us runs,
  the lioness and lion-cubs be ta'en';
  and stretching forth his pitiless talons,
he clutched the one they called Learchus, then
  whirling him round, dashed him against a rock;
  and she with the other drowned herself. And when
by Fortune's wheel the Trojans' haughty stock
  which dared all things was turned to abasement, so
  that king and kingdom perished in the shock,
Hecuba, weeping, captive and brought low,
  after she'd seen Polyxena struck dead,
  and on the beach was ware—to crown her woe—
of her own Polydorus lifeless laid,
  fell on a frenzy and, dog-like, began
  to bark, such aberration grief had bred.
But furies, Theban or of Troy, ne'er ran
  to goad so cruelly any to assail
  beasts, let alone the members of a man,
as I beheld two shades, naked and pale,
  run, like a boar when let out from the sty,
  biting and rending all on whom they fell.
Come to Capocchio, one so fanged him nigh
  the neck-joint that he made his belly grind
  on the hard rock-floor as he dragged him by.
And he of Arezzo, who was left behind,
  trembling, said: '*That* imp's Gianni Schicchi: it's
  his way to maul us in this maniac kind.'
'So may the other's teeth not tear to bits
  thy back,' said I, 'pray tell us, so it prove
  not irksome, who it is, ere hence it flits.'
And he: ' 'Tis she old poets tell us of,
  the soul of Myrrha, sunk so deep in sin,
  that, wooing her father beyond rightful love,
she lay with him, dissembling herself in
  another's person, just as he who went
  his way there, ventured, so that he might win

per guadagnar la donna de la torma,
   falsificare in sè Buoso Donati,
   testando e dando al testamento norma ».   45
E poi che i due rabbiosi fur passati
   sovra cui io avea l'occhio tenuto,
   rivolsilo a guardar gli altri malnati.   48
Io vidi un, fatto a guisa di leuto
   pur ch'egli avesse avuto l'anguinaia
   tronca da l'altro che l'uom ha forcuto.   51
La grave idropisia, che sì dispaia
   le membra, con l'umor che mal converte,
   che il viso non risponde a la ventraia,   54
faceva lui tener le labbra aperte
   come l'etico fa, che per la sete
   l'un verso il mento e l'altro in sù rinverte.   57
« O voi che sanz'alcuna pena siete,
   e non so io perchè, nel mondo gramo »
   diss'egli a noi « guardate ed attendete   60
a la miseria del maestro Adamo:
   io ebbi, vivo, assai di quel ch'io volli;
   e ora, lasso, un gocciol d'acqua bramo.   63
Li ruscelletti che dei verdi colli
   del Casentin discendon giuso in Arno
   facendo i lor canali freddi e molli,   66
sempre mi stanno innanzi, e non indarno,
   chè l'immagine lor vie più m'asciuga
   che il male ond'io nel volto mi discarno.   69
La rigida giustizia che mi fruga
   tragge cagion del loco ov'io peccai
   a metter più li miei sospiri in fuga.   72
Ivi è Romena là dov'io falsai
   la lega suggellata del Battista,
   perch'io il corpo sù arso lasciai.   75
Ma s'io vedessi qui l'anima trista
   di Guido o d'Alessandro o di lor frate,
   per fonte Branda non darei la vista.   78
Dentro c'è l'una già, se l'arrabbiate
   ombre che vanno intorno dicon vero;
   ma che mi val? ch'ho le membra legate!   81

the "stud's queen", in himself to represent
  Buoso Donati, drawing up a will,
  and giving it due form, with that intent.'
My eye, when the mad two, whom it had still
  been following, were gone, from their pursuit
  turned back to watch the others born for ill.
And I beheld one shapen like a lute,
  if he had only had his groin just there
  cut short, where a man's fork is jointed to 't.
The grievous dropsy—which will so dis-pair
  the limbs with fluid it converts to bane,
  that face to paunch doth no proportion bear—
kept his lips parted like the hectic's when,
  by reason of his thirst, he curls the one
  upward and drops the other tow'rds his chin.
'O you that free of punishment are down
  (and why I know not) in the world accurst,'
  he said to us, 'pay heed and gaze upon
woe wherewith Master Adam is amerced:
  I who, alive, had all I wanted, now,
  ah me! for one small drop of water thirst.
The little brooks that into Arno flow
  down from the green hills of the Casentín,
  cooling and making moist their channels, how
they ever, nor in vain, confront my een!
  For the image of them makes me far more dry
  than the ill through which my face is grown so lean.
The rigid justice which I'm goaded by
  uses the place which saw my sin committed
  as means to make my sighs the faster fly.
There lies Romena, where I counterfeited
  the coin stamped with the Baptist: for which thing
  I up there at the stake my body quitted.
But saw I Guy's vile spirit in this ring,
  or Alexander's, or their brother's, I'd
  not give that welcome sight for Branda spring.
One of them is already here inside,
  if the mad shades that rush about speak true,
  but what avails me that, whose limbs are tied?

S'io fossi pur di tanto ancor leggero
  ch'io potessi in cent'anni andare un'oncia
  io sarei messo già per lo sentiero   84
cercando lui tra questa gente sconcia;
  con tutto ch'ella volge undici miglia,
  e men d'un mezzo di traverso non ci ha.   87
Io son per lor tra sì fatta famiglia:
  ei m'indussero a batter li fiorini
  che avevan tre carati di mondiglia».   90
Ed io a lui: « Chi son li due tapini
  che fuman come man bagnata il verno,
  giacendo stretti a' tuoi destri confini?»   93
« Qui li trovai, e poi volta non dierno »
  rispose « quando piovvi in questo greppo;
  e non credo che dieno in sempiterno.   96
L'una è la falsa che accusò Giuseppo;
  l'altro è il falso Sinon greco da Troia:
  per febbre acuta gittan tanto leppo».   99
E l'un di lor, che si recò a noia
  forse d'esser nomato sì oscuro
  col pugno li percosse l'epa croia.   102
Quella sonò come fosse un tamburo;
  e mastro Adamo li percosse il volto
  col braccio suo, che non parve men duro,   105
dicendo a lui: « Ancor che mi sia tolto
  lo mover, per le membra che son gravi,
  ho io il braccio a tal mestiere sciolto».   108
Ond'ei rispose: « Quando tu andavi
  al foco, non l'avei tu così presto,
  ma sì e più l'avei quando coniavi».   111
E l'idropico: « Tu di' ver di questo;
  ma tu non fosti sì ver testimonio
  là 've del ver fosti a Troia richiesto».   114
« S'io dissi il falso, e tu falsasti il conio».
  disse Sinone « e son qui per un fallo,
  e tu per più che alcun altro demonio».   117
« Ricorditi, spergiuro, del cavallo »
  rispose quel che aveva infiata l'epa,
  « e sieti reo che tutto il mondo sallo».   120

Were I but still so light that I could through
  one inch advance in a hundred years, I should,
  to seek him out mid this disfigured crew,
have started long since, though the pit's a good
  eleven miles about, and here must be
  not less than half a mile in latitude.
Through them am I in such a family:
  'twas they induced me strike the florins, so
  that of alloy they'd carats fully three.'
And I to him: 'The two there, lying low,
  who smoke like wet hands when the air is frore,
  close to thy right, who are they? dost thou know?'
'I found them here (and they've not once turned o'er)'
  he answered, 'when I rained into this creek:
  nor do I think they'll stir for evermore.
The one's from Troy: he's Sinon, the false Greek;
  falsehoods 'gainst Joseph did the other launch:
  sharp fever makes them cast so foul a reek.'
And one, when named thus darkly, on his haunch
  turned and, perhaps from outraged self-regard,
  with the fist smote him on the leathery paunch,
which thudded like a drum; and, nowise scared,
  did Master Adam smite him on the face,
  using an arm which seemed no whit less hard,
and saying: 'Though my limbs through heaviness
  refuse to budge, my arm does not decline
  to function, and I hold it ready, in case.'
'Upon thy way to the stake,' did he rejoin,
  'it did not move so promptly at thy behest,
  but quite as promptly, and more, when striking coin.'
And he of the dropsy: 'True is what thou say'st
  of this, but not so true thy witness there
  where to hear truth from thee was Troy's request.'
'If false my words, *as* false' said Sinon, 'were
  thy coins: and I'm here but for *one* fault, thou
  for more than any demon whatsoe'er.'
'Bethink thee, perjurer, of the horse' was how
  he of the swollen belly made reply;
  'may 't plague thee that the whole world knows it now.'

« A te sia rea la sete onde ti crepa »
    disse il greco « la lingua, e l'acqua marcia
    che il ventre innanzi gli occhi sì t'assiepa ».   123
Allora il monetier: « Così si squarcia
    la bocca tua per tuo mal, come suole:
    chè s'io ho sete ed umor mi rinfarcia,   126
tu hai l'arsura e il capo che ti duole,
    e per leccar lo specchio di Narcisso
    non vorresti, a invitar, molte parole ».   129
Ad ascoltarli er'io del tutto fisso,
    quando il maestro mi disse: « Or pur mira!
    ch'è per poco che teco non mi risso! »   132
Quand'io sentii a me parlar con ira,
    volsimi verso lui con tal vergogna
    che ancor per la memoria mi si gira.   135
E qual colui che suo dannaggio sogna,
    che, sognando, desidera sognare,
    sì che quel ch'è, come non fosse, agogna,   138
tal mi fec'io non possendo parlare:
    che disiava scusarmi, e scusava
    me tuttavia, e nol mi credea fare.   141
« Maggior difetto men vergogna lava »
    disse il maestro « che il tuo non è stato;
    però d'ogni tristizia ti disgrava.   144
E fa ragion ch'io ti sia sempre a lato
    se più avvien che fortuna ti coglia
    dove sien genti in simigliante piato: 147
chè voler ciò udire è bassa voglia ».

CANTO 31

Una medesma lingua pria mi morse
    sì che mi tinse l'una e l'altra guancia,
    e poi la medicina mi riporse: 3
così od'io che soleva la lancia
    d'Achille e del suo padre esser cagione
    prima di trista e poi di buona mancia.   6

'And thee may the thirst plague which cracks thy dry
   tongue,' said the Greek, 'and the foul fluid to boot,
   which 'fore thine eyes piles up thy paunch so high.'
The coiner then: 'Still gapes thy mouth to put
   thee at disadvantage, as 'twas wont to do;
   for if I've thirst, and moisture puffs me out,
thou hast thy fever, and the headache too,
   so that to lick Narcissus' looking-glass
   the words thou'dst want to invite thee would be few.'
Listening to them, I was all ears, whenas
   my lord said: 'Now keep looking! and with thee
   I shall fall out, ere many moments pass.'
With such shame, when I heard him speak to me
   in anger, did I tow'rds him turn, that 'tis
   even yet circling in my memory.
And as, while dreaming, he who dreams of his
   own hurt doth wish 'twas but a dream, and so
   desires, as though it were not, that which is,
thus I, while powerless by words to show
   how much I longed to excuse myself, was yet
   all the time doing it, though I did not know.
'Less shame' my master said 'would expiate
   a greater fault than this of thine hath been;
   therefore unload thyself of all regret.
And count on my being always by thee, in
   the event that chance to such a devilish
   dispute as this should bring thee e'er again;
for wishing to hear such things is a low wish.'

CANTO 31

THE selfsame tongue that first had stung me, so
   that it tinged both my cheeks, was then as swift
   the healing balm upon me to bestow.
Thus, so I've heard, the lance that none could lift
   except Achilles and his sire, was source
   first of a sorry, then of a good gift.

Noi demmo il dosso al misero vallone,
   su per la ripa che il cinge d'intorno,
   attraversando sanza alcun sermone.   9
Quivi era men che notte e men che giorno,
   sì che il viso m'andava innanzi poco;
   ma io sentii sonare un alto corno   12
tanto che avrebbe ogni tuon fatto fioco,
   che contra sè, la sua via seguitando,
   dirizzò gli occhi miei tutti ad un loco.   15
Dopo la dolorosa rotta, quando
   Carlo Magno perdè la santa gesta,
   non sonò si terribilmente Orlando.   18
Poco portai in là volta la testa
   che mi parve veder molte alte torri;
   ond'io: « Maestro, di', che terra è questa? »   21
Ed egli a me: « Però che tu trascorri
   per le tenebre troppo da la lungi,
   avvien che poi nel maginare abborri.   24
Tu vedrai ben, se tu là ti congiungi,
   quanto il senso s'inganna di lontano;
   però alquanto più te stesso pungi ».   27
Poi caramente mi prese per mano,
   e disse: « Pria che noi siam più avanti,
   a ciò che il fatto men ti paia strano,   30
sappi che non son torri, ma giganti,
   e son nel pozzo, intorno da la ripa,
   da l'umbilico in giuso tutti quanti ».   33
Come quando la nebbia si dissïpa
   lo sguardo a poco a poco raffigura
   ciò che cela il vapor che l'aere stipa,   36
così, forando l'aùra grossa e scura,
   più e più appressando ver la sponda,
   fuggiemi errore e cresceami paura;   39
però che, come su la cerchia tonda
   Montereggion di torri si corona,
   così la proda che il pozzo circonda   42
torreggiavan di mezza la persona
   gli orribili giganti, cui minaccia
   Giove dal cielo ancora quando tuona.   45

Quitting the vale of woe we shaped our course
   up o'er the bank that girdles it around,
    nor, crossing it, did we of aught discourse.
There less than night and less than day we found,
   so that my sight not far before me went;
    but I could hear the blast of a horn, whose sound
would have made any thunderclap seem faint,
   by which my eyes, that were, to meet it, cast
    in its direction, on one spot were bent.
After the dolorous rout, when fell the last
   devoted paladins of Charlëmain,
    not Roland blew so terrible a blast.
Brief while I'd kept my head turn'd thither, when
   methought I saw many high towers; and 'Sir,
    tell me, what city is this?' I asked him then.
And he to me: 'Because thou fain wouldst fare
   across the gloom from too far off is why
    it comes about that fancy makes thee err.
How much mere distance can deceive the eye
   thou'lt see well, if thou comest to that place:
    so a somewhat sharper spur to thyself apply.'
Then with a loving gesture did he press
   my hand, and added: 'Ere we farther reach,
    so that the strangeness of the fact seem less,
know that they are not towers, but giants, which
   thou seest there, round the bank and in the pit
    set from the navel downward, all and each.'
As, when a fog disperses, bit by bit
   one's gaze gives shape to whatsoe'er the mist
    that thickens the atmosphere conceals from it;
so, as we pierced the dim gross air nor ceas'd
   to approach the edge, my error, point by point
    of our advance, fled, and my fear increas'd;
for, as upon its circular *enceinte*
   Montereggione wears a crown of towers,
    so, round the bank that holds the pit within't,
there towered aloft, with half their bodies, scores
   of those dread giants whose rebellious pride
    Jove threatens still from heav'n when thunder roars.

Ed io scorgevo già d'alcun la faccia,
  le spalle e il petto e del ventre gran parte,
  e per le coste giù ambo le braccia.   48
Natura certo quando lasciò l'arte
  di siffatti animali, assai fe' bene,
  per tòrre tali esecutori a Marte.   51
E s'ella d'elefanti e di balene
  non si pente, chi guarda sottilmente
  più giusta e più discreta la ne tiene;   54
chè dove l'argomento de la mente
  s'aggiunge al mal volere ed a la possa,
  nessun riparo vi può far la gente.   57
La faccia sua mi parea lunga e grossa
  come la pina di San Pietro a Roma,
  ed a sua proporzion eran l'altr'ossa;   60
sì che la ripa, ch'era perizoma
  dal mezzo in giù, ne mostrava ben tanto
  di sopra, che di giungere a la chioma   63
tre Frison s'averien dato mal vanto,
  però ch'io ne vedea trenta gran palmi
  dal luogo in giù dov'uomo affibbia il manto.   66
Raphel maì amech zabi almi
  cominciò a gridar la fiera bocca
  cui non si convenian più dolci salmi.   69
E il duca mio ver lui: « Anima sciocca,
  tienti col corno, e con quel ti disfoga
  quand'ira o altra passion ti tocca.   72
Cercati al collo, e troverai la soga
  che il tien legato, o anima confusa,
  e vedi lui che il gran petto ti doga ».   75
Poi disse a me: « Elli stesso s'accusa:
  questi è Nembrotte, per lo cui mal coto
  pur un linguaggio nel mondo non s'usa.   78
Lasciamlo stare e non parliamo a voto,
  chè così è a lui ciascun linguaggio
  come il suo ad altrui, che a nullo è noto ».   81
Facemmo adunque più lungo viaggio
  volti a sinistra, ed al trar d'un balestro
  trovammo l'altro, assai più fiero e maggio.   84

The face of one already I descried,
   the shoulders, chest, and of the paunch great part,
   and both the arms, which hung down by his side.
Sure, Nature did right well to leave the art
   of beings so made, and take from Mars away
   agents framed so much after his own heart.
And if she rues not whales and to this day
   makes elephants, whoso look subtilly
   deem her for that the wiser, and well may;
since where conjoined is the mind's faculty
   with ill-will and with strength, of no avail
   against them can man's stoutest rampart be.
In length and bulk his face would tally well,
   I reckoned, with St. Peter's pine at Rome:
   and the other bones agreed therewith in scale;
so that the bank, which was his perizome
   from the waist down, showed so much of him there
   above, that from three Frisians would have come
in vain the boast to reach up to his hair:
   for thirty great spans of him did I see,
   downward from where one's cloak is buckled, laid bare.
'Raphèl maỳ amèch zabì almì' —
   the brute began to shout this rigmarole
   in tones too harsh for sweeter psalmody.
Then cried my leader towr'ds him: 'Stupid soul,
   stick to thy horn: vent thee with that, whene'er
   anger or other passion bids thee howl.
Search at thy neck, and thou'lt discover there
   the strap that holds it tied, thou scatterbrain,
   and that it hoops thy great chest be aware.'
'He is his own accuser,' said he then
   to me; 'that's Nimrod, through whose evil thought
   there's not one language, only, in use by men.
Let's waste no words, but leave him, in that aught
   we said were futile, since all tongues to him
   are as to others his, which meaneth nought.'
Pursuing our journey then, by the pit's rim,
   still leftward, at a cross-bow-shot we found
   the next one, bigger far, and much more grim.

A cinger lui qual che fosse il maestro
  non so io dir, ma ei tenea succinto
  dinanzi l'altro e dietro il braccio destro   87
d'una catena che il teneva avvinto
  dal collo in giù, sì che su lo scoperto
  si ravvolgeva infino al giro quinto.   90
« Questo superbo voll'essere sperto
  di sua potenza contro al sommo Giove »
  disse il mio duca « ond'egli ha cotal merto.   93
Fialte ha nome, e fece le gran prove
  quando i giganti fer paura ai Dei;
  le braccia ch'ei menò già mai non move ».   96
Ed io a lui: « S'esser puote, io vorrei
  che de lo smisurato Briareo
  esperienza avesser gli occhi miei ».   99
Ond'ei rispose: « Tu vedrai Anteo
  presso di qui, che parla ed è disciolto,
  che ne porrà nel fondo d'ogni reo.   102
Quel che tu vuoi veder più là è molto,
  ed è legato, e fatto come questo,
  salvo che più feroce par nel volto ».   105
Non fu tremoto già tanto rubesto,
  che scotesse una torre così forte,
  come Fialte a scuotersi fu presto.   108
Allor temetti più che mai la morte,
  e non v'era mestier più che la dotta
  s'io non avessi viste le ritorte.   111
Noi procedemmo più avante allotta,
  e venimmo ad Anteo, che ben cinqu'alle,
  sanza la testa, uscìa fuor de la grotta.   114
« O tu che ne la fortunata valle
  che fece Scipion di gloria reda,
  quando Annibàl co' suoi diede le spalle,   117
recasti già mille lion per preda,
  e che se fossi stato a l'alta guerra
  de' tuoi fratelli, ancor par che si creda   120
che avrebber vinto i figli de la Terra;
  mettine giù e non ten vegna schifo,
  dove Cocito la freddura serra.   123

What master thus could gird him is beyond
  my power to say, but his right arm behind,
  his left in front of, him was tightly bound
with one chain, which about him so was twined
  from the neck down, that on the part display'd
  it did as many as five times round him wind.
'This insolent spirit willed' my leader said
  'to pit his strength against the most high Jove:
  and therefore in these terms is now repaid.
His name's Ephialtes, and none mightier strove,
  what time the giants put the Gods in fear;
  the arms he waved then, nevermore shall move.'
'Were't possible, I would my eyes could here
  have sight of the enormous Bríareus,'
  said I; and he replied: 'Antaeus near
at hand thou'lt see, who speaks and is let loose
  from chains and of whose arm as means to place
  us down at sin's rock-bottom we'll make use.
He, whom to see thou showest such eagerness,
  stands far on, chained and like this one in make,
  save that he looks much fiercer in the face.'
Ne'er of such violence yet was an earthquake,
  that it so mightily shook a tower, as wrath
  made Ephialtes of a sudden shake.
Then was I more than e'er in fear of death
  and, but that I beheld his gyves, the dread
  alone would have sufficed to stop my breath.
We then proceeded farther, and so made
  our way on to Antaeus, who from the well
  emerged a good five ells, besides the head.
'O thou who in the fortune-vexéd vale
  which made of Scipio glory's heir, that day
  when Hannibal with all his host turned tail,
didst once bear off a thousand lions for prey,
  and who if with thy brethren thou hadst gone
  to war 'gainst Heaven, some folk (it seems) still say
the sons of Earth the victory would have won;
  be not disdainful of my plea, but where
  the cold locks up Cocytus set us down.

Non ci far ire a Tizio nè a Tifo:
   questi può dar di quel che qui si brama:
   però ti china e non torcer lo grifo.   126
Ancor ti può nel mondo render fama,
   ch'ei vive, e lunga vita ancora aspetta,
   se innanzi tempo Grazia a sè nol chiama ».   129
Così disse il maestro, e quegli in fretta
   le man distese e prese il duca mio,
   ond'Ercole sentì già grande stretta.   132
Virgilio, quando prender si sentìo,
   disse a me: « Fatti qua sì ch'io ti prenda ».
   Poi fece sì che un fascio era egli ed io.   135
Qual pare a riguardar la Garisenda
   sotto il chinato, quando un nuvol vada
   sovr'essa sì ch'ella in contrario penda,   138
tal parve Anteo a me, che stava a bada
   di vederlo chinare, e fu tal ora
   ch'i' avrei voluto ir per altra strada.   141
Ma lievemente al fondo che divora
   Lucifero con Giuda ci posò;
   nè sì chinato lì fece dimora,   144
e com'albero in nave si levò.

CANTO 32

S'io avessi le rime aspre e chiocce
   come si converrebbe al tristo buco
   sovra il qual pontan tutte l'altre rocce,   3
io premerei di mio concetto il suco
   più pienamente; ma perch'io non l'abbo
   non sanza tema a dicer mi conduco;   6
chè non è impresa da pigliare a gabbo
   descriver fondo a tutto l'universo,
   nè da lingua che chiami *mamma* e *babbo*.   9
Ma quelle donne aiutino il mio verso
   che aiutaro Anfione a chiuder Tebe,
   sì che dal fatto il dir non sia diverso.   12

To Tityus nor to Typhon make us fare;
   this man can give thee of that here hungered for:
   so stoop, and to turn up thy snout forbear.
He yet can fame to thee on earth restore;
   for life still claims him, and long may, unless
   Grace calls him to itself before his hour.'
Thus spoke the master: and he with eagerness
   stretched forth those mighty hands to grasp my guide,
   of which e'en Hercules once felt the stress.
And when he felt them grasp him, Virgil cried
   to me: 'Come close, that I may grasp thee': and so
   himself and me into one bundle tied.
As looks the Carisenda from below
   its leaning side, when over it a cloud
   so goes, that it hangs contrary thereto;
such looked to me Antaeus, as I stood
   watching to see him bend—a moment this,
   when I would fain have gone by another road.
But, delicately, he, within the abyss
   which devours Lucifer with Judas, set
   us down, nor stayed bent, after our release,
but rose and, like a ship's mast, stood up straight.

CANTO 32

Had I harsh rhymes, hacked out of sound that shocks
   the ear, such as would suit the dismal pit,
   down upon which thrust all the other rocks,
I would squeeze out the juice of my conceit
   more fully; but, not having them framed ready,
   not without fear do I dare to speak of it.
For to describe the basis which holds steady
   the entire universe is no child's play,
   nor for a tongue whose cry is 'mummy' and 'daddy'.
But may those ladies help me build my lay
   who helped Amphion wall-in Thebes, that not
   at variance with the fact be aught I say.

Oh sopra tutte mal creata plebe
   che stai nel loco onde parlare è duro,
   me' foste state qui pecore o zebe!   15
Come noi fummo giù nel pozzo scuro,
   sotto i piè del gigante, assai più bassi,
   e io mirava ancora all'alto muro,   18
dicere udimmi: «Guarda come passi:
   va sì che tu non calchi con le piante
   le teste de' fratei miseri lassi».   21
Per ch'io mi volsi, e vidimi davante
   e sotto i piedi un lago che per gelo
   avea di vetro e non d'acqua sembiante.   24
Non fece al corso suo sì grosso velo
   di verno la Danoia in Osterricche
   nè Tanaì là sotto il freddo cielo,   27
com'era quivi; che se Tambernicche
   vi fosse sù caduto, o Pietrapana,
   non avria pur da l'orlo fatto *cricche*.   30
E come a gracidar si sta la rana
   col muso fuor de l'acqua, quando sogna
   di spigolar sovente la villana,   33
livide, insin là dove appar vergogna
   eran l'ombre dolenti ne la ghiaccia,
   mettendo i denti in nota di cicogna.   36
Ognuna in giù tenea volta la faccia;
   da bocca il freddo e da gli occhi il cor tristo
   tra lor testimonianza si procaccia.   39
Quand'io m'ebbi dintorno alquanto visto,
   volsimi ai piedi, e vidi due sì stretti
   che il pel del capo avieno insieme misto. 42
«Ditemi, voi che sì strignete i petti»
   diss'io «chi siete». E quei piegaro i colli;
   e poi ch'ebber li visi a me eretti,   45
gli occhi lor, ch'eran pria pur dentro molli,
   gocciar su per li lab'ri, e il gelo strinse
   le lacrime tra essi, e risserrolli.   48
Con legno legno spranga mai non cinse
   forte così; ond'ei come due becchi
   cozzaro insieme, tanta ira li vinse.   51

Oh rabble above all others misbegot,
  better had ye been up here goats or sheep
  than biding in that hard-to-talk-of spot!
When we were down there in the gloomy deep
  beneath the giant's feet and far more low,
  I, scanning still the wall of that high keep,
heard said to me: 'Look to thy steps; move so
  that with thy soles thou kick not on the head
  the weary brothers lying here in woe.'
Wherefore I turned and saw before me spread
  and 'neath my feet a lake which looked like glass
  not water, so by frost was it bested.
Ne'er did the Danube o'er its current pass
  in wintry Austria a veil so thick,
  nor Tanais yonder, 'neath the cold sky, as
there was here: for, supposing Tambernic
  had fallen on't, or Pietrapán, it would
  not even at the edge have given a creak.
And, as out of the water frogs protrude
  their snouts to croak, what time the village-maid
  goes gleaning in her dreams oft-times renew'd;
blue-pinched up to the place where shame's display'd,
  setting their teeth to the stork's note, thuswise
  wedged in the ice the woeful spirits were laid.
Each kept his face bent downward; by the eyes
  the aching heart, and by the mouth the cold,
  among them witness to itself supplies.
Having looked round awhile did I behold
  two at my feet, so close together press'd,
  that which was either's hair could not be told.
'Tell me,' said I, 'you, clamped thus breast to breast,
  who are you?'—They bent back their necks; and when
  each tow'rd me had raised his face, their eyes express'd
the moisture, only inward until then,
  up through the lids, and the frost failed not to bind
  the tears 'twixt these, and locked them up again.
Plank to plank trennel ne'er so firmly join'd;
  whence, like two goats, they butted each other, stung
  by mutual rage, as fierce as it was blind.

Ed un che avea perduto ambo gli orecchi
  per la freddura, pur col viso in giue,
  disse: « Perchè cotanto in noi ti specchi?   54
Se vuoi saper chi son cotesti due,
  la valle onde Bisenzio si dichina
  del padre loro, Alberto, e di lor fue.   57
D'un corpo usciro, e tutta la Caina
  potrai cercare, e non troverai ombra
  degna più d'esser fitta in gelatina: 60
non quegli a cui fu rotto il petto e l'ombra
  con esso un colpo per la man d'Artù,
  non Focaccia, non questi che m'ingombra   63
col capo sì ch'io non veggio oltre più,
  e fu nomato Sassol Mascheroni:
  se tosco se', ben sai omai chi fu.   66
E perchè non mi metti in più sermoni,
  sappi ch'io fui il Camicion de' Pazzi,
  ed aspetto Carlin che mi scagioni ».   69
Poscia vid'io mille visi cagnazzi
  fatti per freddo; onde mi vien riprezzo,
  e verrà sempre, dei gelati guazzi.   72
E mentre che andavamo in ver lo mezzo,
  al quale ogni gravezza si rauna,
  ed io tremava ne l'eterno rezzo,   75
se voler fu o destino o fortuna
  non so, ma passeggiando tra le teste,
  forte percossi il piè nel viso ad una.   78
Piangendo mi sgridò: « Perchè mi peste?
  se tu non veni a crescer la vendetta
  di Montaperti, perchè mi moleste? »   81
E io: « Maestro mio, or qui m'aspetta,
  sì ch'io esca d'un dubbio per costui:
  poi mi farai quantunque vorrai fretta ».   84
Lo duca stette; e io dissi a colui
  che bestemmiava duramente ancora:
  « Qual sei tu, che così rampogni altrui? »   87
« Or tu chi se', che vai per l'Antenora
  percotendo » rispose « altrui le gote,
  sì che se fossi vivo troppo fora! »   90

And one near by, off whom the cold had wrung
   both his ears, cried out, with his face still down:
   'Why mirrorest thyself in us so long?
If thou wouldst have these two to thee made known,
   the vale down which Bisenzio flows had been
   their father Albert's, ere it was their own.
They issued from one womb; and, search thou e'en
   the entire Caina, thou wilt find there no
   shade more condignly fixed in gelatine;
not him whose breast and shadow at one blow
   were broken by the hand of Arthur; not
   Focaccia; not this one whose head doth so
obstruct me, that I see not past him aught,
   named Sassol Mascheroni; and now thou right
   well know'st, if Tuscan, who he was and what.
And, to save me more blab, know I'm the sprite
   of Camición de' Pazzi, and I await
   Carlín, that he may exculpate me quite.'
Thereafter I saw a thousand faces set
   a-grin with cold; whence o'er me comes, and will
   always, at frozen pools a shuddering fit,
And as we kept advancing, downward still,
   tow'rds the midpoint all weights converge upon,
   and I was shivering in the eternal chill;
whether by will or fate or chance 'twas done
   who knows? but, 'mongst the heads, while going by
   I struck my foot hard on the face of one.
Weeping, he railed at me: 'Why kick me? Why
   molest me, if thou com'st not to increase
   the vengeance wreaked for Montaperti?' And I:
'Now, master, await me here, that I by this
   one's means may issue from a doubt: and then,
   wouldst hurry me on, thou'lt find me not remiss.'
My leader stopped, and I, intent again
   on him who still was cursing fiercely, cried:
   'Who art thou, that so abusest other men?'
'Say, rather, who thyself art, that dost stride
   through Antenora kicking others' cheeks
   harder than wert thou living?' he replied.

« Vivo son io, e caro esser ti puote »
  fu mia risposta « se dimandi fama,
  ch'io metta il nome tuo tra l'altre note ».   93
Ed egli a me: « Del contrario ho brama;
  levati quinci e non mi dar più lagna,
  chè mal sai lusingar per questa lama! »   96
Allor lo presi per la cuticagna
  e dissi: « E' converrà che tu ti nomi,
  o che capel qua sù non ti rimagna ».   99
Ond'egli a me: « Perchè tu mi dischiomi
  nè ti dirò ch'io sia, nè mostrerolti
  se mille fiate in sul capo mi tomi ».   102
Io avea già i capelli in mano avvolti,
  e tratti li n'avea più d'una ciocca,
  latrando lui con gli occhi in giù raccolti,   105
quando un altro gridò: « Che hai tu, Bocca?
  Non ti basta sonar con le mascelle
  se tu non latri? Qual diavol ti tocca? »   108
« Omai » diss'io « non vo' che tu favelle,
  malvagio traditor, ch'a la tua onta,
  io porterò di te vere novelle ».   111
« Va via », rispose « e ciò che tu vuoi conta;
  ma non tacer, se tu di qua entro eschi,
  di quel ch'ebbe or così la lingua pronta.   114
Ei piange qui l'argento dei Francheschi;
  'Io vidi' potrai dir 'quel da Duera
  là dove i peccatori stanno freschi'.   117
Se fossi domandato altri chi v'era,
  tu hai da lato quel di Beccheria
  di cui segò Firenze la gorgiera.   120
Gianni del Soldanier credo che sia
  più là con Ganellone e Tebaldello
  che aprì Faenza quando si dormia ».   123
Noi eravam partiti già da ello,
  ch'io vidi due ghiacciati in una buca
  sì che l'un capo a l'altro era cappello.   126
E come il pan per fame si manduca
  così il sopran li denti a l'altro pose
  là 've il cervel s'aggiunge con la nuca.   129

'I *am* living, and wert thou one that seeks
   fame,' was my answer, 'such thou well might'st have,
   did I thy name to my other notes affix.'
And he to me: ' 'Tis the reverse I crave;
   so pester me no more, but get thee gone:
   ill know'st thou how to gloze in this concave!'
Whereat I seized him by the neck upon
   the nape and said: 'Thou shalt declare thy name
   or of the locks on this be left with none.'
Whence he to me: 'Shouldst tear out all of them,
   yet who I am I'll tell thee not, nor show,
   though at my head a thousand kicks thou aim.'
I had his hair coiled round my hand by now
   and, while he barked and kept his visage held
   still downward, had plucked out a tuft or so,
when 'Heh, what ails thee, Bocca?' another yell'd:
   'enough that with thy jaws thou clatterest: must
   thou bark too? By what devil art thou assail'd?'
'No matter now, curst traitor, if thou dost
   say nought,' said I: 'for I'll bear, to thy shame,
   true news of thee and where thou hast been thrust.'
'Be off,' he snarled, 'and what thou wilt, proclaim;
   but, get'st thou hence, fail not to mention he's
   here too from whom that last glib utterance came.
He rues French *argent* here, a traitor's fees:
   "him of Duera" thou canst say "there too
   I saw, where sinners are laid out to freeze."
Shouldst thou be asked who else was here in view,
   by thee thou hast the Beccería who met
   his end when Florence hewed his gorget through.
John of the Soldanieri, I think, is set
   next him, with Ganellón and Tebaldello,
   who, while men slept, opened Faënza's gate.'
When we had passed on, leaving him to bellow,
   I beheld two, so frozen in one pit
   that the one head was headpiece to its fellow.
And as the starved chew bread, the top one bit
   and savaged with his teeth the one below
   just where the brain and spinal marrow meet.

237

Non altrimenti Tideo si rose
  le tempie a Menalippo per disdegno,
  che quei faceva il teschio e l'altre cose.   132
« O. tu che mostri per sì bestial segno
  odio sovra colui che tu ti mangi,
  dimmi il perchè » diss'io « per tal convegno: 135
che se tu a ragion di lui ti piangi,
  sappiendo chi voi siete e la sua pecca,
  nel mondo suso ancora io te ne cangi,   138
se quella con ch'io parlo non si secca ».

CANTO 33

Lᴀ bocca sollevò dal fiero pasto
  quel peccator, forbendola ai capelli
  del capo ch'egli avea di retro guasto.   3
Poi cominciò: « Tu vuoi ch'io rinnovelli
  disperato dolor, che il cor mi preme,
  già pur pensando, pria ch'io ne favelli.   6
Ma se le mie parole esser déen seme
  che frutti infamia al traditor ch'io rodo,
  parlare e lacrimar vedrai insieme.   9
Io non so chi tu sei nè per che modo
  venuto sei qua giù; ma fiorentino
  mi sembri veramente quand'io t'odo.   12
Tu dei saper ch'io fui conte Ugolino,
  e questi è l'arcivescovo Ruggieri.
  Or ti dirò perch'io son tal vicino.   15
Che per l'effetto de' suoi mai pensieri,
  fidandomi di lui, io fossi preso
  e poscia morto, dir non è mestieri;   18
però quel che non puoi avere inteso,
  cioè come la morte mia fu cruda,
  udirai, e saprai s'ei m'ha offeso.   21
Breve pertugio dentro da la muda
  la qual per me ha il titol de la fame,
  e in che conviene ancor ch'altri si chiuda,   24

The temples of Menelippus even so
  did Tydeus gnaw for sheer despite, as he
  was doing the skull and parts that with it go.
'O thou who showest by such bestial glee
  hatred of him thou munchest, tell my why,'
  I said, 'on this agreement, that, so be
thou hast a just complaint against him, I,
  knowing who you are and *his* crime, when I thither
  go back, requite thee in the world on high,
if that with which I'm speaking does not wither.'

CANTO 33

Lifting his mouth up from the savage feast,
  that sinner wiped it on the hair of the head
  which in its hinder part he had laid waste.
And then 'Thou wilt that I renew' he said
  'a desperate grief, which but to think of, ere
  I speak of it, weighs on my heart like lead.
But if my words are to be seeds to bear
  fruits of ill fame unto this traitor whom
  I'm gnawing, I will with tears the truth declare.
I know not who thou art, nor how thou art come
  down here: but from thy speech it seems to me
  it must be Florence that thou hailest from.
Know, then—I was count Ugolín, and he
  is the archbishop Roger: now I'll tell
  thee why I am to him so neighbourly.
That I, who deemed his word reliable,
  was captured and then died—the effect of his
  ill schemes, why mention? for thou know'st it well.
But that which thou canst *not* have heard, that is,
  how cruel my death was, thou shalt hear, and then
  know if from him I've suffered injuries.
A narrow slit within the mew which men
  now call the "tower of famine" after me,
  and which as prison needs must serve again,

m'avea mostrato per lo suo forame
   più lune già, quand'io feci il mal sonno
   che del futuro mi squarciò il velame.   27
Questi pareva a me maestro e donno
   cacciando il lupo e i lupicini al monte
   per che i Pisan veder Lucca non ponno.   30
Con cagne magre, studiose e conte,
   Gualandi con Sismondi e con Lanfranchi
   s'avea messi dinanzi da la fronte.   33
In picciol corso mi pareano stanchi
   lo padre e i figli, e con l'acute scane
   mi parea lor veder fender li fianchi.   36
Quando fui desto innanzi la dimane
   pianger sentii fra il sonno i miei figliuoli
   ch'eran con meco, e domandar del pane.   39
Ben sei crudel se tu già non ti duoli
   pensando ciò che il mio cor s'annunziava:
   e se non piangi, di che pianger suoli?   42
Già eran desti, e l'ora s'appressava
   che il cibo ne soleva essere addotto,
   e per suo sogno ciascun dubitava;   45
e io sentii chiavar l'uscio di sotto
   a l'orribile torre, ond'io guardai
   nel viso a' miei figliuol sanza far motto.   48
Io non piangeva, sì dentro impietrai;
   piangevan elli, ed Anselmuccio mio
   disse: 'Tu guardi sì, padre: che hai?'   51
Però non lacrimai nè rispos'io
   tutto quel giorno nè la notte appresso,
   infin che l'altro sol nel mondo uscio.   54
Come un poco di raggio si fu messo
   nel doloroso carcere ed io scorsi
   per quattro visi il mio aspetto istesso,   57
ambo le man per lo dolor mi morsi;
   ed ei, pensando che il fessi per voglia
   di manicar, di subito levorsi   60
e disser: 'Padre, assai ci fia men doglia
   se tu mangi di noi: tu ne vestisti
   queste misere carni, e tu le spoglia'.   63

had let me already through its opening see
   many moons, when a nightmare for me drew
   abruptly aside the veil of things to be.
I saw this man as lord and master who
   was chasing wolf and wolf-cubs tow'rds the mount
   which shuts off Lucca from the Pisans' view.
With braches eager, lean and trained to hunt,
   Gualandi and Sismondi he had sent
   before him, with Lanfranchi, on in front.
I saw the father and the sons, forspent,
   being quickly overtaken as they fled,
   and then their flanks by the sharp tushes rent.
When I awoke before the dawn, with dread
   I heard my children moaning in their sleep
   (for they were with me) and demanding bread.
Right cruel thou art, if thou from tears canst keep,
   thinking on what my heart forbode: if thou
   weep'st not, at what, then, dost thou ever weep?
They'd woken, and the hour was nearing now
   when our next meal was due, and his dream stirr'd
   a doubt in each one, which he feared to show;
and at the foot of that grim tower I heard
   the door being nailed up; whence I gazed upon
   the faces of my sons but spake no word.
I wept not, so within I'd turned to stone:
   but *they* wept; and my darling Anselm cried:
   "What ails thee, father? Why look'st thou so wan?"
E'en at this tears I shed not, nor replied
   all that day, nor the following night, until
   the next sun rose upon the world outside.
When a faint ray of light began to steal
   into the woeful prison, and on four
   faces my own looks now were visible,
I bit both hands, my anguish was so sore;
   and they, who deemed I did it to relieve
   my hunger, straightway rising from the floor,
said: "Father, wouldst thou feed on us, we'd grieve
   much less: this sorry flesh in which we're clad
   thou gav'st us: now strip off what thou didst give."

Quetaimi allor per non farli più tristi;
  quel dì e l'altro stemmo tutti muti.
  Ahi, dura terra, perchè non t'apristi?   66
Poscia che fummo al quarto dì venuti,
  Gaddo mi si gettò disteso ai piedi
  dicendo: 'Padre mio, chè non m'aiuti?'   69
Quivi morì. E come tu mi vedi
  vid'io cascar li tre ad uno ad uno
  tra il quinto dì e il sesto, ond'io mi diedi   72
già cieco, a brancolar sopra ciascuno,
  e due dì li chiamai poi che fur morti:
  poscia più che il dolor potè il digiuno».   75
Quand'ebbe detto ciò, con gli occhi torti,
  riprese il teschio misero coi denti,
  che furo all'osso come d'un can forti.   78
Ahi Pisa, vituperio de le genti
  del bel paese là dove il sì suona,
  poi che i vicini a te punir son lenti,   81
movasi la Capraia e la Gorgona,
  e faccian siepe ad Arno in su la foce
  sì ch'elli annieghi in te ogni persona.   84
Che se il conte Ugolino aveva voce
  d'aver tradita te de le castella,
  non dovei tu i figliuoi porre a tal croce.   87
Innocenti facea l'età novella,
  novella Tebe, Uguccione e il Brigata
  e gli altri due che il canto suso appella.   90
Noi passammo oltre, là 've la gelata
  ruvidamente un'altra gente fascia
  non volta in giù, ma tutta riversata.   93
Lo pianto stesso lì pianger non lascia,
  e il duol, che trova in su gli occhi rintoppo,
  si volge in dietro a far crescer l'ambascia;   96
chè le lacrime prime fanno groppo,
  e sì come visiere di cristallo
  riempion sotto il ciglio tutto il coppo.   99
Ed avvegna che sì come d'un callo
  per la freddura ciascun sentimento
  cessato avesse del mio viso stallo,   102

I calmed me then, not to make them more sad:
  both that day and the next we all sat dumb:
  why opened not the hard earth? Would it had!
Gaddo, when to the fourth day we were come,
  flung himself full length at my feet with the cry:
  "My father, food—why dost not give me some?",
and there died; then, as *thou* seest *me*, did I
  between the fifth and sixth day even so
  see the three, one by one, fall down and die.
I crawled among them, groping, being now
  blind, and two days kept calling them though dead:
  then fasting was more powerful than woe.'
Ceasing, he rolled his eyes and again made
  his teeth, strong as a dog's upon the bone,
  meet in the wretched skull on which he fed.
Ah, Pisa, execrated up and down
  the lovely country where the 'sì' doth sound,
  since of thy neighbours punish thee will none,
well, were Capraia and Gorgona found
  to have moved and so blocked up the Arno's mouth,
  that every person in thee had been drown'd!
For if Count Ugolino had in truth
  betrayed thy castles, even as men say,
  why torture thus his children without ruth?
Their tender age, thou new Thebes, proved that they
  were innocent, Brigata and little Hugh
  and those two named already in my lay.
We passed on further, where another crew,
  frozen hard in, though not face-downward this,
  but lying completely upturned, met our view.
The weeping's self there makes the weeping cease,
  and, finding on the eyes a barrier, woe,
  turn'd inward, causes anguish to increase;
for the first tears, congealing, thereby grow
  into a block and, like a visor of glass,
  fill all the hollow up beneath the eyebrow.
And though, as in a callus, it came to pass
  that in my face sensation could not find,
  owing to the cold, the abode it elsewise has,

già mi parea sentire alquanto vento;
 per ch'io: « Maestro mio, questo chi move?
 non è qua giù ogni vapore spento? »   105
Ed egli a me: « Avaccio sarai dove
 di ciò ti farà l'occhio la risposta,
 veggendo la cagion che il fiato piove ».   108
E un dei tristi de la fredda crosta
 gridò a noi: « O anime crudeli
 tanto che data v'è l'ultima posta,   111
levatemi dal viso i duri veli,
 sì ch'io sfoghi il duol che il cor m'impregna
 un poco, pria che il pianto si raggeli ».   114
Per ch'io a lui: « Se vuoi ch'io ti sovvegna,
 dimmi chi sei, e s'io non ti disbrigo
 al fondo de la ghiaccia ir mi convegna ».   117
Rispose dunque: « Io son frate Alberigo;
 io son quel da le frutta del mal orto,
 che qui riprendo dattero per figo ».   120
« Oh » diss'io lui « or sei tu ancor morto? »
 Ed egli a me: « Come il mio corpo stea
 nel mondo sù, nulla scienza porto.   123
Cotal vantaggio ha questa Tolomea,
 che spesse volte l'anima ci cade
 innanzi che Atropòs mossa le dea.   126
E perchè tu più volentier mi rade
 le invetriate lacrime dal volto,
 sappi che tosto che l'anima trade   129
come fec'io, il corpo suo l'è tolto
 da un demonio, che poscia il governa
 mentre che il tempo suo tutto sia volto.   132
Ella ruina in sì fatta cisterna;
 e forse pare ancor lo corpo suso
 de l'ombra che di qua dietro mi verna.   135
Tu il dei saper, se tu vien pur mo giuso:
 egli è ser Branca d'Oria, e son più anni
 poscia passati ch'ei fu sì racchiuso ».   138
« Io credo » dissi lui « che tu m'inganni:
 chè Branca d'Oria non morì unquanche,
 e mangia, e bee, e dorme, e veste panni ».   141

already, so meseemed, I felt some wind;
  whence I: 'Master, who causes this? To an end
  come not, down here, vapours of every kind?'
And he to me: 'Quite soon thou'lt have attain'd
  to a place where answer thee shall thine own eye,
  by seeing the source from which the blast is rain'd.'
And cried to us one wretch encrusted by
  the frost: 'O souls so cruel, that 'tis Hell's
  last dungeon ye've been given wherein to lie,
lift from my countenance the hardened veils,
  that somewhat, ere the tears re-freeze, I so
  may vent the grief with which my bosom swells.'
And I: 'Wouldst have me aid thee, let me know
  who thou art: and, if then I free thee not,
  to the bottom of the ice may I have to go.'
'I'm he of the fruits of the bad orchard-plot,
  the friar, Alberigo,' he then said;
  'to get back dates for figs is here my lot.'
'Oh!' I exclaimed, 'then, art thou already dead?'
  And he to me: 'In sooth I do not know
  how fares my body in the world o'erhead.
This Ptolomea is advantaged so,
  that oftentimes a soul falls hither, ere
  by Atropos 'tis given the sign to go.
And so that thou more willingly mayst clear
  my face of the glazed tear-drops, thou shalt weet
  that the instant any soul has turned betrayer,
like as mine did, its body is snatched from it
  by a fiend, who thenceforth rules it, he alone,
  until its cycle of years be quite complete.
Itself to a tank like this falls headlong down;
  and, haply, on earth one still the body sees
  of the shade wintering here behind my own.
Thou must know, if but just come down, for he's
  Ser Branca d'Oria: years are come and gone,
  since he was thus shut up down here to freeze.'
'I think,' said I, 'thou seek'st to impose upon
  me now; for Branca d'Oria died not e'er,
  but eats and drinks and sleeps and puts clothes on.'

« Nel fosso sù » diss'ei « dei Malebranche,
  là dove bolle la tenace pece,
  non era giunto ancora Michel Zanche,   144
che questi lasciò un diavolo in sua vece
  nel corpo suo, ed un suo prossimano
  che il tradimento insieme con lui fece.   147
Ma distendi oggimai in qua la mano:
  aprimi gli occhi ». E io non glieli apersi,
  e cortesia fu a lui esser villano.   150
Ahi Genovesi, uomini diversi
  d'ogni costume e pien d'ogni magagna,
  perchè non siete voi del mondo spersi?   153
Chè col peggiore spirto di Romagna
  trovai di voi un tal, che per sua opra
  in anima in Cocito già si bagna,   156
ed in corpo par vivo ancor di sopra.

CANTO 34

« *V*exilla regis prodeunt Inferni
  verso di noi; però dinanzi mira »
  disse il maestro mio « se tu il discerni ».   3
Come quando una grossa nebbia spira
  o quando l'emisperio nostro annotta,
  par di lungi un molin che il vento gira,   6
veder mi parve un tal dificio allotta;
  poi per lo vento mi ristrinsi retro
  al duca mio, chè non v'era altra grotta.   9
Già era, e con paura il metto in metro,
  là dove l'ombre tutte eran coperte,
  e trasparien come festuca in vetro.   12
Altre sono a giacere; altre stanno erte,
  quella col capo e quella con le piante;
  altra, com'arco, il volto ai piè rinverte.   15
Quando noi fummo fatti tanto avante
  che al mio maestro piacque di mostrarmi
  la creatura ch'ebbe il bel sembiante,   18

'The trench of the Evilclaws,' he answered, 'where
   the viscous tar is boiling, had as yet
   not seen the arrival of Michael Zanche there,
when this man left his body and therein let
   a devil replace him, as did likewise he,
   his kinsman and in treachery his mate.
But now reach out thy hand here; set thou free
   these eyes of mine.' And free them I did not;
   and churlishness to him was courtesy.
Ah, men of Genoa, ever prone to scout
   good customs, ever to corrupt ones bound,
   why from the world are ye not driven out?
For with Romagna's vilest spirit I found
   one of you, for his deeds so void of worth,
   that, in soul long since in Cocytus drown'd,
he appears in body still alive on earth.

CANTO 34

'*Vexilla regis prodeunt inferni*
   tow'rd *us*,' my lord said: 'look, then, if avails
   thine eye to see him and let it forward journey.'
As through the gloom, when a dense fog exhales
   or when our hemisphere is darkling, men
   discern far off a mill with turning sails;
meseemed 'twas some such structure I saw then;
   and, for the wind, behind my leader I
   shrank back, for there was else no lee in ken.
By now (and this with fear I versify)
   I was where, like to straws seen through a sheet
   of glass, the shades were covered totally.
Some lay recumbent, and on some I lit,
   this on its head, that with an upright stance,
   another, like a bow, bent face to feet.
My master, when he deemed that our advance
   permitted him to show me, clearly view'd,
   the creature of the once fair countenance,

dinanzi mi si tolse e fe' restarmi,
« Ecco Dite » dicendo « ed ecco il loco
ove convien che di fortezza t'armi ».   21

Com'io divenni allor gelato e fioco
no! dimandar, lettor, ch'io non lo scrivo,
però ch'ogni parlar sarebbe poco.   24

Io non morii e non rimasi vivo;
pensa oggimai per te, s'hai fior d'ingegno,
qual io divenni d'uno e d'altro privo.   27

Lo imperador del doloroso regno
da mezzo il petto uscìa fuor de la ghiaccia;
e più con un gigante io mi convègno   30

che i giganti non fan con le sue braccia:
vedi oggimai quant'esser dee quel tutto
che a cosiffatta parte si confaccia.   33

S'ei fu sì bello com'egli è or brutto,
e contro il suo fattore alzò le ciglia,
ben dee da lui procedere ogni lutto.   36

Oh quanto parve a me gran meraviglia
quand'io vidi, tre facce a la sua testa!
L'una dinanzi, e quella era vermiglia;   39

de l'altre due che s'aggiugneano a questa
sovr'esso il mezzo di ciascuna spalla,
e sè giugneano al loco de la cresta,   42

la destra mi parea tra bianca e gialla;
la sinistra a vedere era tal quali
vegnon di là onde il Nilo s'avvalla.   45

Sotto ciascun uscivan due grand'ali
quanto si conveniva a tanto uccello:
vele di mar non vid'io mai cotali.   48

Non avean penne ma di vipistrello
era lor modo; e quelle svolazzava,
sì che tre venti si movean da ello.   51

Quindi Cocito tutto s'aggelava;
con sei occhi piangeva, e per tre menti
gocciava il pianto e sanguinosa bava.   54

Da ogni bocca dirompea coi denti
un peccatore, a guisa di maciulla,
sì che tre ne facea così dolenti.   57

moved away from in front of me, then stood
    beside me and said: 'Lo Dis, and lo the place
    where thou must arm thyself with fortitude.'
How frozen I grew, how weak, through fearfulness,
    ask me not, Reader: wherefore should I strive
    to write what words are powerless to express?
I neither died not yet remained alive:
    hast thou a grain of sense, picture me now,
    whom fear could both of death and life deprive.
The imperial monarch of the realm of woe
    stood forth at midbreast from the ice; and me,
    in size, a giant doth not more outgo
than *his* arms do the giants: thus thou'lt see
    now, how enormous needs must be that whole
    which with a part so fashioned would agree.
If he was once fair, as he now is foul,
    and scorned the Being by whom he had been made,
    well may from him proceed all human dole.
And oh, my astonishment, when on his head
    I saw no fewer than three faces! one
    in front, and that was of vermilion-red;
to this face the two others were joined on
    just midway above 'twixt where begins and ends
    each shoulder, and all three joined at the crown.
The right was coloured of the tint which blends
    yellow with white; the left, of that we find
    in such as come from whence the Nile descends.
Beneath each two great wings came out, design'd
    to fit such a colossal bird: I ne'er
    set eyes on sails at sea of the like kind.
They had no feathers, but in fashion were
    like to a bat's: and these he flapped about,
    so that from him went forth three currents of air,
which caused Cocytus to congeal throughout.
    With six eyes wept he, and o'er three chins beneath
    dripped tears, with slaver, gout on bloody gout.
In each mouth he was bruising with his teeth
    a sinner, as with a brake, and torturer
    he was thuswise of three of them therewith.

A quel dinanzi il mordere era nulla
 verso il graffiar, che talvolta la schiena
 rimanea de la pelle tutta brulla.   60
« Quell'anima là sù ch'ha maggior pena »
 disse il maestro « è Giuda Scariotto,
 che il capo ha dentro e fuor le gambe mena.   63
De gli altri due ch'hanno il capo di sotto,
 quel che pende dal nero ceffo è Bruto:
 vedi come si storce e non fa motto;   66
e l'altro è Cassio che par sì membruto.
 Ma la notte risurge, ed oramai
 è da partir, chè tutto avem veduto ».   69
Come a lui piacque, il collo gli avvinghiai;
 ed ei prese di tempo e loco poste,
 e quando l'ali furo aperte assai,   72
appigliò sè a le vellute coste;
 di vello in vello giù discese poscia
 tra il folto pelo e le gelate croste.   75
Quando noi fummo là dove la coscia
 si volge appunto in sul grosso de l'anche,
 lo duca, con fatica e con angoscia,   78
volse la testa ov'egli avea le zanche
 ed aggrappossi al pel com'uom che sale,
 sì che in Inferno io credea tornar anche.   81
« Attienti ben, chè per cotali scale »
 disse il maestro ansando com'uom lasso
 « conviensi dipartir da tanto male ».   84
Poi uscì fuor per lo foro d'un sasso
 e pose me in su l'orlo a sedere;
 appresso porse a me l'accorto passo.   87
Io levai gli occhi, e credetti vedere
 Lucifero com'io l'avea lasciato,
 e vidili le gambe in sù tenere;   90
e s'io divenni allora travagliato,
 la gente grossa il pensi, che non vede
 qual è quel punto ch'io avea passato.   93
« Levati sù », disse il maestro « in piede:
 la via è lunga e il cammino è malvagio,
 e già il Sole a mezza terza riede ».   96

For him in front the chewing was, in compare,
  nought to the clawing, which sometimes scarified
  his back so, that of skin it was stripped bare.
'The soul up there worst punished,' said my guide,
  'is Judas called Iscariot, who kicks
  his legs without, and has his head inside.
Of the other two, who hang head-downward, fix
  thine eye on him i' the black snout—Brutus, he!
  Look how he writhes, but neither moans nor speaks;
and the other's Cassius, limbed so stalwartly.
  But night is re-ascending, and we now
  must go, for we've seen all there is to see.'
I clasped him round the neck, he showing me how;
  and, having chosen time and place with care,
  when the wings opened wide enough to allow
his clutching of the shaggy flanks, he there
  and then from shag to shag descended by
  this means 'twixt frozen crusts and matted hair.
When we were at the exact point where the thigh
  turns itself, on the thick of the haunch, with strain
  and stress my leader brought round gradually
his head to where Dis had his shanks, and then
  clutched at the hair like one who's climbing, so
  that back to Hell I thought we turned again.
'Hold fast,' the master said, panting as though
  forspent, 'for 'tis by stairs like these that we
  must part from evil and such utter woe.'
Then, issuing where a rock was tunnelled, me
  he placed upon its edge to sit; anon
  himself to where I was stepped cautiously.
I raised my eyes and thought to look upon
  Lucifer standing as I'd seen him last,
  and saw him, legs in air, set upside down.
If this perplexed me and I stared aghast,
  judge they, to whose dull wits it does not pierce
  what point it is which I had just then pass'd.
'Up' said my master 'on thy feet: for there's
  a long way yet to go, and rough the road,
  and the Sun's back already at mid-tierce.'

Non era caminata di palagio
là 'v'eravam, ma natural burella
che avea mal suolo e di lume disagio.   99
« Prima ch'io de l'abisso mi divella,
maestro mio » diss'io quando fui dritto
« a trarmi d'erro un poco mi favella: 102
ov'è la ghiaccia? e questi com'è fitto
sì sottosopra? e come in sì poc'ora
da sera a mane ha fatto il Sol tragitto? »   105
Ed egli a me: « Tu imagini ancora
d'esser di là dal centro, ov'io mi presi
al pel del vermo reo che il mondo fora.   108
Di là fosti cotanto quant'io scesi;
quando mi volsi, tu passasti il punto
al qual si traggon d'ogni parte i pesi.   111
E sei or sotto l'emisperio giunto
ch'è opposto a quel che la gran secca
coperchia, e sotto il cui colmo consunto   114
fu l'uom che nacque e visse sanza pecca.
Tu hai li piedi in su picciola spera
che l'altra faccia fa de la Giudecca.   117
Qui è da man quando di là è sera;
e questi che ne fe' scala col pelo
fitto è ancora sì come prima era.   120
Da questa parte cadde giù dal cielo;
e la terra, che pria di qua si sporse,
per paura di lui fe' dei mar velo   123
e venne a l'emisperio nostro; e forse
per fuggir lui lasciò qui 'l loco voto
quella che appar di qua, e sù ricorse ».   126
Loco è là giù da Belzebù remoto
tanto quanto la tomba si distende,
che non per vista, ma per suono è noto   129
d'un ruscelletto che quivi discende
per la buca d'un sasso, ch'egli ha roso
col corso ch'egli avvolge e poco pende.   132
Lo duca e io per quel cammino ascoso
entrammo, a ritornar nel chiaro mondo;
e sanza cura aver d'alcun riposo   135

It was no palace-chamber where we stood:
　　call it a natural dungeon—scarce a ray
　　of light, the floor to tread on far from good.
'Ere from the abyss I pluck myself away,
　　Master,' when risen to my feet I said,
　　'to clear me of error spare me a word, I pray:
where is the ice? and he, how on his head
　　is he thus fixed? and how in one short hour
　　has the Sun on from eve to morning sped?'
And he to me: 'Thou deem'st thou'rt, as before,
　　yonside the centre, where I grasped the hair
　　of the evil worm which through the world doth bore.
So long as I descended thou wast there;
　　but when I turned myself, thou passedst then
　　the point to which weights draw from everywhere.
Hence, 'neath the counter-hemisphere, 'tis plain,
　　thou now art, and not that whose spans o'ervault
　　the great dry land and 'neath whose zenith was slain
the Man born, as he lived, devoid of fault:
　　'tis on the small sphere, forming the other face
　　of the Judecca, that thy feet now halt.
Here it is morn, when there eve: and the place
　　of him whose hair as ladder served us well
　　he's still, as erstwhile, fixed in, motionless.
On this side headlong out of heav'n he fell;
　　and the land, then on this side prominent,
　　for fear of him made of the sea a veil,
and came to our hemisphere; and, maybe, bent
　　on fleeing from him, that now on this side found
　　left here a void and rushing upward went.'
There is a place down there as far beyond
　　Belzebub stretching as his tomb extends,
　　discovered, not by sight, but by the sound
of a small rivulet which there descends
　　thro' a channel in the rock where it has traced
　　the course down which it gently flows and bends.
My guide and I took that hidd'n way in quest
　　of the bright world, nor, after entering
　　upon it, cared we to seek any rest.

salimmo sù, ei primo ed io secondo,
   tanto ch'io vidi de le cose belle
   che porta il ciel, per un pertugio tondo;   138
e quindi uscimmo a riveder le stelle.

We mounted up, he first, I following,
  till, of the lovely things that heaven bears
  I beheld some, through a round opening;
and thence we emerged to re-behold the stars.

PURGATORY

*

*'Quisque suos patimur manis, exinde per amplum
mittimur Elysium et pauci laeta arva tenemus;
donec longa dies perfecto temporis orbe
concretam exemit labem, purumque relinquit
aetherium sensum atque aurai simplicis ignem.'*

*

PURGATORIO

CANTO 1

Per correr miglior acque alza le vele
    omai la navicella del mio ingegno,
    che lascia dietro a sè mar sì crudele;   3
e canterò di quel secondo regno
    dove l'umano spirito si purga
    e di salire al ciel diventa degno.   6
Ma qui la morta poesì risurga,
    o sante Muse, poi che vostro sono,
    e qui Calliopè alquanto surga   9
seguitando il mio canto con quel suono
    di cui le Piche misere sentiro
    lo colpo tal, che disperar perdono.   12
Dolce color d'oriental zaffiro
    che s'accoglieva nel sereno aspetto
    del mezzo, puro infino al primo giro,   15
a gli occhi miei ricominciò diletto
    tosto ch'io uscii fuor de l'aura morta
    che m'avea contristati gli occhi e il petto.   18
Lo bel pianeta che ad amar conforta
    faceva tutto rider l'oriente,
    velando i Pesci, ch'erano in sua scorta.   21
Io mi volsi a man destra e posi mente
    a l'altro polo, e vidi quattro stelle
    non viste mai fuor che a la prima gente.   24
Goder pareva il ciel di lor fiammelle:
    o settentrional vedovo sito,
    poi che privato sei di mirar quelle!   27
Com'io dal loro sguardo fui partito,
    un poco me volgendo a l'altro polo,
    là onde il Carro già era sparito,   30

PURGATORY

CANTO 1

To scud o'er better waters hoisteth sail
   henceforth the little vessel of my wit,
   which leaves behind her now a sea so fell;
and of that second realm my song will treat,
   which is the human spirit's purifier
   and to ascend to heaven makes it fit.
But here with life dead poesy re-inspire,
   O holy Muses, since to you I'm bound;
   and here Calliope rise somewhat higher,
swelling my song with that full-throated sound
   which smote the wretched Pies and made them own
   their hope of pardon would be fruitless found.
Sweet colour, the translucent tint and tone
   of orient sapphire, gathering high in heaven
   serene, and pure down to the primal zone,
made using of my eyes a joy re-given,
   soon as I issued forth from that dead air
   against whose gloom my eyes and breast had striven.
The radiant planet, love's own comforter,
   was setting all a-laugh the eastern sky,
   veiling the Fishes, that escorted her.
I turned to the right and bent my mind thereby
   on the other pole, and saw four stars, the same
   as, save the first folk, none did e'er espy.
The sky seemed revelling in their brilliant flame:
   O widowed northern clime, bereft indeed,
   in that thou art denied the sight of them!
After mine eyes had ceased thereon to feed,
   turning awhile to the other pole, where shone
   the Wain no more, which 'neath it now lay hid,

vidi presso di me un veglio solo,
  degno di tanta reverenza in vista
  che più non dee a padre alcun figliuolo.   33

Lunga la barba e di pel bianco mista
  portava, a' suoi capelli simigliante,
  de' quai cadeva al petto doppia lista.   36

Li raggi de le quattro luci sante
  fregiavan sì la sua faccia di lume,
  ch'io 'l vedea come il Sol fosse davante.   39

« Chi siete voi, che contro al cieco fiume
  fuggita avete la prigione eterna? »
  diss'ei movendo quelle oneste piume.   42

« Chi v'ha guidati? o che vi fu lucerna
  uscendo fuor de la profonda notte
  che sempre nera fa la valle inferna?   45

Son le leggi d'abisso così rotte?
  o è mutato in ciel novo consiglio,
  che, dannati, venite a le mie grotte? »   48

Lo duca mio allor mi diè di piglio,
  e con parole e con mani e con cenni
  reverenti mi fe' le gambe e il ciglio.   51

Poscia rispose lui: « Da me non venni:
  donna scese dal ciel, per li cui prieghi
  de la mia compagnia costui sovvenni.   54

Ma da che è tuo voler che più si spieghi
  di nostra condizion com'ella è vera,
  esser non puote il mio che a te si nieghi.   57

Questi non vide mai l'ultima sera,
  ma per la sua follia le fu sì presso
  che molto poco tempo a volger era.   60

Sì com'io dissi, fui mandato ad esso
  per lui campare, e non v'era altra via
  che questa per la quale io mi son messo.   63

Mostrata ho lui tutta la gente ria,
  e ora intendo mostrar quelli spirti
  che purgan sè sotto la tua balìa.   66

Com'io l'ho tratto, saria lungo a dirti;
  da l'alto scende virtù che m'aiuta
  conducerlo a vederti ed a udirti.   69

I saw beside me an Ancient, all alone,
   worthy of so much reverence in his mien,
   that more owes not to father any son.
Long and with white hairs mingled therewithin
   his beard was, to his tresses like, and these
   in two strips falling to his breast were seen.
The rays of the four holy luminaries
   so lighted him, that as a face would look
   having the Sun before it, so did his.
'What men are ye, that breasting the blind brook
   have fled the eternal prison-house?' Thus fell
   his words, as he his goodly plumage shook.
'What guide, or what to lamp you, could avail,
   as ye came forth from where the deep night is,
   which evermore makes black the pit of hell?
Are the laws broken that control the abyss?
   or some new counsel changed in heaven to allow
   you, that are damned, to approach my cavities?'
My leader then took hold of me and now
   his words, now hands, now gestures made it clear
   he would to reverence bend my legs and brow.
He answered: 'Of myself I came not here:
   from heaven came down a lady, who beside
   this man besought me as saviour to draw near.
But since 'tis *thy* will to have more supplied
   touching our state, how it truly came to pass,
   mine cannot be, that thou shouldst be denied.
Unto his life's last eve this man that has
   ne'er seen it, yet thro' his folly came so nigh,
   that to turn back brief time indeed there was.
So, even as I have said, despatched was I
   to rescue him, nor was there other way
   than this alone which I have travelled by.
Shown him I have, in their complete array,
   the guilty, and now plan that he shall see
   those spirits who purge themselves beneath thy sway.
Of how I've brought him, long the tale would be;
   power from on high its aid on me bestows
   to guide him to the seeing and hearing thee.

Or ti piaccia gradir la sua venuta:
  libertà va cercando, ch'è sì cara
  come sa chi per lei vita rifiuta.   72
Tu il sai, che non ti fu per lei amara
  in Utica la morte, ove lasciasti
  la vesta che al gran dì sarà sì chiara.   75
Non son gli editti eterni per noi guasti;
  chè questi vive, e Minòs me non lega;
  ma son del cerchio ove son gli occhi casti   78
di Marzia tua, che in vista ancor ti prega,
  o santo petto, che per tua la tegni:
  per lo suo amore adunque a noi ti piega: 81
lasciane andar per li tuoi sette regni;
  grazie riporterò di te a lei,
  se d'esser mentovato là giù degni ».   84
« Marzia piacque tanto a gli occhi miei
  mentre ch'io fui di là » diss'egli allora
  « che quante grazie volle da me, fei.   87
Or che di là dal mal fiume dimora,
  più mover non mi può per quella legge,
  che fatta fu quando me n'uscii fora.   90
Ma se donna del ciel ti move e regge,
  come tu di', non c'è mestier lusinghe:
  bastiti ben che per lei mi richiegge.   93
Va dunque, e fa che tu costui ricinghe
  d'un giunco schietto, e che gli lavi il viso
  sì ch'ogni sucidume quindi stinghe;   96
chè non si converria l'occhio sorpriso
  d'alcuna nebbia, andar dinanzi al primo
  ministro, ch'è di quei di Paradiso.   99
Questa isoletta intorno ad imo ad imo,
  là giù colà dove la batte l'onda,
  porta dei giunchi sovra il molle limo: 102
null'altra pianta che facesse fronda
  o indurasse, vi puote aver vita,
  però che a le percosse non seconda.   105
Poscia non sia di qua vostra reddita:
  lo Sol vi mostrerà, che surge omai,
  prendere il monte a più lieve salita ».   108

Now please thee grace his coming: for he goes
 in search of Liberty, and that how dear,
 he who renounces life for her well knows.
Thou know'st it, who for her sake didst not fear
 in Utica death's sting nor to discard
 the robe which shall at doomsday shine so clear.
For us the eternal edicts are not marred;
 since this man lives, nor me doth Minos bind:
 but mine's the zone where by their chaste regard
thy Marcia's eyes, O holy breast, thou'dst find
 still praying thee to deem her thine again:
 for *her* love's sake, then, be to us inclined,
Let us go through thy seven kingdoms; then
 thanks will I bear back, touching thee, to her,
 if to be mentioned there below thou deign.'
'Marcia so pleased my eyes, while over there
 I sojourned,' he replied, 'that all she would
 that I should do, I did without demur.
Now that she dwells beyond the evil flood,
 the law laid down, when forth from there I came,
 ordains she may no longer sway my mood.
But if that, as thou say'st, a heavenly dame
 moves and directs thee, flattery may be spared:
 suffice it that thou ask me in her name.
Go, then, and be it thy task this man to gird
 with a smooth rush and bathe his face, thuswise
 renewing what all that soils it hath impaired.
For 'twere unseemly aught should cloud his eyes
 the first time that a minister he views
 numbered with those who serve in Paradise.
This islet, where its lowest verges lose
 their vantage o'er the breakers, bears a ring
 of rushes bedded in the muddy ooze.
No other plant that grows a stalk whence spring
 leaves or that hardens, can in that place live,
 because it yields not to the buffeting.
Then do not hitherward your steps retrieve;
 the rising Sun will show you where a way is
 which to the mount will easier access give.'

Così sparì: ed io sù mi levai
    sanza parlare, e tutto mi ritrassi
    al duca mio, e gli occhi a lui drizzai.   111

Ei cominciò: « Seguisci li miei passi:
    volgiamci indietro, chè di qua dichina
    questa pianura a' suoi termini bassi ».   114

L'alba vinceva l'ora mattutina
    che fuggía innanzi, sì che di lontano
    conobbi il tremolar de la marina.   117

Noi andavam per lo solingo piano
    com'uom che torna a la perduta strada,
    che infino ad essa li par d'ire invano.   120

Quando noi fummo là 've la rugiada
    pugna col Sole, e, per essere in parte
    ove adorezza, poco si dirada,   123

ambo le mani in su l'erbetta sparte
    soavemente il mio maestro pose;
    ond'io, che fui accorto di su' arte,   126

porsi ver lui le guance lacrimose;
    ivi mi fece tutto discoperto
    quel color che l'Inferno mi nascose.   129

Venimmo poi in sul lito diserto,
    che mai non vide navigar su' acque
    uomo che di tornar sia poscia esperto.   132

Quivi mi cinse sì com'altrui piacque:
    oh maraviglia! chè qual egli scelse
    l'umile pianta, cotal si rinacque   135

subitamente là onde l'avelse.

CANTO 2

Già era il Sole a l'orizzonte giunto
    lo cui meridian cerchio coperchia
    Ierusalem col suo più alto punto,   3

e la Notte, che opposta a lui cerchia,
    uscìa di Gange fuor con le bilance
    che le caggion di man quando soperchia;   6

He vanished; and nought saying, did I upraise
  and draw me backward, wholly intent upon
  my leader, and to him direct my gaze.
And he began: 'Follow me close, my son:
  let us turn back, for this way steadily
  down doth the plain to its low limits run.'
The matin hour had now begun to flee
  before the advancing dawn, and far away
  I recognized the shimmering of the sea.
We paced the lonely level, like as they
  who, the road lost, go seeking it anew
  and, till they find it, deem they vainly stray.
As soon as we had come to where the dew
  fought with the Sun, since it but slowly there
  evaporated where a cool air blew,
both of his hands outspread with gentle care
  on the fresh herbage did my master place;
  whence I, of his contrivance well aware,
held up to him my tear-bedrabbled face;
  unto my cheeks did he thus quite restore
  that colour of which Hell had left no trace.
Then came we down upon the desert shore,
  which never yet saw mariner so skilled
  as to return who sailed its waters o'er.
There did he gird me as another willed:
  oh marvel! such, as by his hand 'twas torn
  from earth, in that same place which it had filled
the humble plant was instantly re-born.

CANTO 2

By now the Sun was touching with his flame
  the horizon whose meridian, where its height
  is greatest, overhangs Jerusalem;
and circling o'er against him, issued Night
  from Ganges, Scales in hand—the Scales she would
  let fall, what time she gains on him in might;

sì che le bianche e le vermiglie guance,
  là dov'io era, de la bella Aurora,
  per troppa etate divenivan rance.   9
Noi eravam lunghesso il mare ancora.
  come gente che pensa a suo cammino,
  che va col cuore e col corpo dimora;   12
ed ecco, qual, sul presso del mattino,
  per li grossi vapor Marte rosseggia
  giù nel ponente sovra il suol marino,   15
cotal m'apparve, s'io ancor lo veggia,
  un lume per lo mar venir sì ratto
  che il mover suo nessun volar pareggia;   18
dal qual com'io un poco ebbi ritratto
  l'occhio per domandar lo duca mio,
  rividil più lucente e maggior fatto.   21
Poi d'ogni lato ad esso m'appario
  un non sapea che bianco, e di sotto
  a poco a poco un altro a lui uscìo.   24
Lo mio maestro ancor non fece motto
  mentre che i primi bianchi apparser ali;
  allor, che ben conobbe il galeotto,   27
gridò: « Fa, fa che le ginocchia cali:
  ecco l'angel di Dio; piega le mani:
  omai vedrai di sì fatti officiali.   30
Vedi che sdegna gli argomenti umani,
  sì che remo non vuol nè altro velo
  che l'ali sue tra liti sì lontani.   33
Vedi come l'ha dritte verso il cielo
  trattando l'aere con l'eterne penne,
  che non si mutan come mortal pelo ».   36
Poi, come più e più verso noi venne
  l'uccel divino, più chiaro appariva,
  per che l'occhio da presso nol sostenne   39
ma chinail giuso; e quei sen venne a riva
  con un vasello snelletto e leggiero
  tanto che l'acqua nulla ne inghiottiva.   42
Da poppa stava il celestial nocchiero,
  tal che parea beato per iscripto;
  e più di cento spirti entro sediero.   45

so that, as seen from there, where I then stood,
   the fair Aurora's cheeks, all white and red,
   thro' excess of age were growing orange-hued.
We by the margin of the sea yet stay'd,
   like folk who, while their road they ponder o'er,
   linger in body, in heart have onward sped.
And lo! as through thick vapours, just before
   the daybreak, Mars burns with a ruddy glow
   down in the west above the ocean-floor,
such appeared—may I once more see it so!—
   a light that o'er the sea came on: nor flies
   aught that for speed can be compared thereto.
From which when I'd an instant turned my eyes
   to question him who led me, I again
   saw it, now brighter and increased in size.
On either side of it I noticed then
   a something white, and underneath it out
   loomed by degrees another no less plain.
My master all this time had uttered nought,
   until the first white objects showed as wings:
   then, when he knew the pilot past all doubt,
'Bend, bend thy knees,' he cried: 'God hither brings
   his angel: fold thy hands: so fashioned are
   all here appointed to such ministerings.
See how he scorns all man-invented gear,
   so that he wills no oar nor other sail
   than his own pinions between shores so far,
See how he lifts them heavenward and how well
   the air do those eternal feathers ply,
   which unlike mortal hair change not nor fail.'
Then as drew nigh to us and still more nigh
   the bird of God, he yet more brightly shone,
   so that mine eyes endured him not close by,
but down I bent them; he to shore came on
   with a ship, which so swiftly and lightly hied,
   that of its bulk the water swallowed none.
Like one whose bliss by his look seemed ratified,
   on the poop stood the heavenly mariner;
   and more than a hundred spirits sat inside.

In exitu Israel de Aegypto,
   cantavan tutti insieme ad una voce,
   con quanto di quel salmo è poscia scripto.   48
Poi fece il segno lor di santa croce,
   ond'ei si gittar tutti in su la spiaggia;
   ed ei sen gì come venne veloce.   51
La turba che rimase lì, selvaggia
   parea del loco, rimirando intorno
   come colui che nove cose assaggia.   54
Da tutte parti saettava il giorno
   lo Sol, che avea con le saette conte
   di mezzo il ciel cacciato Capricorno,   57
quando la nova gente alzò la fronte
   ver noi dicendo a noi: « Se voi sapete,
   mostratene la via di gire al monte ».   60
E Virgilio rispose: « Voi credete
   forse che siamo esperti d'esto loco;
   ma noi siam peregrin come voi siete.   63
Dianzi venimmo, innanzi a voi un poco,
   per altra via, che fu sì aspra e forte,
   che lo salire omai ne parrà gioco ».   66
L'anime che si fur di me accorte,
   per lo spirare, ch'io era ancor vivo,
   maravigliando diventaro smorte.   69
E come a messagger che porta olivo
   tragge la gente per udir novelle,
   e di calcar nessun si mostra schivo,   72
così al viso mio s'affisar quelle
   anime fortunate tutte quante,
   quasi obliando d'ire a farsi belle.   75
Io vidi una di lor trarresi avante
   per abbracciarmi, con sì grande affetto
   che mosse me a far lo simigliante.   78
Oh ombre, vane fuor che ne l'aspetto!
   tre volte dietro a lei le mani avvinsi,
   e tante mi tornai con esse al petto.   81
Di maraviglia, credo, mi dipinsi;
   per che l'ombra sorrise e si ritrasse;
   e io, seguendo lei, oltre mi pinsi.   84

In éxitu Israël de Aegýpto were
   the words that all were chanting, with the rest
   which in the sequel of that psalm occur.

Then with the sign of the holy cross he bless'd
   them all, whereat they flung themselves ashore;
   and off he sped, as he had come, in haste.

The throng that there remained the aspect bore
   of strangers to the place, and their survey
   resembled his who would new things explore.

On every side shone, arrowing forth the day,
   the Sun, who with his well aimed shafts had now
   from the mid-sky chased Capricorn away,

when the new-comers raised each one his brow
   towards *us*, saying; 'Show us, if ye know,
   of access to the mount the where and how.'

And Virgil answered: 'Though it is not so,
   haply ye deem us expert in this isle,
   but we, like you, do on a journey go.

We came just now, ere you did a brief while,
   by another way, which was so rough and rude,
   we'll deem the ascent now rather play than toil.'

The souls, who from my breathing understood
   that I was still alive, grew pale, thereby
   betraying their wonder and its magnitude.

And as to hear his news the folk crowd nigh
   an envoy with an olive-branch and none
   of trampling on his neighbour seemeth shy,

so on my face those lucky spirits, one
   and all, kept gazing and became almost
   forgetful of going to put their beauty on.

I saw one soul out of the spell-bound host
   advance to embrace me, and thereto so fain,
   that he impelled me to the like accost.

Oh shades, in all but outward aspect, vain!
   Behind him thrice my clasping hands I bent,
   thrice brought them, empty, to my breast again.

My face, I think, revealed my wonderment;
   whereat the spirit smiled and backward drew,
   and I, pursuing it, a step forward went.

Soavemente disse ch'io posasse;
  allor conobbi chi era, e pregai
  che per parlarmi un poco s'arrestasse.   87
Risposemi: « Così com'io t'amai
  nel mortal corpo, così t'amo sciolta:
  però m'arresto; ma tu perchè vai? »   90
« Casella mio, per tornare altra volta
  là dov'io son fo io questo viaggio »
  diss'io; « ma a te com'è tant'ora tolta? »   93
Ed egli a me: « Nessun m'è fatto oltraggio
  se quei che leva quando e cui li piace
  più volte m'ha negato esto passaggio,   96
chè di giusto voler lo suo si face.
  Veramente, da tre mesi egli ha tolto
  chi ha voluto intrar, con tutta pace.   99
Ond'io, ch'or era a la marina volto
  dove l'acqua di Tevere s'insala,
  benignamente fui da lui ricolto.   102
A quella foce ha egli or dritta l'ala,
  però che sempre quivi si ricoglie
  qual verso d'Acheronte non si cala ».   105
E io: « Se nova legge non ti toglie
  memoria o uso a l'amoroso canto
  che mi solea quetar tutte mie voglie,   108
di ciò ti piaccia consolare alquanto
  l'anima mia, che con la mia persona
  venendo qui è affannata tanto! »   111
Amor che ne la mente mi ragiona
  cominciò egli allor sì dolcemente
  che la dolcezza ancor dentro mi suona.   114
Lo mio maestro, e io, e quella gente
  ch'eran con lui parevan sì contenti
  come a nessun toccasse altro la mente.   117
Noi eravam tutti fissi ed attenti
  a le sue note; ed ecco il veglio onesto
  gridando: « Che è ciò, spiriti lenti?   120
qual negligenza, quale stare è questo?
  Correte al monte a spogliarvi lo scoglio
  ch'esser non lascia a voi Dio manifesto! »   123

Gently it bade me pause: and then I knew
   who it was, and begged it, staying awhile, to allow
   us time for talk, ere setting forth anew.
'I in my mortal body loved thee, and now,
   thence freed, I love thee as dearly,' answered he;
   'therefore I stay; but wherefore journeyest thou?'
'Casella mine, that I once more may be
   here where I am, I make this journey,' I said;
   'but how hath so much time been taken from thee?'
And he to me: 'None wronged me, if instead
   of granting, he who embarks both when and whom
   he wills, to me this passage oft forbade;
for 'tis a just will which his own springs from:
   nathless, for these three months past he has ta'en,
   with full consent, all who have wished to come.
Whence I, who to the shore had turned me then,
   where Tiber's water with sea-salt is sown,
   by him was gathered in with heart full fain.
Straight to that river-mouth he now has flown;
   for always, there, assemble such of those
   as do not unto Acheron sink down.'
And I: 'If no new law hath made thee lose
   memory or practice of the song of love
   which used to give all my desires repose,
may it please thee somewhile with the strains thereof
   to soothe my soul, for which its mortal mould
   has made my coming here so toilsome prove!'
'*Love that within my mind doth discourse hold*'
   he then began so sweetly that I hear
   the sound within me still its sweets unfold.
My master, I, and all the folk who there
   were with him seemed as well content as though
   our minds for nothing else had thoughts to spare.
Fixed on the strains, we stood entranced, when lo!
   the venerable Ancient with us is,
   crying; 'How now, ye laggard spirits, how now?
What negligence, what dallying is this?
   Run to the mountain, there to cast aside
   the slough that, clouding God, delays your bliss.'

Come quando, cogliendo biada o loglio,
  li colombi adunati a pastura
  queti, senza mostrar l'usato orgoglio,   126
se cosa appare ond'egli abbian paura
  subitamente lasciano star l'esca
  perchè assaliti son da maggior cura;   129
così vid'io quella masnada fresca
  lasciar lo canto e gire inver la costa,
  com'uom che va nè sa dove riesca;   132
nè la nostra partita fu men tosta.

CANTO 3

Avvegna che la subitana fuga
  dispergesse color per la campagna
  rivolte al monte ove ragion ne fruga,   3
io mi ristrinsi a la fida compagna:
  e come sare' io senza lui corso?
  chi m'avria tratto su per la montagna?   6
Ei mi parea de se stesso rimorso:
  o dignitosa coscienza e netta,
  come t'è picciol fallo amaro morso!   9
Quando li piedi suoi lasciar la fretta,
  che l'onestade ad ogni atto dismaga,
  la mente mia, che prima era ristretta,   12
l'intento rallargò, sì come vaga;
  e diedi il viso mio incontro al poggio
  che inverso il ciel più alto si dislaga.   15
Lo Sol, che dietro fiammeggiava roggio,
  rotto m'era dinanzi alla figura
  che aveva in me de' suoi raggi l'appoggio.   18
Io mi volsi da lato, con paura
  d'essere abbandonato, quand'io vidi
  solo dinanzi a me la terra scura.   21
E il mio conforto: « Perchè pur diffidi? »
  a dir mi cominciò tutto rivolto;
  « Non credi tu me teco e ch'io ti guidi?   24

As pigeons, gathering corn or tares, abide
   together, all assembled at their feed
   quietly, nor display their wonted pride,
if aught be seen from which their fears proceed,
   incontinently leave their food to lie,
   because some greater care compels their heed;
so I that lately-landed company
   saw quit the song and, like one going, yet
   not knowing just whither, tow'rds the hillside fly:
nor was our parting less precipitate.

CANTO 3

THOUGH them the sudden flight dispersed abroad
   racing across the plain, intent to keep
   turned tow'rds the mount where reason is our goad;
I closer hugged the trusty comradeship
   of him, without whom how should I have raced?
   Who would have drawn me up the mountain-steep?
Self-blame, meseemed, was rankling in his breast;
   O honourable conscience and unstain'd
   how tart the smallest fault is to thy taste!
When of that hurry his feet had made an end
   which robs all actions of their dignity,
   my mind, which up till then had been restrain'd,
enlarged its compass, eager to range free,
   and, looking up, I scanned the steep ascent
   which heavenward loftiest rises from the sea.
The Sun, behind me glowing a ruddy tint,
   was brok'n before my person, in that there
   to his rays I was myself the impediment.
On seeing in front of me and not elsewhere
   the ground dark, I turned sideways, terrified,
   deeming myself deserted by my fere;
and, turning quite round, he, my comfort, sighed
   'Why so distrustful?' Then 'Believ'st not thou
   I'm with thee and that I am still thy guide?

Vespero è già colà dov'è sepolto
  lo corpo dentro al quale io facev'ombra:
  Napoli l'ha e da Brandizio è tolto.   27
Ora, se innanzi a me nulla s'aombra,
  non ti maravigliar più che dei cieli
  che l'uno a l'altro raggio non ingombra.   30
A sofferir tormenti e caldi e geli
  simili corpi la Virtù dispone,
  che come fa non vuol che a noi si sveli.   33
Matto è chi spera che nostra ragione
  possa trascorrer l'infinita via
  che tiene una sustanza in tre persone.   36
State contenti, umana gente, al *quia*;
  chè se potuto aveste veder tutto,
  mestier non era parturir Maria;   39
e disiar vedeste sanza frutto
  tai che sarebbe lor disio quetato,
  che eternalmente è dato lor per lutto: 42
io dico d'Aristotile e di Plato
  e di molt'altri». E qui chinò la fronte,
  e più non disse, e rimase turbato.   45
Noi divenimmo intanto a piè del monte.
  Quivi trovammo la roccia sì erta,
  che indarno vi sarien le gambe pronte.   48
Tra Lerici e Turbìa, la più diserta,
  la più rotta ruina è una scala,
  verso di quella, agevole ed aperta.   51
« Or chi sa da qual man la costa cala »
  disse il maestro mio fermando il passo
  « sì che possa salir chi va senz'ala? »   54
E mentre ch'ei, tenendo il viso basso,
  esaminava del cammin la mente,
  e io mirava suso e intorno al sasso,   57
da man sinistra m'apparì una gente
  d'anime che moveano i piè ver noi,
  e non parevan, sì venivan lente.   60
« Leva » diss'io « maestro, gli occhi tuoi:
  ecco di qua chi ne darà consiglio,
  se tu da te medesmo aver nol puoi ».   63

Vesper 'tis now o'er there where lieth low
   the body whence I cast a shadow: laid
   first in Brundisium, Naples has it now.
If, here, in front of me there falls no shade,
   this no more than the heav'ns for wondrous hold,
   whose rays through sphere on sphere pass on unstay'd.
To suffer torments both of heat and cold
   bodies like mine doth that high Power dispose,
   which, how it works, wills not that we be told.
Madness to hope that human reason knows
   how the unending pathway may be track'd,
   by which one Substance in three Persons goes.
Content ye, o human race, with the bare fact;
   for had the power been yours to see the whole,
   then Mary's childing was a needless act;
and ye've seen longing vainly many a soul
   so wise, that else achieved had been the quest
   assigned them now as their eternal dole.
Of Aristotle, Plato and the rest
   I speak—full many'; and here he bowed his head,
   and further spake not, and remained distress'd.
We to the mountain's foot meanwhile had made
   our way and found the cliff so steep, that there
   none by the nimblest legs had profited.
'Twixt Lérici and Turbía, how rough soe'er
   and lonely be the pathway, yet, compared
   with that, 'twould seem an easy and open stair.
'Who knows on which hand the hill slopes,' I heard
   my master murmur, as he paused, 'that one
   may climb, whose way is not the way of a bird?'
And while he kept his countenance cast down
   and closely searched what aids the path allow'd,
   and I looked upward round that wall of stone,
on the left hand there met my view a crowd
   of souls, who moved their feet to us-ward, yet
   seemed motionless, so much their pace had slow'd.
'Master, lift up thine eyes,' I said, 'and let
   us seek advice from those, look —there, upon
   this side—if from thyself thou none canst get.'

Guardò allora, e con libero piglio
  rispose: « Andiamo in là, ch'ei vegnon piano;
  e tu ferma la speme, dolce figlio ».   66
Ancora era quel popol di lontano,
  io dico dopo i nostri mille passi,
  quanto un buon gittator trarria con mano,   69
quando si strinser tutti ai duri massi
  de l'alta ripa, e stetter fermi e stretti,
  come a guardar chi va, dubbiando, stassi.   72
« O ben finiti, o già spiriti eletti »
  Virgilio incominciò, « per quella pace
  ch'io credo che per voi tutti s'aspetti,   75
ditene dove la montagna giace,
  sì che possibil sia l'andare in suso;
  chè perder tempo a chi più sa più spiace ». 78
Come le pecorelle escon del chiuso
  a una, a due, a tre, e l'altre stanno
  timidette, atterrando l'occhio e il muso;   81
e ciò che fa la prima e l'altre fanno,
  addossandosi a lei s'ella s'arresta,
  semplici e quete, e lo perchè non sanno;   84
sì vid'io movere a venir la testa
  di quella mandra fortunata, allotta,
  pudica in faccia e ne l'andare onesta.   87
Come color dinanzi vider rotta
  la luce in terra dal mio destro canto,
  sì che l'ombra era da me a la grotta,   90
restaro, e trasser sè indietro alquanto,
  e tutti gli altri che venieno appresso,
  non sappiendo il perchè, fenno altrettanto. 93
« Sanza vostra domanda io vi confesso
  che questo è corpo uman che voi vedete,
  per che il lume del Sole in terra è fesso.   96
Non vi maravigliate; ma credete
  che non sanza virtù che da ciel vegna
  cerchi di soverchiar questa parete ».   99
Così il maestro; e quella gente degna
  « Tornate » disse « intrate innanzi dunque »
  coi dossi de le man facendo insegna.   102

He eyed them then, and all misgiving gone,
   replied: 'Advance we thither, for full slow
   they move, and thou confirm thy hope, sweet son.'
Still were that company a good stone's throw
   away (I mean, as far away as this,
   after we'd walked a thousand steps or so)
when all drew close up to the precipice
   of towering rock and, huddled together, checked,
   as stops, to look, one who mistrustful is.
'O ye who died well, souls already elect,'
   Virgil began, 'be pleased, by that repose
   which I believe ye one and all expect,
to tell us where the mountain's contour shows
   a way to climb it by a bluff less bold;
   for loss of time most irks whoe'er most knows.'
As sheep that, seeing others quit the fold
   by ones, by twos, by threes, stand hesitant
   and to the ground their eyes and muzzles hold;
and what the first does, the rest do, upon 't
   piling themselves, if it should stop, though why,
   silly and passive, they are ignorant;
so of that lucky flock did I descry
   the head, shamefast in face and dignified
   in carriage, come on and to us draw nigh.
When those in front on my right flank espied
   the sunlight broken on the ground where lay
   my shadow reaching to the steep hillside,
they stopped short, and drew back a little way,
   and all the others following, though left
   in ignorance of the cause, did even as they.
'I, ere it be by question from me reft,
   confess this is a human body ye see,
   by which the Sun's light on the ground is cleft.
Marvel not at it; but believers be,
   that not without power from on high he stands
   here, and would scale this wall of rock and scree.'
The master thus; and that deserving band's
   reply was: 'turn—join and precede us, then:'
   and signal made they with the backs of their hands.

E un di loro incominciò: « Chiunque
  tu sei, così andando volgi il viso:
  pon mente se di là mi vedesti unque ».   105
Io mi volsi ver lui e guardail fiso:
  biondo era e bello e di gentile aspetto,
  ma l'un dei cigli un colpo avea diviso.   108
Quand'io mi fui umilmente disdetto
  d'averlo visto mai, ei disse: « Or vedi »;
  e mostrommi una piaga a sommo il petto.   111
Poi sorridendo disse: « Io son Manfredi,
  nipote di Costanza imperatrice;
  ond'io ti priego che quando tu riedi,   114
vadi a mia bella figlia, genitrice
  de l'onor di Cicilia e d'Aragona,
  e dichi il vero a lei, s'altro si dice.   117
Poscia ch'io ebbi rotta la persona
  di due punte mortali, io mi rendei
  piangendo a quei che volentier perdona.   120
Orribil furon li peccati miei;
  ma la bontà infinita ha sì gran braccia
  che prende ciò che si rivolge a lei.   123
Se il pastor di Cosenza, che a la caccia
  di me fu messo per Clemente, allora
  avesse in Dio ben letta questa faccia,   126
l'ossa del corpo mio sarieno ancora
  in co del ponte presso a Benevento,
  sotto la guardia de la grave mora.   129
Or le bagna la pioggia e move il vento
  di fuor dal Regno, quasi lungo il Verde,
  dov'ei le trasmutò a lume spento.   132
Per lor maledizion sì non si perde
  che non possa tornar l'eterno amore
  mentre che la speranza ha fior del verde.   135
Ver è che quale in contumacia more
  di Santa Chiesa, ancor che al fin si penta,
  star li convien di questa ripa in fore   138
per ogni tempo ch'egli è stato, trenta,
  in sua presunzion, se tal decreto
  più corto per buon prieghi non diventa.   141

'Whoe'er thou art, turn thee about again,
    as thus thou goest,' said one; 'bethink thee now
    if yonder I came e'er within thy ken.'
I turned and scanned him closely, noting how
    that comely he was and blond and nobly graced,
    but by a sword-stroke cleft was one eye-brow.
When I, responding humbly, had confess'd
    never to having seen him, he exclaimed
    'Now look!' and showed me a wound high on his breast.
He added, smiling: 'Manfred am I named,
    a grandson of the Empress Constance's;
    so, prithee, go thou, when by earth reclaimed,
to my fair daughter, who bore Sicily's
    and Aragon's chief honour 'neath her side,
    and, whate'er else be rumoured, tell her this.
When pierced by these two stabs whereof it died
    my body lay, weeping did I commit
    myself to Him whose pardon is ne'er denied.
My sins were horrible; but infinite
    Goodness hath arms so wide that they embrace
    readily whatsoe'er turns back to it.
And if Cosenza's pastor, who in chase
    of me was sent by Clement, then had found
    time to peruse this aspect of God's face,
my body's bones had still lain in the ground
    at the bridge-head near Benevento trenched,
    under the wardship of the high-heaped mound.
Wind moves, rain laves them now, from the Realm wrenched,
    hard by the Verde, whither they had been
    at his command transmuted with light quenched.
But through their malediction none, I ween,
    is e'er so lost, that the eternal Love
    cannot return, while hope has speck of green.
True, such as, though at last they contrite prove,
    in contumacy of Holy Church have died,
    this bank once reached, must stay outside thereof
for thirtyfold the time they willed to bide
    in their presumption, if to abridge this strict
    decree no pious voice on God hath cried.

Vedi oggimai se tu mi puoi far lieto
  rivelando a la mia buona Costanza
  come m'hai visto, ed anche esto divieto;   144
chè qui per quei di là molto s'avanza».

CANTO 4

Quando per dilettanze o ver per doglie
  che alcuna virtù nostra comprenda,
  l'anima bene ad essa si raccoglie,   3
par che a nulla potenza più intenda;
  e questo è contra quello error che crede
  che un'anima sovr'altra in noi s'accenda.   6
E però quando s'ode cosa o vede
  che tenga forte a sè l'anima volta
  vassene il tempo e l'uom non se n'avvede,   9
ch'altra potenza è quella che l'ascolta,
  e altra è quella che ha l'anima intera;
  questa è quasi legata, e quella è sciolta.   12
Di ciò ebb'io esperienza vera
  udendo quello spirto, ed ammirando
  che ben cinquanta gradi salito era   15
lo Sole, e io non m'era accorto, quando
  venimmo dove quell'anime, ad una,
  gridaro a noi: «Qui è vostro dimando».   18
Maggiore aperta molte volte impruna
  con una forcatella di sue spine
  l'uom de la villa quando l'uva imbruna,   21
che non era la calla onde saline
  lo duca mio, ed io appresso, soli,
  come da noi la schiera si partine.   24
Vassi in San Leo e discendesi in Noli,
  montasi su Bismantova in cacume
  con esso i piè, ma qui convien ch'uom voli: 27

My welfare, then, do thou hereafter seek 't
　by telling my good Constance of these wounds
　and how thou'st seen me, and of this interdict;
for here from those o'er there much good redounds.'

CANTO 4

Whene'er through pains or pleasures, grasped by one
　or other of our faculties, the mind
　concentrates its whole self on that alone,
to any other power it seems quite blind;
　and this disproves that, lit within us, rise
　one o'er another several souls combined.
Therefore, if aught be sensed with ears or eyes
　which holds the mind's attention forcibly,
　the time, without one's noticing it, flies;
for that which heeds it is one faculty,
　another that which holds the soul entire:
　bound as it were is this, and that is free.
Experience of this truth did I acquire
　in whom to hear that shade such wonder wrought,
　that fifty full degrees had mounted higher
the Sun, and I had yet perceived it not,
　when thither came we where those spirits cried
　with one voice to us: 'Here is what ye sought.'
A larger opening it may oft betide
　with a small forkful of his thorns a swain
　will hedge up, when the grape grows deeper dyed,
than was the gap through which my leader, when
　the troop had left us, and behind him I,
　began forthwith ascending, just we twain.
Climb to San Leo, drop to Noli, try
　to scale Bismantua to its crest one might
　with only feet; but here was need to fly:

281

dico con l'ali snelle e con le piume
del gran disio, diretro a quel condotto
che speranza mi dava e facea lume. 30
Noi salivam per entro il sasso rotto,
e d'ogni lato ne strignea lo stremo,
e piedi e man voleva il suol di sotto. 33
Poi che noi fummo su l'orlo supremo
de l'alta ripa, a la scoperta piaggia,
« Maestro mio » diss'io « che via faremo ? › 36
Ed egli a me: « Nessun tuo passo caggia;
pur su al monte dietro a me acquista,
fin che n'appaia alcuna scorta saggia ». 39
Lo sommo er'alto che vincea la vista,
e la costa superba più assai
che da mezzo quadrante a centro lista. 42
Io era lasso quando cominciai:
« O dolce padre, volgiti e rimira
com'io rimango sol se non ristai ». 45
« Figliuol mio » disse, « infin quivi ti tira »
additandomi un balzo un poco in sue,
che da quel lato il poggio tutto gira. 48
Sì mi spronaron le parole sue,
ch'io mi sforzai, carpando appresso lui,
tanto che il cinghio sotto i piè mi fue. 51
A seder ci ponemmo ivi ambedui
volti a levante ond'eravam saliti,
chè suole a riguardar giovare altrui. 54
Gli occhi prima drizzai ai bassi liti;
poscia li alzai al Sole, ed ammirava
che da sinistra n'eravam feriti. 57
Ben s'avvide il poeta ch'io stava
stupido tutto al carro de la luce,
ove tra noi e l'Aquilone intrava. 60
Ond'egli a me: « Se Castore e Polluce
fossero in compagnia di quello specchio
che sù e giù del suo lume conduce, 63
tu vedresti il Zodiaco rubecchio
ancora a l'Orse più stretto rotare,
se non uscisse fuor del cammin vecchio. 66

I mean, with the swift wings and feathered flight
  of great desire, following his guidance, who
  both was my source of hope and gave me light.

We toiled up by the chimney cloven through
  the rock, which grazed us on both sides, the ground
  not feet alone but hands requiring too.

When we had scaled the cliff and reached, beyond
  its topmost verge, the open mountain-side:
  'Master,' I said, 'where shall a path be found?'

'Take thou not one step backwards,' he replied:
  'straight up the mountain after me press on,
  until there meet us some experienced guide.'

The summit was so high it had outgone
  all vision, and the slope far steeper than
  a line to centre from mid-quadrant drawn.

I was exhausted, when I thus began:
  'Kind father, turn thee and see how, if thou will
  not stop, I'm left alone, strive as I can.'

'My son,' he said, 'but thus far drag thee still,'
  showing me a ledge a little above us yet,
  which on that side goes circling the whole hill.

His words so spurred me that I did not wait,
  but, clambering, forced my pace to the same measure
  as his, till on the shelf my feet were set.

There we both sat us down and at our leisure
  turned tow'rd the east, whence we had made ascent;
  for to look back is wont to give men pleasure.

My glance at first on the low shores was bent,
  then upward at the Sun, and that his rays
  from the left smote us roused my wonderment.

Well did the poet note my startled gaze
  bewildered at the chariot of the light,
  'tween us and Aquilo going its ways.

Whence he to me: 'Suppose yon mirror bright
  which sheds its radiance up and down were now
  in company with the heavenly Twins, one might

behold the Zodiac with its ruddy glow
  wheeling yet closer to the Bears, unless
  it left the path by which it's wont to go.

Come ciò sia se il vuoi poter pensare,
  dentro raccolto immagina Sion
  con questo monte in su la Terra stare   69
sì ch'ambedue hanno un solo orizzon,
  e diversi emisperi, onde la strada
  che mal non seppe carreggiar Feton,   72
vedrai come a costui che vada
  da l'un quando a colui da l'altro fianco,
  se l'intelletto tuo ben chiaro bada ».   75
« Certo, maestro mio » diss'io, « unquanco
  non vid'io chiaro sì com'or discerno
  là dove mio ingegno parea manco,   78
che il mezzo cerchio del moto superno,
  che si chiama Equatore in alcun'arte
  e che sempre riman tra il Sole e il verno,   81
per la ragion che di' quinci si parte
  verso settentrion, quanto gli Ebrei
  vedevan lui verso la calda parte.   84
Ma se a te piace, volentier saprei
  quanto avemo ad andar, chè il poggio sale
  più che salir non posson gli occhi miei ».   87
Ed egli a me: « Questa montagna è tale
  che sempre al cominciar di sotto è grave,
  e quant'uom più va sù, e men fa male.   90
Però quand'ella ti parrà soave
  tanto, che sù andar ti fia leggiero
  come a seconda giù andar per nave,   93
allor sarai al fin d'esto sentiero:
  quivi di riposar l'affanno aspetta.
  Più non rispondo, e questo so per vero ».   96
E com'egli ebbe sua parola detta,
  una voce di presso sonò: « Forse
  che di sedere in prima avrai distretta! »   99
Al suon di lei ciascun di noi si torse,
  e vedemmo a mancina un gran petrone,
  del qual nè io nè ei prima s'accorse.   102
Là ci traemmo, ed ivi eran persone
  che si stavano a l'ombra dietro al sasso
  come l'uom per negghienza a star si pone.   105

How this may be, if thou wouldst rightly guess,
    think hard, and let thy imagination this
    mount and mount Sion on the Earth so place
that, though in different hemispheres, there is
    for both the same horizon; thus, the road,
    which his ill hap caused Phaëton to miss,
thou'lt see must pass, there being no other mode,
    this mount on one, and that on the other side,
    be careful thought thereon by thee bestow'd.'
'Truly, my Master, never' I replied
    'saw I so clearly as I now descry
    there where my wits seemed wanting as a guide,
that the mid-circle of the motion on high,
    which—in one art as the Equator known—
    doth ever 'twixt the Sun and winter lie,
departeth, for the reason thou hast shown,
    hence tow'rd the north, as far as long ago
    the Hebrews saw it tow'rd the torrid zone.
But, if it please thee, gladly would I know
    how far we have to climb, because the hill
    lifts itself higher than my eyes can do.'
And he: 'This mount is such as always will
    at first, below, prove toilsome in the extreme,
    but, the higher climbed, the less it does one ill.
When, therefore, to thy feet the slope shall seem
    so gentle, that going up it will to thee
    be as easy as gliding in a boat down-stream,
then where this pathway endeth thou wilt be:
    there of thy toil expect thou to be quit.
    Enough—but this I know for verity.'
Such was his speech, and as he ended it,
    a voice from nearby sounded: 'Maybe, ere
    that happens thou wilt oft be forced to sit.'
Hearing it sound, both of us turned, and there
    saw on our left a massive block of stone,
    whereof nor he nor I before was ware.
Thither we drew: and persons had sunk down
    there in the shade behind the rock, like those
    whose indolence is by their posture shown.

E un di lor, che mi sembiava lasso,
  sedeva e abbracciava le ginocchia,
  tenendo il viso giù tra esse basso.   108
« O dolce signor mio » diss'io « adocchia
  colui che mostra sè più negligente
  che se pigrizia fosse sua sirocchia! »   111
Allor si volse a noi e pose mente
  movendo il viso pur su per la coscia,
  e disse: « Or va sù tu che sei valente! »   114
Conobbi allor chi era, e quell'angoscia
  che m'avacciava un poco ancor la lena,
  non m'impedì l'andare a lui; e poscia   117
che a lui fui giunto, alzò la testa appena
  dicendo: « Hai ben veduto come il Sole
  da l'omero sinistro il carro mena? »   120
Gli atti suoi pigri e le corte parole
  mosson le labbra mie un poco a riso;
  poi cominciai: « Belacqua, a me non duole   123
di te omai; ma dimmi: perchè assiso
  quiritta sei? Attendi tu iscorta,
  o pur lo modo usato t'hai ripriso? »   126
Ed egli: « O frate, l'andar sù che porta?
  chè non mi lascerebbe ire ai martiri
  l'angel di Dio che siede in su la porta.   129
Prima convien che tanto il ciel m'aggiri
  di fuor da essa, quanto fece in vita,
  perch'io indugiai al fine i buon sospiri,   132
se orazione in prima non m'aita
  che surga sù di cor che in grazia viva:
  l'altra che val che in ciel non è udita? »   135
E già il poeta innanzi mi saliva
  e dicea: « Vienne omai, vedi ch'è tocco
  meridian dal Sole, ed a la riva   138
copre la notte già col piè Morrocco ».

And one of them, to judge him by his pose,
   seemed weary, for he sat and hugged his knees,
   while low between them bent he held his brows.
'Look, good my lord,' said I, 'if Sloth were his
   own sister, that one, seated there among
   these spirits, could not idlier take his ease.'
Then turned he to us and, his face along
   his thigh just moving, gave us heed, and said:
   'Now go on climbing, thou who art so strong!'
I knew him then; and though exhaustion made
   me somewhat breathless still, it hindered not
   my going to him; he barely raised his head,
when I had reached him, drawling: 'Hast thou got
   it quite clear, how it happens that the Sun
   by thy left shoulder drives his chariot?'
His lazy gestures and curt words upon
   my lips for a brief moment raised a smile;
   then I began; 'Belacqua, from now on
for thee I grieve not: tell me, though, meanwhile,
   why sittest thou just here? await'st thou a guide?
   or hast thou but resumed thy wonted style?'
'Brother, to climb what boots it?' he replied:
   'God's angel, he that keeps the gate, would still
   not let me to the torments pass inside.
Ere that, as long the heav'n must round me wheel
   outside thereof, as in my life it did,
   since I delayed to the end the sighs that heal,
unless for me, ere then, should intercede
   prayers rising from a heart that lives in grace:
   what profit the rest to which Heaven pays no heed?'
The poet, already climbing on apace
   in front, said, 'Come on now, the meridian mark
   is touched, look! by the Sun, and 'neath the trace
of night Morocco's coast is growing dark.'

CANTO 5

Io era già da quell'ombre partito,
  e seguitava l'orme del mio duca,
  quando diretro a me, drizzando il dito,   3
una gridò: « Ve' che non par che luca
  lo raggio da sinistra a quel di sotto,
  e come vivo par che si conduca ».   6
Gli occhi rivolsi al suon di questo motto,
  e vidile guardar per maraviglia
  pur me pur me e il lume ch'era rotto.   9
« Perchè l'animo tuo tanto s'impiglia »
  disse il maestro « che l'andare allenti?
  che ti fa ciò che quivi si pispiglia?   12
Vien dietro a me, e lascia dir le genti:
  sta come torre ferma, che non crolla
  già mai la cima per soffiar di venti;   15
chè sempre l'uomo in cui pensier rampolla
  sopra pensier, da sè dilunga il segno,
  perchè la foga l'un de l'altro insolla ».   18
Che poteva io ridir se non: « Io vegno »?
  Dissolo, alquanto del color cosperso
  che fa l'uom di perdon tal volta degno.   21
E intanto per la costa di traverso
  venivan genti innanzi a noi un poco,
  cantando *Miserere* verso a verso.   24
Quando s'accorser ch'io non dava loco
  per lo mio corpo al trapassar dei raggi,
  mutar lor canto in un *Oh* lungo e roco.   27
E due di loro in forma di messaggi
  corsero incontro a noi e dimandarne:
  « Di vostra condizion fatene saggi ».   30
E il mio maestro: « Voi potete andarne
  e ritrarre a color che vi mandaro
  che il corpo di costui è vera carne.   33
Se per veder la sua ombra restaro,
  com'io avviso, assai è lor risposto;
  faccianli onore, ed esser può lor caro ».   36

CANTO 5

ALREADY with those shades I'd ceased to linger,
  and was pursuing the footsteps of my guide,
  when one behind me, pointing with his finger,
cried: 'See—the lower one there—on his left side
  the ray seems not to shine—and more by token
  he bears himself like one who's not yet died.'
I turned my eyes back, when these words were spoken
  and saw them gazing, struck with awe, at me,
  still me, and at the sunlight that was broken.
'Why strays thy mind in such perplexity'
  the master said, 'that thou art dawdling so?
  The things here whispered, what are they to thee?
Follow thou me, and let them talk: stand thou
  firm as a tower, whose summit totters not
  at any time for all the winds that blow.
For he in whom there springs up thought on thought
  keeps putting ever farther off his aim,
  since the one drives perforce the other out.'
What could I answer but, 'I'm coming,' shame
  tinging me, as I said it, with the hue
  which, claim we pardon, oft makes good the claim?
Meanwhile athwart the slope there came in view,
  chanting a *Miserere* in antiphone,
  some folk a little ahead who tow'rds us drew.
They, when aware that of the sunrays none
  was passing through my body, changed their chant
  into an 'Oh!' prolonged and hoarse in tone.
And of their number two, as were they meant
  for envoys, ran to meet us and thus sued:
  'Of your condition make us cognisant.'
'You may go back and make it understood
  of those who sent you' so my master said,
  'that this man's body is truly flesh and blood.
If, as I think, 'twas seeing his shadow stay'd
  their steps, then this reply is adequate:
  honour they him, they may be well repaid.'

Vapori accesi non vid'io sì tosto
    di prima notte mai fender sereno,
    nè solcando le nuvole d'agosto,   39
che color non tornasser suso in meno;
    e, giunti là, con gli altri a noi dier volta
    come schiera che corre sanza freno.   42
«Questa gente che preme a noi è molta,
    e vegnonti a pregar» disse il poeta:
    « però pur va, ed in andando ascolta ».   45
« O anima che vai per esser lieta
    con quelle membra con le quai nascesti »
    venian gridando, «un poco il passo queta.   48
Guarda se alcun di noi unqua vedesti,
    sì che di lui di là novella porti:
    deh, perchè vai? deh, perchè non t'arresti?   51
Noi fummo già tutti per forza morti,
    e peccatori infino a l'ultim'ora:
    quivi lume del ciel ne fece accorti,   54
sì che, pentendo e perdonando, fora
    di vita uscimmo a Dio pacificati,
    che del disio di sè veder n'accora ».   57
Ed io: « Perchè nei vostri visi guati
    non riconosco alcun; ma se a voi piace
    cosa ch'io possa, spiriti ben nati,   60
voi dite, ed io farò, per quella pace
    che dietro i piedi di sì fatta guida
    di mondo in mondo cercar mi si face ».   63
Ed uno incominciò: « Ciascun si fida
    del beneficio tuo sanza giurarlo,
    pur che il voler nonpossa non ricida.   66
Ond'io che solo innanzi a gli altri parlo,
    ti priego, se mai vedi quel paese
    che siede tra Romagna e quel di Carlo,   69
che tu mi sia de' tuoi prieghi cortese
    in Fano, sì che ben per me s'adori,
    perch'io possa purgar le gravi offese.   72
Quindi fu' io, ma li profondi fori
    onde uscì il sangue in sul quale io sedea,
    fatti mi furo in grembo a gli Antenori   75

Ignited vapours ne'er beheld I yet
   so swiftly at nightfall cleave clear skies in twain
   or furrow August clouds with speed so great,
but what in less time climbed they back again;
   and, once back, with the others to us-ward wheel'd,
   as gallops a squadron without drawing rein.
'These people that press on us are many, and fill'd'
   the bard said 'with desire to make their suit:
   listen, but halt not, nor, if begged to, yield.'
'O spirit bound for bliss and journeying to 't
   with those limbs thou wert born with,' thus did they
   cry as they came, 'a brief while stay thy foot.
Look if thou e'er saw any of us we pray,
   that thou to earth bear news of him from hence:
   ah, why dost thou go on? ah, why not stay?
We all, of old, were slain by violence,
   and went on sinning up to our last hour,
   when Heav'n illumined our intelligence,
so that, both penitent and pardoning, o'er
   death's threshold passed we at peace with God, who's made
   our hearts yearn to behold Him evermore.'
And I: 'Although your faces I've survey'd,
   I recall none; but, spirits born for bliss,
   if aught that I can do will bring you aid,
say *ye*, and I will do it, by that peace
   which I am bounden, following such a guide,
   from world to world to search for without cease.'
And one began: 'We all of us confide
   in thy good office without thy swearing it,
   if to the will the power be not denied.
Whence I, who speak but first of these, entreat
   that, shouldst thou e'er behold that territ'ry
   which lies between Romagna and Charles's seat,
thou with thy prayers so courteous be to me
   at Fano, that the pious may Heav'n invoke
   to grant me power to purge my iniquity.
There was I born: but the deep wounds whence broke
   the life-blood forth which housed my soul, were dealt
   me in the bosom of Antenor's folk,

là dov'io più sicuro esser credea;
   quel da Esti il fe' far, che m'avea in ira
   assai più là che dritto non volea.   78
Ma s'io fossi fuggito in ver la Mira
   quando fui sovraggiunto ad Oriaco,
   ancor sarei di là dove si spira.   81
Corsi al palude, e le cannucce e il braco
   m'impigliar sì, ch'io caddi, e lì vid'io
   de le mie vene farsi in terra laco ».   84
Poi disse un altro: « Deh, se quel disio
   si compia che ti tragge a l'alto monte,
   con buona pietate aiuta il mio.   87
Io fui da Montefeltro, io son Buonconte;
   Giovanna o altri non ha di me cura,
   per ch'io vo tra costor con bassa fronte ».   90
E io a lui: « Qual forza o qual ventura
   ti traviò sì fuor di Campaldino
   che non si seppe mai tua sepoltura? »   93
« Oh! » rispos'egli, « a piè del Casentino
   traversa un'acqua che ha nome l'Archiano,
   che sovra l'Ermo nasce in Apennino.   96
Là 've il vocabol suo diventa vano
   arriva' io, forato ne la gola,
   fuggendo a piede e insanguinando il piano,   99
Quivi perdei la vista, e la parola
   nel nome di Maria finii, e quivi
   caddi, e rimase la mia carne sola.   102
Io dirò il vero, e tu il ridì tra i vivi:
   l'angel di Dio mi prese, e quel d'Inferno
   gridava: 'O tu del ciel, perchè mi privi?   105
Tu te ne porti di costui l'eterno
   per una lacrimetta che il me toglie;
   ma io farò de l'altro altro governo'.   108
Ben sai come ne l'aere si raccoglie
   quell'umido vapor che in acqua riede
   tosto che sale dove il freddo il coglie.   111
Giunse quel mal voler che pur mal chiede,
   con l'intelletto, e mosse il fummo e il vento
   per la virtù che sua natura diede.   114

where, of all spots, I thought to have safest dwelt:
  he of Este had it done, who held me in wrath
  far in excess of any rightly felt.
If tow'rd La Mira I had chosen the path,
  when overtaken at Oriaco, then
  I should be yonder still where men draw breath.
I ran to the marsh and, struggling, but in vain,
  'gainst reeds and mire, I fell, and there saw I
  a pool made by my own veins in the fen.'
Another spake: 'Ah, so be granted thy
  desire which draws thee up the mount, do thou
  pity me and assist my own thereby!
Of Montefeltro I was, Buonconte now
  still am: nor Joan nor others give me a thought,
  whence among these I walk with downcast brow.'
And I to him: 'From Campaldino what
  mischance or blow so far deflected thee,
  that no one of thy burial-place knew aught?'
'Oh, at the Casentino's foot,' said he,
  'crosses a stream, Archiano named, whose source
  in Apennine lies o'er the Hermit'ry.
Just at the junction, where its name perforce
  is lost, I arrived, stabbed in the throat, fordone,
  fleeing on foot and bloodying my course.
There I lost sight, and with my latest groan
  I uttered Mary's name, and there I fell:
  and in that spot remained my flesh alone.
I'll tell the truth: do thou the same re-tell
  'mongst living men; God's angel snatched me, and "Why
  dost rob me, O thou from heav'n?" cried he of hell.
"Thou carriest off and dost to me deny
  this man's eternal part for one small tear:
  but deal with the other otherwise will I."
Thou knowest full well how in the atmosphere
  moist vapours gather and mount skyward till,
  condensed by cold, they turn to water there.
He joined that ill will, which seeks only ill,
  with the intellect, and stirred the fog and blast
  in virtue of power his nature doth instil.

Indi la valle, come il dì fu spento,
   da Pratomagno al gran giogo coperse
   di nebbia, e il ciel di sopra fece intento   117
sì, che il pregno aere in acqua si converse:
   la pioggia cadde, ed ai fossati venne
   di lei ciò che la terra non sofferse;   120
e come ai rivi grandi si convenne,
   ver lo fiume real tanto veloce
   si ruinò, che nulla la ritenne.   123
Lo corpo mio gelato in su la foce
   trovò l'Archian rubesto, e quel sospinse
   ne l'Arno, e sciolse al mio petto la croce   126
ch'io fei di me quando il dolor mi vinse:
   voltommi per le ripe e per lo fondo,
   poi di sua preda mi coperse e cinse».   129
« Deh, quando tu sarai tornato al mondo
   e riposato de la lunga via »
   seguitò il terzo spirito al secondo,   132
« ricorditi di me che son la Pia.
   Siena mi fe', disfecemi Maremma:
   salsi colui che inanellata pria,   135
disposando, m'avea con la sua gemma ».

CANTO 6

Quando si parte il gioco de la zara,
   colui che perde si riman dolente
   ripetendo le volte, e tristo impara.   3
Con l'altro se ne va tutta la gente:
   qual va dinanzi e qual di dietro il prende
   e qual da lato li si reca a mente.   6
Ei non s'arresta, e questo e quello intende;
   a cui porge la man, più non fa pressa;
   e così da la calca si difende.   9

Then he o'erspread the vale, when day was past,
  from Pratomagno to the great range with black
  clouds, and the sky above made overcast,
so that to water the charged air changed back:
  rain fell, and through the gullies foamed in spate
  all of it that the earth refused to take:
as in the great ghylls it converged and met,
  tow'rds the royal river with such boisterous
  speed did it rush, that nought its course could let.
The swol'n Archián at the outlet of its fosse
  found my corpse stiff and pushed it on, thus found,
  to the Arno, and on my breast undid the cross
I'd made of myself when vanquished by the wound:
  it rolled me along its banks and o'er its bed;
  then with its spoils covered and wrapped me round.'
'Ah, when unto the world thou shalt have made
  return, and rested from the way's long strain,'
  the third after the second spirit said,
'me, who am Pia, may'st thou think of then:
  'twas Siena made, Maremma that unmade me:
  he knows it who with his own jewel, when
our mutual troth had first been plighted, wed me.'

CANTO 6

THE loser, when the game at dice breaks up,
  lingers despondent, and repeats the throws
  to learn, in grief, what made his fortune droop;
with the other all the folk depart: one goes
  in front, one plucks him from behind, one near
  his side protests he knew him once: to those,
then these, while halting not, he lends an ear;
  any he gives his hand to, cease to crowd:
  thus from the jostling he at last wins clear.

Tal era io in quella turba spessa,
  volgendo a loro e qua e là la faccia,
  e promettendo mi sciogliea da essa.   12

Quivi era l'Aretin che da le braccia
  fiere di Ghin di Tacco ebbe la morte,
  e l'altro che annegò correndo in caccia.   15

Quivi pregava con le mani sporte
  Federigo Novello, e quel da Pisa
  che fe' parer lo buon Marzucco forte.   18

Vidi Cont'Orso, e l'anima divisa
  dal corpo suo per astio e per inveggia,
  com'ei dicea, non per colpa commisa: 21

Pier da la Broccia, dico; e qui proveggia
  mentr'è di qua la donna di Brabante,
  sì che però non sia di peggior greggia.   24

Come libero fui da tutte quante
  quell'ombre, che pregar pur ch'altri prieghi
  sì che s'avacci lor divenir sante,   27

io cominciai: « E' par che tu mi nieghi,
  o luce mia, espresso in alcun testo
  che decreto del cielo orazion pieghi;   30

e questa gente prega pur di questo:
  sarebbe dunque loro speme vana?
  o non m'è il detto tuo ben manifesto? »   33

Ed egli a me: « La mia scrittura è piana,
  e la speranza di costor non falla
  se ben si guarda con la mente sana.   36

Chè cima di giudizio non s'avvalla
  perchè foco d'amor compia in un punto
  ciò che dee sodisfar chi qui si stalla;   39

e là dov'io fermai cotesto punto,
  non s'ammendava, per pregar, difetto,
  perchè il priego da Dio era disgiunto.   42

Veramente a così alto sospetto
  non ti fermar, se quella nol ti dice
  che lume fia tra il vero e l'intelletto.   45

Non so se intendi; io dico di Beatrice:
  tu la vedrai di sopra in su la vetta
  di questo monte, ridere felice ».   48

So 'twas with me in that dense multitude:
  turning to them now here, now there, my face
  and promising, I passed on unpursued.
There was the Aretine, to death's embrace
  dispatched by Ghin di Tacco's savage blade,
  and the other who was drowned while giving chase.
There supplicated with his hands outspread
  Frederick Novello, and the Pisan who
  caused good Marzucco's phlegm to be display'd.
I saw Count Orso and the spirit through
  sheer hate and envy (so did it aver)
  disbodied, not for aught 'twas sin to do—
Pierre de la Brousse, I mean: and here let her,
  Brabant's great dame, while o'er there, to it see
  that she herd not with worse for this affair.
When I was quit of all that company,
  who only prayed that some one else should pray
  that they might grow in grace more speedily,
'It seems, my Light,' I then began to say,
  'thou hast expressly in some text denied
  that aught decreed by Heav'n to prayer gives way;
yet these folk pray for this and nought beside.
  Can it be, then, that what they hope is vain?
  Or have I missed the sense thy words implied?'
And he to me: 'That which I wrote is plain,
  nor is their hope fallacious, if but well
  considered with a judgment that is sane;
for Justice her high summit doth not vail
  because the fire of love pays in a trice
  the debt each owes who here is doomed to dwell;
and there, too, where my words were so precise,
  prayer by a gulf from reaching God was check'd,
  so that no praying could atone for vice.
But on a question so profound expect
  no certainty, till she instruct thee in this,
  who'll be thy lamp 'twixt truth and the intellect.
Dost understand me? I speak of Beatrice:
  thou wilt behold her up there, on the crest
  of this same mountain, smiling and in bliss.'

E io: « Signore, andiamo a maggior fretta,
  che già non m'affatico come dianzi,
  e vedi omai che il poggio l'ombra getta ».   51
« Noi anderem con questo giorno innanzi »
  rispose « quanto più potremo omai;
  ma il fatto è d'altra forma che non stanzi.   54
Prima che sie là sù, tornar vedrai
  colui che già si copre de la costa,
  sì che i suoi raggi tu romper non fai.   57
Ma vedi là un'anima che, posta
  sola soletta, verso noi riguarda:
  quella ne insegnerà la via più tosta ».   60
Venimmo a lei. O anima lombarda,
  come ti stavi altera e disdegnosa,
  e nel mover de gli occhi onesta e tarda!   63
Ella non ci diceva alcuna cosa,
  ma lasciavane gir, solo sguardando
  a guisa di leon quando si posa.   66
Pur Virgilio si trasse a lei, pregando
  che ne mostrasse la miglior salita;
  e quella non rispose al suo dimando,   69
ma di nostro paese e de la vita
  c'inchiese; e il dolce duca incominciava;
  « Mantova.... » e l'ombra, tutta in sè romita,   72
surse ver lui del loco ove pria stava,
  dicendo: « O Mantovano, io son Sordello,
  de la tua terra!», e l'un l'altro abbracciava.   75
Ahi serva Italia, di dolore ostello,
  nave senza nocchiero in gran tempesta,
  non donna di provincie, ma bordello!   78
Quell'anima gentil fu così presta,
  sol per lo dolce suon de la sua terra,
  di fare al cittadin suo quivi festa;   81
e ora in te non stanno sanza guerra
  li vivi tuoi, e l'un l'altro si rode
  di quei che un muro ed una fossa serra.   84
Cerca, misera, intorno da le prode
  le tue marine, e poi ti guarda in seno,
  se alcuna parte in te di pace gode.   87

And I: 'My lord, let us make greater haste,
  for the fatigue I felt is now less sore,
  and look! the hill now casts shadow manifest.'
'With this day's light we'll climb on as much more
  as we are able'—thus it was he spake—
  'but things are other than thou tak'st them for.
Before thou'rt up there, thou'lt behold him make
  his way back—him, behind the slope now gone
  so that on thee his rays no longer break.
But see yon spirit, placed there quite alone,
  looking in our direction: *it* will show
  us where with most speed we may journey on.'
We came to it. O Lombard spirit, how
  haughty and scornful was thine attitude,
  the movement of thine eyes how grave and slow!
It said no word as we our way pursued,
  but let us still go on, not doing aught
  save watch us, as a couching lion would.
Yet Virgil, drawing close to it, besought
  that it would point us out what we desired,
  the best way up; to which it answered nought,
but of our country and of our life enquired;
  and the loved guide began, at this request:
  'Mantua . . .', and the shade, all self-retired,
rose tow'rds him from where it before was placed
  saying: 'O Mantuan, I'm Sordello of thy
  own city!', and the one the other embraced.
Ah, enslaved Italia, sorrow's mansionry,
  ship without pilot in a raging gale,
  not lady of provinces, but harlots' sty!
Thus did his zeal that noble soul impel,
  merely at the sweet sound of his city's name,
  to bid his fellow-townsman here all-hail;
and now in thee war ceases not to inflame
  thy living men, and one the other devours,
  though the same wall, same moat encloses them.
Search, wretch, thy seaboard, all around its shores,
  then look within thy breast, if any part
  in thee enjoy the boon of peaceful hours.

Che val perchè ti racconciasse il freno
  Giustiniano, se la sella è vota?
  Sanz'esso fora la vergogna meno.   90
Ahi gente che dovresti esser devota
  e lasciar seder Cesare in la sella,
  se bene intendi ciò che Dio ti nota,   93
guarda com'esta fera è fatta fella
  per non esser corretta da li sproni
  poi che ponesti mano a la predella.   96
O Alberto tedesco che abbandoni
  costei ch'è fatta indomita e selvaggia,
  e dovresti inforcar li suoi arcioni,   99
giusto giudicio da le stelle caggia
  sovra il tuo sangue, e sia novo ed aperto
  sì che il tuo successor temenza n'aggia.   102
Chè avete tu e il tuo padre sofferto,
  per cupidigia di costà distretti,
  che il giardin de l'imperio sia diserto.   105
Vieni a veder Montecchi e Cappelletti,
  Monaldi e Filippeschi, uom sanza cura:
  color già tristi e questi con sospetti.   108
Vien, crudel, vieni, e vedi la pressura
  de' tuoi gentili, e cura lor magagne;
  e vedrai Santa Fior come si cura!   111
Vieni a veder la tua Roma che piagne
  vedova e sola, e dì e notte chiama:
  « Cesare mio, perchè non m'accompagne? »   114
Vieni a veder la gente quanto s'ama!
  e se nulla di noi pietà ti move,
  a vergognar ti vien de la tua fama.   117
E se licito m'è, o sommo Giove
  che fosti in Terra per noi crocifisso,
  son li giusti occhi tuoi rivolti altrove?   120
O è preparazion che ne l'abisso
  del tuo consiglio fai, per alcun bene
  in tutto de l'accorger nostro scisso?   123
Chè le città d'Italia tutte piene
  son di tiranni, ed un Marcel diventa
  ogni villan che parteggiando viene.   126

What boots it that for thee Justinian's art
  retrimmed the bit, if no one mounts the steed?
  The shame would, but for that, less keenly smart.
Ah, folk that should be given to prayer, and need
  but to let Caesar fill the saddle again,
  paid ye to God's direction proper heed,
look how this beast, for lack of spurs to train
  and curb its ardour, still more savage grows,
  ever since ye laid hand upon the rein.
O German Albert, who thine eyes dost close
  to her, grown wild and vicious, though by right
  'tis thou who shouldst bestride her saddle-bows,
may a just judgment from the stars alight
  upon thy blood: be't strange and manifest,
  that thy successor may thereat take fright.
For, like thy father, thou—held back, in quest
  of lands o'er there, by greed that nought abates—
  hast let the empire's garden run to waste.
Come and see Montagues and Capulets,
  Monaldi and Filippeschi, O heedless man:
  these dreading ill which those e'en now besets!
Come, cruel! come and see how oppressive can
  thy nobles be, and the ills they've wrought make good;
  and thou'lt see Santafiór, how it needs thy ban!
Come, see thy Rome, in lonely widowhood
  weeping, and calling day and night: 'Oh, why,
  my Caesar, dost thou leave me in solitude?'
Come and see how they love each other, thy
  good folk, and if nought else thy pity move,
  come for thy own repute's sake, shamed thereby.
And, be't lawful for me, O highest Jove
  who wast on Earth for our sake crucified,
  I'll ask, do thy just eyes elsewhither rove?
Or art thou thus preparing, but dost hide
  in thy unfathomed counsel, some good end
  by our weak vision wholly undescried?
For all the lands of Italy now bend
  to tyrants, and no churl exists but he's
  a right Marcellus, be he faction's friend.

Fiorenza mia, ben puoi esser contenta
  di questa digression che non ti tocca
  mercè del popol tuo che s'argomenta.   129
Molti han giustizia in cuore, e tardi scocca
  per non venir sanza consiglio a l'arco;
  ma il popol tuo l'ha in sommo de la bocca.   132
Molti rifiutan lo comune incarco;
  ma il popol tuo sollicito risponde
  sanza chiamare, e grida « Io mi sobbarco!»   135
Or ti fa lieta, che tu hai ben onde:
  tu ricca, tu con pace, tu con senno.
  S'io dico ver, l'effetto nol nasconde.   138
Atene e Lacedemona, che fenno
  l'antiche leggi e furon sì civili,
  fecero al viver bene un piccol cenno   141
verso di te, che fai tanto sottili
  provedimenti, che a mezzo novembre
  non giugne quel che tu d'ottobre fili.   144
Quante volte, del tempo che rimembre,
  legge, moneta, officio e costume
  hai tu mutato, e rinnovato membre!   147
E se ben ti ricordi e vedi lume,
  vedrai te somigliante a quella inferma
  che non può trovar posa in su le piume,   150
ma con dar volta suo dolore scherma.

CANTO 7

Poscia che l'accoglienze oneste e liete
  furo iterate tre e quattro volte,
  Sordel si trasse, e disse: « Voi chi siete?»   3
« Anzi che a questo monte fosser volte
  l'anime degne di salire a Dio,
  fur l'ossa mie per Ottavian sepolte.   6

Thou, my own Florence, well may'st be at ease
  with this digression, withers quite unwrung,
  thanks to thy folk who are so prompt with pleas.
Many love justice, but their bows are strung
  with caution, and they shoot the word with care;
  but *thy* folk have it on the tip of the tongue.
Many refuse the common load to share:
  but *thy* folk eagerly respond, nor wait
  to be asked, but cry: 'For me 'tis light to bear.'
Count thyself—and with reason—fortunate:
  thou wealthy, thou at peace, and thou so wise!
  a truth I leave the facts to demonstrate.
Athens and Lacedaemon, who made rise
  the ancient laws and civic discipline
  scarce showed at all wherein well-living lies,
compared with thee, who of a thread so thin
  dost make provisions, that to mid-November
  lasts not what thou dost in October spin.
How often hast thou, since thou canst remember,
  changed customs, coinage, laws and offices,
  rejointing limbs only to re-dismember!
This called to mind, seeing clearly thy disease,
  thou'lt see thyself resembling that sick dame,
  who, laid on down, by tossing seeks to ease
her aches, but goes on suffering just the same.

CANTO 7

THREE and four times did they with joy renew
  their courtly greetings, after which I heard
  Sordello say, withdrawing, 'But who are *you*?'
'Ere yet to this same mountain had repaired
  the souls deemed worthy of ascent to God,
  my bones had by Octavian been interred.

Io son Virgilio, e per null'altro rio
　　lo ciel perdei che per non aver fe' ».
　　Così rispose allora il duca mio.　　　　　　　9
Qual è colui che cosa innanzi a sè
　　subita vede, ond'ei si maraviglia,
　　che crede e non, dicendo « Ell'è.... non è »,　　12
tal parve quelli; e poi chinò le ciglia,
　　ed umilmente ritornò ver lui,
　　ed abbracciollo ove il minor s'appiglia.　　　15
« O gloria dei Latin » disse « per cui
　　mostrò ciò che potea la lingua nostra,
　　o pregio eterno del loco ond'io fui,　　　　　18
qual merito o qual grazia mi ti mostra?
　　S'io son d'udir le tue parole degno,
　　dimmi se vien d'Inferno, e di qual chiostra ».　21
« Per tutti i cerchi del dolente regno »
　　rispose lui « son io di qua venuto;
　　virtù del ciel mi mosse e con lei vegno.　　　24
Non per far, ma per non fare ho perduto
　　di veder l'alto Sol che tu disiri,
　　e che fu tardi per me conosciuto.　　　　　　27
Loco è là giù non tristo da martiri
　　ma da tenebre solo, ove i lamenti
　　non suonan come guai, ma son sospiri.　　　30
Quivi sto io coi pargoli innocenti
　　dai denti morsi de la morte avante
　　che fosser da l'umana colpa esenti;　　　　　33
quivi sto io con quei che le tre sante
　　virtù non si vestiro, e sanza vizio
　　conobber l'altre e seguir tutte quante.　　　36
Ma se tu sai e puoi, alcun indizio
　　dà noi perchè venir possiam più tosto
　　là dove Purgatorio ha dritto inizio ».　　　39
Rispose: « Loco certo non c'è posto:
　　licito m'è andar suso ed intorno;
　　per quanto ir posso a guida mi t'accosto.　　42
Ma vedi già come dichina il giorno,
　　e andar sù di notte non si puote;
　　però è buon pensar di bel soggiorno.　　　　45

I'm Virgil: and the loss of heav'n I owed
   unto no other crime than lack of faith.'
   Thus answered then he in whose steps I trod.
As one who by a thing he marvelleth
   suddenly to see before him, plunged in both
   belief and doubt, 'it is, nay 'tis not' saith,
such seemed the other:—then bowing his head, as loth
   to exalt his own worth, once more tow'rds him made
   and there embraced him where the inferior doth.
'O glory of the Latin race,' he said,
   'through whom our tongue showed all its mightiness,
   O eternal praise of the spot where I was bred,
what merit of mine shows thee to me, what grace?
   If worthy I am to hear thee, say wherefrom
   thou com'st, and, if from Hell, from what duress?'
'Through all the circles of the realm of gloom,'
   he answered, 'came I hither: it was power
   from heav'n that moved me, and with it I come.
Lost to me, not for doing but on the score
   of *not* doing, was the sight of the high Sun
   I knew too late, which thou art longing for.
A place there is down there the light doth shun
   though darkened not by tortures, where laments
   are sighs: for of loud wailings there is none.
There I'm with those, the little innocents
   nipped by the fangs of death before set free
   from that infection which all men attaints.
There I'm with those who put not on the three
   God-given virtues, but without vice knew
   the rest and practised all unfailingly.
But if thou knowest and canst, give us some clue
   by which we may find out the real gate
   of Purgatory, and sooner come thereto.'
He answered: 'No fixed place for us is set:
   I'm licensed to go upward and around:
   I'll guide thee as far as 'tis legitimate.
But see how day declines now to its bound;
   and climb by night one cannot: it is well
   to think, then, of some pleasant resting-ground.

Anime sono a destra qua remote:
  se mi consenti, io ti merrò ad esse,
  e non sanza diletto ti fien note ».   48
« Com'è ciò? » fu risposto. « Chi volesse
  salir di notte fora egli impedito
  d'altrui, o non sarria chè non potesse? »   51
E il buon Sordello in terra fregò il dito,
  dicendo: « Vedi, sola questa riga
  non varcheresti dopo il Sol partito.   54
Non però ch'altra cosa desse briga
  che la notturna tenebra ad ir suso:
  quella col non poder la voglia intriga.   57
Ben si poria con lei tornare in giuso
  e passeggiar la costa intorno errando,
  mentre che l'orizzonte il dì tien chiuso ».   60
Allora il mio signor, quasi ammirando,
  « Menane dunque, » disse « là 've dici
  che aver si può diletto dimorando ».   63
Poco allungati c'eravam di lici,
  quand'io m'accorsi che il monte era scemo
  a guisa che i vallon li sceman quici.   66
« Colà » disse quell'ombra « n'anderemo
  dove la costa face di sè grembo,
  e là il novo giorno attenderemo ».   69
Tra erto e piano era un sentiero sghembo
  che ne condusse in fianco de la lacca,
  là dove più che a mezzo muore il lembo.   72
Oro ed argento fine, cocco e biacca,
  indaco, legno lucido, sereno,
  fresco smeraldo in l'ora che si fiacca,   75
da l'erba e da li fior, dentro a quel seno
  posti, ciascun saria di color vinto,
  come dal suo maggiore è vinto il meno.   78
Non avea pur Natura ivi dipinto,
  ma di soavità di mille odori
  vi facea uno, incognito e indistinto.   81
Salve Regina in sul verde e in su i fiori
  quivi seder cantando anime vidi,
  che per la valle non parean di fuori.   84

Souls, on the right here, in seclusion dwell:
  I'll bring thee, if thou give me leave, to them;
  not without joy wilt thou their presence hail.'
'How?' came response: 'would others foil the aim
  of him who sought to climb by night, or would
  he have but his own impotence to blame?'
Drawing his finger along the ground, the good
  Sordello said: 'Look, e'en beyond this line,
  the Sun gone, pass nor thou nor any could.
Not that aught save the shades of night define
  a bound beyond which barred is the ascent:
  'tis they that from the will its power disjoin.
Well might with them one's steps be downward bent
  and round the mountain-side at random stray
  while the horizon keeps the dawn close-pent.'
Then did my lord, as if in wonder, say:
  'Bring us then thither, where, as thou hast said,
  we can derive some pleasure from our stay.'
Only a short way thence had we been led,
  when in the hillside I perceived a dip,
  just as by valleys here a dip is made.
'Yonder,' that shade said, 'where the mountain-steep
  makes of itself a lap, we hence will go
  and there for the new day our watch will keep.'
'Twixt steep and level wound a path, which now
  led us along that corrie's flank, to wit
  there where, by more than half, its rim sinks low.
Gold and fine silver, rotten wood self-lit,
  indigo, white lead, cochineal, sky-blue,
  fresh emerald at the instant it is split,
each by the herbage and the flowers which grew
  within that bosom in colour were outdone,
  e'en as its greater doth the less subdue.
Nor in that place had Nature limned alone,
  but from a thousand odours, there allied,
  made one scent, undetermined and unknown.
Here on the flowers and grass I souls espied,
  '*Salve regina*' singing, seated where
  owing to the vale they appeared not from outside.

307

« Prima che il poco sole omai s'annidi »
   cominciò il Mantovan che ci avea volti
   « tra costor non vogliate ch'io vi guidi.   87
Da questo balzo meglio gli atti e i volti
   conoscerete voi di tutti quanti,
   che ne la lama giù tra essi accolti.   90
Colui che più sied'alto e fa sembianti
   d'aver negletto ciò che far dovea,
   e che non move bocca a gli altrui canti,   93
Rodolfo imperador fu, che potea
   sanar le piaghe ch'hanno Italia morta
   sì che tardi per altri si ricrea.   96
L'altro, che ne la vista lui conforta,
   resse la terra dove l'acqua nasce
   che Molta in Albia ed Albia in mar ne porta.   99
Ottachero ebbe nome, e ne le fasce
   fu meglio assai che Venceslao suo figlio
   barbuto, cui lussuria ed ozio pasce.   102
E quel nasetto, che stretto a consiglio
   par con colui ch'ha sì benigno aspetto,
   morì fuggendo e disfiorando il giglio.   105
Guardate là come si batte il petto!
   L'altro vedete che ha fatto a la guancia
   de la sua palma, sospirando, letto.   108
Padre e suocero son del mal di Francia:
   sanno la vita sua viziata e lorda,
   e quindi viene il duol che sì li lancia.   111
Quel che par sì membruto, e che s'accorda
   cantando con colui dal maschio naso,
   d'ogni valor portò cinta la corda;   114
e se re dopo lui fosse rimaso
   lo giovanetto che retro a lui siede,
   ben andava il valor di vaso in vaso: 117
che non si puote dir de l'altre rede;
   Jacomo e Federigo hanno i reami,
   del retaggio miglior nessun possiede.   120
Rade volte risurge per li rami
   l'umana probitate, e questo vuole
   quei che la dà, perchè da lui si chiami.   123

'Before the brief sun nestles in his lair,
  bid me not guide you amid those yonder'; so
  began the Mantuan who had led us there.
'Better from *this* bank will you learn to know
  the looks and acts of each and all, than when
  received amongst them in the dell below.
He who sits highest and, judged by his mien,
  appears to have neglected what he should
  have done, nor moves his mouth to the others' strain,
is Rudolph, who was emperor and could
  have healed Italia, now too mortally
  wounded to have by others her life renew'd.
The next, who seems consoling him, is he
  who ruled the land that gives the water birth
  Which Moldau bears to Elbe, Elbe to the sea.
Named Ottocar, he was of far more worth
  in swaddling clothes than Wenz'las, bearded, is—
  his son, who of sloth and lechery knows no dearth.
Yon Snubnose, whom one close in counsel sees
  with him who looks so kindly, died in flight,
  stripping its blossom from the fleur-de-lice.
Look how he beats his bosom, wretched wight!
  the other, see! has used his palm to lay
  his cheek on, while with sighs he mourns his plight.
Sire and wife's sire o' the Pest of France are they:
  they know his foul and vicious life: and thence
  the grief that to their hearts so stabs its way.
He whose large limbs give him pre-eminence,
  singing in time with him o' the Roman nose,
  wore girt the cord of every excellence.
Had but the youth, whose face behind him shows,
  continued reigning monarch in his stead,
  worth would indeed have passed from vase to vase,
which cannot of the other heirs be said:
  James now and Frederick have the kingdoms got;
  the better share hath none inherited.
Seldom re-mounteth through the branches aught
  of human goodness; and this willeth He
  who gives it, that from Him it may be sought.

Anche al nasuto vanno mie parole,
  non men che a l'altro, Pier, che con lui canta,
  onde Puglia e Provenza già si duole.   126
Tant'è del seme suo minor la pianta,
  quanto più che Beatrice e Margherita,
  Costanza di marito ancor si vanta.   129
Vedete il re de la semplice vita
  seder là solo: Arrigo d'Inghilterra;
  questi ha nei rami suoi migliore uscita.   132
Quel che più basso tra costor s'atterra,
  guardando in suso, è Guglielmo marchese,
  per cui e Alessandria e la sua guerra   135
fa pianger Monferrato e Canavese ».

CANTO 8

Era già l'ora che volge il disio
  ai naviganti e intenerisce il core,
  lo dì che han detto ai dolci amici addio;   3
e che lo novo peregrin d'amore
  punge, se ode squilla di lontano
  che paia il giorno pianger che si more;   6
quand'io incominciai a render vano
  l'udire, ed a mirare una de l'alme
  surta, che l'ascoltar chiedea con mano.   9
Ella giunse e levò ambo le palme,
  ficcando gli occhi verso l'oriente,
  come dicesse a Dio « D'altro non calme ».   12
Te lucis ante si devotamente
  le uscìo di bocca e con sì dolci note,
  che fece me a me uscir di mente.   15
E l'altre poi dolcemente e devote
  seguitar lei pur tutto l'inno intero,
  avendo gli occhi a le superne rote.   18

As to yon Big-nose, so my words may be
    applied to Pedro, who sings with him: whence
    the woes Apulia and Provence now dree.
The seed as far outshines the plant's pretence,
    as, more than Beatrice and Margaret,
    Constance yet vaunts her husband's excellence.
Behold the king whose life was guileless, set
    aloof there, Harry of England: herein blest
    to have for scion issue worthier yet.
He, lowest of all, with gaze to heav'n address'd,
    is Marquis William, for their championship
    of whom the war, by Alexandria press'd,
makes Montferrato and Canavese weep.'

CANTO 8

Now was the hour that shoreward turns the eye
    of men at sea and makes the bosom swell,
    the day they've bidden belovéd friends goodbye;
and stabs with love as tolls a distant bell
    the newly started traveller if he hears
    the sound which seems the dying day to knell;
when I began to disemploy my ears
    and of the souls watch one that I espied
    stand up and beckon for silence to its peers.
Joining and lifting both its palms, it eyed
    with steadfast look the East, as inwardly
    'twere saying to God: 'I care for nought beside.'
'*Te lucis ante*' so melodiously
    poured from its mouth, with such devotion phrased
    that I was rapt into an ecstasy.
And the others then, with voices sweetly raised,
    devoutly followed it the whole hymn through,
    while ever on the heavenly wheels they gazed.

Aguzza qui, lettor, ben gli occhi al vero,
  chè il velo è ora ben tanto sottile,
  certo che il trapassar dentro è leggiero.   21
Io vidi quell'esercito gentile
  tacito poscia riguardare in sue,
  quasi aspettando, pallido ed umile.   24
E vidi uscir de l'alto e scender giue
  due angeli con due spade affocate,
  tronche e private de le punte sue.   27
Verdi come fogliette pur mo nate
  erano in vesti, che da verdi penne
  percosse traean dietro e ventilate.   30
L'un poco sovra noi a star si venne,
  e l'altro scese in l'opposita sponda,
  sì che la gente in mezzo si contenne.   33
Ben discerneva in lor la testa bionda,
  ma ne la faccia l'occhio si smarria,
  come virtù che al troppo si confonda.   36
«Ambo vegnon dal grembo di Maria»
  disse Sordello «a guardia de la valle
  per lo serpente che verrà via via».   39
Ond'io, che non sapeva per qual calle,
  mi volsi intorno, e stretto m'accostai,
  tutto gelato, a le fidate spalle.   42
E Sordello anche: « Or avvalliamo omai
  tra le grandi ombre, e parleremo ad esse:
  grazioso fia lor vedervi assai».   45
Solo tre passi credo ch'io scendesse,
  e fui di sotto, e vidi un che mirava
  pur me, come conoscer mi volesse.   48
Tempo era già che l'aere s'annerava,
  ma non sì che tra gli occhi suoi e i miei
  non dichiarisse ciò che pria serrava.   51
Ver me si fece, ed io ver lui mi fei:
  Giudice Nin gentil, quanto mi piacque
  quando ti vidi non esser tra i rei!   54
Nullo bel salutar fra noi si tacque;
  poi dimandò: «Quant'è che tu venisti
  a piè del monte per le lontane acque?»   57

Sharpen thine eyes here, Reader, to the true
   meaning, because the veil is now so thin,
   that pierce it surely is thing not hard to do.
I saw that noble army then begin
   silently up tow'rds heaven their gaze to bend,
   as if expectant, pale and lowly of mien.
And I saw, issuing from on high, descend
   two angels with two swords of flame, each brand
   broken short off and blunted at the end.
Green as the young leaves, just ere they expand,
   their garb was, and drawn backward through the air
   by the strong pulse of their green pinions fann'd.
One, lighting close above us, halted there;
   one with the hillside opposite made touch,
   so that the folk all in between them were.
Blond were their heads, them saw I clearly as such;
   but at their faces dazzled was the eye,
   like to a power confused by overmuch.
'Both of them,' said Sordello, 'hither fly
   from Mary's bosom, to defend the vale
   against the serpent e'en now drawing nigh.'
Whereat—for whence 'twould come I could not tell—
   I turned me about and, chill with terror, strain'd
   close to the shoulders that I trusted well.
Once more Sordello: 'Let us now descend
   for converse with the mighty shades below:
   much will your presence to their pleasure tend.'
I think but three steps downward did I go
   ere I was with them, and I saw one gaze
   only at me, as fain my face to know.
'Twas growing dark, but not so dim the haze
   that 'twixt his eyes and mine were not display'd
   things hidden before by the light's dwindling rays.
He made tow'rds *me*, tow'rds *him* I likewise made:
   noble Judge Nino, how it cheered my heart
   to see thee, and not amongst the guilty dead!
No courteous greeting lacked on either part;
   then asked he: 'How long since didst thou attain
   this mountain's foot the distant waves athwart?'

« Oh » diss'io lui, « per entro i luoghi tristi
　venni stamane, e sono in prima vita,
　ancor che l'altra sì andando acquisti ».　　60
E come fu la mia risposta udita,
　Sordello ed egli indietro si raccolse,
　come gente di subito smarrita.　　63
L'uno a Virgilio, e l'altro ad un si volse
　che sedea lì, gridando: « Sù, Currado,
　vieni a veder che Dio per grazia volse! »　　66
Poi volto a me: « Per quel singular grado
　che tu dei a colui che sì nasconde
　lo suo primo perchè, che non gli è guado,　　69
quando sarai di là da le larghe onde,
　di' a Giovanna mia che per me chiami
　là dove a gl'innocenti si risponde.　　72
Non credo che la sua madre più m'ami
　poscia che trasmutò le bianche bende,
　le quai convien che, misera, ancor brami.　　75
Per lei assai di lieve si comprende
　quanto in femmina foco d'amor dura
　se l'occhio o il tatto spesso non l'accende.　　78
Non le farà sì bella sepoltura
　la vipera che il Milanese accampa,
　com'avria fatto il gallo di Gallura ».　　81
Così dicea, segnato de la stampa,
　nel suo aspetto, di quel dritto zelo,
　che misuratamente in core avvampa.　　84
Gli occhi miei ghiotti andavan pur al cielo,
　pur là dove le stelle son più tarde
　sì come rota più presso a lo stelo.　　87
E il duca mio: « Figliuol, che là sù guarde? »
　E io a lui: « A quelle tre facelle
　di che il polo di qua tutto quanto arde ».　　90
Ond'egli a me: « Le quattro chiare stelle
　che vedevi staman son di là basse,
　e queste son salite ov'eran quelle ».　　93
Com'ei parlava, e Sordello a sè il trasse
　dicendo: « Vedi là 'l nostro avversaro »;
　e drizzò il dito perchè in là guardasse.　　96

'Oh!' was my answer, 'through the abodes of pain
   I came this morning: in first life am I,
   though the other by so journeying I may gain.'
As soon as they had heard me thus reply,
   he and Sordello backward drew a pace,
   like folk bewildered unexpectedly.
The one to Virgil, th'other turned his face
   to one there seated and: 'Up, Conrad! come
   and see,' he cried, 'this marvel of God's grace.'
Then, to me turning: 'By that untold sum
   of thanks thou owest to Him whose primal ground
   lies at a depth no mortal mind can plumb,
when thou hast crossed again the wide sea-bound,
   bid my Joanna grace for me implore
   where guileless hearts have ever answer found.
I think her mother loves me now no more
   since changing her white wimples, which 'tis meet
   that she, poor soul, should yet be pining for.
Right well from her you learn this truth, to wit,
   how brief a space a woman's love burns on,
   save eye or touch ofttimes rekindle it.
Fair though it look when blazoned bright thereon,
   yet Milan's viper will not grace her tomb
   so well as would Gallura's cock have done.'
As thus he spoke, I saw his face assume
   that mark of righteous zeal which in the soul,
   when in due measure moved, well findeth room.
My greedy eyes went only to the pole,
   there where the constellations move most slow,
   e'en as a wheel nearest the axle-bole.
'My son, what sight in heaven attracts thee so?'
   my guide asked. 'Those three cresset-flames,' I said,
   'with which the zenith here is all aglow.'
Whence he to me: 'Beneath the ocean-bed
   are sunk the stars thou sawest when day was new,
   those radiant four, and these are risen instead.'
As thus he spoke, behold Sordello drew
   him back: 'See there, our adversary!' he cried,
   pointing his finger as a guide thereto.

Da quella parte onde non ha riparo
  la picciola vallea, era una biscia
  forse qual diede ad Eva il cibo amaro.   99
Tra l'erba e i fiori venia la mala striscia
  volgendo ad ora ad or la testa, e il dosso
  leccando come bestia che si liscia.   102
Io non vidi, e però dicer non posso,
  come mosser gli astor celestiali,
  ma vidi bene e l'uno e l'altro mosso.   105
Sentendo fender l'aer a le verdi ali,
  fuggì il serpente, e gli angeli dier volta,
  suso a le poste rivolando iguali.   108
L'ombra che s'era al Giudice raccolta
  quando chiamò, per tutto quell'assalto
  punto non fu da me guardare sciolta.   111
« Se la lucerna che ti mena in alto
  trovi nel tuo arbitrio tanta cera
  quant'è mestieri infino al sommo smalto »   114
cominciò ella, « se novella vera
  di Val di Magra o di parte vicina
  sai, dilla a me che già grande là era.   117
Fui chiamato Currado Malaspina;
  non son l'antico, ma di lui discesi;
  ai miei portai l'amor che qui raffina ».   120
« Oh » diss'io lui, « per li vostri paesi
  già mai non fui, ma dove si dimora
  per tutta Europa ch'ei non sien palesi?   123
La fama che la vostra casa onora
  grida i signori e grida la contrada,
  sì che ne sa chi non vi fu ancora.   126
Ed io vi giuro, s'io di sopra vada,
  che vostra gente onrata non si sfregia
  del pregio de la borsa e da la spada.   129
Uso e natura sì la privilegia,
  che, perchè il capo reo lo mondo torca,
  sola va dritta, e il mal cammin dispregia ».   132
Ed egli: « Or va, che il Sol non si ricorca
  sette volte nel letto che il Montone
  con tutti e quattro i piè copre ed inforca,   135

Upon the little vale's unguarded side
  a snake, perhaps the very one that press'd
  on Eve the bitter food, straight onward hied.
Through flowers and grass, bending at times its crest
  to lick its back, like beast that sleeks its fell,
  the reptile glided on its evil quest.
I did not see, therefore I cannot tell
  how stooped the heavenly goshawks from the height,
  but stoop both did—that I perceived right well.
Hearing their green wings cleave the air, in fright
  the serpent fled, and the angels wheeled about,
  back to their posts soaring in equal flight.
The shade that when he heard the Judge's shout
  had neared him, not one instant turned his eye
  aside from me that whole affray throughout.
'So may thy will in due amount supply
  wax to the lamp that brings thee, till at last
  thy steps attain the enamelled sward on high,'
thus it began, 'if thou sure tidings hast
  of Val di Magra or the parts allied,
  tell me, for I was great there in times past.
Called Conrad Malaspina, 'twas my pride,
  though not the elder, that from him I sprung:
  I bore my folk the love here purified.'
'Oh!' was my answer, 'I was ne'er among
  your domains; but all Europe through, what place
  exists wherein their praises are not sung?
The fame that honours your illustrious race
  so bruits the land, so bruits the lords thereof,
  that strangers to them know them none the less.
I swear to you—so may I mount above—
  your honoured clan whether with purse or sword
  still earns the world's respect, still wins its love.
To it alone nature and use afford
  grace, though the guilty head leads all astray,
  to have kept the right path and the wrong abhorr'd.'
Then he: 'Enough; for ere the Sun shall lay
  himself seven times to rest upon the bed
  the Ram bestrides with all four feet asplay,

che cotesta cortese opinione
   ti fia chiavata in mezzo de la testa
   con maggior chiovi che d'altrui sermone,   138
se corso di giudicio non s'arresta ».

CANTO 9

LA concubina di Titone antico
   già s'imbiancava al balzo d'oriente
   fuor de le braccia del suo dolce amico;   3
di gemme la sua fronte era lucente,
   poste in figura del freddo animale
   che con la coda percuote la gente;   6
e la notte dei passi con che sale
   fatti avea due nel loco ov'eravamo,
   e il terzo già chinava in giuso l'ale,   9
quand'io, che meco avea di quel d'Adamo,
   vinto dal sonno, in su l'erba inchinai
   là 've già tutti e cinque sedevamo.   12
Ne l'ora che comincia i tristi lai
   la rondinella presso a la mattina,
   forse a memoria de' suoi primi guai,   15
e che la mente nostra, peregrina
   più da la carne e men dai pensier presa,
   a le sue vision quasi è divina,   18
in sogno mi parea veder sospesa
   un'aquila nel ciel con penne d'oro,
   con l'ali aperte ed a calare intesa;   21
ed esser mi parea là dove foro
   abbandonati i suoi da Ganimede,
   quando fu ratto al sommo consistoro.   24
Fra me pensava: « Forse questa fiede
   pur qui per uso, e forse d'altro loco
   disdegna di portarne suso in piede ».   27
Poi mi parea che, roteata un poco,
   terribil come folgor discendesse,
   e me rapisse suso infino al foco.   30

this courteous testimony shall in thy head
  be fixed by stouter nails than could by force
  of aught be driven that other folks have said;
if so it be that judgment holds its course.'

CANTO 9

Already, from the amorous arms releas'd
  of old Tithonus, she who shares his bed
  stood glimmering at her window in the east;
the sky that faced her was with gems inlaid
  set in that creature's shape whose blood is cold
  and tail inflicts a blow that people dread;
and of the steps she climbs with, two, all told,
  had Night made at the spot where we then were,
  and the third, now, began its wings to fold;
when I, who bore of Adam's load my share,
  vanquished by sleep, upon the grass reclined,
  all five of us being still seated there.
About the hour which morn comes close behind—
  when the small swallow starts her mournful lays,
  haply to keep her first laments in mind,
and when the soul, since more from flesh it strays,
  and less do thoughts the ranging fancy coop,
  as seer, almost prophetic power displays—
in dream meseemed I saw, as I looked up,
  an eagle in the sky, with plumes of gold,
  with wings wide open, and prepared to stoop;
and there meseemed I was where once of old
  abandoned were his mates by Ganymede
  when rapt to where the gods high council hold.
I thought: 'Perchance, 'tis only here he did
  or e'er does strike: prey he might clutch elsewhere
  he deems, perchance, unworthy of his heed.'
Then seemed he, having wheeled a little there,
  to swoop down, awful as lightning, me his aim,
  and snatch me upward e'en to the fiery sphere.

Ivi pareva ch'ella ed io ardesse;
  e sì l'incendio immaginato cosse,
  che convenne che il sonno si rompesse.   33
Non altrimenti Achille si riscosse,
  gli occhi svegliati rivolgendo in giro
  e non sappiendo là dove si fosse,   36
quando la madre da Chirone a Sciro
  trafugò lui dormendo in le sue braccia,
  là·onde poi li Greci il dipartiro,   39
che mi scoss'io sì come de la faccia
  mi fuggì il sonno, e diventai smorto,
  come fa l'uom che spaventato agghiaccia.   42
Da lato m'era solo il mio conforto,
  e il Sole er'alto già più che due ore,
  e il viso m'era a la marina torto.   45
« Non aver tema » disse il mio signore;
  « fatti secur che noi semo a buon punto:
  non stringer, ma rallarga ogni vigore.   48
Tu sei omai al Purgatorio giunto:
  vedi là il balzo che il chiude dintorno,
  vedi l'entrata là 've par disgiunto.   51
Dianzi, ne l'alba che precede al giorno,
  quando l'anima tua dentro dormia,
  sovra li fiori ond'è là giù adorno   54
venne una donna; e disse: 'Io son Lucia.
  Lasciatemi pigliar costui che dorme:
  sì l'agevolerò per la sua via'.   57
Sordel rimase e l'altre gentil forme.
  Ella ti tolse, e come il dì fu chiaro
  sen venne suso, e io per le sue orme.   60
Qui ti posò, ma pria mi dimonstraro
  gli occhi suoi belli quell'entrata aperta;
  poi ella e il sonno a una se n'andaro ».   63
A guisa d'uom che in dubbio si raccerta,
  e che muta in conforto sua paura
  poi che la verità gli è discoperta,   66
mi cambia' io; e come sanza cura
  vide me il duca mio, sù per lo balzo
  si mosse, ed io di retro, in ver l'altura.   69

There meseemed he, and I too, felt the flame:
   and so the imagined conflagration baked,
   that, broken, sleep perforce to an ending came.
Not otherwise, Achilles, having waked,
   did shudder, and wild glances round him dart,
   not knowing where he was or what to expect
(when him by stealth, press'd sleeping to her heart,
   from Chiron Scyros-wards his mother bore,
   whence the Greeks later caused him to depart),
than shuddered I, as soon as from before
   my face sleep fled; and I turned pale, like one
   who, panic-struck, stands frozen to the core.
Beside me was my Comfort, he alone,
   the Sun already up more than two hours,
   and I now faced and on the sea looked down.
'Fear not, we've reached a point now, which ensures
   thy safety,' said my lord, 'and things look fair:
   relax not, but exert thine utmost powers.
Thou art now come to Purgatory: see where
   the rampart runs which hems it in all round;
   see—where the rock seems cleft—one enters there!
Before this, ere the day had passed beyond
   its dawn, and while thy inner self was laid
   asleep, down there where flowers bedeck the ground,
there came a lady thither, and she said:
   "I am Lucy, let me lift this sleeper, so
   that I may ease his journey by my aid."
Sordello, with those noble forms below,
   remained behind: she took thee, and with day
   came upward; in her tracks I mounted too.
She laid thee here: her lovely eyes, 'twas they
   which showed me first that open entrance, then
   did she and sleep together pass away.'
As one who, doubting, feels assured again,
   and into confidence transmutes his fear,
   when once the truth has been to him made plain,
so changed was I; and, seeing me of good cheer,
   my leader moved on up the rocky steep,
   and I behind, tow'rds where the cliff rose sheer.

Lettor, tu vedi ben com'io innalzo
  la mia materia, e però con più arte
  non ti maravigliar s'io la rincalzo.   72
Noi ci appressammo, ed eravamo in parte
  che là dove pareami prima un rotto
  pur come un fesso che muro diparte,   75
vidi una porta, e tre gradi di sotto
  per gire ad essa, di color diversi,
  ed un portier che ancor non facea motto.   78
E come l'occhio più e più v'apersi,
  vidil seder sovra il grado soprano,
  tal ne la faccia, ch'io non lo soffersi;   81
ed una spada nuda aveva in mano,
  che rifletteva i raggi sì ver noi,
  ch'io dirizzava spesso il viso invano.   84
« Dite costinci: che volete voi? »
  cominciò egli a dire; « Ov'è la scorta?
  guardate che il venir sù non vi nòi ».   87
« Donna del ciel di queste cose accorta »
  rispose il mio maestro a lui « pur dianzi
  ne disse: 'Andate là: quivi è la porta' ».   90
« Ed ella i passi vostri in bene avanzi »
  ricominciò il cortese portinaio;
  « venite dunque ai nostri gradi innanzi ».   93
Là ne venimmo; e lo scaglion primaio
  bianco marmo era sì pulito e terso
  ch'io mi specchiai in esso qual io paio.   96
Era il secondo tinto più che perso,
  d'una petrina ruvida ed arsiccia,
  crepata per lo lungo e per traverso.   99
Lo terzo, che di sopra s'ammassiccia,
  porfido mi parea sì fiammeggiante
  come sangue che fuor di vena spiccia.   102
Sovra questo tenev'ambo le piante
  l'angel di Dio, sedendo in su la soglia,
  che mi sembrava pietra di diamante.   105
Per li tre gradi sù di buona voglia
  mi trasse il duca mio dicendo: « Chiedi
  umilemente che il serrame scioglia ».   108

Reader, well see'st thou how my theme I keep
 exalting: therefore marvel not if I
 support it with more cunning craftsmanship.
We reached a point, as we were drawing nigh,
 from which, where there had first seemed but a breach
 like to a cleft a wall is parted by,
I saw a gateway, and below—by which
 to approach it—three steps, coloured differently,
 and a gate-ward who as yet refrained from speech.
As more and more thereto I oped mine ee
 I saw he sat above the topmost stair,
 such in his visage as I could not dree.
And in his hand a naked sword he bare,
 which back to us-ward so the sunbeams threw,
 that all my attempts to face it fruitless were.
'Speak thence: What will ye? Who escorteth you?'
 he began: 'Look well, lest it be your fate
 to find the ascent a risk ye'll sorely rue.'
'A lady of heaven, well knowing our estate,'
 my master answered him, 'did but just now
 say to us, "Go ye thither, there's the gate".'
'And may she speed your steps in good' was how
 the gatekeeper resumed with courteous mien:
 'Come to our stairs, then; for we so allow.'
There came we, and the first great step had been
 made of white marble, polished with such skill,
 that mirrored was my very self therein.
The second, coloured perse or darker still,
 was of rough stone and calcined as by heat,
 cracked through from side to side and head to heel.
As for the third, whose mass surmounts them, it,
 meseemed, was porphyry, as flaming-red
 as blood one sees a spurting vein emit.
God's angel, both feet planted on this tread,
 was sitting on the threshold: to my view
 this last of solid adamant seemed made.
Over the three steps then my leader drew
 me upward with a good will, saying: 'Entreat
 him humbly now that he the bolt undo.'

Devoto mi gittai ai santi piedi;
　misericordia chiesi che m'aprisse,
　ma pria nel petto tre fiate mi diedi.　　　111
Sette P nella fronte mi descrisse
　col punton della spada, e « Fa che lavi
　quando sei dentro queste piaghe » disse.　　　114
Cenere o terra secca che si cavi
　d'un color fora col suo vestimento;
　e di sotto da quel trasse due chiavi.　　　117
L'una era d'oro e l'altra era d'argento;
　pria con la bianca e poscia con la gialla
　fece a la porta sì ch'io fui contento.　　　120
« Quandunque l'una d'este chiavi falla
　che non si volga dritta per la toppa »
　diss'egli a noi « non s'apre questa calla.　　　123
Più cara è l'una, ma l'altra vuol troppa
　d'arte e d'ingegno avanti che disserri,
　perch'ella è quella che il nodo disgroppa.　　　126
Da Pier le tegno; e dissemi ch'io erri
　anzi ad aprir ch'a tenerla serrata,
　pur che la gente ai piedi mi s'atterri ».　　　129
Poi pinse l'uscio a la porta sacrata;
　dicendo: « Intrate, ma facciovi accorti
　che di fuor torna chi indietro si guata ».　　　132
E quando fur sui cardini distorti
　li spigoli di quella regge sacra
　che di metallo son sonanti e forti,　　　135
non rugghiò sì nè si mostrò sì acra
　Tarpea, come le fu tolto il buono
　Metello, per che poi rimase macra.　　　138
Io mi rivolsi attento, al primo tuono,
　e *Te Deum laudamus* mi parea
　udire in voci miste a dolce suono.　　　141
Tale imagine a punto mi rendea
　ciò ch'io udiva, qual prender si suole
　quando a cantar con organi si stea;　　　144
ch'or sì or no s'intendon le parole.

Devoutly I cast myself at the holy feet:
   in mercy I begged that he would let me in,
   but first upon my bosom thrice I beat.
Seven P's upon my brow, the scars of sin,
   he traced with the sword's point, and 'see that these
   thou wash away,' he said, 'when thou'rt within.'
Ashes, or earth when delved, if dry it is,
   would of one colour with his vesture be,
   and from beneath it he drew forth two keys,
the one of gold, the other of silver; he
   first with the white, then with the yellow, wrought
   so with the gate that he contented me.
'Whene'er the wards of either key get caught
   within the lock so that it turns awry,'
   he said to us, 'this passage opens not.
Costlier the one: but the other, ere thereby
   the lock be turned, needs wisdom and great skill,
   for it is that which doth the knot untie.
From Piers I hold them; nor should I do ill
   he told me, if suppliants at my feet fall prone,
   rather to ope, than keep it bolted still.'
Then of that holy gate he pushed upon
   the valve, saying: 'Enter; but be warned—outside
   must he return whose glance is backward thrown.'
When on the hinges turned, as it swung wide,
   the pivots of that sacred door, which are
   of metal strong and resonantly gride,
not roared so loud, less strident was by far,
   Tarpeia, when wrested from it was the good
   Metellus, and it then was left stripped bare.
I turned attent, at the first sound, and could
   hear *Te Deum laudamus*, so I deemed,
   in accents blent with notes that sweetly flow'd.
That which I heard the like impression seemed
   to give me, as may here oft-times be got
   when, chanted to an organ, what is hymned
is at some moments heard, at others not.

CANTO 10

Poi fummo dentro al soglio de la porta
   che il malo amor de l'anime disusa
   perchè fa parer dritta la via torta,   3
sonando la sentii esser richiusa;
   e s'io avessi gli occhi volti ad essa
   qual fora stata al fallo degna scusa?   6
Noi salivam per una pietra fessa
   che si moveva d'una e d'altra parte,
   sì come l'onda che fugge e s'appressa.   9
« Qui si conviene usare un poco d'arte »
   cominciò il duca mio « in accostarsi
   or quinci or quindi al lato che si parte ».   12
E questo fece i nostri passi scarsi,
   tanto che pria lo scemo de la Luna
   rigiunse al letto suo per ricorcarsi   15
che noi fossimo fuor di quella cruna.
   Ma quando fummo liberi ed aperti,
   sù dove il monte indietro si rauna,   18
io stancato ed ambedue incerti
   di nostra via, ristemmo in su un piano
   solingo più che strade per diserti.   21
Da la sua sponda ove confina il vano
   al piè de l'alta ripa che pur sale,
   misurrebbe in tre volte un corpo umano;   24
e quanto l'occhio mio potea trar d'ale,
   or dal sinistro ed or dal destro fianco,
   questa cornice mi parea cotale.   27
Là sù non eran mossi i piè nostri anco,
   quand'io conobbi quella ripa intorno
   che, dritta, di salita aveva manco,   30
esser di marmo candido e adorno
   d'intagli sì, che non pur Policreto,
   ma la natura lì avrebbe scorno.   33
L'angel che venne in Terra col decreto
   de la molt'anni lacrimata pace,
   che aperse il ciel dal suo lungo divieto,   36

CANTO 10

Wʜᴇɴ we were past the threshold of the gate
    which souls, impelled by evil love, disuse,
    because this makes the crooked way seem straight,
the door, pulled to, so clanged, I could not choose
    but hear; though had I turned my eyes to it,
    what plea had fault so grave sufficed to excuse?
We were ascending through a rock that, split,
    kept moving from the one to the other side,
    like waves that now advance and now retreat.
'Here it behoveth us' began my guide
    'to employ some skill in keeping closely to
    the side, this way or that, which leaves a void.'
And such procedure made our steps so few,
    that the Moon's waning orb had left the sky
    to seek its bed and rest itself anew,
ere we had issued from that needle's eye:
    but when we had won forth to an open space
    above, where draws-in the declivity,
I, weary, and both alike still left to guess
    our way, we stopped on level ground e'en more
    lonely than roads that pave a wilderness.
From where its edge confines the void, this floor
    to that point whence the cliff keeps rising sheer
    would measure a man's body three times o'er.
And to the farthest that my eye could peer,
    whether it leftward flew or tow'rds the right,
    this cornice looked of such width everywhere.
Our feet had not yet moved upon that height,
    when I perceived that, all round, the rock-wall
    (climb which, it being vertical, none might)
was of white marble, decked with carvings, all
    so grav'n that Polyclete nor only he,
    but Nature's self, had there been shamed withal.
The angel who came to Earth with the decree
    establishing the ages-wept-for peace,
    which opened Heav'n, from its long ban set free,

dinanzi a noi pareva sì verace,
quivi intagliato in un atto soave,
che non sembiava imagine che tace.   39
Giurato si saria ch'ei dicesse *Ave*;
perchè ivi era imaginata quella
che ad aprir l'alto amor volse la chiave;   42
e aveva in atto impressa esta favella,
Ecce ancilla Dei, propriamente
come figura in cera si suggella.   45
« Non tener pure ad un loco la mente »
disse il dolce maestro, che m'avea
da quella parte onde il core ha la gente.   48
Per ch'io mi mossi col viso, e vedea
di retro da Maria, da quella costa
onde m'era colui che mi movea,   51
un'altra storia ne la roccia imposta;
per ch'io varcai Virgilio, e feimi presso
a ciò che fosse a gli occhi miei disposta.   54
Era intagliato lì nel marmo stesso
lo carro e i buoi traendo l'arca santa,
per che si teme officio non commesso.   57
Dinanzi parea gente, e, tutta quanta
partita in sette cori, a' due miei sensi
faceva dir l'un « No », l'altro « Sì, canta ».   60
Similemente al fummo de gl'incensi
che v'era imaginato, gli occhi e il naso
ed al sì ed al no discordi fensi.   63
Lì precedeva al benedetto vaso,
trescando alzato, l'umile salmista;
e più e men che re era in quel caso.   66
Di contra, effigiata ad una vista
d'un gran palazzo, Micòl ammirava
sì come donna dispettosa e trista.   69
Io mossi i piè dal loco dov'io stava
per avvisar da presso un'altra storia
che di retro a Micòl mi biancheggiava.   72
Quivi era storiata l'alta gloria
del roman principato il cui valore
mosse Gregorio a la sua gran vittoria: 75

before us stood so carved that none could miss
  to note his gracious attitude, nor fail
  to ejaculate 'No silent image, this!'
One could have sworn that he was crying '*Hail!*';
  for she who turned the key which open laid
  the exalted Love was imaged there as well;
and in her gesture were these words she said,
  '*Ecce ancilla Dei*,' as clearly impressed
  as is in wax the shape a seal hath made.
'Keep not to but *one* spot thy mind addressed'
  my loving master said, who on that side
  of him then had me where man's heart is placed.
Therefore I moved my visage, and descried
  past Mary (on that side of me where he
  was standing with whose charge I thus complied)
placed in the rock another history:
  so, stepping across Virgil, I drew nigh,
  to have it set forth straight in front of me.
There, sculptured in the marble's self, did I
  see wain and oxen drawing the ark of God,
  which makes men of unchartered office shy.
Before it folk appeared: and the whole crowd—
  seven separate choirs—made, of my senses, two
  say, one 'they're mute' and one 'they're singing loud.'
Likewise the smoke that from the censers blew
  was there so imaged, that with 'yea' and 'nay'
  the eyes and nose disputed which spake true.
There in the sacred vessel's van his way,
  leaping girt-high, the humble psalmist took,
  both more and less than king in that array.
Facing him, figured in a window-nook
  of a great palace, Michal, like a vexed
  and scornful dame, stood frowning her rebuke.
I moved from where I was, that I might next
  con close at hand, where it was gleaming white
  past Michal, yet another storied text.
There the exalted glory met my sight
  of Rome's great prince, whose goodness by its power
  moved Gregory to win his noblest fight.

io dico di Traiano imperatore.
 Ed una vedovella gli era al freno,
 di lacrime atteggiata e di dolore.   78
Intorno a lui parea calcato e pieno
 di cavalieri, e l'aquile ne l'oro
 sovr'essi in vista al vento si movieno.   81
La miserella intra tutti costoro
 parea dicer: « Signor, fammi vendetta
 del mio figliuol ch'è morto, ond'io m'accoro ». 84
Ed egli a lei risponder: « Ora aspetta
 tanto ch'io torni ». E quella: « Signor mio »,
 come persona in cui dolor s'affretta,   87
« se tu non torni? » Ed ei: « Chi fia dov'io
 la ti farà ». Ed ella: « L'altrui bene
 a te che fia, se il tuo metti in oblio? » 90
Ond'egli: « Or ti conforta, ch'ei conviene
 ch'io solva il mio dover anzi ch'io mova:
 giustizia vuole e pietà mi ritiene ».   93
Colui che mai non vide cosa nova
 produsse esto visibile parlare,
 novello a noi perchè qui non si trova. 96
Mentr'io mi dilettava di guardare
 le imagini di tante umilitadi,
 e per lo fabbro loro a veder care,   99
« Ecco di qua, ma fanno i passi radi »
 mormorava il poeta « molte genti:
 questi ne invieranno a gli alti gradi ». 102
Gli occhi miei, che a mirare erano intenti,
 per veder novitadi, ond'ei son vaghi,
 volgendosi ver lui non furon lenti.   105
Non vo' però, lettor, che tu ti smaghi
 di buon proponimento, per udire
 come Dio vuol che il debito si paghi. 108
Non attender la forma del martire:
 pensa la succession, pensa che al peggio
 oltre la gran sentenza non può ire.   111
Io cominciai: « Maestro, quel ch'io veggio
 movere a noi non mi sembian persone,
 e non so che, sì nel veder vaneggio ». 114

I speak of Trajan—him, the emperor:
   and a poor widow on his bridle laid
   her hand, in gesture sad and weeping sore.
Round him a press of horsemen was displayed,
   trampling the ground: the eagles, thrid with gold,
   over him to the wind, in seeming, swayed.
Forlorn mid all this pomp she appeared to hold
   him back saying: 'Sire, avenge me for my son
   who is dead, for which I mourn with grief untold';
and he to answer her: 'I shall anon
   return, so wait till then.' And she: 'O sire,'
   like to a person grief keeps egging on,
'if thou return not?' He then: 'Thy desire
   my heir will grant.' And she: 'Will his good deeds
   avail thee aught, if of thy own thou tire?'
Whereupon he: 'Now comfort thee, for needs
   must I discharge my duty ere I go;
   compassion holds me back, and justice bids.'
That Being, who can never see or know
   aught new, produced this visible speaking, new
   to us, because 'tis found not here below.
While I was gazing, as I joyed to do,
   at emblems of such great humilities,
   dear also, for their Craftsman's sake, to view,
'Lo! on this side—but slow their progress is—'
   murmured the poet 'people—a multitude:
   direct us to the lofty steps will these.'
I, who still gazing at the sculpture stood,
   lagged not in turning tow'rds him, greedy-eyed—
   being one to whom new sights are welcome food.
I would not have thee, Reader, turned aside
   from a good resolution for hearing how
   God willeth that the debt be satisfied.
Heed not the torment's form: consider thou
   what follows: bear in mind that, at the worst,
   beyond the last great doom it cannot go.
'Master, yon shapes I see' said I at first
   'which tow'rds us move, do not seem real men,
   nor know I what, I'm so in doubt immers'd.'

Ed egli a me: « La grave condizione
  di lor tormento a terra li rannicchia
  sì che i miei occhi pria n'ebber tenzone.   117
Ma guarda fiso là, e disviticchia
  col viso quel che vien sotto a quei sassi:
  già scorger puoi come ciascun si picchia ».   120
O superbi cristian, miseri lassi,
  che, de la vista de la mente infermi,
  fidanza avete nei retrosi passi,   123
non v'accorgete voi che noi siam vermi
  nati a formar l'angelica farfalla
  che vola a la giustizia sanza schermi?   126
Di che l'animo vostro in alto galla,
  poi siete quasi entómata in difetto
  sì come verme in cui formazion falla?   129
Come per sostentar solaio o tetto
  per mensola talvolta una figura
  si vede giugner le ginocchia al petto,   132
la qual fa del non ver vera rancura
  nascere in chi la vede, così fatti
  vid'io color, quando posi ben cura.   135
Ver è che più e meno eran contratti
  secondo che avean più o meno a dosso;
  e qual più pazienza avea ne gli atti   138
piangendo parea dicer: « Più non posso ».

CANTO 11

« O PADRE nostro che nei cieli stai,
  non circoscritto, ma per più amore
  ch'ai primi effetti di là sù tu hai,   3
laudato sia il tuo nome e il tuo valore
  da ogni creatura, com'è degno
  di render grazie al tuo dolce vapore.   6

And he: 'The grave sin that conditions their pain
   so bows them to the ground that, seeing it, *my*
   eyes too were first subjected to a strain.
But look hard there, and with thy vision try
   to disengage what comes beneath those stones:
   already how each is stricken thou canst descry.'
Ah! ye proud Christians, weary and uttering groans,
   of whom, diseased in mental vision, none,
   tho' his feet turn back, his faith in them disowns,
perceive ye not that we are grubs, each one
   born to produce the angelic butterfly,
   which flies to justice, all its trappings gone?
What is it floats your spirit up so high,
   since ye are, as 'twere, insects incomplete—
   grubs, to their full formation still unnigh?
As, for a corbel, to support the weight
   of roof or ceiling, one may sometimes find
   a figure carved with knees and breast that meet,
which begets real pain, from pain in kind
   unreal, in who sees it; thuswise made
   I saw these, when I gave them my whole mind.
'Tis true that they were more or less downweigh'd
   as more or less the load their shoulders bore;
   and he in whom most patience was display'd,
weeping appeared to say: 'I can no more.'

CANTO 11

'OUR Father, which art in the heav'ns, thereby
   not circumscribed, but only in the sense
   thou lovest more the first effects on high,
praised be thy name and thine omnipotence
   by every creature, even as it is meet
   to render thanks to thy sweet effluence.

Venga ver noi la pace del tuo regno,
　　chè noi ad essa non potem da noi,
　　s'ella non vien, con tutto nostro ingegno.　　　9
Come del suo voler gli angeli tuoi
　　fan sacrificio a te, cantando Osanna,
　　così facciano gli uomini de' suoi.　　　12
Dà oggi a noi la cotidiana manna,
　　sanza la qual per quest'aspro diserto
　　a retro va chi più di gir s'affanna.　　　15
E come noi lo mal che avem sofferto
　　perdoniamo a ciascuno, e tu perdona
　　benigno, e non guardar lo nostro merto.　　　18
Nostra virtù, che di leggier s'adona,
　　non spermentar con l'antico avversaro,
　　ma libera da lui che sì la sprona.　　　21
Quest'ultima preghiera, Signor caro,
　　già non si fa per noi, chè non bisogna,
　　ma per color che dietro a noi restaro ».　　　24
Così a sè e a noi buona ramogna
　　quell'ombre orando, andavan sotto il pondo
　　simile a quel che talvolta si sogna,　　　27
disparmente angosciate tutte a tondo
　　e lasse, su per la prima cornice,
　　purgando la caligine del mondo.　　　30
Se di là sempre ben per noi si dice,
　　di qua che dire e fare a lor si puote
　　da quei ch'hanno al voler buona radice?　　　33
Ben si dee loro atar lavar le note
　　che portar quinci, sì che mondi e lievi
　　possano uscire a le stellate rote.　　　36
« Deh, se giustizia e pietà vi disgrevi
　　tosto, sì che possiate mover l'ala
　　che secondo il disio vostro vi levi,　　　39
mostrate da qual mano inver la scala
　　si va più corto, e se c'è più d'un varco,
　　quel ne insegnate che men erto cala;　　　42
chè questi che vien meco, per l'incarco
　　de la carne d'Adamo onde si veste,
　　al montar sù, contra sua voglia, è parco ».　　　45

Come unto us thy kingdom's peace: for it
 no power of ourselves to attain have we,
 save of itself it comes, with all our wit.

As of their wills thine angels unto thee
 make sacrifice, chanting "*hosanna*," so
 let mankind make of theirs as joyously.

Give us this day our daily manna too,
 without which through this rugged wilderness
 those labouring most to advance but backward go.

And like as we forgive those who transgress
 against ourselves, be not extreme to weigh
 our merit, but forgive thou of thy grace.

Our will-power, lightly worsted in the fray,
 put not to trial with our ancient foe,
 but him, who goads it so, drive thou away.

This last petition, dearest Lord, we know
 is needless for ourselves, but it is made
 for those we've left behind us down below.'

So for themselves and us those spirits prayed
 god-speed, while all, beneath the burden bent
 like that we sometimes dream upon us laid,

unequally tormented, and sore spent,
 kept pacing the first cornice round and round,
 purging away the world's foul sediment.

If there at all times prayers for us abound,
 what can for them be done or uttered here
 by those whose wills are rooted in good ground?

Truly we should assist them to wash clear
 the stains they carried hence, that clean and light
 they may pass forth, each to his starry sphere.

'Ah, so may justice speedily unite
 with mercy to disburden you, that where
 ye long to soar, there ye may wing your flight,

show us on which hand we may reach the stair
 most shortly; and, if more ways there be than one,
 which mounts least steeply I pray you to declare.

For my companion, who is clothed upon
 with Adam's flesh and by its weight oppress'd,
 when climbing grows, against his will, fordone.'

335

Le lor parole, che rendero a queste
   che dette avea colui cui io seguiva,
   non fur da cui venisser manifeste;   48
ma fu detto: « A man destra, per la riva
   con noi venite, e troverete il passo
   possibile a salir persona viva.   51
E s'io non fossi impedito dal sasso
   che la cervice mia superba doma,
   onde portar conviemmi il viso basso,   54
cotesti che ancor vive e non si noma
   guardere' io per veder se il conosco,
   e per farlo pietoso a-questa soma.   57
Io fui latino, e nato d'un gran tosco:
   Guglielmo Aldobrandesco fu mio padre;
   non so se il nome suo già mai fu vosco.   60
L'antico sangue e l'opere leggiadre
   de' miei maggiori mi fer sì arrogante
   che, non pensando alla comune madre,   63
ogni uomo ebbi in dispetto tanto avante
   ch'io ne morii, come i Sanesi sanno,
   e sallo in Campagnatico ogni fante.   66
Io sono Omberto; e non pure a me danno
   superbia fe', chè tutti i miei consorti
   ha ella tratti seco nel malanno.   69
E qui convien ch'io questo peso porti
   per lei, tanto che a Dio si sodisfaccia,
   poi ch'io nol fei tra i vivi, qui tra i morti». 72
Ascoltando, chinai in giù la faccia;
   e un di lor, non questi che parlava,
   si torse sotto il peso che li impaccia,   75
e videmi e conobbemi e chiamava,
   tenendo gli occhi con fatica fisi
   a me, che tutto chin con loro andava.   78
« Oh » diss'io lui, « non sei tu Oderisi,
   l'onor d'Agobbio e l'onor di quell'arte
   che *alluminare* è chiamata in Parisi?»   81
« Frate » diss'egli, « più ridon le carte
   che pennelleggia Franco Bolognese:
   l'onore è tutto or suo, e mio in parte.   84

From whence their words came which were then address'd
   to him I followed who had spoken thus
   asking for guidance, was not manifest;
but this was said: 'Come to the right with us
   along the ledge, and passage ye shall find
   for living man not too precipitous.
And checked me not the stone, by heaven design'd
   to curb my haughty neck and with its weight
   to keep my visage ever down inclined,
this man still living, whose name thou dost not state,
   I would look up at, chance his friendship claim
   and, burdened thus, win him to weep my fate.
Latin was I: a Tuscan known to fame,
   William Aldobrandesco, was my sire;
   I know not if ye ever heard his name.
My forbears' feats set my proud blood on fire:
   forgetting the one womb to which all owe
   their being, to such heights did I aspire,
and such contempt for all men did I show,
   it wrought my death, as the Sienese can tell
   and every wight in Compagnático.
For I am Humbert: and through pride I fell,
   nor I alone, for all my kith and kin
   into disaster has it dragged as well.
Living, I scorned this load and for my sin
   must therefore bear it here among the dead,
   till I at last from God my quittance win.'
While listening I had downward bowed my head:
   and one (not Humbert) twisting as he bent
   beneath the load by which they were bested,
saw me and knew me and, calling, gazed intent,
   holding his eyes with difficulty extreme
   on me, who stooping low still with them went.
'Oh, art *thou* not Oderisi' I said to him,
   'honour of Gubbio, honour of that fine
   art by Parisians called the art "to limn"?'
'Brother,' said he, 'gayer the pages shine
   which Franco of Bologna paints: the whole
   honour is his now and but partly mine.

Ben non sare'io stato sì cortese
  mentre ch'io vissi, per lo gran disio
  de l'eccellenza, ove mio core intese.   87
Di tal superbia qui si paga il fio:
  ed ancor non sarei qui, se non fosse
  che possendo peccar mi volsi a Dio.   90
Oh vana gloria de l'umane posse!
  com' poco verde in su la cima dura,
  se non è giunta da l'etati grosse!   93
Credette Cimabue ne la pittura
  tener lo campo, ed ora ha Giotto il grido,
  sì che la fama di colui oscura.   96
Così ha tolto l'uno a l'altro Guido
  la gloria de la lingua, e forse è nato
  chi l'uno e l'altro caccerà di nido.   99
Non è il mondan romore altro che un fiato
  di vento, ch'or vien quinci ed or vien quindi,
  e muta nome perchè muta lato.   102
Che voce avrai tu più se vecchia scindi
  da te la carne, che se fossi morto
  anzi che tu lasciassi il *pappo* e il *dindi*,   105
pria che passin mill'anni? ch'è più corto
  spazio a l'eterno che un mover di ciglia
  al cerchio che più tardi in cielo è torto.   108
Colui che del cammin sì poco piglia
  dinanzi a me, Toscana sonò tutta,
  ed ora a pena in Siena sen pispiglia,   111
ond'era sire quando fu distrutta
  la rabbia fiorentina, che superba
  fu a quel tempo sì com'ora è putta.   114
La vostra nominanza è color d'erba
  che viene e va, e quei la discolora
  per cui ell'esce da la terra acerba».   117
E io a lui: «Tuo vero dir m'incuora
  buona umiltà, e gran tumor m'appiani;
  ma chi è quei di cui tu parlavi ora?»   120
«Quegli è» rispose «Provenzan Salvani;
  ed è qui perchè fu presuntuoso
  a recar Siena tutta a le sue mani.   123

'Tis true I should have lacked the self-control
  in life to be so courteous, through the keen
  ambition to excel which fired my soul.

Such pride pays forfeit here; nor had I been
  here yet, save that I turned to seek God's grace,
  while still it lay within my power to sin.

Vain glory of human powers, how brief a space
  endures the green thy loftiest twigs unfold,
  save when succeeding times are talentless!

In painting Cimabue thought to hold
  the field, and now hath Giotto all the cry,
  so that the other's fame is less extoll'd.

Thus Guido wrests the glory of poetry
  from Guido; and already born (who knows?)
  is one who shall unnest both by and by.

The reputation which the world bestows
  is like the wind, that shifts now here now there,
  its name changed with the quarter whence it blows.

What more fame will be thine, suppose thou bare
  thyself of flesh when old, than hadst thou died
  before being quit of "pap" and "chink", or e'er

a thousand years pass?—briefer time beside
  the eternal than, beside the sphere that wheels
  slowest in heav'n, the eye takes to blink its lid.

All Tuscany once rang with him who feels
  his slow way there in front of me; and now
  scarce whisper of his name through Siena steals,

which he was lord of, when was struck the blow
  that felled infuriate Florence, who was then
  as proud, as now she's venal and brought low.

Like grass in hue is the renown of men,
  which comes and goes, and he through whom it springs
  green from the earth soon withers it again.'

And I to him: 'Thy truthful discourse brings
  a chastening meekness and pricks swollen pride:
  but who is he of whom thou hast said these things?'

' 'Tis Provenzán Salvani,' he replied,
  'who made all Siena own his mastery,
  for which presumptuous deed he here must bide.

Ito è così e va sanza riposo
  poi che morì: cotal moneta rende
  a sodisfar chi è di là tropp'oso ».   126
Ed io: « Se quello spirito che attende
  pria che si penta l'orlo de la vita
  là giù dimora e qua sù non ascende,   129
se buona orazion lui non aita
  prima che passi tempo quanto visse,
  come fu la venuta a lui largita? »   132
« Quando vivea più glorioso » disse,
  « liberamente nel Campo di Siena,
  ogni vergogna deposta, s'affisse;   135
e lì, per trar l'amico suo di pena
  che sostenea ne la prigion di Carlo,
  si condusse a tremar per ogni vena.   138
Più non dirò, e scuro so che parlo;
  ma poco tempo andrà, che i tuoi vicini
  faranno sì che tu potrai chiosarlo.   141
Quest'opera gli tolse quei confini ».

CANTO 12

Dɪ pari come buoi che vanno a giogo
  m'andava io con quell'anima carca,
  fin chè il sofferse il dolce pedagogo.   3
Ma quando disse: « Lascia lui e varca,
  chè qui è buon con la vela e coi remi
  quantunque può ciascun pinger sua barca »,   6
dritto, siccome andar vuolsi, rife'mi
  con la persona, avvegna che i pensieri
  mi rimanessero e chinati e scemi.   9
Io m'era mosso, e seguia volentieri
  del mio maestro i passi, ed ambedue
  già mostravam com'eravam leggieri.   12

So hath he gone, and so unceasingly
  goes since his death: such compensation pay
  all those who in the world aspire too high.'
And I: 'If every soul who should delay
  repentance, till its life be all but sped,
  ascends not hither, but below must stay,
(unless the good by prayer should lend it aid)
  till time its whole life's length be passed, what right
  the coming here in his case warranted?'
Quoth he: 'When at his glory's topmost height,
  in Siena's great square, of his own free will,
  he took his stand, in ridicule's despite,
and there, to save his friend, who languished still
  in Charles's prison, brought himself to show
  the shame he felt through all his pulses thrill.
Enough! I speak in riddles, as I know;
  but ere thy neighbours help thee by clear signs
  to gloss my words, thou hast not far to go.
This deed delivered him from those confines.'

CANTO 12

Still side by side, like oxen that go yoked,
  I went on with that burdened soul as long
  as the kind pedagogue my action brooked:
but when he said: 'Pass onward; for such strong
  propulsion both with sail and oar all boats
  need here, that not to quit him now were wrong;'
in body the upright pose that best promotes
  the act of walking I resumed, although
  still humbled and abased remained my thoughts.
I had already moved and was with no
  reluctance following in my master's tread,
  both of us showing how nimbly we could go,

Ed ei mi disse: « Volgi gli occhi in giue:
　buon ti sarà per tranquillar la via
　veder lo letto de le piante tue ».　　　　　　15
Come, perchè di lor memoria sia,
　sovra i sepolti le tombe terragne
　portan segnato quel ch'egli eran pria,　　　18
onde lì molte volte se ne piagne
　per la puntura de la rimembranza,
　che solo ai pii dà de le calcagne;　　　　21
sì vid'io lì, ma di miglior sembianza
　secondo l'artificio, figurato
　quanto, per via, di fuor del monte avanza.　24
Vedea colui che fu nobil creato
　più ch'altra creatura, giù dal cielo
　folgoreggiando scendere da un lato.　　　27
Vedeva Briareo, fitto dal telo
　celestial, giacer da l'altra parte,
　grave a la terra per lo mortal gelo.　　　30
Vedea Timbreo, vedea Pallade e Marte,
　armati ancora, intorno al padre loro,
　mirar le membra dei Giganti sparte.　　　33
Vedea Nembrotte a piè del gran lavoro,
　quasi smarrito, riguardar le genti
　che in Sennaàr con lui superbi foro.　　　36
O Niobè, con che occhi dolenti
　vedeva io te segnata in su la strada,
　fra sette e sette tuoi figliuoli spenti!　　39
O Saùl, come su la propria spada
　quivi parevi morto in Gelboè,
　che poi non sentì pioggia nè rugiada!　　42
O folle Aragne, sì vedeva io te
　già mezza ragna, trista in su lo stracci
　de l'opera che mal per te si fè.　　　　45
O Roboam, già non par che minacci
　quivi il tuo segno; ma pien di spavento
　nel porta un carro sanza ch'altri il cacci.　48
Mostrava ancor lo duro pavimento
　come Alcmeone a sua madre fe' caro
　parer lo sventurato adornamento.　　　51

when to me 'Look thou downward now' he said:
  'thou'lt find it good, for easing of the way,
  to scan the bed on which thy soles are laid.'
As o'er the ensepulchred, that so they may
  be called to mind, the pavement-tombstones bear
  figures of what they looked like in their day—
whence comes it that not seldom tears are there
  shed at the prick of memory, though 'tis but
  the pitiful to whom it gives the spur—
so figured, but more life-like, since without
  defects of craftsmanship, did I there see
  all that for pathway from the mount juts out.
Mine eyes saw him, created in degree
  nobler than creatures else, down from the sky
  as lightning fall, on the one side of me.
Mine eyes saw Bríareus, on the other, lie
  cumbering the ground, stone-cold, for all his pride
  felled by the bolt from heaven's artillery.
Mine eyes saw, still armed, at their father's side
  Thymbraeus, Mars and Pallas gazing o'er
  the field with giants' limbs strewn far and wide.
Mine eyes saw, at the foot of his great tower,
  Nimrod, as though bewildered, eyeing the men
  who bragged with him in Shinar of their power.
Ah, Niobe, with eyes how brimmed with pain
  I saw, upon the pavement carved, thee too
  between thy children, seven and seven, all slain!
Ah, Saul, how there on thine own sword pierced through,
  wast thou portrayed, dead in Gilboa, a spot
  which felt thereafter neither rain nor dew!
Ah, vain Arachne, thee I saw distraught,
  already turned half spider, in the shreds
  of that which thou to thine own ill had'st wrought!
Ah, Rehoboam, here thine image sheds
  its air of menace; in a chariot set,
  'tis borne away, ere chased by what it dreads.
Now shown by that hard pavement further yet
  was how Alcmaeon made his mother pay
  right dearly for the luckless carcanet.

Mostrava come i figli si gettaro
  sovra Sennacherib dentro dal tempio,
  e come morto lui quivi lasciaro.   54
Mostrava la ruina e il crudo scempio
  che fe' Tamiri quando disse a Ciro:
  « Sangue sitisti, e io di sangue t'empio ».   57
Mostrava come in rotta si fuggiro
  gli Assiri poi che fu morto Oloferne,
  e anche le reliquie del martiro.   60
Vedeva Troia in cenere e caverne:
  o Ilion, come te basso e vile
  mostrava il segno che lì si discerne!   63
Qual di pennel fu maestro o di stile
  che ritraesse l'ombre e i tratti ch'ivi
  mirar farien ogni ingegno sottile?   66
Morti li morti e i vivi parean vivi:
  non vide me' di me, chi vide il vero,
  quant'io calcai finchè chinato givi.   69
Or superbite, e via col viso altero,
  figliuoli d'Eva, e non chinate il volto
  sì che veggiate il vostro mal sentiero! 72
Più era già per noi del monte volto
  e del cammin del Sole assai più speso
  che non stimasse l'animo non sciolto, 75
quando colui che sempre innanzi atteso
  andava, cominciò: « Drizza la testa,
  non è più tempo di gir sì sospeso.   78
Vedi colà un angel che s'appresta
  per venir verso noi, vedi che torna
  dal servigio del dì l'ancella sesta.   81
Di reverenza il viso e gli atti adorna
  sì che i diletti l'inviarci in suso;
  pensa che questo dì mai non raggiorna ». 84
Io era ben del suo ammonir uso
  pur di non perder tempo, sì che in questa
  materia non potea parlarmi chiuso.   87
A noi venia la creatura bella
  bianco vestita e ne la faccia quale
  par tremolando mattutina stella.   90

Now shown was how his own sons rushed to slay
   Sennacherib within the temple, killed
   him there, and left his body where it lay.
Now shown was the ruin Tómyris wrought, when, steeled
   'gainst pity, she to slaughtered Cyrus said:
   'Blood didst thou crave, with blood shalt thou be filled!'
Now shown was how in rout the Assyrians fled
   at Holofernes' death; there too his spurned
   remains were shown, a trunk without the head.
*M*ine eyes saw Troy, to pits and ashes turned:
   *a*h, Ilion, how debased and mean one saw
   *n*ow shown thine image, as 'tis there discerned!
What master, ever, of brush or point could draw
   figures and lineaments that, as there shown,
   would make the subtlest craftsman gaze with awe?
The dead looked dead, alive the living: none
   that saw the truth itself saw better than I
   all that I trod on, while I walked bent down.
Now be ye proud, advance with head held high,
   you sons of Eve, nor bend your visage low,
   to see the evil path ye are travelling by!
We had gone farther round the mount by now,
   much farther, on his course, the Sun had hied,
   than I had gauged, with mind enfettered so;
when he who still was walking watchful-eyed
   before me, thus began; 'Lift up thy head;
   time lacks now to go thus pre-occupied.
See there an angel who with welcome aid
   prepares to meet us: see, returning too
   from the day's service is the sixth handmaid.
With reverence, then, thine acts and looks endue,
   that he with joy may speed us on the ascent:
   think that this day will never dawn anew.'
Well used was I to his admonishment
   ne'er to lose time, so that familiar
   I found these words, nor hidden their intent.

The lovely creature, now from us not far,
   tow'rds us was coming on, white garmented,
   his visage sparkling as doth morning star.

Le braccia aperse e indi aperse l'ale;
  disse: « Venite, qui son presso i gradi,
  ed agevolemente omai si sale.   93
A questo invito vegnon molto radi:
  o gente umana, per volar sù nata,
  perchè a poco vento così cadi?»   96
Menocci ove la roccia era tagliata;
  quivi mi battè l'ali per la fronte,
  poi mi promise sicura l'andata.   99
Come a man destra, per salire al monte
  dove siede la chiesa che soggioga
  la ben guidata sopra Rubaconte,   102
si rompe del montar l'ardita foga
  per le scalee che si fero ad etade
  ch'era sicuro il quaderno e la doga,   105
così s'allenta la ripa, che cade
  quivi ben ratta da l'altro girone,
  ma quinci e quindi l'alta pietra rade.   108
Noi volgend'ivi le nostre persone,
  Beati pauperes spiritu voci
  cantaron sì che nol diria sermone.   111
Ahi quanto son diverse quelle foci
  da l'infernali! chè quivi per canti
  s'entra, e là giù per lamenti feroci.   114
Già montavam sù per gli scaglion santi,
  ed esser mi parea troppo più lieve
  che per lo pian non mi parea davanti.   117
Ond'io: « Maestro, di', qual cosa greve
  levata s'è da me, che nulla quasi
  per me fatica, andando, si riceve?»   120
Rispose: « Quando i P che son rimasi
  ancor nel volto tuo presso che stinti
  saranno, come l'un, del tutto rasi,   123
fien li tuoi piè dal buon voler sì vinti
  che non pur non fatica sentiranno,
  ma fia diletto lor esser sù spinti ».   126
Allor fec'io come color che vanno
  con cosa in capo non da lor saputa,
  se non che cenni altrui sospecciar fanno,   129

His arms he opened, then his wings, and said:
  'Come; for the stairs are nigh, and henceforth shall
  you unlaborïously mount ahead.

Few, few are they who come unto this call:
  born to fly upward, why, O human breed,
  at but a little wind dost thou so fall?'

To where the rock was cleft we took his lead:
  there with his wings he smote me on the brow,
  then that I safe should travel he guaranteed.

As on one's right, to scale the hill where now
  'bove Rubaconte's bridge the church is set
  which dominates the well-ruled town below,

the bold abruptness of the ascent is met
  and brok'n by steps constructed in the days
  when stave and ledger were inviolate;

so grows less steep the slope, which, other ways,
  falls very sharply here from the next round:
  yet doth the cliff, both sides, the climber graze.

As thither turned we our persons upward bound,
  '*Beati pauperes spiritu*' was sung
  in tones for which no language could be found.

Ah with what different sounds these passes rung
  from those of hell; for here to songs, down there
  to fierce wails, as one enters, give they tongue.

Up by the sacred steps already were
  we mounting, and I felt much lighter e'en
  than when I trod the level path whilere.

Whence I: 'Master, tell me what weight has been
  lifted from me, that climbing seems no strain,
  or almost none, from where these stairs begin?'

He answered: 'When the P's that still remain,
  all but extinguished, on thy face shall be,
  as one has been, erased completely, then

thy feet shall by goodwill so thoroughly
  be mastered, that not only will they not
  feel weary, but, when urged, will mount with glee.'

Then did I as men out walking, who have got
  something upon their head, but if not made
  by others' signs suspicious, know not what;

per che la mano ad accertar s'aiuta,
  e cerca, e trova, e quell'officio adempie
  che non si può fornir per la veduta;   132
e con le dita de la destra, scempie
  trovai pur sei, le lettere che incise
  quel da le chiavi a me sopra le tempie: 135
a che guardando il mio duca sorrise.

CANTO 13

Noi eravamo al sommo de la scala
  dove secondamente si risega
  lo monte che salendo altrui dismala.   3
Ivi così una cornice lega
  dintorno il poggio, come la primaia;
  se non che l'arco suo più tosto piega.   6
Ombra non v'è nè segno che si paia;
  parsi la ripa e parsi la via schietta
  col livido color de la petraia.   9
« Se qui per dimandar gente s'aspetta »
  ragionava il poeta, « io temo forse
  che troppo avrà d'indugio nostra eletta ». 12
Poi fisamente al Sole gli occhi porse;
  fece del destro lato a mover centro
  e la sinistra parte di sè torse.   15
« O dolce lume a cui fidanza i' entro
  per lo novo cammin, tu ne conduci »
  dicea « come condur si vuol quinci entro. 18
Tu scaldi il mondo, tu sovr'esso luci:
  s'altra ragione in contrario non ponta,
  esser den sempre li tuoi raggi duci ». 21
Quanto di qua per un migliaio si conta,
  tanto di là eravam noi già iti
  con poco tempo per la voglia pronta, 24

wherefore the hand, to ascertain, brings aid,
   and seeks and finds, and doth thereby afford
   the service that sight cannot, in its stead;
and, fingers spread wide, my right hand explor'd
   and found but six the letters that erewhile
   he of the keys above my temples scor'd;
which, when he saw it, made my leader smile.

CANTO 13

Upon the stairway's summit now we stood
   where for the second time is cut away
   the mount which, as one climbs, turns bad to good:
there, like the first, a second cornice lay
   girding the hill all round, save that its zone
   doth, as it bends, a sharper curve display.
No shading there, no imagery is shown;
   the cliff has nought, the pathway nought, to entice
   the eye; 'tis all smooth livid-coloured stone.
'If here we wait'—thus spoke the poet's voice—
   'for folk of whom to enquire, I am afraid
   we may perhaps o'erlong delay our choice.'
Then firmly upon the Sun his eyes he stay'd;
   he used as centre of movement his right side,
   and turned his left part on the pivot thus made.
'O kindly Light, in whom I now confide
   as I set forth on this new road, be thou,
   where guidance needful is, thyself our guide.
'Tis thou dost warm the world and o'er it glow:
   save other reason urge the contrary,
   thy beams should always guide us here below.'
A mile, by this world's reckoning, had we
   already gone—and quickly did we move,
   by reason of our will's alacrity—

e verso noi volar furon sentiti,
  non però visti, spiriti parlando
  a la mensa d'amor cortesi inviti: 27
La prima voce che passò volando
  Vinum non habent altamente disse,
  e dietro a noi l'andò reiterando.   30
E prima che del tutto non s'udisse
  per allungarsi, un'altra « Io sono Oreste »
  passò gridando, e anco non s'affisse.   33
« Oh » diss'io, « padre, che voci son queste? »
  E com'io domandai, ecco la terza
  dicendo « Amate da cui male aveste ».   36
E il buon maestro: « Questo cinghio sferza
  la colpa de l'invidia, e però sono
  tratte da amor le corde de la ferza.   39
Lo fren vuol esser del contrario suono,
  credo che l'udirai, per mio avviso,
  prima che giunghi al passo del perdono.   42
Ma ficca il viso per l'aere ben fiso,
  e vedrai gente innanzi a noi sedersi,
  e ciascun è lungo la grotta assiso ».   45
Allora più che prima gli occhi apersi,
  guardaimi innanzi, e vidi ombre con manti
  al color de la pietra non diversi.   48
E poi che fummo un poco più avanti,
  udia gridar: 'Maria ora per noi',
  gridar 'Michele' e 'Pietro' e tutti i santi.   51
Non credo che per terra vada ancoi
  uomo sì duro, che non fosse punto
  per compassion di quel che vidi poi;   54
chè quando fui sì presso di lor giunto
  che gli atti loro a me venivan certi,
  per gli occhi fui di grave dolor munto.   57
Di vil cilicio mi parean coperti,
  e l'un sofferia l'altro con la spalla,
  e tutti da la ripa eran sofferti: 60
così li ciechi a cui la roba falla
  stanno ai perdoni a chieder lor bisogna,
  e l'uno il capo sovra l'altro avvalla,   63

when tow'rds us flying in the air above
  were heard, but not seen, spirits uttering
  a courteous welcome to the feast of love.
The first voice as it passed us on the wing
  '*Vinum non habent*' in loud accents cried,
  and sped to our rear repeating that one thing.
And ere it wholly had on the distance died,
  another passed, in accents no less strong
  crying 'I am Orestes': it too did not bide.
'Oh!' I exclaimed, 'father, to whom belong
  these voices?' And behold, the third, saying e'en
  that instant 'Love ye those who have done you wrong.'
And the good master: 'By this circle the sin
  of envy is chastised, on which account
  'tis Love vibrates the cords of the discipline.
Methinks, if I err not, the curb being wont
  to sound the contrary tone, thou'lt hear it, ere
  thou reach the pass up which the pardoned mount.
But now through space direct thy sight with care,
  and thou wilt see in front of us, each one
  stationed along the cliff, folk seated there.'
I oped my eyes more than before I'd done;
  looking before me, shades did I descry
  in mantles of a hue that matched the stone.
Anon, as drew we a short space more nigh,
  of 'Mary, pray for us,' of 'Michael, pray'
  and 'Peter' and 'All Saints' I heard a cry.
I do not think there walks the earth today
  a man so hard, that he had not been stung
  by pity at what before my eyes then lay;
for when so close to them I passed along,
  that to my vision nought they did came short,
  a grievous anguish from my eyes was wrung.
In hair-cloth seemed they draped, of meanest sort:
  supported one by another's shoulder, all
  leaned likewise 'gainst the cliff-side for support.
So folk who are blind, and destitute withal,
  at pardons sit to beg for what they need,
  and each upon the next his head lets fall,

351

perchè in altrui pietà tosto si pogna
  non pur per lo sonar de le parole,
  ma per la vista, che non meno agogna.   66
E come a gli orbi non approda il Sole,
  così a l'ombre quivi, ond'io parl'ora,
  luce del ciel di sè largir non vuole;   69
chè a tutti un fil di ferro i cigli fora
  e cuce, sì come a sparvier selvaggio
  si fa, però che queto non dimora.   72
A me pareva andando fare oltraggio
  veggendo altrui non essendo veduto:
  perch'io mi volsi al mio consiglio saggio.   75
Ben sapev'ei che volea dir lo muto;
  e però non attese mia dimanda
  ma disse: « Parla, e sii breve ed arguto ».   78
Virgilio mi venia da quella banda
  de la cornice onde cader si puote
  perchè da nulla sponda s'inghirlanda;   81
da l'altra parte m'eran le divote
  ombre, che per l'orribile costura
  premevan sì che bagnavan le gote.   84
Volsimi a loro, e « O gente sicura »
  incominciai « di veder l'alto lume
  che il disio vostro solo ha in sua cura;   87
se tosto grazia risolva le schiume
  di vostra coscienza, sì che chiaro
  per essa scenda de la mente il fiume: 90
ditemi, chè mi fia grazioso e caro,
  s'anima è qui tra voi che sia latina;
  e forse a lei sarà buon s'io l'apparo ».   93
« O frate mio, ciascuna è cittadina
  d'una vera città; ma tu vuoi dire
  che vivesse in Italia pellegrina ».   96
Questo mi parve per risposta udire
  più innanzi alquanto che là dov'io stava,
  ond'io mi feci ancor più là sentire.   99
Tra l'altre vidi un'ombra che aspettava
  in vista; e se volesse alcun dir: 'Come?',
  lo mento a guisa d'orbo in sù levava.   102

that thus the sooner others may take heed,
  to pity moved, not by the sound of words
  alone, but by the looks which no less plead.
And as to sightless men the Sun affords
  no ray, so to the shades placed where I've said,
  heav'n's light no largess of itself accords;
for the eye-lids of them all an iron thread
  bores and sews up, as to a wild sparhawk
  men do, because it stays not quieted.
I—for it seemed an outrage, thus to walk,
  seeing others while myself unseen—drew near
  to my sage counsel, fain therewith to talk.
What the dumb craved to say well knew the seer,
  and therefore for my question did not bide
  but said: 'Speak, and be brief and very clear.'
Virgil was walking by me on that side
  the cornice where, because no parapet
  engarlands it, to fall may well betide;
and on my other hand the shades were set,
  absorbed in prayer and through the frightful seam
  so forcing tears out that their cheeks were wet.
'O folk assured of seeing the light supreme,'
  turning to them I thus began, 'the sum
  of all your prayers and their abiding theme,
so in brief while may grace dissolve the scum
  upon your consciences, that memory
  may, stainless, flowing downward through them come,
say, if 'mongst you some Latin soul I see;
  'twere dear and gracious news for me to ken,
  and, learn I of it, him 'twill help, may be.'
'My brother, we are each a citizen
  of one true city: whereas *thou* mean'st one
  who lived in Italy—a pilgrim then.'
Came this for answer (speaker saw I none)
  from just beyond where I was standing: so
  I made my voice heard somewhat farther on.
'Mongst the other shades I then beheld one who
  expectant looked; were I asked 'how?', the same
  as, when they raise the chin, the sightless do.

« Spirto » diss'io « che per salir ti dome,
   se tu sei quelli che mi rispondesti,
   fammiti conto e per luogo e per nome ».   105
« Io fui sanese » rispose « e con questi
   altri rimondo qui la vita ria
   lacrimando a Colui che sè ne presti.   108
Savia non fui, avvegna che Sapìa
   fossi chiamata, e fui de gli altrui danni
   più lieta assai che di ventura mia.   111
E perchè tu non credi ch'io t'inganni,
   odi s'io fui, com'io ti dico, folle,
   già discendendo l'arco de' miei anni.   114
Erano i cittadin miei presso a Colle
   in campo giunti coi loro avversari,
   e io pregava Iddio di quel ch'Ei volle.   117
Rotti fur quivi e volti ne gli amari
   passi di fuga, e veggendo la caccia
   letizia presi a tutt'altre dispàri   120
tanto ch'io volsi in sù l'ardita faccia
   gridando a Dio 'Omai più non ti temo'
   come fa il merlo per poca bonaccia.   123
Pace volli con Dio in su lo stremo
   de la mia vita; ed ancor non sarebbe
   lo mio dover per penitenza scemo,   126
se ciò non fosse che a memoria m'ebbe
   Pier Pettinaio in sue sante orazioni,
   a cui di me per caritate increbbe.   129
Ma tu chi sei, che nostre condizioni
   vai dimandando, e porti gli occhi sciolti,
   sì com'io credo, e spirando ragioni? »   132
« Gli occhi », diss'io « mi fieno ancor qui tolti,
   ma picciol tempo, chè poco è l'offesa
   fatta per esser con invidia volti.   135
Troppa è più la paura ond'è sospesa
   l'anima mia del tormento di sotto
   che già l'incarco di là giù mi pesa ».   138
Ed ella a me: « Chi t'ha dunque condotto
   qua sù tra noi, se giù ritornar credi? »
   E io: « Costui ch'è meco e non fa motto;   141

'Spirit' said I 'who to ascend dost tame
  thy nature, if 'twas thou that answered, please
  make thyself known to me by place or name.'
'Of Siena I,' it answered, 'and with these
  my sinful life do I here purify,
  praying Him with tears to impart to our life His.
Sapient I was not, though Sapìa I
  was named: and what caused others bitter tears,
  far more than my own welfare, gave me joy.
And lest thou think that I deceive thine ears,
  hear what I tell thee, judge how mad I grew,
  when down already sloped my arch of years.
My fellow-townsmen forth to battle drew,
  near Colle, with their foemen in the field:
  and I what God then willed prayed Him to do.
Defeated were they there and backward wheel'd
  into flight's bitter straits, and, seeing their rout,
  to joy that passed all limits did I yield;
so much so that I dared, head raised, to shout,
  challenging God, "Henceforth I fear thee not,"
  like the merle, if for a little the sun comes out.
Arrived at life's extremity, I sought
  for peace with God; but e'en now of my debt
  would penitence have no reduction brought,
if Peter, the Comb-seller, of my state
  had not been mindful in his holy prayers,
  whom charity made thus compassionate.
But who art *thou*, that makest our affairs
  thy quest and hast thine eyes, I take it, free,
  and speak'st as one in whom his breath yet stirs?'
'Mine eyes' I said, 'will here be ta'en from me
  awhile, but not for long, since erred have they
  but seldom, through their turning enviously.
Far more it irks my soul to hold at bay
  dread of the torment underneath; I feel
  e'en now the load down there upon me weigh.'
She answered: 'Who, then, led thee up the hill
  'mongst *us*, if thou'rt for re-descending it?'
  And I: 'He that stands by me, mute and still.

e vivo sono, e però mi richiedi,
  spirito eletto, se tu vuoi ch'io mova
  di là per te ancor li mortai piedi ».   144
« O questa è ad udir sì cosa nova »
  rispose, « che gran segno è che Iddio t'ami;
  però col prego tuo talor mi giova.   147
E chieggioti, per quel che tu più brami,
  se mai calchi la terra di Toscana,
  che a' miei propinqui tu ben mi rinfami.   150
Tu li vedrai tra quella gente vana
  che spera in Talamone, e perderagli
  più di speranza che a trovar la Diana;   153
ma più vi perderanno gli ammiragli ».

CANTO 14

« Chi è costui che il nostro monte cerchia
  prima che morte gli abbia dato il volo,
  e apre gli occhi a sua voglia e coperchia? »   3
« Non so chi sia, ma so che non è solo;
  domandal tu che più li t'avvicini,
  e dolcemente, sì che parli, acco'lo ».   6
Così due spirti, l'uno a l'altro chini,
  ragionavan di me ivi a man dritta;
  poi fer li visi, per dirmi, supini.   9
E disse l'uno · « O anima che fitta
  nel corpo ancora inver lo ciel ten vai,
  per carità ne consola e ne ditta   12
onde vieni e chi sei; chè tu ne fai
  tanto maravigliar de la tua grazia
  quanto vuol cosa che non fu più mai ».   15
E io: « Per mezza Toscana si spazia
  un fiumicel che nasce in Falterona,
  e cento miglia di corso nol sazia: 18

And I am alive; so ask of me—if meet
 thou deem'st it, spirit elect, that I o'er there
 hereafter move for thee my mortal feet.'
'Oh! news is this' she answered me 'so rare,
 'tis sign God loves thee—proof what need'st thou more?—
 therefore assist me sometimes with thy prayer.
I beg thee by what most thou longest for,
 if e'er thou treadest Tuscan soil again,
 among my kinsmen my good name restore.
Thou'lt see them with that people, of all most vain,
 who hope in Telamone, and will lose
 more hope there than in finding the Diáne;
but more there will the admirals lose than those.'

CANTO 14

'WHO's this that travels round our hill about,
 ere death has given him wings wherewith to fly,
 and can at will open his eyes and shut?'
'I know not, but I know he comes not by
 alone; ask *thou*, who'rt nigher, and be concerned
 to accost him gently, so that he reply.'
Thus from two souls there, on my right, I learned
 how, leaning mouth to ear, they talked of me;
 their faces then, to address me, they upturned.
And the one said: 'O soul that, bodily
 a prisoner still, art journeying heaven-ward,
 tell us—and, telling, our consoler be—
for love's sake, who thou art and whence thou hast fared,
 since the grace done thee stirs our wonderment,
 as needs must thing that else hath ne'er occurred.'
And I: 'Through mid-Toscana flows unpent
 a rill—on Falterona lies its spring—
 nor rests with a course of a hundred miles content.

357

di sovr'esso rech'io questa persona;
 dirvi chi sia saria parlare indarno,
 chè il nome mio ancor molto non suona ».   21
« Se ben l'intendimento tuo accarno
 con l'intelletto » allora mi rispose
 quei che diceva pria, « tu parli d'Arno ».   24
E l'altro disse a lui: « Perchè nascose
 questi il vocabol di quella riviera
 pur com'uom fa de l'orribili cose? »   27
E l'ombra che di ciò domandata era
 si sdebitò così: « Non so, ma degno
 ben è che il nome di tal valle pera.   30
Chè dal principio suo, ov'è sì pregno
 l'alpestro monte ond'è tronco Peloro
 che in pochi luoghi passa oltre quel segno,   33
infin là 've si rende per ristoro
 di quel che il ciel de la marina asciuga
 ond'hanno i fiumi ciò che va con loro,   36
virtù così per nimica si fuga
 da tutti come biscia, o per sventura
 del loco o per mal uso che li fruga;   39
ond'hanno sì mutata lor natura
 gli abitator de la misera valle,
 che par che Circe li avesse in pastura.   42
Tra brutti porci, più degni di galle
 che d'altro cibo fatto in uman uso,
 dirizza prima il suo povero calle.   45
Botoli trova poi, venendo giuso,
 ringhiosi più che non chieda lor possa,
 e da lor disdegnosa torce il muso.   48
Vassi caggendo, e quant'ella più ingrossa
 tanto più trova di can farsi lupi
 la maledetta e sventurata fossa.   51
Discesa poi per più pelaghi cupi,
 trova le volpi sì piene di froda
 che non temono ingegno che le occupi.   54
Nè lascerò di dir perch'altri m'oda,
 e buon sarà a costui s'ancor s'ammenta
 di ciò che vero spirto mi disnoda.   57

From *its* bank comes this body that I bring;
   to tell you who I am were waste of breath,
   since mine's a name none yet goes trumpeting.'
'If with my mind I rightly pierce beneath
   thy meaning,' he that spake before replied,
   ' 'tis Arno which the traits thou mentionest hath.'
And the other asked him: 'Why did this man hide
   that river's name, as men are wont to do
   with things by which they have been horrified?'
Whereat the shade he put this question to
   acquitted himself thus: 'I know not, though
   that perish should this valley's name is true;
for from its starting-point (where swells up so
   the high range, from Pelorus shorn away,
   that past that mark in few spots doth it go),
down to where it surrenders, to repay
   what sky absorbs from sea, whence rivers get
   that which along with them pursues its way,
virtue is fled from like a foe all hate
   as 'twere a snake, be evil habit to blame
   which spurs them, or the place ill-fortunate.
Wherefore so changed their nature have these same
   inhabitants of that most wretched vale
   that Circe, one might think, had pastured them.
Among foul hogs, which acorns should regale
   rather than food prepared for use of men,
   it first directs its trickle for a spell.
Curs, as it comes on downward, finds it then,
   snarling more than their power demands, from which
   it turns aside its muzzle in disdain.
The bigger it grows, as lower its waters reach,
   so much the more the dogs, turned wolves, are found
   by that ill-starred and execrable ditch.
Descending then through many a gorge, beyond,
   it finds the foxes, whom, so wily they,
   no cunning frights: all traps can *they* get round.
I speak on, caring nought who hears my say:
   and since the truth unfolds them, 'twill be wise
   of him there to recall my words some day.

Io veggio tuo nipote che diventa
  cacciator di quei lupi in su la riva
  del fiero fiume, e tutti li sgomenta.   60
Vende la carne loro essendo viva,
  poscia li ancide: come antica belva.
  Molti di vita e sè di pregio priva.   63
Sanguinoso esce de la trista selva;
  lasciala tal, che di qui a mill'anni
  ne lo stato primaio non si rinselva ».   66
Come all'annunzio di dogliosi danni
  si turba il viso di colui che ascolta,
  da qual che parte il periglio lo assanni,   69
così vid'io l'altr'anima, che volta
  stava ad udir, turbarsi e farsi trista,
  poi ch'ebbe la parola a sè raccolta.   72
Lo dir de l'una e de l'altra la vista
  mi fer voglioso di saper lor nomi,
  e dimanda ne fei con prieghi mista.   75
Per che lo spirto che di pria parlomi
  ricominciò : « Tu vuoi ch'io mi deduca
  nel fare a te ciò che tu far non vuo'mi.   78
Ma da che Dio in te vuol che traluca
  tanta sua grazia, non ti sarò scarso;
  però sappi ch'io son Guido del Duca.   81
Fu il sangue mio d'invidia sì riarso
  che se veduto avessi uom farsi lieto
  visto m'avresti di livore sparso.   84
Di mia semente cotal paglia mieto.
  O gente umana, perchè poni il core
  là 'v'è mestier di consorto divieto?   87
Questi è Rinier, questi è il pregio e l'onore
  de la casa da Calboli, ove nullo
  fatto s'è reda poi del suo valore.   90
E non pur lo suo sangue è fatto brullo,
  tra il Po e il monte e la marina e il Reno,
  del ben richiesto al vero ed al trastullo;   93
chè dentro questi termini è ripieno
  di venenosi sterpi, sì che tardi
  per coltivare omai verrebber meno.   96

Along that savage river's bank my eyes
   behold thy grandson, grown a huntsman, drive
   those wolves, and all alike he terrifies.
I see him sell their flesh while yet alive;
   then kill them like old beeves, and equally
   himself of honour and many of life deprive.
Forth from the dismal wood bloodstained comes he,
   and leaves it such that not for a thousand years
   to its first state shall it rewooded be.'
As, when a man of doleful losses hears,
   his face becomes distressed, no matter what
   the quarter whence the peril gores his ears,
so saw I the other soul (who, where he sat,
   had turned to listen) once he'd taken in
   the words, become disturbed and sad thereat.
The one's recital and the other's mien
   made me desire to know their names, so these
   not without prayer I sought from them to win.
Hence he that spake before resumed: 'It is
   thy wish that what thou wilt not do for me
   I now should do for thee, if so I please.
But I'll not stint thee, in that God through thee
   wills that his grace in such large measure shine—
   hast heard of Guy del Duca? I am he.
Envy so fired my blood, that the least sign
   of joy I saw to another's visage leap
   thou'dst seen suffuse with livid colour mine.
Of my own sowing such the straw I reap:
   why set ye there your hearts, O sons of earth,
   where must needs be exclusion of partnership?
This is Rinieri, this is he whose birth
   and genius graced the house of Cálboli,
   where none since hath succeeded to his worth.
Nor, between Po and mount, Reno and sea,
   stripped of the good belonging to earnest and
   to sport is his the only family;
for rank, within these boundaries, is the land
   with stocks so poisonous, 't will be long indeed
   ere they die out beneath the tiller's hand.

Ov'è il buon Lizio ed Arrigo Manardi,
  Pier Traversaro e Guido di Carpigna?
  O Romagnuoli tornati in bastardi!   99
Quando in Bologna un Fabbro si ralligna?
  quando in Faenza un Bernardin di Fosco,
  verga gentil di picciola gramigna?   102
Non ti maravigliar s'io piango, Tosco,
  quando rimembro con Guido da Prata
  Ugolin d'Azzo che vivette nosco,   105
Federigo Tignoso e sua brigata,
  la casa Traversara e gli Anastagi
  (e l'una gente e l'altra è diredata),   108
le donne e i cavalier gli affanni e gli agi
  che ne invogliava amore e cortesia
  là dove i cor son fatti sì malvagi.   111
O Bertinoro, chè non fuggi via,
  poi che gita se n'è la tua famiglia
  e molta gente per non esser ria?   114
Ben fa Bagnacaval che non rifiglia;
  e mal fa Castrocaro e peggio Conio
  che di figliar tai conti più s'impiglia.   117
Ben faranno i Pagan da che il demonio
  lor sen girà; ma non però che puro
  già mai rimagna d'essi testimonio.   120
O Ugolin de' Fantolin, sicuro
  è il nome tuo, da che più non s'aspetta
  chi far lo possa, tralignando, oscuro. 123
Ma va via, Tosco, omai, ch'or mi diletta
  troppo di pianger più che di parlare,
  sì m'ha nostra ragion la mente stretta ». 126
Noi sapevam che quell'anime care
  ci sentivano andar; però tacendo
  facevan noi del cammin confidare.   129
Poi fummo fatti soli procedendo,
  folgore parve quando l'aere fende,
  voce che giunse di contra dicendo: 132
« Anciderammi qualunque m'apprende ».
  E fuggì come tuon che si dilegua
  se subito la nuvola scoscende.   135

Where's Hal Manardi, Lizio good at need,
  Guy of Carpigna and Piers Traversár?
  O Romagnóles, now turned a bastard breed!
When will Bologna another Fabbro rear?
  Faënza another Fosco's Bernardín,
  right noble scion for humble plant to bear?
Marvel not, Tuscan, at my tearful mien
  when I, of our co-evals call to mind
  from Prata Guy, and Azzo's Ugolín,
Frederick Tignoso and, with him conjoin'd,
  the Traversari and Anastagi (names
  of houses to which now no heirs thou'lt find),
the pastimes and the toils, the knights and dames,
  made dear to us by love and courtesy
  where now men's hearts such wickedness inflames.
O Bertinoro, why dost thou not flee
  away, since now thy household from thee runs,
  and much folk, that from guilt they may be free?
Bagnacavál does well to have no more sons;
  and Castrocaro ill, and Cónio worse,
  having such counts, to beget other ones.
And well, when quitted by their Demon-curse,
  will the Pagani do; yet, all the same,
  what clouds their record nought can e'er disperse.
O Ugolín de' Fántolin, *thy* name
  is safe: since it no heir, where none is now
  expected, can by falling off defame.
But go thy way now, Tuscan: in that, so
  has our conversing wrung my mind, I'd far
  rather than speak allow my tears to flow.'
We knew that those dear spirits were aware
  of our departure; hence their silence made
  us sure of the right pathway on from there.
As we proceeded, now uncompaniëd,
  like lightning, when it cleaves the air, came on
  a voice to meet us, and while coming said:
'Whoever finds will slay me': whereupon,
  as thunder does, if suddenly it smash
  the cloud to bits, it scattered and was gone.

Come da lei l'udir nostro ebbe tregua,
 ed ecco l'altra con sì gran fracasso
 che somigliò tonar che tosto segua: 138
« Io sono Aglauro che divenni sasso ».
 Ed allor, per ristrignermi al poeta,
 in destro feci e non innanzi il passo.   141
Già era l'aura d'ogni parte queta,
 ed ei mi disse: « Quel fu il duro camo
 che dovria l'uom tener dentro a sua meta.   144
Ma voi prendete l'esca, sì che l'amo
 de l'antico avversaro a sè vi tira;
 e però poco val freno o richiamo.   147
Chiàmavi il cielo e intorno vi si gira
 mostrandovi le sue bellezze eterne,
 e l'occhio vostro pure a terra mira;   150
onde vi batte chi tutto discerne ».

CANTO 15

QUANTO tra l'ultimar de l'ora terza
 e il principio del dì par de la spera
 che sempre a guisa di fanciullo scherza,   3
tanto pareva già inver la sera
 essere al Sol del suo corso rimaso:
 vespero là e qui mezzanott'era;   6
e i raggi ne ferien per mezzo il naso,
 perchè per noi girato era sì il monte
 che già dritti andavamo inver l'occaso,   9
quand'io sentii a me gravar la fronte
 a lo splendore assai più che di prima,
 e stupor m'eran le cause non conte;   12
ond'io levai le mani inver la cima
 de le mie ciglia, e fecimi il solecchio,
 che del soverchio visibile lima.   15
Come quando da l'acqua o da lo specchio
 salta lo raggio a l'opposita parte,
 salendo sù per lo modo parecchio   18

Scarce had our hearing truce from it, when crash!
   the second voice—resembling, as it cried,
   the thunderclap close following on the flash—
'I am Aglauros who was petrified';
   I stepped to the right, not forward, at the sound,
   thus to press closer to the poet's side.
By now the air was quiet all around;
   and 'That' he said, 'was the hard check that ought
   to keep a man within his proper bound.
But you suck in the bait and thus are caught
   on the hook which the old adversary plies;
   nor curb nor lure avails you then one jot.
The heaven calls you with its wheeling skies
   displaying eternal beauties to your gaze,
   and on the ground alone you fix your eyes:
hence are ye smitten by Him who all surveys.'

CANTO 15

As much as the eye sees, 'twixt the day-spring
   and the third hour's last moment, of the sphere
   which, like a child, is ever frolicking,
so much appeared now of the Sun's career
   still left him as he journeyed to his rest;
   there it was eventide, and midnight here.
Now struck us full on the nose the beams we faced;
   for we had gone on so far round the hill
   as to be walking by this time due west,
when far more than at first I came to feel
   the splendour weigh my forehead down, and I
   was dazed by things to me inscrutable;
on which account I raised my hands as high
   as mine eyebrows, and made myself the screen
   which an excess of light is tempered by.
As when from mirror or from water in
   the opposite direction leaps the ray,
   its rising like as its descent has been

a quel che scende, e tanto si diparte
    dal cader de la pietra, in egual tratta,
    sì come mostra esperienza ed arte;   21
così mi parve da luce rifratta
    quivi dinanzi a me esser percosso,
    per che a fuggir la vista mia fu ratta.   24
« Che è quei, dolce padre, a che non posso
    schermar lo viso tanto che mi vaglia »
    diss'io « e pare inver noi esser mosso? »   27
« Non ti maravigliar se ancor t'abbaglia
    la famiglia del cielo » a me rispose:
    « messo è che viene ad invitar ch'uom saglia.   30
Tosto sarà che a veder queste cose
    non ti fia grave, ma fieti diletto
    quanto natura a sentir ti dispose ».   33
Poi giunti fummo a l'angel benedetto,
    con lieta voce disse: « Intrate quinci
    ad un scaleo vie men che gli altri eretto ».   36
Noi montavam già partiti di linci,
    e *Beati misericordes* fue
    cantato retro, e « Godi tu che vinci ».   39
Lo mio maestro ed io, soli ambedue
    suso andavamo, ed io pensai, andando,
    prode acquistar ne le parole sue;   42
e dirizzaimi a lui sì dimandando:
    « Che volle dir lo spirto di Romagna
    e *divieto* e *consorto* menzionando? »   45
Per ch'egli a me: « Di sua maggior magagna
    conosce il danno; e però non s'ammiri
    se ne riprende perchè men sen piagna.   48
Perchè s'appuntano i vostri disiri
    dove per compagnia parte si scema,
    invidia move il mantaco ai sospiri.   51
Ma se l'amor de la spera suprema
    torcesse in suso il desiderio vostro,
    non vi sarebbe al petto quella tema;   54
chè per quanti si dice lì più *nostro*
    tanto possiede più di ben ciascuno,
    e più di caritate arde in quel chiostro ».   57

and just as far diverges from the way
  a falling stone takes, in an equal space—
  as shown alike by science and by essáy;
so by reflected light, meseemed, the place
  in front of me was smitten; whereupon
  I speedily averted thence my face.
'What is that, dearest father, which undone
  makes all I do to shield me from its glare'
  said I 'and which seems our way coming on?'
'Marvel not, if thou'rt dazzled still, whene'er
  thou seest the heavenly household' he replied;
  'to bid one mount he comes as messenger.
'Twill not be long ere these things, when descried,
  will not grieve but delight thee as much as thou
  to enjoy them art by nature qualified.'
The blesséd angel, whom we had reached by now,
  with a glad voice said: 'Here's the entrance; nor
  is this stair half as steep as the other two.'
Quitting him, we had not climbed far, before
  '*Beati misericordes*' to our rear
  was chanted, and 'Rejoice, thou conqueror!'
My master and I were mounting, none else near;
  and, as we went, I pondered how to make
  his discourse profitable for me to hear;
so, tow'rds him turned, did I thus silence break:
  'What did the spirit from Romagna mean,
  when of "exclusion" and "partnership" he spake?'
Whence he to me: 'Of his own greatest sin
  he knows the cost: no grounds, then, for surprise,
  if he rebukes it, so that it cause less teen.
It is because ye there turn longing eyes
  where through companionship a share is lost,
  that envy works the bellows for your sighs.
But, if love for the sphere that is uppermost
  turned thither your desire with all its powers,
  that fear would no more vex you to your cost;
in that the more there are who there say "ours",
  so much the more of good is owned by each,
  and all with warmer love that cloister dowers.'

« Io son d'esser contento più digiuno »
  diss'io « che se mi fossi pria taciuto,
  e più di dubbio ne la mente aduno.   60
Com'esser puote che un ben distributo
  i più posseditor faccia più ricchi
  di sè, che se da pochi è posseduto? »   63
Ed egli a me: « Però che tu rificchi
  la mente pure a le cose terrene,
  di vera luce tenebre dispicchi.   66
Quello infinito ed ineffabil bene
  che là sù è, così corre ad amore
  come a lucido corpo raggio viene;   69
tanto si dà quanto trova d'ardore,
  sì che quantunque carità si stende
  cresce sovr'essa l'eterno valore;   72
e quanta gente più là sù s'intende,
  più v'è da ben amare e più vi s'ama,
  e come specchio l'uno a l'altro rende.   75
E se la mia ragion non ti disfama,
  vedrai Beatrice, ed ella pienamente
  ti torrà questa e ciascun'altra brama.   78
Procaccia pur che tosto sieno spente,
  come son già le due, le cinque piaghe
  che si richiudon per esser dolente ».   81
Com'io voleva dicer: « Tu m'appaghe »,
  vidimi giunto in su l'altro girone,
  sì che tacer mi fer le luci vaghe.   84
Ivi mi parve in una visione
  estatica di subito esser tratto;
  e vedere in un tempio più persone,   87
ed una donna, in su l'entrar, con atto
  dolce di madre dicer: « Figliuol mio,
  perchè hai tu così verso noi fatto?   90
Ecco, dolenti lo tuo padre ed io
  ti cercavamo ». E come qui si tacque,
  ciò che pareva prima dispario.   93
Indi m'apparve un'altra con quell'acque
  giù per le gote che il dolor distilla
  quando di gran dispetto in altrui nacque,   96

'I'm left more uncontented by thy speech'
   said I 'than if before I'd held my tongue:
   and to yet further doubt my mind doth reach.
How can it be that one good shared among
   many that have it should enrich them more
   than did it but to few of them belong?'
And he to me: 'Because the setting store
   by earthly things alone is thy fixed mood,
   thou gatherest darkness from light's very core.
That infinite and unexpressive Good,
   which up there *is*, to love runneth as fleet
   as to a lucid body a sunbeam would.
As much it giveth as it finds of heat;
   so that, how wide soe'er spreads charity,
   the eternal Worth increases over it.
And the more souls, hearts set on high, there be,
   more are there to love well and more are loved:
   and, mirror-like, they give back mutually.
And if my discourse hath too meagre proved
   to fill thy famine, thou'lt see Beatrice,
   by whom thy cravings will be all removed.
Only strive hard that soon, as two ere this
   have been, the five wounds left be remedied,
   of which contrition the sole healer is.'
'Twas on my lips to say 'I'm satisfied,'
   when on my view lo! the next circle broke,
   so that my eager eyes held me tongue-tied.
There (seemed it) an ecstatic vision took
   me suddenly and before my mind unroll'd
   this scene—a temple, and therein much folk;
and, at its door, with sweetness past aught told
   of mothers else, a lady questioning:
   'Son, why hast thou thus dealt with us? Behold,
thy father and I have sought thee sorrowing.'
   And as she here ceased utterance, from my view
   vanished what I had first been witnessing.
Then saw I another woman, with that dew
   wetting her cheeks which grief distils when great
   despite 'gainst others giveth birth thereto.

e dir: « Se tu sei sire de la villa
  del cui nome ne' Dei fu tanta lite,
  e onde ogni scienza disfavilla, 99
vendica te di quelle braccia ardite
  che abbracciar nostra figlia, o Pisistrato! »
  E il signor mi parea, benigno e mite, 102
risponder lei con viso temperato:
  « Che farem noi a chi mal ne disira,
  se quei che ci ama è per noi condannato? » 105
Poi vidi genti accese in foco d'ira
  con pietre un giovinetto ancider, forte
  gridando a sè pur: « Martira, martira! » 108
E lui vedea chinarsi, per la morte
  che l'aggravava già, in ver la terra,
  ma de gli occhi facea sempre al ciel porte, 111
orando a l'alto Sire, in tanta guerra,
  che perdonasse a' suoi persecutori,
  con quell'aspetto che pietà disserra. 114
Quando l'anima mia tornò di fuori
  a le cose che son fuor di lei vere,
  io riconobbi i miei non falsi errori. 117
Lo duca mio, che mi potea vedere
  far sì com'uom che dal sonno si slega,
  disse: « Che hai che non ti puoi tenere, 120
ma sei venuto più che mezza lega
  velando gli occhi e con le gambe avvolte,
  a guisa di cui vino o sonno piega? » 123
« O dolce padre mio, se tu m'ascolte
  io ti dirò » diss'io « ciò che m'apparve
  quando le gambe mi furon sì tolte ». 126
Ed ei: « Se tu avessi cento larve
  sovra la faccia, non mi sarien chiuse
  le tue cogitazion quantunque parve. 129
Ciò che vedesti fu perchè non scuse
  d'aprir lo core a l'acque de la pace
  che da l'eterno fonte son diffuse. 132
Non dimandai *che hai*? per quel che face
  chi guarda pur con l'occhio che non vede
  quando disanimato il corpo giace; 135

saying: 'If thou over the town art set
   whose name among the Gods caused such dispute,
   and whence the sciences all radiate,
punish, Peisistratus, those dissolute
   arms that embraced our daughter, unashamed.'
To whom, with tranquil look, in tones that suit
therewith, meseemed her lord this answer framed:
   'What shall we do to those that wish us ill,
   if he who loves us is by us condemned?'
Then saw I people, ablaze with anger, fill
   the scene, who stoned a young man, while aloud
   they cried to each other nought but: 'Kill him, kill!'
And by that death I saw him earthward bowed
   which was already weighing upon him; yet
   his eyes he still made doors to the high God,
whom he implored, e'en in so dire a strait,
   to pardon his persecutors, with that look
   which never fails to unlock compassion's gate.
Soon as my mind its inner world forsook,
   turning to things without, I knew aright
   for dreams, not false, what late for real I took.
My leader, who could see me in the plight
   of one who shakes off sleep, exclaimed: 'Come, say
   what ails thee that thou canst not walk upright,
but more than half a league upon thy way
   art come with tottering legs and with eyes veil'd
   like one whom wine or slumber holds in sway?'
'Sweet father, if thine ear be not withheld,
   I'll tell thee' I replied, 'what in this place
   I saw appearing, when my legs thus fail'd.'
'Hadst thou a hundred masks upon thy face,
   thy thoughts, how insignificant soe'er,'
   he answered, 'would be clear to me no less.
The vision was shown thee that thou shouldst not spare
   to let thy heart be flooded by the peace
   spread by the Fount Eternal everywhere.
I asked "What ails thee?" not for the reason this
   is asked by one who looks but with the eye
   whose seeing, when lies the flesh unsouled, doth cease;

371

ma dimandai per darti forza al piede:
   così frugar conviensi i pigri, i lenti,
   ad usar lor vigilia quando riede».   138
Noi andavam per lo vespero, attenti
   oltre quanto potean gli occhi allungarsi
   contra i raggi serotini e lucenti;   141
ed ecco a poco a poco un fummo farsi
   verso di noi come la notte scuro;
   nè da quello era loco da cansarsi.   144
Questo ne tolse gli occhi e l'aer puro.

CANTO 16

Buio d'Inferno e di notte privata
   d'ogni pianeta, sotto pover cielo,
   quant'esser può di nuvol tenebrata,   3
non fece al viso mio sì grosso velo
   come quel fummo ch'ivi ci coperse,
   nè a sentir di così aspro pelo,   6
che l'occhio stare aperto non sofferse;
   onde la scorta mia saputa e fida
   mi s'accostò e l'omero m'offerse.   9
Sì come cieco va dietro a sua guida
   per non smarrirsi e per non dar di cozzo
   in cosa che il molesti o forse ancida,   12
m'andava io per l'aere amaro e sozzo,
   ascoltando il mio duca che diceva
   pur: «Guarda che da me tu non sii mozzo».   15
Io sentia voci, e ciascuna pareva
   pregar per pace e per misericordia
   l'agnel di Dio che le peccata leva.   18
Pure *Agnus Dei* eran le loro esordia;
   una parola in tutte era ed un modo,
   sì che parea tra esse ogni concordia.   21
«Quei sono spirti, maestro, ch'i' odo?»
   diss'io; ed egli a me: «Tu vero apprendi;
   e d'iracundia van solvendo il nodo».   24

I did but ask it, so as to fortify
   thy feet: 'tis thus one spurs the laggard, slow
   when wakefulness returns to profit thereby.'
We were still journeying through the vesper glow,
   with eyes strained forward 'gainst the dazzling flame
   of closing day, as far as they could go;
when, lo, little by little tow'rds us came
   a smoke, thick clouds thereof as dark as night;
   nor was there any place to escape from them.
This took from us the pure air and our sight.

CANTO 16

GLOOM as of Hell and night, night that allow'd
   no planet's gleam, under a straitened sky,
   night to the utmost darkened by dense cloud,
over my sight ne'er spread a canopy
   so thick, of frieze so rasping to the sense,
   as did that smoke we there were covered by,
which suffered not the eye to stay open; whence
   my escort, trusty and sage, drew to my side
   and offered me his shoulder for defence.
Just as, that he may stray not or collide
   with what by chance might injure or, indeed,
   kill him, a blind man walks behind his guide;
through the foul, pungent air did I proceed,
   marking my leader, who ceased not to say:
   'Take heed thou lose not touch with me, take heed.'
I was aware of voices, and that they
   seemed each for peace and mercy to entreat
   the Lamb of God that taketh sins away.
Preluding *Agnus Dei*, nought but it,
   all to the same words the same measure brought,
   so that their concord seemed to be complete.
'Are these spirits, Master, that my ear hath caught?'
   said I. And he: 'Thou deem'st them what they are;
   of anger are they now untying the knot.'

« Or tu chi sei, che il nostro fummo fendi,
  e di noi parli sì come se tue
  partissi ancor lo tempo per calendi? »   27
Così per una voce detto fue;
  onde il maestro mio disse: « Rispondi,
  e domanda se quinci si va sue ».   30
E io: « O creatura che ti mondi
  per tornar bella a colui che ti fece,
  maraviglia udirai se mi secondi ».   33
« Io ti seguiterò quanto mi lece »
  rispose, « e se veder fummo non lascia,
  l'udir ci terrà giunti in quella vece ».   36
Allora incominciai: « Con quella fascia
  che la morte dissolve men vo suso,
  e venni qui per l'infernale ambascia.   39
E se Dio m'ha in sua grazia richiuso
  tanto che vuol ch'io veggia la sua corte
  per modo tutto fuor del modern'uso,   42
non mi celar chi fosti anzi la morte,
  ma dilmi, e dimmi s'io vo bene al varco;
  e tue parole fien le nostre scorte ».   45
«Lombardo fui, e fui chiamato Marco;
  del mondo seppi e quel valore amai
  al quale ha or ciascun disteso l'arco.   48
Per montar sù dirittamente vai ».
  Così rispose e soggiunse: « Io ti prego
  che per me preghi quando sù sarai ».   51
E io a lui: « Per fede mi ti lego
  di far ciò che mi chiedi; ma io scoppio
  dentro ad un dubbio, s'io non me ne spiego.   54
Prima era scempio, ed ora è fatto doppio
  ne la sentenza tua, che mi fa certo
  qui ed altrove quello ov'io l'accoppio.   57
Lo mondo è ben così tutto diserto
  d'ogni virtute, come tu mi suone,
  e di malizia gravido e coverto;   60
ma prego che m'addite la cagione,
  sì ch'io la veggia e ch'io la mostri altrui;
  chè nel ciel uno, ed un quaggiù la pone ».   63

'Now who art thou, cleaving our smoke thus far,
　　and speaking of us just as if for thee
　　time was still measured by the calendar?'
This by a single voice was said; to me
　　therefore my master said: 'Do thou reply,
　　and ask where the way upward hence may be.'
'O creature purifying thyself, thereby
　　unto thy Maker to return all fair,
　　follow me and thou'lt hear a marvel,' said I.
'So far as I'm allowed, thy path I'll share,'
　　it answered, 'and if smoke makes seeing fail.
　　instead of that we'll keep in touch by ear.'
Then I began: 'Still with that swathing veil
　　which death unwraps I take the upward road.
　　and I came hither through the pains of hell.
And if God makes his grace for me abode
　　so wondrous, that he wills I see his court
　　by a way quite outside our modern mode,
hide not, but say, who wast thou, ere cut short
　　by death; and say if to the pass I go
　　aright: and let thy words be our escort.'
'A Lombard I, named Mark; I used to know
　　the world's ways, and that virtue won my love
　　towards which all have now unbent the bow
For mounting, on the right track dost thou move.'
　　Thus he replied, and added: 'Pray for me,
　　I pray thee, when thou findst thyself above.'
And I to him: 'I pledge my word to thee
　　to do thy bidding; but I'm like to burst
　　with inward doubt, unless therefrom set free.
'Tis doubled now, from being single at first,
　　by thine opinion, which corroborates here
　　and elsewhere what I couple it with, that curst
indeed the world is, as thy words make clear,
　　bereft of every virtue, and big with all
　　that's evil, which o'erwhelms it everywhere.
Point me out, prithee, what makes this befall,
　　that I may see and show it to others too;
　　for some deem heav'n, some earth, the criminal.'

Alto sospir, che duolo strinse in 'hui!',
  mise fuor prima, e poi cominciò: « Frate,
  lo mondo è cieco, e tu vien ben da lui.   66
Voi che vivete ogni cagion recate
  pur suso al cielo, sì come se tutto
  movesse seco di necessitate.   69
Se così fosse, in voi fora distrutto
  libero arbitrio, e non fora giustizia
  per ben letizia, e per male aver lutto.   72
Lo cielo i vostri movimenti inizia;
  non dico tutti, ma posto ch'io 'l dica,
  lume v'è dato a bene ed a malizia   75
e libero voler, che se fatica
  ne le prime battaglie col ciel dura,
  poi vince tutto, se ben si nutrica.   78
A maggior forza ed a miglior natura
  liberi soggiacete, e quella cria
  la mente in voi, che il ciel non ha in sua cura.   81
Però se il mondo presente disvia,
  in voi è la cagione, in voi si chieggia;
  ed io te ne sarò or vera spia.   84
Esce di mano a Lui che la vagheggia
  prima che sia, a guisa di fanciulla
  che piangendo e ridendo pargoleggia,   87
l'anima semplicetta, che sa nulla
  salvo che, mòssa da lieto fattore,
  volentier torna a ciò che la trastulla.   90
Di picciol bene in pria sente sapore:
  quivi s'inganna, e dietro ad esso corre,
  se guida o fren non torce su' amore.   93
Onde convenne legge per fren porre,
  convenne rege aver che discernesse
  de la vera città almen la torre.   96
Le leggi son, ma chi pon mano ad esse?
  Nullo, però che il pastor che precede
  ruminar può ma non ha l'unghie fesse.   99
Per che la gente, che sua guida vede
  pure a quel ben ferire ond'ella è ghiotta,
  di quel si pasce e più oltre non chiede.   102

A deep sigh, forced by grief into 'heigh-ho!',
  broke from him first: then 'Brother,' he began,
  'the world is blind, and thence, 'tis clear, com'st thou.
All causes are referred by living man
  to the heav'ns alone, as did they everything
  move with themselves on some predestined plan.
But this, if true, would to destruction bring
  free choice, nor were it justice to requite
  good deeds with joy and ill with suffering.
The heav'ns *do* your first impulses incite;
  I say not all, but, grant it said, e'en then
  to discern good from ill ye are given light
and free will; which, though subject to great strain
  in its first battles with the heav'ns, in the end
  will, if well nourished, total victory gain.
You, free, are by a mightier force constrain'd,
  by a better nature; and through this holds sway
  the mind in you, which the heav'ns lack power to bend.
Hence, if the world at present goes astray,
  in you is the cause, in you it should be sought,
  to which I'll put thee now on the right way.
Forth from His hand, who yearns to her in thought
  ere she exists, comes, like a little maid
  all tears and smiles, eager to play with aught,
the little simple soul, in life unread,
  save that, by her glad Maker moved, with zest
  she turns to that by which her joy is fed.
Of trivial good at first she tries the taste;
  thereby deceived, after it will she scour,
  if guide or curb do not divert her quest.
Whence need of law for curb; and need, moreo'er,
  of one who can, in regal state aloof,
  of the true city glimpse at least the tower.
Laws there *are*, but by what hand put to proof?
  No one's: because the leading shepherd, who
  can chew the cud, lacks the divided hoof;
Wherefore the people, seeing their guide pursue
  only that good whereof their greed is fain,
  pasture on that, and other foods eschew.

Ben puoi veder che la mala condotta
  è la cagion che il mondo ha fatto reo,
  e non natura che in voi sia corrotta.   105
Soleva Roma, che il buon mondo feo,
  due Soli aver, che l'una e l'altra strada
  facean vedere, e del mondo e di Deo.   108
L'un l'altro ha spento, ed è giunta la spada
  col pastorale, e l'un con l'altro insieme
  per viva forza mal convien che vada;   111
però che, giunti, l'un l'altro non teme.
  Se non mi credi, pon mente a la spiga,
  chè ogn'erba si conosce per lo seme.   114
In sul paese ch'Adice e Po riga
  solea valore e cortesia trovarsi
  prima che Federigo avesse briga;   117
or può sicuramente indi passarsi
  da qualunque lasciasse, per vergogna
  di ragionar coi buoni o d'appressarsi.   120
Ben v'èn tre vecchi ancora in cui rampogna
  l'antica età la nova, e par lor tardo
  che Dio a miglior vita li ripogna: 123
Currado da Palazzo e il buon Gherardo
  e Guido de Castel, che me' si noma
  francescamente il semplice Lombardo.   126
Di' oggimai che la chiesa di Roma,
  per confondere in sè due reggimenti,
  cade nel fango, e sè brutta e la soma ».   129
« O Marco mio » diss'io, « bene argomenti;
  e or discerno perchè dal retaggio
  li figli di Levì furono esenti.   132
Ma qual Gherardo è quel che tu per saggio
  di' ch'è rimaso de la gente spenta,
  in rimproverio del secol selvaggio? »   135
« O tuo parlar m'inganna o ei mi tenta »
  rispose a me, « chè, parlandomi tosco,
  par che del buon Gherardo nulla senta.   138
Per altro soprannome io nol conosco,
  s'io nol togliessi da sua figlia Gaia.
  Dio sia con voi, chè più non vegno vosco.   141

Your corrupt nature, then, is not your bane;
  ill-guidance—*that* is why the world hath trod
  the way of sin; see *there* the cause writ plain.
Rome, that once kept the world good by her rod,
  was wont to have two Suns, whose light made clear
  both roads, that of the world and that of God.
One hath the other quenched; to crozier
  hath now been joined the sword, and it must needs
  be ill going, when the two together fare;
for, when joined, neither power the other dreads:
  if still thou doubt, look to the ripened grain,
  since every plant is made known by its seeds.
True worth and courtesy throughout the plain
  watered by Po and Adigé prevailed,
  ere Frederick was involved in his campaign:
Whoso, for shame, from good men's talk hath held
  aloof, nor neared them, can pass thro' it these days
  all fear of meeting any such dispelled.
Three veterans, true, still live, whose old-time ways
  rebuke the new, and it seems hard to them
  that God their call to better life delays:
Palazzo's Conrad, Gerard whom men name
  the Good, and Guy of Castél, better styled
  French-wise "the honest Lombard"—such his fame.
Since in herself she holds unreconciled
  two governments, the church of Rome now say
  is bog-bound, self and burden both defiled.'
'Friend Mark,' said I, 'thou arguest well: that they,
  the sons of Levi, from all heritage
  were rightly barred thou makest clear as day.
But who's the Gerard that thy words allege
  remains a sample of the folk gone by,
  by way of censure, to this barbarous age?'
'Either thou would'st deceive,' was his reply,
  'or test me: for, though speaking Tuscan, thou
  knowest nought of the good Gerard, seemingly.
Him by no other surname do I know
  than what his daughter Gaia might provide.
  Goodbye, for I must leave you now and go.

379

Vedi l'albor che per lo fummo raia
  già biancheggiare; e me convien partirmi
  — l'angelo è ivi — prima ch'io li paia».   144
Così tornò, e più non volle udirmi.

CANTO 17

Rɪᴄᴏʀᴅɪᴛɪ, lettor, se mai nell'alpe
  ti colse nebbia per la qual vedessi
  non altrimenti che per pelle talpe,   3
come, quando i vapori umidi e spessi
  a diradar cominciansi, la spera
  del sol debilemente entra per essi;   6
e fia la tua imagine leggiera
  in giugnere a veder com'io rividi
  lo Sole in pria, che già nel corcar era.   9
Sì, pareggiando i miei coi passi fidi
  del mio maestro, uscii fuor di tal nube
  ai raggi morti già nei bassi lidi.   12
O imaginativa, che ne rube
  tal volta sì di fuor, ch'uom non s'accorge
  perchè dintorno suonin mille tube,   15
chi move te, se il senso non ti porge?
  Moveti lume che nel ciel s'informa
  per sè o per voler che giù lo scorge.   18
De l'empiezza di lei che mutò forma
  ne l'uccel che a cantar più si diletta,
  ne l'imagine mia apparve l'orma;   21
e qui fu la mia mente sì ristretta
  dentro di sè, che di fuor non venia
  cosa che fosse allor da lei recetta.   24
Poi piovve dentro a l'alta fantasia
  un crucifisso dispettoso e fero
  ne la sua vista, e cotal si moria.   27
Intorno ad esso era il grande Assuero,
  Ester sua sposa e il giusto Mardocheo,
  che fu al dire ed al far così intero.   30

Look, through the smoke some light may be descried
  dawning e'en now: I must away, before
  by the angel—he is there—I be espied.'
So he turned back, and would not hear me more.

CANTO 17

Bᴇᴛʜɪɴᴋ thee, Reader, if in the Alps e'er stole
  a mist upon thee, such that thou couldst no
  more through it see than sees thro' its skin a mole,
how, as the dank, thick vapours then by slow
  degrees begin to thin themselves, they let
  the sun's orb, though but feebly, through them show;
and thy imaginative power will straight
  come to behold how I at first beheld
  the Sun again, now on the point to set.
Thus—following, as my faith in him compell'd,
  my master's steps—I emerged from such a cloud
  to sunlight, which on the low shores now failed.
O imagination, oft with power endow'd
  so to transport us that we heed it not,
  though round us blare a thousand trumpets loud,
who moves thee, if no sense affords thee aught?
  A light doth move thee, which is formed in heaven
  by a Will that guides it down, or else self-wrought.
To what I imagined was the outline given
  of *her* crime who was changed into the bird
  by which in song all others are outstriven:
and here so deeply was my mind interr'd
  within itself, that from without obtained
  was nought which then it either saw or heard.
Into my high-raised phantasy next rained
  one, crucified, whose look, that spoke a mood
  of fierce contempt, he still in death retained:
around him great Ahasuerus stood,
  Esther his wife and just Mordecaï, who
  in word and deed was so entirely good.

E come questa imagine rompeo
    sè per se stessa, a guisa d'una bulla
    cui manca l'acqua sotto qual si feo,   33
surse in mia visione una fanciulla
    piangendo forte, e diceva: « O regina,
    perchè per ira hai voluto esser nulla?   36
Ancisa t'hai per non perder Lavina:
    or m'hai perduta. Io son essa, che lutto,
    madre, a la tua pria che a l'altrui ruina ».   39
Come si frange il sonno, ove di butto
    nova luce percuote il viso chiuso,
    che fratto guizza pria che muoia tutto,   42
così l'imaginar mio cadde giuso
    tosto che un lume il volto mi percosse,
    maggior assai che quel che è in nostr'uso.   45
Io mi volgea per vedere ov'io fosse,
    quando una voce disse « Qui si monta »,
    che da ogn'altro intento mi rimosse;   48
e fece la mia voglia tanto pronta
    di riguardar chi era che parlava,
    che mai non posa se non si raffronta.   51
Ma come al Sol che nostra vista grava
    e per soverchio sua figura vela,
    così la mia virtù quivi mancava.   54
« Questo è divino spirito che ne la
    via da ir sù ne drizza sanza priego,
    e col suo lume se medesmo cela.   57
Sì fa con noi come l'uom si fa sego,
    chè quale aspetta prego e l'uopo vede,
    malignamente già si mette al niego.   60
Or accordiamo a tanto invito il piede;
    procacciam di salir pria che s'abbui,
    chè poi non si poria, se il dì non riede ».   63
Così disse il mio duca, ed io con lui
    volgemmo i nostri passi ad una scala;
    e tosto ch'io al primo grado fui,   66
sentiimi presso quasi un mover d'ala
    e ventarmi nel viso e dir: « Beati
    pacifici, che son senz'ira mala ».   69

And as this image, like a bubble whereto
  the water fails that gave it shape and place,
  broke of itself and disappeared from view,
rose on my vision a girl, in deep distress
  sobbing: 'O queen, ah! wherefore didst thou choose
  for wrath to bring thy life to nothingness?
Thou'st lost Lavinia now, whom fear to lose
  made thee a self-slayer! And 'tis I who grieve,
  mother, at thine ere another's death ensues.'
As sleep which, breaking, if new light should give
  a sudden blow to closed eyes, comes and goes
  when broken, ere it takes its final leave;
so lapsed my imagining, as soon as rose
  a light that on my face smote violently,
  brighter by far than that which here one knows.
I turned round to find out where I might be,
  when a voice saying 'Here is the ascent'
  from every other thought diverted me;
and made my wish with such an ardour bent
  upon beholding who it was that spoke,
  as, until face to face, ne'er rests content.
But as at the Sun, which weighs down eyes that look
  to see its shape when dark thro' excess of light,
  so me my power of vision here forsook.
'This is a spirit divine, who tow'rds the right
  way up, unasked, directs us where to go,
  and with his own beams hides himself from sight.
He treats us, as one treats oneself: whoso
  awaits the asking, once the need is shown,
  ill-willed already leans tow'rds answering "no".
With such a welcome bring we our feet in tone:
  climb we with all our might, before the air
  grows dark, for then we could not, till the dawn.'
Thus did my leader speak, and tow'rds a stair
  we turned our steps together, I and he;
  and soon as on the lowest tread we were,
I felt my face fanned by what seemed to be
  a wing-beat, and heard uttered: 'Blessèd are,
  as knowing not evil wrath, *Pacifici!*'

Già eran sopra noi tanto levati
  gli ultimi raggi che la notte segue,
  che le stelle apparivan da più lati.   72
« O virtù mia, perchè sì ti dilegue? »
  fra me stesso dicea, chè mi sentiva
  la possa de le gambe posta in tregue.   75
Noi eravam dove più non saliva
  la scala sù, ed eravamo affissi
  pur come nave che a la piaggia arriva.   78
Ed io attesi un poco s'io udissi
  alcuna cosa nel novo girone;
  poi mi volsi al maestro mio, e dissi: 81
« Dolce mio padre, dì, quale offensione
  si purga qui nel giro dove semo?
  Se i piè si stanno, non stea tuo sermone ».   84
Ed egli a me: « L'amor del bene scemo
  del suo dover quiritta si ristora:
  qui si ribatte il mal tardato remo.   87
Ma perchè più aperto intendi ancora,
  volgi la mente a me, e prenderai
  alcun buon frutto di nostra dimora.   90
Nè Creator nè creatura mai
  — cominciò ei — figliuol, fu sanza amore
  o naturale o d'animo; e tu il sai.   93
Lo naturale è sempre sanza errore;
  ma l'altro puote errar per malo obbietto,
  o per troppo o per poco di vigore.   96
Mentre ch'egli è nel primo ben diretto
  e nei secondi se stesso misura,
  esser non può cagion di mal diletto;   99
ma quando al mal si torce, o con più cura
  o con men che non dee corre nel bene,
  contra il fattore adopra sua fattura.   102
Quinci comprender puoi ch'esser conviene
  amor sementa in voi d'ogni virtute
  e d'ogni operazion che merta pene.   105
Or, perchè mai non può da la salute
  amor del suo subbietto volger viso,
  da l'odio proprio son le cose tute;   108

Above us were by now upreared so far
  the last rays which the night comes close behind,
  that on all sides there twinkled many a star.
'Oh! why, my strength, hast thou so much declin'd?'
  I said within myself, because I found
  my legs had for a while their power resign'd.
A point now which the stair rose not beyond
  we came to, and just there, stuck fast, we stay'd,
  e'en as a ship does when it runs aground.
I listened awhile and close attention paid,
  should aught from this new circle chance to reach
  my ear—then, turning to my master, said:
'Dear father mine, say what the fault is which
  is purged here in the circle where we are?
  Although our feet be stayed, stay not thy speech,'
'Love of the good, which some defect doth mar,'
  he answered, 'is, precisely here, restor'd:
  here is the laggard oar re-plied with care.
But, that more clearly yet thou grasp my word,
  give heed to me, and thou from our delay
  shalt reap some harvest it may well afford'—
'Son,' he began, 'that the Creator, nay
  the creature too, was ne'er devoid of love,
  natural or of the mind, thou'lt not gainsay.
The natural never errs; but it may prove
  that the other errs through a wrong object *or*
  through excess of zeal *or* through defect thereof.
Whilst by the primal Good it sets chief store,
  with due stress on the secondary laid,
  love can cause no delight ye need deplore.
But when 'tis warped to evil, or is led
  or more or less than duly its good to seize,
  against its Maker works the thing he made.
Hence follows that it must be love which is
  the seed in you of every virtue, yet
  of all acts, too, that merit penalties.
Now, inasmuch as love can never let
  its subject's welfare 'scape its fond regard,
  all creatures are exempted from self-hate.

e perchè intender non si può diviso
   e per se stante alcun esser dal primo,
   da quello odiare ogni effetto è deciso.   111
Resta, se dividendo bene estimo,
   che il mal che s'ama è del prossimo; ed esso
   amor nasce in tre modi in vostro limo.   114
È chi per esser suo vicin soppresso
   spera eccellenza, e sol per questo brama
   ch'ei sia di sua grandezza in basso messo;   117
è chi podere, grazia, onore e fama
   teme di perder perch'altri sormonti,
   onde s'attrista sì che il contrar ama;   120
ed è chi per ingiuria par che adonti
   sì che si fa de la vendetta ghiotto,
   e tal convien che il male altrui impronti.   123
Questo triforme amor qua giù di sotto
   si piange: or vo' che tu de l'altro intende,
   che corre al ben con ordine corrotto.   126
Ciascun confusamente un bene apprende
   nel qual si queti l'animo, e disira;
   per che di giunger lui ciascun contende.   129
Se lento amore in lui veder vi tira
   o in lui acquistar, questa cornice,
   dopo giusto penter, ve ne martira.   132
Altro ben è che non fa l'uom felice:
   non è felicità, non è la buona
   essenza, d'ogni ben frutto e radice.   135
L'amor che ad esso troppo s'abbandona
   di sopra a noi si piagne per tre cerchi;
   ma come tripartito si ragiona,   138
tacciolo a ciò che tu per te ne cerchi».

CANTO 18

Posto avea fine al suo ragionamento
   l'alto dottore, ed attento guardava
   ne la mia vista s'io parea contento;   3

And since no being, strive he however hard,
  can stand alone, dissevered from the First,
  from hating *that* all its effects are barr'd.
Remains, if I with nicety have discours'd,
  that 'tis a neighbour's ill that's loved: and know,
  this love in three modes in your clay is nurst.
There are who hope by a neighbour's overthrow
  themselves to excel, on which account alone
  they long to see him from his height brought low;
there are who fear the loss of power, renown,
  favour and honour, if another rise,
  which irks them so that, up, they wish him down;
and there are those who, wronged, seem in such wise
  aggrieved, their thirst for vengeance can be sated
  only if they their neighbour's hurt devise.
Love, in this triple form, is expiated
  below: now turn thy thoughts to the other kind,
  which pursues good in modes ill-regulated.
Vague notions of a good wherein the mind
  may rest ye all have, and this good desire;
  and ways to achieve it all men strive to find.
If sluggish be the love with which ye aspire
  thereto, or grasp it, on repentance due
  this cornice 'tis which racks you, not a higher.
Another good there is, but not the true
  felicity, the good essence, fruit and root
  of all goods: hence it ne'er contenteth you.
Love that of this makes over-keen pursuit,
  above us in three circles pays its score;
  but how 'tis as tripartite reckoned, mute
am I, that by thyself thou search therefór.'

CANTO 18

THE exalted teacher when his argument
  was ended, searched my eyes, should they reveal
  that with his reasoning I appeared content;

387

e io, cui nova sete ancor frugava,
   di fuor taceva, e dentro dicea: « Forse
   lo troppo dimandar ch'io fo li grava ».   6
Ma quel padre verace, che s'accorse
   del timido voler che non s'apriva,
   parlando, di parlare ardir mi porse.   9
Ond'io: « Maestro, il mio veder s'avviva
   sì nel tuo lume, ch'io discerno chiaro
   quanto la tua ragion porti o descriva.   12
Però ti prego, dolce padre caro,
   che mi dimostri amore, a cui riduci
   ogni buono operare e il suo contraro ».   15
« Drizza » disse « ver me l'acute luci
   de l'intelletto, e fieti manifesto
   l'error dei ciechi che si fanno duci.   18
L'animo, ch'è creato ad amar presto,
   ad ogni cosa è mobile che piace
   tosto che dal piacere in atto è desto.   21
Vostra apprensiva da esser verace
   tragge intenzione, e dentro a voi la spiega
   sì che l'animo ad essa volger face;   24
e se, rivolto, in ver di lei si piega,
   quel piegare è amor, quello è natura
   che, per piacer, di novo in voi si lega.   27
Poi, come il foco movesi in altura
   per la sua forma, ch'è nata a salire
   là dove più in sua matera dura,   30
così l'animo preso entra in disire
   ch'è moto spiritale, e mai non posa
   fin che la cosa amata il fa gioire.   33
Or ti puote apparer quant'è nascosa
   la veritate a la gente che avvera
   ciascun amore in sè laudabil cosa,   36
però che forse appar la sua matera
   sempre esser buona; ma non ciascun segno
   è buono, ancor che buona sia la cera ».   39
« Le tue parole e il mio seguace ingegno »
   rispos'io lui « m'hanno amor discoperto;
   ma ciò m'ha fatto di dubbiar più pregno.   42

And I, whom a new thirst was urging still,
   outwardly mute, within was saying: 'May be
   I ask too much, and he will take it ill.'
But that veracious father, prompt to see
   my timid wish, too shy to raise its veil,
   speaking himself, to speak emboldened me.
Hence I said: 'Master, I discern right well
   (so is my vision quickened in thy light)
   all that thy discourse means or fain would tell.
But, prithee, dear sweet father, to my sight
   make plain the love to which thy words refer
   every good action and its opposite.'
'Bring thou thine intellect's keen eyes to bear
   on me,' he said, 'and where the blind have posed
   as leaders thou shalt see how much they err.
The mind, to loving from its birth disposed,
   moves readily to aught of pleasing hue,
   once by the pleasure 'tis to action roused.
Your apprehensive power draws from a true
   existent an impression and makes your mind,
   by unfolding this within you, turn thereto;
and if, when turned, it tow'rds it be inclined,
   so to incline is love: 'tis nature's bent,
   which, so it charms, fresh ties within you bind.
And even as fire flies upward, since ascent
   is of its essence, urging it on high,
   there where it most dwells in its element;
so to desire, the captured mind doth fly,
   which is a motion of the spirit, and ne'er
   rests, till the thing it loves doth give it joy.
Now canst thou see how much from those who aver
   that ev'ry love in itself is worthy praise
   the truth is hidden, even tho' true it were
that love seems in its matter good always,
   as they perchance think; but not ev'ry seal,
   good tho' the wax be, hath no blemishes.'
I answered: 'By thy words and by my skill
   in following them love's nature hath been shown.
   but this with doubt makes me more pregnant still.

Chè se amore è di fuori a noi offerto
  e l'anima non va con altro piede,
  se dritta o torta va non è suo merto ».   45
Ed egli a me: «Quanto ragion qui vede
  dir ti poss'io: da indi in là t'aspetta
  pur a Beatrice, ch'è opra di fede.   48
Ogni forma sustanzial, che setta
  è da materia ed è con lei unita,
  specifica virtù ha in sè colletta   51
la qual sanza operar non è sentita,
  nè si dimostra ma' che per effetto,
  come per verdi fronde in pianta vita: 54
però laonde vegna l'intelletto
  delle prime notizie uom non sape,
  e dei primi appetibili l'affetto,   57
ch'è solo in voi sì come studio in ape
  di far lo mele; e questa prima voglia
  merto di lode o di biasmo non cape.   60
Or perchè a questa ogn'altra si raccoglia,
  innata v'è la virtù che consiglia
  e de l'assenso dee tener la soglia.   63
Quest'è il principio là onde si piglia
  ragion di meritare in voi, secondo
  che buoni o rei amori accoglie o viglia.   66
Color che ragionando andaro al fondo,
  s'accorser d'esta innata libertade,
  però moralità lasciaro al mondo.   69
Onde poniam che di necessitade
  surga ogni amor che dentro a voi s'accende:
  di ritenerlo è in voi la potestade.   72
La nobile virtù Beatrice intende
  per lo libero arbitrio, e però guarda
  che l'abbi a mente se a parlar ten prende ».   75
La luna, quasi a mezzanotte tarda,
  facea le stelle a noi parer più rade,
  fatta come un secchion che tutto arda;   78
e correa contra il ciel per quelle strade
  che il Sole infiamma allor che quel da Roma
  tra i Sardi e i Corsi il vede quando cade.   81

For, be love offered from without alone,
  and if the soul no other footing hath,
  right going or wrong is merit not its own.'
And he: 'As touching this, what reason saith
  I can inform thee; but, beyond that, wait
  on Beatrice, for 'tis a work of faith.
Every substantial form, distinct from, yet
  made one with matter, hath a specific power
  stored up within itself, which, save when set
in operation, is not noticed, nor
  is ever proved but by the effect it shows,
  as life in plants is proved by leaf and flower.
Therefore the fount from which man's knowledge flows
  of the first notions, and that bent of his
  to the first appetibles, no one knows,
which is but in you, as is zeal in bees
  for making honey; and this primal will
  can merit neither meeds nor penalties.
Now that to this all other desires ye feel
  be gathered, the power-that-counsels is innate
  in you, and of assent should hold the sill.
This is the source whence ye the reason get
  of your deserts, according as it fans
  the loves it garners, good or reprobate.
Those who by reasoning fathomed nature's plans
  perceived this innate freedom; therefore they
  bequeathed their ethic, to be thenceforth man's.
Hence, of all loves within you kindled, say
  that each be of necessity what it is:
  there dwells in you the power to curb its sway—
the noble faculty, which Beatrice
  means by free choice, and therefore see that thou
  bear it in mind, if she should speak of this.'
The moon, almost at midnight pacing slow,
  shaped like a copper bucket all ablaze,
  made the stars seem less numerous to us now;
and moved against the heav'n along those ways
  the Sun inflames, when one descries from Rome
  'twixt Sards and Corsicans his dying rays;

E quell'ombra gentil per cui si noma
   Pietola più che villa mantovana,
   del mio carcar deposta avea la soma;   84
per ch'io, che la ragione aperta e piana
   sopra le mie questioni avea ricolta,
   stava com'uom che sonnolento vana.   87
Ma questa sonnolenza mi fu tolta
   subitamente da gente che dopo
   le nostre spalle a noi era già volta.   90
E quale Ismeno già vide ed Asopo
   lungo di sè di notte furia e calca
   pur che i Teban di Bacco avesser uopo,   93
cotal per quel giron suo passo falca,
   per quel ch'io vidi di color venendo,
   cui buon volere e giusto amor cavalca.   96
Tosto fur sovra noi, perchè correndo
   si movea tutta quella turba magna;
   e due dinanzi gridavan piangendo: 99
« Maria corse con fretta a la montagna;
   e Cesare per soggiogare Ilerda
   punse Massilia e poi corse in Ispagna ».   102
« Ratto, ratto, che il tempo non si perda
   per poco amor » gridavan gli altri appresso,
   « chè studio di ben far grazia rinverda ».   105
« O gente in cui fervore acuto adesso
   ricompie forse negligenza e indugio
   da voi per tepidezza in ben far messo,   108
questi che vive, e certo io non vi bugio,
   vuole andar sù pur che il Sol ne riluca;
   però ne dite ond'è presso il pertugio ».   111
Parole furon queste del mio duca;
   e un di quelli spirti disse: « Vieni
   di retro a noi e troverai la buca.   114
Noi siam di voglia a moverci sì pieni
   che restar non potem; però perdona
   se villania nostra giustizia tieni.   117
Io fui abate in San Zeno a Verona
   sotto l'imperio del buon Barbarossa,
   di cui dolente ancor Milan ragiona.   120

and he, through whom Piétola has become
   famed 'bove all Mantuan towns, that gentle shade,
   had doffed the load I'd made so burdensome;
whence I, who'd to my questions harvested
   elucidation frank as it was plain,
   remained like one who nods through drowsihead—
drowsihead on a sudden from me ta'en
   by folk, who, travelling round the hill about
   behind our backs, tow'rds us had turned just then.
And as of old by night a fury and rout
   along Ismenus and Asopus hied,
   if but the Thebans aid from Bacchus sought,
just such a rout, by what I there descried,
   of those along that round, curvetting, swept,
   whom a good will and righteous love bestride.
And soon were they upon us, for they kept
   still moving at the run, that mighty train;
   and two in front were shouting while they wept:
'Mary ran fast to the hill country'; then
   'Caesar, that he might crush Ilerda, stung
   Marseilles, and thence ran onward into Spain.'
'Swift, swift, for fear that dallying overlong
   diminish love,' the rest cried in their wake,
   'for zeal in well-doing renders grace more strong.'
'O folk, in whom keen fervour now doth make
   up haply for the negligence and delay
   ye showed when in well-doing but half-awake,
this man who lives and breathes—I lie not, nay—
   would climb, if but the Sun renew his light;
   is the opening near, then, and if so, which way?'
Words of my guide were these; to which one sprite
   among them made reply: 'Tread hard upon
   our heels, and soon the gap will come in sight.
Forgive us, if thou deem'st our penance none
   too courteous: for we cannot stop, so keen
   is our desire to keep still moving on.
I was the abbot of San Zeno in
   Verona, when the empire was the brave
   Redbeard's, of whom Milan still talks with teen.

E tale ha un piede già dentro alla fossa
  che tosto piangerà quel monastero,
  e tristo fia d'avervi avuto possa;   125

perchè suo figlio, mal del corpo intero
  e de la mente peggio, e che mal nacque,
  ha posto in loco di suo pastor vero ».   126

Io non so se più disse o s'ei si tacque,
  tanto era già di là da noi trascorso;
  ma questo intesi e ritener mi piacque.   129

E quei che m'era ad ogni uopo soccorso
  disse: « Volgiti in qua: vedine due
  venire dando all'accidia di morso ».   132

Diretro a tutti dicean: « Prima fue
  morta la gente a cui il mar s'aperse,
  che vedesse Jordan le rede sue.   135

E quella che l'affanno non sofferse
  fino a la fine col figlio d'Anchise,
  sè stessa a vita sanza gloria offerse ».   138

Poi quando fur da noi tanto divise
  quell'ombre, che veder più non potersi,
  novo pensiero dentro a me si mise,   141

dal qual più altri nacquero e diversi;
  e tanto d'uno in altro vaneggiai,
  che gli occhi per vaghezza ricopersi   144

e il pensamento in sogno trasmutai.

CANTO 19

Ne l'ora che non può il calor diurno
  intepidar più il freddo de la Luna,
  vinto da Terra e talor da Saturno;   3

quando i geomanti lor Maggior Fortuna
  veggiono in oriente innanzi a l'alba
  sorger per via che poco resta bruna;   6

mi venne in sogno una femmina balba,
  ne gli occhi guercia, sovra i piè distorta,
  con le man monche e di colore scialba.   9

And there's a man with one foot in the grave
  e'en now, who soon shall mourn that monast'ry,
  and rue the power which there he used to have,
because in place of its true pastor he
  has put his son, deformed in body—and add,
  maimed worse in mind—who was born bastardly.'
If more he spake, or haste more speech forbad,
  I know not, so far past us had he sped;
  but this I heard, and to retain was glad.
And he, who was in every need my aid,
  said: 'Turn thyself to this side: see yon two
  come on, defying the sloth which they upbraid.'
In rear of all they cried: 'The people who
  saw the sea cleave apart were dead, or e'er
  Jordan beheld his heirs come into view;
and they, who the affliction could not bear
  unto the end with famed Anchisiades,
  did willingly inglorious life prefer.'
Then, when those shades from us by distances
  so great were parted, that they could no more
  be seen, within me rose new thoughts, and these
gave birth to diverse others; and to explore
  now this, now that, my mind so idly ranged,
  that through thus straying my eyes I covered o'er
and meditation into dreaming changed.

CANTO 19

About the hour when, vanquished by the Earth
  or whiles by Saturn, the diurnal heat
  ebbs, and the Moon is colder for its dearth—
when geomancers see the sign, to wit
  their 'Greater Luck', rise in the east ere dawn
  by a path which will not long stay dark for it;
I dreamt a woman nigh to me had drawn,
  halting of speech, on feet distorted, eyes
  asquint, with hands maimed, and in colour wan.

Io la mirava; e come il Sol conforta
  le fredde membra che la notte aggrava,
  così lo sguardo mio le facea scorta   12
la lingua, e poscia tutta la drizzava
  in poco d'ora, e lo smarrito volto
  come amor vuol così le colorava.   15
Poi ch'ella avea 'l parlar così disciolto,
  cominciava a cantar sì che con pena
  da lei avrei mio intento rivolto.   18
« Io son » cantava, « io son dolce sirena
  che i marinari in mezzo mar dismago,
  tanto son di piacere a sentir piena.   21
Io volsi Ulisse del suo cammin vago
  al canto mio; e qual meco si aùsa
  rado sen parte, sì tutto l'appago ».   24
Ancor non era sua bocca richiusa,
  quando una donna apparve santa e presta
  lunghesso me, per far colei confusa.   27
« O Virgilio, o Virgilio, chi è questa? »
  fieramente diceva; ed ei venia
  con gli occhi fitti pure in quella onesta.   30
L'altra prendeva, e dinanzi l'apria
  fendendo i drappi e mostrandomi il ventre:
  quel mi svegliò col puzzo che n'uscìa.   33
Io mossi gli occhi; e il buon maestro: « Almen tre
  voci t'ho messe! » dicea. « Surgi e vieni:
  troviam l'aperta per la qual tu entre ».   36
Sù mi levai, e tutti eran già pieni
  dell'alto dì i giron del sacro monte,
  e andavam col Sol novo a le reni.   39
Seguendo lui, portava la mia fronte
  come colui che l'ha di pensier carca,
  che fa di sè un mezz'arco di ponte;   42
quand'io udii: « Venite, qui si varca »
  parlar in modo soave e benigno,
  qual non si sente in questa mortal marca.   45
Con l'ali aperte, che parean di cigno,
  volseci in sù colui che sì parlonne
  tra i due pareti del duro macigno.   48

I gazed at her; and as the Sun supplies
   fresh strength to cold limbs weighed down by the night,
   so of her tongue my look unloosed the ties
that bound it, then in brief while set upright
   her crippled frame, and dyed her pallid cheek
   the colour in which lovers most delight.
When thus unfettered was her power to speak,
   she fell to singing so, that had I willed
   to pay no heed my will had proved too weak.
'I'm,' she sang, 'I'm the sweet-voiced Siren skilled
   to enchant mariners in mid-ocean, so
   with pleasing magic is my utterance filled.
I turned Ulysses from his course, to go
   after my song: to me once closely bound,
   few quit me, such contentment do they know.'
Nor had her mouth yet closed upon the sound,
   when at my side a saintly dame appear'd
   with all speed her bewitchments to confound.
'O Virgil, Virgil, who is this?' I heard
   her fiercely say: and he, with eyes intent
   upon that guileless one—her only—near'd
then seized the other and her drapery rent
   in front and thereby bared her belly; me
   this wakened with the stench that from it went.
I turned to the good master: 'At least three
   calls have I given thee; rise and come,' he said;
   'find we the opening to thine entrance free.'
I rose: broad daylight now had overspread
   the sacred mountain, gilding every ledge:
   and, the new Sun behind us, on we sped.
While following him, as one who is the siege
   of thoughts wherewith his brow is charged and who
   makes of himself a half-arch of a bridge,
I heard 'Here is the gap one passes through'
   breathed in low tones and kindly, such as none
   in this our mortal march e'er listened to.
With wings spread wide, that seemed a swan's, the one
   who thus spoke turned us to the upward way
   between the two walls of unyielding stone.

Mosse le penne poi e ventilonne,
   Qui lugent affermando esser beati,
   che avran di consolar l'anime donne.   51
« Che hai che pure inver la terra guati? »
   la guida mia incominciò a dirmi,
   poco ambedue da l'angel sormontati.   54
E io: « Con tanta suspizion fa irmi
   novella vision che a sè mi piega
   sì ch'io non posso dal pensar partirmi ».   57
« Vedesti » disse « quell'antica strega
   che sola sopra noi omai si piagne;
   vedesti come l'uom da lei si slega.   60
Bastiti, e batti a terra le calcagne:
   gli occhi rivolgi al logoro che gira
   lo rege eterno con le rote magne ».   63
Quale il falcon, che prima ai piè si mira,
   indi si volge al grido e si protende
   per lo disio del pasto che là il tira,   66
tal mi fec'io; e tal quanto si fende
   la roccia per dar via a chi va suso,
   n'andai infin dove il cerchiar si prende.   69
Com'io nel quinto giro fui dischiuso,
   vidi gente per esso che piangea,
   giacendo a terra tutta volta in giuso.   72
Adhaesit pavimento anima mea
   sentia dir lor con sì alti sospiri
   che la parola a pena s'intendea.   75
« O eletti di Dio li cui soffriri
   e giustizia e speranza fa men duri,
   drizzate noi verso gli alti saliri ».   78
« Se voi venite dal giacer sicuri
   e volete trovar la via più tosto,
   le vostre destre sien sempre di furi ».   81
Così pregò il poeta, e sì risposto
   poco dinanzi a noi ne fu, per ch'io
   nel parlare avvisai l'altro nascosto;   84
e volsi gli occhi a gli occhi al signor mio;
   ond'elli m'assentì con lieto cenno
   ciò che chiedea la vista del disio.   87

He waved his feathers then, and fanned us, they
 'qui lugent' he assured us being blest,
 whose souls o'er consolation shall hold sway.
'What ails thee that thou only studiest
 the ground?' began my leader, when we twain
 up past the angel had some way progress'd.
And I: ' 'Tis a new vision doth constrain
 me thus to bend, mistrustful, 'neath the stress
 of thoughts whereof I cannot rid my brain.'
'Thou sawest' he said 'that ancient sorceress,
 sole cause above us from now on of dole:
 thou sawest how man breaks free from her embrace.
Enough! Strike heels to earth, and turn thy whole
 attention to the lure the eternal King
 whirls with the great wheels that before thee roll.'
Like to the falcon, first contémplating
 its feet, then stretching forward at the call,
 fain of the food which spurs it to take wing,
became I and, so far as the rock-wall
 was cleft as passage for one upward bound,
 climbed, till I reached the circling pedestal.
When I had issued thus to the fifth round,
 I beheld folk along it weeping sore,
 who lay, turned wholly downwards, on the ground.
'Adhaesit pavimento,' o'er and o'er,
 'anima mea,' so loudly I heard them sigh,
 that what was said it well nigh overbore.
'O elect of God, whom for your agony
 justice and hope alike have fortified,
 direct us tow'rds the other ways on high.'
'If, spared prostration, ye have hither hied,
 and wish to find the way with greater speed,
 keep ye your right hands to the outer side.'
So prayed the poet and so, to meet our need,
 came words from just in front of us; and I,
 since in them I had marked the wish they hid,
turned back mine eyes unto my lord's, whereby
 observing what my eager look besought,
 he nodded his assent to me with joy.

Poi ch'io potei di me fare a mio senno,
   trassimi sovra quella creatura
   le cui parole pria notar mi fenno,   90
dicendo: « Spirto in cui pianger matura
   quel sanza il quale a Dio tornar non puossi,
   sosta un poco per me tua maggior cura.   93
Chi fosti e perchè volti avete i dossi
   al sù mi di', e se vuoi ch'io t'impetri
   cosa di là ond'io vivendo mossi ».   96
Ed egli a me: « Perchè i nostri diretri
   rivolga il cielo a sè, saprai; ma prima
   scias quod ego fui successor Petri.   99
Intra Siestri e Chiaveri s'adima
   una fiumana bella, e del suo nome
   lo titol del mio sangue fa sua cima.   102
Un mese e poco più provai io come
   pesa il gran manto a chi dal fango il guarda,
   che piuma sembran tutte l'altre some.   105
La mia conversione, omè, fu tarda;
   ma come fatto fui roman pastore
   così scopersi la vita bugiarda: 108
vidi che lì non si quetava il core,
   nè più salir poteasi in quella vita;
   per che di questa in me s'accese amore.   111
Fino a quel punto misera e partita
   da Dio anima fui, del tutto avara:
   or, come vedi, qui ne son punita.   114
Quel che avarizia fa, qui si dichiara
   in purgazion de l'anime converse;
   e nulla pena il monte ha più amara.   117
Sì come l'occhio nostro non s'aderse
   in alto, fisso a le cose terrene,
   così giustizia qui a terra il merse.   120
Come avarizia spense a ciascun bene
   lo nostro amore, onde operar perdèsi,
   così giustizia qui stretti ne tiene   123
nei piedi e ne le man legati e presi;
   e quanto fia piacer del giusto sire,
   tanto staremo immobili e distesi ».   126

I, thus empowered to do the thing I thought,
   neared and stood o'er that creature who whilere
   had by those words of his my notice caught,
saying: 'Spirit, in whom thy tears mature what ne'er,
   till ripe, lets man to God his steps re-track,
   suspend awhile for me thy greater care.
Say who thou wast, why ye lie each with back
   upturned, and if thou'dst have me obtain for thee
   there, whence I living moved, aught thou dost lack.'
'Why Heav'n turns our backparts to itself thou'lt be
   duly informed,' he answered; 'but foremost,
   scias quod ego Petri successor fui.
'Twixt Sestri and Chiáveri to the coast
   flows a fair river, called by a name whence get
   my kin the title, of which in chief they boast.
One month, scarce more, I proved how weighs the great
   mantle on him who guards it from the mire:
   all burdens else seem but a feather's weight.
To be converted, woe's me, my desire
   lagged long, but when to shepherd Rome they chose
   me at length, I found out life to be a liar.
I saw that there the heart found no repose,
   nor in that life could one mount higher; in me
   therefore of this a burning love arose.
Up to that point, wretched, from God cut free,
   my soul was wholly given to avarice,
   now punished for it here, as thou dost see.
What avarice does is here declared in this
   purgation of the souls who turn again;
   nor has the mount more bitter penalties.
E'en as our eyes refused to look up, when
   they could, but were on earthly objects bent,
   so justice here to earth has sunk their ken.
As avarice quenched our love for all that lent
   life value, hence for working left no place,
   so justice here doth hold us in restraint,
with hands and feet fast bound, in close duress:
   and for so long as pleases the just Lord,
   we shall remain outstretched and motionless.'

Io m'era inginocchiato, e volea dire;
  ma com'io cominciai, ed ei s'accorse
  solo ascoltando, del mio riverire,   129
« Qual cagion », disse, « in giù così ti torse? »
  Ed io a lui: « Per vostra dignitate
  mia coscienza dritto mi rimorse ».   132
« Drizza le gambe, levati sù, frate! »
  rispose; « Non errar: conservo sono
  teco e con gli altri ad una potestate.   135
Se mai quel santo evangelico suono
  che dice *Neque nubent* intendesti,
  ben puoi veder perch'io così ragiono.   138
Vattene omai: non vo' che più t'arresti,
  chè la tua stanza mio pianger disagia
  col qual maturo ciò che tu dicesti.   141
Nepote ho io di là che ha nome Alagia,
  buona da sè, pur che la nostra casa
  non faccia lei per esempio malvagia;   144
e questa sola di là m'è rimasa ».

CANTO 20

Contra miglior voler voler mal pugna;
  onde, contra il piacer mio, per piacerli
  trassi de l'acqua non sazia la spugna.   3
Mossimi, e il duca mio si mosse, per li
  luoghi spediti, pur lungo la roccia,
  come si va per muro stretto ai merli;   6
chè la gente che fonde goccia a goccia
  per gli occhi il mal che tutto il mondo occupa,
  da l'altra parte in fuor troppo s'approccia.   9
Maledetta sie tu, antica lupa
  che più di tutte l'altre bestie hai preda
  per la tua fame sanza fine cupa.   12
O ciel, nel cui girar par che si creda
  la condizion di qua giù trasmutarsi,
  quando verrà per cui questa disceda?   15

I'd fallen on my knees, but ere the word
  I purposed could be spoken, he was ware
  of my obeisance, tho' by him but heard;
'What cause,' he said, 'has bent thee downward there?'
  And I: 'By reason of your high estate
  my conscience pricked me: stand I did not dare.'
'Unbend thy legs, brother, stand thou up straight!'
  he answered; 'Err not: with thee and the rest
  I'm servant of the self-same Potentate.
If ever thou did'st read and well digest
  "neque nubent", that holy gospel-text,
  why thus I reason will be manifest.
Tarry not now: but go, because thou make'st,
  by staying, it hard for me to shed the tears
  with which I ripen that whereof thou spake'st.
A niece have I o'er there—the name she bears,
  Alagia—in herself good, if the ill
  character of our house corrupt not hers:
and she alone o'er there is left me still.'

CANTO 20

Matched 'gainst a better will the will must yield;
  against my pleasure, then, to pleasure him,
  the sponge was from the water drawn unfill'd.
I moved; and my guide moved, with care extreme
  along the cliff-side, by the spots left clear,
  as on a wall one hugs the embattled rim;
for those who from their eyes are, tear by tear,
  wringing the ill that doth all lands invade,
  on the other side approach the edge too near.
Accurs'd be thou, old She-wolf who hast made
  more than all other beasts the world thy prey,
  since craves thy maw without end to be fed!
O heaven, whose revolutions (some would say)
  change the condition of things here below,
  when will he come who'll drive this scourge away?

403

Noi andavam con passi lenti e scarsi,
   e io attento a l'ombre, ch'io sentia
   pietosamente piangere e lagnarsi.   18
E per ventura udii: « Dolce Maria »
   dinanzi a noi chiamar così nel pianto
   come fa donna che in parturir sia;   21
e seguitar: « povera fosti tanto
   quanto veder si può per quell'ospizio
   dove sponesti il tuo portato santo ».   24
Seguentemente intesi: « O buon Fabrizio,
   con povertà volesti anzi virtute
   che gran ricchezza posseder con vizio ».   27
Queste parole m'eran sì piaciute,
   ch'io mi trassi oltre per aver contezza
   di quello spirto onde parean venute.   30
Esso parlava ancor de la larghezza
   che fece Niccolò a le pulcelle
   per condurre ad onor lor giovinezza.   33
« O anima che tanto ben favelle,
   dimmi chi fosti » dissi, « e perchè sola
   tu queste degne lode rinnovelle.   36
Non fia sanza mercè la tua parola
   s'io ritorno a compièr lo cammin corto
   di quella vita che al termine vola ».   39
Ed egli: « Io ti dirò, non per conforto
   ch'io attenda di là, ma perchè tanta
   grazia in te luce prima che sie morto.   42
Io fui radice de la mala pianta
   che la terra cristiana tutta aduggia
   sì che buon frutto raro se ne schianta. 45
Ma se Doagio, Lilla, Guanto e Bruggia
   potesser, tosto ne saria vendetta;
   ed io la chieggo a Lui che tutto giuggia. 48
Chiamato fui di là Ugo Ciapetta:
   di me son nati i Filippi e i Luigi
   per cui novellamente è Francia retta.   51
Figliuol fui d'un beccaio di Parigi.
   Quando li regi antichi venner meno
   tutti, fuor ch'un renduto in panni bigi, 54

We picked our path with measured steps and slow,
    I on the shades intent and nought beside,
    their piteous sobs and plaining touched me so;
and as it chanced I heard 'Sweet Mary!' cried
    in front of us amidst the general moan
    as by a woman whom child-birth may betide;
and further: 'Poor thou wast—how poor is shown
    by thy reception at the humble inn
    where thou didst lay thy holy burden down.'
'O good Fabricius,' followed next, 'to win
    virtue with poverty didst thou prefer
    rather than to possess great wealth with sin.'
These words so pleasing for their import were,
    that I pressed forward fain to know the truth
    about the soul that seemed their utterer.
It now was telling of the boon which ruth
    made Nicholas bestow upon the maids,
    that unto honour he might guide their youth.
'O soul, whose speech so great a good pervades,
    who wast thou?' I asked: 'and why renewest thou
    such praises meet, alone of all these shades?
If I return to tread the short way now
    remaining of that life which soon is sped,
    not unrewarded shall thine answer go.'
And he: 'I'll tell thee, not for any aid
    I hope for thence, but because grace in thee
    in such large measure shines ere thou art dead.
I was the root of that malignant tree
    by which all Christendom is shadowed o'er,
    so that good fruit plucked thence men seldom see.
But if Douai, Lille, Ghent and Bruges had power
    sufficient, soon were vengeance on it ta'en;
    and I entreat the Judge of all therefór.
Of me, called Hugh Capét by mortal men,
    were born the Lewises and Philips, they
    who recently have held in France their reign.
A Paris butcher sired me. From that day
    when to their end had come the kings of old,
    all except one who frocked himself in grey,

trovaimi stretto ne le mani il freno
  del governo del regno, e tanta possa
  di novo acquisto, e sì d'amici pieno   57
che a la corona vedova promossa
  la testa di mio figlio fu, dal quale
  cominciar di costor le sacrate ossa.   60
Mentre che la gran dote provenzale
  al sangue mio non tolse la vergogna,
  poco valea, ma pur non facea male.   63
Lì cominciò con forza e con menzogna
  la sua rapina; e poscia, per ammenda,
  Pontiè e Normandia prese, e Guascogna.   66
Carlo venne in Italia, e, per ammenda,
  vittima fe' di Curradino, e poi
  ripinse al ciel Tommaso, per ammenda.   69
Tempo vegg'io, non molto dopo ancoi,
  che tragge un altro Carlo fuor di Francia,
  per far conoscer meglio e sè e i suoi.   72
Sanz'arme n'esce e solo con la lancia
  con la qual giostrò Giuda, e quella ponta
  sì che a Fiorenza fa scoppiar la pancia.   75
Quindi non terra, ma peccato ed onta
  guadagnerà, per sè tanto più grave
  quanto più lieve simil danno conta.   78
L'altro, che già uscì preso di nave,
  veggio vender sua figlia e patteggiarne
  come fanno i corsar de l'altre schiave.   81
O avarizia, che puoi tu più farne
  poscia ch'hai il mio sangue a te sì tratto
  che non si cura de la propria carne?   84
Perchè men paia il mal futuro e il fatto,
  veggio in Alagna entrar lo fiordaliso
  e nel vicario suo Cristo esser catto.   87
Veggiolo un'altra volta esser deriso;
  veggio rinnovellar l'aceto e il fele,
  e tra vivi ladroni essere anciso.   90
Veggio il novo Pilato sì crudele
  che ciò nol sazia, ma sanza decreto
  porta nel Tempio le cupide vele.   93

my hands, I found, had got so firm a hold
  on the realm's guiding reins, power newly won
  so great was mine, such friends had I enroll'd,
that to the widowed crown it was my son
  whose temples were promoted: from the same
  began the anointed bones I've touched upon.
My race, while not as yet from sense of shame
  by the great dowry of Provence set free,
  tho' of small worth, still none found cause to blame.
There it began with force and perfidy
  its rapine: and thereafter, for amends,
  seized Normandy, Ponthieu and Gascony.
Charles entered Italy, and, for amends,
  victimized Conradín and, after this,
  back into heav'n pushed Thomas, for amends.
I see a time, nor long from now it is,
  which draws from France another Charles, athirst
  to make more widely known both him and his.
Unarmed he comes, save with the lance that erst
  Judas went tilting with, and thrusts it so
  at Florence, that he makes her paunch to burst.
Thence will he gain, not territory, no!
  but sin and shame, the worse for him, as more
  the cost of crimes like this he reckons low.
I see the third, who once from ship to shore
  stepped prisoner, sell his daughter as pirates would
  a slave-girl, and her value haggled o'er.
O Avarice, what canst thou more? Subdued
  my race so wholly to thyself thou hast,
  it takes no thought for its own flesh and blood.
That evil may seem less, to come or past,
  I see Alagna to the Lily yield,
  and, in his vicar, Christ held captive fast.
I see him mocked again; I see it filled
  again, the sponge, with vinegar and gall,
  and him 'twixt living malefactors killed.
I see the modern Pilate's cruelty, all
  unglutted by these crimes, without decree
  with greedy sails upon the Temple fall.

O Signor mio, quando sarò io lieto
  a veder la vendetta, che, nascosa,
  fa dolce l'ira tua nel tuo secreto?   96
Ciò ch'io dicea di quell'unica sposa
  de lo Spirito Santo, e che ti fece
  verso me volger per alcuna chiosa,   99
tanto è disposto a tutte nostre prece,
  quanto il dì dura; ma com'ei s'annotta
  contrario suon prendiamo in quella vece.   102
Noi ripetiam Pigmalione allotta,
  cui traditore e ladro e parricida
  fece la voglia sua de l'oro ghiotta;   105
e la miseria de l'avaro Mida
  che seguì a la sua dimanda ingorda,
  per la qual sempre convien che si rida.   108
Del folle Acam ciascun poi si ricorda
  come furò le spoglie, sì che l'ira
  di Josuè qui par che ancor lo morda.   111
Indi accusiam col marito Safira,
  lodiamo i calci ch'ebbe Eliodoro,
  ed in infamia tutto il monte gira   114
Polinestor che ancise Polidoro.
  Ultimamente ci si grida: 'Crasso,
  dicci, chè il sái: di che sapore è l'oro?'   117
Talor parla l'un alto e l'altro basso,
  secondo l'affezion, che a dir ci sprona
  ora a maggiore ed ora a minor passo.   120
Però al ben che il dì ci si ragiona
  dianzi non era io sol, ma qui da presso
  non alzava la voce altra persona».   123
Noi eravam partiti già da esso,
  e brigavam di soperchiar la strada
  tanto quanto al poter n'era permesso,   126
quand'io sentii come cosa che cada
  tremar lo monte, onde mi prese un gelo
  qual prender suol colui che a morte vada. 129
Certo non si scotea sì forte Delo
  pria che Latona in lei facesse il nido
  a parturir li du' occhi del cielo.   132

O Lord my God, when shall I joy to see
   thy vengeance which, albeit undescried,
   makes sweet thine anger in thy secrecy?
What I was saying of that only bride
   of the Holy Spirit and which tow'rds me made
   thee turn, to have some gloss thereon supplied,
has been prescribed to all the prayers here prayed
   while daylight lasts; but when the night comes on,
   we take a contrary strain up in its stead.
Pygmalion's story then we dwell upon,
   whom his unsatiable lust for gold
   made traitor, thief and parricide; anon
of avaricious Midas, too, is told
   the misery his greedy prayer entail'd,
   which men will always in derision hold.
In memory, next, is Achan's folly held,
   how he purloined the spoils: thus here, e'en yet,
   by Joshua's biting wrath he seems assail'd.
Then we accuse Sapphira with her mate;
   we praise the kicks which Heliodorus rued;
   and Polymnestor's shame we circulate
hill-wide, his shedding Polydorus' blood:
   latest of all is cried here "Crassus, thou
   who knowest the taste of gold, say is it good?"
At times we talk, one loud, another low,
   according as our feelings spur us on
   to speak by being now forceful, now less so.
Hence deem not that just now I was alone
   in crying the goodness we rehearse by day;
   but of loud voices, near, there else was none.'
We had already left him, and our way
   were striving to o'ercome, picking our path
   according to such power as in us lay,
when, as a thing ere falling tottereth,
   I felt the mountain quake; and shuddered, even
   as shuddereth one who goes to meet his death.
To Delos, sure, no shock so hard was given,
   ere by Latona 'twas as nest employ'd
   wherein to bring forth the two eyes of heaven.

Poi cominciò da tutte parti un grido
 tal, che il maestro inverso me si feo,
 dicendo: « Non dubbiar mentr'io ti guido ».   135
Gloria in excelsis tutti *Deo*
 dicean, per quel ch'io da vicin compresi
 onde intender lo grido si poteo.   138
Noi stavamo immobili e sospesi
 come i pastor che prima udir quel canto,
 fin che il tremar cessò ed ei compiesi.   141
Poi ripigliammo nostro cammin santo
 guardando l'ombre che giacean per terra
 tornate già in su l'usato pianto.   144
Niuna ignoranza mai con tanta guerra
 mi fe' desideroso di sapere,
 se la memoria mia in ciò non erra,   147
quanta pareami allor, pensando, avere;
 nè per la fretta dimandare era oso,
 nè per me lì potea cosa vedere: 150
così m'andava timido e pensoso.

CANTO 21

La sete natural che mai non sazia
 se non con l'acqua onde la femminetta
 samaritana domandò la grazia,   3
mi travagliava, e pungeami la fretta
 per l'impacciata via dietro al mio duca,
 e condoleami a la giusta vendetta.   6
Ed ecco, sì come ne scrive Luca
 che Cristo apparve ai due ch'erano in vìa,
 già surto fuor de la sepulcral buca,   9
ci apparve un'ombra, e dietro a noi venia
 dal piè guardando la turba che giace;
 nè ci addemmo di lei, sì parlò pria   12
dicendo: « Frati miei, Dio vi dea pace ».
 Noi ci volgemmo subito, e Virgilio
 rendegli il cenno che a ciò si conface.   15

Then there began a shout from every side,
   such that my master tow'rds me was not slow
   to draw near, saying: 'Fear nought, whilst I'm thy guide.'
That *'Gloria in excelsis'* all *'Deo'*
   were saying, from close at hand I comprehended
   whence what was being shouted one could know.
We halted motionless, with breath suspended.
   like to the shepherds who first heard that song,
   until the quaking ceased and the cry ended.
Then we resumed our sacred way among
   the shades, and watched them lying on the ground,
   their wonted plaints again employing each tongue.
No ignorance I've e'er within me found,
   with war so fierce made me desire to know
   (if that my memory here be not unsound),
as then I seemed, in thought, to undergo;
   nor, for our haste, dared I to ask him aught,
   nor, of myself, could aught discern there: so
I took my way, timid and deep in thought.

CANTO 21

The thirst that nature prompts and which alone
   that water satisfies whereof the poor
   woman of Samaria once craved the boon,
tortured me, and haste pricked me onward o'er
   the encumbered path behind my guide, and ruth
   for the just vengeance made my heart feel sore;
and lo, as Luke records for us the truth
   that to the two wayfarers Christ drew near,
   when newly risen from the tomb's dark mouth,
a shade appeared to us, coming from our rear
   and eyeing the crowd that 'neath it prostrate lay;
   nor, till it spoke, perceived we it was there.
'God give you peace, my brothers' did it say.
   We turned forthwith, and Virgil, thus address'd,
   made it the countersign in the due way.

Poi cominciò: « Nel beato concilio
   ti ponga in pace la verace corte
   che me rilega ne l'eterno esilio ».   18
« Come! » diss'egli; e parte andavam forte:
   « se voi siet'ombre che Dio sù non degni,
   chi v'ha per la sua scala tanto scorte? »   21
E il dottor mio: « Se tu riguardi i segni
   che questi porta e che l'angel profila,
   ben vedrai che coi buon convien ch'ei regni.   24
Ma perchè lei che dì e notte fila
   non gli avea tratta ancora la conocchia
   che Cloto impone a ciascuno e compila,   27
l'anima sua, ch'è tua e mia sirocchia,
   venendo sù non potea venir sola,
   però che al nostro modo non adocchia.   30
Ond'io fui tratto fuor de l'ampia gola
   d'Inferno per mostrarli, e mostrerolli
   oltra quanto il potrà menar mia scola.   33
Ma dimmi, se tu sai, perchè tai crolli
   diè dianzi il monte, e perchè tutti ad una
   parver gridare infino a' suoi piè molli ».   36
Sì mi diè, dimandando, per la cruna
   del mio disio, che pur con la speranza
   si fece la mia sete men digiuna.   39
Quei cominciò: « Cosa non è che sanza
   ordine senta la religione
   de la montagna, o che sia fuor d'usanza.   42
Libero è qui da ogni alterazione:
   di quel che il ciel da sè in sè riceve
   esser ci puote, e non d'altra cagione.   45
Per che non pioggia, non grando, non neve,
   non rugiada, non brina più sù cade
   che la scaletta di tre gradi breve;   48
nuvole spesse non paion nè rade,
   nè corruscar, nè figlia di Taumante,
   che di là cangia sovente contrade;   51
secco vapor non surge più avante
   che al sommo dei tre gradi ch'io parlai,
   dov'ha il vicario di Pietro le piante.   54

Then he began: 'To the council of the Blest
   may'st thou be brought in peace by that true court
   which bids me in eternal exile rest.'
'How!' cried he, as on we strode in manful sort,
   'if ye be shades, whose rise God would not deign,
   who up his stairs thus far was your escort?'
'If thou,' my teacher said, 'the marks writ plain
   on this man by the angel have in sight,
   thou'lt see that with the good he needs must reign.
But, because she who spinneth day and night
   had not for him yet drawn off all the flax
   which Clotho loads for each man and packs tight,
his soul, thy sister and mine, was bound to o'ertax
   its strength, if, climbing, it had climbed alone,
   since power to see things, as do we, it lacks.
Whence I from out hell's ample throat was drawn
   to show, and still will show, him how one goes,
   so far as by my school it can be shown.
But tell me, if thou know'st, why with such throes
   the mountain just now shook, and with one cry
   all seemed to shout, down to its basic ooze?'
Thus asking, did he thread the needle's eye
   of my desire, and merely with the hope
   the thirst that parched my mind became less dry.
'Nought,' he began, 'which lies outside the scope
   of its own usage and established laws,
   affects the ritual of this mountain-slope.
'Tis free from any change: what Heaven draws
   from itself *to* itself, and that alone
   can in this region operate as cause.
Wherefore no rain, nor hail, is ever known
   to fall, nor snow, nor dew, nor rime, above
   the short stair-way that hath three steps thereon.
Here is no cloud nor slightest film thereof,
   nor lightning, nor the daughter of Thaumas, she
   who yonder oft from place to place doth rove.
No higher than the topmost of the three
   steps that I spoke of, where the feet are set
   of Peter's Vicar, can dry vapour be.

Trema forse più giù poco od assai;
  ma per vento che in terra si nasconda,
  non so come, qua sù non tremò mai.   57
Tremaci quando alcun'anima monda
  sentasi sì che surga o che si mova
  per salir sù; e tal grido seconda.   60
De la mondizia sol voler fa prova,
  che tutto libero a mutar convento
  l'alma sorprende, e di voler le giova.   63
Prima vuol ben, ma non lascia il talento
  che divina giustizia contra voglia,
  come fu al peccar, pone al tormento.   66
Ed io, che son giaciuto a questa doglia
  cinquecent'anni e più, pur mo' sentii
  libera volontà di miglior soglia;   69
però sentisti il tremoto e li pii
  spiriti per lo monte render lode
  a quel Signor, che tosto sù li invii».   72
Così ne disse, e però ch'ei si gode
  tanto del ber quant'è grande la sete,
  non saprei dir quant'ei mi fece prode.   75
E il savio duca: « Omai veggio la rete
  che qui v'impiglia e come si scalappia,
  perchè ci trema e di che congaudete.   78
Ora chi fosti piacciati ch'io sappia,
  e perchè tanti secoli giaciuto
  qui sei, ne le parole tue mi cappia ».   81
« Nel tempo che il buon Tito, con l'aiuto
  del sommo rege, vendicò le fora
  onde uscì il sangue per Giuda venduto,   84
col nome che più dura e che più onora
  era io di là » rispose quello spirto,
  « famoso assai ma non con fede ancora.   87
Tanto fu dolce mio vocale spirto,
  che, tolosano, a sè mi trasse Roma,
  dove mertai le tempie ornar di mirto.   90
Stazio la gente ancor di là mi noma.
  Cantai di Tebe e poi del grande Achille,
  ma caddi in via con la seconda soma.   93

It quakes, perhaps, with movement little or great
  lower down; but ne'er from wind some power conceals
  in the earth (I know not how) here quaked it yet.
It quakes here every time that a soul feels
  itself clean and is, therefore, moved to ascend,
  or rises: then this shout, to speed it, peals.
Of cleanness proof is from the will obtain'd
  alone, by which, all free to change its mates,
  the soul's surprised and in volition sustain'd.
True, it wills to rise before, but the impulse lets
  it not, which divine justice 'gainst the will,
  as 'twas to sinning, to the torment sets.
And I, who in this sorrow have lain still
  five hundred years and more, felt but just now
  a free volition for a better sill.
That's why thou felt'st the earth quake and heardest how
  the pious spirits throughout the mount gave praise
  to God—them, too, to rise may he soon allow!'
Thus spake he to us; and as drink conveys
  joy, matching what one's thirst was, in degree,
  the good he did me exceeds my power to phrase.
And the sage leader: 'Now I clearly see
  the net that snares you, how 'tis escaped from, why
  it quakes here, and the cause of your joint glee.
Now who thou wast please tell me: and be it in thy
  own words expounded wherefore thou hast stay'd
  here prostrate, while whole centuries rolled by.'
'Of yore, when the good Titus, with the aid
  of heaven's King, avenged the wounds that wet
  with the blood were, which Judas had betray'd,
the name whence, longest, men most honour get
  was mine,' that spirit answered, 'there beneath,
  where I was famed, though not a Christian yet.
Rome—so melodious was my vocal breath—
  to itself drew me, a Toulousian, where
  I earned, to deck my brows, the myrtle wreath.
Statius the people call me still o'er there;
  Thebes, then the great Achilles, did I sing,
  but fell by the way—his weight too great to bear.

415

Al mio ardor fur seme le faville,
  che mi scaldar de la divina fiamma
  onde sono allumati più di mille: 96
de l'Eneida, dico, la qual mamma
  fummi, e fummi nutrice poetando;
  sanz'essa non formai peso di dramma.   99
E per esser vivuto di là quando
  visse Virgilio, assentirei un sole
  più che non deggio, al mio uscir di bando».   102
Volser Virgilio a me queste parole
  con viso che, tacendo, disse «Taci!»
  ma non può tutto la virtù che vuole;   105
chè riso e pianto son tanto seguaci
  a la passion di che ciascun si spicca,
  che men seguon voler nei più veraci.   108
Io pur sorrisi come l'uom che ammicca;
  per che l'ombra si tacque, e riguardommi
  ne gli occhi, ove il sembiante più si ficca;   111
e «Se tanto lavoro in bene assommi»
  disse, «perchè la faccia tua testeso
  un lampeggiar di riso dimostrommi?»   114
Or son io d'una parte e d'altra preso:
  l'una mi fa tacer, l'altra scongiura
  ch'io dica; ond'io sospiro, e sono inteso   117
dal mio maestro, e «Non aver paura»
  mi dice «di parlar; ma parla, e digli
  quel ch'ei dimanda con cotanta cura».   120
Ond'io: «Forse che tu ti maravigli,
  antico spirto, del rider ch'io fei;
  ma più d'ammirazion vo' che ti pigli.   123
Questi che guida in alto gli occhi miei
  è quel Virgilio dal qual tu togliesti
  forza a cantar de gli uomini e de' dei.   126
Se cagion altra al mio rider credesti,
  lasciala per non vera, ed esser credi
  quelle parole che di lui dicesti».   129
Già s'inchinava ad abbracciar li piedi
  al mio dottor, ma ei li disse: «Frate,
  non far, chè tu sei ombra ed ombra vedi».   132

Seed to my ardour were the sparks that spring,
   enkindling, from the flame divine, whence light
   thousands have caught for their illumining:
I mean the *Aeneid*, nurse to me and right
   good mother, since my poesy began,
   and but for which I were not worth a mite.
And, to have been on earth a living man
   with Virgil, I'd consent to one sun more
   than I am due ere coming forth from ban.'
These words turned Virgil's face to me: it wore
   a look that mutely said to me 'Be mute!';
   but there are things beyond volition's power;
for smiles and tears come in such close pursuit
   of feelings whence they spring, as least to obey
   the will in those whose minds with truth most suit.
I did but smile, as one by winking may,
   wherefore the shade broke off, and at me gazed
   in the eyes, where what we feel we most display.
'So mayst thou to thy toiled-for weal be raised,
   why from thy face this moment just gone by
   flashed there a smile?' he asked, like one amazed.
Now caught on this side and on that am I:
   one says 'Be mute', the other, no less clear,
   conjures me 'Speak'; so that I heave a sigh:
my master understands me and 'Do not fear'
   he says 'to speak; but speak; tell him the thing
   he asks, and is so much concerned to hear.'
Whence I: 'It may be thou art marvelling,
   O ancient spirit, at the smile I gave;
   but I'll a greater marvel upon thee spring.
Who guides my eyes aloft no being save
   that Virgil is, by whom to sing of men
   and gods thy timid muse was rendered brave.
If on some other ground thou didst explain
   my smile, believe it's not true, and that it
   was only what thou said'st of him just then.'
Already he'd stooped to embrace my teacher's feet:
   but 'Brother, do it not' he said to him,
   'for, shade thyself, 'tis shade thine eyes now greet.'

Ed ei surgendo: « Or puoi la quantitate
  comprender de l'amor che a te mi scalda,
  quand'io dismento nostra vanitate   135
trattando l'ombre come cosa salda ».

CANTO 22

Già era l'angel dietro a noi rimaso,
  l'angel che n'avea volti al sesto giro
  avendomi dal viso un colpo raso;   3
e quei ch'hanno a giustizia lor disiro
  detti n'avea beati, e le sue voci
  con *sitiunt*, sanz'altro, ciò forniro.   6
E io più lieve che per l'altre foci
  m'andava, sì che sanz'alcun labore
  seguiva in sù li spiriti veloci;   9
quando Virgilio incominciò: « Amore
  acceso di virtù, sempre altro accese
  pur che la fiamma sua paresse fore.   12
Onde da l'ora che tra noi discese
  nel limbo de l'Inferno Giovenale,
  che la tua affezion mi fe' palese,   15
mia benvoglienza inverso te fu quale
  più strinse mai di non vista persona,
  sì ch'or mi parran corte queste scale.   18
Ma dimmi (e come amico mi perdona
  se troppa sicurtà m'allarga il freno,
  e come amico omai meco ragiona):   21
come potè trovar dentro al tuo seno
  loco avarizia, tra cotanto senno
  di quanto per tua cura fosti pieno? »   24
Queste parole Stazio mover fenno
  un poco a riso pria; poscia rispose:
  « Ogni tuo dir d'amor m'è caro cenno.   27
Veramente più volte appaion cose
  che dànno a dubitar falsa matera
  per le vere cagion che son nascose.   30

And he, uprising: 'Now canst thou the extreme
　　love comprehend which warms me to thee and brings
　　me to forget our emptiness and deem
shades could be touched, as were they solid things.'

CANTO 22

By now the angel was behind us left,
　　the angel who, to the sixth round our guide,
　　had first a swordstroke from my visage reft,
and unto us 'Blesséd are those' had cried
　　'whose desire is for justice,' worded so
　　that *sitiunt* he with nought else amplified.
And lighter through this passage did I go
　　than through the others and with ease could move
　　upward behind the spirits, who went not slow.
Then Virgil thus resumed the converse: 'Love,
　　kindled by virtue, never fails to ignite
　　another, if but seen be the flame thereof.
Hence, ever since came down to share our plight
　　in Limbo Juvenal, who brought report
　　of my especial dearness in thy sight,
hath my good will tow'rds thee been of such sort
　　as ne'er bound any yet to one not seen,
　　so that to me these stairs will now seem short.
But tell me—and let me a friend's forgiveness win,
　　if too much confidence relax my rein,
　　and as a friend to speak with me begin—
how in thy breast could any room remain
　　for avarice mid all the sound good sense
　　which thou hadst been so diligent to gain?'
These words caused Statius some amusement; hence
　　he smiled a little at first, and then replied:
　　'Thine every saying is love's dear evidence.
Truly we often see things which provide
　　false matter for misdoubting, just because
　　their real causes deep within them hide.

419

La tua dimanda tuo creder m'avvera
  esser ch'io fossi avaro in l'altra vita,
  forse per quella cerchia dov'io era.   33
Or sappi che avarizia fu partita
  troppo da me, e questa dismisura
  migliaia di lunari hanno punita.   36
E se non fosse ch'io drizzai mia cura
  quand'io intesi là dove tu chiame,
  crucciato quasi a l'umana natura: 39
'Per che non reggi tu, o sacra fame
  de l'oro, l'appetito dei mortali?'
  voltando sentirei le giostre grame.   42
Allor m'accorsi che troppo aprir l'ali
  potean le mani a spendere, e pente'mi
  così di quel come de gli altri mali.   45
Quanti risurgeran coi crini scemi,
  per ignoranza, che di questa pecca
  toglie il penter vivendo e ne li stremi!   48
E sappi che la colpa che rimbecca
  per dritta opposizione alcun peccato,
  con esso insieme qui suo verde secca.   51
Però, s'io son tra quella gente stato
  che piange l'avarizia, per purgarmi,
  per lo contrario suo m'è incontrato».   54
« Or quando tu cantasti le crude armi
  de la doppia tristizia di Iocasta»
  disse il cantor dei bucolici carmi,   57
« per quello che Cliò teco lì tasta,
  non par che ti facesse ancor fedele
  la fede sanza qual ben far non basta.   60
Se così è, qual Sole o quai candele
  ti stenebraron sì che tu drizzasti
  poscia diretro al pescator le vele?»   63
Ed egli a lui: « Tu prima m'inviasti
  verso Parnaso a ber ne le sue grotte,
  e prima appresso a Dio m'illuminasti.   66
Facesti come quei che va di notte,
  che porta il lume dietro, e sè non giova,
  ma dopo sè fa le persone dotte,   69

That I was avaricious (thy question shows)
  in the other life is what thou dost believe,
  it may be, from that circle where I was.
But avarice, I'd have thee now conceive,
  was all too far from me, for which excess
  thousands of moons to me were punitive.
And were it not that I corrected this,
  when pondering those lines of thine which cry,
  as wert thou enraged by human wickedness,
"O curséd hunger after gold, whereby
  dost thou *not* sway the greed of mortal men?"
  tourneying now in the grim jousts were I.
The hands could spread their wings (I saw it plain)
  too much in spending: nor of that alone,
  of other sins did I repent me then.
How many will rise again with a shorn crown
  through ignorance, which lets them not repent
  this sin in life and when life's almost gone!
And know thou that the fault that by its bent
  directly opposes any sin, with it
  here of its green dries up the over-extent.
If, then, I've been mid yonder folk, to wit
  those that rue avarice, to cleanse my stains,
  this hath befallen me for its opposite.'
'Now at the time thou sangest the twin banes
  Jocasta bore and the fell hosts they led,'
  said then the bard of the bucolic strains,
'It seems, from what there Clio with thee essay'd,
  thou had'st not by the faith, without which no
  good works suffice, as yet been faithful made.
But, in that case, what sun or candle so
  undarkened thee, that thou didst from that day
  into the Fisher's wake direct thy prow?'
And he: 'Thy self first set me on the way
  tow'rds the deep springs that on Parnassus rise,
  and up tow'rds God first lit me with thy ray.
Like a night-walker thou, who onward hies
  bearing a light behind him, useless to
  himself, but making those who follow wise.

quando dicesti: 'Secol si rinnova;
 torna giustizia e primo tempo umano,
 e progenie discende dal ciel nova'.   72
Per te poeta fui, per te cristiano.
 Ma perchè veggi me' ciò ch'io disegno,
 a colorar distenderò la mano.   75
Già era il mondo tutto quanto pregno
 de la vera credenza, seminata
 per li messaggi de l'eterno regno;   78
e la parola tua sopra toccata
 si consonava ai novi predicanti;
 ond'io a visitarli presi usata.   81
Vennermi poi parendo tanto santi,
 che quando Domizian li perseguette,
 sanza mio lacrimar non fur lor pianti;   84
e mentre che di là per me si stette
 io li sovvenni, e lor dritti costumi
 fer dispregiare a me tutt'altre sette.   87
E pria ch'io conducessi i Greci ai fiumi
 di Tebe poetando, ebb'io battesmo,
 ma per paura chiuso cristian fu'mi   90
lungamente mostrando paganesmo;
 e questa tepidezza il quarto cerchio
 cerchiar mi fe' più che il quarto centesmo.   93
Tu dunque che levato m'hai 'l coperchio
 che m'ascondeva quanto bene io dico,
 mentre che del salire avem soverchio,   96
dimmi dov'è Terenzio nostro antico;
 Cecilio e Plauto e Vario, se lo sai:
 dimmi se son dannati, ed in qual vico».   99
« Costoro, e Persio, e io, e altri assai »
 rispose il duca mio « siam con quel greco
 che le Muse lattar più ch'altri mai,   102
nel primo cinghio del carcere cieco;
 spesse fiate ragioniam del monte
 che le nutrici nostre ha sempre seco.   105
Euripide v'è nosco, ed Antifonte,
 Simonide, Agatone, ed altri piue
 greci che già di lauro orna la fronte.   108

what time thou said'st: "A new world comes in view;
   Justice returns, and the first age of man,
   and Heaven sends down an offspring that is new."
Through thee became I poet and Christian:
   but now, to paint this outline in, I'll blend
   hues that will make it easier to scan.
Already was the whole wide world impregn'd
   with the one true belief, which had been sown
   by heralds of the realm that hath no end.
And that same saying I touched on of thy own
   so chimed with what those novel preachers taught,
   that I to visit them had accustomed grown.
Their patent holiness on me so wrought
   at last, that when Domitian harassed them,
   to their sad plaints my tears were wanting not;
and while life yonder still was mine, I came
   to their assistance, and their upright way
   caused me all other doctrines to contemn.
And ere I'd led the Greek host, in my lay,
   to Thebes's streams, I was baptized: although
   through fear a secret Christian did I stay,
of paganism long while making show:
   which tepidness round the fourth circle made
   me circle four whole centuries and moe.
Thou, then, who hast lifted that which overlaid
   and hid from me the good whereof I've told,
   while for the ascent we still have time ahead,
tell me, where Terence is, our bard of old,
   Caecilius, Plautus, Varius, if thou know'st:
   tell me if they are damned, and in what hold?'
'They, Persius, I, and others—a great host—'
   answered my guide, 'are with that Greek confined,
   whom of all men the Muses suckled most,
in the first circle of the prison blind:
   oft talk we of the mountain slopes whereon
   have dwelt our nurses from time out of mind.
Euripides is there, with Antiphon
   Simónides, Agathón and many more—
   Greeks, crowned of yore with laurels they had won.

Quivi si veggion de le genti tue
  Antigone, Deifile ed Argia,
  ed Ismene sì trista come fue.   111
Vedesi quella che mostrò Langìa;
  evvi la figlia di Tiresia, e Teti,
  e con le suore sue Deidamia».   114
Tacevansi ambedue già li poeti,
  di novo attenti a riguardar dintorno,
  liberi dal salire e da pareti.   117
E già le quattro ancelle eran del giorno
  rimase addietro, e la quinta era al temo,
  drizzando pur in sù l'ardente corno,   120
quando il mio duca: « Io credo che a lo stremo
  le destre spalle volger ne convegna,
  girando il monte come far solemo».   123
Così l'usanza fu lì nostra insegna,
  e prendemmo la via con men sospetto
  per l'assentir di quell'anima degna.   126
Elli givan dinanzi, ed io soletto
  di retro, ed ascoltava i lor sermoni,
  che a poetar mi davano intelletto.   129
Ma tosto ruppe le dolci ragioni
  un alber che trovammo in mezza strada,
  con pomi a odorar soavi e buoni.   132
E come abete in alto si digrada
  di ramo in ramo, così quello in giuso:
  cred'io perchè persona sù non vada.   135
Dal lato onde il cammin nostro era chiuso
  cadea da l'alta roccia un liquor chiaro
  e si spandeva per le foglie suso.   138
Li due poeti a l'alber s'appressaro;
  ed una voce per entro le fronde
  gridò: « Di questo cibo avrete caro ».   141
Poi disse: « Più pensava Maria onde
  fosser le nozze orrevoli ed intere,
  che alla sua bocca, ch'or per voi risponde. 144
E le Romane antiche per lor bere
  contente furon d'acqua; e Daniello
  dispregiò cibo ed acquistò sapere.   147

There are seen people known to thy own lore,
   Antigone, Deïphile and Argía:
   there too, Ismene mournful as of yore.
Seen there is she who pointed out Langía:
   there is Teiresias' daughter, and there too
   Thetis and, with her sisters, Deïdamía.'
Fell silent now both bards, intent to view
   afresh the prospect: for we'd reached our bourn,
   the climb accomplished and the walls passed through.
By now, four of the handmaids of the morn
   were left behind: the fifth, at the car's beam,
   directed upward still its blazing horn.
My leader then: 'To the outer edge, I deem,
   we ought to turn here our right shoulders, thus
   circling the mount, as doth our wont beseem.'
So on we went with custom guiding us:
   and since that worthy soul to ours inclined
   his judgment, found we doubt less onerous.
They walked in front, I by myself behind,
   listening their talk that gave me, by its wit,
   for poesy an understanding mind.
Dear parley, but soon interrupted it
   a tree we found mid-way, with a brave show
   of fruit thereon, which smelt both good and sweet.
And as a fir-tree tapers upward, so
   downward did that, from branch to branch, thereby
   to ensure, I think, that none should up it go.
There fell clear liquid from the cliff-top, high
   on that side where we could no progress make,
   sprinkling the leaves above unceasingly.
Both poets neared the tree; and from it brake
   a voice forth—whose it was, the foliage hid—
   that cried: 'Of this food spare ye to partake.'
Then it said: 'More thought Mary of the need
   to make the wedding seemly and complete
   than of her own lips, which for you now plead.
Women drank water, being content with it,
   in ancient Rome; and Daniel, we are told,
   acquired his wisdom by despising meat.

Lo secol primo quant'oro fu bello,
  fe' saporose con fame le ghiande,
  e nettare con sete ogni ruscello.   150
Miele e locuste furon le vivande
  che nutriro il Battista nel deserto;
  per ch'egli è glorioso e tanto grande   153
quanto per l'Evangelio v'è aperto ».

CANTO 23

Mentre che gli occhi per la fronda verde
  ficcava io sì come far suole
  chi dietro a gli uccellin sua vita perde,   3
lo più che padre mi dicea: « Figliuole,
  vienne oramai, chè il tempo che n'è imposto
  più utilmente compartir si vuole ».   6
Io volsi il viso, e il passo non men tosto,
  appresso i savi, che parlavan sie
  che l'andar mi facean di nullo costo.   9
Ed ecco piangere e cantar s'udie
  Labia mea Domine per modo
  tal che diletto e doglia parturie.   12
« O dolce padre, che è quel ch'i' odo? »
  comincia' io. Ed egli: « Ombre che vanno
  forse di lor dover solvendo il nodo ».   15
Sì come i peregrin pensosi fanno
  giugnendo per cammin gente non nota,
  che si volgono ad essa, e non ristanno,   18
così di retro a noi, più tosto mota
  venendo e trapassando, ci ammirava
  d'anime turba tacita e devota.   21
Ne gli occhi era ciascuna oscura e cava,
  pallida ne la faccia, e tanto scema
  che da l'ossa la pelle s'informava.   24
Non credo che così a buccia strema
  Erisitone fosse fatto secco
  per digiunar, quando più n'ebbe tema.   27

The primal age, which was as fair as gold,
　　with hunger made the acorn delicate,
　　and every brook with thirst a nectar hold.
Locusts and honey were the viands set
　　before the Baptist in the wilderness,
　　for which cause he is glorious, and as great
as in the Gospel ye may find express.'

CANTO 23

Whilst I on the green foliage fixed my gaze,
　　searching its depths, as is the wont of one
　　who chasing little birds consumes his days,
my more than father said to me: 'Dear son,
　　come on now, for to better use we ought
　　to put the time we here may count upon.'
My eyes and steps, together turning, sought
　　the sages who conversed, as on they fared,
　　with such charm that the going cost me nought.
And　suddenly, both wept and sung was heard
　　'*Labia mea, Domine*,' to the ear
　　such that at once delight and dole it stirred.
'Belovéd father, what is that I hear?',
　　thus I; and 'Shades' he answered: 'haply they
　　go loosening the knot of debt they bear.'
Like travellers deep in thought, who on their way,
　　when overtaking strangers, turn about
　　and tow'rds them only look, and do not stay,
came up behind us, glanced at us in doubt,
　　and—for they moved more quickly—past us hied
　　a throng of spirits, silent and devout.
Pallid of face and dark and hollow-eyed
　　was each one, and so wasted that the skin
　　took its shape from the bones it failed to hide.
That thus reduced to the mere rind was e'en
　　Erysichthon by hunger, when most sick
　　with fear thereof, could scarce be true, I ween.

Io dicea fra me stesso pensando: « Ecco
   la gente che perdè Ierusalemme
   quando Maria nel figlio diè di becco ».   30
Parean l'occhiaie anella sanza gemme;
   chi nel viso de gli uomini legge *omo*
   ben avria quivi conosciuta l'emme.   33
Chi crederebbe che l'odor d'un pomo
   sì governasse, generando brama,
   e quel d'un'acqua, non sappiendo como?   36
Già era in ammirar che sì li affama,
   per la cagione ancor non manifesta
   di loro magrezza e di lor trista squama,   39
ed ecco dal profondo de la testa
   volse a me gli occhi un'ombra e guardò fiso;
   poi gridò forte: « Qual grazia m'è questa! »   42
Mai non l'avrei riconosciuto al viso,
   ma ne la voce sua mi fu palese
   ciò che l'aspetto in sè avea conquiso.   45
Questa favilla tutta mi raccese
   mia conoscenza a la cangiata labbia,
   e ravvisai la faccia di Forese.   48
« Deh, non contendere a l'asciutta scabbia
   che mi scolora » pregava « la pelle,
   nè a difetto di carne ch'i' abbia;   51
ma dimmi il ver di te, e chi son quelle
   du' anime che là ti fanno scorta:
   non rimaner che tu non mi favelle! »   54
« La faccia tua, ch'io lacrimai già morta,
   mi dà di pianger mo' non minor doglia »
   rispos'io lui « veggendola sì torta.   57
Però mi di', per Dio, che sì vi sfoglia;
   non mi far dir mentr'io mi maraviglio,
   chè mal può dir chi è pien d'altra voglia ».   60
Ed egli a me: « De l'eterno consiglio
   cade virtù ne l'acqua e ne la pianta
   rimasa dietro, ond'io sì m'assottiglio.   63
Tutt'esta gente che piangendo canta,
   per seguitar la gola oltre misura
   in fame e in sete qui si rifà santa.   66

The thought unuttered rose within me quick:
  'Behold the folk who lost Jerusalem,
  when Miriam in her own child fleshed her beak.'
Each eye-pit seemed a ring without the gem;
  he that reads 'omo' in the human face
  would here with ease have recognized the M.
Who, unless told the cause thereof, would guess
  that the mere smell of fruit and of a spring
  had thus wrought, by engendering greediness?
Not knowing what made them lean, or what could bring
  their skin to peel so sorely, I did not cease
  to wonder why they thus were famishing,
when from his head's deep-sunken cavities
  turn'd tow'rds me his eyes a shade, intently gazed,
  then cried aloud: 'What grace to me is this?'
Ne'er by his looks had I been aught but mazed:
  but in his voice was rendered manifest
  what in itself his aspect had erased.
This was the spark that, kindling in my breast,
  quickened my knowledge of the altered mien,
  and 'twas Forese who there stood confess'd.
'Ah, stare not,' he entreated, 'at my skin
  robbed by these dry scabs of its natural hue,
  nor at the fleshless state that I am in;
But tell me the truth about thyself, and who
  those two souls are, by whom thy steps are led:
  stay not, but speak, oh! speak, I implore thee, do!'
'Thy face, which once I wept for when 'twas dead,
  now gives me cause to weep with no less care,'
  I answered, 'seeing it so disfiguréd.
For God's sake, tell me what so strips you bare:
  make me not talk while wonder grips my mind;
  ill can he talk whose wish is turned elsewhere.'
'Into the tree and spring we've left behind,
  by the eternal counsel,' he replied,
  'a virtue falls, and thence I am thus pined.
These weeping singers all pursued outside
  due bounds their appetite: therefore are they
  in thirst and hunger here re-sanctified.

Di bere e di mangiar n'accende cura
   l'odor ch'esce del pomo, e de lo sprazzo
   che si distende su per la verdura.   69
E non pur una volta questo spazzo
   girando si rinfresca nostra pena:
   io dico pena, e dovrei dir sollazzo,   72
chè quella voglia a gli alberi ci mena
   che menò Cristo lieto a dire *Elì*
   quando ne liberò con la sua vena ».   75
Ed io a lui: « Forese, da quel dì
   nel qual mutasti mondo a miglior vita
   cinqu'anni non son volti infino a qui.   78
Se prima fu la possa in te finita
   di peccar più, che sorvenisse l'ora
   del buon dolor che a Dio ne rimarita,   81
come sei tu qua sù venuto? Ancora
   io ti credea trovar là giù di sotto
   dove tempo per tempo si ristora ».   84
Ond'egli a me: « Sì tosto m'ha condotto
   a ber lo dolce assenzio dei martìri
   la Nella mia con suo pianger dirotto.   87
Con suoi preghi divoti e con sospiri
   tratto m'ha de la costa ove s'aspetta
   e liberato m'ha de gli altri giri.   90
Tant'è a Dio più cara e più diletta
   la vedovella mia, che molto amai,
   quanto in bene operare è più soletta.   93
Chè la Barbagia di Sardigna assai
   ne le femmine sue è più pudica
   che la Barbagia dov'io la lasciai.   96
O dolce frate, che vuoi tu ch'io dica?
   Tempo futuro m'è già nel cospetto,
   cui non sarà quest'ora molto antica,   99
nel qual sarà in pergamo interdetto
   a le sfacciate donne fiorentine
   l'andar mostrando con le poppe il petto. 102
Quai barbare fur mai, quai saracine,
   cui bisognasse, per farle ir coperte,
   o spiritali o altre discipline?   105

The scent, emitted by the fruit and spray
   spread o'er the foliage, whets an eagerness
   to eat and drink, whereof we are the prey.
And not once only, as around this space
   we circle, is renewed our penalty:
   our penalty? nay, call it our solace;
for the same longing leads us to each tree
   which led Christ, when with bleeding veins he won
   our freedom, to cry out with joy "Elì".'
And I: 'Forese, since that day, whereon
   thy change of world to better life was made,
   not five years up till now their course have run.
If power, then, to commit more sin was sped
   in thy case, ere the hour of pious woe
   had struck by which to God we are re-wed,
how hast thou climbed up here? Still down below
   I thought to find thee, where the rule obtains
   that time must pay the debt that time doth owe.'
He answered: ' 'Twas my Nella's potent strains
   of grief that brought me here so speedily
   to drink of the sweet wormwood of these pains.
By her devout prayers and her sighs did she
   withdraw me from the slope where one delays,
   and from the other circles set me free.
So much to God more dear and worthier praise
   is my poor widow, once my fondest care,
   as stands she lonelier in good offices.
For the Barbagia of Sardinia ne'er
   had women so immodest as are they
   of the Barbagia where I quitted her.
Brother belov'd, what wilt thou have me say?
   E'en now a coming time my vision meets,
   from which this hour shall not be far away,
when the unblushing women, in the streets
   of Florence, pulpit-bans shall disallow
   to expose their bosoms even to the teats.
What Berber women, in past times or now,
   what Saracen, e'er needed Church or State
   to enforce their dressing chastely? None, I trow.

431

Ma se le svergognate fosser certe
  di quel che il ciel veloce loro ammanna,
  già per urlare avrien le bocche aperte;   108
chè se l'antiveder qui non m'inganna,
  prima fien triste che le guance impeli
  colui che mo si consola con nanna.   111
Deh, frate, or fa che più non mi ti celi:
  vedi che non pur io, ma questa gente
  tutta rimira là dove il Sol veli».   114
Per ch'io a lui: « Se ti riduci a mente
  qual fosti meco e qual io teco fui,
  ancor fia grave il memorar presente.   117
Di quella vita mi volse costui
  che mi va innanzi, l'altr'ier, quando tonda
  vi si mostrò la suora di colui »   120
e il Sol mostrai. « Costui per la profonda
  notte menato m'ha dei veri morti,
  con questa vera carne che il seconda.   123
Indi m'han tratto sù li suoi conforti,
  salendo e rigirando la montagna
  che drizza voi che il mondo fece torti.   126
Tanto dice di farmi sua compagna
  che io sarò là dove fia Beatrice:
  quivi convien che sanza lui rimagna.   129
Virgilio è questi che così mi dice »
  e additailo; « e quest'altro è quell'ombra
  per cui scosse dianzi ogni pendice   132
lo vostro regno, che da sè lo sgombra ».

CANTO 24

Nè il dir l'andar, nè l'andar lui più lento
  facea; ma ragionando andavam forte
  sì come nave pinta da buon vento.   3
E l'ombre, che parean cose rimorte,
  per le fosse de gli occhi ammirazione
  traean di me, di mio vivere accorte.   6

But if the shameless creatures knew the fate
   the swift heav'n holds in store for them, to howl
   they'd have their mouths e'en now wide open set.
For, doth our foresight here not cheat my soul,
   they'll be in tears, ere he, whom lullabies
   are soothing now, shall have grown hair on jowl.
Now, brother, prithee, off with thy disguise!
   see, not I only, but all these combined
   to where thou veil'st the Sun direct their eyes.'
Then I to him: 'If thou bring back to mind
   what thou with me wast and what I with thee,
   still grievous wilt thou the remembrance find.
From that same life the other day did he
   in front there turn me, what time fully round
   the sister shone of him we yonder see,'
I pointed to the Sun. 'Through the profound
   night of the really dead led down was I,
   to this real flesh that follows him still bound.
Thence have his comforts drawn me up thus high,
   climbing and circling round the mountain-side,
   which straightens you whom the world bent awry.
So long, he says, we two shall go allied,
   till I shall be where will be Beatrice:
   there it behoves that I without him bide.
Virgil'—and I pointed to him—'is this
   who tells me so; this other is that shade,
   for whom in all your realm's declivities
it just now shook, counting his quittance paid.'

CANTO 24

Speech stayed not progress, nor did this in turn
   stay speech: but, still conversing, on we sped,
   e'en as a ship does, with the wind astern.
Meanwhile the shades, tho' seeming things twice dead,
   to my being still alive now wide awake,
   through their eye-pits on me their wonder fed.

E io, continuando il mio sermone,
  dissi: « Ella sen va sù forse più tarda
  che non farebbe, per altrui cagione.   9
Ma dimmi, se tu sai, dov'è Piccarda;
  dimmi s'io veggio da notar persona
  tra questa gente che sì mi riguarda ».   12
« La mia sorella, che tra bella e buona
  non so qual fosse più, trionfa lieta
  ne l'alto Olimpo già di sua corona ».   15
Sì disse prima. E poi: « Qui non si vieta
  di nominar ciascun, da che è sì munta
  nostra sembianza via per la dieta.   18
Questi » e mostrò col dito « è Bonagiunta,
  Bonagiunta da Lucca; e quella faccia
  di là da lui più che l'altre trapunta   21
ebbe la Santa Chiesa in le sue braccia;
  dal Torso fu, e purga per digiuno
  l'anguille di Bolsena e la vernaccia ».   24
Molti altri mi nomò ad uno ad uno;
  e del nomar parean tutti contenti,
  sì ch'io però non vidi un atto bruno.   27
Vidi per fame a voto usar li denti
  Ubaldin de la Pila, e Bonifazio
  che pasturò col rocco molte genti.   30
Vidi messer Marchese, ch'ebbe spazio
  già di bere a Forlì con men secchezza,
  e sì fu tal che non si sentì sazio.   33
Ma come fa chi guarda e poi fa prezza
  più d'un che d'altro, fe' io a quel da Lucca
  che più parea di me aver contezza.   36
Ei mormorava, e non so che *Gentucca*
  sentiva io là ov'ei sentia la piaga
  de la giustizia che sì li pilucca.   39
« O anima » diss'io « che par sì vaga
  di parlar meco, fa sì ch'io t'intenda,
  e te e me col tuo parlare appaga ».   42
« Femmina è nata, e non porta ancor benda »
  cominciò ei, « che ti farà piacere
  la mia città, come ch'uom la riprenda.   45

And I, without a pause, thus further spake:
  'He, as he climbs, it may be goes more slow
  than he would else do, for another's sake.
But where's Piccarda? Tell me, if thou dost know:
  tell me if I see any whom their renown
  marks out among these folk who eye me so.'
'My sister—which the more to write her down,
  or fair or good, I know not—triumphs on high
  Olympus, joying already in her crown.'
So said he first, and then: 'To identify
  each one by name nought here forbids: we've been
  in visage so by abstinence milked dry.
This'—pointing to him—'is Bonagiunta, I mean
  Bonagiunta of Lucca: that—the face
  beyond him and than all the rest more lean—
once held the Holy Church in his embrace.
  He was from Tours: for the eels, Bolsena's pride,
  in vernage cooked, his fasting makes redress.'
Names many other, one by one, he cried;
  nor did I see among them one dark look,
  but to be named all seemed well satisfied.
As bit they the air for hunger, note I took
  of Ubaldín o' the Pile and Boniface,
  who pastured many people with his crook.
I saw Messér Marchese, who had space
  once at Forlì for drinking with a throat
  less dry, yet with his thirst could ne'er keep pace.
But as, mid many, a gazer takes chief note
  of one, at him from Lucca did I stare,
  whom most, it seemed, some memory of me smote.
He muttered something, and methought from there
  I heard 'Gentucca' where he felt the wound
  made by the justice which so plucks them bare.
'O soul,' said I, 'who seemingly hast ground
  for word with me, be thou articulate,
  that in thy words peace for us both be found.'
'A woman's born and wears no wimple yet,'
  began he, 'who will make thee glad to stay
  within my city, howe'er men blame its state.

Tu te n'andrai con questo antivedere:
  se nel mio mormorar prendesti errore
  dichiareranti ancor le cose vere.   48
Ma di' s'io veggio qui colui che fore
  trasse le nove rime, cominciando
  Donne ch'avete intelletto d'amore».   51
Ed io a lui: « Io mi son un che quando
  Amor mi spira, noto, ed a quel modo
  ch'ei ditta dentro vo significando ».   54
« O frate, issa vegg'io » diss'egli « il nodo
  che il Notaro e Guittone e me ritenne
  di qua dal dolce stil novo ch'i' odo.   57
Io veggio ben come le vostre penne
  di retro al dittator sen vanno strette,
  che de le nostre certo non avvenne;   60
e qual più a riguardar oltre si mette,
  non vede più da l'uno a l'altro stilo ».
  E, quasi contentato, si tacette.   63
Come gli augei che vernan lungo il Nilo
  alcuna volta in aere fanno schiera,
  poi volan più in fretta e vanno in filo,   66
così tutta la gente che lì era,
  volgendo il viso, raffrettò suo passo,
  e per magrezza e per voler leggiera.   69
E come l'uom che di trottare è lasso
  lascia andar li compagni, e si passeggia
  finchè si sfoghi l'affollar del casso,   72
sì lasciò trapassar la santa greggia
  Forese, e dietro meco sen veniva
  dicendo: « Quando fia ch'io ti riveggia ?» 75
« Non so » rispos'io lui « quant'io mi viva,
  ma già non fia 'l tornar mio tanto tosto,
  ch'io non sia col voler prima a la riva,   78
però che il loco u' fui a viver posto
  di giorno in giorno più di ben si spolpa,
  e a trista ruina par disposto ».   81
« Or va » diss'ei, « che quei che più n'ha colpa
  vegg'io a coda d'una bestia tratto
  inver la valle ove mai non si scolpa.   84

With this for presage go thou on thy way;
 did aught I muttered puzzling to thee prove,
 the facts themselves will make all clear some day.
But say if I see here the evoker of
 those rhymes in novel fashion, which begin
 "*Ladies, who understand the lore of love*"?'
And I to him: 'I'm, meseems, one who, when
 addressed by Love, am careful to give ear
 and but so write as he dictates within.'
'Brother,' said he, 'now is the hindrance clear
 that kept the Notary and Guittóne and me
 from reaching the sweet new style which I hear.
I see well how, as closely as it might be,
 your pens pursuing the dictator went,
 which happed not with our own, most certainly.
And he who's most on further searching bent
 sees nought else parting one from the other style';
 thereat he held his peace and seemed content.
As birds that winter on the banks o' the Nile
 at one time form a squadron in the air,
 then fly in greater haste and go in file;
so all the people who had gathered there
 faced round and, stepping faster, onward press'd,
 agile as they through zeal and leanness were.
And as the runner who becomes distrest
 lets his companions pass nor deems it wrong
 to walk, till he have eased his panting chest;
so did Forese let the holy throng
 pass by, and walked beside me, saying then:
 'When shall we meet again? Will it be long?'
'My life,' I answered, 'ends I know not when:
 but, sooth, right soon though my return be, yet
 still sooner will my heart the shore regain;
because the place wherein my life was set
 strips itself more of good from day to day
 and seems to dismal ruin predestinate.'
'Courage!' said he, 'for him, on whom doth weigh
 the guilt most, I behold at a beast's tail
 dragged tow'rds the pit where sinners bide for aye.

437

La bestia ad ogni passo va più ratto,
  crescendo sempre, fin ch'ella il percote,
  e lascia il corpo vilmente disfatto.   87
Non hanno molto a volger quelle rote».
  e drizzò gli occhi al ciel «che ti fia chiaro
  ciò che il mio dir più dichiarar non puote.   90
Tu ti rimani omai chè il tempo è caro
  in questo regno, sì ch'io perdo troppo
  venendo teco sì a paro a paro».   93
Qual esce alcuna volta di galoppo
  lo cavalier di schiera che cavalchi,
  e va per farsi onor del primo intoppo,   96
tal si partì da noi con maggior valchi;
  e io rimasi in via con esso i due
  che fur del mondo sì gran marescalchi.   99
E quando innanzi a noi intrato fue
  che gli occhi miei si fero a lui seguaci
  come la mente a le parole sue,   102
parvermi i rami gravidi e vivaci
  d'un altro pomo, e non molto lontani,
  per esser pure allora volto in laci.   105
Vidi gente sott'esso alzar le mani
  e gridar non so che verso le fronde
  quasi bramosi fantolini e vani,   108
che pregano e il pregato non risponde,
  ma, per far esser ben la voglia acuta,
  tien alto lor disio e nol nasconde.   111
Poi si partì sì come ricreduta;
  e noi venimmo al grand'arbore adesso,
  che tanti preghi e lagrime rifiuta.   114
«Trapassate oltre sanza farvi presso:
  legno è più sù che fu morso da Eva,
  e questa pianta si levò da esso».   117
Sì tra le frasche non so chi diceva;
  per che Virgilio e Stazio e io, ristretti,
  oltre andavam, dal lato che si leva.   120
«Ricordivi» dicea «dei maledetti
  nei nuvoli formati, che, satolli,
  Teseo combatter coi doppi petti;   123

The beast at every step with speed more fell
  goes faster, till it strikes him, blow on blow,
  and of the man leaves but his broken shell.
Yon wheels in circling have not far to go'—
  and he glanced sky-ward—'ere thou'lt clearly see
  that which my discourse may not further show.
Stay now behind, for in this kingdom we
  so highly value time, that I've disburs'd
  o'ermuch already in keeping step with thee.'
As sometimes at a gallop a knight will burst
  forth from a troop of horse, his only care
  to charge, and be for honour's sake the first;
so, lengthening his stride, he left us there:
  and I went on my way with but those twain,
  who of the world such mighty marshals were.
And when my eyes had seen him on us gain
  so much ground that he baffled their pursuit,
  e'en as my mind pursued his words in vain,
I noticed, nor far distant—in that tó it
  I had but just then turned—another tree,
  its branches thick with leaves and laden with fruit.
And 'neath it folk with hands raised did I see,
  who tow'rds the foliage cried I know not what,
  like greedy children who, though vain their plea,
beseech, nor answers he that is besought,
  but holds aloft, to make their longing keen,
  the thing they yearn for and conceals it not.
Then they, as had they disillusioned been,
  moved off, and we to the great tree came now,
  which mocks at prayers so many and so much teen.
'Pass farther on, without drawing near, and go
  higher up; there stands the stock whereof Eve chose
  to eat, and thence did this, its scion, grow.'
Thus spake I know not who among the boughs;
  so Virgil, Statius, and myself, close join'd,
  advanced along the side that upward goes.
'Call,' he was saying, 'those curséd ones to mind,
  formed in the clouds, who, having gorged their fill,
  with Theseus fought—man's breast with brute's combined;

439

e de gli Ebrei che al ber si mostrar molli,
  per che no i volle Gedeon compagni
  quando ver Madian discese i colli».   126

Sì, accostati a l'un de' due vivagni,
  passammo, udendo colpe de la gola
  seguite già da miseri guadagni.   129

Poi, rallargati per la strada sola,
  ben mille passi e più ci portar oltre,
  contemplando ciascun sanza parola.   132

« Che andate pensando sì voi sol tre?»
  subita voce disse; ond'io mi scossi
  come fan bestie spaventate e poltre.   135

Drizzai la testa per veder chi fossi;
  e già mai non si videro in fornace
  vetri o metalli sì lucenti e rossi,   138

com'io vidi un che dicea: « S'a voi piace
  montare in sù, qui si convien dar volta;
  quinci si va, chi vuol andar per pace».   141

L'aspetto suo m'avea la vista tolta;
  per ch'io mi volsi dietro ai miei dottori,
  com'uom che va secondo ch'egli ascolta.   144

E quale, annunziatrice de gli albori,
  l'aura di maggio movesi ed olezza
  tutta impregnata de l'erba e dai fiori,   147

tal mi sentii un vento dar per mezza
  la fronte, e ben sentii mover la piuma,
  che fe' sentir d'ambrosia l'orezza.   150

E sentii dir: « Beati cui alluma
  tanto di grazia, che l'amor del gusto
  nel petto lor troppo disir non fuma,   153

esuriendo sempre quanto è giusto».

CANTO 25

Ora era onde il salir non volea storpio,
  chè il Sole aveva il cerchio di merigge
  lasciato al Tauro e la notte a lo Scorpio;   3

the Hebrews too, in drinking soft of will,
   whom Gideon, therefore, would not take with him,
   when towards Midian he came down the hill.'
Thus keeping close to the path's inner rim
   we passed, and ever tales of gluttons heard,
   who gained the wages that their sin beseem.
Then, as at large on the blank road we fared,
   more than a thousand paces bore us on,
   each deeply plunged in thought without a word.
'What go ye pondering so, ye three alone?'
   a sudden voice said; whence I swerved aside,
   like torpid beasts when into panic thrown.
I raised my head to see who thus had cried;
   and in a furnace ne'er was seen to glow
   metal or glass so bright, so rubified,
as I beheld one who was saying: 'If so
   it pleases you to mount, here must ye turn:
   this way go all who in quest of peace would go.'
His look was such, that I could nought discern;
   so I turned to walk behind my teachers, as
   does one who would by ear his pathway learn.
And as, announcers of the dawn, there pass
   soft breaths of air in May-time that smell sweet,
   all impregnated by the flowers and grass;
so did I sense, just where mine eyebrows meet,
   a wind, and well I sensed the pinion's touch,
   and sensed the ambrosial odour accompanying it.
And 'Blest are they,' I heard said, 'whom so much
   of grace enlightens, that in them the pleasure
   of taste reeks not with greed too strong, being such
as always hunger only in due measure.'

CANTO 25

THE hour was one forbade our climbing slow,
   for now the Sun had left the meridian ring
   to Taurus, as had Night, to Scorpio:

per che, come fa l'uom che non s'affigge,
  ma vassi a la via sua, che che gli appaia,
  se di bisogno stimolo il trafigge,   6
così entrammo noi per la callaia,
  uno innanzi altro prendendo la scala
  che per artezza i salitor dispaia.   9
E quale il cicognin che leva l'ala
  per voglia di volare, e non s'attenta
  d'abbandonar lo nido, e giù la cala,   12
tal era io con voglia accesa e spenta
  di dimandar, venendo infino a l'atto
  che fa colui che a dicer s'argomenta.   15
Non lasciò, per l'andar che fosse ratto,
  lo dolce padre mio, ma disse: « Scocca
  l'arco del dir, che infino al ferro hai tratto ».   18
Allor sicuramente aprii la bocca
  e cominciai: « Come si può far magro
  là dove l'uopo di nodrir non tocca? »   21
« Se t'ammentassi come Meleagro
  si consumò al consumar d'un stizzo,
  non fora » disse « a te questo sì agro;   24
e se pensassi come al vostro guizzo
  guizza dentro a lo specchio vostra imago,
  ciò che par duro ti parrebbe vizzo.   27
Ma perchè dentro a tuo voler t'adage,
  ecco qui Stazio; e io lui chiamo e prego
  che sia or sanator de le tue piage ».   30
« Se la veduta eterna li dislego »
  rispose Stazio « là dove tu sie,
  discolpi me non potert'io far niego ».   33
Poi cominciò: « Se le parole mie,
  figlio, la mente tua guarda e riceve,
  lume ti fieno al come che tu die.   36
Sangue perfetto che mai non si beve
  da l'assetate vene, e si rimane
  quasi alimento che di mensa leve,   39
prende, nel cuore, a tutte membra umane
  virtute informativa, come quello
  che a farsi quelle per le vene vane.   42

Wherefore, as he does who, whate'er the thing
  that meets his eye, halts not, but moves in haste,
  if of some goading need he feels the sting,
so through the gap we entered, and address'd
  ourselves in single file to take the stair,
  which was too strait to let men climb abreast.
And as the fledgling stork that does not dare
  to leave the nest, though with the wish to fly,
  lets the wing droop it raised but now in the air;
even so the wish, kindled and quenched, had I
  to ask a question, and as far had gone
  as he who speaks not, yet to speech comes nigh.
Forbore not, fast though we were hurrying on,
  my gentle father, but he said to me: 'Loose
  thy bow of speech which to the barb is drawn.'
Thus, then, my mouth I opened, bidding truce
  to my reluctance: 'How can one grow lean
  there where for nourishment one finds no use?'
'Would'st thou recall how Meleager seen
  to waste was, with the wasting brand,' said he,
  'this problem's edge would seem to thee less keen.
Think, too, how in the glass, whene'er start ye,
  your image starts likewise, and thou'dst have grounds
  for finding softened what seems hard to thee.
But, to grant all that to thine ease redounds,
  here's Statius, and on him I call, and pray
  that he be now a healer of thy wounds.'
'If', Statius answered, 'things seen in the way
  God sees them I reveal while *thou* art here,
  my excuse must be I cannot say thee nay.'
Then he began: 'Son, if thou persevere
  in marking well and taking-in my word
  its light will make the "how" thou askest clear.
Blood that is perfect, which is never pour'd
  into the thirsty veins, and still remains
  like food which thou removest from the board,
within the heart for all man's limbs obtains
  virtue informative, as being that flood
  which, to become those limbs, pervades the veins.

Ancor digesto, scende ov'è più bello
   tacer che dire; e quindi poscia geme
   sovr'altrui sangue in natural vasello.   45
Ivi s'accoglie l'uno e l'altro insieme,
   l'un disposto a patire, e l'altro a fare
   per lo perfetto loco onde si preme;   48
e, giunto lui, comincia ad operare
   coagulando prima, e poi avviva
   ciò che per sua matera fe' constare.   51
Anima fatta la virtute attiva
   qual d'una pianta, in tanto differente
   che questa è in via e quella è già a riva,   54
tanto ovra poi, che già si move e sente
   come fungo marino; e indi imprende
   ad organar le posse ond'è semente.   57
Or si spiega, figliuolo, or si distende
   la virtù ch'è dal cor del generante,
   dove natura a tutte membra intende.   60
Ma come d'animal divenga fante
   non vedi tu ancor: quest'è tal punto,
   che più savio di te fe' già errante,   63
sì che per sua dottina fe' disgiunto
   da l'anima il possibile intelletto,
   perchè da lui non vide organo assunto.   66
Apri a la verità che viene il petto;
   e sappi che sì tosto come al feto
   l'articular del cerebro è perfetto,   69
lo motor primo a lui si volge lieto
   sovra tant'arte di natura, e spira
   spirito novo di virtù repleto,   72
che ciò che trova attivo quivi, tira
   in sua sustanzia, e fassi un'alma sola,
   che vive, e sente, e sè in sè rigira.   75
E perchè meno ammiri la parola,
   guarda il calor del Sol che si fa vino
   giunto a l'umor che de la vite cola.   78
E quando Lachesis non ha più lino,
   solvesi da la carne, ed in virtute
   ne porta seco l'umano e il divino: 81

Re-distilled, it descends where seemlier would
   silence than speech be, trickling thence to where
   it meets in nature's vessel another's blood.
The one commingles with the other there,
   this fitted to be passive, active that,
   owing to the perfect place whence it doth fare;
and, so joined, it begins to operate,
   first curdling and then quickening more and more
   what for its matter it has caused to set.
Thus grown into a soul, the active power—
   like to a plant's, but so far differing,
   that this has reached and that still makes for shore—
so works that it becomes a sponge-like thing,
   which moves and feels; and then not long deprived
   of organs are the powers that from it spring.
Now, son, dilates, now spreads the power derived
   from the begetter's heart, where, as design'd
   by nature, all man's members are contrived.
But how from animal is born the mind
   thou seest not yet: this is a point that made
   a wiser man than thou erewhile go blind;
for, since he saw no organ (so he said)
   which it assumed, the possible intellect
   was from the soul by him disseveréd.
Open thy heart now and the truth expect;
   and know that to the *fœtus*, once the brain
   is shaped there in each last minute respect,
the primal Mover turns himself, full fain
   of nature's masterpiece, a work so fair,
   and inbreathes a new spirit, which draws amain,
replete with power, all it finds active there
   into its substance and becomes but one
   quick, sentient soul, of its own self aware.
To make my words less marvellous, let the Sun
   remind thee how its heat turns into wine,
   when blent with juice which from the vine doth run.
The soul, when Lachesis has no more twine,
   sheds the flesh, bearing thence potentially
   the human with itself, and the divine:

l'altre potenze tutte quante mute;
　memoria intelligenza e voluntade
　in atto, molto più che prima acute. 84
Senza restarsi, per se stessa cade
　mirabilmente ad una de le rive:
　quivi conosce prima le sue strade. 87
Tosto che loco lì la circunscrive,
　la virtù informativa raggia intorno,
　così e quanto ne le membra vive; 90
e come l'aere, quando è ben piorno,
　per l'altrui raggio che in sè si riflette
　di diversi color diventa adorno, 93
così l'aere vicin quivi si mette
　in quella forma che in lui suggella
　virtualmente l'alma che ristette; 96
e simigliante poi a la fiammella
　che segue il foco là ovunque si muta,
　segue lo spirto sua forma novella. 99
Però che quindi ha poscia sua paruta,
　è chiamata ombra, e quindi organa poi
　ciascun sentire, infino a la veduta. 102
Quindi parliamo e quindi ridiam noi,
　quindi facciam le lagrime e i sospiri
　che per lo monte aver sentiti puoi. 105
Secondo che ci affiggono i disiri
　e gli altri affetti, l'ombra si figura;
　e questa è la cagion di che tu miri». 108
E già venuto all'ultima tortura
　s'era per noi e volto a la man destra,
　ed eravamo attenti ad altra cura. 111
Quivi la ripa fiamma in fuor balestra,
　e la cornice spira fiato in suso
　che la riflette, e via da lei sequestra; 114
ond'ir ne convenia dal lato schiuso
　ad uno ad uno, e io temeva il foco
　quinci, e quindi temea cader giuso. 117
Lo duca mio dicea: «Per questo loco
　si vuol tenere a gli occhi stretto il freno,
　però che errar potrebbesi per poco». 120

mute now being every other faculty;
   but memory, intelligence and will
   in act far keener than they used to be.
Falling in wondrous wise, it rests not, till,
   self-moved, it gains the one or the other shore:
   there it first learns which road awaits it still.
Once place there circumscribes it, doth the power
   that shaped its living limbs radiate around,
   as, and as much as, e'er it did before.
And as the air, when charged with rain, is found,
   owing to another's rays reflected in 't,
   to adorn itself, with various colours crown'd;
so does the soul that halted, there imprint
   its virtual form upon the neighbouring air,
   which thus assumes apparent shape and tint.
Thereafter, like the flamelet which, where'er
   the fire may shift, goes after it, e'en so
   its new form with the soul goes everywhere.
Since thence it hath henceforth its outward show,
   'tis called a shade; and thence an organ then
   it hath for each sense, even for vision too.
Thence do we speak, thence laugh, and thence obtain
   the wherewithal to make the tears and sighs
   thou may'st have heard, as on the mount we plain.
The shade takes shape according as modifies
   us that which we desire and else may feel;
   and this it is that causes thy surprise.'
To the last terrace winding round the hill
   we now were come, turning to our right hand,
   and to our eyes new objects made appeal.
Here the bank shoots forth flames, and 'tis so plann'd
   that from the cliff's edge wind shall upward blow,
   which beats them back and from it keeps them bann'd;
thus on the unfenced brink we needs must go
   one after the other; and I feared the fire
   leftward, and rightward feared to fall below.
My guide kept saying: 'This pathway will require
   that on our eyes we keep a tightened rein,
   for of the least slip here the effect were dire.'

Summae Deus clementiae nel seno
  del grande ardore allora udii cantando,
  che di volger mi fe' caler non meno;   123
e vidi spirti per la fiamma andando;
  per ch'io guardava a loro ed a' miei passi
  compartendo la vista a quando a quando.   126
Appresso al fine che a quell'inno fassi
  gridavan alto: *Virum non cognosco*;
  indi ricominciavan l'inno bassi.   129
Finitolo, anco gridavano: « Al bosco
  si tenne Diana, ed Elice caccionne
  che di Venere avea sentito il tosco ».   132
Indi al cantar tornavano; indi donne
  gridavano e mariti che fur casti
  come virtute e matrimonio imponne.   135
E questo modo credo che lor basti
  per tutto il tempo che il foco li abbrucia.
  Con tal cura conviene e con tai pasti   138
che la piaga da sezzo si ricucia.

CANTO 26

Mentre che sì per l'orlo uno innanzi altro
  ce n'andavamo, spesso il buon maestro
  diceva: « Guarda, giovi ch'io ti scaltro ».   3
Feriami il Sole in su l'omero destro,
  che già, raggiando, tutto l'occidente
  mutava in bianco aspetto di cilestro;   6
ed io facea con l'ombra più rovente
  parer la fiamma, e pur a tanto indizio
  vidi molt'ombre, andando, poner mente.   9
Questa fu la cagion che diede inizio
  loro a parlar di me; e cominciarsi
  a dir: « Colui non par corpo fittizio ».   12
Poi verso me, quanto potevan farsi,
  certi si feron, sempre con riguardo
  di non uscir dove non fosser arsi.   15

'*Summae Deus clementiae*' heard I then
   sung in the core of that enormous heat,
   which to turn tow'rds it made me not less fain;
and, having turned, I saw in the midst of it
   souls walking; and, divided 'twixt the two,
   looked now at them, now where I placed my feet.
They, after that whole hymn had been sung through,
   first '*Virum non cognosco*' cried aloud;
   then, in soft tones, they sang the hymn anew.
That done, again they shouted: 'To the wood
   Diana kept, and thence chased Helicé,
   who'd felt the poison of Venus in her blood.'
Then they resumed their song; then wives did they
   cry out aloud and husbands who were chaste,
   as virtue and strict wedlock point the way.
From song and shout, I ween, they never rest
   throughout the time they endure their burning pain:
   with such a cure, with diet of such taste
the wound will be at last stitched up again.

CANTO 26

As thus along the edge in single file
   we went, and the good master 'Profit by
   my warnings and take heed' kept saying the while,
the Sun, whose radiance all the western sky
   was turning now to white from palest blue,
   struck me on my right shoulder, so that I
made the flame with my shadow a ruddier hue;
   and as the shades passed by, I could perceive
   the hint, though slight, was marked by not a few.
'Twas this that did to them the occasion give
   for talk of me; and one to another turned,
   saying: '*His* body seems not make-believe.'
Anon, so far as each the way discerned,
   some made tow'rds me, while always giving heed
   not to come out where they could not be burned.

« O tu che vai, non per esser più tardo
   ma forse reverente, a gli altri dopo,
   rispondi a me che in sete e in foco ardo.   18
Nè solo a me la tua risposta è uopo,
   chè tutti questi n'hanno maggior sete
   che d'acqua fredda Indo o Etiòpo.   21
Dinne com'è che fai di te parete
   al Sol, pur come tu non fossi ancora
   di morte intrato dentro da la rete ».   24
Sì mi parlava un d'essi, ed io mi fora
   già manifesto, s'io non fossi atteso
   ad altra novità che apparse allora.   27
Chè per lo mezzo del cammino acceso
   venne gente col viso incontro a questa,
   la qual mi fece a rimirar sospeso.   30
Lì veggio d'ogni parte farsi presta
   ciascun'ombra e baciarsi una con una
   sanza restar, contente a breve festa.   33
Così per entro loro schiera bruna
   s'ammusa l'una con l'altra formica,
   forse a spiar lor via e lor fortuna.   36
Tosto che parton l'accoglienza amica,
   prima che il primo passo lì trascorra,
   sopraggridar ciascuna s'affatica: 39
la nova gente « Soddoma e Gomorra »,
   e l'altra « Ne la vacca entra Pasife
   perchè il torello a sua lussuria corra ».   42
Poi come grue che a le montagne Rife
   volasser parte e parte inver l'arene,
   queste del gel, quelle del sole schife,   45
l'una gente sen va, l'altra sen viene,
   e tornan lacrimando ai primi canti
   e al gridar che più lor si conviene.   48
E raccostarsi a me come davanti
   essi medesmi che m'avean pregato,
   attenti ad ascoltar nei lor sembianti.   51
Io, che due volte avea visto lor grato,
   incominciai: « O anime sicure
   d'aver quando che sia di pace stato,   54

'O thou who walkest—not that less thy speed,
  but, chance, from reverence—in the others' wake,
  reply to me athirst in this glowing gleed:
reply not needed only for my sake,
  since all these thirst therefór, as ne'er did yet
  Indian or Ethiop for cool water-break.
Tell us how comes it that thou here art set
  a wall to sunlight, as if still unmewed
  by death within the meshes of his net.'
Thus one of them addressed me: and I should
  have made me known at once, had not just then
  another sight my wonderment renewed.
For midmost of that path of fiery pain
  came on, encountering this, another band
  of souls that made me pause with eyes a-strain.
I see there all the shades on either hand
  in haste exchanging kisses, each with each,
  content with brief salute, nor making stand.
Thus in their dusky troop do emmets, which
  touch each another's snout, perhaps thereby
  to enquire the way or what their luck may teach.
Their friendly greeting ended, instantly
  ere thence a single footstep bears them on,
  each party strives to outdo the other's cry;
'Sodom, Gomorrah' shout the new folk: 'Gone
  within the heifer is Pasiphaé'
  the rest, 'that to her rut the young bull may run.'
Then, like to cranes which flying some might be
  to the Riphaeans, some tow'rd the sandy waste,
  these from the frost, those from the sun to flee;
the one band going, the other coming, haste
  to turn with tears to their first songs again,
  and to the cry which suits them each the best;
and close beside me drew up, now as then,
  those same who had addressed to me their prayer,
  intent on listening, as their looks made plain.
I, who had twice seen what their wishes were,
  began: 'O souls, assured of entering
  a state of peace, come that time whensoe'er.

non son rimase acerbe nè mature
  le membra mie di là, ma son qui meco
  col sangue suo e con le sue giunture. 57
Quinci vo sù per non esser più cieco;
  donna è di sopra che m'acquista grazia
  per che il mortal pel vostro mondo reco. 60
Ma se la vostra maggior voglia sazia
  tosto divegna, sì che il ciel v'alberghi
  ch'è pien d'amore e più ampio si spazia, 63
ditemi, a ciò che ancor carte ne verghi,
  chi siete voi e chi è quella turba
  che se ne va di retro ai vostri terghi ». 66
Non altrimenti stupido si turba
  lo montanaro e rimirando ammuta,
  quando rozzo e salvatico s'inurba, 69
che ciascun'ombra fece in sua paruta;
  ma poi che furo di stupore scarche,
  lo qual ne gli alti cor tosto s'attuta, 72
« Beato te che ne le nostre marche »
  ricominciò colei che pria m'inchiese
  « per morir meglio esperienza imbarche! 75
La gente che non vien con noi, offese
  di ciò per che già Cesar, trionfando,
  regina contra sè chiamar s'intese. 78
Però si parton *Soddoma* gridando,
  rimproverando a sè com'hai udito,
  ed aiutan l'arsura vergognando. 81
Nostro peccato fu ermafrodito,
  ma perchè non servammo umana legge,
  seguendo come bestie l'appetito, 84
in obbrobrio di noi per noi si legge,
  quando partiamci, il nome di colei
  che s'imbestiò ne l'imbestiate schegge. 87
Or sai nostri atti e di che fummo rei:
  se forse a nome vuoi saper chi semo,
  tempo non è di dire, e non saprei. 90
Farotti ben di me volere scemo:
  son Guido Guinizelli, e già mi purgo
  per ben dolermi prima che a lo stremo ». 93

not left behind on earth or in their spring
  or winter are my limbs, but here with me
  these with their blood and with their joints I bring.
Long blind, by climbing thus I learn to see:
  I owe it to a heavenly lady's grace
  that of your world my mortal is made free.
But—so may what ye most wish soon take place,
  in such wise that the heaven may be your inn
  which full of love and amplest is in space—
tell me, that I may write it yet within
  my pages, who are you and who the throng
  going off behind your backs, and what their sin?'
Not otherwise, when first he goes among
  townsfolk, does some wild hillman, roughly bred,
  stand wonderstruck and, staring, hold his tongue,
than each soul did in the aspect it display'd;
  but once of their amazement they were quit
  (which in a noble heart is soon allay'd),
'O happy thou, who gain'st, to grow more fit
  for dying,' resumed my previous questioner,
  'experience of our coasts, and shippest it!
The folk who come not with us, used to err
  in that for which once Caesar, triumphing,
  heard "Queen" against him shouted: whence at their
departure from us they, to feel the sting
  of self-reproof, shout "Sodom", as thou'st heard,
  and on the fire their shame as fuel fling.
Though *our* sin was hermaphrodite, we err'd
  since beast-like we pursued the lust of sense,
  and this to keeping human law preferr'd;
therefore, to our own shame, when parting hence,
  we cite the name of her who bestialized
  herself within the beast-shaped wicker-fence.
Now of our deeds, and guilt, art thou apprised:
  wouldst haply know by name who we here are,
  time fails me, nor thereof am I advised.
Me would'st thou know, to that there is no bar;
  I'm Guido Guinicelli, and purge me now,
  since I repented, when from death not far.'

453

Quali ne la tristizia di Licurgo
　si fer due figli a riveder la madre,
　tal mi fec'io, ma non a tanto insurgo, 96
quand'io udii nomar se stesso il padre
　mio e de gli altri miei miglior che mai
　rime d'amore usar dolci e leggiadre; 99
e sanza udire e dir pensoso andai
　lunga fiata rimirando lui,
　nè per lo foco in là più m'appressai. 102
Poi che di riguardar pasciuto fui,
　tutto m'offersi pronto al suo servigio
　con l'affermar che fa credere altrui. 105
Ed egli a me: « Tu lasci tal vestigio,
　per quel ch'i' odo, in me, e tanto chiaro,
　che Letè nol può torre nè far bigio. 108
Ma se le tue parole or ver giuraro,
　dimmi che è cagion per che dimostri
　nel dire e nel guardare avermi caro ». 111
E io a lui: « Li dolci detti vostri,
　che quanto durerà l'uso moderno
　faranno cari ancora i loro inchiostri ». 114
« O frate », disse, « questi ch'io ti cerno
　col dito », e additò uno spirto innanzi,
　« fu miglior fabbro del parlar materno. 117
Versi d'amore e prose di romanzi
　soverchiò tutti; e lascia dir li stolti
　che quel di Lemosì credon che avanzi. 120
A voce più che al ver drizzan li volti,
　e così ferman sua opinione,
　prima ch'arte o ragion per lor s'ascolti. 123
Così fer molti antichi di Guittone,
　di grido in grido pur lui dando pregio,
　fin che l'ha vinto il ver con più persone. 126
Or se tu hai sì ampio privilegio
　che licito ti sia l'andare al chiostro
　nel quale è Cristo abate del collegio, 129
falli per me un dir di paternostro,
　quanto bisogna a noi di questo mondo,
　dove poter peccar non è più nostro ». 132

As, while Lycurgus raged with grief, her two
  sons felt, to re-behold their mother's face,
  felt I, to hear—though not transported so—
him name himself who fathered me, nor less
  others as well, my betters, all that e'er
  used rhymes of love with sweet and tender grace.
And, hearing not nor speaking, did I fare,
  deep in my thoughts and gazing long at him,
  nor, for the flames, durst I approach more near.
Anon, full fed with looking, my extreme
  desire I stressed to serve him every way,
  adding the oath which men most cogent deem.
And he to me: 'By what I hear thee say
  is left on me an imprint, stamped so clear,
  that Lethe cannot rase nor turn it grey.
But if the oath thou sworest was sincere,
  pray tell me what it is that makes me think,
  judging by word and look, thou hold'st me dear?'
I answered: ' 'Tis the words with words you link
  so sweetly, which will still, if nothing breach
  the modern use, endear their very ink.'
'O brother,' he replied, 'yon spirit which
  I point to'—and he showed me one ahead—
  'forged with yet greater skill his mother-speech.
Of prose-romancers and love-poets he led
  the field, and quite outdistances the bard
  named "of Limoges", whatever fools have said.
Rumour it is, not truth, that they regard;
  fixed in their own opinions, they disown
  reason and art, which speak but are not heard.
Thus, in old times, did many with Guittón,
  praising but him, from mouth to mouth, till now
  truth, with most minds, has come into its own.
But, if so highly privileged art thou
  that thou may'st to the cloister go, wherein
  Christ is the college-abbot, prithee vow
to say me there a paternoster, in
  so far as we of this world need such aid,
  where 'tis no more within our power to sin.'

Poi, forse per dar luogo altrui secondo,
   che presso avea, disparve per lo foco
   come per l'acqua pesce andando al fondo.   135
Io mi feci al mostrato avanti un poco,
   e dissi che al suo nome il mio disire
   apparecchiava grazioso loco.   138
Ei cominciò liberamente a dire:
   « Tan m'abellis vostre cortes deman,
   qu'ieu no me puesc ni voill a vos cobrire: 141
ieu sui Arnaut, que plor e vau cantan.
   Consiros vei la pasada folor,
   e vei jausen lo joi qu'esper denan.   144
Ara vos prec, per aquella valor
   que vos guida al som de l'escalina,
   sovenha vos a temps de ma dolor ».   147
Poi s'ascose nel foco che li affina.

CANTO 27

Sì come quando i primi raggi vibra
   là dove il suo fattor lo sangue sparse,
   cadendo Ibero sotto l'alta Libra,   3
e l'onde in Gange da nona riarse,
   sì stava il Sole; onde il giorno sen giva,
   quando l'angel di Dio lieto ci apparse.   6
Fuor de la fiamma stava in su la riva,
   e cantava *Beati mundo corde*
   con voce assai più che la nostra viva.   9
Poscia: « Più non si va se pria non morde,
   anime sante, il foco: intrate in esso,
   ed al cantar di là non siate sorde »,   12
ci disse come noi li fummo presso;
   per ch'io divenni tal quando lo intesi
   qual è colui che ne la fossa è messo.   15
In sù, le man commesse, mi protesi
   guardando il foco e immaginando forte
   umani corpi già veduti accesi.   18

Then, haply, to leave others room who made
   their way close by, he vanished through the fire,
   like fish that, diving, in deep water fade.
To the soul shown me I drew a little nigher,
   and said my wish to know his name was well
   arraying a place for it, and none was higher.
And he without reserve took up his tale:
   'Swich is my plesure in youre curteis ple,
   that I ne can ne will my name concele.
Ich am Arnaut, who wepynge, syngynge se
   in mynde past folie and, bifore me playne,
   with joye se my longe soght felicite.
Now, preie you, by that power whiche not in vayn
   up this high montaigne-staire hath lad you sure,
   bethynke you in due sesoun of my payne!'
Then hid he in the fire that makes them pure.

CANTO 27

As when, where bled his Maker, he assails
   the world at that spot with his earliest rays,
   the Ebro lying beneath the lofty Scales,
and Ganges scorching in the noontide blaze,
   so stood the sun; hence nigh day's-end we were
   when blithe in mien God's angel met our gaze,
forth of the flame, on the cliff, singing there
   Beati mundo corde with such art
   as made his voice than ours far livelier.
Then 'None goes farther, save he feel the smart
   of the fire, blest spirits: go ye into it,
   nor let your ears from yonder singing part.'
Us, as we neared him, did he thuswise greet;
   whereupon, when I heard him, I became
   like as one placed in the execution-pit.
Hands clasped, I rose to full height, at the same
   time eyeing the fire and picturing vividly
   men's bodies seen before this wrapped in flame.

Volsersi verso me le buone scorte;
  e Virgilio mi disse: « Figliuol mio,
  qui può esser tormento, ma non morte.   21
Ricorditi, ricorditi! ... E se io
  sovresso Gerion ti guidai salvo,
  che farò ora, presso più a Dio?   24
Credi per certo che se dentro a l'alvo
  di questa fiamma stessi ben mill'anni,
  non ti potrebbe far d'un capel calvo.   27
E se tu forse credi ch'io t'inganni,
  fatti ver lei, e fatti far credenza
  con le tue mani al lembo de' tuoi panni.   30
Pon giù omai, pon giù ogni temenza:
  volgiti in qua, vieni ed entra sicuro ».
  Ed io pur fermo, e contra a coscienza.   33
Quando mi vide star pur fermo e duro,
  turbato un poco disse: « Or vedi, figlio,
  tra Beatrice e te è questo muro ».   36
Come al nome di Tisbe aperse il ciglio
  Piramo in su la morte, e riguardolla,
  allor che il gelso diventò vermiglio,   39
così, la mia durezza fatta solla,
  mi volsi al savio duca, udendo il nome
  che ne la mente sempre mi rampolla.   42
Ond'ei crollò la fronte e disse: « Come?
  volemci star di qua? » Indi sorrise
  come al fanciul si fa ch'è vinto al pome.   45
Poi dentro al foco innanzi mi si mise,
  pregando Stazio che venisse retro,
  che pria per lunga strada ci divise.   48
Sì com fui dentro, in un bogliente vetro
  gittato mi sarei per rinfrescarmi,
  tanto er'ivi l'incendio sanza metro.   51
Lo dolce padre mio per confortarmi
  pur di Beatrice ragionando andava,
  dicendo: « Gli occhi suoi già veder parmi ».   54
Guidavaci una voce che cantava
  di là; e noi, attenti pur a lei,
  venimmo fuor là ove si montava.   57

My kindly escorts turned themselves tow'rds me,
  and Virgil thus addressed me: 'O my son,
  here may be torment, death there cannot be.

Think, think again! and if I, even upon
  the back of Geryon, led thee safely there,
  how not now, when to God much nearer drawn?

Deem this for certain: if thy body were
  for full a thousand years wombed in this flame,
  it could not rob thy head of a single hair.

And if perchance thou deem that 'tis my aim
  to trick thee, tow'rds it draw and credence get
  with thine own hands upon thy garment's hem.

Have done henceforth, have done with fears: and set
  thy face this way, come and go in, secure.'
  But, 'gainst my conscience, I still obdurate!

He, when he saw me still stand fixed and dour,
  somewhat perturbed, said: 'Son, this rampart lies
  'twixt Beatrice and thee; of that be sure!'

As Pyramus, at the point of death, his eyes
  opened at Thisbe's name and looked on her,
  what time the mulberry donned its crimson guise;

So to my wise guide I, without demur,
  turned at the name which ever firmer root
  takes in my memory and burgeons there.

He shook his head, saying: 'What? still resolute
  in staying this side?' then smiled, as one would smile
  at a small boy, won over by a fruit.

Then entered he the fire before me, while
  praying Statius to come on behind, whereas
  till then he'd walked between us many a mile.

Once in it, I would into boiling glass
  have flung myself to cool me: in such wise
  the heat burned as all measure to surpass.

My kindly father, fain to exorcize
  my fear, kept talking only of Beatrice,
  saying: 'E'en now, methinks, I see her eyes.'

On the far side a voice was chanting: this
  served as our guide and, looking but that way,
  we came forth there, where the path-upward is.

Venite, benedicti patris mei!
  sonò dentro ad un lume che lì era,
  tal che mi vinse e guardar nol potei.   60
« Lo Sol sen va » soggiunse « e vien la sera:
  non v'arrestate, ma studiate il passo,
  mentre che l'occidente non s'annera ».   63
Dritta salia la via per entro il sasso,
  verso tal parte, ch'io toglieva i raggi
  dinanzi a me del Sol ch'era già basso.   66
E di pochi scaglion levammo i saggi,
  che il Sol corcar, per l'ombra che si spense,
  sentimmo dietro e io e li miei saggi.   69
E pria che in tutte le sue parti immense
  fosse orizzonte fatto d'un aspetto,
  e notte avesse tutte sue dispense,   72
ciascun di noi d'un grado fece letto;
  chè la natura del monte ci affranse
  la possa del salire più e il diletto.   75
Quali si stanno ruminando manse
  le capre, state rapide e proterve
  sovra le cime avanti che sien pranse,   78
tacite a l'ombra, mentre che il Sol ferve,
  guardate dal pastor, che in su la verga
  poggiato s'è e lor di posa serve;   81
e quale il mandrian che fuori alberga,
  lungo il peculio suo queto pernotta,
  guardando perchè fiera non lo sperga;   84
tali eravam noi tutti e tre allotta,
  io come capra ed ei come pastori,
  fasciati quinci e quindi d'alta grotta.   87
Poco parer potea lì del di fuori,
  ma per quel poco, vedea io le stelle
  di lor solere e più chiare e maggiori.   90
Sì ruminando e sì mirando in quelle,
  mi prese il sonno: il sonno che sovente
  anzi che il fatto sia sa le novelle.   93
Ne l'ora, credo, che de l'oriente
  prima raggiò nel monte Citerea,
  che di foco d'amor par sempre ardente,   96

'*Venite, benedicti patris mei!*'
    sang one within a splendour there, so bright
    it conquered me and held my gaze at bay.
'The Sun is sinking fast,' he added; 'night
    is coming, tarry not, make haste and go,
    before the West is wholly void of light.'
Straight-up the path rose through the rock, and so
    directed, that I broke the radiance, square
    before me, of the Sun, already low.
And but few steps had we essayed, or e'er
    I and my sages knew the Sun had set
    behind us, seeing my shadow disappear.
And ere the horizon had one aspect yet
    assumed in all its parts, unlimited,
    and night dispensed a darkness without let,
each one of us made of a step his bed;
    because the power to climb more, and the zest,
    owing to the mountain's nature from us fled.
Like as, while ruminating, glad to rest,
    goats that, ere they had browsed their fill, ceased not
    to scour the hill-tops in their impetuous haste,
lie quiet in the shade, while the Sun's hot,
    and leaning on his staff, alert of eye,
    the shepherd serves them the repose they sought;
and as the herdsman 'neath the open sky,
    passes the night beside his tranquil flock,
    watching lest wolf to scatter it come nigh;
such were we then all three, in that still nook,
    I like a goat, like shepherds they, hemmed in
    on this side and on that by towering rock.
Of things without but little could be seen,
    but through that little I beheld the stars,
    larger than usual and of brighter sheen.
So ruminant, so gazing, it appears
    sleep took me, sleep, which oft-times makes acquist
    of some event, ere it in fact occurs.
About the hour, I think, when from the East
    by Cytherea's first rays, who seems to flame
    with ever-burning love, the mount was kiss'd,

giovane e bella in sonno mi parea
  donna vedere andar per una landa
  cogliendo fiori, e cantando dicea: 99
«Sappia qualunque il mio nome dimanda
  ch'io mi son Lia e vo movendo intorno
  la belle mani a farmi una ghirlanda.   102
Per piacermi a lo specchio qui m'adorno,
  ma mia suora Rachel mai non si smaga
  dal suo miraglio e siede tutto il giorno.   105
Ell'è de' suoi begli occhi veder vaga
  com'io de l'adornarmi con le mani:
  lei lo vedere e me l'oprare appaga ».   108
E già per li splendori antelucani,
  che tanto ai pellegrin sorgon più grati
  quanto tornando albergan men lontani, 111
le tenebre fuggian da tutti i lati,
  e il sonno mio con esse; ond'io leva'mi
  vedendo i gran maestri già levati.   114
« Quel dolce pome che per tanti rami
  cercando va la cura dei mortali,
  oggi porrà in pace le tue fami ».   117
Virgilio inverso me queste cotali
  parole usò, e mai non furon strenne
  che fosser di piacere a queste uguali.   120
Tanto voler sopra voler mi venne
  de l'esser sù, che ad ogni passo poi
  al volo mi sentia crescer le penne.   123
Come la scala tutta sotto noi
  fu corsa, e fummo in sul grado superno,
  in me ficcò Virgilio gli occhi suoi,   126
e disse: « Il temporal foco e l'eterno
  veduto hai, figlio, e sei venuto in parte
  dov'io per me più oltre non discerno.   129
Tratto t'ho qui con ingegno e con arte;
  lo tuo piacere omai prendi per duce:
  fuor sei de l'erte vie, fuor sei de l'arte. 132
Vedi lo Sol che in fronte ti riluce;
  vedi l'erbetta, i fiori e gli arbuscelli
  che qui la terra sol da sè produce.   135

I dreamt I saw a young and lovely dame
  who, culling blossoms, through a meadow went,
  and from her, as she sang, these words there came:
'Whoso should ask my name I would acquaint
  that I am Leah; to make me a wreath with these
  my lovely busy hands is my intent.
I deck me here at the glass, myself to please:
  but from her mirror at no time will rise
  my sister Rachel: there all day she is.
She is as fain to gaze at her fair eyes
  as I to deck me with my hands am drawn:
  her seeing, and *me* working, satisfies.'
Now through the splendours that precede the dawn,
  whose rise wayfarers the more gladly greet
  as, homing, lodge they a stage farther on,
the dark was fleeing on all sides, and with it
  fled sleep from me; whence to my feet I rose,
  seeing the great masters risen to their feet.
'That sweet fruit, which the care of mortals goes
  in search of along branches numberless,
  today shall set at rest thy hunger-throes.'
With words like these did Virgil's voice address
  itself tow'rds me; and never Easter-gift
  was there to match them for delightfulness.
So much I longed, and longed again, to lift
  me heavenward, that thereafter I was ware
  how at each step my pinions grew more swift.
When, quickly scaled, beneath us all the stair
  now lay, and on the topmost step we stood,
  on me did Virgil fix his eyes, and there
thus spoke: 'My son, the temporal thou hast view'd
  and the eternal fire, and reached a place
  where vision of mine no farther may intrude.
I've drawn thee here with judgment and address;
  take thine own pleasure now for leader: forth
  from the steep ways thou art, the strait no less.
See there the Sun shine, fronting thee, the earth
  gay with young grass and flowers and springing trees,
  to which the soil here, of itself, gives birth.

Mentre che vegnan lieti gli occhi belli
  che lacrimando a te venir mi fenno,
  seder ti puoi e puoi andar tra elli.   138
Non aspettar mio dir più nè mio cenno:
  libero, dritto e sano è tuo arbitrio,
  e fallo fora non fare a suo senno: 141
per ch'io te sovra te corono e mitrio ».

CANTO 28

VAGO già di cercar dentro e dintorno
  la divina foresta spessa e viva
  che a gli occhi temperava il novo giorno,   3
sanza più aspettar lasciai la riva,
  prendendo la campagna lento lento
  su per lo suol che d'ogni parte auliva.   6
Un'aura dolce, sanza mutamento
  avere in sè, mi feria per la fronte
  non di più colpo che soave vento,   9
per cui le fronde, tremolando pronte,
  tutte quante piegavano a la parte
  u' la prim'ombra gitta il santo monte;   12
non però dal lor esser dritte sparte
  tanto, che gli augelletti per le cime
  lasciasser d'operare ogni lor arte;   15
ma con piena letizia l'ore prime,
  cantando, riceveano intra le foglie,
  che tenevan bordone a le sue rime,   18
tal qual di ramo in ramo si raccoglie
  per la pineta in sul lito di Chiassi,
  quand'Eolo scirocco fuor discioglie.   21
Già m'avean trasportato i lenti passi
  dentro a la selva antica, tanto ch'io
  non potea rivedere ond'io m'intrassi,   24
ed ecco più andar mi tolse un rio
  che in ver sinistra con sue picciol'onde
  piegava l'erba che in sua ripa uscio.   27

While the fair eyes are coming, now at ease,
    which, weeping, made me come to thee, 'tis thine
    to sit and thine to wander among these.
Expect no longer word from me, nor sign:
    thy will could not be sounder, freër, uprighter;
    'twere fault henceforth its fiat to decline:
thee o'er thyself I therefore crown and mitre.'

CANTO 28

Eager forthwith to enter and survey
    the divine forest, quick with foliage, meet
    for tempering to the eye the new-born day,
I lingered not, but making haste to quit
    the edge, I took the plain by slow degrees
    o'er soil that from all sides was smelling sweet.
A soft air, having no inconstancies
    within itself, was smiting on my brow
    but no more roughly than a gentle breeze;
wherewith in tremulous accord each bough
    was thither bending where the sacred hill
    casts its first shadow on the world below;
yet not so far deflected, but that still
    the little birds upon the topmost sprays
    could without pausing ply their varied skill;
which with their song were welcoming the day's
    first hours exultantly among the leaves,
    that kept a burden to their roundelays,
such as from branch to branch the ear perceives
    gathering among the pines on Chiassi's shore,
    when Aeolus freedom to Scirocco gives.
By now my feet, tho' slow, had paced the floor
    of that primeval wood so far, that I
    to whence I'd entered could look back no more,
and lo! my farther going was halted by
    a stream, which leftward with its ripples plied
    the herbage that upon its bank grew high.

Tutte l'acque che son di qua più monde
   parrieno avere in sè mistura alcuna
   verso di quella, che nulla nasconde   30
avvegna che si mova bruna bruna
   sotto l'ombra perpetua, che mai
   raggiar non lascia Sole ivi nè Luna.   33
Coi piè ristetti, e con gli occhi passai
   dì là dal fiumicello, per mirare
   la gran variazion dei freschi mai;   36
e là m'apparve, sì com'egli appare
   subitamente cosa che disvia
   per maraviglia tutt'altro pensare,   39
una donna soletta che si gìa
   cantando e scegliendo fior da fiore
   ond'era pinta tutta la sua via.   42
«Deh, bella donna, che ai raggi d'amore
   ti scaldi, s'io vo' credere ai sembianti,
   che soglion esser testimon del core,   45
vègnati voglia di trarreti avanti»
   diss'io a ́lei «verso questa rivera
   tanto ch'io possa intender che tu canti.   48
Tu mi fai rimembrar dove e qual era
   Proserpina nel tempo che perdette
   la madre lei ed ella primavera».   51
Come si volge con le piante strette
   a terra ed intra sè donna che balli,
   e piede innanzi piede appena mette,   54
volsesi in su i vermigli ed in su i gialli
   fioretti verso me, non altrimenti
   che vergine che gli occhi onesti avvalli;   57
e fece i prieghi miei esser contenti
   sì appressando sè, che il dolce suono
   veniva a me co' suoi intendimenti.   60
Tosto che fu là dove l'erbe sono
   bagnate già da l'onde del bel fiume,
   di levar gli occhi suoi mi fece dono.   63
Non credo che splendesse tanto lume
   sotto le ciglia a Venere trafitta
   dal figlio fuor di tutto suo costume.   66

All waters here, e'en the most purified,
   would from some mixture fail to seem immune,
   compared with that one, which doth nothing hide
though dark its movement, very dark, in tune
   with the perpetual shade, which ne'er to cast
   one ray allows the Sun there, nor the Moon.
I stayed my feet, but with my eyes I passed
   beyond the brook, so as to let them dwell
   on the may-boughs in daedal verdure massed;
and, there, to me appeared, as things may well
   suddenly appear, that for sheer wonderment
   all other thinking from the mind dispel,
a lady, quite alone, who onward went
   singing, and choosing blossoms, flower by flower,
   which all along her way their colours blent,
'Ah, lovely lady, who, if looks have power
   to bear true witness of the heart within,
   art basking in the rays that love doth shower,
may the wish come to thee,' did I begin,
   'that I may understand what thou dost sing,
   to draw towards this river closer in.
Back to my mind Prosérpine dost thou bring,
   where and what then she looked like, when bereft
   the mother was of her, and she of spring.'
Like as a lady turns, at dancing deft,
   feet close to earth, the space between them slight,
   scarcely advancing now the right, now left,
she turned tow'rds me upon the herbage, dight
   with red and yellow flowerets, dropping low
   her modest eyes, as some fair virgin might;
and made my prayers content, approaching so
   that not alone the dulcet sound attain'd
   my ears but therewithal its meaning too.
When she was where the grass began to blend
   already with the waves of the fair stream
   to raise her eyes she then did condescend.
Less light, methinks, did 'neath the eye-lids beam
   of Venus, wounded by her son's own hand,
   that time his wonted skill deserted him.

Ella ridea da l'altra riva dritta,
    trattando più color con le sue mani,
    che l'alta terra sanza seme gitta.   69
Tre passi ci facea 'l fiume lontani;
    ma Ellesponto, la 've passò Serse,
    ancora freno a tutti orgogli umani,   72
più odio da Leandro non sofferse
    per mareggiare intra Sesto ed Abido
    che quel da me perchè allor non s'aperse.   75
«Voi siete novi, e forse perch'io rido»
    cominciò ella «in questo loco, eletto
    a l'umana natura per suo nido,   78
maravigliando tienvi alcun sospetto;
    ma luce rende il salmo *Delectasti*
    che puote disnebbiar vostro intelletto.   81
E tu che sei dinanzi e mi pregasti,
    di', s'altro vuoli udir, ch'io venni presta
    ad ogni tua question tanto che basti».   84
« L'acqua » diss'io « e il suon de la foresta
    impugnan dentro me novella fede
    di cosa ch'io udii contraria a questa».   87
Ond'ella: «Io dicerò come procede
    per sua cagion ciò che ammirar ti face,
    e purgherò la nebbia che ti fiede.   90
Lo sommo ben, che solo esso a sè piace,
    fece l'uom buono e a bene, e questo loco
    diede per arra a lui d'eterna pace.   93
Per sua diffalta qui dimorò poco;
    per sua diffalta in pianto ed in affanno
    cambiò onesto riso e dolce gioco.   96
Perchè il turbar che sotto da sè fanno
    l'esalazion de l'acqua e de la terra,
    che quanto posson dietro al calor vanno,   99
a l'uomo non facesse alcuna guerra,
    questo monte salio verso il ciel tanto,
    e libero n'è indi ove si serra.   102
Or perchè in circuito tutto quanto
    l'aere si volge con la prima volta,
    se non gli è rotto il cerchio d'alcun canto,   105

She smiled, erect, upon the farther strand,
   still plaiting with her hands the colours pied,
   produced without seed in that lofty land.
Between us flowed the brook three paces wide;
   but Hellespont, where Xerxes crossed—whilere,
   and even now, a curb to human pride—
tholed not more hatred from Leander, where
   it surged 'twixt Sestos and Abydos, than
   from me this, that it clave not then and there.
'Newcomers ye! and, haply,' she began,
   'that I stand smiling in this place elect,
   expressly made to be the nest of man,
may make you, through surprise, my aim suspect;
   but the psalm *Delectasti* well may grant
   a light that will uncloud your intellect.
And thou, the foremost, and my suppliant,
   would'st know more? For I came here to supply,
   so far as may suffice, thy every want.'
'The sound the forest makes, this stream,' said I
   'impugn a doctrine that I heard of late
   and thought was true, to which they give the lie.'
Then she: 'If I the cause before thee set
   of that which makes thee wonder, then will this
   the fog that now assails thee dissipate.
The highest Good, sole source of its own bliss,
   to man, for good created good, this lief
   abode as pledge gave of eternal peace.
By his default his sojourn here was brief:
   by his default he changed his blameless mirth
   and playful pastimes to distress and grief.
That tumults, which below it owe their birth
   to exhalations (wont to follow hard
   upon the heat) from water and from the earth,
might not make war on man, this mount was rear'd
   so high tow'rds heaven and from storms is free
   from that point upward where the way is barr'd.
Now, seeing that with the *primum mobile*
   the whole air ever smoothly circles round,
   save by some point its circuit broken be,

in quest'altezza, che tutta è disciolta
  ne l'aer vivo, tal moto percuote,
  e fa sonar la selva perch'è folta.   108
E la percossa pianta tanto puote
  che de la sua virtute l'aura impregna,
  e quella poi, girando intorno, scuote;   111
e l'altra terra, secondo ch'è degna
  per sè e per suo ciel, concepe e figlia
  di diverse virtù diverse legna.   114
Non parrebbe di là poi maraviglia,
  udito questo, quando alcuna pianta
  sanza seme palese vi s'appiglia.   117
E saper dei che la campagna santa
  dove tu sei d'ogni semenza è piena,
  e frutto ha in sè che di là non si schianta.   120
L'acqua che vedi non surge di vena
  che ristori vapor, che gel converta,
  come fiume che acquista e perde lena,   123
ma esce di fontana salda e certa
  che tanto dal voler di Dio riprende
  quant'ella versa da due parti aperta.   126
Da questa parte con virtù discende
  che toglie altrui memoria del peccato,
  da l'altra d'ogni ben fatto la rende.   129
Quinci Letè; così da l'altro lato
  Eunoè si chiama, e non adopra
  se quinci e quindi pria non è gustato.   132
A tutt'altri sapori esto è di sopra.
  Ed avvegna che assai possa esser sazia
  la sete tua per ch'io più non ti scopra,   135
darotti un corollario ancor per grazia;
  nè credo che il mio dir ti sia men caro
  se oltre promission teco si spazia.   138
Quelli che anticamente poetaro
  l'età de l'oro e suo stato felice,
  forse in Parnaso esto loco sognaro.   141
Qui fu innocente l'umana radice,
  qui primavera sempre ed ogni frutto,
  nettare è questo, di che ciascun dice ».   144

such motion strikes upon this height, that bound
  knows none in the live air, and makes the wood
  (so dense its foliage) to intone a sound;
and with such power is every plant endued
  when smitten, that its virtue impregns the breeze,
  by revolution whereof 'tis then far-strewed;
and all the earth else, as it worthy is
  in itself and in clime, conceives and brings
  to birth from divers virtues divers trees.
This known, it should not yonder class with things
  to wonder at, when there a plant takes root,
  though no seed be apparent whence it springs.
The holy plain whereon thou settest foot
  know, too, doth every kind of seed contain,
  and hath its own, on earth ne'er gathered, fruit.
The stream thou seëst wells not from a vein
  whose volume mists, by cold condensed, enforce,
  like rivers that now lose in breath, now gain,
but issues from a sure, unfailing source,
  which as much back, by God's own will, receives
  as it pours out on a divided course.
On this side it descends with power that leaves
  in human minds no memory of sin;
  on the other, that of aught well done retrieves.
Here Lethe: so on that side is its twin
  called Eúnoë, which, if tasted not both this
  and that side first, will its effect not win.
This of all other savours sovereign is.
  And though now fully quenched thy thirst may be,
  so that, if told no more, thou'dst nothing miss,
I'll add, of pure grace, a corollary,
  nor do I think my words will prove less dear
  for going yet farther than I promised thee.
Perhaps those, who long since the poets were
  of the age of gold and of its blissful state,
  dreamed on Parnassus of this region fair.
Here, in his innocence, man's root was set;
  here spring is, aye, and fruits in plenitude;
  the nectar this, that they all celebrate.'

Io mi rivolsi in dietro allora tutto
  a miei poeti, e vidi che con riso
  udito aveano l'ultimo costrutto.   147
Poi a la bella donna tornai 'l viso.

CANTO 29

Cantando come donna innamorata,
  continuò, col fin di sue parole:
  Beati quorum tecta sunt peccata.   3
E come ninfe che si givan sole
  per le salvatiche ombre, disiando
  qual di veder qual di fuggir lo Sole,   6
allor si mosse contra il fiume, andando
  su per la riva; ed io pari di lei,
  picciol passo con picciol seguitando.   9
Non eran cento tra i suoi passi e i miei,
  quando le ripe igualmente dier volta,
  per modo che a levante mi rendei.   12
Nè anco fu così nostra via molta,
  quando la donna tutta a me si torse
  dicendo: « Frate mio, guarda ed ascolta ». 15
Ed ecco un lustro subito trascorse
  da tutte parti per la gran foresta,
  tal che di balenar mi mise in forse.   18
Ma perchè il balenar come vien resta,
  e quel, durando, più e più splendeva,
  nel mio pensar dicea: « Che cosa è questa? » 21
E una melodia dolce correva
  per l'aere luminoso; onde buon zelo
  mi fe' riprender l'ardimento d'Eva,   24
che là dove ubbidia la Terra e il Cielo,
  femmina sola e pur testè formata
  non sofferse di star sotto alcun velo: 27
sotto il qual se divota fosse stata.
  avrei quelle ineffabili delizie
  gustate prima e più lunga fiata.   30

Then turned I about to where my poets stood,
  and saw how to their lips a smile there came
  at her last words, as they their sense construed;
I turned my visage then to the fair dame.

CANTO 29

Singing like one enamoured, she, when át a
  conclusion were her words, forthwith went on:
  Beati quorum tecta sunt peccata.
And like to nymphs, whose wont it was to shun
  the haunts of men and roam the woodland shade,
  some fain to see, some to avoid the Sun,
she then upstream along the margin made
  her way, and I the while kept pace with her,
  my small by her small steps being onward led.
Not five-score had we taken between us, ere
  both banks made correspondingly a bend,
  so that my course lay eastward on from there.
Nor had we yet that way much distance gain'd,
  before the lady, facing full tow'rds me,
  exclaimed: 'My brother, look thou and attend.'
And lo, through the great forest suddenly
  a lustre ran, so bright I could not miss
  to think at first that it must lightning be.
But since the lightning, as it comes, doth cease,
  and that stayed, more and more illuminative,
  I said within myself: 'What thing is this?'
Then did a melody its sweetness give
  to the far-shining air; whence righteous zeal
  made me reproach the hardihood of Eve,
who there, where Heaven and Earth obeyed God's will,
  a woman, she only, and but newly made,
  brooked not that any veil should aught conceal;
under which veil, had she submissive stay'd,
  I should on those ineffable delights
  have supped before and on them longer fed.

Mentr'io m'andava fra tante primizie
  de l'eterno piacer tutto sospeso
  e disioso ancora a più letizie,   33
dinanzi a noi tal quale un foco acceso
  ci se fe' l'aere sotto i verdi rami,
  e il dolce suon per canto era già inteso.   36
O sacrosante vergini, se fami,
  freddi o vigilie mai per voi soffersi,
  cagion mi sprona ch'io mercè vi chiami.   39
Or convien ch'Elicona per me versi,
  e Urania m'aiuti col suo coro
  forti cose a pensar mettere in versi.   42
Poco più oltre sette alberi d'oro
  falsava nel parere il lungo tratto
  del mezzo ch'era ancor tra noi e loro;   45
ma quando fui sì presso di lor fatto
  che l'obietto comun, che il senso inganna,
  non perdea per distanza alcun suo atto,   48
la virtù che a ragion discorso ammanna
  sì com'egli eran candelabri apprese,
  e ne le voci del cantare *Osanna*.   51
Di sopra fiammeggiava il bell'arnese
  più chiaro assai che Luna per sereno
  di mezza notte nel suo mezzo mese.   54
Io mi rivolsi d'ammirazion pieno
  al buon Virgilio, ed esso mi rispose
  con vista carca di stupor non meno.   57
Indi rendei l'aspetto a l'alte cose,
  che si movieno incontra noi sì tardi
  che foran vinte da novelle spose.   60
La donna mi sgridò: « Perchè pur ardi
  sì ne l'aspetto de le vive luci,
  e ciò che vien di retro a lor non guardi? » 63
Genti vid'io allor, come a lor duci,
  venire appresso, vestite di bianco;
  e tal candor di qua giammai non fuci.   66
L'acqua splendeami dal sinistro fianco
  e rendea a me la mia sinistra costa
  s'io riguardava in lei, come specchio, anco. 69

As I mid these prelusive sounds and sights
  of bliss eternal walked on, all amazed,
  in joy that reached out to yet higher heights,
before us, like a fire enkindled, blazed
  the air beneath the green boughs, and now grew
  the sweet sound to a chant, distinctly phrased.
O virgins sacrosanct, if e'er for you
  I've suffered vigils, fasts and cold, therefór
  need spurs me now to claim the guerdon due.
For me must Helicon its springs outpour,
  and with her choir Urania lend me aid
  to put in verse things hard for thought to explore.
A short way on, seven trees of gold were made
  to seem, though falsely, such by the wide tract
  which between us and them still lay outspread;
but having neared the things they were in fact—
  the common object, which to our sense tells lies,
  thus gaining detail it through distance lacked—
I, through the power which with discourse supplies
  the reason, saw that candlesticks they were,
  and in the singing heard 'hosanna' rise.
Above was blazing the equipment fair,
  much brighter than, in her mid-month, we see
  the Moon at midnight, when the sky is bare.
I turned me round, wonder o'ercoming me,
  to the good Virgil, and his look replied
  charged with amazement in no less degree.
To the high things reverting, I descried
  them moving tow'rds us at a pace so slow,
  that faster would have stepped a new-wed bride.
The lady chid me: 'Why still burnst thou so
  to keep in view the living lights, and in
  what comes behind them wilt no interest show?'
Folk saw I then, as had their leaders been
  the lights, behind these coming, garbed in white:
  such whiteness on this earth was never seen.
The water on my left cast back the light
  and, if I gazed therein, reflected too
  my own left side, as a clear mirror might.

Quand'io da la mia riva ebbi tal posta
  che solo il fiume mi facea distante,
  per veder meglio ai passi diedi sosta;   72
e vidi le fiammelle andar davante,
  lasciando dietro a sè l'aere dipinto;
  e di tratti pennelli avean sembiante,   75
sì che lì sopra rimanea distinto
  di sette liste, tutte in quei colori
  onde fa l'arco il Sole e Delia il cinto.   78
Questi ostendali dietro eran maggiori
  che la mia vista; e quanto a mio avviso
  dieci passi distavan quei di fuori.   81
Sotto così bel ciel com'io diviso,
  ventiquattro seniori, a due a due,
  coronati venien di fiordaliso.   84
Tutti cantavan: « Benedetta tue
  ne le figlie d'Adamo, e benedette
  sieno in eterno le bellezze tue ».   87
Poscia che i fiori e l'altre fresche erbette
  a rimpetto di me da l'altra sponda
  libere fur da quelle genti elette,   90
sì come luce luce in ciel seconda
  vennero appresso a lor quattro animali,
  coronati ciascun di verde fronda.   93
Ognuno era pennuto di sei ali;
  le penne piene d'occhi, e gli occhi d'Argo
  se fosser vivi sarebber cotali.   96
A descriver lor forme più non spargo
  rime, lettor, ch'altra spesa mi strigne
  tanto che a questa non posso esser largo;   99
ma leggi Ezechiel che li dipigne
  come li vide da la fredda parte
  venir con vento e con nube e con igne;   102
e quali i troverai ne le sue carte
  tali eran quivi, salvo che a le penne
  Giovanni è meco e da lui si diparte.   105
Lo spazio dentro a lor quattro contenne
  un carro, in su due rote, triunfale,
  che al collo d'un grifon tirato venne.   108

Then on my bank up to a point I drew,
   where nothing parted us except the brook,
   and halted there to obtain a better view,
and saw that, as the flamelets onward took
   their way, the air behind them tinted shone
   and like to drawn-out pennons made them look;
so that it overhead went stretching on
   striped with seven bands, all in those hues of which
   the Solar bow is made and Delia's zone.
These standards far beyond my vision's reach
   streamed backward: and ten paces, I should say,
   parted the two outside ones each from each.
Beneath so fair a sky as I portray,
   marching in pairs and crowned with fleur-de-lys
   came four and twenty elders on their way.
And all were chanting: 'Blest eternally
   art thou among the daughters of Adam, blest
   be evermore the beauties found in thee!'
Then, when the flowers and tender herbs that dress'd
   in front of me the other river's-edge
   were of those chosen people dispossess'd,
as star on star in heaven's equipage,
   next after them four living Creatures came,
   crowned each alike with verdant foliage.
Feathered with six wings was each one of them,
   the feathers full of eyes; could they still wake,
   the eyes of Argus would look much the same.
Reader, if to describe their forms I make
   these rhymes suffice, 'tis outlay elsewhere due
   that bids me here my bounty keep in check;
but read Ezekiel, who their picture drew
   as he beheld them come from northern cold
   with fire and cloud what time the whirlwind blew;
and as thou'lt find them on his page enscroll'd,
   such were they there, save John is on my side
   as to their wings, and not with him doth hold.
A car, two-wheeled, triumphal, occupied
   the space between the four of whom I sing:
   drawn at a Griffin's neck it onward hied.

Esso tendeva in sù l'una e l'altr'ale
  tra la mezzana e le tre e tre liste,
  sì che a nulla fendendo facea male.   111
Tanto salivan che non eran viste;
  le membra d'oro avea quanto era uccello,
  e bianche l'altre di vermiglio miste.   114
Non che Roma di carro così bello
  rallegrasse Affricano ovvero Augusto,
  ma quel del Sol saria pover con ello: 117
quel del Sol che, sviando, fu combusto
  per l'orazion de la Terra devota,
  quando fu Giove arcanamente giusto.   120
Tre donne in giro da la destra rota
  venian danzando: l'una tanto rossa
  che a pena fora dentro al foco nota;   123
l'altra era come se le carni e l'ossa
  fossero state di smeraldo fatte;
  la terza parea neve testè mossa.   126
E or parevan da la bianca tratte,
  or da la rossa; e dal canto di questa
  l'altre togliean l'andare o tarde o ratte.   129
Da la sinistra quattro facean festa
  in porpora vestite, dietro al modo
  d'una di lor che avea tre occhi in testa.   132
Appresso tutto il pertrattato nodo
  vidi due vecchi in abito dispàri,
  ma pari in atto, ed onesto e sodo.   135
L'un si mostrava alcun dei familiari
  di quel sommo Ippocràte, che natura
  a gli animali fe' ch'ella ha più cari.   138
Mostrava l'altro la contraria cura
  con una spada lucida ed acuta,
  tal che di qua dal rio mi fe' paura.   141
Poi vidi quattro in umile paruta;
  e di retro da tutti un veglio solo
  venir dormendo con la faccia arguta.   144
E questi sette col primaio stuolo
  erano abituati, ma di gigli
  dintorno al capo non facevan brolo,   147

He stretched aloft the one and the other wing
  between the mid-band and the three and three,
  which thus he cut through without injuring.
They rose beyond a point that eye could see;
  his limbs were gold, so far as he was bird,
  and white the rest, mingled with cramoisie.
Never did car so rich, by Rome conferr'd,
  grace Africanus, e'en Augustus: nay,
  the Sun's own car were mean, with that compared:
the Sun's own car, which, having gone astray,
  was burnt up at the Earth's devout appeal,
  when Jove's mysterious justice had its way.
Three ladies in a ring at the right wheel
  came dancing; one so fiery red that, given
  for background fire, she were discerned but ill.
Another shone as had the emerald striven
  to make her flesh and bones with itself glow:
  the third appeared like unto snow new-driven;
and to the red one's song—as now she, now
  the white one (so it seemed) the others led—
  they timed their movement, whether quick or slow.
On the left, four, in purple habited,
  made festival; and of their steps the guide
  was one of them with three eyes in her head.
Behind all those here mentioned I descried
  two agéd men, unlike in dress, in mood
  and gesture like, both grave and dignified.
One was familiar, as his aspect show'd,
  of that supreme Hippocrates, design'd
  by Nature for her best-loved creatures' good.
The other's care seemed opposite in kind:
  he bore a sword so bright and sharp, that e'en
  this side the stream fear of it seized my mind.
Then I beheld four more, of humble mien;
  and behind all an agéd man, alone,
  come walking in a trance, with visage keen.
Garbed were these seven as was the troop I've shown
  that foremost filed, except that they in lieu
  of lilies round the head wore each a crown

anzi di rose e d'altri fior vermigli:
   giurato avria poco lontano aspetto
   che tutti ardesser di sopra dai cigli.   150
E quando il carro a me fu a rimpetto
   un tuon s'udì, e quelle genti degne
   parvero aver l'andar più interdetto,   153
fermandosi ivi con le prime insegne.

CANTO 30

Quando il Settentrion del primo cielo,
   che nè occaso mai seppe nè orto
   nè d'altra nebbia che di colpa velo,   3
e che faceva lì ciascuno accorto
   di suoi dover, come il più basso face
   qual timon gira per venire a porto,   6
fermo s'affisse, la gente verace
   venuta prima tra il grifone ed esso
   al carro volse sè come a sua pace: 9
e un di loro, quasi di ciel messo,
   Veni, sponsa, de Libano cantando
   gridò tre volte, e tutti gli altri appresso.   12
Quali i beati al novissimo bando
   surgeran presti ognun di sua caverna,
   la rivestita voçe alleluiando,   15
cotali in su la divina basterna
   si levar cento, *ad vocem tanti senis*,
   ministri e messagger di vita eterna.   18
Tutti dicean *Benedictus qui venis*,
   e, fior gittando di sopra e dintorno,
   Manibus o date lilia plenis.   21
Io vidi già nel cominciar del giorno
   la parte oriental tutta rosata
   e l'altro ciel di bel sereno adorno;   24

of roses and like flowers of vermeil hue;
   one would have sworn that they were all aflame
   above the eyebrows, till quite close they drew.
The car once over against myself, there came
   a thunderclap, and all those stately folk
   there, with the ensigns which preceded them,
their onward march, as were it forbidd'n them, broke.

CANTO 30

Wʜᴇɴ the Septentrion of the primal heaven,
   which never sets nor rises nor is veil'd
   'neath other cloud than sin—that starry 'seven'
which held each person there, and kept them held,
   true to his course, as here the lower one does,
   for such as steer back thither whence they sail'd—
when this stood still, of truth's own people those
   who'd first between the Griffin come and it,
   turned to the car, as if to their repose;
and one, as sent from heaven, a singer sweet,
   Veni, sponsa, de Libano then cried
   three times, and this did all the rest repeat.
As at the last trump shall arise, o'erjoyed,
   each from his tomb, with re-clad voices blending
   their alleluias, the Beatified,
so rose up, o'er the heavenly wain ascending,
   a hundred spirits *ad vocem tanti senis,*
   heralds and ministers of life unending.
And all were shouting: '*Benedictus qui venis!*'
   and, as they flowers up and around it threw,
   cried: '*Manibus o date lilia plenis!*'
I've seen ere now, as the dawn brighter grew,
   the eastern parts all rosy, and elsewhere
   the heaven arrayed in a deep, tranquil blue,

e la faccia del Sol nascere ombrata,
 sì che, per temperanza di vapori,
 l'occhio la sostenea lunga fiata.   27
Così, dentro una nuvola di fiori
 che da le mani angeliche saliva
 e ricadeva giù dentro e di fuori,   30
sovra candido vel cinta d'oliva
 donna m'apparve, sotto verde manto
 vestita del color di fiamma viva.   33
E lo spirito mio, che già cotanto
 tempo era stato che a la sua presenza
 non era di stupor tremando affranto,   36
sanza de gli occhi aver più conoscenza,
 per occulta virtù che da lei mosse,
 d'antico amor sentì la gran potenza.   39
Tosto che ne la vista mi percosse
 l'alta virtù che già m'avea trafitto
 prima ch'io fuor di puerizia fosse,   42
volsimi a la sinistra col rispitto
 col quale il fantolin corre alla mamma
 quando ha paura o quand'egli è afflitto, 45
per dicere a Virgilio: « Men che dramma
 di sangue m'è rimaso che non tremi;
 conosco i segni de l'antica fiamma! »   48
Ma Virgilio n'avea lasciati scemi
 di sè: Virgilio, dolcissimo padre;
 Virgilio, a cui per mia salute die'mi;   51
nè quantunque perdeo l'antica madre
 valse a le guance nette di rugiada
 che lacrimando non tornasser adre.   54
« Dante, perchè Virgilio se ne vada
 non pianger anco, non piangere ancora,
 chè pianger ti convien per altra spada ». 57
Quasi ammiraglio che in poppa od in prora
 viene a veder la gente che ministra
 per gli altri legni ed a ben far l'incuora, 60
in su la sponda del carro sinistra,
 quando mi volsi al suon del nome mio,
 che di necessità qui si registra,   63

and the Sun's face come forth, the misty air
  his beams so tempering, that the visual powers
  found them, a long while, not too bright to bear;
unto me thus, within a cloud of flowers,
  which, by angelic hands tossed upward, came
  falling back on, and round, the car in showers,
wreathed, o'er a white veil, with an olive stem
  a lady appeared, under a cloak of green
  apparelled in the hue of living flame.
Straightway my spirit—which so long had been
  free from the crushing stupor that, before,
  would make it tremble in her presence—e'en
tho' the eyes revealed but thus much and no more,
  through hidden virtue which from her flowed out,
  of by-gone love now felt the o'ermastering power.
So soon as that exalted virtue smote
  my vision, which already, ere I was done
  with boyhood's days, had caught me by the throat,
I turned me leftward, as a child will run
  to its mummy trustfully, when 'tis its aim
  to escape some fear or grief it fain would shun,
intent on saying to Virgil: 'Barely a drachm
  of blood that trembles not is left me still:
  I recognize the signs of the ancient flame!'
But Virgil had forsaken us, my leal
  companion: Virgil, sweetest father; he,
  Virgil, to whom I gave me for my weal;
nor to my cheeks, dew-cleansed, could all that she,
  man's ancient mother, lost, avail that they
  should not with tears once more polluted be.
'Dante, for all that Virgil goes his way,
  not yet, weep thou not yet; for needs must thou
  weep when thou feel'st another sword in play.'
Like to an admiral who on poop or prow
  comes to inspect and hearten crews on board
  of other ships, that they their best may do;
at the car's left-hand rim—when to the word
  I turned which is my own name, and which here
  only because I must do I record—

vidi la donna che pria m'appario
  velata sotto l'angelica festa
  drizzar gli occhi ver me di qua dal rio,   66
tutto che il vel che le scendea di testa
  cerchiato de le fronde di Minerva
  non la lasciasse parer manifesta.   69
Regalmente ne l'atto ancor proterva
  continuò come colui che dice
  e il più caldo parlar dietro riserva: 72
« Guardami ben! Ben son, ben son Beatrice!
  Come degnasti d'accedere al monte?
  non sapei tu che qui è l'uom felice? »   75
Gli occhi mi cadder giù nel chiaro fonte,
  ma veggendomi in esso i trassi a l'erba,
  tanta vergogna mi gravò la fronte.   78
Così la madre al figlio par superba
  com'ella parve a me; perchè d'amaro
  sente il sapor de la pietate acerba.   81
Ella si tacque, e gli angeli cantaro
  di subito *In te, Domine, speravi*;
  ma oltre *pedes meos* non passaro.   84
Sì come neve tra le vive travi
  per lo dosso d'Italia si congela,
  soffiata e stretta da li venti schiavi;   87
poi liquefatta in sè stessa trapela,
  pur che la terra che perde ombra spiri,
  sì che par foco fonder la candela;   90
così fui sanza lacrime e sospiri
  anzi il cantar di quei che notan sempre
  dietro a le note de gli eterni giri;   93
ma poi che intesi ne le dolci tempre
  lor compatire a me, più che se detto
  avesser: « Donna, perchè sì lo stempre? »,   96
lo gel che m'era intorno al cor ristretto
  spirito ed acqua fessi, e con angoscia
  da la bocca e da gli occhi uscì del petto.   99
Ella, pur ferma in su la detta coscia
  del carro stando, a le sustanzie pie
  volse le sue parole così poscia: 102

I saw the lady, seen of me whilere
   veiled 'neath the angelic festival, had stay'd
   her eyes on me this side the barrier,
albeit the veil descending from her head,
   encircled with Minerva's leaf, remain'd
   such that her face and form were not display'd.
In queenly wise still haughty, yet she deign'd
   to speak on, like to one who does not cease
   from words, but keeps her warmest for the end:
'Look at me well! Yes I'm, yes I'm Beatrice!
   How durst thou approach the mountain? Didst, then, thou
   not know that here man finds himself in bliss?'
I dropped my eyes to the clear fount below,
   but, seeing myself therein, drew them anon
   to the green turf, such shame oppressed my brow.
Harsh as is deemed the mother by the son
   I deemed her; for the taste of love when blent
   with sternness takes a tang of tartness on.
She ceased; and the angels sang incontinent
   '*In te, Domine, speravi*', but their song
   no farther than to *pedes meos* went.
Like snow, that mid the living beams along
   Italy's spine congeals, as drives and packs
   it tight the *bora*, when its blast is strong,
then, melting, if but breathes the land that lacks
   a shadow, and trickling through itself, appears
   as 'twere a candle which the fire attacks:
even so was I devoid of sighs and tears
   ere they began to sing whose notes always
   echo *their* notes who roll the eternal spheres;
but instantly, when in their dulcet lays
   I heard their pity for me, more than if they
   had asked her: 'Lady, wherefore such dispraise?'
the ice that clamped my heart, without more stay
   turning to breath and water, from my breast
   through mouth and eyes with anguish forced its way.
She, on the same side of the car still placed,
   stood moveless, and thereafter her discourse
   to the compassionate spirits thus address'd:

« Voi vigilate ne l'eterno die,
  sì che notte nè sonno a voi non fura
  passo che faccia il secol per sue vie;   105
onde la mia risposta è con più cura
  che m'intenda colui che di là piagne,
  perchè sia colpa e duol d'una misura.   108
Non pur per opra de le rote magne
  che drizzan ciascun seme ad alcun fine
  secondo che le stelle son compagne,   111
ma per larghezza di grazie divine,
  che sì alti vapori hanno a lor piova
  che nostre viste là non van vicine,   114
questi fu tal ne la sua vita nova
  virtualmente, che ogni abito destro
  fatto averebbe in lui mirabil prova.   117
Ma tanto più maligno e più silvestro
  si fa il terren col mal seme non cólto,
  quant'egli ha più di buon vigor terrestro.   120
Alcun tempo il sostenni col mio vólto:
  mostrando gli occhi giovinetti a lui
  meco il menava in dritta parte vòlto.   123
Sì tosto come in su la soglia fui
  di mia seconda etade e mutai vita,
  questi si tolse a me e diessi altrui.   126
Quando di carne a spirto ero salita
  e bellezza e virtù cresciuta m'era,
  fu'io a lui men cara e men gradita;   129
e volse i passi suoi per via non vera,
  imagini di ben seguendo false
  che nulla promission rendono intera.   132
Nè l'impetrare ispirazion mi valse,
  con le quali, ed in sogno ed altrimenti,
  lo rivocai: sì poco a lui ne calse.   135
Tanto giù cadde, che tutti argomenti
  a la salute sua eran già corti,
  fuor che mostrargli le perdute genti.   138
Per questo visitai l'uscio dei morti,
  ed a colui che l'ha qua sù condotto
  li preghi miei piangendo furon porti.   141

486

'Ye, where the day eternal hath its source
   keep watch, so that from you nor sleep nor night
   can steal one step of the ages in their course;
hence with more care I pick my words to indict
   him who on yon bank weeps disconsolate,
   that fault with sorrow may be matched aright.
Not only through the working of the great
   wheels which direct each seed unto some end
   according to the stars that with it mate,
but through largess of graces which descend
   rained down by God from clouds enskied so high,
   that never mortal sight thereto attain'd,
this man in his new life potentially
   was such that each right habit would have wrought
   in him a wondrous harvest by and by.
But all the more malign and rank a plot
   of ground becomes with bad seed, if untilled,
   the more good earthy vigour it hath got.
Awhile my face was both his strength and shield:
   and, showing him my youthful eyes, I led
   him with me, in the right direction held.
So soon as of my second age I made
   to cross the threshold and changed life, he then
   abandoned me and after others stray'd.
When I had risen from flesh to spirit, and when
   my beauty and virtue had increased, not more
   but less he loved them, less thereof was fain.
A way not true he turned his steps to explore,
   phantoms of good pursuing that were lies,
   such as no promise of fulfilment bore.
Nor helped it that in dreams and otherwise,
   conveyed through inspirations sought by prayer,
   I called him back: such did he little prize.
So low he fell, that insufficient were
   by then all means of saving him, except
   to show him those who of being saved despair.
For this I visited the portal kept
   for the dead, and his guide up hither not
   unheedful of my prayer was, when I wept.

L'alto fato di Dio sarebbe rotto
  se Letè si passasse e tal vivanda
  fosse gustata, sanza alcuno scotto   144
di pentimento che lacrime spanda ».

CANTO 31

« O tu che sei di là dal fiume sacro »
  volgendo suo parlare a me per punta,
  che pur per taglio m'era paruto acro,   3
ricominciò, seguendo sanza cunta,
  « di', di' se questo è vero: a tanta accusa
  tua confession convien esser congiunta ».   6
Era la mia virtù tanto confusa,
  che la voce si mosse, e pria si spense
  che da gli organi suoi fosse dischiusa.   9
Poco sofferse; poi disse: « Che pense?
  Rispondi a me, chè le memorie triste
  in te non sono ancor da l'acqua offense ».   12
Confusione e paura insieme miste
  mi pinsero un tal *sì* fuor de la bocca
  al qual intender fur mestier le viste.   15
Come balestro frange, quando scocca
  da troppa tesa, la sua corda e l'arco,
  e con men foga l'asta il segno tocca,   18
sì scoppia' io sott'esso il grave carco,
  fuori sgorgando lacrime e sospiri,
  e la voce allentò per lo suo varco.   21
Ond'ella a me: « Per entro i miei disiri,
  che ti menavano ad amar lo bene
  di là dal qual non è a che s'aspiri,   24
quai fossi attraversati o quai catene
  trovasti, perchè del passare innanzi
  dovessiti così spogliar la spene?   27
E quali agevolezze o quali avanzi
  ne la fronte de gli altri si mostraro,
  perchè dovessi lor passeggiare anzi? »   30

God's high decree were to annulment brought,
  if Lethe should be crossed and viand so
  delicious tasted without any scot
of penitence which may cause tears to flow.'

CANTO 31

'Ho! thou yon-side the sacred rivulet'—
  turning her discourse with its point tow'rds me,
  sharp tho' I'd found it when but edgeways set—
she thus resumed, continuing instantly:
  'Say, say, is 't true? For with so grave a charge
  'tis meet thy own confession should agree.'
So baffled was my power, that to the marge
  of utterance rose my voice, but then died down,
  ere from its organs it was set at large.
Whiles she forbore, then said: 'Why silent? Own
  thy guilt; for by the water in no wise
  have thy sad memories yet been overthrown.'
Fear and confusion, miserable allies,
  forced from my mouth a 'yes', but breathed so low,
  that to perceive it there was need of eyes.
As an arblast that snaps both string and bow,
  when it goes off from being too tightly drawn,
  and the bolt hits the mark with feebler blow,
thus I, by that sore burden weighed upon,
  broke down, outpouring sighs and tears, which drown'd
  my voice so, that it barely a passage won.
Whence she: ' 'Mongst those desires that had their ground
  in me, and led thee on to love the Good
  which to all aspiration sets a bound,
what crossed thy way that forced thee to denude
  thyself of hope of pressing still ahead?
  what dikes or what chains sapped thy fortitude?
And what advantages, what charms display'd
  upon the face of the others, lured thine eye,
  that unto *them* thy court was to be paid?'

Dopo la tratta d'un sospiro amaro,
  appena ebbi la voce che rispose,
  (e le labbra a fatica la formaro),   33
piangendo dissi: « Le presenti cose
  col falso lor piacer volser miei passi
  tosto che il vostro viso si nascose ».   36
Ed ella: « Se tacessi o se negassi
  ciò che confessi, non fora men nota
  la colpa tua, da tal giudice sassi.   39
Ma quando scoppia da la propria gota
  l'accusa del peccato, in nostra corte
  rivolge sè contra il taglio la rota.   42
Tuttavia, perchè me' vergogna porte
  del tuo errore, e perchè altra volta
  udendo le sirene sii più forte,   45
pon giù il seme del piangere, ed ascolta:
  sì udirai come in contraria parte
  mover doveati mia carne sepolta.   48
Mai non t'appresentò natura o arte
  piacer quanto le belle membra in ch'io
  rinchiusa fui, e sono in terra sparte;   51
e se il sommo piacer sì ti fallìo
  per la mia morte, qual cosa mortale
  dovea poi trarre te nel suo disio?   54
Ben ti dovevi, per lo primo strale
  de le cose fallaci, levar suso
  di retro a me che non era più tale.   57
Non ti dovea gravar le penne in giuso,
  ad aspettar più colpi, o pargoletta
  o altra vanità con sì brev'uso.   60
Novo augelletto due o tre aspetta,
  ma dinanzi da gli occhi dei pennuti
  rete si spiega indarno o si saetta ».   63
Quali i fanciulli, vergognando, muti
  con gli occhi a terra stannosi, ascoltando
  e sè riconoscendo e ripentuti,   66
tal mi stav'io: ed ella disse: « Quando
  per udir sei dolente, alza la barba
  e prenderai più doglia riguardando ».   69

After the heaving of one bitter sigh
  scarcely my voice found utterance, and my lips
  with difficulty framed words to make reply.
Weeping, I said: 'The present world that steeps
  things in a false light turned my steps aside,
  when once your countenance was in eclipse.'
And she: 'Hadst thou kept silent or denied
  what thou confessest, not less fully known,
  thy fault were: 'tis by such a judge descried.
But when there breaks forth from the sinner's own
  mouth his self-accusation, in our court
  turns counter to the edge the grinding-stone.
Yet now, that better with thine error comport
  thy shame, and that in future, if thou hear
  the Sirens, thou behave in manlier sort,
put by the seed of weeping, and give ear:
  so shalt thou learn how contrary was in worth
  the course my buried flesh should have made thee steer.
Nought to which art or nature e'er gave birth,
  so pleased thee as did the fair limbs wherein I
  was prisoned—limbs resolved now into earth;
and if that, through my death, the sovereign joy
  thus failed thee, how should mortal things so much
  have lured thee that thou wert bewitched thereby?
Thou ought'st indeed, when stung by the first touch
  of things fallacious, to have soared aloft
  after myself who was no longer such.
Nor should thy wings have drooped, to wait with soft
  compliance for more blows from some light girl
  or vain thing else, no sooner donned than doff'd.
The young bird waits, when first his plumes uncurl,
  for two or three; but before those full-fledged
  in vain ye spread the net, the missile hurl.'
As children, after hearing some keen-edged
  reproof, stand dumb, ashamed, with eyes downcast,
  owning with sorrow to the fault alleged,
even so stood I; and she: 'If cause thou hast
  to grieve through hearing, do but lift thy beard
  and greater grief through looking shalt thou taste.'

Con men di resistenza si dibarba
   robusto cerro, o vero al nostral vento
   o vero a quel de la terra di Iarba,   72
ch'io non levai al suo comando il mento;
   e quando per la barba il viso chiese,
   ben conobbi il velen de l'argomento.   75
E come la mia faccia si distese,
   posarsi quelle prime creature
   da loro aspersion l'occhio comprese;   78
e le mie luci, ancor poco sicure,
   vider Beatrice volta in su la fera
   ch'è sola una persona in due nature.   81
Sotto il suo velo ed oltre la riviera
   vincer pareami più se stessa antica
   che vincer l'altre qui quand'ella c'era.   84
Di penter sì mi punse ivi l'ortica,
   che di tutt'altre cose, qual mi torse
   più nel su' amor più mi si fe' nemica.   87
Tanta riconoscenza il cor mi morse
   ch'io caddi vinto, e quale allora femmi
   salsi colei che la cagion mi porse.   90
Poi, quando il cor virtù di fuor rendemmi,
   la donna ch'io avea trovata sola
   sopra me vidi, e dicea: « Tiemmi, tiemmi ».   93
Tratto m'avea nel fiume infin la gola,
   e tirandosi me dietro, sen giva
   sovr'esso l'acqua lieve come spola.   96
Quando fui presso a la beata riva,
   Asperges me sì dolcemente udissi
   ch'io nol so rimembrar, non ch'io lo scriva.   99
La bella donna ne le braccia aprissi,
   abbracciommi la testa e mi sommerse,
   ove convenne ch'io l'acqua inghiottissi.   102
Indi mi tolse, e bagnato m'offerse
   dentro a la danza de le quattro belle;
   e ciascuna del braccio mi coperse.   105
« Noi siam qui ninfe e nel ciel siamo stelle;
   pria che Beatrice discendesse al mondo
   fummo ordinate a lei per sue ancelle.   108

With less resistance, when 'tis blowing hard
   in Europe or the land Iarbas sway'd,
   uproots itself an oak tree, stoutly rear'd,
than I my chin then lifted, as she bade;
   and when by 'beard' she asked for visage, there
   well did I note the venom in what she said.
And when my countenance was all laid bare,
   that now those first-created substances
   had ceased from scattering flowers, my sight was ware;
and then my eyes, still little at their ease,
   saw Beatrice turned tow'rds the Creature—him
   who in two natures one sole person is.
Tho' veiled and on the far side of the stream,
   to excel her former self, yea, even more
   than here she excelled all others, did she seem.
Thereat remorse with nettle-sting so sore
   my conscience pricked, that aught else which to its love
   most wrenched me, that the most did I abhor.
Into my heart such self-conviction drove
   its barb, that I fell conquered: and my last
   state she alone knows who was cause thereof.
Then, when new life from heart to eye had pass'd,
   I saw the dame I'd found uncompanied,
   above me saying: 'Hold me, hold me fast.'
Into the stream she'd drawn me save my head,
   pulling me through the water in her train,
   while, lightly as a shuttle, she o'er it sped.
Nearing the blissful snore, I heard the strain
   '*Asperges me*' in tones so passing sweet,
   my mind recalls them not, much less my pen.
Opening her arms the lovely lady knit
   them round my head, dipped me, and towed me through
   the water where I needs must swallow it,
then drew me forth and offered me, made new,
   to the four lovely dancers at the car's
   left side; and each an arm about me threw.
'Here we are nymphs and in the heaven are stars:
   ere Beatrice went down on earth to dwell,
   we were ordained, as handmaids, to be her's.

Merrenti a gli occhi suoi, ma nel giocondo
lume ch'è dentro aguzzeranno i tuoi
le tre di là, che miran più profondo».   111

Così cantando cominciaro, e poi
al petto del grifon seco menarmi,
ove Beatrice stava volta a noi.   114

Disser: « Fa che le viste non risparmi:
posto t'avem dinanzi a li smeraldi
onde Amor già ti trasse le sue armi ».   117

Mille disiri più che fiamma caldi
strinsermi gli occhi a gli occhi rilucenti
che pur sopra il grifone stavan saldi.   120

Come in lo specchio Sol, non altrimenti
la doppia fiera dentro vi raggiava
or con gli uni or con gli altri reggimenti.   123

Pensa, lettor, s'io mi maravigliava
quando vedea la cosa in sè star queta
e ne l'idolo suo si trasmutava.   126

Mentre che piena di stupore e lieta
l'anima mia gustava di quel cibo
che saziando di sè di sè asseta,   129

sè dimostrando di più alto tribo
ne gli atti, l'altre tre si fero avanti
danzando al loro angelico caribo.   132

« Volgi, Beatrice, volgi gli occhi santi »
era la sua canzone « al tuo fedele
che per vederti ha mosso passi tanti.   135

Per grazia fa noi grazia che disvele
a lui la bocca tua, sì che discerna
la seconda bellezza che tu cele ».   138

O isplendor di viva luce eterna,
chi pallido si fece sotto l'ombra
sì di Parnaso o bevve in sua cisterna,   141

che non paresse aver la mente ingombra
tentando a render te qual tu paresti,
là dove armonizzando il Ciel t'adombra,   144
quando ne l'aere aperto ti solvesti?

We'll lead thee to her eyes; but sharpen well
    thine for the light that maketh hers joyous
    shall yon three, who its deeper meaning spell.'
Me, after they had started singing thus,
    up to the Griffin's breast with them they led,
    where Beatrice was standing turned tow'rds us,
and 'Be not chary of thy looks' they said:
    'we've set thee now before the emeralds whence
    Love drew the shafts he once against thee sped.'
A thousand yearnings, past all flame intense,
    bound fast mine eyes to the relucent eyes
    fixed on the Griffin and ne'er moving thence.
As in the glass the sun, not otherwise
    the two-fold Animal within them beamed,
    with each, in turn, of both Authorities.
Think, Reader, what strange thoughts within me teemed,
    on seeing that in itself the thing stayed still,
    and in its image self-transmuting seemed.
While, filled with awe and joy unspeakable,
    my soul thus tasted of the food which they
    still pine for, who have ate of it their fill,
showing their higher status by the way
    they bore themselves, the other three came on,
    dancing to their angelic roundelay.
'Turn, Beatrice, turn thy holy eyes upon
    thy liegeman' was their ode, 'who, that he might
    behold thee, hath so many footsteps gone!
Of grace so grace us that for his delight
    thou unveil thy mouth, that he may there discern
    the second beauty thou conceal'st from sight.'
O splendour of the living Light eterne,
    who, on Parnassus, in the umbered glen
    e'er so grew pale, or drunk of its cistern,
that he in mind would sink not 'neath the strain
    of trying to paint thee as thou appearedst there
    where Heaven, concordant, adumbrates thee, when
thou didst disclose thyself in the free air?

CANTO 32

Tant'eran gli occhi miei fissi ed attenti
　　a disbramarsi la decenne sete,
　　che gli altri sensi m'eran tutti spenti. 3
Ed essi quinci e quindi avean parete
　　di non caler: così lo santo riso
　　a sè traeali con l'antica rete! 6
Quando per forza mi fu volto il viso
　　ver la sinistra mia da quelle dee,
　　perch'io udii da loro un « Troppo fiso! »; 9
e la disposizion ch'a veder èe
　　negli occhi pur testè da Sol percossi,
　　sanza la vista alquanto esser mi fèe. 12
Ma poi che al poco il viso riformossi
　　(io dico al poco per rispetto al molto
　　sensibile onde a forza mi rimossi), 15
vidi sul braccio destro esser rivolto
　　lo glorioso esercito, e tornarsi
　　col Sole e con le sette fiamme al volto. 18
Come sotto li scudi per salvarsi
　　volgesi schiera, e sè gira col segno
　　prima che possa tutta in sè mutarsi, 21
quella milizia del celeste regno
　　che precedeva, tutta trapassonne
　　pria che piegasse il carro il primo legno. 24
Indi a le rote si tornar le donne,
　　e il grifon mosse il benedetto carco
　　sì che però nulla penna crollonne. 27
La bella donna che mi trasse al varco
　　e Stazio e io seguitavam la rota
　　che fè l'orbita sua con minor arco. 30
Sì passeggiando l'alta selva vota,
　　colpa di quella che al serpente crese,
　　temprava i passi un'angelica nota. 33
Forse in tre voli tanto spazio prese
　　disfrenata saetta quanto eramo
　　rimossi, quando Beatrice scese. 36

CANTO 32

So firmly fixed my eyes were and so full
    of eagerness to slake their ten years' thirst,
    that every other sense was rendered null.
The holy smile into the toils that erst
    had snared them still so drew them as to raise
    round them a wall of unconcern, dispers'd
only when leftward by those goddesses
    I was compelled to turn aside my face,
    hearing them murmur a 'Too fixed thy gaze!';
and that condition for seeing which takes place
    in eyes but just now smitten by the Sun
    left me without sight for a little space.
But when my sight re-shaped itself to con
    of sensibles the *less* bright (less, I mean,
    than the great one whence I'd perforce withdrawn),
the glorious army now of me was seen
    its steps retracing, having rightward wheel'd,
    fronting the Sun and sevenfold candle-sheen.
As for its safety, each man 'neath his shield,
    a squadron wheels, its colours on beyond,
    ere it can all change front throughout the field,
those soldiers of the heavenly kingdom wound
    their way on past us with their van, before
    its pole as yet had turned the chariot round.
Then to the wheels the ladies went once more:
    the Griffin—but in such wise that he shook
    not one plume—moved the blessèd charge he bore.
The fair dame who had towed me across the brook
    followed, with Statius and myself, the wheel
    that traced the smaller arc of the course it took.
Thus threading the tall forest, empty still—
    her fault who in the snake had credit shown—
    we timed our steps to the angels' canticle.
Maybe as far as, loosened thrice, had flown
    an arrow from the bow-string, had we now
    moved on from there, when Beatrice stepped down.

497

Io sentii mormorare a tutti *Adamo*;
   poi cerchiaro una pianta dispogliata
   di foglie e d'altra fronda in ciascun ramo.   39
La chioma sua, che tanto si dilata
   più quanto più è sù, fora da gl'Indi
   nei boschi lor per altezza ammirata.   42
« Beato sei, grifon, che non discindi
   col becco d'esto legno dolce al gusto,
   poscia che mal si torce il ventre quindi ».   45
Così dintorno a l'arbore robusto
   gridaro gli altri; e l'animal binato:
   « Sì si conserva il seme d'ogni giusto ».   48
E volto al temo ch'egli avea tirato
   trasselo al piè de la vedova frasca,
   e quel di lei a lei lasciò legato.   51
Come le nostre piante quando casca
   giù la gran luce mischiata con quella
   che raggia dietro a la celeste lasca   54
turgide fansi, e poi si rinnovella
   di suo color ciascuna pria che il Sole
   giunga li suoi corsier sott'altra stella,   57
men che di rose e più che di viole
   colori aprendo, s'innovò la pianta
   che prima avea le ramora sì sole.   60
Io non l'intesi, nè qui non si canta
   l'inno che quella gente allor cantaro;
   nè la nota soffersi tutta quanta.   63
S'io potessi ritrar come assonnaro
   gli occhi spietati udendo di Siringa,
   gli occhi a cui più vegghiar costò sì caro,   66
come pintor che con esemplo pinga
   disegnerei com'io m'addormentai;
   ma qual vuol sia che l'assonnar ben finga.   69
Però trascorro a quando mi svegliai,
   e dico che un splendor mi squarciò il velo
   del sonno, e un chiamar: « Surgi, che fai? »   72
Quali a veder dei fioretti del melo
   che del suo pomo gli angeli fa ghiotti
   e perpetue nozze fa nel cielo,   75

'Adam' I heard by each one murmured low;
   then round a tree they gathered, which was bare
   of blossom and aught else leafy in every bough.
Its branches, which the loftier they were
   spread wider, would to see them rise so high
   have made the Indian in his forest stare.
'Blest art thou, Griffin, that thou nought with thy
   beak dost tear off from this sweet-tasting wood,
   in that the belly is ill racked thereby.'
Thus cried they, as round the stalwart tree they stood;
   and the two-natured Animal replied:
   'So of all justice is the seed kept good.'
And, turning to the pole he'd drawn, beside
   and 'neath the widowed branch he dragged it; then
   to this by means of this he left it tied.
As in our world the trees start budding when
   the great light downward falls in combination
   with that which beams in the heavenly Roach's train,
and each is then engaged in renovation
   of its own colour, ere the Sun shall yoke
   his coursers 'neath another constellation,
not rose, not violet, but a tint that spoke
   somewhat of both disclosing, the whole tree,
   erstwhile so bare, into new life outbroke.
I understood it not, nor may the glee
   which then that people sang be chanted here,
   nor bore I to the end its melody.
Could I portray how drowsy, when the ear
   heard tell of Syrinx, grew the ruthless eyes,
   eyes which too long a vigil cost so dear,
as one whose painting with his model vies,
   I'd draw how I fell asleep; but let him make
   sure he can well limn drowsing, whoever tries.
Therefore I pass to when my slumber brake;
   I say, then, that a splendour rent the veil
   of sleep, and a loud crying: 'What dost thou? Wake!'
As Peter, James and John for a brief spell
   were led to view some flowerets of the tree
   whose apples, by the angels craved, regale

Pietro, Giovanni e Giacomo condotti
  e vinti, ritornaro a la parola
  da la qual furon maggior sonni rotti,   78
e videro scemata loro scuola
  così di Moisè come d'Elia,
  ed al maestro suo cangiata stola;   81
tal torna' io, e vidi quella pia
  sovra me starsi, che conducitrice
  fu de' miei passi lungo il fiume pria.   84
E tutto in dubbio dissi: « Ov'è Beatrice? »
  Ond'ella: « Vedi lei, sotto la fronda
  nova, sedere in su la sua radice;   87
vedi la compagnia che la circonda;
  gli altri dopo il grifon sen vanno suso
  con più dolce canzone e più profonda ».   90
E se più fu lo suo parlar diffuso
  non so, però che già ne gli occhi m'era
  quella che ad altro intender m'avea chiuso.   93
Sola sedeasi in su la terra vera,
  come guardia lasciata lì del plaustro
  che legar vidi a la biforme fiera.   96
In cerchio le facevan di sè claustro
  le sette ninfe con quei lumi in mano
  che son sicuri d'Aquilone e d'Austro.   99
« Qui sarai tu poco tempo silvano,
  e sarai meco sanza fine cive
  di quella Roma onde Cristo è romano.   102
Però, in pro del mondo che mal vive,
  al carro tieni or gli occhi, e quel che vedi,
  ritornato di là fa che tu scrive ».   105
Così Beatrice; e io che tutto ai piedi
  de' suoi comandamenti era divoto,
  la mente e gli occhi ov'ella volle diedi.   108
Non scese mai con sì veloce moto
  foco di spessa nube quando piove
  da quel confine che più va remoto,   111
com'io vidi calar l'uccel di Giove
  per l'alber giù, rompendo de la scorza,
  non che dei fiori e de le foglie nove;   114

God's wedding-guests in Heaven perpetually;
 and as, when tranced, they came to at the word
 by which far deeper sleeps were made to flee,
and saw their school to its former size restor'd
 by being bereft alike of Moses and
 Elias, and changed the garment of its Lord;
so came I to myself, and o'er me stand
 saw the compassionate lady who ere this
 had led my steps along the river-strand.
I, all in doubt, said: 'Where is Beatrice?'
 and she: 'Look yonder, seated on its root
 under the tree's new foliage, there she is.
Those that surround her let thy gaze salute;
 the rest, pursuing the Griffin, mount on high
 with sweeter odes that deeper meanings suit.'
And whether more at large she spake do I
 not know, because that being I had espied
 who closed my mind to aught else when she was by.
On the bare ground she sat with none beside,
 as if left there to guard the wain I'd seen
 by the two-formed wild-beast securely tied.
The seven nymphs stood round and closed her in,
 holding those lights, of which, be it Auster's, be
 it Aquilo's, no blast can quench the sheen.
'Brief while a woodman here, and endlessly
 a citizen of that same Rome of which
 the Christ is Roman shalt thou be with me.
Therefore, that thou mayst profit by thy speech
 an ill world, watch the car; and all thou see'st,
 when thou art back there, by thy writings teach.'
So Beatrice: and I, who to the least
 of her commands stooped all devoted, sight
 and mind as bidd'n directing, nothing miss'd.
Never descended with so swift a flight
 fire from a dense cloud, when the skies above
 pour down the rain from heav'ns remotest height,
as I saw downward swoop the bird of Jove
 right through the tree, rending some bark away,
 not the flowers only and new leaves thereof.

e ferì il carro di tutta sua forza,
  ond'ei piegò come nave in fortuna
  vinta da l'onda, or da poggia or da orza.   117
Poscia vidi avventarsi ne la cuna
  del triunfal veicolo una volpe
  che d'ogni pasto buon parea digiuna.   120
Ma riprendendo lei di laide colpe
  la donna mia la volse in tanta futa
  quanta sofferser l'ossa sanza polpe.   123
Poscia per indi ond'era pria venuta
  l'aquila vidi scender giù ne l'arca
  del carro e lasciar lei di sè pennuta;   126
e qual esce di cor che si rammarca
  tal voce uscì del cielo, e cotal disse:
  « O navicella mia, com mal sei carca! »   129
Poi parve a me che la terra s'aprisse
  tr'ambo le rote, e vidi uscirne un drago
  che per lo carro sù la coda fisse;   132
e come vespa che ritragge l'ago,
  a sè traendo la coda maligna
  trasse del fondo, e gissen vago vago.   135
Quel che rimase, come da gramigna
  vivace terra, de la piuma, offerta
  forse con intenzion sana e benigna,   138
si ricoperse, e funne ricoperta
  e l'una e l'altra rota e il temo, in tanto
  che più tiene un sospir la bocca aperta.   141
Trasformato così, 'l dificio santo
  mise fuor teste per le parti sue,
  tre sovra il temo e una in ciascun canto.   144
Le prime eran cornute come bue,
  ma le quattro un sol corno avean per fronte:
  simile mostro visto ancor non fue.   147
Sicura quasi rocca in alto monte,
  seder sovr'esso una puttana sciolta
  m'apparve, con le ciglia intorno pronte.   150
E come perchè non li fosse tolta,
  vidi di costa a lei dritto un gigante;
  e baciavansi insieme alcuna volta.   153

He smote the car full force and made it sway,
  as in a storm a ship goes staggering
  now windward, leeward now, the wild waves' prey.
Then I beheld into the cradle spring
  of the triumphal car a fox, so lean
  she seemed for lack of good food famishing.
But, chiding her for many a loathsome sin,
  my lady turned her to as swift a flight
  as aught could bear that was but bones and skin.
Anon, from there whence first he'd come in sight,
  I saw the eagle stoop at the waggon's ark
  and leave it with his own plumes richly dight.
And, such as issues from a bosom stark
  with grief, a voice thuswise from heaven fell:
  'How ill thou'rt laden, O my little barque!'
The earth between the wheels—I saw it well—
  then opened, and a dragon emerged and through
  the chariot's floor thrust up his deadly tail;
and, as a wasp her sting, he then withdrew
  into himself his tail and partly rent
  the floor away, and off at random flew.
That which remained, like ground alive with bent,
  with the eagle's plumage—offered, one would fain
  believe, with honest and benign intent—
re-clothed itself: and clothed therewith again
  were both wheels and the pole: so quick 'twas done,
  a sigh to pass the lips had longer ta'en.
The holy fabric, thus transformed, upon
  its several parts protruded heads, to wit,
  three on the pole, and at each corner one.
Such horns had those as well might oxen fit,
  these each but one horn on the forehead bore:
  never was monster seen resembling it.
Firm as a mountain-citadel before
  me sat thereon, with eyes alert to glance
  in all directions, a dishevelled whore.
As if on guard against their severance,
  I saw a giant standing at her side,
  and oft they kissed in shameful dalliance.

Ma perchè l'occhio cupido e vagante
  a me rivolse, quel feroce drudo
  la flagellò dal capo infin le piante.   156
Poi di sospetto pieno e d'ira crudo,
  disciolse il mostro e trassel per la selva
  tanto, che sol di lei mi fece scudo   159
a la puttana ed a la nova belva.

CANTO 33

DEUS, venerunt gentes, alternando
  or tre or quattro dolce salmodia,
  le donne incominciaro, e lacrimando;   3
e Beatrice, sospirosa e pia,
  quelle ascoltava sì fatta, che poco
  più alla croce si cambiò Maria.   6
Ma poi che l'altre vergini dier loco
  a lei di dir, levata dritta in piè,
  rispose, colorata come fuoco: 9
Modicum et non videbitis me;
  et iterum, sorelle mie dilette,
  modicum et vos videbitis me.   12
Poi le si mise innanzi tutte e sette,
  e dopo sè, solo accennando, mosse
  me e la donna e il savio che ristette.   15
Così sen giva, e non credo che fosse
  lo decimo suo passo in terra posto,
  quando con gli occhi gli occhi mi percosse;   18
e con tranquillo aspetto « Vien più tosto »
  mi disse « tanto che s'io parlo teco
  ad ascoltarmi tu sie ben disposto ».   21
Sì com'io fui, com'io doveva, seco,
  dissemi: « Frate, perchè non t'attenti
  a domandarmi omai, venendo meco? »   24

But when with lustful, roving looks she eyed
  and ogled me, that savage paramour
  from head to heel his lash upon her plied.
Next, wild with rage and jealousy, he tore
  the monster loose and through the trees then drew't
  so far, that they alone sufficed him for
shielding from me the whore and the strange brute.

CANTO 33

'*DEUS, venerunt gentes*' thus, now three,
  now four, the ladies raised in antiphon,
  weeping the while, their dulcet psalmody;
and as she listened, Beatrice made moan
  and looked so wondrous sad, that at the rood
  scarce greater change in Mary's face was shown.
But when the other virgins made as would
  they yield her place that she might have her say,
  she rose full height and answered, fiery-hued:
'*Modicum, et non videbitis me*;
  et iterum, O ye my sisters dear,
  modicum, et vos videbitis me.'
Then set she all the seven in front of her,
  and made the lady and me by a mere sign
  with him, the sage still left, to close the rear.
Thus she advanced, nor had she, I opine,
  planted ten steps upon the ground she paced,
  before she turned her eyes to strike on mine;
and with a calm demeanour: 'Make more haste,'
  she enjoined me, 'so that, if I speak with thee,
  thou hear me better by being better placed.'
Once by her side, as duty bade me be,
  she asked me: 'Brother, why attemptest thou
  no questions now thou walkest here with me?'

Come a color che troppo reverenti
   dinanzi a' suoi maggior parlando sono,
   che non traggon la voce viva ai denti,   27
avvenne a me, che sanza intero suono
   incominciai: « Madonna, mia bisogna
   voi conoscete, e ciò che ad essa è buono ».   30
Ed ella a me: « Da tema e da vergogna
   voglio che tu omai ti disviluppe,
   sì che non parli più com'uom che sogna.   33
Sappi che il vaso che il serpente ruppe
   fu e non è, ma chi n'ha colpa creda
   che vendetta di Dio non teme suppe.   36
Non sarà tutto tempo sanza reda
   l'aquila che lasciò le penne al carro,
   per che divenne mostro e poscia preda;   39
ch'io veggio certamente, e però il narro,
   a darne tempo già stelle propinque,
   secure d'ogni intoppo e d'ogni sbarro,   42
nel quale un cinquecento dieci e cinque
   messo di Dio, anciderà la fuia
   con quel gigante che con lei delinque.   45
E forse che la mia narrazion, buia
   qual Temi o Sfinge, men ti persuade
   perchè a lor modo l'intelletto attuia;   48
ma tosto fien li fatti le Naiade
   che solveranno quest'enigma forte,
   sanza danno di pecore o di biade.   51
Tu nota, e sì come da me son porte
   così queste parole segna ai vivi
   del vivere ch'è un correre alla morte.   54
E aggi a mente, quanto tu le scrivi,
   di non celar quale hai vista la pianta
   ch'è or due volte dirubata quivi.   57
Qualunque ruba quella o quella schianta,
   con bestemmia di fatto offende Dio,
   che solo a l'uso suo la creò santa.   60
Per morder quella, in pena ed in disio
   cinquemil'anni e più l'anima prima
   bramò colui che il morso in sè punio.   63

As haps with those who excess of reverence show
  in speech before their betters, so that o'er
  the teeth the voice drags, and its tones are low,
such case was mine, and with imperfect power
  of utterance I began: 'Lady, my need
  you know yourself, and what is good therefór.'
'Alike of shame and fear,' did she proceed,
  'I'd have thee, from now on, strip off the cloak,
  and speak no more as one whom dreams mislead.
Know that the vessel which the serpent broke
  was, and is not: nor let the culprit say
  sops will avert the heaven's avenging stroke.
Not for all time without an heir shall stay
  the eagle who left his plumage on the car,
  whereby 'twas made a monster, then a prey.
For I discern in sooth, and hence declare,
  stars that to mark a time shall soon arrive,
  secure from every hindrance, every bar,
a time when a "five hundred, ten and five",
  sent down from God, shall kill the robber dame,
  nor leave that giant who sinned with her alive.
Maybe my utterance, dark as that which came
  from Themis and the Sphinx, persuades thee less,
  dimming thy mind as minds were dimmed by them;
but, before long, the facts themselves in place
  of Naiads will solve this knotty riddle, nor scaith
  to harvest do nor cause the sheep distress.
Take note, and e'en as each word issueth
  from me, pass thou it on to those who live
  the life which is a racing unto death.
And, when thou writest, strict attention give
  to hiding not how stands it with the tree,
  which here, twice o'er, thou hast seen the spoiler reave.
Whoever robs that plant or rends it, he
  blasphemes in act against God, who created
  it holy, for his own sole use to be.
For biting of 't, in pain and longing waited
  five thousand years and more the soul, first-made,
  for Him whose self that same bite expiated.

Dorme l'ingegno tuo se non estima
   per singular cagione esser eccelsa
   lei tanto, e sì travolta ne la cima.   66
E se stati non fossero acqua d'Elsa
   li pensier vani intorno a la tua mente,
   e il piacer loro un Piramo a la gelsa,   69
per tante circostanze solamente
   la giustizia di Dio ne l'interdetto
   conosceresti a l'arbor moralmente.   72
Ma perch'io veggio te ne l'intelletto
   fatto di pietra e, impetrato, tinto,
   sì che t'abbaglia il lume del mio detto,   75
voglio anco, e se non scritto almen dipinto,
   che il te ne porti dentro a te, per quello
   che si reca il bordon di palma cinto».   78
E io: « Sì come cera da suggello,
   che la figura impressa non trasmuta,
   segnato è or da voi lo mio cervello.   81
Ma perchè tanto sovra mia veduta
   vostra parola disiata vola,
   che più la perde quanto più s'aiuta?»   84
« Perchè conoschi » disse « quella scuola
   ch'ai seguitata, e veggi sua dottrina
   come può seguitar la mia parola;   87
e veggi vostra via da la divina
   distar cotanto, quanto si discorda
   da Terra il ciel che più alto festina ».   90
Ond'io risposi lei: « Non mi ricorda
   ch'io straniassi me già mai da voi
   nè honne coscienza che rimorda ».   93
« E se tu ricordar non te ne puoi »
   sorridendo rispose, « or ti rammenta
   come bevesti di Letè ancoi;   96
e se dal fummo foco s'argomenta,
   cotesta oblivion chiaro conclude
   colpa ne la tua voglia altrove attenta.   99
Veramente oramai saranno nude
   le mie parole, quanto converrassi
   quelle scovrire a la tua vista rude ».   102

Thy wits sleep, if to them still undisplay'd
   the special reason be for which so high
   it rises and its top is so dispread.
And if, like Elsa's water, did not lie
   vain thoughts about thy mind, and their delight
   were not a Pyramus to the mulberry,
from all these incidents alone how right
   God's justice was in ruling none should touch
   the tree were plain now to thy moral sight.
But since in intellect I see thee such
   as stone is and, thus stony, dyed withal,
   so that my discourse dazzles thee o'ermuch,
I yet would have thee bear it hence, tho' all
   unwritten, at least pictured in thy breast,
   as palmer's staff brings home its coronal.'
And I: 'Like wax whereon unchanged doth rest
   the figure by a signet stamped, my brain
   has now by you been durably impress'd.
But wherefore fly so high above my ken
   the wishéd words you utter, that the more
   I seek their aid the more I find it vain?'
'That thou mayst know,' she said, 'the kind of lore
   thy school pursued, and see its doctrine—how,
   pursuing my words, it lacks the power to soar;
and see, too, that the way ye mortals go
   is as far off from God's, as is disjoin'd
   the heav'n that highest speeds, from Earth below.'
I answered her: 'It comes not to my mind
   that I did e'er estrange myself from you:
   no guilty sense thereof do I in me find.'
'That thou canst not remember it, is true:
   but call to mind,' such was her smiling word,
   'the draught thy lips today from Lethe drew;
and as from smoke a fire may be inferr'd,
   so this forgetfulness of thine, 'tis clear,
   proves that thy will, in turning elsewhere, err'd.
But verily my words shall be stripped bare
   henceforward, in so far as it be meet
   to unveil their charms to such a raw-eyed seer.'

E più corusco e con più lenti passi
    teneva il Sole il cerchio di merigge,
    che qua e là come gli aspetti fassi,   105
quando s'affisser, sì come s'affigge
    chi va dinanzi a gente per iscorta
    se trova novitate in sue vestigge,   108
le sette donne al fin d'un'ombra smorta,
    qual sotto foglie verdi e rami nigri
    sovra suoi freddi rivi l'Alpe porta.   111
Dinanzi ad esse Eufratès e Tigri
    veder mi parve uscir d'una fontana,
    e quasi amici dipartirsi pigri.   114
« O luce, o gloria de la gente umana,
    che acqua è questa che qui si dispiega
    da un principio, e sè da sè lontana?»   117
Per cotal priego detto mi fu: « Prega
    Matelda che il ti dica». E qui rispose
    come fa chi da colpa si dislega   120
la bella donna: « Questo ed altre cose
    dette li son per me; e son sicura
    che l'acqua di Letè non gliel nascose».   123
E Beatrice: « Forse maggior cura,
    che spesse volte la memoria priva,
    fatt'ha la mente sua ne gli occhi oscura.   126
Ma vedi Eunoè che là diriva:
    menalo ad esso, e, come tu sei usa,
    la tramortita sua virtù ravviva».   129
Come anima gentil, che non fa scusa,
    ma fa sua voglia de la voglia altrui,
    tosto che è per segno fuor dischiusa,   132
così, poi che da essa preso fui,
    la bella donna mossesi, ed a Stazio
    donnescamente disse: « Vien con lui ».   135
S'io avessi, lettor, più lungo spazio
    da scrivere, io pur cantere' in parte
    lo dolce ber che mai non m'avria sazio;   138
ma perchè piene son tutte le carte
    ordite a questa cantica seconda
    non mi lascia più ir lo fren de l'arte.   141

With slower steps and with more radiant heat
  the sun now held the meridian ring, which changes
  its place, as here or there one looks at it,
when halted, just as halts a man who ranges
  ahead of people he escorts, to urge
  their notice, if he comes on aught that strange is,
the seven dames at a dim shadow's verge,
  such as, 'neath black boughs and green undergrowth,
  the Alp casts, over where its cold brooks surge.
Before them Tigris and Euphrates both,
  meseemed, were welling from a single vein
  like parting friends, who yet to part seem loth.
'O light, O glory of the race of men,
  what may this water be that breaks its way
  from one source and divides itself in twain?'
To this my prayer there came the answer: 'Pray
  Matilda that she tell thee'; straight replied
  like one, who, blamed, can well the charge gainsay,
the lovely lady: 'This and much beside
  he *has* been told by me: and I could swear
  it was not hidd'n from him by Lethe's tide.'
And Beatrice: 'Perhaps some greater care,
  which oft-times takes away the memory,
  has in his mental vision caused a blur.
But Eúnoë, look, is gushing here close by:
  lead him to *it* and as thy custom is,
  revive his powers upon the point to die.'
Like as a gentle soul who makes no pleas,
  but wills another's will, so it doth seem,
  as soon as but a hint thereof it sees;
so, after she had gripped me, to the stream
  the beauteous lady moved, with queenly grace
  saying to Statius: 'Come thou, too, with him.'
If only, Reader, I had ampler space
  for writing, I would sing at least in part
  that sweet which, quaffed, one thirsts for none the less;
but, full being all the sheets which at the start
  were laid in warp for this my second Lay,
  I'm checked here by the bridle of my art.

Io ritornai da la santissim'onda
  rifatto sì come piante novelle
  rinnovellate di novella fronda,   144
puro e disposto a salire a le stelle.

From that most holy wave I came away
 refashioned, like new plants no blemish mars,
 made new again with new leaves: pure as they,
and ready now for mounting to the stars.

PARADISE

*

'*They live aye in one beauty that is brighter sevenfold, and sheener than the sun; and ever in one strength, to do without labour all that they will; and ever more in one stay, in all that ever good is, without waning, without anything that may harm or ail, in all that ever is soft and sweet. Their life is the sight of God, and the knowledge of God, as our Lord said: "that is", said he, "eternal life, to see and know the sooth God, and Him whom He hath sent, Jesus Christ our Lord, for our redemption". Therefore they are like him, in the same beauty that he is, for they see him as he is, face to face. They are so wise that they know all God's redes, and his runes, and his dooms that derne be, and deeper than any sea-dingle.*'

*

PARADISO

CANTO 1

La gloria di colui che tutto move
  per l'Universo penetra, e risplende
  in una parte più e meno altrove.   3
Nel ciel, che più de la sua luce prende,
  fu'io, e vidi cose che ridire
  nè sa nè può qual di là sù discende;   6
perchè appressando sè al suo disire
  nostro intelletto si profonda tanto
  che dietro la memoria non può ire.   9
Veramente, quant'io del regno santo
  ne la mia mente potei far tesoro
  sarà ora materia del mio canto.   12
O buon Apollo, a l'ultimo lavoro
  fammi del tuo valor sì fatto vaso
  come dimandi a dar l'amato alloro.   15
Infino a qui l'un giogo di Parnaso
  assai mi fu, ma or con amendue
  m'è uopo entrar ne l'aringo rimaso.   18
Entra nel petto mio, e spira tue
  sì come quando Marsia traesti
  da la vagina de le membra sue.   21
O divina virtù, se mi ti presti
  tanto che l'ombra del beato regno
  segnata nel mio capo io manifesti,   24
venir vedraimi al tuo diletto legno
  e coronarmi allor di quelle foglie
  che la materia e tu mi farai degno.   27
Sì rade volte, padre, se ne coglie
  per trionfare o Cesare o poeta,
  colpa e vergogna de l'umane voglie,   30

PARADISE

CANTO 1

His glory, in whose being all things move,
　　pervades Creation and, here more there less
　　resplendent, shines in every part thereof.
Within the heaven his brightest beams caress
　　was I, and things beheld which none returning
　　to earth hath power or knowledge to express;
because, when near the object of its yearning,
　　our understanding is for truths made strong,
　　which memory is too feeble for relearning.
Yet of the realm that saints and angels throng
　　so much as I could treasure up in mind
　　shall now be made the matter of my song.
Apollo, to my crowning task be kind;
　　make me thy chosen vessel, round whose brow
　　thy darling bay might fitly be entwined.
So far with one Parnassian peak hast thou
　　met all my needs: but I require the twain,
　　to dare the arena that awaits me now.
Enter my breast in such a mood as when
　　thou from the scabbard of his limbs didst tear
　　forth Marsyas; breathe in me that matchless strain.
O power divine, let me but so far share
　　thyself, that I, dim memory though it be,
　　the blesséd kingdom may in words declare,
and thou shalt see me come to thy loved tree
　　and crown myself with laurel, then indeed
　　made fit to wear it by my theme and thee.
So seldom, Father, has it been for meed
　　of bard or Caesar's triumph culled of late
　　(man's fault, who to his shame pays it no heed),

517

che parturir letizia in su la lieta
  delfica deità dovria la fronda
  peneia, quando alcun di sè asseta.   33
Poca favilla gran fiamma seconda:
  forse di retro a me con miglior voci
  si pregherà perchè Cirra risponda.   36
Surge ai mortali per diverse foci
  la lucerna del mondo, ma da quella
  che quattro cerchi giugne con tre croci   39
con miglior corso e con migliore stella
  esce congiunta, e la mondana cera
  più a suo modo tempera e suggella.   42
Fatto avea di là mane e di qua sera
  tal foce, e quasi tutto era là bianco
  quello emispero, e l'altra parte nera,   45
quando Beatrice in sul sinistro fianco
  vidi rivolta a riguardar nel Sole:
  aquila sì non li s'affisse unquanco.   48
E sì come secondo raggio suole
  uscir del primo e risalire in suso,
  pur come pellegrin che tornar vuole,   51
così de l'atto suo, per gli occhi infuso
  ne l'imagine mia, il mio si fece;
  e fissi gli occhi al Sole oltre nostr'uso.   54
Molto è licito là, che qui non lece
  a le nostre virtù, mercè del loco
  fatto per proprio de l'umana spece.   57
Io nol soffersi molto, nè sì poco
  ch'io nol vedessi sfavillar dintorno
  qual ferro che bogliente esce dal foco;   60
e di subito parve giorno a giorno
  essere aggiunto, come quei che puote
  avesse il ciel d'un altro Sole adorno.   63
Beatrice tutta ne l'eterne rote
  fissa con gli occhi stava, ed io in lei
  le luci fissi, di là su rimote.   66
Nel suo aspetto tal dentro mi fei
  qual si fe' Glauco nel gustar de l'erba
  che il fe' consorto in mar de gli altri Dei.   69

that the Peneian leaves should generate
  gladness in the glad Delphic deity,
  when they, in any, a thirst for them create.
From tiny spark a flame may leap full high:
  haply some bard, praying in worthier wise,
  may after me from Cirrha win reply.
Through divers openings dawns on mortal eyes
  the lamp of the world; but that we see display
  four circles with three crosses joined, supplies
his beams with happier course, wherein, with ray
  of happier star conjoined, he mouldeth fair
  the mundane wax more after his own way.
This point, or near it, had caused morning there,
  here eve: and all of half the heavens were white
  on that side, and on this all darkling were,
when I saw Beatrice, with visage bright
  turned leftward, gazing full upon the Sun:
  eagle thereon so never fixed his sight.
As from the first the second ray will run
  and upward re-ascend, like traveller fain
  to turn home, when his outward voyage is done,
so to her gesture, through the eyesight ta'en
  into my fancy, was my own inclined,
  and I gazed Sunward, past the wont of men.
There much is granted, which our senses find
  denied them here, through virtue of the spot
  fashioned of old expressly for mankind.
So long I gazed—tho' long I bore it not—
  as to perceive him sparkling all around,
  like iron which from the furnace flows white-hot;
and suddenly the light of day I found
  increased twofold, as though the Omnipotent
  the heaven with a second Sun had crown'd.
Beatrice stood with gaze still wholly bent
  upon the eternal wheels; and I on her
  fixed mine, withdrawn now from the firmament.
So gazing did I feel in me the stir
  that Glaucus felt, when he consumed of yore
  the grass which made him as the sea-gods were.

Trasumanar significar *per verba*
  non si porìa; però l'esempio basti
  a cui esperienza grazia serba.   72
S'io era sol di me quel che creasti
  novellamente, amor che il ciel governi,
  tu il sai, che col tuo lume mi levasti.   75
Quando la rota che tu sempiterni
  desiderato, a sè mi fece atteso
  con l'armonia che temperi e discerni,   78
parvemi tanto allor del cielo acceso
  de la fiamma del Sol, che pioggia o fiume
  lago non fece mai tanto disteso.   81
La novità del suono e il grande lume
  di lor cagion m'accesero un disio
  mai non sentito di cotanto acume;   84
ond'ella, che vedea me sì com'io,
  a quietarmi l'animo commosso
  pria ch'io a dimandar la bocca aprìo,   87
e cominciò: « Tu stesso ti fai grosso
  col falso imaginar, sì che non vedi
  ciò che vedresti se l'avessi scosso.   90
Tu non se' in Terra, sì come tu credi;
  ma folgore fuggendo il proprio sito
  non corse come tu che ad esso riedi ».   93
S'io fui del primo dubbio disvestito
  per le sorrise parolette brevi,
  dentro ad un nuovo più fui irretito;   96
e dissi: « Già contento requievi
  di grande ammirazion, ma ora ammiro
  com'io trascenda questi corpi lievi ».   99
Ond'ella, appresso d'un pio sospiro,
  gli occhi drizzò ver me con quel sembiante
  che madre fa sovra figlio deliro,   102
e cominciò: « Le cose tutte quante
  hanno ordine tra loro, e questo è forma
  che l'Universo a Dio fa simigliante.   105
Qui veggion l'alte creature l'orma
  de l'eterno valore, il quale è fine
  al quale è fatta la toccata norma.   108

Transhuman change none hath *per verba* power
   to express; so let the example satisfy
   him for whom grace the experience holds in store.
O Love, the lord of heaven, if nought was I
   of self save what in man thou new-createst
   thou know'st, whose light it was that raised me on high.
Whenas the wheel which thou for aye rotatest
   by being desired thereof, had charmed my ear
   with tones which thou, its tuner, modulatest,
I saw such vast fields of the atmosphere
   lit by the Solar flame, that neither flood
   nor deluge ever formed so wide a mere.
The unwonted sound, the light's great magnitude
   kindled in me such ardour to cognise
   their cause, as ne'er till then had fired my blood.
Then she, who saw me as with my own eyes,
   opened her mouth to calm my troubled mind,
   ere I to frame a question, and thuswise
began: 'Thine own false fancies make thee blind;
   hence unperceived are things thou wouldst perceive,
   hadst thou but left thy vain conceits behind.
Thou'rt not on Earth still, as thou dost believe;
   but lightning, fleeing its proper home, ne'er tore
   as thou art thine now rushing to retrieve.'
Stript of my first doubt by the dulcet lore
   that, smilingly, these few brief words supplied,
   I in a new one was enmeshed the more;
and said: 'Awhile I rested, satisfied,
   from my great wonder; but I wonder yet,
   how up through these light bodies I can glide.'
My question with a pitying sigh she met,
   then eyed me with a mother's anxious care
   for child whose brain delirious dreams beset,
and began thuswise: 'All things whatsoe'er
   have order among themselves, and this indeed
   is form, which makes the World God's image bear.
Herein do the higher beings the impress read
   of that eternal Worth, which is the end
   whereto the aforesaid rule has been decreed.

Ne l'ordine ch'io dico sono accline
  tutte nature per diverse sorti
  più al principio loro e men vicine;   111
onde si movono a diversi porti
  per lo gran mar de l'essere, e ciascuna
  con istinto a lei dato che la porti.   114
Questo ne porta il foco in ver la Luna,
  questo nei cor mortali è permotore,
  questo la Terra in sè stringe e aduna.   117
Nè pur le creature che son fuore
  d'intelligenza quest'arco saetta,
  ma quelle ch'hanno intelletto ed amore.   120
La provedenza che cotanto assetta,
  del suo lume fa il ciel sempre quieto
  nel qual si volge quel ch'ha maggior fretta;   123
ed ora lì come a sito decreto
  cen porta la virtù di quella corda
  che ciò che scocca drizza in segno lieto.   126
Vero è che come forma non s'accorda
  molte fiate a l'intenzion de l'arte,
  perchè a risponder la materia è sorda,   129
così da questo corso si diparte
  talor la creatura, ch'ha potere
  di piegar, così pinta, in altra parte;   132
e sì come veder si può cadere
  foco da nube, sì l'impeto primo,
  s'a Terra è torto da falso piacere.   135
Non dei più ammirar, se bene estimo,
  lo tuo salir, se non come d'un rivo
  se d'alto monte scende giuso ad imo.   138
Maraviglia sarebbe in te, se, privo
  d'impedimento, giù ti fossi assiso,
  come a terra quiete in foco vivo ».   141
Quinci rivolse inver lo cielo il viso.

In this same order ranked, all natures bend
   their several ways, through divers lots, as near
   and farther from the source whence all descend;
thus onward unto divers ports they steer
   through the great sea of being, each impell'd
   by instinct, given to make it persevere.
This tow'rd the Moon keeps blazing fire upheld;
   this is in mortal hearts what makes them move;
   this doth the Earth into one structure weld:
nor only creatures void of reason prove
   this bow's impelling force, but every soul
   that is endowed with intellect and love.
The providence, which rules this ordered whole,
   keeps making ever tranquil with its light
   the heaven wherein the swiftest sphere doth roll;
and thither, as to pre-appointed site,
   that bow-string which doth all its arrows shoot
   at happy mark, now speeds us by its might.
'Tis true that, as a form will oft ill-suit
   with the result which art would fain effect,
   the stuff being deaf, hence unresponsive to it,
so from this course the creature may deflect
   itself at whiles; for, though thus urged on high,
   its power to swerve aside remains uncheck'd
(even as fire may oft be seen to fly
   down from a cloud), should the first impulse bring
   it Earthward, by false pleasure wrenched awry.
If I deem right, thou shouldst be wondering
   no more at thine ascent, than at a rill
   for rushing downward from its mountain-spring.
Marvel it were in thee, if, with a will
   unhindered, thou hadst hugged a lower plane,
   as in quick fire on earth, if it kept still.'
Therewith she turned her face to heaven again.

CANTO 2

O voi che siete in piccioletta barca,
desiderosi d'ascoltar, seguìti
dietro al mio legno che cantando varca,   3
tornate a riveder li vostri liti,
non vi mettete in pelago, chè forse
perdendo me rimarreste smarriti.   6
L'acqua ch'io prendo già mai non si corse:
Minerva spira e conducemi Apollo
e nove Muse mi dimostran l'Orse.   9
Voi altri pochi che drizzaste il collo
per tempo al pan de gli angeli, del quale
vivesi qui, ma non sen vien satollo,   12
metter potete ben per l'alto sale
vostro navigio, servando mio solco
dinanzi a l'acqua che ritorna eguale: 15
quei gloriosi che passaro a Colco
non s'ammiraron come voi farete,
quando Iason vider fatto bifolco.   18
La concreata e perpetua sete
del deiforme regno cen portava
veloci quasi come il ciel vedete.   21
Beatrice in suso e io in lei guardava,
e forse in tanto in quanto un quadrel posa
e vola e da la noce si dischiava,   24
giunto mi vidi ove mirabil cosa
mi torse il viso a sè; e però quella
cui non potea mia cura essere ascosa,   27
volta ver me sì lieta come bella
« Drizza la mente in Dio grata » mi disse
« che n'ha congiunti con la prima stella ».   30
Pareva a me che nube ne coprisse
lucida, spessa, solida e polita,
quasi adamante che lo Sol ferisse.   33
Per entro sè l'eterna margarita
ne ricevette com'acqua recepe
raggio di luce permanendo unita.   36

CANTO 2

ALL ye, that in your little boat, full fain
  to listen, have pursued upon its way
  my gallant ship that singing cleaves the main,
put back to your own shores, while yet ye may:
  tempt not the deep; or, venturing too far,
  ye well might lose me and be left astray.
The seas I sail as yet untravelled are:
  Minerva wafts me, and Apollo steers,
  and all his Nine point me to either Bear.
But ye, the few, who from your earliest years
  have held up eager mouths for angels' bread,
  sole food on earth that cloys not whom it cheers,
may safely seaward turn your vessel's head,
  if close upon my furrowed wake ye stand,
  or e'er its ridges back to smoothness fade.
More shall ye marvel than the glorious band
  that voyaged to Colchis, when with wondering eyes
  they stared at Jason toiling plough in hand.
The concreate, perpetual thirst to rise
  to the deiform realm ceased not to bear
  us on with speed that well-nigh matched the sky's.
Beatrice upward gazed, and I on her;
  and as a quarrel finds the mark, takes wing,
  and quits the peg, so quick or quicklier
arrived I saw me, where a marvellous thing
  wrenched to itself my gaze; and therefore she
  who saw full well my secret wondering,
bending, as blithe as fair, her looks on me,
  cried, ' 'Tis the first star! Turn thee, as thou art bound,
  in thanks to God, that joined therewith are we.'
It seemed to me that cloud had wrapped us round:
  luminous, solid, dense and smooth, it best
  were likened to a sunlit diamond.
The sempiternal pearl held us encased
  within itself, as water holds a ray
  of light, itself remaining undisplaced.

S'io era corpo, e qui non si concepe
  come una dimensione altra patìo,
  ch'esser convien se corpo in corpo repe,   39
accender ne dovria più il disio
  di veder quell'essenza in che si vede
  come nostra natura a Dio s'unìo.   42
Lì si vedrà ciò che tenem per fede,
  non dimostrato, ma per sè fia noto
  a guisa del ver primo che l'uom crede.   45
Io risposi: « Madonna, sì devoto
  com'esser posso più, ringrazio lui
  lo qual dal mortal mondo m'ha remoto.   48
Ma ditemi, che son li segni bui
  di questo corpo, che là giuso in Terra
  fan di Cain favoleggiare altrui? »   51
Ella sorrise alquanto, e poi « S'egli erra
  l'opinion » mi disse « dei mortali
  dove chiave di senso non disserra,   54
certo non ti dovrien punger li strali
  d'ammirazione omai poi dietro ai sensi
  vedi che la ragione ha corte l'ali.   57
Ma dimmi quel che tu da te ne pensi ».
  E io: « Ciò che n'appar qua sù diverso
  credo che 'l fanno i corpi rari e densi ».   60
Ed ella: « Certo assai vedrai sommerso
  nel falso il creder tuo, se bene ascolti
  l'argomentar ch'io li farò avverso.   63
La spera ottava vi dimostra molti
  lumi, li quali e nel quale e nel quanto
  notar si posson di diversi volti.   66
Se raro e denso ciò facesser tanto,
  una sola virtù sarebbe in tutti
  più e men distribuita ed altrettanto: 69
virtù diverse esser convegnon frutti
  di principii formali, e quei, fuor ch'uno,
  seguiterieno a tua ragion distrutti.   72
Ancor, se raro fosse di quel bruno
  cagion che tu dimandi, od oltre, in parte,
  fora di sua materia sì digiuno   75

If I was body—and none here can say
  how mass could suffer mass, as must ensue,
  if body into body steals its way—
so much the rather should we burn to view
  that essence which alone discovereth
  how the divine was yet made human too.
There will be seen that which we hold by faith,
  not proven, nay, but of itself made plain,
  like those first truths which no one questioneth.
I answered: 'Lady, I with heart as fain,
  as heart can be, pay reverent thanks to Him
  who hath removed me from the world of men.
But tell me what the spots are which bedim
  this body's surface and down there on Earth
  cause folk to make of Cain a fable's theme.'
She smiled a little; then, 'If, where key held forth
  by sense unlocks not, man's opinioning
  so errs' she said 'as to be void of worth,
surely the shafts of wonder should not sting
  thee now, who seëst that, following after sense,
  reason hath, even so, too short a wing.
But tell me what thyself thou deemest: whence
  come they?' And I: 'This mottled aspect here
  I think is caused by bodies rare and dense.'
And she: 'Doubt not thy thought shall soon appear
  in error drowned, if to the proofs I'll bring
  against it thou but lend attentive ear.
By the eighth Sphere displayed, past numbering,
  are luminaries, which differ to your eyes
  in the amount and kind of light they fling.
Did this from rare and dense alone arise,
  one virtue only would in all be found
  in greater, less and equal quantities.
Virtues that differ needs must have their ground
  in formal causes, all of which, save one,
  would be destroyed, suppose thy reasoning sound.
Besides, if rarity produced that dun
  effect whose cause thou'dst fain investigate,
  either, right through, this orb in part would run

527

esto pianeta, o sì come comparte
  lo grasso e il magro un corpo, così questo
  nel suo volume cangerebbe carte.   78
Se il primo fosse, fora manifesto
  ne l'eclissi del Sol, per trasparere
  lo lume come in altro raro ingesto.   81
Questo non è; però è da vedere
  de l'altro; e s'egli avvien ch'io l'altro cassi,
  falsificato fia lo tuo parere.   84
S'egli è che questo raro non trapassi,
  esser conviene un termine da onde
  lo suo contrario più passar non lassi,   87
e indi l'altrui raggio si rifonde
  così come color torna per vetro
  lo qual diretro a sè piombo nasconde.   90
Or dirai tu ch'ei si dimostra tetro
  ivi lo raggio più che in altre parti
  per esser lì refratto più a retro.   93
Da questa instanza può deliberarti
  esperienza, se già mai la provi,
  ch'esser suol fonte ai rivi di vostr'arti.   96
Tre specchi prenderai, e i due rimovi
  da te d'un modo, e l'altro, più rimosso,
  tr'ambo li primi gli occhi tuoi ritrovi.   99
Rivolto ad essi, fa che dopo il dosso
  ti stea un lume che i tre specchi accenda
  e torni a te da tutti ripercosso.   102
Ben che nel quanto tanto non si stenda
  la vista più lontana, lì vedrai
  come convien ch'igualmente risplenda.   105
Or, come ai colpi de li caldi rai
  de la neve riman nudo il suggetto
  e del colore e del freddo primai,   108
così rimaso te ne l'intelletto
  voglio informar di luce sì vivace
  che ti tremolerà nel suo aspetto.   111
Dentro dal ciel de la divina pace
  si gira un corpo ne la cui virtute
  l'esser di tutto suo contento giace.   114

short of its matter, or as lean and fat
　are interchanged in bodies, so would this
　the leaves within its volume alternate.
We could accept the first hypothesis,
　if at the Sun's eclipse the light shone through,
　as through all other tenuous substances.
This is not so: and hence we must review
　the other theory which if I refute,
　then thy opinion will be proved untrue.
Suppose this rareness not to pass right thro' it,
　the dense must form a limit beyond which
　it will its contrary's further path dispute;
and thence reflected are the rays that reach
　it from without, as colours are through glass
　that hides behind it lead they cannot breach.
This reflex radiance (now thou'lt argue) has
　less brilliance than the rest, because it starts
　from deeper down within the lunar mass.
From this demur experiment imparts
　the lore to free thee, wilt thou but essay
　that wonted fountainhead of all your arts.
Take *three* mirrors; move two of them away
　like distance from thee, and let the third be seen
　'twixt both the first, but farther off then they.
Then, facing tow'rds them, have a lamp brought in
　behind thy back to illumine them, that so
　all may return thee its reflected sheen.
Albeit the farther mirror will not show
　so wide a surface, yet thou'lt there behold
　how it must needs with equal splendour glow.
Now, even as some snow-encumbered wold,
　when warm beams strike it, doth dismantled lie
　of that which lately made it white and cold,
so thee, dismantled in thy mind, will I
　inform with light so lively it shall shine
　before thee sparkling like a star on high.
Within the heaven of the peace divine
　revolves a body in whose virtue lies
　the being of all things which its bounds confine.

Lo ciel seguente, che ha tante vedute,
   quell'esser parte per diverse essenze
   da lui distinte e da lui contenute.   117
Gli altri giron, per varie differenze,
   le distinzion che dentro da sè hanno
   dispongono a lor fini e lor semenze.   120
Questi organi del mondo così vanno,
   come tu vedi omai, di grado in grado,
   che di sù prendono e di sotto fanno.   123
Riguarda bene omai sì come io vado
   per questo loco al vero che disiri,
   sì che poi sappi sol tener lo guado.   126
Lo moto e la virtù dei santi giri,
   come dal fabbro l'arte del martello
   dai beati motor convien che spiri;   129
e il ciel cui tanti lumi fanno bello
   da la mente profonda che lui volve
   prende l'image e fassene suggello.   132
E come l'alma dentro a vostra polve
   per differenti membra, e conformate
   a diverse potenze, si risolve,   135
così l'intelligenza sua bontate
   multiplicata per le stelle spiega,
   girando sè sopra sua unitate.   138
Virtù diversa fa diversa lega
   col prezioso corpo ch'ella avviva,
   nel qual, sì come vita in voi, si lega.   141
Per la natura lieta onde deriva,
   la virtù mista per lo corpo luce
   come letizia per pupilla viva.   144
Da essa vien ciò che da luce a luce
   par differente, non da denso e raro;
   essa è il formal principio che produce,   147
conforme a sua bontà, lo turbo e il chiaro ».

The heaven that follows, bright with myriad eyes,
   divides that being mid diverse essences,
   from it distinct, but which its terms comprise.
The other gyres in various degrees
   dispose to their due ends their own innate
   distinctions and the germs contained in these.
Thus, as thou seëst now, in grades rotate
   these organs of the world, since, from above
   acted upon, below they actuate.
Now mark me crossing by this ford to prove
   the truth thou cravest: then, no aid required,
   thyself with boldness through the shallows move.
The holy spheres, with virtue and motion fired,
   like hammer guided by the workman's skill,
   by their blest movers needs must be inspired;
and from the deep Mind, causing it to wheel,
   the heav'n so many lights make beautiful
   its image takes and makes thereof a seal.
And as in your material frame the soul,
   through different members fashioned to comply
   with different potencies, informs the whole,
so the intelligence unfolds on high
   its goodness through the stars: thus multiplied,
   revolving still on its own unity.
Virtue diverse is diversely alloyed
   with the rich mass it quickens, in whose frame,
   as life in yours, its being is closely tied.
True to the joyous nature whence it came,
   this virtue, like the joy in sparkling eyes,
   once blent therewith doth all the mass enflame.
From this, and not from rare and dense, arise
   the differences observed 'twixt light and light:
   this is the formal cause whence spring likewise,
agreeable to its boon, the dull and bright.'

531

CANTO 3

Quel Sol che pria d'amor mi scaldò il petto,
 di bella verità m'avea scoperto,
 provando e riprovando, il dolce aspetto;   3
e io, per confessar corretto e certo
 me stesso, tanto quanto si convenne
 levai il capo, a proferer, più erto;   6
ma visione apparve che ritenne
 a sè me tanto stretto, per vedersi,
 che di mia confession non mi sovvenne.   9
Quali per vetri trasparenti e tersi,
 ovver per acque nitide e tranquille
 non sì profonde che i fondi sien persi,   12
tornan dei nostri visi le postille
 debili sì, che perla in bianca fronte
 non vien men tosto a le nostre pupille;   15
tali vid'io più facce a parlar pronte:
 per ch'io dentro a l'error contrario corsi
 a quel che accese amor tra l'uomo e il fonte.   18
Subito sì com'io di lor m'accorsi,
 quelle stimando specchiati sembianti,
 per veder di cui fosser gli occhi torsi;   21
e nulla vidi, e ritorsili avanti,
 dritti nel lume de la dolce guida,
 che sorridendo ardea ne gli occhi santi.   24
« Non ti maravigliar perch'io sorrida »
 mi disse « appresso il tuo pueril coto,
 poi sopra il vero ancor lo piè non fida,   27
ma te rivolve, come suole, a vòto:
 vere sustanze son ciò che tu vedi,
 qui rilegate per manco di vóto.   30
Però parla con esse, e odi, e credi;
 chè la verace luce che le appaga
 da sè non lascia lor torcer li piedi ».   33
Ed io a l'ombra che parea più vaga
 di ragionar drizza' mi, e cominciai
 quasi com'uom cui troppa voglia smaga: 36

CANTO 3

THAT Sun which first inflamed my breast with love
   had thus, to proof and disproof paying heed,
   shown me fair truth and the sweet look thereof;
and I, to own myself convinced and freed
   from error, lifted more erect my head
   to speak, just in so far as there was need;
but there appeared a sight which in me bred
   such wonder, that mine eyes stayed fixed thereto
   and my avowal, forgotten, remained unsaid.
As through transparent sheets of glass, or through
   bright, tranquil water, not so deep withal
   as that its bottom should be lost to view,
come jottings of our features back, yet all
   so faint, that pearls, on a white forehead gleaming,
   would not less quickly on our pupils fall;
such I beheld a group of faces seeming
   eager to speak, and erred in counter-wise
   to that which set the fountain-lover dreaming.
No sooner seen, than I, in swift surmise
   that they were mirrored images, to know
   whose they might be, cast back inquiring eyes,
saw nothing, forward looked again, and so
   gazed full into the light of my sweet guide,
   who smiling stood, her holy eyes aglow.
'Be not astonished that I smile,' she cried,
   'after thy childish thought, which, even now
   in solid truth unwilling to confide,
sinks thee in error, as it well knows how:
   true substances are these thou dost perceive,
   consigned here for the failure of some vow.
So speak with them and listen and believe;
   for the true light which fills them with content
   unto itself compels their steps to cleave.'
And I unto the shade which seemed most bent
   on converse, turned me and thus began, like one
   so eager that he feels bewilderment:

« O ben creato spirito, che ai rai
 di vita eterna la dolcezza senti
 che, non gustata, non s'intende mai,   39
grazioso mi fia se mi contenti
 del nome tuo e de la vostra sorte».
  Ond'ella, pronta e con occhi ridenti: 42
« La nostra carità non serra porte
 a giusta voglia, se non come quella
 che vuol simile a sè tutta sua corte.   45
Io fui nel mondo vergine sorella,
 e se la mente tua ben si riguarda,
 non mi ti celerà l'esser più bella   48
ma riconoscerai ch'io son Piccarda,
 che, posta qui con questi altri beati,
 beata sono in la spera più tarda.   51
Li nostri affetti, che solo infiammati
 son nel piacer de lo Spirito Santo,
 letizian del su' ordine formati;   54
e questa sorte che par giù cotanto
 però n'è data perchè fur negletti
 li nostri vóti, o vòti in alcun canto».   57
Ond'io a lei: « Nei mirabili aspetti
 vostri risplende non so che divino
 che vi trasmuta dai primi concetti: 60
però non fui a rimembrar festino;
 ma or m'aiuta ciò che tu mi dici,
 sì che raffigurar m'è più latino.   63
Ma dimmi: voi che siete qui felici,
 desiderate voi più alto loco
 per più vedere e per più farvi amici?»   66
Con quelle altr'ombre pria sorrise un poco;
 da indi mi rispose tanto lieta
 ch'arder parea d'amor nel primo foco: 69
« Frate, la nostra volontà quieta
 virtù di carità, che fa volerne
 sol quel ch'avemo, e d'altro non ci asseta.   72
Se disiassimo esser più superne,
 foran discordi li nostri disiri
 dal voler di colui che qui ne cerne: 75

'O spirit born for bliss, who in the sun
  of life eternal dost the sweetness try
  which, save by taste, is understood of none,
'twould please me well if thou wouldst satisfy
  my wish to know thy name and your estate.'
  Whence she with laughing eyes made prompt reply:
'To rightful wish our love unlocks the gate
  freely as His doth, whose own graciousness
  he wills that all his courtiers imitate.
On earth I was a virgin-votaress;
  and if thou search thy memory 'twill be clear
  to thee despite my greater loveliness
that thou behold'st Piccarda, stationed here
  among these other blessèd ones, and blest
  myself too in the slowest-moving sphere.
Our hearts, aflame with joy, which draws its zest
  from the Holy Ghost alone, are glad to be
  formed to his order, here where we are placed.
And giv'n us is this station, seemingly
  so low, because our vows, since we had paid
  less than we vow'd, were void to some degree.'
Whence I to her: 'Your faces, thus array'd,
  glow with I know not what of heavenly sheen,
  making one's former notions of you fade:
hence was my recollection not so keen;
  but now thy words awake old memories,
  so that more clearly I reshape thy mien.
But tell me, ye who tarry here in bliss,
  would ye not fain ascend to regions higher,
  to see more, and be loved more, than in this?'
All smiled at first to hear me thus inquire;
  then with such radiant gladness she replied,
  methought her burning in love's primal fire:
'Brother, our will is wholly pacified
  by virtue of love, which makes us will alone
  what we possess, and thirst for nought beside.
Wished we to make a loftier seat our own,
  our wish discordant with His will would be,
  who hath assigned this planet for our throne;

535

che vedrai non capere in questi giri,
  s'essere in carità è qui necesse,
  e se la sua natura ben rimiri.   78
Anzi è formale ad esto beato esse
  tenersi dentro a la divina voglia
  perch'una fansi nostre voglie istesse,   81
sì che come noi sem di soglia in soglia
  per questo regno, a tutto il regno piace
  come a lo re che a suo voler ne invoglia.   84
E'n la sua volontade è nostra pace:
  ella è quel mare al qual tutto si move
  ciò ch'ella cria e che natura face».   87
Chiaro mi fu allor come ogni dove
  in cielo è Paradiso, etsi la grazia
  del sommo ben d'un modo non vi piove.   90
Ma sì com'egli avvien, se un cibo sazia
  e d'un altro rimane ancor la gola,
  che quel si chiede e di quel si ringrazia,   93
così fec'io con atto e con parola
  per apprender da lei qual fu la tela
  onde non trasse infino al co la spola.   96
« Perfetta vita ed alto merto inciela
  donna più sù » mi disse « a la cui norma
  nel vostro mondo giù si veste e vela   99
perchè fino al morir si vegli e dorma
  con quello sposo che ogni voto accetta
  che caritate a suo piacer conforma.   102
Dal mondo, per seguirla, giovinetta
  fuggi'mi, e nel suo abito mi chiusi,
  e promisi la via de la sua setta.   105
Uomini poi a mal più ch'a bene usi
  fuor mi rapiron de la dolce chiostra:
  Iddio si sa qual poi mia vita fusi.   108
E quest'altro splendor che ti si mostra
  da la mia destra parte e che s'accende
  di tutto il lume de la spera nostra,   111
ciò ch'io dico di me di sè intende:
  sorella fu, e così le fu tolta
  di capo l'ombra de le sacre bende.   114

the which these orbs admit not, as thou'lt see,
   if here to be in love must needs befall,
   and thou regard love's nature carefully.
Nay, 'tis essential to the being we call
   blest, that it should the will of God fulfil,
   so making one the very wills of all:
therefore, our being thus, from sill to sill
   this whole realm through, alike the realm doth please
   and Ruler who in-wills us to his will.
And solely in his will exists our peace;
   it is that sea to which flows whatsoe'er
   it creates or of Nature's making is.'
Thus learned I how in heaven every 'where'
   is Paradise, *etsi* the highest good
   sheds not its grace in one sole fashion there.
But as may be if, sated with one food
   and greedy for another, we have pled
   for this, and shown for that our gratitude,
such was my gesture, such the words I said,
   to learn from her what web it was wherethrough
   she had not drawn the shuttle to the head.
'Shines higher enskied,' quoth she, 'as guerdon due
   to perfect life and high desert, a dame
   whose rule on earth girls, robed and veiled, pursue,
that so till death, both day and night the same,
   they may attend that Spouse who will reject
   no vows, if love to his will conformeth them.
Fleeing the world, did I in youth elect
   to follow her; and, in her habit wrapt,
   I pledged me to the pathway of her sect.
Thereafter men, for ill than good more apt,
   forth snatched me from the cloister's peaceful ways;
   and God knows on what later life I happ'd.
And lo, this other splendour who displays
   her beauty on my right and whom our sphere
   lights up with the full brilliance of its rays,
knows that my story to her own comes near:
   she too a nun, her brows were forced to part
   with the o'ershadowing coif she held so dear.

Ma poi che pur al mondo fu rivolta
  contra suo grado e contra buona usanza,
  non fu dal vel del cor già mai disciolta.   117
Questa è la luce de la gran Costanza,
  che del secondo vento di Soave
  generò il terzo e l'ultima possanza».   120
Così parlommi, e poi cominciò *Ave*
  Maria cantando, e cantando vanio,
  come per acqua cupa cosa grave.   123
La vista mia, che tanto la seguìo
  quanto possibil fu, poi che la perse
  volsesi al segno di maggior disio,   126
e a Beatrice tutta si converse;
  ma quella folgorò ne lo mio sguardo
  sì, che da prima il viso nol sofferse: 129
e ciò mi fece a domandar più tardo.

CANTO 4

Intra due cibi distanti e moventi
  d'un modo, prima si morria di fame
  che liber uomo l'un recasse ai denti;   3
sì si starebbe un agno intra due brame
  di fieri lupi igualmente temendo;
  sì si starebbe un cane intra due dame: 6
per che s'io mi tacea, me non riprendo,
  da li miei dubbi d'un modo sospinto,
  poi ch'era necessario, nè commendo.   9
Io mi tacea, ma il mio disir dipinto
  m'era nel viso, e il dimandar con ello,
  più caldo assai che per parlar distinto.   12
Fe' sì Beatrice qual fe' Daniello
  Nabuccodonosor levando d'ira
  che l'avea fatto ingiustamente fello;   15
e disse: « Io veggio ben come ti tira
  uno e altro disio, sì che tua cura
  se stessa lega sì che fuor non spira.   18

Yet, when against her will—and though to thwart
   that will was sin—she found herself re-cast
   upon the world, she stayed still veiled in heart.
This light is the great Constance: from one blast,
   the second Swabian, did she generate
   the third imperial whirlwind, and the last.'
Thus she addressed me and, beginning straight
   to sing *Hail, Mary*, singing, did not stay
   but sank, as through deep water heavy weight.
So long as possible did I essay
   to keep her form in view: when she was gone,
   to the more longed-for mark I turned away,
and Beatrice my whole attention won;
   but for a while my vision lacked the power
   to gaze at her, so dazzling bright she shone:
which made me in my questioning the slower.

CANTO 4

Between two foods, equally tempting, set
   equally near, a man, tho' free to choose,
   would starve before his teeth in either met;
so would a lamb, fearing alike both foes,
   stay fixed between two ravening wolves; and so
   a hound would hesitate between two does:
Wherefore, if I was silent, cast I no
   blame on myself, by equal doubts impelled,
   since it was necessary, nor praise bestow.
Silent I was, but my desire, unquelled,
   limned, on my face, my question fervently,
   far warmlier than the plain words I withheld.
Beatrice did as Daniel did, when he
   Nebuchadnezzar from an anger freed
   which drove him to unrighteous cruelty.
'Plainly,' she said, 'thy two desires impede
   each one the other; hence thy troubled thought
   so binds itself it breathes not forth its need.

Tu argomenti: 'Se il buon voler dura,
  la violenza altrui per qual ragione
  di meritar mi scema la misura?'   21
Ancor di dubitar ti dà cagione
  parer tornarsi l'anime a le stelle
  secondo la sentenza di Platone.   24
Queste son le question che nel tuo velle
  pontano igualmente; e però pria
  tratterò quella che più ha di felle.   27
Dei Serafin colui che più s'indìa,
  Moisè, Samuel, e quel Giovanni
  che prender vuoli, io dico non Maria,   30
non hanno in altro cielo i loro scanni
  che questi spirti che mo' t'appariro,
  nè hanno a l'esser lor più o meno anni;   33
ma tutti fanno bello il primo giro,
  e differentemente han dolce vita
  per sentir più o men l'eterno spiro.   36
Qui si mostraro non perchè sortita
  sia questa spera a lor, ma per far segno
  de la celestial ch'ha men salita.   39
Così parlar conviensi al vostro ingegno,
  però che solo da sensato apprende
  ciò che fa poscia d'intelletto degno.   42
Per questo la scrittura condescende
  a vostra facultate, e piedi e mano
  attribuisce a Dio, e altro intende;   45
e Santa Chiesa con aspetto umano
  Gabriel e Michel vi rappresenta,
  e l'altro che Tobia rifece sano.   48
Quel che Timeo de l'anime argomenta
  non è simile a ciò che qui si vede,
  però che come dice par che senta: 51
dice che l'alma a la sua stella riede,
  credendo quella quindi esser decisa
  quando natura per forma la diede.   54
E forse sua sentenza è d'altra guisa
  che la voce non suona, ed esser puote
  con intenzion da non esser derisa: 57

Thou arguest: "if the good will fails in nought,
  why should my merit be accounted less,
  because of violence by others wrought?"
It further gives thee cause for doubtfulness
  that seemingly, as Plato fancied, all
  disbodied souls to stars their path retrace.
These are the questions which alike bethrall
  thy will; hence, though thou'rt equally engross'd
  by both, I'll treat first that which hath more gall.
Of Seraphs not the one ingodded most,
  not Moses, Samuel nor whichever John
  thou choose, not even Mary, have their post
in other heaven than those spirits just gone
  from hence, nor to their being have they there
  more years or fewer in comparison;
but the first circle each and all make fair,
  breathing a life diversely sweet, as they
  or more or less the eternal spirit share.
Nor did they in this sphere their forms display
  as were it their portion, but to betoken thus
  the grade which least reflects the heavenly ray.
So to address your wit behoveth us,
  for sole from object sensed it grasps what then
  to intellect it renders luminous.
This is why Scripture condescends to feign
  for your behoof, though meaning otherwise,
  that God hath hands and feet, like mortal men;
and Holy Church depicts in human guise
  Gabriel and Michael, and that other too,
  who restored vision unto Tobit's eyes.
As for Timaeus touching souls, his view
  resembles not that which one here discerns,
  since what he says he seems to think is true.
He says the soul to its own star returns,
  deeming it severed thence, when nature gave
  it for substantial form—a view one spurns;
but haply his opinion he might save
  from mere derision, could his language claim
  a meaning other than it seems to have.

s'elli intende tornare a queste rote
    l'onor de l'influenza e il biasmo, forse
    in alcun vero su' arco percuote.   60
Questo principio, male inteso, torse
    già tutto il mondo quasi, sì che Giove
    Mercurio e Marte a nominar trascorse.   63
L'altra dubitazion che ti commove
    ha men velen, però che sua malizia
    non ti porìa menar da me altrove: 66
parere ingiusta la nostra giustizia
    ne gli occhi dei mortali, è argomento
    di fede e non d'eretica nequizia.   69
Ma perchè puote vostro accorgimento
    ben penetrare a questa veritate,
    come disiri ti farò contento.   72
Se violenza è quando quel che pate
    niente conferisce a quel che sforza,
    non fur quest'alme per essa scusate,   75
chè volontà, se non vuol, non s'ammorza
    ma fa come natura face in foco
    se mille volte violenza il torza;   78
per che s'ella si piega assai o poco,
    segue la forza: e così queste fero
    possendo rifuggir nel santo loco.   81
Se fosse stato lor volere intero
    come tenne Lorenzo in su la grada
    e fece Muzio a la sua man severo,   84
così l'avria ripinte per la strada
    ond'eran tratte, come furo sciolte;
    ma così salda voglia è troppo rada.   87
E per queste parole, se ricolte
    l'hai come dei, è l'argomento casso
    che t'avria fatto noia ancor più volte.   90
Ma or ti s'attraversa un altro passo
    dinanzi a gli occhi, tal, che per te stesso
    non ne usciresti, pria saresti lasso: 93
io t'ho per certo ne la mente messo
    ch'alma beata non poria mentire,
    però ch'è sempre al primo vero appresso;   96

Means he that to these wheels return the blame
  and honour of their influence, then maybe
  some truth he strikes, at which his bow took aim.
This lore, mis-learned, perverted formerly
  well nigh the whole world, causing it to err
  by invoking Jove and Mars and Mercury.
The other doubt thou feel'st within thee stir
  is less envenomed, for it could not blind
  thine eyes to me nor lead thee otherwhere.
Theirs is no wicked heresy who find
  seeming injustice in our justice—nay,
  this should but make them more to faith inclined.
But seeing that to this truth there leads a way
  which by your intellect might well be used,
  all thou wouldst have me tell I now will say.
If it be violence when the one abused
  to that which forces him contributes nil,
  these souls were not on that account excused;
for nought can quench the unconsenting will:
  'tis like to fire which, beaten from its track
  a thousand times, by nature seeks it still.
Hence, if it yields at all through growing slack,
  will abets force, as these did, who, with power
  to turn back to the cloister, turned not back.
Had but their will been whole, like that which o'er
  the grid held Laurence and made Mucius stern
  to his own hand, they would, when free once more,
have been compelled by it to make return
  thither, whence they were dragged by violence;
  but in too few doth will so steadfast burn.
And thus, if thou hast duly gleaned their sense,
  my words refute the reasoning which might yet
  full many a time have caused thee grave offence.
But now before thee winds another strait,
  such that to issue thence would sorely try
  thy own unaided skill, however great.
Firmly impressed it on thy mind have I,
  that, since to primal truth 'tis alway near,
  no soul that dwells in bliss could ever lie;

e poi potesti da Piccarda udire
  che l'affezion del vel Costanza tenne;
  sì ch'ella par qui meco contraddire.   99
Molte fiate già, frate, addivenne
  che per fuggir periglio, contra grato
  si fe' di quel che far non si convenne;   102
come Almeone, che, di ciò pregato
  dal padre suo, la propria madre spense,
  per non perder pietà si fe' spietato.   105
A questo punto voglio che tu pense
  che la forza al voler si mischia, e fanno
  sì che scusar non si posson l'offense.   108
Voglia assoluta non consente al danno,
  ma consentevi in tanto in quanto teme,
  se si ritrae, cadere in più affanno.   111
Però quando Piccarda quello spreme,
  de la voglia assoluta intende, e io
  de l'altra: sì che ver diciamo insieme».   114
Cotal fu l'ondeggiar del santo rio
  che uscì del fonte onde ogni ver deriva;
  tal pose in pace uno ed altro disio.   117
« O amanza del primo amante, o diva »
  diss'io appresso « il cui parlar m'inonda
  e scalda sì che più e più m'avviva,   120
non è l'affezion mia tanto profonda
  che basti a render voi grazia per grazia;
  ma quei che vede e puote a ciò risponda.   123
Io veggio ben che già mai non si sazia
  nostro intelletto, se il ver non lo illustra
  di fuor dal qual nessun vero si spazia.   126
Posasi in esso come fera in lustra
  tosto che giunto l'ha, e giugner puollo,
  se non ciascun disio sarebbe frustra.   129
Nasce per quello, a guisa di rampollo,
  a piè del vero il dubbio; ed è natura
  che al sommo pinge noi di collo in collo.   132
Questo m'invita, questo m'assicura
  con reverenza, donna, a dimandarvi
  d'un'altra verità che m'è oscura.   135

whereas Piccarda made it no less clear,
  that Constance for the veil her love retain'd;
  so that she seems to contradict me here.
Brother, ofttimes 'twill hap, that to forfend
  a danger, what men should not, men will do,
  e'en while they hate the means which serve their end;
thus, being by his father urged thereto,
  Alcmaeon, not to fail in filial love,
  hardened his heart and his own mother slew.
Bethink thee that such actions clearly prove
  that force with will is mixed, annulling so
  all pleas which might the taint of guilt remove.
Tempted to sin, absolute will says "no",
  but in so far consents, as it may dread,
  through drawing back, to incur some greater woe.
Now, in Piccarda's speech the reference made
  to will was to the absolute will, in mine
  to the other; hence in both the truth was said.'
Thus rippling from the fountainhead divine
  of every truth, the holy rill supplied
  to both my doubts the longed-for anodyne.
'O loved of the first lover,' then I cried,
  'O deity whose speech doth more and more
  refresh me with its warm, full-flowing tide,
to render grace for grace my own poor store
  of love will reach not; but may He requite
  your bounty, who both sees and hath the power.
I see well that apart from that true light
  which comprehends all truth, the minds of men
  can never sate themselves with full insight.
They rest in truth as wild beast in its den,
  when once they have attained it; and they may
  attain it: else were all desires in vain.
Whence at the foot of truth springs up a spray
  of doubt; and we are pushed, from peak to peak,
  up to the topmost in the natural way.
This bids me, this emboldens me to seek
  with reverence, lady, for your aid anent
  another truth of which my grasp is weak.

Io vo' saper se l'uom può sodisfarvi
   ai voti manchi, sì con altri beni
   che a la vostra statera non sien parvi ».   138
Beatrice mi guardò con gli occhi pieni
   di faville d'amor, così divini,
   che, vinta, mia virtute diè le reni,   141
e quasi mi perdei, con gli occhi chini.

CANTO 5

« S' io ti fiammeggio nel caldo d'amore
   di là dal modo che in Terra si vede
   sì che de gli occhi tuoi vinco il valore,   3
non ti maravigliar, chè ciò procede,
   da perfetto veder, che come apprende
   così nel bene appreso move il piede.   6
Io veggio ben sì come già risplende
   ne l'intelletto tuo l'eterna luce
   che, vista, sola e sempre amore accende;   9
e s'altra cosa vostro amor seduce,
   non è se non di quella alcun vestigio
   mal conosciuto, che quivi traluce.   12
Tu vuoi saper se con altro servigio
   per manco voto si può render tanto
   che l'anima sicuri di litigio ».   15
Sì cominciò Beatrice questo canto;
   e sì com'uom che suo parlar non spezza
   continuò così il processo santo: 18
« Lo maggior don che Dio per sua larghezza
   fesse creando, ed a la sua bontate
   più conformato e quel ch'ei più apprezza,   21
fu de la volontà la libertate,
   di che le creature intelligenti
   e tutte e sole furo e son dotate.   24

Fain would I know if man can supplement
  his broken vows by other deeds well done,
  which in your scales may be equivalent.'
Beatrice gazed at me with eyes which shone
  sparkling with love, so divine, it was past
  my power to bear them, and I stood like one
well-nigh bereft of sense, with eyes downcast.

CANTO 5

'If that I flame upon thee in ardent love
  surpassing aught beheld in mortal mien,
  so that thine eyes bear not the blaze thereof,
marvel thou not; for such hath ever been
  the effect of perfect sight, which, as it sees,
  so moves its foot nearer the blessing seen.
The eternal Light—and this alone it is,
  which, once beheld, enkindles love alway—
  now visibly thy mind from darkness frees;
and if aught else doth lead your love astray,
  'tis but some vestige of that Light, which ye
  ill recognize, transmitting there its ray.
Thou askest if for broken vows may be
  with other service such requital made,
  as may secure the soul from further plea.'
So Beatrice this canto preluded;
  and, like some fluent speaker's, onward flowed
  her sacred argument, as thus she said:
'Of all the gifts a bounteous God bestowed
  at the creation, that which made appeal
  most to himself, and most his goodness showed,
and hence the best, was freedom of the will;
  which to all thinking creatures, and alone
  to them, was granted, and is granted still.

Or ti parrà, se tu quinci argomenti,
   l'alto valor del voto, s'è sì fatto
   che Dio consenta quando tu consenti;   27
chè nel fermar tra Dio e l'uomo il patto,
   vittima fassi di questo tesoro
   tal qual io dico, e fassi col suo atto.   30
Dunque che render puossi per ristoro?
   Se credi bene usar quel ch'hai offerto,
   di mal tolletto vuoi far buon lavoro.   33
Tu sei omai del maggior punto certo;
   ma perchè Santa Chiesa in ciò dispensa,
   che par contra lo ver ch'io t'ho scoverto,   36
convienti ancor sedere un poco a mensa,
   però che il cibo rigido ch'hai preso
   richiede ancora aiuto a sua dispensa.   39
Apri la mente a quel ch'io ti paleso
   e fermalvi entro, chè non fa scienza,
   sanza lo ritenere, aver inteso.   42
Due cose si convegnono a l'essenza
   di questo sacrificio: l'una è quella
   di che si fa, l'altra è la convenenza.   45
Quest'ultima già mai non si cancella,
   se non servata: ed intorno di lei
   sì preciso di sopra si favella: 48
però necessità fu a gli Ebrei
   pur l'offerere, ancor che alcuna offerta
   si permutasse, come saper déi.   51
L'altra, che per materia t'è aperta,
   puote ben esser tal, che non si falla
   se con altra materia si converta;   54
ma non trasmuti carco a la sua spalla
   per suo arbitro alcun, sanza la volta
   e de la chiave bianca e de la gialla;   57
e ogni permutanza credi stolta,
   se la cosa dimessa in la sorpresa
   come il quattro nel sei non è raccolta.   60
Però qualunque cosa tanto pesa
   per suo valor che tragga ogni bilancia,
   sodisfar non si può con altra spesa.   63

By argument, thus based, is clearly shown
  the vow's high value, if thou so contract
  with God, that his contracting seals thy own;
for in the very closing of the pact
  between God and the man, this precious thing
  is made a victim, and by its own act.
What compensation, therefore, canst thou bring?
  Thou'dst fain do alms with stolen wealth, if thou
  to good use think to turn thine offering.
So the main point is clear; but since it now
  seems counter to the truth as just express'd
  that Holy Church dispenses from a vow,
thou must at table keep thy seat as guest
  a little longer, for this solid meal
  needs further help to make it well digest.
Open thy mind to what I now reveal:
  there store it closely; for to have understood,
  but not retained, as knowledge counts for nil.
This sacrifice in essence doth include
  two things, of which the service vowed is one,
  and one the covenant thereby made good.
This last is never cancelled, save alone
  by being kept; and hence, just now, my care
  in making so precise my comment thereon:
hence were the Hebrews still obliged to bear
  an offering, though some offered things allowed
  of permutation, as thou'rt well aware.
The other, which I called "the service vowed,"
  can well be such as without fault may be
  exchanged for service other than is owed.
E'en so, let none regard himself as free
  to shift his shoulder's burden, ere the door
  be unlocked by both the white and the yellow key;
and let him every thought of change give o'er,
  unless the burden taken up comprise
  the one laid down, as six containeth four.
Hence there can be no charge which satisfies
  the claim of thing so precious, that its weight
  must still o'erbalance every counterpoise.

Non prendan li mortali il voto a ciancia:
 siate fedeli, ed a ciò far non bieci,
 come Ieptè a la sua prima mancia;   66
cui più si convenia dicer 'Mal feci'
 che servando far peggio; e così stolto
 ritrovar puoi lo gran duca dei Greci,   69
onde pianse Ifigènia il suo bel volto,
 e fe' pianger di sè i folli e i savi
 che udîr parlar di così fatto colto.   72
Siate, cristiani, a movervi più gravi;
 non siate come penna ad ogni vento,
 e non crediate che ogni acqua vi lavi.   75
Avete il novo e il vecchio Testamento
 e il Pastor de la Chiesa che vi guida:
 questo vi basti a vostro salvamento.   78
Se mala cupidigia altro vi grida,
 uomini siate e non pecore matte,
 sì che il Giudeo di voi tra voi non rida.   81
Non fate come agnel che lascia il latte
 de la sua madre, e semplice e lascivo
 seco medesmo a suo piacer combatte».   84
Così Beatrice a me com'io scrivo;
 poi si rivolse tutta disiante
 a quella parte ove il mondo è più vivo.   87
Lo suo tacere e il trasmutar sembiante
 poser silenzio al mio cupido ingegno
 che già nuove questioni avea davante;   90
e sì come saetta che nel segno
 percuote pria che sia la corda queta,
 così corremmo nel secondo regno.   93
Quivi la donna mia vid'io sì lieta,
 come nel lume di quel ciel si mise,
 che più lucente se ne fe' il pianeta.   96
E se la stella si cambiò e rise,
 qual mi fec'io, che pur di mia natura
 trasmutabile son per tutte guise!   99
Come in peschiera ch'è tranquilla e pura
 traggonsi i pesci a ciò che vien di fuori
 per modo che lo stimin lor pastura,   102

Then, mortals, vow not lightly: pay your debt,
    keeping your word, but not with the blurred look
    of Jephthah pledged to kill what first he met;
who should have cried, "Wrong was the vow I took",
    and not sinned worse by keeping it; no less
    insensate can'st thou find the Greeks' great duke,
whence Iphigénia rued her lovely face,
    and made both wise and simple share her teen,
    who heard that rite so foul had e'er ta'en place.
Tread, Christians, firmlier the way ye are in:
    be not, as feathers, sport of every breeze,
    nor think that every water laves you clean.
Both Testaments are yours, whene'er ye please;
    the Church's Shepherd leaves you not forlorn:
    for your salvation rest content with these.
If wicked greed cry to you aught else, turn
    ye not; be men, not silly sheep, that so
    the Jew among you laugh you not to scorn.
Do not as doth the lamb, which will forgo
    its mother's milk to enjoy the empty bliss
    of fighting with itself, a wanton foe!'
Such were the very words of Beatrice;
    then, all consumed with keen desire, she turned
    to that part where the world most quickened is.
Her silence and the change which I discerned
    upon her face my eager mind forbade
    to ask the further things it fain had learned;
and swift as shaft which strikes the quarry dead,
    before the bow-string ceases to vibrate,
    so to the second kingdom on we sped.
I saw my lady there so radiate
    joy, as within that shining heaven she passed,
    that the bright planet grew thence brighter yet.
And if the star was changed and laughed, how was't
    with me, who am obnoxious, of my mere
    nature, to change of every shade and cast!
As in a fish-pond that is calm and clear,
    to aught that enters seeming like to prove
    good for their nourishment the fish draw near,

sì vid'io ben più di mille splendori
   trarsi ver noi, ed in ciascun s'udia:
   « Ecco chi crescerà li nostri amori ».   105
E sì come ciascuno a noi venia,
   vedeasi l'ombra piena di letizia
   nel fulgor chiaro che di lei uscìa.   108
Pensa, lettor, se quel che qui s'inizia
   non procedesse, come tu avresti
   di più sapere angosciosa carizia;   111
e per te vederai come da questi
   m'era in disio d'udir lor condizioni
   sì come a gli occhi mi fur manifesti.   114
« O bene nato, a cui veder li troni
   del trionfo eternal concede grazia
   prima che la milizia s'abbandoni,   117
del lume che per tutto il ciel si spazia
   noi semo accesi, e però se disii
   di noi chiarirti, a tuo piacer ti sazia ».   120
Così da un di quelli spirti pii
   detto mi fu; e da Beatrice: « Dì, dì
   sicuramente, e credi come a dii ».   123
« Io veggio ben sì come tu t'annidi
   nel proprio lume, e che da gli occhi il traggi
   perch'ei corusca sì come tu ridi;   126
ma non so chi tu sei, nè perchè aggi,
   anima degna, il grado de la spera
   che si vela a' mortai con altrui raggi ».   129
Questo diss'io diritto a la lumiera
   che pria m'avea parlato; ond'ella fessi
   lucente più assai di quel ch'ell'era.   132
Sì come il Sol che si cela elli stessi
   per troppa luce, come il caldo ha rose
   le temperanze di vapori spessi,   135
per più letizia sì mi si nascose
   dentro al suo raggio la figura santa;
   e così chiusa, chiusa mi rispose   138
nel modo che il seguente canto canta.

so did I see a swarm of splendours move
    to us-ward, and in each was heard the cry:
    'Lo here, to increase our loves, another love!'
And as towards us each of them drew nigh,
    in the clear luminance with which it shone
    was visible the shade full filled with joy.
Think, Reader, if the tale I've here begun
    were not continued, with what anxious prayer
    thou would'st forthwith implore me to go on;
and hence imagine what my feelings were,
    who longed to ask them how and what they did,
    the moment that mine eyes beheld them there.
'O happy-born, to whom grace doth concede
    sight of the thrones of endless victory,
    ere from thine earthly warfare thou art freed,
lit by the light that floods all heaven are we;
    if, therefore, thou would'st have thy need supplied,
    ask freely, and thou shalt enlightened be.'
One of those gracious souls it was that cried
    these words to me; then Beatrice: 'Fear nought,
    speak to them, speak, and as in gods confide!'
'I see the nest of light thou hast round thee wrought;
    and since thine eyes, whene'er thou smilest, blaze,
    thou drawest this light through them, I may not doubt;
but who thou art, O spirit all-worthy praise,
    I know not, nor why graded in the sphere
    that's veiled to mortals by another's rays.'
Unto the light which first had hailed my ear
    I thus addressed me; whereupon it grew
    far brighter than I'd seen it erst appear.
Like to the Sun who hides himself from view
    thro' excess of light, when the heat has gnawed away
    the mantle which thick vapours round him drew;
so was that holy shape in its own ray
    through mere increase of gladness quite concealed;
    and, thus enveloped, did it say its say,
more fit in fytte ensuing to be revealed.

CANTO 6

« Poscia che Costantin l'aquila volse
　　contro al corso del ciel, ch'ella seguio
　　dietro a l'antico che Lavina tolse, 　　　　　　3
cento e cent'anni e più l'uccel di Dio
　　ne lo stremo d'Europa si ritenne,
　　vicino ai monti de' quai prima uscìo; 　　　　6
e sotto l'ombra de le sacre penne
　　governò il mondo lì di mano in mano,
　　e, sì cangiando, in su la mia pervenne. 　　　9
Cesare fui, e son Giustiniano,
　　che, per voler del primo amor ch'io sento,
　　d'entro le leggi trassi il troppo e il vano. 　12
E prima ch'io a l'opra fossi attento,
　　una natura in Cristo esser, non piue,
　　credeva, e di tal fede era contento; 　　　　15
ma il benedetto Agapito, che fue
　　sommo pastore, a la fede sincera
　　mi dirizzò con le parole sue. 　　　　　　18
Io li credetti, e ciò che in sua fede era
　　veggio ora chiaro sì come tu vedi
　　ogni contradizione e falsa e vera. 　　　　21
Tosto che con la Chiesa mossi i piedi,
　　a Dio per grazia piacque d'ispirarmi
　　l'alto lavoro, e tutto a lui mi diedi; 　　　24
ed al mio Belisar commendai l'armi,
　　cui la destra del ciel fu sì congiunta
　　che segno fu ch'io dovessi posarmi. 　　　27
Or qui a la question prima s'appunta
　　la mia risposta; ma sua condizione
　　mi stringe a seguitare alcuna giunta, 　　　30
perchè tu veggi con quanta ragione
　　si move contra il sacrosanto segno
　　e chi il s'appropria e chi a lui s'oppone. 　33
Vedi quanta virtù l'ha fatto degno
　　di reverenza; e cominciò da l'ora
　　che Pallante morì per darli regno. 　　　　36

CANTO 6

'After that Constantine the eagle had driven
    back on the course which it pursued of yore
    behind Lavinia's spouse, who marched with heaven,
the bird of God two hundred years and more
    on Europe's utmost verge its seat maintain'd
    nigh to the mountains where it learned to soar;
there, shadowed by the sacred plumes, it reign'd
    over the world from hand to hand, and then,
    thus changing, did at last on mine descend.
Caesar I was, Justinian I remain,
    whom that prime love which fires me now, impell'd
    to rid the laws of what was gross and vain.
And ere this labour summoned me, I held
    that Christ of but one nature was possess'd—
    a faith wherein I long contented dwell'd;
but Agapetus—name for ever blest—
    who was chief shepherd, by his reasoning drew
    me on, till I the untainted faith confess'd.
Him I believed and now as clearly view
    the inward of his faith, as in thy sight
    all contradictories are both false and true.
So soon as with the Church I stepped aright,
    God's grace to that high task my heart inclined
    which I pursued thenceforth with all my might;
arms to my Belisarius I resign'd;
    and heaven to him proved such a staunch ally,
    'twas sign I was to rest in peace of mind.
Here, then, to thy first question my reply
    were ended, did its tenor not disclose
    a sequel, which I needs must amplify,
that thou mayst see what right men have to oppose
    the sacred standard, be they what they may,
    its jealous claimants or its bitter foes.
Behold the power for which all ought to pay
    it homage; and thereof began the tale
    from the hour when Pallas died to give it sway.

Tu sai ch'ei fece in Alba sua dimora
   per trecent'anni e oltre, infino al fine
   che i tre e i tre pugnar per lui ancora.   39
E sai che fe' dal mal de le Sabine
   al dolor di Lucrezia, in sette regi,
   vincendo intorno le genti vicine.   42
Sai quel che fe' portato da gli egregi
   Romani incontro a Brenno, incontro a Pirro,
   incontro a gli altri principi e collegi;   45
onde Torquato, e Quinzio che dal cirro
   negletto fu nomato, e i Deci, e i Fabi
   ebber la fama che volentier mirro.   48
Esso atterrò l'orgoglio de gli Aràbi
   che diretro ad Annibale passaro
   l'alpestre rocce, Po, di che tu labi.   51
Sott'esso giovinetti trionfaro
   Scipione e Pompeo; ed a quel colle
   sotto il qual tu nascesti parve amaro.   54
Poi, presso al tempo che tutto il ciel volle
   ridur lo mondo a suo modo sereno,
   Cesare per voler di Roma il tolle.   57
E quel che fe' da Varo infino al Reno,
   Isara vide ed Era e vide Senna
   e ogni valle onde Rodano è pieno.   60
Quel che fe' poi ch'egli uscì di Ravenna
   e saltò Rubicon, fu di tal volo
   che nol seguiteria lingua nè penna.   63
Inver la Spagna rivolse lo stuolo,
   poi ver Durazzo, e Farsaglia percosse
   sì che al Nil caldo si sentì del duolo.   66
Antandro e Simoenta onde si mosse
   rivide, e là dov'Ettore si cuba;
   e mal per Tolomeo poi si riscosse.   69
Da indi scese folgorando a Iuba,
   onde si volse nel vostro occidente
   ove sentia la pompeiana tuba.   72
Di quel ch'ei fe' col bàiulo seguente
   Bruto con Cassio ne l'Inferno latra,
   e Modena e Perugia fu dolente.   75

Thou knowest that Alba was its citadel
  three hundred years and more, till at last found
  were three 'gainst three contending for it still:
and knowest what exploits made its name resound,
  from the rape o' the Sabines down to Lucrece' woe,
  'neath seven kings subduing the tribes around:
knowest how it did with Roman champions go
  forth to meet Brennus, Pyrrhus and a throng
  of others, single prince or leaguéd foe;
whence won Torquatus, Quinctius of the long
  rough locks, the Decii, Fabii far and wide
  the fame which I rejoice to embalm in song.
It struck to earth the Arabs in their pride
  who followed Hannibal what time he scaled
  the Alpine crags, whence, Po, thy waters glide.
Under it in their glorious youth prevailed
  Scipio and Pompey; and the self-same hill
  that crests thy home it bitterly assailed.
Then, near the time when it was Heaven's will
  to spread, the whole world through, calm like its own,
  Caesar laid hold of it on Rome's appeal.
And what it wrought from Var to Rhine did Saône
  and Isère witness, witnessed likewise Seine
  and every vale whose tribute brims the Rhône.
What then it wrought when, swooping south again,
  it left Ravenna, leaped the Rubicon,
  is flight too swift for any tongue or pen.
Tow'rds Spain it turned the legions back, sped on
  then tow'rd Dyrrhachium, and so sorely smote
  Pharsalia that it made the warm Nile groan.
Antandros, its own Simois and the spot
  where lieth Hector it revisited;
  and shook its plumes, with ill for Ptolemy fraught.
From him to Juba lightning-swift it sped;
  and thence when the Pompeian trumpet blew,
  back to your west it turned, unweariéd,
With him who bore it next, the flight it flew
  Brutus and Cassius howl of, down in Hell,
  and Modena, with Perugia, learned to rue.

Piangene ancor la trista Cleopatra,
  che, fuggendogli innanzi, dal colubro
  la morte prese subitana ed atra. 78
Con costui corse infino al lito rubro;
  con costui pose il mondo in tanta pace
  che fu serrato a Iano il suo delubro. 81
Ma ciò che il segno che parlar mi face
  fatto avea prima e poi era fatturo
  per lo regno mortal che a lui soggiace, 84
diventa in apparenza poco e scuro
  se in mano al terzo Cesare si mira
  con occhio chiaro e con affetto puro: 87
chè la viva giustizia che m'ispira
  li concedette, in mano a quel ch'io dico,
  gloria di far vendetta a la sua ira. 90
Or qui t'ammira in ciò ch'io ti replìco:
  poscia con Tito a far vendetta corse
  de la vendetta del peccato antico. 93
E quando il dente longobardo morse
  la Santa Chiesa, sotto le sue ali
  Carlo Magno, vincendo, la soccorse. 96
Omai puoi giudicar di quei cotali
  ch'io accusai di sopra, e di lor falli
  che son cagion di tutti i vostri mali: 99
l'uno al pubblico segno i gigli gialli
  oppone, e l'altro appropria quello a parte,
  sì ch'è forte a veder qual più si falli. 102
Faccian li Ghibellin, faccian lor arte
  sott'altro segno, chè mal segue quello
  sempre chi la giustizia e lui diparte; 105
e non l'abbatta esto Carlo novello
  coi Guelfi suoi, ma tema de gli artigli
  che a più alto leon trasser lo vello. 108
Molte fiate già pianser li figli
  per la colpa del padre, e non si creda
  che Dio trasmuti l'arme pe' suoi gigli. 111
Questa picciola stella si correda
  dei buoni spirti che son stati attivi
  perchè onore e fama li succeda; 114

Still doth the tragic Cleopatra wail
   because thereof, who, fleeing its path before,
   took from the adder death, instant and fell.
With him it swept even to the Red Sea shore;
   with him it on the world such peace conferr'd
   that locked on Janus was his temple-door.
But all yet wrought by this imperial bird,
   all it was yet to achieve by sea or land
   among the nations which obey its word,
seems paltry and obscure, if it be scann'd
   with pure affection and unclouded eye
   as it appears in the third Caesar's hand;
for in that hand it was the means whereby
   the living justice, my life-breath, decreed
   its wrath should be avenged so gloriously.
With Titus next—and do thou here give heed
   to my strange replication—it was sent
   to avenge the avenging of the old misdeed.
And when the Holy Church lay gored and rent
   by the fierce Lombard's tusk, beneath its wings
   Charlemain, in triumph, to her rescue went.
Judge now of those my late indictment brings
   before thee, what they are—their sin how great
   who are the cause of all your sufferings.
Against the public standard some would set
   the yellow lilies: some—no less to blame—
   would to themselves its power appropriate,
Go, play, ye Ghibellines, play your cunning game
   beneath some other standard; who divide
   this one from justice ever do it shame.
Nor with his Guelfs let this young Charles deride
   its power, but fear its talons, lest he be
   stripped, as was prouder lion, of his hide.
Oft wailing for their father's fault we see
   the sons; nor let him madly dream that Heaven
   will change its scutcheon for his fleur-de-lis!
Adornment to this little star is given
   by noble souls, who through laborious days
   for honour and undying fame have striven:

e quando li disiri poggian quivi,
    sì disviando, pur convien che i raggi
    del vero amore in sù poggin men vivi.   117
Ma nel commensurar dei nostri gaggi
    col merto, è parte di nostra letizia,
    perchè non li vedem minor nè maggi.   120
Quindi addolcisce la viva giustizia
    in noi l'affetto sì, che non si puote
    torcer già mai ad alcuna nequizia.   123
Diverse voci fanno dolci note;
    così diversi scanni in nostra vita
    rendon dolce armonia tra queste rote.   126
E dentro a la presente margarita
    luce la luce di Romeo, di cui
    fu l'opra grande e bella mal gradita.   129
Ma i Provenzai che fecer contra lui
    non hanno riso, però mal cammina
    qual si fa danno del ben fare altrui.   132
Quattro figlie ebbe, e ciascuna reina,
    Raimondo Beringhieri, e ciò li fece
    Romeo, persona umìle e peregrina.   135
E poi il mosser le parole biece
    a dimandar ragione a questo giusto,
    che gli assegnò sette e cinque per diece   138
Indi partissi povero e vetusto;
    e se il mondo sapesse il cor ch'egli ebbe
    mendicando sua vita a frusto a frusto,   141
assai lo loda e più lo loderebbe».

CANTO 7

« *H*OSANNA, *sanctus Deus sabaoth,*
    superillustrans claritate tua
    felices ignes horum malacoth».   3
Così, volgendosi alla nota sua,
    fu viso a me cantare essa sustanza,
    sopra la qual doppio lume s'addua;   6

and when desires have clomb thereto by ways
   thus errant, the true love must needs have soar'd
   unto its goal emitting feebler rays.
Yet in the balancing of our reward
   with our desert lies part of our delight,
   because we see them in complete accord.
Hence doth the living justice so make right
   our hearts within us, that we have no fears
   of wishing now aught sinful in God's sight.
As diverse voices make in mortal ears
   sweet music, so our diverse seats combine
   to make sweet harmony among these spheres.
And closed within this pearl, the sheen doth shine
   of Romeo, whose fair deeds of goodly worth
   were guerdoned with ingratitude malign.
But small cause have the Provençáls for mirth
   who wrought his ruin; ill fares the man, I ween,
   who makes from others' riches his own dearth.
Four daughters, and each one a wedded queen,
   had Raymond Berenger, taught thus to thrive
   by Romeo, a mere stranger poor and mean.
Then crooked tongues made him inquisitive
   to probe the accounts of this just man and good,
   who rendered him full six for every five.
Old and in rags he parted thence: and could
   the world but know the gallant heart he bore,
   as, crust by crust, he begged his livelihood,
much as it lauds him it would laud him more.'

CANTO 7

'Hosanna, Sanctus Deus sabaoth!
   Thine are these realms, their blessèd fires are thine,
   for super-illumined by thy beams are both.'
Revolving thus to its own note divine
   I saw that substance chanting, on which two
   bright aureoles, a double splendour, shine;

ed essa e l'altre mossero a sua danza,
 e quasi velocissime faville
 mi si velar di subita distanza.   9
Io dubitava, e dicea « Dille, dille »
 fra me « dille » dicea, a la mia donna
 che mi disseta con le dolci stille;   12
ma quella reverenza che s'indonna
 di tutto me pur per *Be* e per *ice*,
 mi richinava come l'uom che assonna.   15
Poco sofferse me cotal Beatrice;
 e cominciò, raggiandomi d'un riso
 tal, che nel foco faria l'uom felice: 18
« Secondo mio infallibile avviso,
 come giusta vendetta giustamente
 punita fosse, t'ha in pensier miso;   21
ma io ti solverò tosto la mente;
 e tu ascolta, chè le mie parole
 di gran sentenza ti faran presente.   24
Per non soffrire a la virtù che vuole
 freno a suo prode, quell'uom che non nacque
 dannando sè dannò tutta sua prole;   27
onde l'umana specie inferma giacque
 già per secoli molti in grande errore
 fin che al Verbo di Dio di scender piacque, 30
u' la natura che dal suo fattore
 s'era allungata, unì a sè in persona,
 con l'atto sol del su' eterno amore.   33
Or drizza il viso a quel ch'or si ragiona:
 questa natura al suo fattore unita,
 qual fu creata fu sincera e buona;   36
ma per se stessa fu ella sbandita
 di Paradiso, però che si torse
 da via di verità e da sua vita   39
La pena dunque che la croce porse,
 se a la natura assunta si misura,
 nulla già mai sì giustamente morse;   42
e così nulla fu di tanta ingiura
 guardando a la persona che sofferse
 in che era contratta tal natura.   45

and it and the others to their dance withdrew,
  and like exceedingly quick sparks, straightway
  by distance from me veiled, were lost to view.
A doubt within me 'Say it,' whispered, 'say,
  oh, say it to my lady! Be it confess'd
  to her whose gentle dews my thirst allay.'
But that dumb awe which queens it o'er my breast
  wholly, at the mere sound of *Be* and *ice*,
  still bowed me low as one by sleep possess'd.
Not long was I so left by Beatrice,
  who, flashing at me such a smile as might,
  e'en at the stake, have plunged one's soul in bliss,
began, 'If I, who cannot err, deem right,
  how a just vengeance could with justice be
  punished, confounds thee in thine own despite;
but I from doubt thy mind will quickly free;
  and to the words I speak do thou give heed,
  for weighty doctrine shall they impart to thee.
Because his will brooked not a curb decreed
  for his own good, the man no woman bore
  damned in his own damnation all his seed;
whence humankind on earth in error sore
  lay sick for ages, till from heaven above
  God's Word came down the nature to restore,
which from its author stood at far remove,
  and made it with himself in person one
  by the sole act of his eternal love.
Now see what follows now and gaze thereon:
  one with its Maker, such as it was first
  created, pure and good this nature shone;
but through itself alone, because it durst
  turn from the way of truth where its life lay,
  from Paradise 'twas driven forth accurst.
By the adopted nature, then, assay
  the cross as penalty and thou wilt find
  that never doom so justly gripped its prey;
and likewise none to justice was so blind,
  if thou the sufferer's person contemplate,
  in whom this human nature was combined.

Però d'un atto uscir cose diverse:
    che a Dio e ai Giudei piacque una morte;
    per lei tremò la Terra e il Ciel s'aperse.   48
Non ti deve oramai parer più forte
    quando si dice che giusta vendetta
    poscia vengiata fu da giusta corte.   51
Ma io veggio or la tua mente ristretta
    di pensiero in pensier dentro ad un nodo
    del qual con gran disio solver s'aspetta.   54
Tu dici: 'Ben discerno ciò ch'i'odo;
    ma perchè Dio volesse m'è occulto
    a nostra redenzion pur questo modo'.   57
Questo decreto, frate, sta sepulto
    a gli occhi di ciascuno il cui ingegno
    ne la fiamma d'amor non è adulto.   60
Veramente, però che a questo segno
    molto si mira e poco si discerne,
    dirò perchè tal modo fu più degno.   63
La divina bontà, che da sè sperne
    ogni livore, ardendo in sè, sfavilla
    sì che dispiega le bellezze eterne: 66
ciò che da lei sanza mezzo distilla
    non ha poi fine, perchè non si move
    la sua imprenta quando ella sigilla;   69
ciò che da essa sanza mezzo piove
    libero è tutto, perchè non soggiace
    a la virtute de le cose nove;   72
più l'è conforme, e però più le piace,
    chè l'ardor santo ch'ogni cosa raggia,
    ne la più somigliante è più vivace.   75
Di tutte queste dote s'avvantaggia
    l'umana creatura; e s'una manca
    di sua nobilità convien che caggia.   78
Solo il peccato è quel che la disfranca
    e falla dissimìle al sommo bene;
    per che del lume suo poco s'imbianca;   81
ed in sua dignità mai non riviene
    se non riempie, dove colpa vota,
    contra mal dilettar con giuste pene.   84

Thus issued from one act things disparate:
   God and the Jews with the same death were pleased;
   it shook the earth, of Heav'n set wide the gate.
In future, then, no more with doubts be teased,
   when hearing that a just tribunal wrought
   vengeance for one whom vengeance justly seized.
But now, thy mind enmeshed by thought on thought,
   I see thee waiting with attentive ear
   for clue from me that shall untie the knot.
Thou sayst: "I well discern what now I hear;
   but wherefore God ordained this means alone
   for our redemption—that is far from clear."
Too deeply buried, brother, to be shown
   is this decree, except to those whose wit
   within the flame of love is fully grown.
But, inasmuch as many fain would hit
   this mark, and but few strike it, thou shalt learn
   wherefore the method chosen was most fit.
The divine goodness from itself doth spurn
   all envy, so that, sparkling, it reveals
   the eternal beauties that within it burn.
Whate'er from it immediately distils
   endures then endlessly, for there is no
   impression lost when it is God who seals.
Whate'er from him immediately doth flow
   is wholly free, not subject to the might
   of causes which from other causes grow.
As like him more, it gives him more delight;
   for in what most resembles it, most lives
   the holy flame which maketh all things bright.
Such is the birthright that his Maker gives
   to man; who must, if even one should fail,
   lose with it all these high prerogatives.
'Tis sin alone can freedom's loss entail
   and mar man's likeness to the sovereign Good,
   causing its light, which lightens him, to pale—
loss irretrievable, except he should
   refill the void his guilty pleasures made,
   with righteous pains of equal magnitude.

Vostra natura, quando peccò tota
nel seme suo, da queste dignitadi,
come di Paradiso, fu remota;   87
nè ricovrar potiensi, se tu badi
ben sottilmente, per alcuna via
sanza passar per l'un di questi guadi: 90
o che Dio solo per sua cortesia
dimesso avesse, o che l'uom per sè isso
avesse sodisfatto a sua follia.   93
Ficca mo l'occhio per entro l'abisso
de l'eterno consiglio, quanto puoi
al mio parlar distrettamente fisso.   96
Non potea l'uomo nei termini suoi
mai sodisfar, per non potere ir giuso
con umiltate obediendo poi   99
quanto disobediendo intese ir suso;
e questa è la cagion perchè l'uom fue
da poter sodisfar per sè, dischiuso.   102
Dunque a Dio convenia con le vie sue
riparar l'uomo a sua intera vita,
dico con l'una o ver con ambedue.   105
Ma perchè l'opra è tanto più gradita
da l'operante, quanto più appresenta
de la bontà del core ond'ella è uscita,   108
la divina bontà che il mondo imprenta,
di proceder per tutte le sue vie,
a rilevarvi suso, fu contenta;   111
nè tra l'ultima notte e il primo die
sì alto o sì magnifico processo,
o per l'una o per l'altra, fu o fie: 114
chè più largo fu Dio a dar se stesso,
per far l'uom sufficiente a rilevarsi,
che s'egli avesse sol da sè dimesso,   117
e tutti gli altri modi erano scarsi
a la giustizia, se il Figliuol di Dio
non fosse umiliato ad incarnarsi.   120
Or per empierti bene ogni disio,
ritorno a dichiarare in alcun loco
perchè tu veggi lì così com'io.   123

Your nature, when it all had disobey'd
   in its first germ, was, as from Paradise
   removed, so of these honours disarray'd;
nor could regain them, if thou scrutinize
   the matter subtly, save by crossing one
   of these two fords—thus, or not otherwise:
either that of his courtesy alone
   God should remit, or, failing this, that man
   should for his folly of himself atone.
Within the abyss of heaven's eternal plan
   fix now thine eye, and bid thy subtle mind
   cling to my words as closely as it can.
Never could man, in human bounds confined,
   have paid his debt, because he could not stoop
   low by obeying, after he had sinned,
so far as upward it was erst his hope
   to mount by disobeying: this is why
   man with his debt, unaided, could not cope.
God it behoved, then, his own ways to try
   and thus—I mean, by one or both the same—
   to restore man to his integrity.
But as the doer's deed will more proclaim
   its graciousness the more that it displays
   the goodness of the heart from whence it came,
the divine goodness, which its imprint lays
   upon the world, to lift you from your fall
   was minded to proceed by all its ways.
Nor 'tween the last night and first day of all
   shall be, by either way, or has been yet,
   process so high or so magnifical.
for God more richly all requirements met,
   giving himself to give man power to rise,
   than had his simple fiat annulled the debt;
and heav'n no other method could devise
   which squared with justice, save that God's own Son
   himself should stoop to put on mortal guise.
Now to leave nought of all thy wish undone,
   I turn me back to illumine a certain place,
   that therein thou and I may see as one.

Tu dici: 'Io veggio l'acqua, io veggio il foco,
  l'aere, la terra e tutte lor misture
  venire a corruzione e durar poco;   126
e queste cose pur furon creature;
  per che se ciò ch'è detto è stato vero,
  esser dovrien da corruzion secure'.   129
Gli angeli, frate, e il paese sincero
  nel qual tu sei, dir si posson creati
  sì come sono in lor essere intero;   132
ma gli elementi che tu hai nomati
  e quelle cose che di lor si fanno,
  da creata virtù sono informati: 135
creata fu la materia ch'egli hanno,
  creata fu la virtù informante
  in queste stelle che intorno a lor vanno.   138
L'anima d'ogni bruto e de le piante
  di complession potenziata tira
  lo raggio e il moto de le luci sante;   141
ma vostra vita sanza mezzo spira
  la somma beninanza, e la innamora
  di sè sì che poi sempre la disira.   144
E quinci puoi argomentare ancora
  vostra resurrezion, se tu ripensi
  come l'umana carne fessi, allora   147
che li primi parenti entrambi fensi».

CANTO 8

Solea creder lo mondo in suo periclo
  che la bella Ciprigna il folle amore
  raggiasse, volta nel terzo epiciclo;   3
per che non pure a lei faceano onore
  di sacrificio e di votivo grido
  le genti antiche ne l'antico errore;   6
ma Dione onoravano e Cupido,
  quella per madre sua questo per figlio;
  e dicean ch'ei sedette in grembo a Dido;   9

Thou say'st: "I see air, I see fire no less
    than water, earth and all their mixtures grow
    corrupted, and endure but little space;
yet these were creatures, hence should never know
    corruption, but should bide therefrom secure,
    if what thou saidst was true be really so."
The angels, brother, and the region pure
    wherein thou art, were framed (as all agree)
    in their whole being, as they still endure;
but those four elements just named by thee,
    and whatsoever thence is born and bred,
    through some created virtue came to be.
Created was the stuff whereof they are made;
    created was the informing power in these
    revolving constellations round them spread.
The motion and ray o' the holy luminaries
    draw out from a complexion apt therefór
    what soul in plants and every brute there is;
but into you the sovereign Good doth pour
    your life direct, and makes it so to love
    himself, that it desires him evermore.
And hence thou canst by further reasoning prove
    your resurrection, if thou call to mind
    how human flesh was made, what time thereof
were made the two first parents of mankind.'

CANTO 8

'Twas the fair Cyprian, pagans once believed,
    who, whirled in the third epicycle, rayed
    love-frenzy down on mortals; whence, deceived
by the ancient fancy, ancient peoples made
    their offerings, and their votive shouts addressed
    not to her only, but like honours paid
to Cupid and Dione, this confessed
    her mother, that her son; and they were wont
    to say he was on Dido's lap caressed;

e da costei ond'io principio piglio
  pigliavano il vocabol de la stella
  che il Sol vagheggia or da coppa or da ciglio.   12
Io non m'accorsi del salire in ella,
  ma d'esservi entro mi fe' assai fede
  la donna mia ch'io vidi far più bella.   15
E come in fiamma favilla si vede
  e come in voce voce si discerne,
  quand'una è ferma e l'altra va e riede,   18
vid'io in essa luce altre lucerne
  moversi in giro più e men correnti,
  al modo, credo, di lor viste eterne.   21
Di fredda nube non disceser venti,
  o visibili o no, tanto festini,
  che non paressero impediti e lenti   24
a chi avesse quei lumi divini
  veduti a noi venir, lasciando il giro
  pria cominciato in gli alti Serafini.   27
E dentro a quei che più innanzi appariro
  sonava *Osanna* sì, che unque poi
  di riudir non fui sanza disiro.   30
Indi si fece l'un più presso a noi
  e solo incominciò: « Tutti sem presti
  al tuo piacer perchè di noi ti gioi.   33
Noi ci volgiam coi Principi celesti
  d'un giro, d'un girare e d'una sete,
  ai quali tu dal mondo già dicesti   36
Voi che intendendo il terzo ciel movete;
  e sem sì pien d'amor, che per piacerti
  non fia men dolce un poco di quiete ».   39
Poscia che gli occhi miei si furo offerti
  a la mia donna reverenti, ed ella
  fatti li avea di sè contenti e certi,   42
rivolsersi a la luce che promessa
  tanto s'avea, e: « Deh, chi sei tu? » fue
  la voce mia, di grande affetto impressa.   45
E quanta e quale vid'io lei far piue
  per allegrezza nova che s'accrebbe,
  quand'io parlai, a l'allegrezze sue!   48

and after her upon whose name I count
  to adorn this proem did they name the star
  which the Sun woos, now behind, now in front.
That in it now was I the proof was clear
  because, tho' all unconscious that we rose,
  I saw my lady's face had grown more fair.
And even as in flame a sparkle shows,
  and as in voice a voice is heard, when one
  is steady, and the other comes and goes;
I in that light saw other lamps which shone
  revolving, some with less, some greater speed,
  as urged, I trow, by Him they gaze upon.
Never descended winds, or seen or hid,
  from chill cloud, but would slow and hindered seem
  to one who had beheld, as I now did,
those heavenly radiances to us-ward stream,
  quitting the circle where they had till then
  been dancing with the exalted Seraphim.
And from the foremost pealed in loud refrain
  such an 'Hosanna' as thereafter I
  was ne'er without the wish to hear again.
Then one alone, yet closer drawing nigh,
  began: 'We all stand ready at thy beck
  to serve thee, that thou mayest of us have joy.
We in one circle roll, one circling make,
  one thirst with those high Princes share above,
  whom from the world thyself erewhile bespake
as "Spirits that by understanding move
  the third heaven", now for thee not less content
  to pause awhile, so full we are of love.'
Mine eyes, which first with reverence were bent
  upon my lady, turned as soon as she
  had made them glad and sure of her assent,
back to the light, which had on terms so free
  proffered itself, and: 'Oh, who art thou?' I cried
  in tones that spoke my affection forcibly.
How by new gladness, when I spoke, beside
  its other gladnesses I saw it grow
  enlarged, its light how much intensified!

571

Così fatta, mi disse: « Il mondo m'ebbe
  giù poco tempo, e se più fosse stato,
  molto sarà di mal che non sarebbe.   51
La mia letizia mi ti tien celato,
  che mi raggia dintorno e mi nasconde
  quasi animal di sua seta fasciato.   54
Assai m'amasti, e n'avesti ben onde;
  chè s'io fossi giù stato, io ti mostrava
  di mio amor più oltre che le fronde.   57
Quella sinistra riva che si lava
  di Rodano poi ch'è misto con Sorga,
  per suo signore a tempo m'aspettava;   60
e quel corno d'Ausonia che s'imborga
  di Bari, di Gaeta e di Catona,
  da ove Tronto e Verde in mare sgorga.   63
Fulgeami già in fronte la corona
  di quella terra che il Danubio riga
  poi che le ripe tedesche abbandona.   66
E la bella Trinacria, che caliga
  tra Pachino e Peloro, sopra il golfo
  che riceve da Euro maggior briga,   69
non per Tifeo ma per nascente solfo,
  attesi avrebbe li suoi regi ancora
  nati per me di Carlo e di Rodolfo,   72
se mala signoria, che sempre accora
  li popoli soggetti, non avesse
  mosso Palermo a gridar *Mora, mora!*   75
E se mio frate questo antivedesse,
  l'avara povertà di Catalogna
  già fuggiria perchè non gli offendesse;   78
chè veramente provveder bisogna
  per lui o per altrui, sì ch'a sua barca
  carcata, più di carco non si pogna.   81
La sua natura, che di larga parca
  discese, avria mestier di tal milizia
  che non curasse di mettere in arca ».   84
« Però ch'io credo che l'alta letizia
  che il tuo parlar m'infonde, signor mio,
  là 've ogni ben si termina e s'inizia   87

Thus changed, it said to me: 'Short while below
  the world retained me; had it longer been,
  much would be spared of fast impending woe.
My happiness envelops me within
  the beams it sheds, concealing me from view,
  like creature swathed in silk its self doth spin.
Thou lov'dst me well and with good reason too;
  for had I stayed below, thou hadst been shown
  more of my love than to mere leafage grew.
The region watered on his left by Rhône,
  beyond the point where Sorgue is mixed with him,
  me for its sovereign was prepared to own;
so too Ausonia's horn, about whose rim
  Bari, Gaëta and Catona stand,
  whence Verde seaward falls and Tronto's stream.
Upon my brow the crown of that fair land
  already shone which is by Danube bathed,
  when he hath quitted either German strand.
And beautiful Trinacria. cloud-enswathed
  between Pachynus and Pelore, along
  the bay which Eurus never leaves unscathed
(cloud by up-steaming sulphur round it hung,
  not by Typhoeus), had awaited still
  its kings through me of Charles and Rudolf sprung,
if evil lordship, ever prone to fill
  with fury subject peoples, had not made
  Palermo clamour fiercely: "Kill them, kill!"
And if my brother this foresaw, in dread
  lest, through her greedy want, grave ill betide,
  he'd now be shunning Catalonia's aid;
for truly need there is that he provide,
  or others for him, that with further freight
  his over-freighted vessel be not plied.
His nature which is mean, though derivate
  from bounteous, were best served by soldiery
  careless in well-lined chests to hoard more yet.'
'Since I believe the high felicity
  which these thy words infuse in me, Your Grace,
  as *I* see 't in myself, is seen by *thee*

per te si veggia come la vegg'io,
   grata m'è più, ed anco questo ho caro
   perchè il discerni rimirando in Dio.   90
Fatto m'hai lieto, e così mi fa chiaro,
   perchè parlando a dubitar m'hai mosso
   com'escir può di dolce seme amaro».   93
Questo io a lui; ed egli a me: «S'io posso
   mostrarti un vero, a quel che tu domandi
   terrai 'l viso come tieni il dosso.   96
Lo ben che tutto il regno che tu scandi
   volge e contenta, fa esser virtute
   sua providenza in questi corpi grandi;   99
e non pur le nature provedute
   sono in la mente ch'è da sè perfetta,
   ma esse insieme con la lor salute: 102
per che quantunque quest'arco saetta
   disposto cade a preveduto fine,
   sì come cocca in suo segno diretta.   105
Se ciò non fosse, il ciel che tu cammine
   producerebbe sì li suoi effetti,
   che non sarebber arti ma ruine;   108
e ciò esser non può se gl'intelletti
   che movon queste stelle non son manchi,
   e manco il primo che non li ha perfetti.   111
Vuoi tu che questo ver più ti s'imbianchi?»
   E io: «Non già; chè impossibil veggio
   che la natura in quel ch'è uopo stanchi». 114
Ond'egli ancora: «Or dì, sarebbe il peggio
   per l'uomo in Terra se non fosse cive?»
   «Sì» rispos'io «e qui ragion non cheggio». 117
«E può egli esser se giù non si vive
   diversamente per diversi offici?
   No, se il maestro vostro ben vi scrive».   120
Sì venne deducendo infino a quici.
   Poscia conchiuse: «Dunque esser diverse
   convien de' vostri effetti le radici;   123
per ch'un nasce Solone ed altro Serse,
   altro Melchisedech ed altro quello
   che volando per l'aere il figlio perse.   126

where all goods have their goal and starting-place,
  my joy's the more; and this, too, I hold dear—
  that thou discern'st it, gazing on God's face.
Thou'st made me glad, now likewise, make me clear
  since thou hast stirred a doubt within my mind,
  how a sweet seed a bitter fruit can bear.'
Thus I to him; and he to me: 'Thou art blind
  to a truth, which can I show thee, then thine eyes
  will have before them what is now behind.
The Good that wheels and wholly satisfies
  the realm thou'rt climbing, makes its foresight be
  virtue within these mighty luminaries.
The all-perfect Mind doth in itself foresee
  not the mere natures only, but with them
  all that combines for their security:
thus whatsoe'er this bow lets fly, the same
  prevision to a destined mark doth bring,
  like missile loosed with an unerring aim.
Or else the heaven which thou art traversing
  would so produce the effects it does, that these
  would not be works of art, but ruins—a thing
that cannot be, if the Intelligences
  who move these stars have no defect, and none
  the First; for, could they fail, the fault were his.
Wilt thou that on this truth more light be thrown?'
  And I: 'Not so; for Nature, I concede,
  can ne'er grow tired in what must needs be done.'
Whence he again: 'On Earth, should men not lead
  a civic life, would they be worse off so?'
  'Yes' answered I; 'and this no proof doth need.'
'And could they lead it, but that life below
  for divers functions is diversely suited?
  Consult your master, and he tells you "no".'
Thus came he, having point by point disputed,
  to his conclusion—'Therefore,' did it run,
  'effects in you must needs be divers-rooted:
hence one is Solon born, one Xerxes, one
  Melchizedec, one he who sought to win
  his way by air, and, flying, lost his son.

575

La circular natura, ch'è suggello
  a la cera mortal, fa ben su' arte,
  ma non distingue l'un da l'altro ostello;   129
quinci addivien che Esaù si diparte
  per seme da Iacobbe, e vien Quirino
  da sì vil padre che si rende a Marte.   132
Natura generata il suo cammino
  simil farebbe sempre ai generanti
  se non vincesse il provveder divino.   135
Or quel che t'era dietro t'è davanti;
  ma perchè sappi che di te mi giova,
  un corollario voglio che t'ammanti.   138
Sempre natura, se fortuna trova
  discorde a sè, com'ogni altra semente
  fuor di sua region, fa mala prova.   141
E se il mondo là giù ponesse mente
  al fondamento che natura pone,
  seguendo lui avria buona la gente.   144
Ma voi torcete a la religione
  tal che fia nato a cingersi la spada,
  e fate re di tal ch'è da sermone: 147
onde la traccia vostra è fuor di strada».

CANTO 9

Da poi che Carlo tuo, bella Clemenza,
  m'ebbe chiarito, mi narrò gl'inganni
  che ricever dovea la sua semenza;   3
ma disse: «Taci e lascia volger gli anni»;
  sì ch'io non posso dir se non che pianto
  giusto verrà di retro ai vostri danni.   6
E già la vita di quel lume santo
  rivolta s'era al Sol che la riempie
  come quel ben che ad ogni cosa è tanto.   9
Ahi anime ingannate e fatture empie
  che da sì fatto ben torcete i cuori,
  drizzando in vanità le vostre tempie!   12

Nature that, as she wheels, hath ever been
  stamp to your wax, plies well her craft and yet
  favours not one above another inn.
Hence Esau is by seed made separate
  from Jacob; hence Quirinus comes of blood
  so base, that men from Mars his lineage date.
Without the o'erruling providence of God
  begotten nature would forever tread
  the self-same track that the begetters trod.
What was behind thee fronts thee now instead:
  but for a proof of my affection bind
  this, for corollary, about thine head.
Ever with Nature, if she fortune find
  discordant with herself, it goeth hard,
  as with all other seeds in soil unkind.
And if the world down there paid due regard
  to the foundation Nature lays, content
  to build on that, the race were nobly rear'd.
But ye to monkhood twist from his true bent
  the stripling born to gird himself with sword,
  and make a king of one for preaching meant:
thus with the road your foot-prints ill accord.'

CANTO 9

AFTER thy Charles, fair Clemence, thus had freed
  my mind of all obscurity, he spake
  next of the wiles which should defraud his seed;
but he 'Keep silent' said, 'and let time take
  its destined course'; so I can say but this—
  just woe will follow in your losses' wake.
Now to the Sun which fills it aye with bliss
  that holy lantern's life had turned again,
  as to that good which all-sufficing is.
Ah, souls deceived and creatures how profane,
  from good so great to turn your hearts aside,
  setting your thoughts on things that are but vain!

Ed ecco un altro di quelli splendori
ver me si fece, e il suo voler piacermi
significava nel chiarir di fuori.   15

Gli occhi di Beatrice, ch'eran fermi
sovra me, come pria di caro assenso
al mio disio certificato fermi.   18

« Deh metti al mio voler tosto compenso,
beato spirto » dissi « e fammi prova
ch'io possa in te rifletter quel ch'io penso ».   21

Onde la luce che m'era ancor nova,
del suo profondo, ond'ella pria cantava,
seguette come a cui di ben far giova: 24

« In quella parte de la terra prava
italica che siede tra Rialto
e le fontane di Brenta e di Piava,   27

si leva un colle, e non surge molt'alto,
là onde scese già una facella
che fece a la contrada grande assalto.   30

D'una radice nacqui ed io ed ella:
Cunizza fui chiamata, e qui refulgo
perchè mi vinse il lume d'esta stella.   33

Ma lietamente a me medesma indulgo
la cagion di mia sorte, e non mi noia:
che parria forse forte al vostro vulgo.   36

Di questa luculenta e cara gioia
del nostro cielo che più m'è propinqua,
grande fama rimase, e pria che muoia   39

questo centesim'anno ancor s'incinqua:
vedi se far si dee l'uomo eccellente
sì ch'altra vita la prima relinqua.   42

E ciò non pensa la turba presente
che Tagliamento e Adice richiude,
nè per esser battuta ancor si pente.   45

Ma tosto fia che Padova al palude
cangerà l'acqua che Vicenza bagna,
per essere al dover le genti crude.   48

E dove Sile e Cagnan s'accompagna,
tal signoreggia e va con la test'alta,
che già per lui carpir si fa la ragna.   51

And of those splendours lo, another hied
   tow'rds me, and by becoming e'en brighter yet
   its will to please me clearly signified.
The eyes of Beatrice, as erstwhile, set
   firmly on mine, the loved assurance brought
   that my desire with her approval met.
'Ah, blesséd spirit,' I cried, 'delay thou not,
   but to my wish grant speedy recompense,
   and prove thou canst be mirror to my thought!'
Whereat the light out of its own depth whence
   it sang before, and still concealed therein,
   went on, as joying in its beneficence:
'Within that region of the land of sin
   called Italy, which 'tween Rialto lies
   and where the Piava and Brenta both begin,
uplifts itself a hill of no great size,
   whence hurtling once a little firebrand came
   which smote the country round with fierce emprise.
One root produced both me and it: my name
   know for Cunizza, and that here I shine
   because o'ermastered by this planet's flame.
But gladly for what made this lot be mine
   I grant (though your gross minds may wonder why)
   myself forgiveness, nor thereat repine.
Of this bright, precious jewel of our sky
   which glitters next to me, is left alive
   a fame on earth so great that, ere it die,
this century shall lengthen into five:
   see then if man should aim not so to excel
   that in a second life the first survive.
So think not they, the rabble that now dwell
   'twixt Tagliamento and Adigé, nor rue
   they yet their sins, tho' oft chastiséd well.
But soon shall Padua at the marsh imbrue
   the waves that lap Vicenza, since undone
   its folk still leave the thing they ought to do.
And where Cagnán meets Sile, lords it one
   stalking with head held high, for whom the net
   to catch him in is even now begun.

Piangerà Feltre ancora la diffalta
  de l'empio suo pastor, che sarà sconcia
  sì, che per simil non s'entrò in Malta.   54
Troppo sarebbe larga la bigoncia
  che ricevesse il sangue ferrarese,
  e stanco chi il pesasse a oncia a oncia,   57
che donerà questo prete cortese
  per mostrarsi di parte; e cotai doni
  conformi fieno al viver del paese.   60
Sù sono specchi, voi dicete Troni,
  onde refulge a noi Dio giudicante;
  sì che questi parlar ne paion buoni».   63
Qui si tacette, e fecemi sembiante
  che fosse ad altro volta, per la rota
  in che si mise com'era davante.   66
L'altra letizia, che m'era già nota
  per cara cosa, mi si fece in vista
  qual fin balascio in che lo Sol percuota.   69
Per letiziar là sù fulgor s'acquista
  sì come riso qui: ma giù s'abbuia
  l'ombra di fuor, come la mente è trista.   72
« Dio vede tutto, e tuo veder s'inluia »
  diss'io, « beato spirto, sì, che nulla
  voglia di sè a te puot'esser fuia.   75
Dunque la voce tua, che il ciel trastulla
  sempre col canto di quei fuochi pii
  che di sei ali fannosi coculla,   78
perchè non satisface a' miei disii?
  già non attendere' io tua dimanda,
  s'io m'intuassi come tu t'immii ».   81
« La maggior valle in che l'acqua si spanda »
  incominciaro allor le sue parole
  « fuor di quel mar che la terra inghirlanda,   84
tra i discordanti liti contro al Sole
  tanto sen va, che fa meridiano
  là dove l'orizzonte pria far suole.   87
Di quella valle fu' io litorano
  tra Ebro e Macra, che per cammin corto
  parte lo Genovese dal Toscano.   90

Its wicked pastor's crime will Feltro yet
  bewail, and such shall be his turpitude,
  that Malta for the like ne'er oped her gate.
The vat which should contain Ferrara's blood
  were wide indeed, and weary he that strove
  to weigh it ounce by ounce—so large the flood,
which this obliging priest will give to prove
  himself a partisan; and gifts like his
  will suit the country and the ways thereof.
Aloft are mirrors—"Thrones" your saying is—
  which unto us God's judgments clearly show;
  so that we all approve these utterances.'
Therewith she ceased, and semblance made as though
  her thoughts had elsewhere turned, because she flew
  back to the ring where she had wheeled but now.
The other joy, which I already knew
  to be a thing of worth, the look now had
  of a fine balas by the Sun struck through.
Effulgence comes, up there, of being glad,
  as laughter here: but, lower, the shade bedims
  its outward aspect as the mind is sad.
'God sees all, and thy sight so itself in-Hims,'
  said I, 'blest spirit, that from thee can nought
  escape, not e'en one's lightest wish or whims.
Thou with those genial fires, whose cowl is wrought
  of wings sixfold, divert'st unceasingly
  the heaven with song; then why, ere thus besought,
dost thou not give contentment to my plea?
  to thine long since my answer had been made,
  if I in-thee'd me, as thou in-meëst thee.'
'The largest vale where water lies outspread,
  drawn from that sea,' he then began to say,
  'wherewith the whole earth is engarlanded,
'twixt shores discordant, 'gainst the solar ray
  stretches so far, it makes the zenith lie
  where at its outset the horizon lay.
A dweller on that valley's coast was I,
  between the Ebro and where the Magra's short
  descent parts Genoa from Tuscany.

Ad un occaso quasi e ad un orto
   Buggea siede e la terra ond'io fui,
   che fe' del sangue suo già caldo il porto.   93
Folco mi disse quella gente a cui
   fu noto il nome mio; e questo cielo
   di me s'imprenta com'io fei di lui.   96
Chè più non arse la figlia di Belo,
   noiando ed a Sicheo ed a Creusa,
   di me, infin che si convenne al pelo;   99
nè quella Rodopea che delusa
   fu da Demofoonte, nè Alcide
   quando Iole nel core ebbe rinchiusa.   102
Non però qui si pente, ma si ride:
   non della colpa, che a mente non torna,
   ma del valore che ordinò e provvide.   105
Qui si rimira ne l'arte che adorna
   cotanto effetto, e discernesi il bene
   per che il mondo di sù quel di giù torna.   108
Ma perchè tutte le tue voglie piene
   ten porti, che son nate in questa spera,
   procedere ancor oltre mi conviene.   111
Tu vuoi saper chi è in questa lumera
   che qui appresso me così scintilla
   come raggio di sole in acqua mera.   114
Or sappi che là entro si tranquilla
   Raab; ed a nostr'ordine congiunta,
   di lei nel sommo grado si sigilla.   117
Da questo cielo, in cui l'ombra s'appunta
   che il vostro mondo face, pria ch'altr'alma
   del trionfo di Cristo fu assunta.   120
Ben si convenne lei lasciar per palma
   in alcun cielo de l'alta vittoria
   che s'acquistò con l'una e l'altra palma,   123
perch'ella favorò la prima gloria
   di Iosuè in su la Terra Santa,
   che poco tocca al papa la memoria.   126
La tua città, che di colui è pianta
   che pria volse le spalle al suo fattore
   e di cui è l'invidia tanto pianta,   129

Well nigh the same meridian runs athwart
   Bougiah and the city whence I came,
   which with its own blood once made warm the port.
To those that knew it Folco was my name;
   and now with me are stamped this heaven's rays
   in the like manner that I was with them;
for fiercelier did not Belus' daughter blaze,
   wronging Sicheus and Crëusa too,
   than I, till graying hair reformed my ways;
nor that fair Rhodopean, doomed to rue
   Demophoön's guile, nor he, Alcides hight,
   when Iole into his heart he drew.
Yet here repent we not, but feel delight,
   not for the sin, which none remembers now,
   but for God's overruling and foresight.
Here we examine the art which worketh so
   effectively, and here discern the weal
   for which the world above shapes that below.
But that, ere hence thou goest, I may fulfil
   all of thy wishes born within this sphere,
   I must proceed a little farther still.
Fain wouldst thou learn who is it radiant here
   beside me in this glittering splendour dress'd,
   like sunbeams glancing on a crystal mere.
Know, then, that in it Rahab findeth rest;
   who being to our order joined, 'tis shown
   as with her seal conspicuously impress'd.
Unto this heaven, where the shadow thrown
   by your world comes to a point, the first was she
   of souls Christ's triumph raised up with his own.
Right meet it was to leave her, so it be
   somewhere in heaven, as palm of victory gain'd
   by the two palms uplifted on the tree,
because she favoured the first glory obtain'd
   by Joshua o'er the Holy Land, a place
   whereon the pope but little thought doth spend.
Thy city, sprung from him, of all his race
   the first that turned against his Maker's power,
   and from whose envy comes such dire distress,

produce e spande il maledetto fiore
  ch'ha disviate le pecore e gli agni,
  però che ha fatto lupo del pastore.   132
Per questo l'Evangelio e i dottor magni
  son derelitti, e solo ai Decretali
  si studia, sì che pare ai lor vivagni.   135
A questo intende il papa e i cardinali:
  non vanno i lor pensieri a Nazarette,
  là dove Gabriello aperse l'ali.   138
Ma Vaticano e l'altre parti elette
  di Roma che son state cimitero
  a la milizia che Pietro seguette,   141
tosto libere fien de l'adultèro».

CANTO 10

Guardando nel suo Figlio con l'amore
  che l'uno e l'altro eternalmente spira,
  lo primo ed ineffabile valore   3
quanto per mente e per loco si gira
  con tant'ordine fe', ch'esser non puote
  sanza gustar di lui chi ciò rimira.   6
Leva, dunque, lettore, a l'alte rote
  meco la vista, dritto a quella parte
  dove l'un moto e l'altro si percuote,   9
e lì comincia a vagheggiar ne l'arte
  di quel maestro che dentro a sè l'ama
  tanto che mai da lei l'occhio non parte.   12
Vedi come da indi si dirama
  l'obliquo cerchio che i pianeti porta
  per sodisfare al mondo che li chiama.   15
E se la strada lor non fosse torta,
  molta virtù nel Ciel sarebbe in vano
  e quasi ogni potenza qua giù morta;   18
e se dal dritto più o men lontano
  fosse il partire, assai sarebbe manco
  e sù e giù de l'ordine mondano.   21

brings forth and spreads abroad the accurséd flower
   which sheep and lambs alike hath led astray,
   making him wolf that shepherd was before.
For this deserted are the fathers, nay
   the Gospels too, and Canon Law alone
   is studied, as its margins well display.
For this the pope and cardinals disown
   all else, nor ever think on Nazareth,
   where once the wingéd Gabriel flew down.
But Rome and all the tombs in it, by faith
   held sacred, with the Vatican, where lie
   the saints who fought with Peter to the death,
shall soon be freed from the adultery.'

CANTO 10

THE ineffable and uncreated Worth
   gazing with Love upon his Son's dear face—
   the Love that each eternally breathes forth,
hath all things that revolve through mind and place
   with so much order made, that none can view
   his works and taste not of his graciousness.
Raise, then, thy vision, Reader, as I do,
   unto the lofty wheels, straight to that part
   where the one motion strikes the other through;
and there with joy begin to admire the art
   of Him whose eye is never turned aside
   from masterpiece framed after his own heart.
See how the circle where the planets glide
   thence branches off obliquely, with the intent
   that Earth, which calls them, may be satisfied.
And had their pathway not been thus-wise bent,
   vain were much heavenly virtue and well nigh
   all potencies down here would pine and faint;
and were it farther or less far to lie
   out of the straight, in either hemisphere
   grave loss of order would be caused thereby.

Or ti riman, lettor, sopra il tuo banco
  dietro pensando a ciò che si preliba,
  s'esser vuoi lieto assai prima che stanco.   24

Messo t'ho innanzi: omai per te ti ciba,
  chè a sè torce tutta la mia cura
  quella materia ond'io son fatto scriba.   27

Lo ministro maggior de la natura
  che del valor del Ciel lo mondo imprenta
  e col suo lume il tempo ne misura,   30

con quella parte che sù si rammenta
  congiunto, si girava per le spire
  in che più tosto ognora s'appresenta;   33

c io era con lui, ma del salire
  non m'accors'io se non com'uom s'accorge
  anzi il primo pensier, del suo venire.   36

È Beatrice quella che si scorge
  di bene in meglio sì subitamente
  che l'atto suo per tempo non si sporge.   39

Quant'esser convenia da sè lucente
  quel ch'era dentro al Sol dov'io entra'mi,
  non per color, ma per lume parvente!   42

Perch'io l'ingegno e l'arte e l'uso chiami,
  sì nol direi che mai s'immaginasse;
  ma creder puossi e di veder si brami.   45

E se le fantasie nostre son basse
  a tanta altezza, non è maraviglia,
  chè sopra il Sol non fu occhio che andasse.   48

Tal era quivi la quarta famiglia
  de l'alto Padre, che sempre la sazia
  mostrando come spira e come figlia.   51

E Beatrice cominciò: « Ringrazia,
  ringrazia il Sol de gli angeli, che a questo
  sensibil t'ha levato per sua grazia ».   54

Cor di mortal non fu mai sì digesto
  a divozione ed a rendersi a Dio
  con tutto il suo gradir cotanto presto   57

come a quelle parole mi fec'io,
  e sì tutto il mi' amore in lui si mise
  che Beatrice eclissò nell'oblio.   60

Now, Reader, in the banquet persevere,
  reflecting on this foretaste of the meat,
  if, unfatigued, thou would'st enjoy good cheer.
I've set the board: henceforth 'tis yours to eat;
  since all the care I lavish on my rhyme
  is claimed now by the theme whereof I treat.
Of nature's servants, he, the most sublime,
  who stamps with heavenly worth the mundane clay
  and gives us light as means to measure time,
conjoined with that part thou hast heard me say,
  circled the spirals wherein earlier
  his orb presents itself from day to day;
and I was with him; yet no more aware
  of my ascension, than a man may know
  the thought within his brain before it's there.
'Tis Beatrice, 'tis she who guideth so
  from good to better by such instant flight,
  that, to record it, time is far too slow.
How needs must that have been itself most bright,
  which, entering the Sun, I there saw shine
  distinguished, not by colour, but by light!
How, e'er, to image it no skill of mine,
  no wit and usage I invoked, could show;
  but men may trust and for that vision pine.
Nor marvel if, to reach thus high, too low
  our fancies are, for up to light which bates
  the sun's, was never yet eye that could go.
With such, here, the high Father satiates
  his fourth family, to their endless bliss,
  by showing how he breathes and how begets.
'To him, the angels' Sun, who unto this,
  the Sun of sense, hath raised thee by his grace,
  give thanks, give thanks,' commanded Beatrice.
Never was mortal so disposed to place
  his mind on God, and none surrendered e'er
  his heart to God with so much willingness,
as I did, when I heard that call to prayer;
  and so on Him was all my longing stayed,
  that Beatrice, eclipsed, seemed no more there.

Non le dispiacque, ma sì se ne rise
  che lo splendor de gli occhi suoi ridenti
  mia mente unita in più cose divise.   63
Io vidi più fulgor vivi e vincenti
  far di noi centro e di sè far corona,
  più dolci in voce che in vista lucenti: 66
così cinger la figlia di Latona
  vedem talvolta, quando l'aere è pregno
  sì, che ritenga il fil che fa la zona.   69
Ne la corte del cielo, ond'io rivegno,
  si trovan molte gioie care e belle
  tanto che non si posson trar del Regno;   72
e il canto di quei lumi era di quelle;
  chi non s'impenna sì che là sù voli,
  dal muto aspetti quindi le novelle.   75
Poi sì cantando quegli ardenti soli
  si fur girati intorno a noi tre volte
  come stelle vicine ai fermi poli,   78
donne mi parver non da ballo sciolte,
  ma che s'arrestin tacite, ascoltando
  fin che le nuove note hanno ricolte.   81
E dentro a l'un sentii cominciar: « Quando
  lo raggio de la grazia, onde s'accende
  verace amore e che poi cresce amando,   84
moltiplicato in te tanto risplende
  che ti conduce sù per quella scala
  u' sanza risalir nessun discende,   87
qual ti negasse il vin de la sua fiala
  per la tua sete, in libertà non fora
  se non com'acqua che al mar non si cala.   90
Tu vuoi saper di quai piante s'infiora
  questa ghirlanda che intorno vagheggia
  la bella donna che al ciel t'avvalora.   93
Io fui de gli agni de la santa greggia
  che Domenico mena per cammino
  u' ben s'impingua se non si vaneggia.   96
Questi che m'è a destra più vicino
  frate e maestro fummi, ed esso Alberto
  è di Cologna, e io Tomas d'Aquino.   99

No whit displeased, she laughed, and laughter made
   her eyes so splendid, that my mind compelled
   to quit one object, was distributed
mid many dazzling lights I now beheld
   forming a halo, which encircled us
   with radiance, by their song alone excelled.
The daughter of Latona cinctured thus
   we see at times, when vapour fills the sky
   and makes her girdle's texture luminous.
In the celestial court, where once was I,
   are many jewels so precious, that in vain
   one seeks to pluck them from the Realm on high;
and of their number was that heavenly strain:
   who thither soars not on the wings of yearning
   may of a dumb man news from thence obtain.
When, chanting thus melodiously, those burning
   suns had wheeled thrice about us where we stood—
   like stars which round the steady poles keep turning,
ladies they seemed, for dancing still in mood,
   who pause in silence at the measure's close,
   listening, till they have caught the strain renew'd.
And, from the depth of one, these accents rose:
   'In that the beam of grace, which lights and tends
   true love and then, by dint of loving, grows,
multiplied now in thee, so far resplends,
   that it conducts thee upward by that stair,
   which save to re-ascend it none descends,
whoso refused thee, for thy thirst, a share
   of wine from his own vial were no more free
   than water is which doth not seaward fare.
Fain wouldst thou know what blossoms these may be,
   engarlanding and with such joy surveying
   the fair dame, who for heaven doth strengthen thee.
I was a lamb of the holy flock, obeying
   that Dominic, who hath a pathway shown,
   where is good fattening, if there be no straying.
My brother and my master, of Cologne,
   neighbours me on my right: Albert his name,
   and Thomas, called Aquinas, is my own.

Se sì di tutti gli altri esser vuoi certo,
  di retro al mio parlar ten vien col viso
  girando su per lo beato serto.   102

Quell'altro fiammeggiare esce del riso
  di Grazian, che l'uno e l'altro foro
  aiutò sì che piace in Paradiso.   105

L'altro che appresso adorna il nostro coro
  quel Pietro fu che con la poverella
  offerse a Santa Chiesa il suo tesoro.   108

La quinta luce, ch'è tra noi più bella,
  spira di tale amor, che tutto il mondo
  là giù ne gola di saper novella.   111

Entro v'è l'alta mente u' sì profondo
  saper fu messo, che se il vero è vero
  a veder tanto non surse il secondo.   114

Appresso vedi il lume di quel cero
  che giù, in carne, più a dentro vide
  l'angelica natura e il ministero.   117

Ne l'altra piccioletta luce ride
  quell'avvocato dei tempi cristiani
  del cui latino Augustin si provvide.   120

Or se tu l'occhio de la mente trani
  di luce in luce dietro le mie lode,
  già de l'ottava con sete rimani.   123

Per vedere ogni ben dentro vi gode
  l'anima santa che il mondo fallace
  fa manifesto a chi di lei ben ode.   126

Lo corpo ond'ella fu cacciata giace
  giuso in Cieldauro, ed essa da martiro
  e da esilio venne a questa pace.   129

Vedi oltre fiammeggiar l'ardente spiro
  d'Isidoro, di Beda e di Riccardo,
  che a considerar fu più che viro.   132

Questi onde a me ritorna il tuo riguardo,
  è il lume d'uno spirto che, in pensieri
  gravi, a morir li parve venir tardo.   135

Essa è la luce eterna di Sigieri,
  che leggendo nel Vico de li strami
  sillogizzò invidiosi veri».   138

If knowledge of the rest be now thine aim,
  around the blissful garland with thine eyes
  follow my speech, as I their worth proclaim.
Those flames, that come next, from the laughter rise
  of Gratian, who to either forum lent
  such aid as causeth joy in Paradise.
Behold in him, our choir's next ornament,
  that Peter who, at Holy Church's need,
  like the poor widow, all his treasure spent.
The rays of the fifth—our fairest light—proceed
  from such a love, that there is none below
  but longs with news of it to sate his greed.
It veils the mind inspired with wisdom so
  profound, that ne'er arose, if truth be true,
  a second who could boast as much to know.
Beside him the bright taper meets thy view,
  who gained, while in the flesh, his deep insight
  into what angels be and what they do.
There laughs within that other tiny light
  the champion of the Christian ages, one
  whose studied discourse helped Augustine write.
Now, an thou let thy mental vision run
  from light to light, as I record their praise,
  thou art left thirsting for the eighth bright sun.
Within it on all good delights to gaze
  the saintly soul, which unto ears that cease
  mishearing shows the world's deceitful ways.
Down in Cieldauro, where it found release,
  it left its tortured body, thence to soar
  from martyrdom and exile to this peace.
See, blazing yonder, fervent Isidore,
  Bede and that Richard who, as pensive seer,
  was all that a mere man can be, and more.
The flame from which thy glance reverteth here
  shines from a soul who, in deep thinking drown'd,
  complained that all too slowly death drew near:
it is Sigiér's eternal light, once found
  teaching in Straw Street, there intent to prove
  that truths which brought him enmity were sound.'

Indi, come orologio che ne chiami
  ne l'ora che la sposa di Dio surge
  a mattinar lo sposo perchè l'ami,   141
che l'una parte l'altra tira e urge,
  tin tin sonando, con sì dolce nota
  che il ben disposto spirto d'amor turge,   144
così vid'io la gloriosa rota
  moversi e render voce a voce, in tempra
  ed in dolcezza ch'esser non può nota   147
se non colà dove il gioir s'insempra.

CANTO 11

O INSENSATA cura dei mortali,
  quanto son difettivi sillogismi
  quei che ti fanno in basso batter l'ali!   3
Chi dietro a iura e chi ad aforismi
  sen giva, e chi seguendo sacerdozio,
  e chi regnar per forza o per sofismi,   6
e chi rubare, e chi civil negozio;
  chi nel diletto de la carne involto
  s'affaticava, e chi si dava all'ozio;   9
quand'io, da tutte queste cose sciolto,
  con Beatrice m'era suso in cielo
  cotanto gloriosamente accolto!   12
Poi che ciascuno fu tornato ne lo
  punto del cerchio in che avanti s'era,
  fermossi, come a candelier candelo.   15
Ed io sentii dentro a quella lumera
  che pria m'avea parlato, sorridendo
  incominciar facendosi più mera: 18
« Così com'io del suo raggio risplendo,
  sì, riguardando ne la luce eterna,
  li tuoi pensieri onde cagioni apprendo. 21
Tu dubbi, ed hai voler che si ricerna
  in sì aperta e in sì distesa lingua
  lo dicer mio, che al tuo sentir si sterna, 24

Then, as a clock that summons us to move
   at the hour the Bride of God is roused from bed
   to woo, with matin song, her Bridegroom's love,
and, this part drawing and pushing that, is made
   to sound 'ding-ding' which swells—so sweet its tone—
   with love all hearts that ever truly pray'd;
so unto me the glorious wheel was shown
   revolving, voice to voice attuned, and blending
   in sweet harmonious melody unknown
save yonder where delight is never-ending.

CANTO 11

O WITLESS care of mortals, still the dupe
   of that vain reasoning from false premises,
   which makes thy beating pinions downward droop!
One searched the statutes, one Hippocrates
   his maxims: on the priesthood one was bent,
   and one on rule by force or sophistries:
one was on robbery, and one intent
   on civic business: one was wearily given
   to sensual joys, one lying indolent,
while I, from all these things released, was even
   thus gloriously made welcome by a band
   of shining saints, with Beatrice, in heaven.
When round the circle each, on either hand
   returning, had attained his former room,
   he stopped, like candle fixed in candle-stand.
And I perceived the radiancy from whom
   speech had already issued, smiling, grow
   more radiant still, and heard it thus resume:
'As I reflect its glory, even so
   in that eternal light whereon I gaze,
   I know thy thoughts and whence they rise I know.
Thou doubtest, and wouldst have me sift my ways
   of speech and choose large language, adequate
   to thy perception baffled by the phrase,

ove dinanzi dissi *U' ben s'impingua*,
  e là u' dissi *Non surse il secondo*;
  e qui è uopo che ben si distingua.   27
La provedenza, che governa il mondo
  con quel consiglio nel quale ogni aspetto
  creato è vinto pria che vada al fondo,   30
però che andasse ver lo suo diletto
  la sposa di colui che ad alte grida
  disposò lei col sangue benedetto   33
in sè sicura e anche a lui più fida,
  due prìncipi ordinò in suo favore
  che quinci e quindi le fosser per guida.   36
L'un fu tutto serafico in ardore,
  l'altro per sapienza in Terra fue
  di cherubica luce uno splendore.   39
De l'un dirò, però che d'amendue
  si dice l'un pregiando, quale uom prende,
  perchè ad un fine fur l'opere sue.   42
Intra Tupino e l'acqua che discende
  del colle eletto dal beato Ubaldo,
  fertile costa d'alto monte pende   45
onde Perugia sente freddo e caldo
  da Porta Sole; e di retro le piange
  per grave giogo Nocera con Gualdo.   48
Di questa costa, là dov'ella frange
  più sua rattezza, nacque al mondo un Sole
  come fa questo talvolta di Gange;   51
però chi d'esto loco fa parole,
  non dica Ascesi, che direbbe corto,
  ma Oriente, se proprio dir vuole.   54
Non era ancor molto lontan da l'orto,
  ch'ei cominciò a far sentir la Terra
  de la sua gran virtute alcun conforto;   57
chè per tal donna, giovinetto, in guerra
  del padre, corse, a cui, come a la morte,
  la porta del piacer nessun disserra;   60
e dinanzi a la sua spiral corte
  et coram patre le si fece unito;
  poscia di dì in dì l'amò più forte.   63

"Where is good fattening," which I used of late,
   and by that other, "Second ne'er arose":
   here let me, then, a clear distinction state.
The providence, which rules the world and shows
   its ways to none, for they are past descrying
   by created sight, however deep it goes,
in order that the bride of him, who, crying
   "with a loud voice", wed her with his dear blood,
   might seek her joy both on herself relying
and also with her faith in him renewed,
   for her behoof ordained two chiefs of might
   on either hand to lead her into good.
The one burned all seraphically bright;
   the other for his wisdom was on Earth
   a very splendour of cherubic light.
Of one I'll speak, for whoso tells the worth
   of one, whiche'er he take, is both commending,
   because one purpose to their deeds gave birth.
'Twixt the Tupino and the brook descending
   the blesséd Ubald's chosen hill one sees
   a fruitful slope from a high mount depending,
whence on Perugia's Porta Sol the breeze
   blows hot and cold; rearward her irksome sway
   makes Nócera with Gualdo ill at ease.
From this same slope, just where it breaks away
   most gently, to the world was born a Sun,
   as this from Ganges on the timeful day.
Therefore, whene'er the place is named, let none
   call it "Ascesi"—word of meagre sense;
   but "the East" should its title rightly run.
Since there he rose, nor far had travelled thence,
   when to the Earth he 'gan to impart some measure
   of comfort from his mighty influence.
For, still mere stripling, he was quick to treasure,
   to his father's wrath, a dame to whom the door,
   as were she death, no man unlocks with pleasure;
but he, full fain, his bishop's court before
   et coram patre took her for his own;
   thereafter day by day he loved her more.

Questa, privata del primo marito,
  mille e cent'anni e più, dispetta e scura,
  fino a costui si stette sanza invito;   66
nè valse udir che la trovò sicura
  con Amiclate, al suon de la sua voce,
  colui che a tutto il mondo fe' paura;   69
nè valse esser costante nè feroce
  sì, che dove Maria rimase giuso
  ella con Cristo pianse in su la croce.   72
Ma perch'io non proceda troppo chiuso,
  Francesco e Povertà per questi amanti
  prendi oramai nel mio parlar diffuso.   75
La lor concordia e i lor lieti sembianti
  amore e maraviglia e dolce sguardo
  facean esser cagion di pensier santi;   78
tanto che il venerabile Bernardo
  si scalzò prima, e dietro a tanta pace
  corse, e correndo li parve esser tardo.   81
Oh ignota ricchezza, o ben ferace!
  Scalzasi Egidio, scalzasi Silvestro
  dietro a lo sposo, sì la sposa piace.   84
Indi sen va quel padre e quel maestro
  con la sua donna e con quella famiglia
  che già legava l'umile capestro.   87
Nè li gravò viltà di cor le ciglia
  per esser fi' di Pietro Bernardone,
  nè per parer dispetto a maraviglia;   90
ma regalmente sua dura intenzione
  ad Innocenzio aperse, e da lui ebbe
  primo sigillo a sua religione.   93
Poi che la gente poverella crebbe
  dietro a costui, la cui mirabil vita
  meglio in gloria del ciel si canterebbe,   96
di seconda corona redimita
  fu, per Onorio, da l'eterno Spiro
  la santa voglia d'esto archimandrita.   99
E poi che per la sete del martiro
  ne la presenza del Soldan superba
  predicò Cristo e gli altri che il seguiro,   102

Bereaved of her first husband, scorned, unknown,
  more than a thousand and an hundred years
  she lived unwooed, till sought by him alone.

In vain the story that she felt no fears,
  but with Amyclas unperturbed had stood,
  when the world-terror's voice assailed her ears;

in vain the loyal, the matchless fortitude
  with which, while even Mary stayed below,
  she wept with Christ upon the very rood.

But lest too little of my meaning show,
  Francis and Poverty henceforward take
  at large for this fond pair and call them so.

Their concord and glad looks availed to make
  love, wonderment and contemplation sweet
  cause holy thoughts to blossom in their wake.

The venerable Bernard bared his feet
  first, and ran after peace so great with speed
  he deemed o'erslow, yet was his footing fleet.

O unknown riches! O prolific seed!
  barefoot tears Giles, barefoot Silvester tears
  after—so charms the bride—the bridegroom's lead.

Thenceforth that lord and father onward fares
  with his dear lady and that household, now
  bound with the cord, which each so humbly wears.

Nor did a sense of shame weigh down his brow,
  that he was Peter Bernardone's son,
  and was, to look at, passing mean and low;

but he revealed, as might a king have done,
  his stern resolve to Innocent, who granted
  its first seal to his order thus begun.

As multiplied the humble souls that wanted
  to follow one, whose marvellous life were theme
  in the empyréan heav'n more fitly chanted,

the eternal Spirit made Honorius deem
  the moment wise to crown yet once again
  this archimandrite's consecrated scheme.

Next, in the Soldan's haughty presence, fain
  of martyrdom, behold him, dauntless stand,
  preaching of Christ and those, his saintly train;

597

e, per trovare a conversione acerba
troppo la gente, per non stare indarno
reddissi al frutto de l'italica erba,   105
nel crudo sasso intra Tevere ed Arno
da Cristo prese l'ultimo sigillo,
che le sue membra du' anni portarno.   108
Quando a colui che a tanto ben sortillo
piacque di trarlo suso a la mercede
ch'ei meritò nel suo farsi pusillo,   111
ai frati suoi sì come a giuste rede
raccomandò la sua donna più cara,
e comandò che l'amassero a fede;   114
e dal suo grembo l'anima preclara
mover si volle tornando al suo regno,
ed al suo corpo non volle altra bara.   117
Pensa oramai qual fu colui che degno
collega fu a mantener la barca
di Piero in alto mar per dritto segno: 120
e questi fu il nostro patriarca;
per che qual segue lui com'ei comanda,
discerner puoi che buona merce carca.   123
Ma il suo peculio di nova vivanda
è fatto ghiotto, sì ch'esser non puote
che per diversi salti non si spanda;   126
e quanto le sue pecore remote
e vagabunde più da esso vanno,
più tornano a l'ovil di latte vote.   129
Ben son di quelle che temono il danno
e stringonsi al pastor, ma son sì poche
che le cappe fornisce poco panno.   132
Or se le mie parole non son fioche,
se la tua udienza è stata attenta,
se ciò che ho detto a la mente rivoche,   135
in parte fia la tua voglia contenta,
perchè vedrai la pianta onde si scheggia,
e vedrai il corregger che argomenta   138
U' ben s'impingua se non si vaneggia».

but, loth to waste his labours on a land
 unripe for harvest, he returned to reap
 the Italian crop now ready for his hand,
then took from Christ upon the rocky steep,
 'twixt Arno reared and Tiber, his last seal—
 marks that his limbs were two whole years to keep.
When he who chose him for so great a weal
 was pleased at length to raise him to the height
 which he had earned by his self-humbling zeal,
unto his brethren, as to heirs by right,
 he recommended his own lady dear
 and bade each love her as her faithful knight;
and from her bosom to its kingly sphere
 on high his fulgent spirit willed to flee,
 and for his corpse would brook no other bier.
Bethink thee now how great a saint was he,
 his worthy colleague found, to hold the boat
 of Peter on a straight course in mid-sea.
Such was our patriarch; and therefore note,
 that whoso follows him the way he bids
 hath with him goodly merchandise afloat.
But now it lusteth so, the flock he leads,
 for new fare, that it cannot help but stray
 to alien pastures, careless where it feeds,
although the more his sheep forsake the way
 nor heed the shepherd, by so much the more
 devoid of milk they come home day by day.
Some, fearing loss, cleave to him as before;
 yea, but so few in number, that of stuff
 to make them cowls there needs but scanty store.
Now, if my words have been distinct enough,
 if they have sunk in thine attentive ear,
 if from thy memory they meet no rebuff,
in part thou hast thy wish: for both are clear—
 the plant from which they're splintered and the saying
 with its implied rebuke, repeated here:
"Where is good fattening, if there be no straying".'

CANTO 12

Sɪ tosto come l'ultima parola
   la benedetta fiamma per dir tolse,
   a rotar cominciò la santa mola;   3
e nel suo giro tutta non si volse
   prima che un'altra di cerchio la chiuse,
   e moto a moto e canto a canto colse: 6
canto che tanto vince nostre muse,
   nostre sirene, in quelle dolci tube,
   quanto primo splendor quel ch'ei refuse.   9
Come si volgon per tenera nube
   due archi paralleli e concolori,
   quando Iunone a su' ancella iube,   12
nascendo di quel d'entro quel di fuori,
   a guisa del parlar di quella vaga
   che amor consunse come il Sol vapori;   15
e fanno qui la gente esser presaga,
   per lo patto che Dio con Noè pose,
   del mondo che giammai più non s'allaga;   18
così di quelle sempiterne rose
   volgeansi circa noi le due ghirlande,
   e sì l'estrema a l'intima rispose.   21
Poi che il tripudio e l'alta festa grande,
   sì del cantare e sì del fiammeggiarsi
   luce con luce gaudiose e blande,   24
insieme a punto ed a voler quetarsi,
   pur come gli occhi, che al piacer che i move
   conviene insieme chiudersi e levarsi,   27
dal cor de l'una de le luci nuove
   si mosse voce che l'ago a la stella
   parer mi fece in volgermi al suo dove;   30
e cominciò: « L'amor che mi fa bella
   mi tragge a ragionar de l'altro duca
   per cui del mio sì ben ci si favella.   33
Degno è che dov'è l'un l'altro s'induca;
   sì che, com'elli ad una militaro,
   così la gloria loro insieme luca.   36

CANTO 12

So spake the blesséd flame and then was still,
    but, ere its final word had ceased to sound,
    already wheeling was the holy mill,
nor yet had once revolved, when, circling round,
    another compassed it in such a way
    that dance to dance and song to song was bound;
song that in those sweet pipes the loveliest lay
    of earthly muse or siren doth excel
    as much as primary light the reflex ray.
E'en as, both limned alike and parallel,
    two bows are drawn o'er softly clouded skies,
    should Juno's hest her handy-maid impel,
the inner to the outer giving rise,
    like to that errant damsel's voice, who died,
    consumed by love, as Sun-kissed vapour dies;
which make men augur that, whate'er betide,
    by reason of God's pact with Noah made,
    the world from flood shall ever safe abide;
so, curving round us, those two wreaths display'd
    their sempiternal roses, and so shone
    the inmost in the outmost re-portray'd.
Dance and sublime festivity went on,
    alike of flame that flashed and song that soared,
    light blent with light in smooth, glad unison,
till both together ceased with one accord,
    as eyes perforce together ope and close
    obedient to the will that is their lord;
then issued from the heart of one of those
    new lights a voice, whereto I turned me, as sways
    the needle thither where the pole-star glows;
and it began: 'The love wherewith I blaze
    bids me the other leader celebrate,
    on whose account my own hath won such praise.
'Tis just, where one is named, to name his mate;
    that, as both waged their warfare to one end,
    so should like glory on their triumph wait.

L'esercito di Cristo, che sì caro
  costò a riarmar, dietro a l'insegna
  si movea tardo sospeccioso e raro,   39
quando l'imperador che sempre regna
  provvide a la milizia ch'era in forse,
  per sola grazia, non per esser degna;   42
e, com'è detto, a sua sposa soccorse
  con due campioni, al cui fare, al cui dire
  lo popol disviato si raccorse.   45
In quella parte ove surge ad aprire
  Zefiro dolce le novelle fronde
  di che si vede Europa rivestire,   48
non molto lungi al percoter de l'onde
  dietro a le quali per la lunga foga
  lo Sol talvolta ad ogni uom si nasconde, 51
siede la fortunata Calaroga,
  sotto la protezion del grande scudo
  in che soggiace il leone e soggioga.   54
Dentro vi nacque l'amoroso drudo
  de la fede cristiana, il santo atleta
  benigno a' suoi ed ai nemici crudo.   57
E come fu creata, fu repleta
  sì la sua mente di viva virtute
  che, ne la madre, lei fece profeta.   60
Poi che le sposalizie fur compiute
  al sacro fonte in tra lui e la fede,
  u' si dotar di mutua salute,   63
la donna che per lui l'assenso diede
  vide nel sonno il mirabile frutto
  che uscir dovea di lui e de le rede: 66
e perchè fosse qual era in costrutto,
  quinci si mosse spirito a nomarlo
  del possessivo di cui era tutto: 69
Domenico fu detto, ed io ne parlo
  sì come de l'agricola che Cristo
  elesse a l'orto suo per aiutarlo.   72
Ben parve messo e familiar di Cristo,
  chè il primo amor che in lui fu manifesto
  fu al primo consiglio che diè Cristo: 75

Christ's army, which at such dear cost obtain'd
  fresh weapons, moved thin-ranked and slow of pace
  behind the standard, for their faith had wan'd,
when the ever-ruling Emperor, in face
  of their sore peril, sent his soldiers aid,
  not through their merit, but of his pure grace,
and, as thou heardest, for his spouse array'd
  two champions, by whose words and by whose deeds
  the folk were rallied that had erred and stray'd.
Set in that quarter, whence at first proceeds
  sweet Zephyr, at whose breath new leaves are bidden
  clothe Europe when she casts her winter weeds,
not very far from where the coast is chidden
  by waves behind which, of their amplitude
  grown tired, the Sun is whiles from all men hidden,
the happy Calaruega long hath stood,
  guarded by the great shield on which appear
  two lions, one subduing and one subdued.
In that same town was born the amorous fere
  of the true faith, the holy athlete, kind
  unto his own and to his foes severe.
And, scarce conceived, so lively was his mind,
  that, through its power, his mother prophesied,
  while he was yet within her womb confined.
When at the hallowed font he took for bride
  the Faith, and both had pledged themselves to keep
  each other safe, by vows there ratified,
the dame, who was his surety, saw in sleep
  the marvellous fruit one day to issue forth
  from him and from his great companionship.
And, that he might be parsed at his true worth,
  a spirit moved hence to give the child a name
  derived from His who owned him from his birth.
Dominic was he called; whom I proclaim
  as fellow-labourer chosen out by Christ
  to dress his garden and to keep the same.
True envoy seemed he, and true friend, of Christ,
  since from the first he loved, and was intent
  to follow, the first counsel given by Christ.

spesse fiate fu tacito e desto
  trovato in terra da la sua nutrice,
  come dicesse: 'Io son venuto a questo.'   78
Oh padre suo veramente Felice!
  oh madre sua veramente Giovanna,
  se, interpretata, val come si dice!   81
Non per lo mondo, per cui mo' s'affanna
  diretro ad Ostiense ed a Taddeo,
  ma per amor de la verace manna,   84
in picciol tempo gran dottor si feo,
  tal che si mise a circuir la vigna
  che tosto imbianca se il vignaio è reo.   87
E a la sedia che fu già benigna
  più ai poveri giusti, non per lei
  ma per colui che siede e che traligna,   90
non dispensare o due o tre per sei,
  non la fortuna di prima vacante,
  non *decimas quae sunt pauperum Dei*   93
addimandò; ma contro al mondo errante
  licenza di combatter per lo seme
  del qual ti fascian ventiquattro piante.   96
Poi, con dottrina e con volere insieme,
  con l'officio apostolico si mosse,
  quasi torrente che alta vena preme;   99
e ne li sterpi eretici percosse
  l'impeto suo, più vivamente quivi
  dove le resistenze eran più grosse.   102
Di lui si fecer poi diversi rivi
  onde l'orto cattolico si riga,
  sì che i suoi arbuscelli stan più vivi.   105
Se tal fu l'una rota de la biga
  in che la Santa Chiesa si difese
  e vinse in campo la sua civil briga,   108
ben ti dovrebbe assai esser palese
  l'eccellenza de l'altra, di cui Tomma
  dinanzi al mio venir fu sì cortese.   111
Ma l'orbita che fe' la parte somma
  di sua circonferenza è derelitta,
  sì ch'è la muffa dov'era la gromma.   114

Full many a time his nurse would find him bent
  in silence on the ground, awake all night,
  as who should say: "For this end was I sent."
Oh truly Felix was his father! Quite
  as truly Joan, his mother, if to *Joan*,
  interpreted, the meaning given be right!
Not like our worldlings toiling for their own
  gain at Thaddéus and the Ostian,
  but out of love for the true manna, grown
full soon a mighty doctor, he began
  to make inspection of that goodly vine,
  which, if ill tended, quickly turneth wan.
And from the see, no longer now benign
  to the honest poor (not thro' its own fault, nay,
  to its base occupant all blame assign!)
not power to give mere halves or thirds away,
  not promise of the first rich vacant see,
  not *decimas, quae sunt pauperum Dei*,
did he demand; but nought save liberty
  'gainst the erring world to battle for the seed
  whence sprang the twice-twelve scions engirdling thee.
Then forth he fared with mind and will agreed,
  confirmed apostle, as from its high source
  a torrent bursts, which nothing can impede,
and mid the stocks of heresy with force
  o'erwhelming rushed—where chief resistance showed,
  thither directing first his furious course.
From him thereafter various rillets flowed
  watering the catholic garden near and far,
  whereby fresh life is on its shrubs bestowed.
If such one wheel of the two-wheeléd car,
  wherein the Holy Church made her defence,
  and won in open field her civil war,
thou should'st admit the other's excellence,
  of which, before my coming, Thomas told,
  making thereto such courteous reference.
But, where its felly's topmost portion rolled,
  the rut thus formed thou wilt deserted find,
  so that where once was crust there now is mould.

La sua famiglia, che si mosse dritta
· coi piedi a le sue orme, è tanto volta
che quel dinanzi a quel di retro gitta.   117
E tosto si vedrà ne la ricolta
de la mala coltura, quando il loglio
sì lagnerà che l'arca li sia tolta.   120
Ben dico, chi cercasse foglio a foglio
nostro volume, ancor troveria carta
u' leggerebbe 'Io mi son quel che soglio';   123
ma non fia da Casal nè d'Acquasparta,
là onde vegnon tali a la scrittura,
ch'uno la fugge e l'altro la coarta.   126
Io son la vita di Bonaventura
da Bagnoregio, che nei grandi offici
sempre posposi la sinistra cura.   129
Illuminato ed Augustin son quici
che fur dei primi scalzi poverelli
che nel capestro a Dio si fero amici.   132
Ugo da San Vittore è qui con elli,
e Pietro Mangiadore e Pietro Ispano,
lo qual giù luce in dodici libelli;   135
Natan profeta e il metropolitano
Crisostomo ed Anselmo e quel Donato
che a la prim'arte degnò porre mano.   138
Rabano è qui, e lucemi da lato
il calavrese abate Giovacchino
di spirito profetico dotato.   141
Ad inneggiar cotanto paladino
mi mosse l'infiammata cortesia
di fra Tommaso e il discreto latino;   144
e mosse meco questa compagnia ».

CANTO 13

IMAGINI chi bene intender cupe
quel ch'io or vidi, e ritenga l'image,
mentre ch'io dico, come ferma rupe,   3

His household, which set out with feet aligned
  on the prints made by his, so much hath wheeled,
  it thrusts the forward foot tow'rds that behind.
And soon the harvesting clear proof shall yield
  of the bad tillage, when the tares complain
  they are left out, what time the barns are filled.
I grant that whoso searched and searched again
  our volume, still might find some page whereon
  'twas writ, "As I was wont, so I remain";
but from Casál and Acquasparta none
  so minded hails: for the due discipline
  is shirked by this, by that is overdone.
In me doth the life of Bonavénture shine,
  of Bagnoregio, who the temporal end
  put last in each great office that was mine.
To Illuminato and Austen next attend;
  among his first bare-footed bedesmen these,
  who, girded with the cord, made God their friend.
Hugh of St. Victor here beside them is,
  and Piers, called Mangiador, and Piers of Spain,
  shining on earth from his twelve treatises;
Nathan the prophet, metropolitane
  Chrysostom, Anselm and Donatus, he
  that stooped to teach the first great art to men.
Raban is here, and, shining next to me,
  Calabria's abbot, Joachim, the seer
  who was endowed with the spirit of prophecy.
To emulous praise of such a valiant peer
  the courteous ardour and discreet address
  of brother Thomas moved me, and hath here
moved with me this fair company no less.'

CANTO 13

LET him imagine, who would visualize
  what I now saw, and let the image stay
  firm, while I speak, as rock before his eyes—

quindici stelle che in diverse plage
  lo cielo avvivan di tanto sereno
  che soperchia de l'aere ogni compage;   6
imagini quel carro a cui il seno
  basta del nostro cielo e notte e giorno,
  sì che al volger del temo non vien meno;   9
imagini la bocca di quel corno
  che si comincia in punta de lo stelo
  a cui la prima rota va dintorno,   12
aver fatto di sè due segni in cielo
  qual fece la figliuola di Minoi
  allora che sentì di morte il gelo,   15
e l'un ne l'altro aver li raggi suoi,
  ed ambedue girarsi per maniera
  che l'uno andasse al prima e l'altro al poi;   18
ed avrà quasi l'ombra de la vera
  costellazione e della doppia danza
  che circulava il punto dov'io era;   21
poi ch'è tanto di là da nostra usanza,
  quanto di là dal mover de la Chiana
  si move il ciel che tutti gli altri avanza.   24
Lì si cantò non Bacco, non Peana,
  ma tre persone in divina natura,
  ed in una persona essa e l'umana.   27
Compiè il caṇtare e il volger sua misura,
  ed attesersi a noi quei santi lumi
  felicitando sè di cura in cura.   30
Ruppe il silenzio nei concordi numi
  poscia la luce in che mirabil vita
  del poverel dì Dio narrata fumi,   33
e disse: « Quando l'una paglia è trita,
  quando la sua semenza è già riposta,
  a batter l'altra dolce amor m'invita.   36
Tu credi che nel petto onde la costa
  si trasse per formar la bella guancia
  il cui palato a tutto il mondo costa,   39
ed in quel che, forato de la lancia,
  e poscia e prima tanto satisfece
  che d'ogni colpa vince la bilancia,   42

the fifteen stars we see in heaven display
   in divers regions such a living light,
   that not the thickest air can quench their ray;
imagine too the wain which day and night
   doth still the bosom of our skies adorn
   so that its pole wheels ever all in sight;
imagine too the opening of the horn
   which springs from where the axle-point doth lie
   round about which the primal wheel is borne,
to have fashioned of themselves two signs on high,
   such as the daughter of king Minos made,
   when, seized with mortal chill, she came to die;
one by the other's beams encompassèd,
   and both so whirling as that one should pass
   me swifter, and one slower, as round they sped;
and he will see, though darkly as in a glass,
   the very constellation and the dance
   two-fold, which circled round me where I was;
for things as much exceed our cognisance
   there, as the sphere, above all spheres supreme
   in speed, outstrips the Chiana's slow advance.
No Paean there they raise, no Bacchic hymn,
   but 'in one God three persons' and 'in one
   person two natures' are their endless theme.
When dance and song had their due measure run,
   to us paid heed those shining ministers,
   winning new joy from each new task begun.
Broke silence then 'mongst the concordant peers
   that luminary in which the wondrous tale
   of God's own bedesman had entranced mine ears,
and thus it spoke: 'Since I have threshed out well
   one sheaf and stored its grain, on the other too
   sweet love invites me now to ply the flail.
Thou thinkest that the breast from which God drew
   the rib to form the woman fair of mien
   whose palate all mankind so dearly rue,
and His which, when the spear was thrust therein,
   alike for past and future made the great
   atonement, far outweighing every sin,

quantunque a la natura umana lece
  aver di lume, tutto fosse infuso
  da quel valor che l'uno e l'altro fece;   45
e però miri a ciò ch'io dissi suso,
  quando narrai che non ebbe il secondo
  lo ben che ne la quinta luce è chiuso.   48
Or apri gli occhi a quel ch'io ti rispondo,
  e vedrai il tuo credere e il mio dire
  nel vero farsi come centro in tondo.   51
Ciò che non muore e ciò che può morire
  non è se non splendor di quella idea
  che partorisce amando il nostro sire;   54
chè quella viva luce che sì mea
  dal suo lucente, che non si disuna
  da lui nè da l'amor che a lor s'intrea,   57
per sua bontate il suo raggiare aduna
  quasi specchiato, in nove sussistenze,
  eternalmente rimanendosi una.   60
Quindi discende a l'ultime potenze,
  giù d'atto in atto tanto divenendo,
  che più non fa che brevi contingenze: 63
e queste contingenze esser intendo
  le cose generate che produce,
  con seme e sanza seme, il ciel movendo.   66
La cera di costoro e chi la duce
  non sta d'un modo, e però sotto il segno
  ideal poi più e men traluce;   69
ond'egli avvien che un medesimo legno
  secondo specie, peggio e meglio frutta,
  e voi nascete con diverso ingegno.   72
Se fosse a punto la cera dedutta
  e fosse il cielo in sua virtù suprema,
  la luce del suggel parrebbe tutta;   75
ma la natura la dà sempre scema,
  similemente operando a l'artista
  che ha l'abito de l'arte e man che trema.   78
Però se il caldo Amor, la chiara Vista
  e la prima Virtù dispone e segna,
  tutta la perfezion quivi s'acquista.   81

were by the power, whose virtue did create
    one and the other, filled with all the light
    that is permitted to man's natural state;
hence wonderest thou if lately I was right
    in saying no second e'er so wise was found,
    as he whom the fifth lustre veils from sight.
Now mark my words, and thou wilt soon be bound
    to acknowledge that thy thought and my reply
    meet in the truth as centre in the round.
That which dies not and that which must needs die
    are but splendour of that idea which owes
    its birth unto our Father's love on high;
because that living Brightness which so flows
    from its bright Source that one therewith it stays
    and with the Love which is intrined with those,
of its own goodness doth collect its rays
    as it were glassed—itself remaining one
    eternally—in nine subsistences.
And thence from act to act it passes down
    to the last potencies and brings about
    at length mere brief contingencies alone;
and these contingencies, I make no doubt,
    are things engendered, caused by the heaven to grow,
    of its own motion, with seed or without.
Their wax, and that which moulds it, varies so,
    that 'neath the impress of the idea, we find
    this more and less thereafter shining through:
whence comes it that of trees the same in kind
    one better fruit, another worse, doth bear;
    and you are born with differing powers of mind.
Were the wax moulded perfectly and were
    the heaven its highest influence to exert,
    nothing would then the signet's light impair;
but nature never gives it save in part,
    like to the artist whose unsteady hand
    betrays him in the practice of his art.
Yet if the warm Love, the clear Vision and
    the primal Power dispose and seal—this done,
    the work acquires all the perfection planned.

Così fu fatta già la terra degna
  di tutta l'animal perfezione,
  così fu fatta la Vergine pregna: 84
sì ch'io commendo tua opinione
  che l'umana natura mai non fue
  nè fia, qual fu in quelle due persone.   87
Or s'io non procedessi avanti piue,
  'Dunque come costui fu sanza pare?'
  comincerebber le parole tue.   90
Ma perchè paia ben ciò che non pare,
  pensa chi era e la cagion che il mosse,
  quando fu detto *Chiedi*, a dimandare.   93
Non ho parlato sì che tu non posse
  ben veder ch'ei fu re, che chiese senno
  a ciò che re sufficiente fosse;   96
non per sapere il numero in che enno
  li motor di qua sù, o se *necesse*
  con contingente mai *necesse* fenno;   99
non *si est dare primum motum esse*,
  o se nel mezzo cerchio far si puote
  triangol sì che un retto non avesse.   102
Onde, se ciò ch'io dissi e questo note,
  regal prudenza è quel vedere impari
  in che lo stral di mia intenzion percuote;   105
e se al *surse* drizzi gli occhi chiari,
  vedrai aver solamente rispetto
  ai regi, che son molti e i buon son rari.   108
Con questa distinzion prendi il mio detto;
  e così puote star con quel che credi
  del primo padre e del nostro Diletto.   111
E questo ti sia sempre piombo ai piedi
  per farti mover lento com'uom lasso
  e al sì e al no che tu non vedi: 114
chè quegli è tra li stolti bene a basso
  che sanza distinzione afferma e nega
  così ne l'un come ne l'altro passo;   117
perch'egli incontra che più volte piega
  l'opinion corrente in falsa parte,
  e poi l'affetto l'intelletto lega.   120

Thus moulded once to form that paragon
    of living creatures was "the dust of the ground";
    thus was the Virgin made to bear a Son:
so that I grant thy opinion to be sound,
    that those two persons' equal among men
    was never yet and never shall be found.
Now if from further speech I should refrain,
    "How was that other, then, without a peer?"
    forthwith thou wouldest urge me to explain.
But to make quite clear that which is not clear,
    bethink thee who he was and wherefore he
    begged what he did, when "Ask" rang in his ear.
Not so I've argued, that thou canst not see
    clearly, he was a king, who begged good sense
    that he as king might all-sufficient be;
not for to know how many powers dispense
    their motion to these heavens, or whether "may"
    with "must" can e'er give "must" as consequence;
not, if a "first moved" one can rightly say
    exists, or if in circle, when bisected,
    triangle, not right-angled, ever lay.
So, hast thou on this and what I said reflected,
    royal prudence is that "wisdom" past compare
    at which my intention's arrow is directed;
and if to "arose" thou look with vision that's clear,
    to kings alone thou'lt see 'tis apposite,
    of whom be many, but the good are rare.
Draw this distinction, and my words are quite
    consistent, taken thus, with thy conceit
    of the first father and of our Delight.
And be this ever clog unto thy feet,
    to make thee like a weary man move slow
    tow'rds both the "yea" and "nay" that pose thy wit:
for he among the fools is very low
    in either case, who, not distinguishing,
    asserts "it is" or else "it is not so";
since oft-times doth a hasty judgment swing
    to the wrong side, and then doth blind self-will
    about the intellect its fetters fling.

Vie più che indarno da riva si parte,
   perchè non torna tal qual ei si move,
   chi pesca per lo vero e non ha l'arte.   123
E di ciò sono al mondo aperte prove
   Parmenide, Melisso, e Brisso, e molti
   li quali andavano e non sapean dove.   126
Sì fe' Sabellio e Arrio e quelli stolti
   che furon come spade a le Scritture
   in render torti li diritti volti.   129
Non sien le genti ancor troppo sicure
   a giudicar, sì come quei che stima
   le biade in campo pria che sien mature: 132
ch'i' ho veduto tutto il verno prima
   lo prun mostrarsi rigido e feroce,
   poscia portar la rosa in su la cima;   135
e legno vidi già dritto e veloce,
   correr lo mar per tutto suo cammino,
   perire al fine a l'entrar de la foce.   138
Non creda donna Berta e ser Martino,
   per vedere un furare, altro offerere,
   vederli dentro al consiglio divino;   141
chè quel può surgere e quel può cadere ».

CANTO 14

Dal centro al cerchio e sì dal cerchio al centro
   movesi l'acqua in un ritondo vaso,
   secondo ch'è percosso fuori o dentro.   3
Ne la mia mente fe' subito caso
   questo ch'io dico, sì come si tacque
   la gloriosa vita di Tommaso,   6
per la similitudine che nacque
   del suo parlare e di quel di Beatrice,
   a cui sì cominciar, dopo lui, piacque: 9
« A costui fa mestieri, e nol vi dice
   nè con la voce nè pensando ancora,
   d'un altro vero andare a la radice.   12

He pushes off from shore far vainlier still,
  since he returns not such as forth he went,
  who angles for the truth and lacketh skill.
This to the world make plainly evident
  Parmenides, Melissus, Bryson—all
  who, travelling, knew not whither they were bent.
Sabellius, too, and Arius I recall
  with other fools, who were to Holy Writ
  as swords that did its comely features maul.
Let not the people too securely sit
  in judgment, like the man who, while it grows,
  values his corn ere time hath ripened it:
for I have seen the briar no leaves unclose,
  but bristling stand, while a whole winter passed,
  yet, later, on its summit bear the rose;
and once I saw a ship sail straight and fast
  through all her voyage, across smooth seas and fair,
  to perish in the harbour-mouth at last.
So let dame Joan and gaffer Giles beware
  of thinking to see men with God's clear eyes,
  seeing one steal, another offerings bear;
for the saint yet may fall, the sinner rise.'

CANTO 14

In a round vessel water moves about
  'twixt centre and circumference to or fro,
  as smitten from within or from without.
This thought, as here 'tis imaged, even so
  flashed o'er me, when from out the glory shed
  by the life of Thomas words had ceased to flow,
by reason of the like effect then made
  by his discourse and that which, after his,
  flowed graciously from Beatrice, who said:
'Need hath this man, although what need it is
  his voice declares not nor his thoughts as yet,
  to probe one more of heaven's mysteries.

615

Diteli se la luce onde s'infiora
  vostra sustanza rimarrà con voi
  eternalmente sì com'ella è ora;   15
e se rimane, dite come, poi
  che sarete visibili rifatti,
  esser potrà che al veder non vi nòi».   18
Come, da più letizia pinti e tratti,
  a la fiata quei che vanno a rota
  levan la voce e rallegrano gli atti,   21
così, a l'orazion pronta e devota,
  li santi cerchi mostrar nova gioia
  nel torneare e ne la mira nota.   24
Qual si lamenta, perchè qui si muoia
  per viver colassù, non vide quive
  lo refrigerio de l'eterna ploia.   27
Quell'uno e due e tre che sempre vive
  e regna sempre in tre e in due e in uno,
  non circoscritto e tutto circoscrive,   30
tre volte era cantato da ciascuno
  di quelli spirti con tal melodia
  che ad ogni merto sarìa giusto muno.   33
E io udii ne la luce più dia
  del minor cerchio una voce modesta,
  forse qual fu da l'angelo a Maria,   36
risponder: « Quanto fia lunga la festa
  di Paradiso, tanto il nostro amore
  si raggerà dintorno cotal vesta.   39
La sua chiarezza seguita l'ardore,
  l'ardor la visione, e quella è tanta
  quanto ha di grazia sopra suo valore.   42
Come la carne gloriosa e santa
  fia rivestita, la nostra persona
  più grata fia per esser tutta quanta: 45
per che s'accrescerà ciò che ne dona
  di gratuito lume il sommo bene,
  lume che a lui veder ne condiziona;   48
onde la vision crescer conviene,
  crescer l'ardor che di quella s'accende,
  crescer lo raggio che da esso viene.   51

Tell him if these bright beams that emanate
   now from your substance will emblossom you
   as radiantly in your eternal state;
and tell him how their brilliance, if they do,
   shall not perforce work injury to your sight,
   when once again ye are disclosed to view.'
As, urged and drawn by increase of delight,
   with one accord the partners in a reel
   in louder song and livelier dance unite,
so, at her eager and devout appeal,
   by their gyrations and their wondrous strain
   new gladness did those holy cirques reveal.
Whoso laments one here must die to gain
   the life on high hath there not seen the way
   souls are refreshed by the eternal rain.
That One and Two and Three which lives for aye
   and for aye reigns in Three and Two and One,
   bounding all things, while bound *It* nothing may,
was thrice hymned by each spirit in a tone
   so passing sweet, that full reward were found
   for every merit in that song alone.
And from the divinest light of the inner round
   I heard a modest voice, e'en such, may be,
   as the angel's unto Mary, thuswise sound
in answer: 'Long as e'er the festal glee
   of Paradise endures, so long a space
   our love shall swathe us round thus gloriously.
Its brightness with the fervour shall keep pace;
   the fervour with the vision, and that is keen
   as, o'er its proper worth, 'tis granted grace.
When the transfigured, holy flesh has been
   assumed once more, our persons, being brought
   to entire perfection, will more favour win:
whereby shall be increased the light, unbought,
   which we receive from God's own excellence,
   light without which we should behold him not;
so that the vision must needs grow more intense,
   warmer the love enkindled by the same,
   brighter the radiance which proceedeth thence.

Ma sì come carbon che fiamma rende
  e per vivo candor quella soperchia,
  sì che la sua parvenza si difende,   54
così questo fulgor che già ne cerchia
  fia vinto in apparenza da la carne
  che tuttodì la terra ricoperchia;   57
nè potrà tanta luce affaticarne,
  chè gli organi del corpo saran forti
  a tutto ciò che potrà dilettarne».   60
Tanto mi parver subiti ed accorti
  e l'uno e l'altro coro a dicer *Amme!*
  che ben mostrar disio dei corpi morti;   63
forse non pur per lor, ma per le mamme,
  per li padri e per gli altri che fur cari
  anzi che fosser sempiterne fiamme.   66
Ed ecco, intorno di chiarezza pari,
  nascere un lustro sopra quel che v'era,
  per guisa d'orrizzonte che rischiari.   69
E sì come al salir di prima sera
  comincian per lo ciel nuove parvenze,
  sì che la vista pare e non par vera,   72
parvemi lì novelle sussistenze
  cominciare a vedere, e fare un giro
  di fuor da l'altre due circonferenze.   75
Oh vero sfavillar del Santo Spiro!
  come si fece subito candente
  a gli occhi miei! che, vinti, nol soffriro.   78
Ma Beatrice sì bella e ridente
  mi si mostrò, che tra quelle vedute
  si vuol lasciar che non seguir la mente.   81
Quindi ripreser gli occhi miei virtute
  a rilevarsi, e vidimi traslato
  sol con mia donna in più alta salute.   84
Ben m'accors'io ch'io era più levato,
  per l'affocato riso de la stella,
  che mi parea più roggio che l'usato.   87
Con tutto il core e con quella favella
  ch'è una in tutti, a Dio feci olocausto
  qual conveniasi a la grazia novella.   90

But even as a coal that gives forth flame
   outshines it by a livelier, whiter glow,
   and thus its own clear presence doth proclaim,
so this effulgence which enfolds us now,
   will yield in brightness to the flesh which lies
   all this while covered by the earth below;
nor will excess of glory vex our eyes;
   because the body's organs shall be then
   made strong for all delights that heaven supplies.'
So eager and alert to cry 'Amen!'
   seemed either chorus, that their keen desire
   for their dead bodies was thereby made plain;
nor might mere self-regard that cry inspire,
   but thoughts of fathers, mothers and all those
   they loved, ere yet they flamed with deathless fire.
And lo, o'er what was there, a lustre rose,
   equally bright all round, and spreading wide,
   like an horizon as it brighter grows.
And as at rise of early eventide
   new things-to-see, such that the sight seems true
   and yet not true, in heav'n are dim-descried,
meseemed that I began to see there new
   subsistences who in a shining host
   were wheeling round outside the other two.
Oh very sparkling of the Holy Ghost!
   how quickly it with intense brilliance blazed,
   straining my eyes beyond their uttermost!
But with a smile so fair my lady gazed
   upon me that I needs must reckon this
   among those sights from memory erased.
Anon, their strength renewed by Beatrice
   I raised my eyes and found myself up-caught
   alone with her to more exalted bliss.
Clear proof to me of my ascent was brought
   by the star's burning smile, which glowed with flame
   more ruddy than of wont, or so I thought.
With full heart and that speech which is the same
   in all, I made the holocaust I owed
   for this fresh grace, to Him from whom it came.

E non er'anco dal mio petto esausto
l'ardor del sacrificio, ch'io conobbi
esso litare stato accetto e fausto;   93
chè con tanto lucore e tanto robbi
m'apparvero splendor dentro a due raggi
ch'io dissi: « Oh Elios che sì li addobbi! »   96
Come distinta da minori e maggi
lumi biancheggia tra i poli del mondo
Galassia sì che fa dubbiar ben saggi,   99
sì costellati facean nel profondo
Marte quei raggi il venerabil segno
che fan giunture di quadranti in tondo.   102
Qui vince la memoria mia l'ingegno,
chè in quella croce lampeggiava Cristo
sì ch'io non so trovare esemplo degno;   105
ma chi prende sua croce e segue Cristo
ancor mi scuserà di quel ch'io lasso,
vedendo in quell'albor balenar Cristo.   108
Di corno in corno e tra la cima e il basso
si movean lumi, scintillando forte
nel congiungersi insieme e nel trapasso: 111
così si veggion qui diritte e torte,
veloci e tarde, rinnovando vista,
le minuzie dei corpi, e lunghe e corte,   114
moversi per lo raggio onde si lista
tal volta l'ombra che per sua difesa
la gente con ingegno ed arte acquista.   117
E come giga o arpa, in tempra tesa
di molte corde, fa dolce tintinno
a tal da cui la nota non è intesa,   120
così dai lumi che lì m'apparinno
s'accogliea per la croce una melode
che mi rapiva sanza intender l'inno.   123
Ben m'accors'io ch'egli era d'alte lode,
però che a me venia *Risurgi* e *Vinci*,
come a colui che non intende e ode.   126
Io m'innamorava tanto quinci,
che infino a lì non fu alcuna cosa
che mi legasse con sì dolci vinci.   129

Nor had the heat wherewith the offering glowed
   yet faded from my breast ere I could know
   the rite accepted and the omens good;
for with such mighty sheen, such ruddy glow
   splendours appeared within two rays, that I
   'Oh Helios,' said, 'who glorifiest them so!'
As, 'tween the poles of the world, the Galaxy
   gleams white, distinct with less and greater stars,
   making the sagest wonder how and why;
thus constellated in the depth of Mars,
   those rays described the venerable sign
   formed in a round by the four quadrant bars.
Here wit to follow memory must decline;
   for beaconing so upon that cross was Christ,
   that, to depict it, find I nought condign:
but whoso takes his cross and follows Christ,
   will pardon me for what I leave unsaid,
   when flashing in that dawn he beholds Christ.
From horn to horn and 'twixt the foot and head
   moved lights, which sparkled vividly whene'er
   one with another met, or past it sped:
even so on earth do atoms in the air,
   aslant and level, slow and rapid, none
   like-sized, remaining never as they were,
move through the ray of light we notice run
   at times athwart the shade which men devise
   with cunning art to screen them from the sun.
And as, with many strings which harmonize,
   viol and harp din sweetly on an ear
   too gross to catch their subtle melodies,
so from the lights before me did I hear
   throughout the cross enrapturing music swell,
   though what the hymn they carolled was not clear.
'Twas of high praises, for I heard right well
   the words 'Arise' and 'Conquer', even as he
   who hears, but what he heareth cannot tell.
I fell in love so with their minstrelsy,
   that naught whereof this poem yet hath told
   had with so sweet a bondage fettered me.

Forse la mia parola par tropp'osa
  posponendo il piacer de gli occhi belli
  ne' quai mirando mio disio ha posa;   132
ma chi s'avvede che i vivi suggelli
  d'ogni bellezza più fanno più suso,
  e ch'io non m'era lì rivolto a quelli,   135
escusar puommi di quel ch'io m'accuso
  per escusarmi, e vedermi dir vero;
  chè il piacer santo non è qui dischiuso   138
perchè si fa montando più sincero.

CANTO 15

Benigna volontate, in che si liqua
  sempre l'amor che drittamente spira,
  come cupidità fa ne l'iniqua,   3
silenzio pose a quella dolce lira,
  e fece quietar le sante corde
  che la destra del Cielo allenta e tira.   6
Come saranno ai giusti preghi sorde
  quelle sustanze che, per darmi voglia
  ch'io le pregassi, a tacer fur concorde?   9
Ben è che sanza termine si doglia
  chi, per amor di cosa che non duri
  eternamente, quell'amor si spoglia.   12
Quale per li seren tranquilli e puri
  discorre ad ora ad or sùbito foco,
  movendo gli occhi che stavan sicuri,   15
e pare stella che tramuti loco,
  se non che da la parte ond'ei s'accende
  nulla sen perde, ed esso dura poco,   18
tale dal corno che in destro si stende
  al piè di quella croce corse un astro
  de la costellazion che lì risplende;   21
nè si partì la gemma dal suo nastro,
  ma per la lista radial trascorse,
  che parve foco dietro ad alabastro.   24

It may be that my words seem overbold,
  as did they the fair eyes depreciate,
  whose charm it stills my longing to behold:
But who notes that more power, the higher they get,
  to the live seals of every beauty accrues,
  and that to them I'd there not turned back yet,
he'll excuse me for that whereof I accuse,
  to excuse, myself, and see how verily
  the holy charm doth here its place not lose,
for, as it mounts, it grows in purity.

CANTO 15

Benign will, issuing as it ever must
  from righteous love, as cupidous desire
  resolves itself into the will unjust,
silence imposed on that melodious lyre,
  and hushed the sacred chords, now loose, now taut,
  as Heav'n's right hand which tunes them may require.
How unto righteous prayers shall hearken not
  those substances, who, to prompt me to pray
  to them, were one and all to silence brought?
Well may he mourn for ever and for aye
  who, for the love of thing which hath nowise
  eternal value, casts that love away.
As through the clear and tranquil evening skies
  there shoots at times a sudden trail of light,
  stirring to movement the late listless eyes,
which well might be a star that takes to flight,
  save that from where it first was kindled none
  is missing, and it quickly fades from sight,
so from the horn which to the right doth run
  darting adown that cross to its foot there came
  a star, of those that cluster bright thereon.
Nor parted from its riband was the gem,
  but like fire behind alabaster, sped
  along the radial shaft its eager flame.

Sì pia l'ombra d'Anchise si porse,
    se fede merta nostra maggior musa,
    quando in Eliso del figlio s'accorse.   27
« O sanguis meus, o superinfusa
    gratia Dei, sicut tibi cui
    bis umquam coeli ianua reclusa?»   30
Così quel lume, ond'io m'attesi a lui;
    poscia rivolsi a la mia donna il viso,
    e quinci e quindi stupefatto fui;   33
chè dentro a gli occhi suoi ardeva un riso
    tal, ch'io pensai co' miei toccar lo fondo
    da la mia grazia e del mio paradiso.   36
Indi, a udire ed a veder giocondo,
    giunse lo spirto al suo principio cose
    ch'io non intesi, sì parlò profondo;   39
nè per elezion mi si nascose,
    ma per necessità, chè il suo concetto
    al segno dei mortal si sovrappose.   42
E quando l'arco de l'ardente affetto
    fu sì sfogato che il parlar discese
    inver lo segno del nostro intelletto,   45
la prima cosa che per me s'intese
    « Benedetto sii tu » fu « trino ed uno,
    che nel mio seme sei tanto cortese ».   48
E seguitò: « Grato e lontan digiuno
    tratto leggendo nel magno volume
    u' non si muta mai bianco nè bruno,   51
soluto hai, figlio, dentro a questo lume
    in ch'io ti parlo, mercè di colei
    che all'alto volo ti vestì le piume.   54
Tu credi che a me tuo pensier mei
    da quel ch'è primo, così come raia
    da l'un se si conosce, il cinque e il sei;   57
e però chi mi sia e perch'io paia
    più gaudioso a te, non mi domandi,
    che alcun altro in questa turba gaia.   60
Tu credi il vero, chè i minori e i grandi
    di questa vita miran ne lo speglio
    in che prima che pensi il pensier pandi.   63

With equal love reached forth Anchises' shade,
   if worthy of credit be our greatest *musa*,
   on seeing his son in the Elysian glade.
'*O sanguis meus, O superinfusa*
   gratia Dei, sicut tibi cui
   bis umquam coeli ianua reclusa?'
The light thus, so on it I fixed mine eye
   then turned, my lady's face to scrutinize,
   and on both sides was awestruck equally;
for such a smile was blazing in her eyes
   methought that mine had touched the deepest ground
   both of my grace and of my paradise.
Then, glad alike in aspect and in sound,
   that spirit spake such further things as I
   could understand not, they were too profound;
nor did it hide its thought deliberately,
   but could no other, for its argument
   soared, for the mark of mortal minds, too high.
But when the bow, by warm affection bent,
   was so far slackened that its utterance now
   within our mental range had made descent,
the first I understood was: 'Blest be thou,
   threefold and one, who graciously art pleased
   unto my seed such courtesy to show!'
And it pursued: 'My son, thou hast appeased
   in him thou hearest speaking from this light
   a pleasing, long-felt thirst, which on me seized
when reading in the mighty tome, where white
   and dusky never change—and all by grace
   of her who fledged thee for thy lofty flight.
Thou deemest that to me thy thought doth pass
   from primal thought, as "one," if rightly known,
   is of both "five" and "six" the starting-place;
hence askest not my name, nor to be shown
   why in this blithe assemblage of the blest
   the joy of none seems equal to my own.
Thou deemest rightly; for both mightiest
   and humblest here into the mirror gaze
   where thou, ere thinking, hast thy thought express'd.

Ma perchè il sacro amore in che io veglio
  con perpetua vista, e che m'asseta
  di dolce disiar, s'adempia meglio,   66
la voce tua, sicura, balda e lieta,
  suoni la volontà, suoni 'l disio
  a che la mia risposta è già decreta ».   69
Io mi volsi a Beatrice, e quella udìo
  pria ch'io parlassi, ed arrisemi un cenno
  che fece crescer l'ali al voler mio.   72
Poi cominciai così: « L'affetto e il senno,
  come la prima egualità v'apparse,
  d'un peso per ciascun di voi si fenno,   75
però che il Sol che v'allumò ed arse,
  col caldo e con la luce è sì eguali
  che tutte simiglianze sono scarse.   78
Ma voglia ed argomento nei mortali,
  per la cagion ch'a voi è manifesta,
  diversamente son pennuti in ali;   81
ond'io, che son mortal, mi sento in questa
  diseguaglianza, e però non ringrazio
  se non col cuore a la paterna festa.   84
Ben supplico io te, vivo topazio
  che questa gioia preziosa ingemmi,
  che tu mi facci del tuo nome sazio ».   87
« O fronda mia in che io compiacemmi
  pure aspettando, io fui la tua radice »:
  cotal principio rispondendo femmi.   90
Poscia mi disse: « Quel da cui si dice
  tua cognazione, e che cent'anni e piue
  girato ha il monte in la prima cornice,   93
mio figlio fu e tuo bisavol fue;
  ben si convien che la lunga fatica
  tu li raccorci con l'opere tue.   96
Fiorenza, dentro da la cerchia antica
  ond'ella toglie ancora e terza e nona,
  si stava in pace, sobria e pudica.   99
Non avea catenella, non corona,
  non gonne contigiate, non cintura
  che fosse a veder più che la persona.   102

But, that the sacred love which keeps always
   my vision watchful, causing me to pine
   with sweet desire, may yet more brightly blaze,
securely, frankly, blithely be it thine
   to voice the will, voice the desire whereto
   my answer stands decreed by will divine!'
I turned to Beatrice, but she foreknew
   my thought ere uttered, and a smile bestowed
   whereby the wings of my volition grew.
Then I began, 'When unto you there showed
   itself the Prime Equality, your wit
   shone in like measure as your feeling glowed;
because the Sun by whom ye are warmed and lit,
   with light and warmth so equally doth glow,
   that all similitudes fall short of it.
But in mankind—and well the cause ye know—
   wish and the means to give that wish effect
   have pinions which diversely plumaged grow.
I too by this disparity am check'd,
   as man: hence for thy fatherly accost
   no other thanks than of the heart expect.
I implore thee, living topaz-stone that dost
   ingem this precious jewel, satisfy
   me with thy name: 'tis that I long for most.'
'O leaf of mine, in whom well-pleased was I
   while but awaiting thee, I was thy stem':
   such was the preface to its prompt reply.
Then it said: 'He that gave thy clan its name,
   who after more than five-score years doth yet
   toil round the mount's first cornice—even the same
my son was, and thy grandsire did beget:
   well may thy prayers, as it is meet they should,
   the long term of his weariness abate.
Florence within her old enclosure stood,
   whence tierce and nones she still hears daily tolled,
   and dwelt in peace, sober and chaste and good.
No bracelet did she have, no crown of gold,
   no highly-broidered gowns, no girdle in hue
   more striking than its wearer to behold.

Non faceva nascendo ancor paura
  la figlia al padre, chè il tempo e la dote
  non fuggien quinci e quindi la misura.   105
Non avea case di famiglia vote;
  non v'era giunto ancor Sardanapalo
  a mostrar ciò che in camera si puote.   108
Non era vinto ancora Montemalo
  dal vostro Uccellatoio, che com'è vinto
  nel montar sù, così sarà nel calo.   111
Bellincion Berti vid'io andar cinto
  di cuoio e d'osso, e venir da lo specchio
  la donna sua sanza il viso dipinto;   114
e vidi quel de' Nerli e quel del Vecchio
  esser contenti a la pelle scoperta,
  e le sue donne al fuso ed al pennecchio.   117
Oh fortunate! ciascuna era certa
  de la sua sepoltura, ed ancor nulla
  era per Francia nel letto diserta.   120
L'una vegghiava a studio de la culla,
  e, consolando, usava l'idioma
  che prima i padri e le madri trastulla;   123
l'altra, traendo a la rocca la chioma,
  favoleggiava con la sua famiglia
  dei Troiani, di Fiesole e di Roma.   126
Saria tenuta allor tal maraviglia
  una Cianghella, un Lapo Salterello,
  qual or saria Cincinnato e Corniglia.   129
A così riposato, a così bello
  viver di cittadini, a così fida
  cittadinanza, a così dolce ostello,   132
Maria mi diè, chiamata in alte grida;
  e ne l'antico vostro Battisteo
  insieme fui cristiano e Cacciaguida.   135
Moronto fu mio frate, ed Eliseo.
  Mia donna venne a me di Val di Pado,
  e quindi il soprannome tuo si feo.   138
Poi seguitai l'imperador Corrado,
  ed ei mi cinse de la sua milizia,
  tanto per bene ovrar li venni in grado.   141

No father yet found reason to beshrew
  a daughter's birth; for dower and age to wed
  'scaped not, on either hand, the measure due.
No houses then stood uninhabited;
  no Sardanapálus yet was come to show
  what gallant hearts by chambering are bred.
Nor yet defeat did Montemalo know
  by your Uccellatoi'—to be acquainted,
  swift tho' it rise, with swifter overthrow.
Bellinción Berti saw I pass, contented
  with belt of bone and leather, and his dame
  leaving the mirror with her face unpainted;
saw Nerli's lord and Vecchio's, chiefs of fame,
  content with plain buff coats, their wives withal
  of handling flax and distaff think no shame.
Oh happy they! Each sure of burial
  in her own tomb, none fated yet to lie
  deserted in her bed, at France's call.
One, o'er the cradle, crooned a lullaby,
  using the idiom which in every home
  fathers and mothers first delight to employ;
another to the youngsters bidden come
  and gather round her spinning-wheel would tell
  tales of the Trojans, Fiesole and Rome.
Cornelia and Cincinnatus might as well
  be found among you now, as then had been
  such as Cianghella and Lapo Salterel.
Me to a life so lovely, so serene,
  of fellowship with citizens so staid,
  a hostelry so good to sojourn in,
did Mary give, when loudly called to aid;
  and, in your ancient Baptistery, there
  was I both Christ's and Cacciaguida made.
Moronto and Eliséo my brothers were:
  my wife came to me from the vale of Po;
  whence was derived the surname thou dost bear.
Anon with the emperor Conrad did I go
  crusading; and in time he dubbed me knight,
  my gallant deeds of arms had pleased him so.

629

Dietro gli andai incontro a la nequizia
  di quella legge il cui popolo usurpa,
  per colpa dei pastor, vostra giustizia.   144
Quivi fu' io da quella gente turpa
  disviluppato dal mondo fallace
  lo cui amor molt'anime deturpa;   147
e venni dal martiro a questa pace ».

CANTO 16

O POCA nostra nobiltà di sangue,
  se gloriar di te la gente fai
  qua giù dove l'affetto nostro langue,   3
mirabil cosa non mi sarà mai;
  chè là dove appetito non si torce,
  dico nel cielo, io me ne gloriai.   6
Ben sei tu manto che tosto raccorce,
  sì che se non s'appon di dì in die
  lo tempo va dintorno con le force.   9
Dal *voi* che prima Roma sofferie,
  in che la sua famiglia men persevra,
  ricominciaron le parole mie;   12
onde Beatrice, ch'era un poco scevra,
  ridendo parve quella che tossìo
  al primo fallo scritto di Ginevra.   15
Io cominciai: « Voi siete il padre mio;
  voi mi date a parlar tutta baldezza;
  voi mi levate sì ch'io son più ch'io.   18
Per tanti rivi s'empie d'allegrezza
  la mente mia, che di sè fa letizia
  perchè può sostener che non si spezza.   21
Ditemi dunque, cara mia primizia,
  quai fur li vostri antichi, e quai fur gli anni
  che si segnaro in vostra puerizia: 24
ditemi de l'ovil di San Giovanni
  quanto era allora, e chi eran le genti
  tra esso degne di più alti scanni ».   27

With him I fought that law's nefarious might
  whose people, by the pastors' fault, the place
  have long usurped which should be yours by right.
There was I at the hands of that foul race
  dismantled of the world's deceitful shows,
  the love of which doth many a soul debase;
and came from martyrdom to this repose.'

CANTO 16

O PALTRY heritage, our noble blood,
  if that to glory in thee thou movest men
  down here where we but feebly will the good,
no marvel shall I deem it ever again;
  for there, where right affection never veers,
  I mean in heaven, myself thereof grew vain.
Truly thou art a cloak one soon outwears;
  so that, if nought be added day by day,
  time doth go round about thee with his shears.
With plural 'you,' in the old courtly way
  permitted first by Rome, whose sons appear
  to use it less now, I resumed my say;
whence Beatrice, who stood aloof though near,
  laughing, resembled her whose cough gave sign
  of the first fault that's written of Guinevere.
I thus began: 'You are my father, mine;
  you give me boldness to speak all my thought;
  you adorn me so that I myself outshine.
My spirit through so many rills is fraught
  with gladness, that it joyeth in its own joy
  at being so filled therewith and bursting not.
Thus, then, my dear first stock, the time employ:
  tell me your ancestry, and what was done
  that marked the years, while you were yet a boy:
tell me about the sheepfold of St. John—
  its size, and which were then the families
  whose worth the highest seats in it had won.'

Come s'avviva a lo spirar dei venti
  carbone in fiamma, così vid'io quella
  luce risplendere a' miei blandimenti;   30
e come a gli occhi miei si fe' più bella,
  così con voce più dolce e soave,
  ma non con questa moderna favella,   33
dissemi: « Da quel dì che fu detto *Ave*
  al parto in che mia madre, ch'è or santa,
  s'alleviò di me, ond'era grave,   36
al suo Leon cinquecento cinquanta
  e trenta fiate venne questo foco
  a rinfiammarsi sotto la sua pianta.   39
Gli antichi miei e io nacqui nel loco
  dove si trova pria l'ultimo sesto
  da quei che corre il vostro annual gioco.   42
Basti de' miei maggiori udirne questo:
  chi ei si fosser e onde venner quivi
  più è tacer che ragionare onesto.   45
Tutti color che a quel tempo eran ivi
  da poter arme, tra Marte e il Battista,
  erano il quinto di quei che son vivi.   48
Ma la cittadinanza ch'è or mista
  di Campi, di Certaldo e di Figline,
  pura vedeasi ne l'ultimo artista.   51
Oh quanto fora meglio esser vicine
  quelle genti ch'io dico, ed al Galluzzo
  e a Trespiano aver vostro confine,   54
che averle dentro, e sostener lo puzzo
  del villan d'Aguglion, di quel da Signa
  che già per barattare ha l'occhio aguzzo!   57
Se la gente che al mondo più traligna
  non fosse stata a Cesare noverca,
  ma come madre a suo figliuol benigna,   60
tal fatto è fiorentino e cambia e merca,
  che si sarebbe volto a Simifonti,
  là dove andava l'avolo a la cerca;   63
sariesi Montemurlo ancor dei Conti,
  sarieno i Cerchi nel pivier d'Acone,
  e forse in val di Greve i Buondelmonti.   66

I saw the lustre glow on hearing these
  my blandishments, as charcoal to a blaze
  is quickened at the breath of passing breeze.
And as it grew yet fairer to my gaze,
  so with a sweeter, softer voice it made
  reply, but not in this our modern phrase,
with these words: 'From the day when "Hail" was said,
  to that when my now sainted mother's womb
  was of myself, its burden, lightenéd,
to its own Lion had this planet come
  five hundred, fifty and thirty times, its flame
  beneath his burning paw to re-illume.
My ancestors were born and I, like them,
  there, where encountered first is the last ward
  by him who runneth in your annual game.
Suffice it of my forbears to record
  that much: their names, and what their origin,
  rather than mentioned here, were best ignor'd.
All those who at that time were there, between
  Mars and the Baptist, fit for arms were man
  for man the fifth of those to-day there seen.
Yet was the commune—now a mongrel clan
  mixed with Figline, with Certaldo mix'd
  and Campi—pure to the last artisan.
Oh how much better ye should dwell betwixt
  those folk as neighbours, and your boundary
  have at Galluzzo and at Trespiano fix'd,
than have them in and thole the stench thereby
  of Aguglione's boor, of Signa's hind,
  whose eye e'en now is sharp for barratry!
If of all folk the most depraved in mind
  had not the stepdame unto Caesar play'd,
  but as a mother to her son been kind,
there's one, made Florentine, doth truck and trade,
  who would have been thrust back to Simifonti,
  where erst his grandfather went begging bread;
held yet were Montemurlo by the Conti;
  the Cerchi would Acone's parish hold,
  and Valdigreve, chance, the Buondelmonti.

Sempre la confusion de le persone
  principio fu del mal de la cittade,
  come del corpo il cibo che s'appone;   69
e cieco toro più avaccio cade
  che cieco agnello; e molte volte taglia
  più e meglio l'una che le cinque spade.   72
Se tu riguardi Luni ed Urbisaglia
  come son ite, e come se ne vanno
  di retro ad esse Chiusi e Sinigaglia,   75
udir come le schiatte si disfanno
  non ti parrà nova cosa nè forte,
  poscia che le cittadi termine hanno.   78
Le vostre cose tutte hanno lor morte
  sì come voi; ma celasi in alcuna
  che dura molto, e le vite son corte.   81
E come il volger del ciel de la Luna
  copre e discopre i liti sanza posa,
  così fa di Fiorenza la fortuna;   84
per che non dee parer mirabil cosa
  ciò ch'io dirò degli alti Fiorentini
  onde è la fama nel tempo nascosa.   87
Io vidi gli Ughi e vidi i Catellini,
  Filippi, Greci, Ormanni e Alberichi,
  già nel calare, illustri cittadini;   90
e vidi così grandi come antichi
  con quel de la Sannella quel de l'Arca,
  e Soldanieri e Ardinghi e Bostichi.   93
Sovra la porta che al presente è carca
  di nova fellonia di tanto peso
  che tosto fia iattura de la barca,   96
erano i Ravignani, ond'è disceso
  il conte Guido e qualunque del nome
  de l'alto Bellincione ha poscia preso.   99
Quel de la Pressa sapeva già come
  regger si vuole, ed avea Galigaio
  dorata in casa sua già l'elsa e il pome.   102
Grande era già la colonna del vaio,
  Sacchetti, Giuochi, Fifanti e Barucci
  e Galli e quei che arrossan per lo staio.   105

Source of the public ill was, from of old,
  in th' intermingling of men's persons found,
  as food makes sick, if greed be uncontroll'd.
And the blind bull more headlong falls to the ground
  than the blind lamb, and than five swords doth one
  ofttimes inflict more cuts and deeplier wound.
Consider Luni, how she·is past and gone,
  and Urbisaglia; and after them how go
  Chiusi and Sinigaglia: think thereon,
and, inasmuch as cities perish so,
  not hard thou'lt deem it or a strange report
  to hear that families enfeebled grow.
All your belongings in the last resort
  die, as do ye; but some their death conceal
  by enduring long; and human lives are short.
And as the turning of the lunar wheel
  in ceaseless rhythm veils and unveils the shore,
  even so with Florence too doth Fortune deal;
hence that should not be thing to marvel o'er,
  which I will tell of many a Florentine
  great house that, hidden by time, is famed no more.
I saw the Ughi, I saw the Ormanni shine;
  Catalíns, Filippi, Greci and Alberics were
  still glorious, though already in decline;
I saw both l'Arca and la Sanéll', a pair
  as mighty, as for ancient blood renown'd,
  Bosticchi, too, Ardinghi and Soldaniér.
Close to the gate, with felony, beyond
  aught known before, now so o'erladen, that soon
  the barque will have its cargo jettison'd,
the Ravignani dwelt, from whom come down
  Count Guido and whosoe'er from then till now
  has taken the name of the high Bellinción.
He of la Pressa knew already how
  to rule, and Galigaio's house yet claimed
  by gilded hilt and pommel its worth to show.
The pale of vair was then already famed,
  Sacchetti, Giuochi, Fifanti, Barucci
  and Galli and those the bushel makes ashamed.

Lo ceppo di che nacquero i Calfucci
  era già grande, e già eran tratti
  a le curule Sizii ed Arrigucci.   108
Oh quali io vidi quei che son disfatti
  per lor superbia! e le palle de l'oro
  fiorian Fiorenza in tutti i suoi gran fatti!   111
Così faceano i padri di coloro
  che sempre che la vostra chiesa vaca,
  si fanno grassi stando a consistoro.   114
L'oltracotata schiatta che s'indraca
  dietro a chi fugge, ed a chi mostra il dente
  o ver la borsa come agnel si placa,   117
già venia sù, ma di piccola gente,
  sì che non piacque ad Ubertin Donato
  che poi il suocero il fe' lor parente.   120
Già era il Caponsacco nel Mercato
  disceso giù da Fiesole, e già era
  buon cittadino Giuda ed Infangato.   123
Io dirò cosa incredibile e vera:
  nel picciol cerchio s'entrava per porta
  che si nomava da quei de la Pera.   126
Ciascun che de la bella insegna porta
  del gran barone il cui nome e 'l cui pregio
  la festa di Tommaso riconforta,   129
da esso ebbe milizia e privilegio;
  avvegna che col popol si rauni
  oggi colui che la fascia col fregio.   132
Già eran Gualterotti ed Importuni;
  ed ancor saria Borgo più quieto
  se di novi vicin fosser digiuni.   135
La casa di che nacque il vostro fleto,
  per lo giusto disdegno che v'ha morti,
  e pose fine al vostro viver lieto,   138
era onorata, essa e i suoi consorti;
  o Buondelmonte, quanto mal fuggisti
  le nozze sue per gli altrui conforti!   141
Molti sarebber lieti che son tristi
  se Dio t'avesse conceduto ad Ema
  la prima volta che a città venisti.   144

Famed was the stock, whence issued the Calfucci,
  already, and to curule chairs the hour
  had drawn already Sizii and Arrigucci.
Oh, how I saw those mighty who from power
  through pride have fallen! and the balls of gold
  in all their doughty deeds made Florence flower.
Such sires had they, who now consistory hold
  whene'er your church is vacant, and there stay
  and make them fat—such sires were theirs of old.
The o'erweening tribe that will the dragon play
  to him that flees, but doth he turn and show
  his teeth, or purse, no lamb so mild as they,
were on the rise, but still of blood so low,
  that Ubertín Donato grudged it, when
  his father-in-law had made him kin thereto.
The Caponsacchi had come down by then
  from Fiesole to the market; Giuda too
  with Infangato, was good citizen.
Named of la Pera was a port wherethrough
  one entered the small circuit—of all things
  I've told thee yet, least credible, but true!
Each one who bears the sightly quarterings
  of the great peer whose name and whose renown
  the feast of Thomas to your memory brings,
was for his knight and for his liegeman known;
  though he that with a bordure rings them round
  to-day has made the people's cause his own.
In Borgo already were Importuni found,
  and Gualterotti—a more tranquil place
  now, did it with new neighbours less abound.
The proud house that gave birth to your distress,
  through the just anger which hath been your bane,
  and put a period to your happiness,
itself was honoured, and its consorts, then:
  O Buondelmonte, when by others' rede
  thou fledst its nuptials, little didst thou gain!
Many would have rejoiced, whose hearts now bleed,
  if God in Ema's flood had let thee drown,
  when to the city thou didst first proceed.

Ma conveniasi a quella pietra scema
  che guarda il ponte, che Fiorenza fesse
  vittima, ne la sua pace postrema.   147
Con queste genti, e con altre con esse,
  vid'io Fiorenza in sì fatto riposo
  che non avea cagione onde piangesse;   150
con queste genti vid'io glorioso
  e giusto il popol suo, tanto che il giglio
  non era ad asta mai posto a ritroso,   153
nè per division fatto vermiglio ».

CANTO 17

Qual venne a Climenè per accertarsi
  di ciò che avea incontro a sè udito
  quei che ancor fa li padri ai figli scarsi,   3
tal era io e tale era sentito
  e da Beatrice e da la santa lampa
  che pria per me avea mutato sito.   6
Per che mia donna: « Manda fuor la vampa
  del tuo disio » mi disse, « sì ch'ell'esca
  segnata bene de l'interna stampa;   9
non perchè nostra conoscenza cresca
  per tuo parlare, ma perchè t'aùsi
  a dir la sete sì che l'uom ti mesca ».   12
« O cara piota mia, che sì t'insusi
  che come veggion le terrene menti
  non capere in triangol due ottusi,   15
così vedi le cose contingenti
  anzi che sieno in sè, mirando il punto
  a cui tutti li tempi son presenti;   18
mentre ch'io era a Virgilio congiunto
  su per lo monte che l'anime cura
  e discendendo nel mondo defunto,   21

But Florence by that mutilated stone
   which guards the bridge was doomed in those, the last
   days of her peace to strike a victim down.
With these and other houses in times past,
   beheld I Florence live days so serene,
   that she no occasion had to be downcast:
with these beheld her folk such glory win,
   that, as befitting those whom justice rules,
   the lily on the staff was never seen
reversed, nor through division tinctured gules.'

CANTO 17

As came to Clymene, intent to clear
   his name of slander, he who still doth make,
   when sons entreat them, fathers slow to hear;
e'en such was I, and such did Beatrice take
   note that I was, as did the holy lamp
   which late had changed its station for my sake.
Wherefore my lady thus: 'In nowise damp
   the flame of thy desire, but flash it out
   imprinted clearly by the inward stamp;
not that thy speech may banish any doubt
   of ours, but that thou train thyself thereby
   to tell thy need, that one may slake thy drought.'
'Dear turf from which I sprang, now raised so high,
   that, as man's mind sees that, of angles, two
   obtuse in a triangle cannot lie,
so unto thee, who hast the point in view
   which sees all times as present, are display'd
   contingent things ere they in fact come true;
whilst I, with Virgil as companion, made
   my way up o'er the mount that souls doth heal
   and downwards in the world that lieth dead,

dette mi fur di mia vita futura
  parole gravi, avvegna ch'io mi senta
  ben tetragono ai colpi di ventura;   24
per che la voglia mia sarìa contenta
  d'intender qual fortuna mi s'appressa,
  chè saetta prevista vien più lenta ».   27
Così diss'io a quella luce stessa
  che pria m'avea parlato, e come volle
  Beatrice fu la mia voglia confessa.   30
Nè per ambage, in che la gente folle
  già s'inviscava pria che fosse anciso
  l'Agnel di Dio che le peccata tolle,   33
ma per chiare parole e con preciso
  latin rispose quell'amor paterno,
  chiuso e parvente del suo proprio riso: 36
« La contingenza, che fuor del quaderno
  de la vostra materia non si stende,
  tutta è dipinta nel cospetto eterno;   39
necessità però quindi non prende
  se non come dal viso in che si specchia
  nave che per corrente giù discende.   42
Da indi, sì come viene ad orecchia
  dolce armonia da organo, mi viene
  a vista il tempo che ti s'apparecchia.   45
Qual si partì Ippolito d'Atene
  per la spietata e perfida noverca,
  tal di Fiorenza partir ti conviene.   48
Questo si vuole e questo già si cerca,
  e tosto verrà fatto a chi ciò pensa
  là dove Cristo tutto dì si merca.   51
La colpa seguirà la parte offensa
  in grido, come suol, ma la vendetta
  fia testimonio al ver, che la dispensa.   54
Tu lascerai ogni cosa diletta
  più caramente, e questo è quello strale
  che l'arco de l'esilio pria saetta.   57
Tu proverai sì come sa di sale
  lo pane altrui e come è duro calle
  lo scendere e 'l **salir** per l'altrui scale.   60

pronounced were grave words, tending to reveal
  my future life, albeit I feel me now
  right four-square to the blows that chance may deal.
Wherefore my wish were granted, wouldst thou show
  what storm is drawing nigh me, and from where;
  since bolt foreseen strikes a less painful blow.'
Thus spake I to the light which had whilere
  addressed me, and did thus the will obey
  of Beatrice, and my strong wish declare.
Nor by such riddles as fond folk, of a day
  long vanished, were belimed with, ere was slain
  the Lamb of God that taketh sins away,
but in clear words and Latin no less plain
  did that paternal love, which veiled, yet show'd,
  itself in its own smile, thus speak again:
'Contingency, which stretches not its mode
  past the brief page where mortal lives are writ,
  is all depicted in the vision of God;
yet thence derives necessity no whit
  more than the movement of a ship that steers
  downstream depends on the eye that mirrors it.
From thence, e'en as there stealeth on the ears
  sweet harmony from organ, comes to me
  a vision of thy life in future years.
As his stepmother's wiles and cruelty
  from Athens drove Hippolytus, likewise
  thyself from Florence driven forth must be.
This would they, this already they devise,
  and soon will do it he that plots it there
  where Christ is daily hawked as merchandise.
The side wronged will, as wont, in rumour bear
  the blame; yet shall the vengeance testify
  unto the truth, whereof 'tis minister.
Thou shalt leave each thing that most tenderly
  thou lov'st; and this, of arrows from the bow
  of exile, is the first that it lets fly.
Thou shalt make proof how salt the taste doth grow
  of others' bread, and how it tires the feet
  still up, still down, by others' stairs to go.

E quel che più ti graverà le spalle
  sarà la compagnia malvagia e scempia
  con la qual tu cadrai in questa valle;   63
che tutta ingrata, tutta matta ed empia
  si farà contra te; ma poco appresso
  ella, non tu, n'avrà rossa la tempia.   66
Di sua bestialità il suo processo
  farà la prova; sì che a te fia bello
  l'averti fatto parte per te stesso.   69
Lo primo tuo rifugio e 'l primo ostello
  sarà la cortesia del gran Lombardo
  che in su la scala porta il santo uccello;   72
che in te avrà sì benigno riguardo,
  che del dare e del chieder, tra voi due
  fia primo quel che tra gli altri è più tardo.   75
Con lui vedrai colui che impresso fue,
  nascendo, sì da questa stella forte,
  che mirabili fien l'opere sue.   78
Non se ne son le genti ancora accorte
  per la novella età, chè pur nov'anni
  son queste rote intorno di lui torte;   81
ma pria che il Guasco l'alto Arrigo inganni
  parran faville de la sua virtute
  in non curar d'argento nè d'affanni.   84
Le sue magnificenze conosciute
  saranno ancora sì, che i suoi nemici
  non ne potran tener le lingue mute.   87
A lui t'aspetta ed a' suoi benefici:
  per lui fia trasmutata molta gente,
  cambiando condizion ricchi e mendici.   90
E porteraine scritto ne la mente
  di lui, e nol dirai ». E disse cose
  incredibili a quei che fia presente.   93
Poi giunse: « Figlio, queste son le chiose
  di quel che ti fu detto; ecco le insidie
  che dietro a pochi giri son nascose.   96
Non vo' però che a' tuoi vicini invidie,
  poscia che s'infutura la tua vita
  vie più là che il punir di lor perfidie ».   99

And what shall gall thee most, will be to meet
   the company, stupid and evil swine,
   with whom thou shalt be cast into this pit;
who, all mad, all as thankless as malign,
   will turn 'gainst thee; but ere much time hath flown,
   theirs shall the crimsoned forehead be, not thine.
So shall their brutishness in deeds be shown,
   that 'twill become thee well to have preferred
   to form a party of thyself alone.
First refuge and first inn for thee prepared
   shall be the mighty Lombard's courtesy,
   who on the ladder bears the sacred bird;
who shall have such benign regard for thee,
   that, counter to men's wont, between you two
   the granting shall before the asking be.
With him shalt thou behold the mortal who,
   at birth, was so impressed by this strong star,
   that wondrous are the deeds which he shall do.
Still unobserved of men his merits are,
   by reason of his youth; for this bright coil
   has round him wheeled but nine brief years so far:
but ere the Gascon the great Harry foil,
   some sparkles of his temper will he show
   in caring not for money or for toil.
Hereafter shall his deeds be bruited so
   for their magnificence, that they shall let
   no tongue be silent, even of his foe.
Him look to, and upon his favours wait;
   through him shall many be transformed in kind,
   rich men and beggars, changing their estate.
And thou shalt bear hence, written in thy mind
   of him, but tell it not'—and he told things
   which those who see them past belief shall find.
He added: 'Son, these on the happenings
   foretold thee are the glosses: lo, concealed
   by a few turns o' the year, what ambushings!
Yet to no envy of thy neighbours yield,
   in that thy future life shall long outlast
   the doom by which their treachery shall be sealed.'

Poi che tacendo si mostrò spedita
  l'anima santa di metter la trama
  in quella tela ch'io le porsi ordita,   102
io cominciai, come colui che brama,
  dubitando, consiglio da persona
  che vede e vuol dirittamente ed ama: 105
« Ben veggio, padre mio, sì come sprona
  lo tempo verso me, per colpo darmi
  tal, ch'è più grave a chi più s'abbandona,   108
per che di provedenza è buon ch'io m'armi,
  sì che, se il loco m'è tolto più caro,
  io non perdessi gli altri per miei carmi.   111
Giù per lo mondo sanza fine amaro
  e per lo monte del cui bel cacume
  gli occhi de la mia donna mi levaro,   114
e poscia per lo Ciel di lume in lume,
  ho io appreso quel che s'io ridico,
  a molti fia sapor di forte agrume;   117
e s'io al vero son timido amico,
  temo di perder vita tra coloro
  che questo tempo chiameranno antico ».   120
La luce in che rideva il mio tesoro
  ch'io trovai lì, si fe' prima corusca
  quale a raggio di sole specchio d'oro.   123
Indi rispose: « Coscienza fusca
  o de la propria o de l'altrui vergogna
  pur sentirà la tua parola brusca.   126
Ma nondimen, rimossa ogni menzogna,
  tutta tua vision fa manifesta,
  e lascia pur grattar dov'è la rogna;   129
chè se la voce tua sarà molesta
  nel primo gusto, vital nutrimento
  lascerà poi, quando sarà digesta.   132
Questo tuo grido farà come vento
  che le più alte cime più percuote;
  e ciò non fia d'onor poco argomento.   135
Però ti son mostrate in queste rote,
  nel monte e ne la valle dolorosa
  pur l'anime che son di fama note,   138

When, having now from speech to silence pass'd,
    that sainted soul thus showed the web, whereof
    I'd stretched the warp, with woof inwoven fast,
I spake as one who, doubting, fain would prove
    the wisdom of some friend and such doth seek
    as sees and wills uprightly and doth love:
'Father, 'tis clear indeed, how time doth prick
    towards me, such an arrow to let fly
    as woundeth sorest him of eye least quick;
'tis good to be armed with foresight, then, that I,
    if robbed of the place wherein I most delight,
    lose not the others through my poetry.
Down in the world of sorrows infinite,
    and on the mountain from whose lovely crest
    my lady's eyes upbore me by their might,
and, afterwards, through Heaven, as on I pressed
    from light to light, I've learned what, if retold,
    would have for many a harsh pot-herb taste.
And if to truth my friendship turneth cold,
    I fear that I may perish among those
    who will describe these as "the days of old".'
The light that by its smile I knew to enclose
    my late-found treasure flashed with such a beam
    as back to the sun a golden mirror throws,
and then replied: 'To conscience rendered dim
    by its own or others' shame (no matter which)
    'tis true that sharp will much thou sayest seem;
but, notwithstanding, see there be no breach
    with truth, but publish thou thy vision whole;
    which done, e'en let them scratch who feel the itch.
For though thy voice may cause the palate dole
    at the first taste, 'twill later leave behind,
    when well digested, that which feeds the soul.
This cry of thine shall do as doth the wind,
    which hardest strikes upon the loftiest hills;
    and that is no small proof of noble mind.
Hence have no souls been shown thee in these wheels,
    or on the mount, or in the dolorous vale,
    save those whose names the trump of fame yet peals,

che l'animo di quel ch'ode, non posa
   nè ferma fede, per esempio ch'aia
   la sua radice incognita e nascosa,   141
nè per altro argomento che non paia ».

CANTO 18

Già si godeva solo del suo verbo
   quello specchio beato, ed io gustava
   lo mio, temprando il dolce con l'acerbo.   3
E quella donna che a Dio mi menava
   disse: « Muta pensier; pensa ch'io sono
   presso a colui ch'ogni torto disgrava ».   6
Io mi rivolsi a l'amoroso suono
   del mio conforto; e qual io allor vidi
   ne gli occhi santi amor, qui l'abbandono;   9
non perch'io pur del mio parlar diffidi,
   ma per la mente che non può reddire
   sovra sè tanto, s'altri non la guidi.   12
Tanto poss'io di quel punto ridire,
   che rimirando lei lo mio affetto
   libero fu da ogni altro disire,   15
fin che il piacere eterno, che diretto
   raggiava in Beatrice, dal bel viso
   mi contentava col secondo aspetto.   18
Vincendo me col lume d'un sorriso,
   ella mi disse: « Volgiti ed ascolta,
   chè non pur ne' miei occhi è paradiso ».   21
Come si vede qui alcuna volta
   l'affetto ne la vista, s'egli è tanto
   che da lui sia tutta l'anima tolta,   24
così nel fiammeggiar del fulgor santo,
   a ch'io mi volsi, conobbi la voglia
   in lui di ragionarmi ancora alquanto.   27
Ei cominciò: « In questa quinta soglia
   de l'albero che vive de la cima
   e frutta sempre e mai non perde foglia,   30

because the hearer's mind can never dwell
  content, or fix its faith, on instance ta'en
  from root unknown or else invisible,
nor yet on other proof which is not plain.'

CANTO 18

THAT blessed mirror now enjoyed alone
  his word within himself, and I too fed,
  tempering the sweet with bitter, on my own.
And she by whom my steps were Godward led
  cried: 'Change thy thought: bethink thee that I dwell
  with Him by whom all wrongs are lightenèd.'
I turned me, as those loving accents fell,
  unto my comfort; and how blazed with love
  her holy eyes just then, I may not tell;
not only that I trust not speech thereof,
  but to such heights o'er itself the mind in vain
  seeks to return, save guided from above.
This only in my memory lives again,
  that my affection, as I gazed on her,
  was free from every other longing then,
when the eternal Pleasure, raying square
  on Beatrice, contented me, her eyes
  reflecting it, I seeing it mirrored there.
She bade me turn and, smiling in such wise
  that I was dazzled, said: 'Give heed; and know,
  not in my eyes alone is paradise.'
As here at times we see the features show
  the affection, if so mightily this fill
  the spirit as to set it all aglow,
so did the holy light reveal its will,
  whose flame, to which I turned, now made me see
  that it desired some converse with me still.
And it began: 'This fifth grade of the Tree
  which draws life from its summit and ne'er knows **dearth**
  of fruitage nor shall ever leafless be,

spiriti son beati, che giù, prima
    che venissero al Ciel, fur di gran voce,
    sì ch'ogni musa ne sarebbe opima. 33
Però mira nei corni de la croce:
    quello ch'io nomerò, lì farà l'atto
    che fa in nube il suo foco veloce». 36
Io vidi per la croce un lume tratto
    dal nomar Iosuè, com'ei si feo;
    nè mi fu noto il dir prima che il fatto. 39
Ed al nome de l'alto Maccabeo
    vidi moversi un altro roteando,
    e letizia era ferza del paleo. 42
Così per Carlo Magno e per Orlando
    due ne seguì lo mio attento sguardo
    com'occhio segue suo falcon volando. 45
Poscia trasse Guglielmo e Rinoardo
    e il duca Gottifredi la mia vista
    per quella croce, e Ruberto Guiscardo. 48
Indi, tra l'altre luci mota e mista,
    mostrommi l'alma che m'avea parlato
    qual era tra i cantor del cielo artista. 51
Io mi rivolsi dal mio destro lato
    per vedere in Beatrice il mio dovere
    o per parlare o per atto segnato; 54
e vidi le sue luci tanto mere,
    tanto gioconde, che la sua sembianza
    vinceva gli altri e l'ultimo solere. 57
E come per sentir più dilettanza
    bene operando l'uom, di giorno in giorno
    s'accorge che la sua virtute avanza, 60
sì m'accors'io che il mio girar d'intorno
    col cielo insieme avea cresciuto l'arco.
    veggendo quel miracol più adorno. 63
E qual è il trasmutare in picciol varco
    di tempo in bianca donna, quando il volto
    suo si discarchi di vergogna il carco, 66
tal fu ne gli occhi miei, quando fui volto,
    per lo candor de la temprata stella
    sesta, che dentro a sè m'avea ricolto. 69

holds blesséd spirits, who while down on earth,
    before they came to Heaven, had won such fame
    that every muse would grow rich by their worth.
Look, therefore, on the horns of the cross; the flame
    that darts in cloud doth not so swiftly dart
    as there the soul will, whom I now shall name.'
Straight I beheld a lustre drawn athwart
    the cross by Joshua's name: he spake, 'twas done;
    nor could I tell the word and deed apart.
He called great Maccabeus, and thereupon
    I saw shoot by another whirling light;
    joy was the whip that made the top spin on.
Two more I thus pursued with eager sight,
    answering to Roland and to Charlëmain,
    as falconer's eye pursues its bird in flight.
Thereafter William and Rainouart, and then
    duke Godfrey to the cross compelled mine eye;
    last, Robert Guiscard flashed upon my ken.
The soul who spake with me then passed on high,
    where mingled with the other lights he plied
    his art among the minstrels of the sky.
I turned me round unto the right-hand side
    to see in Beatrice what I ought to do,
    whether by word or gesture signified;
and in her eyes beheld new radiance, new
    delight, so pure that she in this array
    surpassed her former wont, her latest too.
And as a man, through feeling day by day
    more joy in doing good, will thence suspect
    the measure of his advance on virtue's way;
so, wheeling with the heaven, did I detect
    a widening of the arc we swept through space,
    on seeing that miracle more brightly decked.
And such a change as quickly taketh place
    in fair-complexioned lady, when its load
    of bashfulness is put from off her face,
now, as I turned, in all the prospect showed,
    by reason of the mild sixth star, whose white
    radiance it was, that round me softly glowed.

Io vidi in quella giovial facella
  lo sfavillar de l'amor che lì era
  segnare a gli occhi miei nostra favella.   72
E come augelli surti di riviera,
  quasi congratulando a lor pasture,
  fanno di sè or tonda or lunga schiera,   75
sì dentro ai lumi sante creature
  volitando cantavano, e faciensi
  or D, or I, or L, in sue figure.   78
Prima, cantando, a sua nota moviensi,
  poi, diventando l'un di questi segni,
  un poco s'arrestavano e taciensi.   81
O diva Pegasea, che gl'ingegni
  fai gloriosi e rendili longevi,
  ed essi teco le cittadi e i regni,   84
illustrami di te sì ch'io rilevi
  le lor figure com'io l'ho concette:
  paia tua possa in questi versi brevi.   87
Mostrarsi dunque in cinque volte sette
  vocali e consonanti, ed io notai
  le parti sì come mi parver dette.   90
Diligite iustitiam primai
  fur verbo e nome di tutto il dipinto;
  qui iudicatis Terram fur sezzai.   93
Poscia ne l'emme del vocabol quinto
  rimasero ordinate, sì che Giove
  pareva argento lì d'oro distinto.   96
E vidi scendere altre luci dove
  era il colmo de l'emme, e lì quetarsi,
  cantando, credo, il ben che a sè le move.   99
Poi, come nel percuoter dei ciocchi arsi
  surgono innumerabili faville,
  onde li stolti sogliono augurarsi,   102
resurger parver quindi più di mille
  luci, e salir qual assai e qual poco,
  sì come il Sol che le accende sortille;   105
e quietata ciascuna in suo loco,
  la testa e il collo d'un'aquila vidi
  rappresentare a quel distinto foco,   108

I saw within that Jovial torch the light,
　　all sparkling, of the love which in it lies
　　trace out our human language clear to sight.

And as birds, when from river-bank they rise,
　　as if congratulant to their pastures, do
　　their flying now in line, now circlewise,

so, light-enveloped, holy creatures flew
　　hither and thither, singing, and now *D*,
　　now *I*, now *L* in their own figures drew.

First, chanting, moved they to their measured glee;
　　then at each letter, when 'twas wholly writ,
　　they paused awhile and hushed their psalmody.

O Pegasea divine, who to the wit
　　of men giv'st glory and length of years, as they
　　to cities and to realms, an thou permit,

lighten me with thyself, that so I may
　　carve out their shapes according to my thought:
　　in these scant verses all thy power display!

Five times seven, then, were the signs they wrought,
　　both consonants and vowels; as each passed,
　　I noted well what every portion taught.

'*DILIGITE IUSTITIAM*', these, cast
　　together, verb and noun, were the first told;
　　'*QUI IUDICATIS TERRAM*' were the last.

Next, in the *M* of the fifth word enscrolled,
　　awhile they lingered; so that Jupiter
　　seemed silver at that point inlaid with gold.

And on the *M*'s crest descend, and settling there,
　　more lights I saw that, chanting, seemed to sing
　　the Good which bids them to itself repair.

Then, as from burning logs, when beaten, spring
　　innumerable sparks which often lend
　　excuse to fools for fortune-mongering,

more than a thousand lights appeared to ascend
　　from there again and mount, some lower, some higher,
　　e'en as the Sun who kindles them ordain'd;

and each alighting where it did require,
　　the head and neck of an eagle I descried
　　distinctly pictured by that inlaid fire.

Quei che dipinge lì non ha chi il guidi,
　　ma esso guida, e da lui si rammenta
　　quella virtù ch'è forma per li nidi.　　　　　111
L'altra beatitudo, che contenta
　　pareva prima d'ingigliarsi l'emme,
　　con poco moto seguitò l'imprenta.　　　　　114
O dolce stella, quali e quante gemme
　　mi dimostraro che nostra giustizia
　　effetto sia del ciel che tu ingemme!　　　　　117
Per ch'io prego la mente in che s'inizia
　　tuo moto e tua virtute, che rimiri
　　ond'esce il fummo che il tuo raggio vizia;　　　120
sì che un'altra fiata omai s'adiri
　　del comperare e vender dentro al templo
　　che si murò di segni e di martìri.　　　　　123
O milizia del ciel, cu' io contemplo,
　　adora per color che sono in Terra
　　tutti sviati dietro al malo esemplo!　　　　　126
Già si solea con le spade far guerra;
　　ma or si fa togliendo or qui or quivi
　　lo pan che il pio padre a nessun serra.　　　　129
Ma tu che sol per cancellare scrivi,
　　pensa che Pietro e Paolo, che moriro
　　per la vigna che guasti, ancor son vivi.　　　132
Ben puoi tu dir: « Io ho fermo il disiro
　　sì a colui che volle viver solo
　　e che per salti fu tratto al martiro,　　　　　135
ch'io non conosco il pescator nè Polo ».

CANTO 19

Parea dinanzi a me con l'ali aperte
　　la bella image che, nel dolce frui
　　liete, facevan l'anime conserte.　　　　　　3
Parea ciascun rubinetto in cui
　　raggio di Sole ardesse, sì acceso
　　che ne' miei occhi rifrangesse lui.　　　　　6

Who painteth there hath none to guide him; guide
  himself is, and by him that power of mind
  known as the nesting instinct is supplied.
The other beatitude which seemed inclined
  at first to stay enlilying the *M*,
  by moving slightly, with the print combined.
Oh lovely star, how many a precious gem
  showed me that 'tis the heaven whose jewel thou art
  which dowers the just with all that honours them!
Therefore I pray the mind whence issuing start
  thy power and motion, that it look whence blows
  the fog thy radiance fails to cleave apart;
so that once more it may be wroth with those
  who buy and sell within the temple-gate—
  that temple built with signs and martyrs' throes.
O soldiery of the heaven I contemplate,
  pray thou for those on Earth who all misled
  by evil ensample, love what they should hate!
Aforetime waged with swords, war now is made
  by banning, as man listeth, what the kind
  Father locks up from none—his gift of bread.
But thou who writest but to erase, shalt find
  that Paul and Peter, for the vineyard slain
  which thou layest waste, live yet: bear that in mind.
Well canst thou say: 'Of him, who willed from men
  to live apart and at a caperer's call
  was dragged to martyrdom, my heart's so fain,
that I know not the Fisherman nor Poll.'

CANTO 19

Confronting me appeared with wings outspread
  the fair image which, revelling in their sweet
  fruition, the souls thus interwoven made.
Each seemed a little ruby, a sunbeam lit
  with flame so intensely bright I well might say
  the Sun's self was to my eyes thrown back by it.

E quel che mi convien ritrar testeso
 non portò voce mai, nè scrisse inchiostro,
 nè fu per fantasia già mai compreso: 9
ch'io vidi e anche udii parlar lo rostro,
 e sonar ne la voce e *io* e *mio*,
 quand'era nel concetto *noi* e *nostro*.   12
E cominciò: « Per esser giusto e pio
 son io qui esaltato a quella gloria
 che non si lascia vincere a disio;   15
ed in Terra lasciai la mia memoria
 sì fatta, che le genti lì malvage
 commendan lei ma non seguon la storia ». 18
Così un solo calor di molte brage
 si fa sentir, come di molti amori
 usciva solo un suon di quella image.   21
Ond'io appresso: « O perpetui fiori
 de l'eterna letizia, che pur uno
 parer mi fate tutti i vostri odori,   24
solvetemi, spirando, il gran digiuno
 che lungamente m'ha tenuto in fame
 non trovandoli in Terra cibo alcuno.   27
Ben so io che se in Cielo altro reame
 la divina giustizia fa suo specchio,
 che il vostro non l'apprende con velame. 30
Sapete come attento io m'apparecchio
 ad ascoltar; sapete qual è quello
 dubbio che m'è digiun cotanto vecchio ». 33
Quasi falcone ch'esce dal cappello,
 move la testa e con l'ali si plaude,
 voglia mostrando e facendosi bello,   36
vid'io farsi quel segno, che di laude
 de la divina grazia era contesto,
 con canti quai si sa chi là sù gaude.   39
Poi cominciò: « Colui che volse il sesto
 a lo stremo del mondo, e dentro ad esso
 distinse tanto occulto e manifesto,   42
non potè suo valor sì fare impresso
 in tutto l'universo, che il suo verbo
 non rimanesse in infinito eccesso;   45

And what it now behoves me to portray
  voice never spake, nor ink writ, nor did power
  of fancy ever grasp until this day:
for the beak clearly spoke and, furthermore,
  there sounded in the voice both 'I' and 'my',
  when in conception it was 'we' and 'our';
beginning: 'Just and merciful was I;
  hence am I here exalted to that glory
  which overtops desire however high;
and there, on Earth, I left no transitory
  record, but such as e'en the bad think fit
  to praise, although they follow not the story.'
As there is felt from many coals one heat,
  thus from that image one sole utterance came,
  though many were the loves that spoke from it.
Then cried I: 'O perpetual flowers, aflame
  with the eternal joy, who to my sense
  cause all your odours to appear the same,
break with your breath the stubborn abstinence,
  which, finding no relief on Earth, hath held
  my hungry spirit in such long suspense.
Your kingdom, well I know, hath never failed,
  e'en if the mirror of God's justice shine
  elsewhere in Heaven, to see its light unveiled.
Ye know how eagerly I now incline
  to listen; and the doubt which hath for years
  been unto me a fast ye well divine.'
As, when the hood is slipped, a falcon rears
  his head and claps his wings, eager to fly,
  and vaunts himself as a bird that hath no peers,
so moved that emblem, woven of revelry
  in the divine grace and with praises fraught
  such as they sing who there rejoice on high.
Then, 'He whose compass,' were the words I caught,
  'outlined the world, and who within that space
  so much in open and in secret wrought,
could not his power after suchwise impress
  on all the universe, but that his word
  must still remain in infinite excess.

e ciò fa certo, che il primo superbo,
    che fu la somma d'ogni creatura,
    per non aspettar lume cadde acerbo.   48
E quinci appar ch'ogni minor natura
    è corto recettacolo a quel bene
    che non ha fine e sè con sè misura.   51
Dunque nostra veduta, che conviene
    essere alcun dei raggi de la mente
    di che tutte le cose son ripiene,   54
non può da sua natura esser possente
    tanto, che suo principio non discerna
    molto di là da quel che l'è parvente;   57
però ne la giustizia sempiterna
    la vista che riceve il vostro mondo
    com'occhio per lo mare entro s'interna,   60
che ben che da la proda veggia il fondo,
    in pelago nol vede; e nondimeno
    ègli, ma cela lui l'esser profondo.   63
Lume non è se non vien dal sereno
    che non si turba mai; anzi è tenebra
    o ombra de la carne, o suo veleno.   66
Assai t'è mo aperta la latebra
    che t'ascondeva la giustizia viva
    di che facei question cotanto crebra.   69
Chè tu dicevi: 'Un uom nasce a la riva
    de l'Indo, e quivi non è chi ragioni
    di Cristo, nè chi legga nè chi scriva;   72
e tutti i suoi voleri ed atti buoni
    sono, quanto ragione umana vede,
    sanza peccato in vita od in sermoni.   75
Muore non battezzato e sanza fede:
    ov'è questa giustizia che il condanna?
    ov'è la colpa sua, se ei non crede?'   78
Or tu chi se' che vuoi sedere a scranna,
    per giudicar di lungi mille miglia
    con la veduta corta d'una spanna?   81
Certo, a colui che meco s'assottiglia,
    se la Scrittura sovra voi non fosse
    da dubitar sarebbe a maraviglia.   84

In proof whereof, he who through pride first erred
   fell immature, through waiting not for light,
   though, once, above all creatures else preferred;
hence, clearly, lesser natures are but slight
   containers for that good which is alone
   with itself measured, being infinite.
Therefore our vision, which must needs be one
   or other of the rays shed by the mind
   which fills all things that know or may be known,
can never be so strong, of its own kind,
   but that, compared with its great origin,
   it still must seem in countless matters blind.
Therefore the sight your world receives, within
   the eternal justice penetrates no more
   than into the sea's depth the eye may win;
which, though it see the bottom near the shore,
   on the wide ocean looks for it in vain;
   yet it exists, but the depth veils it o'er.
Light is not, save from that serene domain
   which nought e'er clouds; rather 'tis darkness all,
   or shadow of the flesh, or else its bane.
Enough now have I drawn aside the pall
   that hid the living justice from thy sight,
   which thou so often wouldst in question call.
For thou wouldst say: "A man first sees the light
   beside the Indus, where is none who could
   discourse of Christ or read of him or write;
all his volitions and his acts are good,
   so far as human reason sees, nor fail,
   in life or speech, of perfect rectitude.
He dies unchristened and an infidel:
   where is this justice that condemns the man?
   where, if without faith, is he culpable?"
Now who art thou, to assume the bench and scan
   for judgment things a thousand miles away
   with sight restricted to a single span?
The man whose thoughts with me so subtly play,
   truly would wondrous cause for doubting find,
   if over you the Scripture held not sway.

Oh terreni animali, o menti grosse!
   La prima volontà, ch'è da sè buona,
   da sè, ch'è sommo ben, mai non si mosse: 87
cotanto è giusto quanto a lei consuona;
   nullo creato bene a sè la tira,
   ma essa, radiando, lui cagiona».   90
Quale sovresso il nido si rigira
   poi c'ha pasciuti la cicogna i figli,
   e come quel ch'è pasto la rimira,   93
cotal si fece (e sì levai li cigli)
   la benedetta imagine, che l'ali
   movea sospinte da tanti consigli.   96
Roteando cantava, e dicea: « Quali
   son le mie note a te, che non le intendi,
   tal è il giudizio eterno a voi mortali».   99
Poi si quetaron quei lucenti incendi
   de lo Spirito Santo, ancor nel segno
   che fe' i Romani al mondo reverendi,   102
esso ricominciò: « A questo regno
   non salì mai chi non credette in Cristo,
   vel pria vel poi ch'ei si chiavasse al legno.   105
Ma vedi: molti gridan *Cristo! Cristo!*
   che saranno in giudicio assai men prope
   a lui, che tal che non conosce Cristo;   108
e tai cristiani dannerà l'Etiope
   quando si partiranno i due collegi,
   l'uno in eterno ricco e l'altro inope.   111
Che potran dir li Persi ai vostri regi,
   come vedranno quel volume aperto
   nel qual si scrivon tutti suoi dispregi?   114
Lì si vedrà, tra l'opere d'Alberto,
   quella che tosto moverà la penna
   per che il regno di Praga fia diserto.   117
Lì si vedrà il duol che sovra Senna
   induce falseggiando la moneta
   quel che morrà di colpo di cotenna.   120
Lì si vedrà la superbia che asseta,
   che fa lo Scotto e l'Inghilese folle,
   sì che non può soffrir dentro a sua meta.   123

Oh animals of earth, oh dull of mind!
  Good of itself, the primal Will hath never
  from its own self, the highest good, declined.
What chimes with it alone is just: nor ever
  aught to created goodness doth it owe,
  but, by its rays, itself thereof is giver.'
As o'er her nest the stork will circling go,
  when she hath fed her brood, and as the one
  just fed looks up towards her from below,
thus moved the blessèd image, and thereon
  thus looked I, as above me it swept round,
  urged by so many wills in unison.
And, wheeling, thus it sang: 'E'en as beyond
  thy grasp my notes are, so for mortal ken
  the eternal judgment is too deep to sound.'
Those bright fires of the Holy Spirit then
  grew quiet, forming still the Sign, once held
  in awe by Rome's world-empire; then again
It began: Never to this realm prevail'd
  any to rise who believed not in Christ,
  vel ere *vel* after He'd on cross been nail'd.
But behold: many now exclaim "Christ! Christ ,
  who shall at judgment find themselves far more
  estranged from him than such as knows not Christ;
Christians like these shall the Ethiop triumph o'er,
  what time the two assemblies separate,
  the one forever rich, the other poor.
What may the Persians say to incriminate
  your kings, when with that open volume faced
  which registers their failings, small and great?
Read, there, shall be, mid deeds that have disgraced
  Albert, the one—now soon to stir the pen—
  through which the realm of Prague shall be laid waste.
Read, there, shall be the woe which on the Seine,
  through the false coinage far and wide dispers'd,
  he brings, who'll die of blow from a pig's skin.
Read, there, shall be the pride that quickens thirst,
  which makes the Scot and Englishman so mad,
  that each would through his proper frontier burst.

Vedrassi la lussuria e il viver molle
  di quel di Spagna e di quel di Boemme,
  che mai valor non conobbe nè volle.   126

Vedrassi al Ciotto di Gerusalemme
  segnata con un i la sua bontate
  quando il contrario segnerà un emme.   129

Vedrassi l'avarizia e la viltate
  di quei che guarda l'isola del foco
  ove Anchise finì la lunga etate.   132

E a dare ad intender quanto è poco,
  la sua scrittura fien lettere mozze
  che noteranno molto in parvo loco.   135

E parranno a ciascun l'opere sozze
  del barba e del fratel, che tanto egregia
  nazione e due corone han fatte bozze.   138

E quel di Portogallo e di Norvegia
  lì si conosceranno, e quel di Rascia
  che male ha visto il conio di Vinegia.   141

Oh beata Ungheria se non si lascia
  più malmenare! e beata Navarra
  se s'armasse del monte che la fascia!   144

E creder dee ciascun che già, per arra
  di questo, Nicosia e Famagosta
  per la lor bestia si lamenti e garra,   147
che dal fianco de l'altre non si scosta ».

CANTO 20

Quando colui che tutto il mondo alluma
  da l'emisperio nostro sì discende
  che il giorno d'ogni parte si consuma,   3
lo ciel, che sol di lui prima s'accende,
  subitamente si rifà parvente
  per molte luci, in che una risplende.   6

E quest'atto del ciel mi venne a mente
  come il segno del mondo e de' suoi duci
  nel benedetto rostro fu tacente;   9

On view shall be the sensual, silken-clad
   life of the Spaniard, the Bohemian's too,
   who valour never wished nor ever had.
On view an "I", to the one merit due
   of him, the Cripple of Jerusalem,
   while to his faults an "M" will give the clue.
On view the cowardice and the greed which shame
   him in whose wardship is the Isle of Fire,
   where to his long life's end Anchises came.
To set his paltry value yet in higher
   relief, the script shall have its letters maimed,
   which for much import little space require.
To all shall be, for their foul deeds, proclaimed
   his nuncle and his brother, who so fair
   a lineage and a double crown have shamed.
Two kings, both Portugal's and Norway's, there
   and with them likewise Rascia's shall be shown,
   for whom an ill sight coins of Venice were.
Oh happy Hungary, if she suffers none
   to ill-treat her further! happy too Navarre,
   made she a rampart of her mountain-zone!
Of this see earnest in the times that are,
   when Nicosía with Famagosta weeps
   and chides by reason of their beast, who, far
from parting with the rest, beside them keeps.'

CANTO 20

When he who floods the whole, wide world with light
   so far beneath our hemisphere is gone,
   that day on every side melts into night,
the sky, lit up before by him alone,
   suddenly yet again begins to shine
   with many lights, which but reflect the one:
and this sky-change I thought of, when the sign,
   by which the world and the world's lords are sway'd,
   at length was silent in the beak divine;

però che tutte quelle vive luci,
  vie più lucendo, cominciaron canti
  da mia memoria labili e caduci.   12
O dolce amor che di riso t'ammanti,
  quanto parevi ardente in quei flailli
  che aveano spirto sol di pensier santi!   15
Poscia che i cari e lucidi lapilli
  ond'io vidi ingemmato il sesto lume
  poser silenzio agli angelici squilli,   18
udir mi parve un mormorar di fiume
  che scenda chiaro giù di pietra in pietra
  mostrando l'ubertà del suo cacume.   21
E come suono al collo de la cetra
  prende sua forma, e sì come al pertugio
  de la sampogna vento che penetra,   24
così, rimosso d'aspettare indugio,
  quel mormorar de l'aquila salissi
  su per lo collo, come fosse bugio,   27
fecesi voce quivi e quindi uscissi
  per lo becco in forma di parole,
  quali aspettava il core, ov'io le scrissi.   30
« La parte in me che vede e pate il Sole
  ne l'aquile mortali » incominciommi,
  « or fisamente riguardar si vuole;   33
perchè dei fuochi ond'io figura fommi,
  quelli onde l'occhio in testa mi scintilla
  ei di tutti i lor gradi sono i sommi.   36
Colui che luce in mezzo per pupilla
  fu il cantor de lo Spirito Santo,
  che l'Arca traslatò di villa in villa: 39
ora conosce il merto del suo canto,
  in quanto effetto fu del suo consiglio,
  per lo remunerar, ch'è altrettanto.   42
Dei cinque che gli fan cerchio per ciglio,
  colui che più al becco mi s'accosta
  la vedovella consolò del figlio: 45
ora conosce quanto caro costa
  non seguir Cristo, per l'esperienza
  di questa dolce vita e de l'opposta.   48

for all those living lights began to shed
   far brighter radiance and made heaven resound
   with songs which from my memory fall and fade.
O sweet Love, that with smiles dost wrap thee round,
   how in those flutes whose holy musing owns
   their sole inspirer, did thy warmth abound!
After those precious and clear shining stones
   with which I saw enjewelled the sixth light,
   had stilled the chime of their angelic tones,
methought I heard a stream that, crystal bright,
   falls murmuring, down from rock to rock, and shows
   how rich the spring that pours it from the height.
And as the sound that from a zittern flows
   forms at the neck thereof, and as at vent
   of reedpipe does the wind that through it blows,
so, with no time in tedious waiting spent,
   that murmuring of the eagle, louder grown.
   up through the neck, as it were hollow, went.
There it became a voice and thence was thrown
   from out its beak in words, such in all ways
   as the heart looked for, where I wrote them down.
'The part in me which sees, and bears the rays
   o' the Sun in mortal eagles,' so it said,
   'must now be noted with a steadfast gaze;
for, of the fires that shape me, in their grade
   those are supreme, those I would have thee mark,
   wherewith the eye doth glitter in my head.
He who as pupil forms the central spark,
   the Holy Spirit's minstrel was on earth,
   who from one town to another bore the Ark:
now knows he, by the guerdon to its worth
   proportioned, the true merit of his song,
   so far as his own counsel gave it birth.
Next, of the five that form the curve along
   mine eyebrow, nearest to the beak is he
   who did the widow justice for her wrong:
now knows he what it costeth not to be
   a Christian, from his own experience
   of this sweet life and of its contrary.

E quel che segue, in la circonferenza
  di che ragiono, per l'arco superno,
  morte indugiò per vera penitenza: 51
ora conosce che il giudicio eterno
  non si trasmuta quando degno preco
  fa crastino là giù de l'odierno.   54
L'altro che segue, con le leggi e meco,
  sotto buona intenzion che fe' mal frutto,
  per cedere al pastor si fece greco: 57
ora conosce come il mal dedutto
  dal suo bene operar non gli è nocivo,
  avvegna che sia 'l mondo indi distrutto.   60
E quel che vedi ne l'arco declivo,
  Guglielmo fu, cui quella terra plora
  che piagne Carlo e Federigo vivo: 63
ora conosce come s'innamora
  lo ciel del giusto rege, ed al sembiante
  del suo fulgore il fa vedere ancora.   66
Chi crederebbe giù nel mondo errante
  che Rifeo Troiano in questo tondo
  fosse la quinta de le luci sante?   69
Ora conosce assai di quel che il mondo
  veder non può de la divina grazia,
  ben che sua vista non discerna il fondo».   72
Quale allodetta che in aere si spazia
  prima cantando, e poi tace, contenta
  de l'ultima dolcezza che la sazia,   75
tal mi sembiò l'imago de l'imprenta
  de l'eterno piacere, al cui disio
  ciascuna cosa quale ell'è diventa.   78
Ed avvegna ch'io fossi al dubbiar mio
  lì quasi vetro a lo color ch'el veste,
  tempo aspettar tacendo non patio,   81
ma de la bocca: «Che cose son queste?»
  mi pinse con la forza del suo peso:
  per ch'io di coruscar vidi gran feste.   84
Poi appresso, con l'occhio più acceso,
  lo benedetto segno mi rispose
  per non tenermi in ammirar sospeso: 87

And he who follows in the circumference
   I speak of, on the curve that upward sways,
   put death off by unfeignéd penitence:
now knows he that the eternal judgment stays
   unaltered, when on earth a worthy prayer
   doth make tomorrow's that which is today's.
Who follows next, with good intent which bare
   ill fruit, to leave the shepherd room, transferred
   me and the laws to Greece and settled there:
now knows he how the evil, first incurred
   through his well-doing, harms him not, although
   the world be now destroyed because he erred.
And he thou seëst on the downward bow,
   was William, whose decease that land bewails
   which Charles and Frederick, living, plunge in woe:
now knows he how a righteous king compels
   the love of heaven, and the consciousness
   thereof his glorious semblance yet forthtells.
Who in the erring world below would guess,
   that Trojan Rhipeus should be, in this round,
   the fifth among these lights of holiness?
Now knows he much of what the world hath found
   past understanding in the grace of God,
   e'en though his sight its bottom cannot sound.'
Like a small lark who in the air rangeth abroad,
   first singing, then, contented, holds his peace,
   cloyed with the sweetness of his last sweet ode,
so seemed the image satiate with its bliss,
   imprint of His, at whose desire whate'er
   exists becomes such as it truly is.
And though there to my doubt I was, as 'twere,
   glass to the colour that it clothes, to eschew
   speech and bide time was more than it could bear,
but from my lips, 'How can these things be true?'
   was forced out by sheer pressure of its weight;
   at which a riot of sparkling met my view.
Then straightway, with its eye enkindled yet
   more brightly, the blest emblem made reply,
   to keep my thoughts no longer in debate:

« Io veggio che tu credi queste cose
  perch'io le dico, ma non vedi come,
  sì che, se son credute, sono ascose.   90
Fai come quei che la cosa per nome
  apprende ben, ma la sua quiditate
  veder non può se altri non la prome.   93
Regnum coelorum violenza pate
  da caldo amore e da viva speranza
  che vince la divina volontate: 96
non a guisa che l'uomo a l'uom sobranza,
  ma vince lei perchè vuole esser vinta;
  e vinta, vince con sua beninanza.   99
La prima vita del ciglio e la quinta
  ti fa maravigliar, perchè ne vedi
  la region de gli angeli dipinta.   102
Da' corpi suoi non uscir, come credi,
  gentili, ma cristiani, in ferma fede
  quel dei passuri e quel dei passi piedi.   105
Chè l'una de l'Inferno, u' non si riede
  già mai a buon voler, tornò a l'ossa;
  e ciò di viva spene fu mercede: 108
di viva spene, che mise la possa
  nei prieghi fatti a Dio per suscitarla,
  sì che potesse sua voglia esser mossa.   111
L'anima gloriosa onde si parla,
  tornata ne la carne, in che fu poco,
  credette in lui che poteva aiutarla;   114
e credendo s'accese in tanto foco
  di vero amor, che a la morte seconda
  fu degna di venire a questo gioco.   117
L'altra per grazia che da sì profonda
  fontana stilla, che mai creatura
  non pinse l'occhio infino a la prima onda,   120
tutto su' amor là giù pose a drittura;
  per che, di grazia in grazia, Dio gli aperse
  l'occhio a la nostra redenzion futura;   123
ond'ei credette in quella, e non sofferse
  da indi il puzzo più del paganesmo,
  e riprendiene le genti perverse.   126

'I see that thou believ'st them, since 'tis I
    who say these things, but thou discern'st not how;
    so that they, if believed, still hidden lie.
Thou dost as one who something well doth know
    by name, but of its essence nought can see,
    unless another should that essence show.
Heaven's kingdom suffers violence willingly
    from ardent love and lively hope: by these
    alone the will divine may vanquished be;
not like to man's o'er man that victory is,
    but won because the vanquished wills defeat,
    and, vanquished, by its mercy vanquishes.
There are two lives it staggers thee to meet
    decking the angels' realm, to wit the first
    and fifth that in the eyebrow have their seat.
Not Gentiles did they quit the body, as erst
    thou deem'dst, but firm believers in our Lord,
    one after, one before, his feet were pierced.
For one from Hell, whence none was e'er restored
    to righteous willing, to his bones returned;
    and that of lively hope was the reward;
of lively hope, inspiring prayers that earned
    the power from God to raise him, and thus made
    him able to will that for which he yearned.
The glorious soul of whom these words are said,
    when re-incarnate a brief while on earth,
    believed in Him who had the power to aid;
and, in believing, to such fire gave birth
    of very love that, when it died again,
    worthy it was of joining in our mirth.
The other, moved by grace which from a vein
    so deep distils that never yet to sight
    of creature was its primal source made plain,
set all his love below on just and right;
    wherefore from grace to grace God oped his eye
    to see, before it dawned, redemption's light:
whence he believed therein, and the foul sty
    of paganism could no longer bear;
    and 'gainst the froward nations raised his cry.

667

Quelle tre donne li fur per battesmo
   che tu vedesti de la destra rota,
   dinanzi al battezzar più d'un millesmo.   129
O predestinazion, quanto remota
   è la radice tua da quegli aspetti
   che la prima cagion non veggion tota!   132
E voi mortali, tenetevi stretti
   a giudicar; chè noi che Dio vedemo
   non conoscemo ancor tutti gli eletti;   135
ed enne dolce così fatto scemo,
   perchè il ben nostro in questo ben s'affina
   che quel che vuole Dio, e noi volemo ».   138
Così da quella imagine divina,
   per farmi chiara la mia corta vista
   data mi fu soave medicina.   141
E come a buon cantor buon citarista
   fa seguitar lo guizzo de la corda,
   in che più di piacer lo canto acquista,   144
sì, mentre che parlò sì mi ricorda
   ch'io vidi le due luci benedette,
   pur come batter d'occhi si concorda,   147
con le parole mover le fiammette.

CANTO 21

Già eran gli occhi miei rifissi al volto
   de la mia donna, e l'animo con essi,
   e da ogni altro intento s'era tolto.   3
E quella non ridea, ma « S'io ridessi »
   mi cominciò, « tu ti faresti quale
   fu Semelè quando di cener fessi;   6
chè la bellezza mia, che per le scale
   de l'eterno palazzo più s'accende,
   com'hai veduto, quanto più si sale,   9
se non si temperasse, tanto splende
   che il tuo mortal potere al suo fulgore
   sarebbe fronda che tuono scoscende.   12

For baptism, a good millennium ere
   men knew baptising, those three ladies, seen
   of thee at the right wheel, his proxies were.
Predestination, oh what worlds between
   thy root and those extend who cannot see
   the primal cause, entire, with mortal een!
Judge, then, you mortals, with restraint; for we,
   to whom the sight of God is granted, still
   know not how many the elect will be:
and us this very lack with joy doth fill,
   because we find our crowning good herein,
   that what is willed by God we also will.'
Thus, by that form divine, sweet medicine
   was giv'n me, from mine eyes to clear the mist,
   that so they might to purer vision win.
And e'en as to good voice good lutanist
   by perfect timing makes the chord vibrate,
   whereby the song's enjoyment is increas'd,
so, while it spoke, do I remember yet
   that, even as one's eyes blink in accord,
   I saw the two enraptured stars equate
their twinkles to its utterance, flame to word.

CANTO 21

Now on my lady's face again intent
   mine eyes were, and, like them my thoughts, concerned
   with nothing else, on her alone were bent.
And yet no smile upon her visage burned;
   but 'Did I smile' she said 'thou wouldst be e'en
   as Semele when she to ashes turned;
because my beauty, which, as thou hast seen,
   on this eternal palace-stair, the higher
   one climbs, hath ever more enkindled been,
if not subdued, would prove itself as dire
   (such its effulgence) to thy mortal might,
   as to a bough the thunderbolt's quick fire.

Noi sem levati al settimo splendore,
  che sotto il petto del Leone ardente
  raggia mo misto giù del suo valore.   15
Ficca di retro a gli occhi tuoi la mente,
  e fa di quelli specchio a la figura
  che in questo specchio ti sarà parvente».   18
Chi sapesse qual era la pastura
  del viso mio ne l'aspetto beato
  quand'io mi trasmutai ad altra cura,   21
conoscerebbe quanto m'era a grato
  ubbidire a la mia celeste scorta,
  contrappesando l'un con l'altro lato.   24
Dentro al cristallo che il vocabol porta,
  cerchiando il mondo, del suo caro duce
  sotto cui giacque ogni malizia morta,   27
di color d'oro in cui raggio traluce
  vid'io uno scaleo eretto in suso
  tanto, che nol seguiva la mia luce.   30
Vidi anche per li gradi scender giuso
  tanti splendor, ch'io pensai che ogni lume
  che par nel ciel quindi fosse diffuso.   33
E come, per lo natural costume,
  le pole insieme al cominciar del giorno
  si movono a scaldar le fredde piume;   36
poi altre vanno via sanza ritorno,
  altre rivolgon sè onde son mosse,
  e altre roteando fan soggiorno;   39
tal modo parve a me che quivi fosse
  in quello sfavillar che insieme venne,
  sì come in certo grado si percosse;   42
e quel che presso più ci si ritenne
  si fe' sì chiaro, ch'io dicea pensando:
  «Io veggio ben l'amor che tu m'accenne».   45
Ma quella ond'io aspetto il come e il quando
  del dire e del tacer, si sta; ond'io,
  contra il disio, fo ben ch'io non dimando.   48
Per ch'ella, che vedeva il tacer mio
  nel veder di colui che tutto vede,
  mi disse: «Solvi il tuo caldo disio».   51

We are exalted to the seventh light,
   which now beneath the burning Lion's breast,
   mixed with his power, sheds down its radiance bright.
Behind thine eyes now let thy mind be placed,
   and be in turn the image mirrored there
   which in this mirror thou shalt see expressed.'
He that should know with what delicious fare
   her blesséd look my vision satisfied
   when I transferred me to another care,
would recognize, by weighing the one side
   against the other, how it charmed me still
   to do the bidding of my heavenly guide.
Within the crystal, named, as it doth wheel
   about the world, of him—the world's dear king,
   'neath whom no power could live that worketh ill,
coloured like gold, translucent, glittering,
   I saw a stairway reaching up so high,
   that to my sight it was past following.
I saw, moreover, coming down thereby,
   of splendours, such a multitude untold,
   meseemed it shone with every star in the sky.
And as the jackdaws, gathering by an old
   instinctive custom at the break of day
   flutter about to warm their feathers cold;
then some, without returning, fly away,
   some to their starting-point again repair,
   and others wheeling round and round it stay;
so meseemed did that sparkling I saw there
   arrive in company, then discombine
   when it had struck upon a certain stair.
One, nearest to us, then began to shine
   so brightly, that I said in thought: ' 'Tis plain
   thou lovest me, for well I see the sign.'
But she from whom I await the 'how' and 'when'
   of silence or of speech, is mute; whence I
   do well to ask not, though of asking fain.
She, therefore, when I spoke not, seeing why
   in the clear seeing of Him who all things sees,
   said: 'Loose thy warm desire': encouraged whereby

Ed io incominciai: « La mia mercede
   non mi fa degno de la tua risposta;
   ma per colei che il chieder mi concede,   54
vita beata che ti stai nascosta
   dentro a la tua letizia, fammi nota
   la cagion che sì presso mi t'ha posta;   57
e di' perchè si tace in questa rota
   la dolce sinfonia di Paradiso
   che giù per l'altre suona sì devota ».   60
« Tu hai l'udir mortal sì come il viso »
   rispose a me; « onde qui non si canta
   per quel che Beatrice non ha riso.   63
Giù per li gradi de la scala santa
   discesi tanto sol per farti festa
   col dire e con la luce che m'ammanta;   66
nè più amor mi fece esser più presta,
   chè più e tanto amor quinci sù ferve,
   sì come il fiammeggiar ti manifesta;   69
ma l'alta carità che ci fa serve
   pronte al consiglio che il mondo governa,
   sorteggia qui sì come tu osserve ».   72
« Io veggio ben » diss'io, « sacra lucerna,
   come libero amore in questa corte
   basta a seguir la provedenza eterna;   75
ma questo è quel che a cerner mi par forte:
   perchè predestinata fosti sola
   a questo officio tra le tue consorte ».   78
Nè venni prima a l'ultima parola,
   che del suo mezzo fece il lume centro,
   girando sè come veloce mola.   81
Poi rispose l'amor che v'era dentro:
   « Luce divina sopra me s'appunta,
   penetrando per questa in ch'io m'inventro,   84
la cui virtù, col mio veder congiunta,
   mi leva sopra me tanto, ch'io veggio
   la somma essenza de la quale è munta.   87
Quinci vien l'allegrezza ond'io fiammeggio,
   perchè a la vista mia, quant'ella è chiara,
   la chiarità de la fiamma pareggio.   90

I thus began: 'Not mine the merit is,
  which makes me worthy of thine answer; yet,
  if her who allows my question thou wouldst please,
blest life that art concealed within the great
  effulgence of thy joy, do thou make known
  the cause which thee so near to me hath set;
and say why silent in this wheel alone
  is the sweet symphony of Paradise,
  chanted with such devotion lower down.'
'Thine ears,' it answered me, 'are, like thine eyes,
  mortal; hence here we sing not for the same
  reason that Beatrice her smile denies.
Down by the steps of the holy stair I came
  thus far, only to greet thee with discourse
  and with the light that wraps me in its flame;
neither in me was greater love the source
  of greater zeal; for love up there doth burn
  (witness the flames) with like and greater force.
But the high charity, which makes us yearn
  to serve the all-ruling will with instant speed,
  casts the lot here, e'en as thou dost discern.'
'O sacred lamp' said I, ''tis clear indeed
  how love, unbidden, in this court will do
  what'er the eternal foresight hath decreed;
but to this harder knot I find no clue—
  wherefore predestined thou alone shouldst be,
  of all thy peers, this office to pursue.'
Nor had I ended, ere, as one may see
  a millstone doing, that which there illumed
  us whirled upon its centre rapidly.
Anon, the love within it thus resumed:
  'Focused on me eternal light doth blaze,
  piercing through this wherein I am enwombed,
whose virtue, with my vision conjoined, doth raise
  me above myself so far, that the divine
  essence which it is milked from meets my gaze.
Hence comes this flaming gladness that is mine;
  for, as my sight is clear, thereto I even
  the clearness of the flame with which I shine.

Ma quell'alma nel ciel che più si schiara,
  quel Serafin che in Dio più l'occhio ha fisso
  a la domanda tua non satisfara;   93
però che sì s'inoltra ne l'abisso
  de l'eterno statuto quel che chiedi,
  che da ogni creata vista è scisso.   96
Ed al mondo mortal, quando tu riedi,
  questo rapporta, sì che non presumma
  a tanto segno più mover li piedi.   99
La mente, che qui luce, in Terra fumma;
  onde riguarda come può là giue
  quel che non puote perchè il Ciel l'assumma ».   102
Sì mi prescrisser le parole sue
  ch'io lasciai la questione, e mi ritrassi
  a dimandarla umilmente chi fue.   105
« Tra' due liti d'Italia surgon sassi,
  e non molto distanti a la tua patria
  tanto, che i tuoni assai suonan più bassi;   108
e fanno un gibbo che si chiama Catria,
  di sotto al quale è consecrato un ermo
  che suol esser disposto a sola làtria ».   111
Così ricominciommi il terzo sermo;
  e poi continuando disse: « Quivi
  al servigio di Dio mi fei sì fermo   114
che pur con cibi di liquor d'ulivi
  lievemente passava caldi e geli,
  contento nei pensier contemplativi.   117
Render solea quel chiostro a questi cieli
  fertilemente, ed ora è fatto vano,
  sì che tosto convien che si riveli.   120
In quel loco fu' io Pietro Damiano,
  e Pietro Peccator fui ne la casa
  di Nostra Donna in sul lito adriano.   123
Poca vita mortal m'era rimasa,
  quando fui chiesto e tratto a quel cappello
  che pur di male in peggio si travasa.   126
Venne Cefas e venne il gran vasello
  de lo Spirito Santo, magri e scalzi,
  prendendo il cibo di qualunque ostello;   129

But by that most enlightened soul in heaven,
   that Seraph who on God most pins his glance,
   to thy demand no answer could be given;
seeing that in the eternal ordinance
   so deeply plunged doth that thou askest lie,
   'tis hid from all created cognisance.
When thou returnest, carry this reply
   back to your world, that none henceforth may dare
   to move his feet unto a goal so high.
The mind, here bright, is dimmed by smoke down there;
   how may it, then, on Earth do things that pass
   its power to do e'en tho' to Heaven it fare?'
From further question I refrained, whenas
   it spake these words—they overawed me so—
   and did but ask it humbly who it was.
' 'Twixt Italy's two shores a rocky brow,
   not much removed from thine own land, doth rise
   so high, the thunders mutter far below,
and forms a hump, called Catria: 'neath it lies
   a hermitage, which sacred was of yore
   to prayer alone and holy ministries.'
A third time thus it spoke, then added more
   after this fashion: 'There, in service done
   to God, I such a steadfast spirit bore,
that I with viands, olive-oiled, else none,
   easily passed through seasons hot and cold,
   content in thoughts contemplative alone.
Rich harvest did that cloister yield of old
   unto these heavens; a harvest grown so spare
   now, that its barrenness must soon be told.
I was entitled Peter Damian there,
   and in Our Lady's house by the Adrian sea
   Peter the Sinner was the name I bare.
When I was nearing death, they summoned me,
   nay, dragged me to the hat, that is from sin
   to greater sin passed on successively.
Came Cephas, came the mighty vessel wherein
   the Holy Spirit dwelt, lean and unshod,
   taking their food from whatsoever inn.

or voglion quinci e quindi chi i rincalzi
   li moderni pastori, e chi li meni,
   tanto son gravi, e chi diretro li alzi;   132
copron dei manti lor li palafreni,
   sì che due bestie van sotto una pelle:
   oh pazienza che tanto sostieni! »   135
A questa voce vid'io più fiammelle
   di grado in grado scendere e girarsi,
   ed ogni giro le facea più belle.   138
Dintorno a questa vennero a fermarsi,
   e fero un grido di sì alto suono,
   che non potrebbe qui assomigliarsi;   141
nè io lo intesi, sì mi vinse il tuono.

CANTO 22

Oppresso di stupore, a la mia guida
   mi volsi, come pargol che ricorre
   sempre colà dove più si confida;   3
e quella, come madre che soccorre
   subito al figlio pallido ed anelo
   con la sua voce che il suol ben disporre,   6
mi disse: « Non sai tu che tu se' in cielo?
   e non sai tu che il cielo è tutto santo,
   e ciò che ci si fa vien da buon zelo?   9
come t'avrebbe trasmutato il canto
   e io ridendo, mo pensar lo puoi,
   poscia che il grido t'ha mosso cotanto;   12
nel qual, se inteso avessi i prieghi suoi,
   già ti sarebbe nota la vendetta
   che tu vedrai innanzi che tu muoi.   15
La spada di qua sù non taglia in fretta
   nè tardo, ma' che al parer di colui
   che disiando o temendo l'aspetta.   18
Ma rivolgiti omai inverso altrui,
   chè assai illustri spiriti vedrai
   se com'io dico l'aspetto redui ».   21

Now on both sides our bloated men of God
   need one to prop them, one to lift their train,
   one to precede them with a verger's rod.
Their mantles drape their palfreys, so that then
   two beasts pace onwards 'neath a single hide:
   O patience, what a load dost thou sustain!'
And at these words more flamelets I espied
   from step to step descending and whirling round,
   and every whirl their beauty intensified.
Round this they thronged, and stayed them, and with sound
   so loud, so awful shouted, that no wonder
   if here no likeness for it may be found:
nor grasped I aught; so vanquished me the thunder.

CANTO 22

Unto my guide, in blank amazement lost
   I turned me, like a child who always there
   for refuge runneth where it trusteth most;
and she, like mother who is quick to bear
   her pale and gasping son the succour given
   by her familiar voice, which soothes his fear,
said to me: 'Know'st not thou that thou'rt in heaven?
   and heaven all holy is, nor does one aught
   here, save thereto by righteous ardour driven?
How great a change in thee the song had wrought,
   and I by smiling, now right well appears,
   since thou art moved so deeply by the shout;
wherein, couldst thou have understood its prayers,
   to thee already were the vengeance known
   which thou shalt witness in thy mortal years.
The sword of heaven, save in their view alone
   who wish or fear its advent, is not slack,
   nor yet in haste, to strike the wicked down.
But turn round now to the others; for no lack
   of many illustrious spirits wilt thou see,
   if as I say thou cast thy glances back.'

Come a lei piacque gli occhi ritornai,
  e vidi cento sperule che insieme
  più s'abbellivan con mutui rai. 24

Io stava come quei che in sè ripreme
  la punta del disio, e non s'attenta
  di domandar, sì del troppo si teme; 27

e la maggiore e la più luculenta
  di quelle margherite innanzi fessi,
  per far di sè la mia voglia contenta. 30

Poi dentro a lei udii: « Se tu vedessi
  com'io la carità che tra noi arde,
  li tuoi concetti sarebbero espressi. 33

Ma perchè tu aspettando non tarde
  a l'alto fine, io ti farò risposta
  pur al pensier, da che sì ti riguarde. 36

Quel monte a cui Cassino è ne la costa
  fu frequentato già in su la cima
  da la gente ingannata e mal disposta; 39

e quel son io che sù vi portai prima
  lo nome di colui che in Terra addusse
  la verità che tanto ci sublima; 42

e tanta grazia sovra me rilusse,
  ch'io ritrassi le ville circostanti
  da l'empio culto che il mondo sedusse. 45

Questi altri fuochi tutti contemplanti
  uomini foro, accesi di quel caldo
  che fa nascere i fiori e i frutti santi. 48

Qui è Macario, qui è Romualdo,
  qui son li frati miei che dentro ai chiostri
  fermar li piedi e tennero il cor saldo ». 51

E io a lui: « L'affetto che dimostri
  meco parlando, e la buona sembianza
  ch'io veggio e noto in tutti gli ardor vostri, 54

così m'ha dilatato mia fidanza
  come il Sol fa la rosa, quando, aperta,
  tanto divien quanto ell'ha di possanza; 57

però ti priego, e tu, padre, m'accerta
  s'io posso prender tanta grazia, ch'io
  ti veggia con imagine scoperta ». 60

I turned my eyes, as she directed me,
  and saw a hundred little globes, their fire
  made lovelier through their mutual brilliancy.
I stood as one who on his keen desire,
  lest it exceed due limit, such restraint
  imposes, that he dares not to enquire.
And of those pearls the one pre-eminent
  in size and lustre drew from out the rest,
  to render of itself my wish content.
Then heard I from within it: 'Wert thou blest
  with sight, as I am, of the charity
  we burn with, thy conceits had been express'd.
But that thou wait not and retard thereby
  thy lofty aim, to what thy doubts disguise,
  e'en to thy secret thought, I'll make reply.
The mountain on whose slope Cassino lies,
  was, on its top, much visited of yore
  by ill-disposed, deluded votaries;
and it was I that first up thither bore
  the name of Him who down to Earth convey'd
  the truth which so sublimes us by its power;
and such abundant grace on me was shed,
  that I reclaimed the hamlets scattered round
  from the impious worship that the world misled.
These other fires their happiness all found
  in contemplation, kindled by the heat
  which maketh holy flowers and fruits abound.
Here Romualdus, here Macarius meet
  my brethren, those who in their cells below
  with persevering courage fixed their feet.'
And I to him: 'The affection thou dost show
  in speaking with me, and the kindly mien
  I see and note in all your ardours glow,
swelling my confidence, have made it e'en
  as the Sun makes the rose, when he doth swell
  her calyx till its inmost heart is seen.
Hence I entreat thee, and thou, father, tell
  me truly, if on me such grace can shine,
  that I may see thy shape without a veil.'

Ond'elli: « Frate, il tuo alto disio
   s'adempierà in su l'ultima spera,
   ove s'adempion tutti gli altri e il mio.   63
Ivi è perfetta, matura ed intera
   ciascuna disianza, in quella sola
   è ogni parte là ove sempr'era,   66
perchè non è in loco e non s'impola;
   e nostra scala infino ad essa varca,
   onde così dal viso ti s'invola.   69
Infin là sù la vide il patriarca
   Iacobbe porger la superna parte,
   quando gli apparve d'angeli sì carca.   72
Ma per salirla mo nessun diparte
   da terra i piedi, e la regola mia
   rimasa è per danno de le carte.   75
Le mura che solean esser badia
   fatte sono spelonche, e le cocolle
   sacca son piene di farina ria.   78
Ma grave usura tanto non si tolle
   contra il piacer di Dio quanto quel frutto
   che fa il cor dei monaci sì folle;   81
chè quantunque la Chiesa guarda, tutto
   è de la gente che per Dio dimanda,
   non di parenti, nè d'altro più brutto.   84
La carne dei mortali è tanto blanda,
   che giù non basta buon cominciamento
   dal nascer de la quercia al far la ghianda.   87
Pier cominciò sanz'oro e sanz'argento,
   e io con orazione e con digiuno,
   e Francesco umilmente il suo convento.   90
E se guardi il principio di ciascuno,
   poscia riguardi là dov'è trascorso,
   tu vederai del bianco fatto bruno.   93
Veramente Iordan volto retrorso
   più fu, e il mar fuggir, quando Dio volse,
   mirabile a veder, che qui il soccorso ».   96
Così mi disse, e indi si raccolse
   al suo collegio, e il collegio si strinse,
   poi, come turbo, in sù tutto s'avvolse.   99

He therefore: 'Like all others and like mine,
  thy lofty wish shall be fulfilled whenas
  thou attainest, brother, to the sphere divine.

There only all we long for comes to pass:
  there only all is perfect, ripe and whole,
  and every part is where it always was,

for it lies not in space, nor has it pole;
  and this our stairway up to it doth go,
  whence thus thine eyes it cheateth of their goal.

Thither the patriarch Jacob saw it throw
  its upper span, when it appeared to him
  laden with angels passing to and fro.

But now, for climbing it, doth no one dream
  of lifting foot from earth; and, unobeyed,
  my rule does but a waste of paper seem.

The walls that were for monastery made,
  are turned now into dens; the cowls are sacks
  crammed full of meal, and all of it gone bad.

But the usurer's greed, however gross it wax,
  doth not so much for God's displeasure call
  as that which makes the monkish heart so lax;

for what the Church in keeping hath, should all
  to those who in the name of God make suit,
  not to one's kin, or viler claimants, fall.

The flesh of man is grown so dissolute,
  that good beginnings with their goodness part,
  ere comes to bearing acorns the oak-shoot.

With gold and silver none did Peter start
  his convent; I, with prayers and fasting, mine;
  and Francis his, in humbleness of heart.

And if of each thou mark the first design,
  then mark again to where it thence hath stray'd,
  thou wilt behold that dim, which used to shine.

And yet the sea, when God so willed it, fled,
  and Jordan was turned backward—both, to view,
  more wondrous, than if here his hand should aid.'

Thus spake he to me, and anon withdrew
  to his college; and the college, flame to flame,
  closed up; then all, like whirlwind, upward flew.

La dolce donna dietro a lor mi pinse
sol con un cenno sù per quella scala,
sì sua virtù la mia natura vinse;   102
nè mai qua giù, dove si monta e cala
naturalmente, fu sì ratto moto
che agguagliar si potesse a la mi' ala.   105
S'io torni mai, lettore, a quel devoto
triunfo per lo quale io piango spesso
le mie peccata e il petto mi percuoto,   108
tu non avresti in tanto tratto e messo
nel foco il dito, in quanto io vidi il segno
che segue il Tauro e fui dentro da esso.   111
O gloriose stelle, o lume pregno
di gran virtù, dal quale io riconosco
tutto, qual che si sia, il mio ingegno,   114
con voi nasceva e s'ascondeva vosco
quelli ch'è padre d'ogni mortal vita,
quand'io sentii da prima l'aer tosco;   117
e poi, quando mi fu grazia largita
d'entrar ne l'alta rota che vi gira
la vostra region mi fu sortita.   120
A voi divotamente ora sospira
l'anima mia per acquistar virtute
al passo forte che a sè la tira.   123
« Tu sei sì presso a l'ultima salute »
cominciò Beatrice, « che tu dèi
aver le luci tue chiare ed acute.   126
E però, prima che tu più t'inlei,
rimira in giù, e vedi quanto mondo
sotto li piedi già esser ti fei;   129
sì che il tuo cor quantunque può giocondo
s'appresenti a la turba trionfante
che lieta vien per quest'ètera tondo ».   132
Col viso ritornai per tutte quante
le sette spere, e vidi questo globo
tal ch'io sorrisi del suo vil sembiante;   135
e quel consiglio per migliore approbo
che l'ha per meno, e chi ad altro pensa
chiamar si puote veramente probo.   138

And, with a single gesture, my sweet dame
  behind them up that stairway thrust me on,
  so much her power my nature overcame;
nor here below, where men go up and down
  by natural means, was e'er such rapid flight,
  as with my wing could bear comparison.
So, Reader, may I once again have sight
  of that devout triumph, for whose sake my sin
  ofttimes do I bewail and bosom smite,
thou hadst not dipped thy finger out and in
  the fire so quickly, as I saw the sign
  which follows Taurus and was therewithin.
O glorious stars, O radiancy divine
  pregnant with mighty power, to which is due
  all of whatever genius may be mine,
the father of every mortal life with you
  was born, with you was setting, at the time
  when first on me the Tuscan breezes blew;
and, after, when within the wheel sublime
  that whirls you grace was granted me thuswise
  to enter, yours was my allotted clime.
Yea, and for strength to meet the hard emprise
  that draws her to itself, my soul no less
  to you now, even now, devoutly sighs.
'Thou art so near the final blessedness'
  Beatrice began, 'that it is requisite
  thine eyes the utmost clearness should possess.
So, ere thou wend yet farther into it,
  look down once more, and the vast world survey,
  by me already placed beneath thy feet;
thus shall thy heart, with all the joy it may,
  greet the triumphant throng which, full of cheer,
  through this round aether now is on its way.'
In vision I re-travelled, sphere by sphere,
  the seven heavens, and saw this globe of ours
  such, that I smiled, so mean did it appear;
and highest I esteem his mental powers
  who rates it least; and him, whose thoughts elsewhere
  are fixed, good sense with truest wisdom dowers.

Vidi la figlia di Latona incensa
    sanza quell'ombra che mi fu cagione
    per che già la credetti rara e densa.   141
L'aspetto del tuo nato, Iperione,
    quivi sostenni, e vidi com' si muove
    circa e vicino a lui, Maia e Dione.   144
Quindi m'apparve il temperar di Giove
    tra il padre e 'l figlio; e quindi mi fu chiaro
    il variar che fanno di lor dove.   147
E tutti e sette mi si dimostraro
    quanto son grandi e quanto son veloci,
    e come sono in distante riparo.   150
L'aiuola che ci fa tanto feroci
    volgendom'io con gli eterni Gemelli
    tutta m'apparve dai colli a le foci.   153
Poscia rivolsi gli occhi a gli occhi belli.

CANTO 23

Come l'augello, intra l'amate fronde
    posato al nido de' suoi dolci nati
    la notte che le cose ci nasconde,   3
che per veder gli aspetti disiati
    e per trovar lo cibo onde li pasca,
    in che gravi labor gli sono aggrati,   6
previene il tempo in su l'aperta frasca,
    e con ardente affetto il Sole aspetta,
    fiso guardando pur che l'alba nasca,   9
così la donna mia si stava eretta
    ed attenta, rivolta in ver la plaga
    sotto la quale il Sol mostra men fretta;   12
sì che, veggendol' io sospesa e vaga,
    fecemi qual è quei che disiando
    altro vorria, e sperando s'appaga.   15
Ma poco fu tra l'uno e l'altro quando,
    del mio attender, dico, e del vedere
    lo ciel venir più e più rischiarando.   18

I saw Latona's daughter shining bare
  of all the shadow which some while agone
  had caused me to suppose her dense and rare.
Thine offspring's countenance, Hyperion,
  there I endured and saw how, circling, move
  near him thy child, Dione, and, Maia, thy son.
From here I saw the tempering of Jove
  between his sire and son, from here could trace
  their true positions and each change thereof.
Likewise did all the seven, how swift their pace,
  how vast their size, unto my vision show,
  and each from each how far removed in space.
As for the threshing-floor that mads us so,
  I, rolling with the timeless Twins, discerned
  it all, from the hills to where its streams outflow.
Then to the beauteous eyes mine eyes returned.

CANTO 23

Like to the bird, among the leaves she loves
  stilled on the nest of her sweet progeny
  by night, which all things from our vision removes,
who, to behold their wishèd looks and fly
  in search of food as wherewithal to stay
  their hunger (hard, though grateful, task to ply),
foreruns the time upon the open spray
  and waits there for the Sun with fervent zest,
  fixedly watching for the birth of day,
so stood my lady erect, her gaze address'd
  intently tow'rds the tract beneath which hies
  the Sun, when on his course he shows less haste;
so that I, seeing her rapt in fond surmise,
  became like one who, in desire, would fain
  have what he has not, and on hope relies.
Yet was the time but short 'twixt either 'when',
  I mean, 'twixt my expecting and seeing o'erhead
  the heaven still more and more in brightness gain.

E Beatrice disse: « Ecco le schiere
   del triunfo di Cristo, e tutto il frutto
   ricolto del girar di queste spere ».   21
Pareami che il suo viso ardesse tutto,
   e gli occhi avea di letizia sì pieni,
   che passar mi convien sanza costrutto.   24
Quale nei plenilunii sereni
   Trivia ride tra le ninfe eterne
   che dipingon lo ciel per tutti i seni,   27
vidi sopra migliaia di lucerne
   un Sol che tutte quante le accendea,
   come fa il nostro le viste superne;   30
e per la viva luce trasparea
   la lucente sustanza tanto chiara
   nel viso mio, che non la sostenea.   33
Oh Beatrice dolce guida e cara!
   Ella mi disse: « Quel che ti sobranza
   è virtù da cui nulla si ripara.   36
Quivi è la sapienza e la possanza
   che aprì le strade tra il Cielo e la Terra,
   onde fu già sì lunga disianza ».   39
Come foco di nube si disserra
   per dilatarsi, sì che non vi cape
   e fuor di sua natura in giù s'atterra,   42
la mente mia così, tra quelle dape
   fatta più grande, di se stessa uscìo,
   e che si fesse rimembrar non sape.   45
« Apri gli occhi e riguarda qual son io:
   tu hai vedute cose, che possente
   sei fatto a sostener lo riso mio ».   48
Io era come quei che si risente
   di visione oblìta, e che s'ingegna
   indarno di ridurlasi a la mente,   51
quand'io udii questa profferta, degna
   di tanto grado, che mai non s'estingue
   dal libro che il preterito rassegna.   54
Se mo sonasser tutte quelle lingue
   che Polinnìa con le suore fero
   del latte lor dolcissimo più pingue,   57

And Beatrice cried: 'Behold the legions led
  by the triumphant Christ, and all the fruit
  by these revolving spheres safe harvested!'
Her visage blazed, and joy so absolute
  beamed in her eyes, that to depict such heights
  of bliss words fail me, and I must stay mute.
As in serene and fullmooned summer nights
  Trivia smiles 'mongst her eternal train
  of nymphs who paint the heaven through all its bights,
outshining myriad lamps beheld I then
  one Sun who kindled each and all, as ours
  kindles the stars that throng his high domain;
and through the rays, poured down in living showers,
  the radiant substance, blazing on me, tried
  my mortal vision far beyond its powers.
Oh Beatrice, beloved and loving guide!
  She said: 'That power by which thine own is quell'd,
  is such as nought created may abide.
Here is the might and wisdom which avail'd,
  'twixt Heaven and Earth to open every road
  so long from yearning human hearts withheld.'
As lightning from a cloud must needs explode
  through room too strait to hold the swelling flame,
  which falls to earth against its natural mode,
even so then did my spirit burst its frame,
  grown greater at those banquets through excess
  of sweets, and it forgets what it became.
'Open thine eyes to my true loveliness:
  thou hast seen things, from which thou shalt derive
  the strength to bear the smile upon my face.'
I was like one who, eager to revive
  some long-forgotten dream, with all his wit
  strives to recall it, yet doth vainly strive,
when I this invitation heard, so meet
  for largest thanks, that it shall aye be found
  traced in the volume where my past is writ.
Should now to aid me all the tongues resound
  which Polyhymnia and her sisterhood
  have with their sweetest milk made most abound,

per aiutarmi al millesmo del vero
   non si verrìa cantando il santo riso
   e quanto il santo aspetto facea mero.   60
E così, figurando il Paradiso,
   convien saltar lo sacrato poema
   come chi trova suo cammin reciso.   63
Ma chi pensasse il ponderoso tema
   e l'omero mortal che se ne carca,
   nol biasmerebbe se sott'esso trema: 66
non è pileggio di picciola barca
   quel che fendendo va l'ardita prora
   nè da nocchier che a se medesmo parca.   69
« Perchè la faccia mia sì t'innamora
   che tu non ti rivolgi al bel giardino
   che sotto i raggi di Cristo s'infiora?   72
Quivi è la rosa in che il verbo divino
   carne si fece; quivi son li gigli
   al cui odor si prese il buon cammino ».   75
Così Beatrice; ed io che a' suoi consigli
   tutto era pronto, ancora mi rendei
   a la battaglia dei debili cigli.   78
Come a raggio di Sol che puro mei
   per fratta nube, già prato di fiori
   vider, coperti d'ombra, gli occhi miei,   81
vid'io così più turbe di splendori
   fulgurate di sù da raggi ardenti,
   sanza veder principio di fulgori.   84
O benigna virtù che sì li imprenti!
   sù t'esaltasti per largirmi loco
   a gli occhi lì che non eran possenti.   87
Il nome del bel fior ch'io sempre invoco
   e mane e sera, tutto mi ristrinse
   l'animo ad avvisar lo maggior foco.   90
E come ambo le luci mi dipinse
   il quale e il quanto de la viva stella
   che là sù vince come qua giù vinse,   93
per entro il cielo scese una facella
   formata in cerchio a guisa di corona,
   e cinsela, e girossi intorno ad ella.   96

when chanting of her holy smile they would
  not even a thousandth of its charm portray,
  nor how therewith her holy visage glow'd.

So too the sacred poem, which would essay
  to picture Paradise, must jump, like him
  who finds an interruption to his way.

But none who ponders on the weighty theme,
  which a mere man sustains, will take amiss
  his staggering under burden so extreme.

No sea-way for a bauble-boat is this
  cut by my daring prow, but one to prove
  the steersman's mettle in extremities.

'Why with my face art thou so much in love,
  that thou turn'st not to the fair garden where
  it blossoms beneath Christ who shines above?

The rose which bore the incarnate Word is there:
  there are the lilies whose sweet odour gave
  men strength along the narrow way to fare.'

Thus Beatrice; and I, the willing slave
  of her injunctions, set myself anew
  to make my frail lids for the contest brave.

As in a Sun-ray, slanting undimmed through
  a broken cloud, erewhile a flowery field,
  myself in shadow, I have chanced to view,

saw I more throngs of splendours thus reveal'd,
  irradiated by a downward flow
  of intense brilliance from a source conceal'd.

O kindly power whose signet stamps them so!
  thou rosest higher expressly to afford
  mine eyes more scope, else dazzled by thy glow.

The name of that fair flower, by me implor'd
  morning and evening, made me concentrate
  upon the fire whence the most radiance pour'd.

And as on both mine eyes 'twas limned how great
  and glorious is the living star who there
  shines, as she shone on earth, supreme in state,

there fell through heaven a torch, which as it were
  a crown—for, whirling, such the shape it bore—
  straightway encircled and revolved round her.

Qualunque melodia più dolce sona
   qua giù e più a sè l'anima tira,
   parrebbe nube che squarciata tuona   99
comparata al sonar di quella lira
   onde si coronava il bel zaffiro
   del quale il ciel più chiaro s'inzaffira.   102
« Io sono amore angelico che giro
   l'alta letizia che spira del ventre
   che fu albergo del nostro disiro;   105
e girerommi, Donna del Ciel, mentre
   che seguirai tuo figlio, e farai dia
   più la spera suprema perchè gli entre ».   108
Così la circulata melodia
   si sigillava, e tutti gli altri lumi
   facean sonare il nome di Maria.   111
Lo real manto di tutti i volumi
   del mondo, che più ferve e più s'avviva
   ne l'alito di Dio e nei costumi,   114
avea sopra di noi l'interna riva
   tanto distante, che la sua parvenza
   là dov'io era ancor non appariva;   117
però non ebber gli occhi miei potenza
   di seguitar la coronata fiamma
   che si levò appresso sua semenza.   120
E come fantolin che inver la mamma
   tende le braccia come il latte prese,
   per l'animo che infin di fuor s'infiamma,   123
ciascun di quei candori in sù si stese
   con la sua fiamma, sì che l'alto affetto
   ch'elli aveano a Maria mi fu palese.   126
Indi rimaser lì nel mio cospetto,
   Regina coeli cantando sì dolce
   che mai da me non si partì il diletto.   129
Oh quanta è l'ubertà che si soffolce
   in quell'arche ricchissime che foro
   a seminar qua giù buone bobolce!   132
Quivi si vive e gode del tesoro
   che s'acquistò piangendo ne l'esilio
   di Babilon, ove si lasciò l'oro.   135

The sweetest tune that on this earthly shore
  most draws to itself the soul in fond desire,
  would seem a splitting thunder-cloud's harsh roar,
matched with the tones of that melodious lyre
  wherewith I saw the lovely sapphire crown'd
  which floods the brightest heav'n with its sapphire.
'Angelic love am I who circle round
  the exalted joy breathed from the womb, yea thine,
  in which the world's desire fit lodging found:
and here to circle, Lady of Heaven, is mine,
  till, following thy son, thou enterest
  the heaven of heavens to make it more divine.'
Thus on the circling music was impress'd
  its seal, and 'Mary' was the name that rung
  through heaven, by all the other lights confess'd.
The mantle royal round all the swathings flung
  that wrap the world, in God's ways most alight,
  in God's breath most alive, all spheres among,
upreared its inner shore to such a height
  above us as, from where I was, to make
  no aspect of it yet appear in sight:
hence did the crownéd flame ere long forsake
  the range of my weak vision, as it rose
  on high, while following in its offspring's wake.
And as an infant to its mummy throws
  its little arms out, when the breast is drained,
  for thus the love flames forth which in it glows,
each of those starry splendours upward strained
  its flame, whereby they visibly display'd
  how all to Mary yearned with love unfeigned.
Anon, still present to my sight they stay'd,
  chanting '*Regina coeli*' in a strain
  so sweet, my joy thereat can never fade.
Oh, how abundant is the garnered grain
  stored in those richest coffers which in sowing
  proved themselves here on earth good husbandmen!
Here live they and enjoy the overflowing
  wealth, which with tears, exiled in Babylon,
  spurning its gold, they gained beyond their knowing.

Quivi triunfa sotto l'alto filio
  di Dio e di Maria, di sua vittoria,
  e con l'antico e col novo concilio,   138
colui che tien le chiavi di tal gloria.

CANTO 24

« O SODALIZIO eletto a la gran cena
  del benedetto agnello, il qual vi ciba
  sì, che la vostra voglia è sempre piena,   3
se per grazia di Dio questi preliba
  di quel che cade de la vostra mensa
  prima che morte tempo gli prescriba,   6
ponete mente a l'affezione immensa
  e roratelo alquanto: voi bevete
  sempre del fonte onde vien quel ch'ei pensa ».   9
Così Beatrice; e quell'anime liete
  si fero spere sopra fissi poli,
  fiammando, volte, a guisa di comete.   12
E come cerchi in tempra d'oriuoli
  si giran sì che il primo, a chi pon mente,
  quieto pare, e l'ultimo che voli;   15
così quelle, carole differente-
  mente danzando, de la sua ricchezza
  mi si facean stimar, veloci o lente.   18
Di quella che notai di più carezza
  vid'io uscire un foco sì felice
  che nullo vi lasciò di più chiarezza;   21
e tre fiate intorno di Beatrice
  si volse, con un canto tanto divo
  che la mia fantasia nol mi ridice.   24
Però salta la penna e non lo scrivo,
  che l'imagine nostra a cotai pieghe,
  non che il parlare, è color troppo vivo.   27
« O santa suora mia che sì ne prieghe
  divota, per lo tuo ardente affetto
  da quella bella spera mi disleghe ».   30

There, under God's and Mary's lofty Son,
  triumphs, together with the consistóry
  both old and new alike, as victor, one
who holds the keys of such transcendent glory.

CANTO 24

'O COMPANY whom the blesséd Lamb so feeds
  at the great supper he hath called you to,
  that ever satisfied are all your needs,
if by divine grace, ere his term be due
  prescribed by death, this man foretasteth aught
  spilled from the board so richly spread for you,
mindful of his immeasurable drought,
  shed some few drops upon him: ye for aye
  drink of the fountain whence proceeds his thought.'
Thus Beatrice; and those joyful spirits straightway
  made themselves spheres on fixéd poles, thereby
  flashing, revolved, with a comet's fiery ray.
And as in clockwork, when with heedful eye
  you watch the wheels, the first seems motionless,
  so slow its movement, and the last to fly;
thus, by the varied measure of their pace-
  enwoven dances, whether swift or slow,
  those carols made me gauge their wealthiness.
From that which I remarked the richest, lo,
  a fire emerged of such resplendent bliss
  that none it left there shone with livelier glow;
and three times it revolved round Beatrice
  with so divine a song, that fancy keeps
  no record of those subtle melodies.
Therefore my pen describes them not, but skips;
  since for such folds our imagination were
  too crude a colourist, much more our lips.
'O holy sister mine, thine earnest prayer,
  enkindled by thy burning love, hath made
  me unloose myself from yonder circle fair.'

Poscia fermato, il foco benedetto
  a la mia donna dirizzò lo spiro,
  che favellò così com'io ho detto.   33
Ed ella: « O luce eterna del gran viro
  a cui Nostro Signor lasciò le chiavi
  ch'ei portò giù di questo gaudio miro,   36
tenta costui dei punti lievi e gravi,
  come ti piace, intorno de la fede
  per la qual tu su per lo mare andavi.   39
S'egli ama bene e bene spera e crede,
  non t'è occulto, perchè il viso hai quivi
  dove ogni cosa dipinta si vede;   42
ma perchè questo regno ha fatto civi
  per la verace fede, a gloriarla,
  di lei parlare è ben che a lui arrivi ».   45
Sì come il baccellier s'arma, e non parla
  fin che il maestro la question propone,
  per approvarla, non per terminarla,   48
così m'armava io d'ogni ragione,
  mentre ch'ella dicea, per esser presto
  a tal querente ed a tal professione.   51
« Di': buon cristiano fatti manifesto:
  fede che è? »; ond'io levai la fronte
  in quella luce onde spirava questo.   54
Poi mi volsi a Beatrice, ed essa pronte
  sembianze femmi perch'io spandessi
  l'acqua di fuor del mio interno fonte.   57
« La grazia che mi dà ch'io mi confessi »
  comincia' io « da l'alto primipilo,
  faccia li miei concetti bene espressi ».   60
E seguitai: « Come il verace stilo
  ne scrisse, padre, del tuo caro frate
  che mise teco Roma nel buon filo,   63
fede è sustanza di cose sperate
  e argomento de le non parventi;
  e questa pare a me sua quiditate ».   66
Allora udii: « Dirittamente senti,
  se bene intendi perchè la ripose
  tra le sustanze e poi tra gli argomenti ».   69

Such were the words with which, when it had stay'd
   its dance, I heared the blesséd fire begin
   to address my lady; whereupon she said:
'O eternal light of the great paladin
   to whom Our Lord bequeathed the keys which he
   brought down, that men this wondrous joy might win,
examine this man, as seemeth good to thee,
   on points both light and grave, touching the faith,
   by which of old thou walkedst on the sea.
If rightly he loves, and hopeth rightly, and hath
   a sound belief, to thee e'en now is shown
   in Him, who all that is discovereth;
but since by the true faith, and that alone,
   this realm hath gained its citizens, 'tis meet
   it fall to him to make its glory known.'
As, till the master states the *quodlibet*,
   to be argued, not conclusively defined,
   the bachelor in silence arms his wit,
so did I arm myself with every kind
   of reason, while she spoke, for such a creed
   and such a querist to be ready in mind,
'Good Christian, speak: show thyself such indeed;
   Faith, what *is* it?' Whereon I raised my brow
   unto the light which bade me thus proceed;
then turned to Beatrice, who was quick to show
   clear tokens that from out their secret place
   within me I should let the waters flow.
'May the same grace which grants me to confess
   before the chief centurion, in my mouth
   put words that shall my notions well express.'
Thus I, then added: 'Father, as with sooth
   thy brother wrote, who was thy loved ally
   in setting Rome upon the way to truth,
"Faith is the substance of things hoped for, ay
   and argument withal of things not seen";
   and this I take to be its quiddity.'
Then heard I: 'Thou thereof dost rightly ween,
   if, when he terms it first a substance, then
   an argument, thou knowest what he doth mean.'

E io appresso: « Le profonde cose
 che mi largiscon qui la lor parvenza
 a gli occhi di là giù son sì ascose,   72
che l'esser loro v'è in sola credenza,
 sopra la qual si fonda l'alta spene;
 e però di sustanza prende intenza.   75
E da questa credenza ci conviene
 sillogizzar, sanz'avere altra vista;
 però l'intenza d'argomento tiene ».   78
Allora udii: « Se quantunque s'acquista
 giù per dottrina fosse così inteso,
 non gli avria loco ingegno di sofista ». 81
Così spirò da quell'amore acceso;
 indi soggiunse: « Assai bene è trascorsa
 d'esta moneta già la lega e il peso;   84
ma dimmi se tu l'hai ne la tua borsa ».
 Ond'io: « Sì, l'ho, sì lucida e sì tonda
 che nel suo conio nulla mi s'inforsa ». 87
Appresso uscì da la luce profonda
 che lì splendeva: « Questa cara gioia
 sopra la quale ogni virtù si fonda,   90
onde ti venne? » E io: « La larga ploia
 de lo Spirito Santo, ch'è diffusa
 in su le vecchie e in su le nuove cuoia, 93
è sillogismo che la m'ha conchiusa
 acutamente sì, che inverso d'ella
 ogni dimostrazion mi pare ottusa ».   96
Io udii poi: « L'antica e la novella
 proposizion che così ti conchiude
 perchè l'hai tu per divina favella? »   99
E io: « La prova che il ver mi dischiude
 son l'opere seguite, a che natura
 non scaldò ferro mai nè battè incude ». 102
Risposto fummi: « Di', chi t'assicura
 che quell'opere fosser? Quel medesmo
 che vuol provarsi, non altri, il ti giura ». 105
« Se il mondo si rivolse al cristianesmo »
 diss'io « sanza miracoli, quest'uno
 è tal che gli altri non sono il centesmo; 108

'The deep things,' so I answered him again,
  'which to my vision here are freely shown,
  down there are so concealed from mortal ken,
that they exist there in belief alone,
  to which the intention of substance well applies,
  because the exalted hope is based thereon.
And since from faith, as wanting other eyes,
  we needs must make our syllogisms start,
  it holds the intention of argument likewise.'
Then heard I: 'If all lore, in learning's mart
  acquired below, were thuswise understood,
  no room were left there for the sophist's art.'
So breathed that kindled love, and then pursued:
  'Right well we've now assayed this coin throughout,
  both in alloy and weight, and found it good:
but is it in thy purse?' Whence I: 'Without
  question it is, and that so bright and round,
  that in its stamp there is no shade of doubt.'
Forthwith there issued from the light profound
  that shone there: 'This inestimable gem
  which is of every virtue the sole ground,
whence came it to thee?' And I: 'From him it came,
  the Holy Spirit, whose abundant rain
  flooding the parchments, old and new, in them
is syllogism which by proof so plain
  concludes it for me, that in point and force
  all others, when with that compared, seem vain.'
'Why hold'st thou,' heard I then from the same source,
  'the elder premise, and the new, whose might
  doth so persuade thee, for divine discourse?'
And I: 'The proof which brings the truth to light
  are the works consequent, which nature ne'er
  made iron hot for, nor did anvil smite.'
Came answer: 'That those same works ever were
  who vouches? Save the writ that seeks thereby
  to prove itself, none else to them doth swear.'
'If the world turned to Christianity,'
  I answered, 'without miracles, this one
  doth all the rest a hundredfold outvie;

697

chè tu entrasti povero e digiuno
   in campo, a seminar la buona pianta
   che fu già vite ed ora è fatta pruno ».   111
Finito questo l'alta corte santa
   risonò per le spere un *Dio laudamo !*
   ne la melode che là sù si canta.   114
E quel baron che sì di ramo in ramo,
   esaminando, già tratto m'avea
   che a l'ultime fronde appressavamo,   117
ricominciò: « La grazia che donnea
   con la tua mente, la bocca t'aperse
   infino a qui come aprir si dovea;   120
sì ch'io approvo ciò che fuori emerse.
   Ma or conviene esprimer quel' che credi,
   e onde a la credenza tua s'offerse ».   123
« O santo padre, spirito che vedi
   ciò che credesti sì, che tu vincesti
   ver lo sepulcro più giovani piedi »   126
comincia' io « tu vuoi ch'io manifesti
   la forma qui del pronto creder mio;
   e anche la cagion di lui chiedesti.   129
E io rispondo: Io credo in uno Dio
   solo ed eterno, che tutto il ciel move,
   non moto, con amore e con desio.   132
Ed a tal creder non ho io pur prove
   fisiche e metafisiche, ma dalmi
   anche la verità che quinci piove   135
per Moisè, per profeti e per Salmi,
   per l'Evangelio, e per voi che scriveste
   poi che l'ardente Spirto vi fe' almi.   138
E credo in tre persone eterne, e queste
   credo un'essenza sì una e sì trina
   che soffera congiunto *sono* ed *este*.   141
De la profonda condizion divina
   ch'io tocco mo', la mente mi sigilla
   più volte l'evangelica dottrina.   144
Quest'è il principio, questa è la favilla
   che si dilata in fiamma poi vivace,
   e come stella in cielo in me scintilla ».   147

for thou, both poor and fasting, wentest down
  into the field to sow the goodly plant,
    which, once a vine, is now a bramble grown.'
This ended, straightway such a jubilant
  '*Te Deum*' rang through heaven from star to star,
    as only its courtiers have the power to chant.
That baron who from branch to branch so far
  by examining had led me, that we now
    unto the topmost fronds were drawing near,
began once more: 'The grace, which loves to woo
  thy mind, thus far hath oped thy lips and made
    them give the answer it behoved them to;
I approve, therefore, that which they have said;
  but now 'tis meet that thou declare thy creed,
    and whence to such belief thy thoughts were led.'
'O holy father, spirit that for thy meed
  here seest what thou didst so believe, that thou
    didst younger feet to the sepulchre outspeed,'
I thus began, 'since here thou'dst have me show
  the essentials of my faith, and tell thee why
    I hold them with full confidence, then know
that I believe in one, sole Deity
  eternal, who, himself unmoved, doth move
    with love and longing all that wheels on high.
Such is my creed, and ample proof thereof
  nature supplies, and reason more, but most
    the truth which raineth down from here above
through Moses, through the Psalms and through a host
  of Prophets, through the Gospel and through you
    when quickened by the fire of the Holy Ghost.
Three eternal Persons I believe in too;
  I believe these an essence, one yet trine,
    so that thereof both "sunt" and "est" are true.
Of the mysterious estate divine
  I touch on now, my mind doth bear the mark
    impressed on it by many a gospel line.
From this beginning, from this pregnant spark
  the lively flame dilates and, glittering clear
    like to a star in heaven, dispels my dark.'

Come il signor che ascolta quel che i piace,
   da indi abbraccia il servo, gratulando
   per la novella, tosto ch'ei si tace,   150
così, benedicendomi cantando,
   tre volte cinse me, sì com'io tacqui,
   l'apostolico lume al cui comando   153
io avea detto, sì nel dir gli piacqui.

CANTO 25

Se mai continga che il poema sacro
   al quale ha posto mano e Cielo e Terra,
   sì che m'ha fatto per più anni macro,   3
vinca la crudeltà che fuor mi serra
   dal bell'ovile ov'io dormii agnello,
   nimico ai lupi che li danno guerra,   6
con altra voce omai, con altro vello,
   ritornerò poeta, ed in sul fonte
   del mio battesmo prenderò il cappello;   9
però che ne la Fede che fa conte
   l'anime a Dio quivi entra' io, e poi
   Pietro per lei sì mi girò la fronte.   12
Indi si mosse un lume verso noi
   di quella spera onde uscì la primizia
   che lasciò Cristo dei vicari suoi.   15
E la mia donna, piena di letizia,
   mi disse: « Mira, mira: ecco il barone
   per cui là giù si visita Galizia ».   18
Sì come quando il colombo si pone
   presso al compagno, e l'uno a l'altro pande
   girando e mormorando l'affezione,   21
così vid'io l'uno da l'altro grande
   principe glorioso essere accolto,
   laudando il cibo che là sù li prande.   24

Then as a lord who from his page doth hear
 good news, when he hath heard it, moved by strong
 delight, embraces him and holds him dear;
thus, pouring benediction forth with song,
 thrice wheeled about me, as I silent fell,
 the apostolic radiance who my tongue
had prompted; so its utterance pleased him well!

CANTO 25

If e'er it fortune that the sacred lay
 at which both Heaven and Earth co-workers are,
 so that it long hath worn my flesh away,
o'ercome the cruel hearts which 'gainst me bar
 the lovely sheepfold, where, a lamb, I grew
 up guileless, foe to the wolves that give it war,
with other voice, with fleece of other hue
 I shall return a Poet, and at my own
 baptismal font receive a laureate's due;
for on the Faith which maketh spirits known
 to God I there embarked, and Peter then
 for sake of it thus made himself my crown.
Next moved a light towards us once again
 out of that circle whence had issued forth
 the first-fruit of Christ's vicars among men.
'Look, look: behold the baron who on earth
 draws pilgrims to Galicia'—thus, elate,
 my lady made me know that spirit's worth.
As when the ring-dove settles near his mate,
 circling and cooing, each the affection shows
 which mutual love doth in their hearts beget;
so welcomed of each other saw I those
 two great and glorious princes, while in praise
 they chanted of the food which heaven bestows.

Ma poi che il gratular si fu assolto,
  tacito *coram me* ciascun s'affisse,
  ignito sì che vinceva il mio volto.   27
Ridendo allora Beatrice disse:
  « Inclita vita per cui la larghezza
  de la nostra basilica si scrisse,   30
fa risonar la spene in quest'altezza:
  tu sai che tante fiate la figuri
  quante Gesù ai tre fe' più chiarezza ».   33
« Leva la testa e fa che t'assicuri;
  chè ciò che vien qua sù dal mortal mondo
  convien che ai nostri raggi si maturi ».   36
Questo conforto dal foco secondo
  mi venne; ond'io levai gli occhi ai monti
  che l'incurvaron pria col troppo pondo.   39
« Poi che per grazia vuol che tu t'affronti
  lo nostro imperadore anzi la morte
  ne l'aula più secreta co' suoi conti,   42
sì che, veduto il ver di questa corte,
  la spene che là giù bene innamora
  in te ed in altrui di ciò conforte,   45
di' quel ch'ell'è, e come se ne infiora
  la mente tua, e di' onde a te venne ».
  Così seguì 'l secondo lume ancora.   48
E quella pia che guidò le penne
  de le mie ali a così alto volo,
  a la risposta così mi prevenne: 51
« La Chiesa militante alcun figliuolo
  non ha con più speranza, com'è scritto
  nel Sol che raggia tutto nostro stuolo: 54
però gli è conceduto che d'Egitto
  venga in Gerusalemme, per vedere
  anzi che il militar gli sia prescritto.   57
Gli altri due punti, che non per sapere
  son dimandati, ma perch'ei rapporti
  quanto questa virtù t'è in piacere,   60
a lui lasc'io, chè non li saran forti
  nè di iattanza; ed egli a ciò risponda,
  e la grazia di Dio ciò gli comporti ».   63

But both, when once these glad assurances
   were ended, *coram me* in silence glow'd,
   so burning bright as to o'ercome my gaze.
Beatrice smiled, then spake after this mode:
   'Renowned life, of the largess called to write
   which is by our basilica bestow'd,
make hope resound on this celestial height:
   thou canst, who as oft-times its figure art
   as Jesus on the three shed greater light.'
'Lift up thy head and be thou of good heart;
   for what mounts hither from the world below
   will ripen in the warmth our beams impart.'
Thus strengthened me the second fire; and so
   I lifted up mine eyes unto the hills
   whose weight, till then o'erheavy, had made them bow.
'Seeing that of his grace our Emperor wills
   that thou, ere death, shouldst with his lords consort
   in the most secret hall his presence fills,
so that this vision of our very court
   may strengthen in thyself and others too
   hope, which doth men to a right love exhort,
say what it is, how in thy mind it grew
   and blossoms there, and whence to thee it came.'
   Thus did the second light its speech pursue.
That generous one who to so high an aim
   my wings had guided, with this quick riposte
   prevented me, ere I could answer frame:
'No son of the Church militant can boast
   of having fuller hope, as may be read
   in Him whose beams enlighten all our host:
therefore he hath by special grace been led
   from Egypt to Jerusalem, its bliss
   to see, or e'er his fighting days be sped.
The two remaining points, which not to increase
   thy knowledge have been asked, but that he may
   report how dear to thee this virtue is,
I leave to him; not difficult are they,
   nor theme for self-praise; and let *him* reply
   God helping him, to both in his own way.'

Come discente che a dottor seconda
   pronto e libente in quel ch'egli è esperto,
   perchè la sua bontà si disasconda: 66
« Spene » diss'io « è un attender certo
   de la gloria futura, il qual produce
   grazia divina e precedente merto.   69
Da molte stelle mi vien questa luce,
   ma quei la distillò nel mio cor pria
   che fu sommo cantor del sommo duce.   72
'*Sperent in te*' ne la sua teodia
   dice, 'color che sanno il nome tuo';
   e chi nol sa s'egli ha la fede mia?   75
Tu mi stillasti con lo stillar suo
   ne l'epistola poi; sì ch'io son pieno
   ed in altrui vostra pioggia repluo ».   78
Mentr'io diceva, dentro al vivo seno
   di quell'incendio tremolava un lampo
   subito e spesso a guisa di·baleno.   81
Indi spirò: « L'amore ond'io avvampo
   ancor ver la virtù che mi seguette
   infin la palma ed a l'uscir del campo,   84
vuol ch'io rispiri a te che ti dilette
   di lei, ed emmi a grato che tu diche
   quello che la speranza ti promette ».   87
Ed io: « Le nuove e le scritture antiche
   porgono il segno — ed esso lo mi addita —
   de l'anime che Dio s'ha fatte amiche: 90
dice Isaia che ciascuna vestita
   ne la sua terra fia di doppia vesta,
   e la sua terra è questa dolce vita;   93
e il tuo fratello assai vie più digesta,
   là dove tratta de le bianche stole,
   questa rivelazion ci manifesta ».   96
E prima, appresso al fin d'este parole,
   sperent in te di sopra noi s'udì,
   a che risposer tutte le carole;   99
poscia tra esse un lume si schiarì
   sì, che se il Cancro avesse un tal cristallo,
   l'inverno avrebbe un mese d'un sol dì.   102

As practised scholar, who would fain thereby
  reveal his worth, displays an eager spirit
  in seconding his teacher, 'Hope', said I,
'is of the glory that we shall inherit
  a sure expectancy, the fruit withal
  of grace divine and of preceding merit.
On me from many stars this light doth fall;
  but the chief captain's chief musician, he
  distilled it in my heart the first of all.
"*Sperent in te*" so runs his theody
  "who know thy name"; and what man knows it not,
  dwells but in him the faith that dwells in me?
Drenching me fell, dew of his dew begot,
  thine own epistle next; and now to pour
  your rain on others is in turn my lot.'
As thus I spoke, quick flashes o'er and o'er
  repeated, as of sudden lightning, shone
  within that conflagration's living core.
Then it breathed forth: 'The love that still burns on
  within me for the virtue which pursued
  my steps till palm and foughten field were won,
bids me respond to thee as one imbued
  with it, and I would have thee now unfold
  what it doth promise thee of future good.'
And I: 'The latter scriptures and the old
  offer the sign—which to me makes it clear—
  of souls whom God doth in his friendship hold.
Isaiah says, in their own land they wear
  each one a double robe; and their own land
  is the existence ye delight in here.
Which revelation hath thy brother's hand
  depicted in far clearer imagery
  there where he treateth of the white-robed band.'
And when these words were ended, instantly
  '*Sperent in te*' rang o'er us from the height;
  unto which all the carols made reply.
Then in their midst a star became so bright,
  that if in Cancer sparkled such a gem,
  winter would have a month without a night.

705

E come surge e va ed entra in ballo
   vergine lieta sol per fare onore
   a la novizia, non per alcun fallo,   105
così vid'io lo schiarato splendore
   venire ai due, che si volgeano a nota
   qual conveniesi al loro ardente amore.   108
Misesi lì nel canto e ne la rota;
   e la mia donna in lor tenea l'aspetto,
   pur come sposa tacita ed immota.   111
« Questi è colui che giacque sopra il petto
   del nostro pellicano; e questi fue
   di su la croce al grande ufficio eletto ». 114
La donna mia così : nè però piue
   mosser la vista sua di stare attenta
   poscia che prima le parole sue.   117
Qual è colui che adocchia e s'argomenta
   di vedere eclissar lo Sole un poco,
   che per veder non vedente diventa,   120
tal mi fec'io a quell'ultimo foco,
   mentre che detto fu: « Perchè t'abbagli
   per veder cosa che qui non ha loco?   123
In Terra, terra è 'l mio corpo, e saragli
   tanto con gli altri, che il numero nostro
   con l'eterno proposito s'agguagli.   126
Con le due stole nel beato chiostro
   son le due luci sole che saliro;
   e questo apporterai nel mondo vostro ». 129
A questa voce l'infiammato giro
   si quietò con esso il dolce mischio
   che si facea nel suon del trino spiro; 132
sì come, per cessar fatica o rischio,
   li remi, pria ne l'acqua ripercossi,
   tutti si posano al sonar d'un fischio.   135
Ahi quanto ne la mente mi commossi
   quando mi volsi per veder Beatrice,
   per non poter vedere, ben ch'io fossi   138
presso di lei e nel mondo felice!

And as a blithe girl, moved by nought to blame,
   but solely to do honour to the bride,
    where folk dance, ups and runs and joins with them,

so saw I that embrightened splendour glide
   up to the other twain, whose whirling pace
    was such as with their ardent love complied.

In song and wheel it took its own due place;
   the while my lady, gazing at them, stood
    as stands a bride, silent and motionless.

'Lo, this is he o'er whom most loved to brood
   our pelican; and this is he who bore
    the mighty charge laid on him from the rood.'

My lady thus; nor, for all that, the more
   was she withdrawn from her intent regard
    by that she spake, thereafter than before.

As one who'd fain contrive, by looking hard,
   to see the Sun eclipsed in some degree,
    by dint of seeing finds his seeing marr'd;

so, before that last fire, it happed with me,
   till this was said: 'Why dazzlest thou thine eye
    in seeking that which is not here to see?

In earth, earth is my body and there will lie
   with the others, till our number fills the tale
    which shall the eternal purpose satisfy.

With the two vestures in the heavenly pale
   are the two lights alone which have ascended;
    and this report to the world wherein ye dwell.'

This utterance checked the fiery reel and ended
   therewith the sweet harmonious rise and fall
    of sound in which the trinal breath was blended,

even as, fatigue or danger to forestall,
   the oars, which smote the waves a moment past,
    stop all together at a whistle's call.

Ah into what a stir my mind was cast,
   whenas I turned me to see Beatrice,
    for lack of power to see, though I was fast

beside her still, and in the world of bliss!

CANTO 26

Mentr'io dubbiava per lo viso spento,
  da la fulgida fiamma che lo spense
  uscì uno spiro che mi fece attento,   3
dicendo: « Intanto che tu ti risense
  de la vista che hai in me consunta,
  ben è che ragionando la compense.   6
Comincia dunque, e di' ove s'appunta
  l'anima tua, e fa ragion che sia
  la vista in te smarrita e non defunta;   9
perchè la donna che per questa dia
  region ti conduce, ha ne lo sguardo
  la virtù ch'ebbe la man d'Anania ».   12
Io dissi: « Al suo piacere, o tosto o tardo
  vegna rimedio a gli occhi che fur porte
  quand'ella entrò col foco ond'io sempr'ardo.   15
Lo ben che fa contenta questa corte
  Alfa ed Omega è di quanta scrittura
  mi legge amore o lievemente o forte ».   18
Quella medesma voce che paura
  tolta m'avea del subito abbarbaglio,
  di ragionare ancor mi mise in cura;   21
e disse: « Certo a più angusto vaglio
  ti conviene schiarar: dicer convienti
  chi drizzò l'arco tuo a tal bersaglio ».   24
Ed io: « Per filosofici argomenti
  e per l'autorità che quinci scende
  cotale amor convien che in me s'imprenti.   27
Chè il bene, in quanto ben, come s'intende
  così accende amore, e tanto maggio
  quanto più di bontade in sè comprende.   30
Dunque a l'essenza ov'è tanto avvantaggio
  che ciascun ben che fuor di lei si trova
  altro non è che un lume di suo raggio,   33
più che in altra convien che si muova
  la mente, amando, di ciascun che cerne
  il vero in che si fonda questa prova.   36

CANTO 26

WHILE, blinded thus, I strove to banish fear,
  there issued from the radiancy intense
  which blinded me a voice that held my ear,
breathing these words: 'Till thou regain the sense
  of vision which thou hast consumed on me,
  'tis well that thou in speech find recompense.
Begin then; and declare what is for thee
  thy soul's chief aim, and reckon that not dead,
  but only wildered, is thy power to see;
for in her look the lady who hath led
  thee through this realm divine, hath virtue as great
  as once the hand of Ananias had.'
I answered: 'To the eyes which were the gate
  what time she entered with her quenchless fire,
  come healing, as she wills, or soon or late.
The good, which in this court fulfils desire,
  is Alpha and Omega of aught, writ with pen,
  teaching me love, be't easy or hard to acquire.'
The same voice which had just relieved me when
  oppressed by fear o' the sudden dazzle, now
  inspired me with the wish to speak again;
and said: 'In sooth with finer sieve must thou
  make clear this matter: it is meet thou tell
  who made thee at such a target aim thy bow?'
And I: 'Philosophy must needs avail
  to stamp me with such love, and to that end
  authority comes down from here as well.
For good, *qua* good, even as we apprehend
  it truly, kindles love, and that the more
  as more of goodness is therein contained.
Hence to the essence which contains such store
  of goodness that all good outside it found
  does but reflect the ray itself doth pour,
more than to others must, in love, be bound
  the mind of whosoe'er distinguishes
  the truth which is this demonstration's ground.

Tal vero a l'intelletto mio sterne
  colui che mi dimostra il primo amore
  di tutte le sustanze sempiterne.
      39
Sternel la voce del verace autore
  che dice a Moisè, di sè parlando:
  'Io ti farò vedere ogni valore.'
      42
Sternilmi tu ancora, incominciando
  l'alto preconio che grida l'arcano
  di qui là giù sovra ogni altro bando ».
      45
E io udii: « Per intelletto umano
  e per autoritadi a lui concorde
  de' tuoi amori a Dio guarda il sovrano.
      48
Ma di' ancor se tu senti altre corde
  tirarti verso lui, sì che tu suone
  con quanti denti quest'amor ti morde ».
      51
Non fu latente la santa intenzione
  de l'aquila di Cristo, anzi m'accorsi
  dove volea menar mia professione.
      54
Però ricominciai: « Tutti quei morsi
  che posson far lo cor volgere a Dio
  a la mia caritade son concorsi;
      57
chè l'essere del mondo e l'esser mio,
  la morte ch'ei sostenne perch'io viva,
  e quel che spera ogni fedel com'io,
      60
con la predetta conoscenza viva,
  tratto m'hanno del mar de l'amor torto
  e del diritto m'han posto a la riva.
      63
Le fronde onde s'infronda tutto l'orto
  de l'ortolano eterno, amo io cotanto
  quanto da lui a lor di bene è porto ».
      66
Sì com'io tacqui, un dolcissimo canto
  risonò per lo cielo, e la mia donna
  dicea con gli altri: « Santo, Santo, Santo! »
      69
E come a lume acuto si dissonna
  per lo spirto visivo che ricorre
  a lo splendor che va di gonna in **gonna**,
      72
e lo svegliato ciò che vede abborre
  sì nescia è la sua subita vigilia,
  fin che la stimativa non soccorre;
      75

He to my understanding well displays
   the truth concerned who shows me the first love
   of all the sempiternal substances.
Displays it the true word of One above,
   who, speaking of himself, to Moses saith:
   "I in thy sight will all my goodness prove."
Displays it further that which preludeth
   thine own great gospel, chief of all to cry
   in mortal ears the mysteries of the faith.'
'The human intellect,' so came reply,
   'and consonant authorities unite
   to fix thy sovran love on the Most High.
But say if other cords there be, of might
   to draw thee tow'rds him, so that thou mayst show
   what the teeth are wherewith this love doth bite.'
Nor could I not the holy intention know
   of the eagle of Christ—rather, divined therein
   the way which he would have my avowal go.
Hence I resumed: 'All bitings which can win
   the heart to turn towards God have, each one,
   unto my charity concurrent been;
in that the world's existence and my own,
   the death He tholed that I may live, moreo'er
   what all the faithful hope, not I alone,
joined to that lively knowledge named before,
   have, from the sea of passion men miscall
   love, of the right love set me on the shore.
I love the leaves, wherewith enleaved is all
   the garden by the eternal Gardener tended,
   in measure as on each His dew doth fall.'
A song most sweet, soon as my words were ended,
   made the whole heaven resound, and with the rest
   my lady's 'Holy, holy, holy!' blended.
And as, when a light flashes, sleep is chased
   away from the eyes, because their spirit runs
   to meet the glare that spreads from vest to vest,
and the roused sleeper what he seëth shuns,
   until the power of judgment comes to aid
   the sense which that abrupt awakening stuns;

così de gli occhi miei ogni quisquilia
  fugò Beatrice col raggio de' suoi,
  che rifulgea da più di mille milia;   78
onde me' che dinanzi vidi poi;
  e quasi stupefatto domandai
  d'un quarto lume ch'io vidi con noi.   81
E la mia donna: « Dentro da que' rai
  vagheggia il suo fattor l'anima prima
  che la prima virtù creasse mai ».   84
Come la fronda che flette la cima
  nel transito del vento e poi si leva
  per la propria virtù che la sublima,   87
fec'io in tanto in quanto ella diceva,
  stupendo, e poi mi rifece sicuro
  un disio di parlare ond'io ardeva.   90
E cominciai: « O pomo che maturo
  solo prodotto fosti, o padre antico
  a cui ciascuna sposa è figlia e nuro,   93
divoto quanto posso a te supplìco
  perchè mi parli: tu vedi mia voglia,
  e per udirti tosto non la dico ».   96
Talvolta un animal coverto broglia,
  sì che l'affetto convien che si paia
  per lo seguir che face a lui la invoglia;   99
e similmente l'anima primaia
  mi facea trasparer per la coperta
  quant'ella a compiacermi venia gaia.   102
Indi spirò: « Sanz'essermi profferta
  da te, la voglia tua discerno meglio
  che tu qualunque cosa t'è più certa;   105
perch'io la veggio nel verace speglio
  che fa di sè pareglio a l'altre cose,
  e nulla face a lui di sè pareglio.   108
Tu vuoi udir quant'è che Dio mi pose
  ne l'eccelso giardino ove costei
  a così lunga scala ti dispose,   111
e quanto fu diletto a gli occhi miei,
  e la propria cagion del gran disdegno,
  e l'idioma che usai e ch'io fei.   114

thus from my eyes drove Beatrice every shred
  of cloud away by radiance which her own
  more than a thousand miles around her spread:
whence I saw better now than I had done
  before, and asked, as though in deep amaze,
  touching a fourth light which among us shone.
My lady then: 'Concealed in yonder rays
  the first soul ever framed by the first might
  regards its Maker with adoring gaze.'
E'en as a leafy bough, that bends its light
  crest in a passing breeze, then backward swayed
  by its own virtue raises it upright,
so I while she was speaking bowed my head,
  awe-stricken; and then, stronger than my awe,
  these words so burned within me that I said:
'O thou sole fruit that the world ever saw
  produced already ripe, O sire of old
  who in ev'ry bride hast daughter and daughter-in-law,
devoutly as I may, I implore thee hold
  converse with me; thou seëst my wish, and I,
  to hear thee sooner, leave it all untold.'
An animal which under wraps doth lie,
  sometimes by wriggling makes its impulse plain,
  since with it move the folds 'tis covered by;
just so that first of all the souls of men
  made clear to me through its integument
  how it to do my pleasure was full fain.
Then breathed it: 'That whereon thy mind is bent,
  tho' untold by thee, is clearer to my view
  than unto thine a fact self-evident;
because I see it in the mirror true,
  itself reflecting all things whatsoe'er,
  while reflect *it* is that which nought can do.
How long is it since God, thou fain wouldst hear,
  in the high garden placed me whither came
  she, who disposed thee for so long a stair,
and how long did mine eyes enjoy the same,
  and what was the true cause of the great wrath
  and what tongue did I speak and, myself, frame.

713

Or, figliuol mio, non il gustar del legno
    fu per sè la cagion di tanto esilio,
    ma solamente il trapassar del segno.   117
Quindi onde mosse tua donna Virgilio
    quattromila trecento e due volumi
    di Sol desiderai questo concilio;   120
e vidi lui tornare a tutti i lumi
    de la sua strada novecento trenta
    fiate, mentre ch'io in Terra fumi.   123
La lingua ch'io parlai fu tutta spenta
    innanzi che all'ovra inconsummabile
    fosse la gente di Nembrotte attenta;   126
chè nullo effetto mai razionabile,
    per lo piacere uman che rinnovella
    seguendo il cielo, sempre fu durabile.   129
Opera naturale è ch'uom favella;
    ma così o così natura lascia
    poi fare a voi, secondo che v'abbella.   132
Pria ch'io scendessi all'infernale ambascia
    I s'appellava in Terra il sommo bene
    onde vien la letizia che mi fascia;   135
e *El* si chiamò poi: e ciò conviene,
    chè l'uso dei mortali è come fronda
    in ramo, che sen va e l'altra viene.   138
Nel monte che si leva più da l'onda
    fu' io, con vita pura e disonesta,
    da la prim'ora a quella che seconda,   141
come il Sol muta quadra, l'ora sesta».

CANTO 27

Aʟ Padre, al Figlio, a lo Spirito Santo
    cominciò *Gloria* tutto il Paradiso
    sì che m'inebriava il dolce canto.   3
Ciò ch'io vedeva mi sembrava un riso
    de l'universo, perchè mia ebbrezza
    entrava per l'udire e per lo viso.   6

Mankind, my son, for its long exile hath
  to blame, not the mere tasting of the tree,
  but that it crossed the bound set to its path.
I for this council yearned four thousand, three
  hundred and two years in the place below
  whence Virgil set forth at thy lady's plea;
to all the lights that on his pathway glow
  nine hundred and thirty times I saw the Sun
  return, whilst I on Earth went to and fro.
The language which I spoke was all fordone
  long ere the work they could not consummate
  by Nimrod's people was as yet begun;
for nought of reason born was ever yet
  perdurable, since human liking still
  keeps changing with the stars, which rise and set.
In speaking, man doth Nature's law fulfil;
  but in this way or that she then doth leave
  to you to do, after your own sweet will.
Ere thither I went down where spirits grieve,
  JAH was the name on Earth of the chief good
  whose rays this light of gladness round me weave;
and *EL* men called him, as 'tis meet they should
  thereafter; in that, like to leaves on spray,
  their habits pass and are, like leaves, renew'd.
On the highest of sea-girt mountains did I stay,
  pure to begin with, then in guiltiness,
  from the first hour to that which, as the day
shifts quadrant, makes the sixth hour yield it place.'

CANTO 27

'GLORY' to Father, Son, and Holy Spirit
  all Paradise 'gan chanting in a style
  so passing sweet, it made me drunk to hear it.
What I was seeing appeared to me a smile
  of the universe; for that my drunkenness
  through eyes and ears kept entering all the while.

Oh gioia! oh ineffabile allegrezza!
  oh vita intera d'amore e di pace!
  oh sanza brama sicura ricchezza!   9
Dinanzi a gli occhi miei le quattro face
  stavano accese; e quella che pria venne
  incominciò a farsi più vivace,   12
e tal ne la sembianza sua divenne
  qual diverrebbe Giove s'egli e Marte
  fossero augelli e cambiassersi penne.   15
La providenza, che quivi comparte
  vice ed officio, nel beato coro
  silenzio posto aveva d'ogni parte,   18
quand'io udii: « Se io mi trascoloro
  non ti maravigliar, chè dicend'io
  vedrai trascolorar tutti costoro.   21
Quelli che usurpa in Terra il loco mio,
  il loco mio, il loco mio, che vaca
  ne la presenza del Figliuol di Dio,   24
fatt'ha del cimitero mio cloaca
  del sangue e de la puzza; onde il perverso
  che cadde di qua sù là giù si placa ».   27
Di quel color che per lo Sole avverso
  nube dipigne da sera e da mane,
  vid'io allora tutto il ciel cosperso.   30
E come donna onesta che permane
  di sè secura, e per l'altrui fallanza,
  pur ascoltando, timida si fane,   33
così Beatrice trasmutò sembianza;
  e tale eclissi credo che in ciel fue
  quando patì la suprema possanza.   36
Poi procedetter le parole sue,
  con voce tanto da sè trasmutata
  che la sembianza non si mutò piue: 39
« Non fu la sposa di Cristo allevata
  del sangue mio, di Lin, di quel di Cleto,
  per essere ad acquisto d'oro usata;   42
ma per acquisto d'esto viver lieto
  e Sisto e Pio e Calisto ed Urbano
  sparser lo sangue dopo molto fleto.   45

Oh joy! Oh mirth no words have power to express!
  oh perfect life, fulfilled of love and peace!
  Oh wealth unlosable and limitless!
Stood the four torches, flaming without cease,
  before mine eyes, and that which first had shone,
  in brilliancy began now to increase.
And such an aspect did it then put on,
  as Jupiter would do, if he and Mars
  were birds and should each other's plumage don.
The providence, which all particulars
  of function here assigns and service due,
  had silenced all those blissful choristers,
When this I heard: 'Marvel not if my hue
  is changed, for, while I'm speaking, thou wilt see
  all of these hallows change their colour too.
He who usurps on Earth the place by me,
  by me, by me first occupied, now rated
  vacant before the Son of the Deity,
hath made my cemetery a sewer of fetid
  filth and of blood; wherewith the renegade
  who fell from up here is down there placated.'
With colour such as that by the Sun laid
  on cloud it fronts at dawn and close of day,
  beheld I then all heaven overspread.
And as a modest damsel, in no way
  doubtful of her own virtue, yet at bare
  report of other's fault, reveals dismay,
thus Beatrice was changed in look and air;
  and thus methinks, what time the Almighty bore
  the pains of death, the heavens eclipséd were.
His voice went on, but not now as before,
  since from itself so great a change it show'd,
  that even his semblance did not alter more:
'The bride of Christ was never with my blood,
  with that of Linus and of Cletus fed,
  to find in gain of gold her highest good;
but Sextus, Pius and Calixtus bled,
  and Urban, after weeping tears untold,
  to gain thereby this happy life instead.

Non fu nostra intenzion che a destra mano
  dei nostri successor parte sedesse,
  parte da l'altra del popol cristiano;   48
nè che le chiavi che mi fur concesse
  divenisser segnacolo in vessillo
  che contra a battezzati combattesse;   51
ne ch'io fossi figura di sigillo
  a privilegi venduti e mendaci,
  ond'io sovente arrosso e disfavillo.   54
In vesta di pastor lupi rapaci
  si vedon di qua sù per tutti i paschi:
  o difesa di Dio, perchè pur giaci?   57
Del sangue nostro Caorsini e Guaschi
  s'apparecchian di bere; o buon principio,
  a che vil fine convien che tu caschi!   60
Ma l'alta provedenza che con Scipio
  difese a Roma la gloria del mondo,
  soccorrà tosto, sì com'io concipio.   63
E tu, figliuol, che per lo mortal pondo
  ancor giù tornerai, apri la bocca
  e non asconder quel ch'io non ascondo ».   66
Sì come di vapor gelati fiocca
  in giuso l'aer nostro, quando il corno
  de la capra del ciel col Sol si tocca,   69
in sù vid'io così l'ètera adorno
  farsi e fioccar di vapor trionfanti
  che fatto avean con noi quivi soggiorno.   72
Lo viso mio seguiva i suoi sembianti,
  e seguì fin che il mezzo, per lo molto,
  li tolse il trapassar del più avanti.   75
Onde la donna che mi vide assolto
  de l'attendere in sù mi disse: « Adima
  il viso, e guarda come tu sei volto ».   78
Da l'ora ch'io avea guardato prima
  io vidi mosso me per tutto l'arco
  che fa dal mezzo al fine il primo clima;   81
sì ch'io vedea di là da Gade il varco
  folle d'Ulisse, e di qua presso il lito
  nel qual si fece Europa dolce carco.   84

No intention was 't of ours that of Christ's fold
  one part should sit on our successors' right,
  the other on the left its station hold;
nor that upon a banner men should write
  as crest the keys entrusted unto me,
  and against folk baptized, bear it in fight;
nor that I should myself as signet see
  to false and venal privileges set,
  whence oft I redden and glow indignantly.
In every pasture hence our eyes are met
  by ravening wolves garbed in what shepherds wear;
  O God our strength, why dost thou linger yet?
Sons of Cahors and Gascony prepare
  to drink our blood: oh, that so vile a doom
  must needs await thee, promise once so fair!
But that high providence which saved for Rome
  the glory of the world by Scipio's sword,
  will, if I err not, soon bid succour come.
And thou, son, who to Earth must be restor'd
  by reason of thy mortal burden, hide
  nought that I hide not; tell it, word for word.'
As, when the she-goat's horn is so enskied
  that it doth touch the Sun, downwards our air
  is flaked with frozen vapours far and wide,
upwards saw I the ether thus made fair
  and flaked thick with triumphant vapours who
  had sojourned for a season with us there.
My sight pursued, and ceased not to pursue,
  their semblances till height on heights beyond
  of intervenient space obscured its view.
Wherefore the lady, who my visage found
  absolved from gazing up, said 'Downward cast
  thy sight, and see how thou hast circled round.'
Since the hour when I'd first looked, I saw I'd passed
  all round so much of the first 'climate' as
  extends between its mid-point and its last;
hence saw I, that side Gades, the mad pass
  Ulysses dared, and, this side, nigh the shore
  where once Europa a sweet burden was.

E più mi fora discoperto il sito
　di quest'aiuola, ma il Sol procedea
　sotto i miei piedi un segno e più partito.　　87
La mente innamorata, che donnea
　sempre con la mia donna, di redure
　ad essa gli occhi più che mai ardea;　　90
e se natura o arte fe' pasture
　da pigliare occhi per aver la mente,
　in carne umana o ne le sue pitture,　　93
tutte adunate parrebber niente
　ver lo piacer divin che mi refulse
　quando mi volsi al suo viso ridente.　　96
E la virtù che lo sguardo m'indulse,
　del bel nido di Leda mi divelse
　e nel ciel velocissimo m'impulse.　　99
Le parti sue vivissime ed eccelse
　sì uniforme son, che non so dire
　qual Beatrice per loco mi scelse.　　102
Ma ella, che vedeva il mio disire,
　incominciò, ridendo tanto lieta
　che Dio parea nel suo volto gioire:　　105
« La natura del mondo, che quieta
　il mezzo, e tutto l'altro intorno move,
　quinci comincia come da sua meta.　　108
E questo cielo non ha altro dove
　che la mente divina in che s'accende
　l'amor che il volge e la virtù ch'ei piove.　　111
Luce ed amor d'un cerchio lui comprende
　sì come questo gli altri; e quel precinto
　colui che il cinge solamente intende.　　114
Non è suo moto per altro distinto,
　ma gli altri son misurati da questo
　sì come dieci da mezzo e da quinto.　　117
E come il tempo tenga in cotal testo
　le sue radici e ne gli altri le fronde,
　omai a te può esser manifesto.　　120
Oh cupidigia che i mortali affonde
　sì sotto te, che nessuno ha podere
　di trarre gli occhi fuor de le tue onde!　　123

And further had this little threshing-floor
   been shown me; but the Sun beneath my feet
   was rolling on a sign away and more.
My enamoured mind, which ever found it sweet
   to woo my lady, never more her wooer
   than now, burned once again her glance to meet.
If nature or if art e'er fashioned lure
   to catch the eyes, and so the mind possess,
   in human flesh or in its portraiture,
all such combined would nothing seem, or less,
   to the divine delight which on me shone
   when I had turned me to her smiling face.
Such virtue from that radiant look I won,
   as tore me forth from Leda's lovely nest
   and to the swiftest heaven thrust me on.
Its parts, supreme in height and liveliest,
   so correspond in form, I cannot tell
   which for my entrance Beatrice deemed best.
But she, who my desire perceived full well,
   smiling the while, with so much gladness spake,
   that her delight seemed God's, made visible:
'The nature of the world, that fixed doth make
   the centre, and all circling it constrains
   to move, from here its starting-point doth take.
No other "where" than God's own mind contains
   this heaven, for in that mind alone is lit
   the love that rolls it, and the power it rains.
Around it light and love in circle meet,
   as it does round the rest; and sole presides
   o'er that engirdment he who girdeth it.
Measured itself by none, this heaven decides
   the motion, swift or slow, of all the rest,
   as ten into its half and fifth divides.
And how in this same flower-pot have been placed
   time's roots, and in the rest its leafage lies,
   will henceforth unto thee be manifest.
Oh covetousness that mortals in such wise
   dost whelm beneath thy billows, that no power
   is left to any thence to lift his eyes!

Ben fiorisce ne gli uomini il volere,
  ma la pioggia continua converte
  in bozzacchioni le susine vere.   126
Fede ed innocenzia son reperte
  solo nei pargoletti; poi ciascuna
  pria fugge che le guance sian coperte.   129
Tale, balbuziendo ancor, digiuna,
  che poi divora, con la lingua sciolta,
  qualunque cibo per qualunque luna;   132
e tal, balbuziendo, ama ed ascolta
  la madre sua, che, con loquela intera,
  desira poi di vederla sepolta: 135
così si fa la pelle bianca nera
  nel primo aspetto de la bella figlia
  di quei che apporta mane e lascia sera.   138
Tu, perchè non ti facci meraviglia,
  pensa che in Terra non è chi governi,
  onde si svia l'umana famiglia.   141
Ma prima che gennaio tutto si sverni
  per la centesma ch'è là giù negletta,
  raggeran sì questi cerchi superni,   144
che la fortuna che tanto s'aspetta
  le poppe volgerà u' son le prore,
  sì che la classe correrà diretta;   147
e vero frutto verrà dopo il fiore ».

CANTO 28

Poscia che incontro a la vita presente
  dei miseri mortali, aperse il vero
  quella che imparadisa la mia mente,   3
come in lo specchio fiamma di doppiero
  vede colui che se n'alluma retro,
  prima che l'abbia in vista od in pensiero,   6
e sè rivolge per veder se il vetro
  li dice il vero, e vede ch'el s'accorda
  con esso come nota con suo metro;   9

The will in men bursts into glorious flower;
  but the true plums a never-ceasing rain
  turns into prunes all blighted to the core.
To look for faith and innocence were vain
  except in children; later on, we find
  both fled, before on cheeks the down be plain.
One that, while lisping yet, observes the enjoin'd
  fast-days, will later, when his tongue's unbound,
  'neath any moon wolf food of any kind;
and one, while lisping, is his mother's fond
  obedient child, who, when he speaks aright,
  longs then to see her dead and laid in ground.
Thus soon becomes the white skin dark as night
  in the first aspect of His daughter fair,
  who adds the morning to the evening light.
Do thou, lest thou shouldst marvel at it, bear
  in mind that Earth no ruler hath to show
  the human family how it doth err.
But ere that through the hundredth, down below
  neglected, January shall have passed
  clean out of winter, these high spheres will so
ray, that the longed-for tempest, come at last,
  shall whirl the vessel, poop to prow, right round,
  so that the fleet shall run on straight and fast;
and after blossom true fruit shall abound.'

CANTO 28

Wᴴᴇɴ she whose charms imparadise my mind
  had—ah, the contrast!—bared in all its shame
  the present life of miserable mankind,
as in the looking-glass a candle's flame
  is seen of one it lighteth from the rear,
  ere he beholds or dreameth of the same,
who turns to see if real flame be there
  to match the image and finds this agree
  with that, as to its words is set the air;

723

così la mia memoria si ricorda
  ch'io feci, riguardando nei begli occhi
  onde a pigliarmi amor fece la corda.   12
E com'io mi rivolsi e furon tocchi
  li miei da ciò che pare in quel volume
  quandunque nel suo giro ben s'adocchi,   15
un punto vidi che raggiava lume
  acuto sì, che il viso ch'egli affoca
  chiuder conviensi per lo forte acume;   18
e quale stella par quinci più poca
  parrebbe luna locata con esso
  come stella con stella si colloca.   21
Forse cotanto quanto pare appresso
  alo cinger la luce che il dipigne,
  quando il vapor che il porta più è spesso,   24
distante, intorno al punto un cerchio d'igne
  si girava sì ratto che avria vinto
  quel moto che più tosto il mondo cigne;   27
e questo era d'un altro circumcinto,
  e quel dal terzo, e il terzo poi dal quarto,
  dal quinto il quarto, e poi dal sesto il quinto.   30
Sopra seguiva il settimo, sì sparto
  già di larghezza, che il messo di Iuno
  intero a contenerlo sarebb'arto.   33
Così l'ottavo e il nono; e ciascheduno
  più tardo si movea secondo ch'era
  in numero distante più da l'uno;   36
e quello avea la fiamma più sincera
  cui men distava la favilla pura;
  credo però che più di lei s'invera.   39
La donna mia, che mi vedeva in cura
  forte sospeso, disse: « Da quel punto
  dipende il Cielo e tutta la natura.   42
Mira quel cerchio che più gli è congiunto;
  e sappi che il suo movere è sì tosto
  per l'affocato amore ond'egli è punto ».   45
E io a lei: « Se il mondo fosse posto
  con l'ordine ch'io veggio in quelle rote,
  sazio m'avrebbe ciò che m'è proposto;   48

even thus, I well remember, did I see
   a brightness mirrored in those beauteous eyes
   whence Love had made the noose to capture me.
And as I turned and mine were touched likewise
   by what within that volume leaps to sight,
   when its rotation well we scrutinise,
I saw a Point, which radiated light
   so sharp, no eye on which the ray is thrown
   can bear its keenness, past conception bright:
and of all stars in heaven the smallest known,
   as seen from earth, beside it set, as star
   is set by star, in size would seem a moon.
Maybe as distant thence, as seemeth far
   the halo from the light whose tints attire
   the mists that form it, when these thickest are,
there whirled about the Point a ring of fire,
   more rapid than the motion which around
   the world revolveth with the swiftest gyre.
Another this enringed, the which I found
   girt by the third, that by the fourth, outside
   the fourth the fifth, which by the sixth was bound.
Followed the seventh now spread out so wide,
   that Juno's herald, if her course were run
   entire, would not contain it though she tried.
So too the eighth and ninth; and of them none
   but slower moved according as its post
   was numbered farther from the central one;
and of the clearest radiance that could boast
   which from the pure Spark stood at least remove,
   I think, because it shares its essence most.
My lady, who perceived the doubts that strove
   within me, said: 'On yonder Point depend
   the Heavens and nature, with all parts thereof.
Observe the circle which doth round it bend
   most closely, and know it burns with love, the spur
   whereby its rapid motion is maintain'd.'
'Did the world-order,' I replied, 'concur
   with that to which I see those wheels are brought,
   I should accept thy words without demur;

ma nel mondo sensibile si puote
  veder le volte tanto più divine
  quant'elle son dal centro più remote.   51
Onde, se il mio disio dee aver fine,
  in questo miro ed angelico templo
  che solo amore e luce ha per confine,   54
udir convienmi ancor come l'esemplo
  e l'esemplato non vanno d'un modo;
  chè io per me indarno a ciò contemplo».   57
« Se li tuoi diti non sono a tal nodo
  sufficienti, non è maraviglia,
  tanto, per non tentare, è fatto sodo».   60
Così la donna mia; poi disse: « Piglia
  quel ch'io ti dicerò, se vuoi saziarti;
  ed intorno da esso t'assottiglia.   63
Li cerchi corporai son ampi ed arti
  secondo il più e il men de la virtute
  che si distende per tutte lor parti.   66
Maggior bontà vuol far maggior salute:
  maggior salute maggior corpo cape,
  s'egli ha le parti ugualmante compiute.   69
Dunque costui che tutto quanto rape
  l'alto universo seco, corrisponde
  al cerchio che più ama e che più sape.   72
Per che se tu a la virtù circonde
  la tua misura, non a la parvenza
  de le sustanze che t'appaion tonde,   75
tu vederai mirabil conseguenza
  di maggio a più e di minore a meno,
  in ciascun cielo, a sua intelligenza».   78
Come rimane splendido e sereno
  l'emisperio de l'aere quando soffia
  Borea da quella guancia ond'è più leno,   81
per che si purga e risolve la roffia
  che pria turbava, sì che il ciel ne ride
  con le bellezze d'ogni sua paroffia;   84
così fec'io poi che mi provide
  la donna mia del suo risponder chiaro,
  e come stella in cielo il ver si vide.   87

but in the world of sense one can but note
  God makes the revolutions more his own,
  as from the centre they are more remote.

To show me, then, all I would fain be shown
  within this wondrous and angelic shrine
  which hath for boundaries love and light alone,

I needs must further hear why in design
  model and copy tally not: for I
  gaze, but myself no reason can divine.'

'That thy own fingers lack the skill to untie
  this knot, should cause thee no astonishment;
  so hard 'tis grown through lack of will to try!'

My lady thus; then, 'Wouldst thou rest content,'
  she added, 'lay these words of mine to heart;
  and on them whet thy subtle argument.

Ample and narrow are the spheres which dart
  material light, as more the power or less
  which permeates them all in every part.

The greater good will work more blessedness;
  more blessedness the greater bulk enclose,
  if like perfection all its parts possess.

Hence this one which sweeps with it as it goes
  the whole creation, corresponds, 'tis clear,
  unto the sphere that most loves and most knows.

Measure the virtue, then, which doth inhere
  within these rings, not their circumference—
  that which they are, not that which they appear,

and straightway will a marvellous congruence
  of more with more and less with less be seen,
  in every heaven, with its intelligence.'

As, when from out his milder cheek the keen
  North-Easter blows a blast that scours the sky,
  our air is left transparent and serene,

and heaven, because it sees the rack whereby
  'twas overcast dissolved and put to rout,
  smiles on us, decked in all its pageantry;

just so did I, when Beatrice my doubt
  had by her lucid answer quite dispelled,
  and like a star in heaven the truth shone out.

E poi che le parole sue restaro,
  non altrimenti ferro disfavilla
  che bolle, come i cerchi sfavillaro;   90
l'incendio suo seguiva ogni scintilla,
  ed eran tante, che il numero loro
  più che il doppiar de li scacchi s'immilla.   93
Io sentiva osannar di coro in coro
  al punto fisso che li tiene a l'ubi,
  e terrà sempre, nel qual sempre foro.   96
E quella che vedeva i pensier dubi
  ne la mia mente, disse: « I cerchi primi
  t'hanno mostrati Serafi e Cherubi.   99
Così veloci seguono i suoi vimi
  per somigliarsi al punto quanto ponno;
  e posson quanto a veder son sublimi.   102
Quegli altri amor che dintorno gli vonno
  si chiaman Troni del divino aspetto,
  per che il primo ternaro terminonno.   105
E dei saper che tutti hanno diletto
  quanto la sua veduta si profonda
  nel vero in che si queta ogn'intelletto.   108
Quinci si può veder come si fonda
  l'esser beato ne l'atto che vede,
  non in quel ch'ama, che poscia seconda;   111
e del vedere è misura mercede,
  che grazia partorisce e buona voglia;
  così di grado in grado si procede.   114
L'altro ternaro, che così germoglia
  in questa primavera sempiterna
  che notturno Ariete non dispoglia,   117
perpetualemente *Osanna* sverna
  con tre melode, che suonano in tree
  ordini di letizia onde s'interna.   120
In essa gerarchia son l'altre dee:
  prima Dominazioni e poi Virtudi;
  l'ordine terzo di Podestadi èe.   123
Poscia ne' due penultimi tripudi
  Principati ed Arcangeli si girano;
  l'ultimo è tutto d'angelici ludi.   126

After her words were ended, I beheld
   the spheres emitting sparks, as iron, when
   it's molten, sparkles; and no sparkle failed
to accompany its own blazing circle's train;
   in number such, that they out-thousanded
   the chequers doubled o'er and o'er again.
From choir to choir I heard hosanna sped,
   as ever thus the fixéd Point they hymn,
   which aye will stay them where they've aye been stayed.
And she who saw my understanding dim
   with doubt, said: 'The two rings that met thy view
   first, are the Seraphim and the Cherubim.
Thus swiftly their own bonds do they pursue,
   to grow as like the one Point as they may;
   and may, the higher for seeing they're raised thereto.
Those other loves that round them go their way
   (bringing thereby the first trine to a close)
   are called Thrones; for God's judgment-seat are they.
And know thou that the joy which through them flows
   is as the depth to which they penetrate
   into the truth in which all minds repose.
Hence may it be seen, the beatific state
   has its foundation in the act of sight,
   and not of love, which must on seeing wait;
and, for this seeing, merit supplies the light.
   and merit is born of grace and of goodwill:
   'tis thus that one proceeds from height to height.
The second triad, which, in like manner still,
   doth burgeon in this sempiternal spring
   whose buds no nightly Ram can spoil or kill,
is with three melodíes unwintering
   for aye 'Hosanna' warbled in the trine
   orders of joy which make their threefold ring.
The three within this hierarchy divine
   are, first, Dominions; Virtues after these,
   then Powers, which here the third in order shine.
Ranked last but one, the Principalities
   and the Archangels whirl in measured dance;
   Angels at play the whole last circle is.

Questi ordini di sù tutti s'ammirano,
  e di giù vincon sì che verso Dio
  tutti tirati sono e tutti tirano.   129

E Dionisio con tanto disio
  a contemplar questi ordini si mise,
  che li nomò e distinse com'io.   132

Ma Gregorio da lui poi si divise;
  onde sì tosto come gli occhi aperse
  in questo ciel, di sè medesmo rise.   135

E se tanto secreto ver proferse
  mortale in Terra, non voglio che ammiri,
  chè chi il vide qua sù gliel discoperse   138
con altro assai del ver di questi giri ».

CANTO 29

Quando ambedue li figli di Latona
  coperti del Montone e de la Libra
  fanno de l'orizzonte insieme zona,   3

quant'è dal punto che il zenit i libra
  infin che l'uno e l'altro da quel cinto,
  cambiando l'emispero, si dilibra,   6

tanto, col volto di riso dipinto,
  si tacque Beatrice, riguardando
  fisso nel punto che m'aveva vinto.   9

Poi cominciò: « Io dico e non domando
  quel che tu vuoi udir, perchè l'ho visto
  là 've s'appunta ogni ubi ed ogni quando. 12

Non per avere a sè di bene acquisto,
  ch'esser non può, ma perchè suo splendore
  potesse, risplendendo, dir *Subsisto*,   15

in sua eternità, di tempo fuore,
  fuor d'ogni altro comprender, come i piacque,
  s'aperse in nuovi amor l'eterno amore.   18

Nè prima quasi torpente si giacque,
  chè nè prima nè poscia procedette
  lo discorrer di Dio sopra quest'acque.   21

All, as they wheel in order, upward glance,
  and downward so prevail, that, as all find
  themselves entranced by God, so all entrance.
And Denis with such passion set his mind
  to contemplate these orders, that he styled
  them all as I do, and their ranks defined.
But Gregory was in later times beguiled
  by other views; and, when he oped his eyes
  within this heaven, at his own error smiled.
Nor marvel that a truth which hidden lies
  with God, was by a man on Earth forthtold;
  for one who saw it here did him apprise
of this and of much else these circles hold.'

CANTO 29

WHEN of Latona's twins the one is found
  beneath the Ram, the other 'neath the Scales,
  and with the horizon both at once are zoned,
long as from when the equipoise prevails
  between them which the zenith makes, until,
  their hemispheres exchanged, the balance fails,
so long, her features painted with a smile,
  full on the Point whose beams I could not bear
  gazed Beatrice; so long her voice was still.
Then she began: 'Since there I've seen it where
  all *ubi's* and all *quando's* have their tryst,
  what thou would'st learn, I ask not, but declare.
Not that his proper good might be increas'd,
  which cannot be, but that his sheen might of
  itself, in shining back, say, "I subsist",
shrined in his own eternity, above
  all time, all limits, as it pleased him, shone
  unfolded in new loves the eternal Love.
Nor before lay he, as with nothing done;
  for ere God moved upon these waters, know
  that of "befores" and "afters" there was none

731

Forma e materia, congiunte e purette,
  usciro ad esser che non avea fallo,
  come d'arco tricorde tre saette.   24
E come in vetro, in ambra od in cristallo
  raggio risplende sì, che dal venire
  a l'esser fratto non è intervallo,   27
così 'l triforme effetto del suo sire
  ne l'esser suo raggiò insieme tutto,
  sanza distinzione in esordire.   30
Concreato fu ordine e costrutto
  a le sustanze; e quelle furon cima
  del mondo in che puro atto fu produtto;   33
pura potenza tenne la parte ima;
  nel mezzo strinse potenza con atto
  tal vime che già mai non si divima.   36
Ieronimo vi scrisse lungo tratto
  di secoli degli angeli creati
  anzi che l'altro mondo fusse fatto;   39
ma questo vero è scritto in molti lati
  da li scrittor de lo Spirito Santo;
  e tu te n'avvedrai se bene agguati;   42
e anche la ragione il vede alquanto,
  che non concederebbe che i motori
  sanza sua perfezion fosser cotanto.   45
Or sai tu dove e quando questi amori
  furon creati e come; sì che spenti
  nel tuo disio già sono tre ardori.   48
Nè giugneriesi, numerando, al venti
  sì tosto, come de gli angeli parte
  turbò il suggetto dei vostri elementi.   51
L'altra rimase, e cominciò quest'arte
  che tu discerni, con tanto diletto
  che mai da circuir non si diparte.   54
Principio del cader fu il maledetto
  superbir di colui che tu vedesti
  da tutti i pesi del mondo costretto.   57
Quelli che vedi qui furon modesti
  a riconoscer sè da la bontate
  che li avea fatti a tanto intender presti;   60

Simple and mixed did form and matter go
   forth to a being which had no defect,
   like to three arrows from a three-stringed bow.
And as, if ye a beam of light project
   on crystal, glass or amber, they its fire,
   when it comes, instantaneously reflect,
so the triform creation from its sire
   into existence leapt, with no degrees
   in its beginning, but rayed forth entire.
Concreate and stablished with the substances
   was order; some were made pure act, and heaven
   as summit of the world appointed these;
pure potency the lowest place was given;
   midway was potency with act clinched fast
   by such a rivet as may ne'er be riven.
In Jerome's writings you are told of vast
   aeons thro' which the angels lived, or e'er,
   for the world else, one moment's life had pass'd;
yet do the Holy Ghost's own scribes declare
   in many a text that what I say is true;
   as thou'lt discover, if thou search with care;
and reason, in some measure, sees it too,
   which would not grant their movers could have stayed
   short of perfection all those ages through.
Now knowest thou where and when these loves were made,
   as well as how; and thus in thy desire
   already have three ardours been allay'd.
One would, in counting, not count up to higher
   than twenty, ere of the angels no small part
   convulsed what lies 'neath water, air and fire.
The others, standing firm, were prompt to start
   the work thou seëst, which they love so well,
   that thus forever round and round they dart.
'Twas by the accurséd arrogance they fell
   of him thou sawest crushed by all the weight
   of all the universe in deepest hell.
Those here thou seëst, humbly owned their state
   dependent on the Goodness which alone
   had framed them for intelligence so great;

per che le viste lor furo esaltate
  con grazia illuminante e con lor merto,
  sì c'hanno ferma e piena volontate.   63
E non voglio che dubbi, ma sie certo
  che ricever la grazia è meritorio,
  secondo che l'affetto l'è aperto.   66
Omai dintorno a questo consistorio
  puoi contemplare assai, se le parole
  mie son ricolte, sanz'altro aiutorio.   69
Ma perchè in Terra per le vostre scuole
  si legge che l'angelica natura
  è tal che intende e si ricorda e vuole,   72
ancor dirò, perchè tu veggi pura
  la verità che là giù si confonde,
  equivocando in sì fatta lettura.   75
Queste sustanze, poi che fur gioconde
  de la faccia di Dio, non volser viso
  da essa, da cui nulla si nasconde;   78
però non hanno vedere interciso
  da novo obbietto, e però non bisogna
  rimemorar per concetto diviso.   81
Sì che là giù, non dormendo, si sogna,
  credendo e non credendo dicer vero;
  ma ne l'uno è più colpa e più vergogna.   84
Voi non andate giù per un sentiero
  filosofando, tanto vi trasporta
  l'amor de l'apparenza e il suo pensiero.   87
Ed ancor questo qua sù si comporta
  con men disdegno che quando è posposta
  la divina scrittura o quando è torta.   90
Non vi si pensa quanto sangue costa
  seminarla nel mondo, e quanto piace
  chi umilmente con essa s'accosta.   93
Per apparer ciascun s'ingegna e face
  sue invenzioni; e quelle son trascorse
  dai predicanti, e il Vangelo si tace.   96
Un dice che la Luna si ritorse
  ne la passion di Cristo e s'interpose,
  per che il lume del Sol giù non si porse;   99

thus by enlightening grace and by their own
  desert their vision was uplifted so,
  that will in them is full and steadfast grown.
Nor would I have thee doubt, but surely know,
  that to receive grace is a virtuous deed,
  in measure as the heart inclines thereto.
Henceforth, if thou hast culled my words with heed,
  around this sacred college take thy fill
  of gazing; for no further help thou'lt need.
But since on Earth your schoolmen argue still
  that the angelic nature is possess'd
  of understanding, memory and will,
this will I add yet further, that thou mayst
  see in its purity a truth down there
  confused, when thus equivocally expressed.
Since first they found the face of God so fair,
  these substances have ne'er turned eyes aside
  from it, from which there's nought hid anywhere.
Therefore no object not before descried
  cuts off their vision, nor need they to recall
  by abstraction aught to present sight denied.
Thus folk down there are waking dreamers all,
  some holding true, some not, the words they say;
  though these into the viler sin do fall.
Ye men in your philosophising stray
  down by-paths many; so much do love and thought
  of vain appearance carry you away!
This, tho' it angers heaven, provokes it not
  so much as when the holy scripture stands
  neglected or its doctrines are mistaught.
What blood the sowing thereof throughout all lands
  doth cost ye care not, nor how blest is he
  who humbly strives to do as it commands.
Each aims at outward show and fain would see
  his own inventions preached; which being done,
  the Gospel is passed over silently.
One says that when Christ's passion was begun
  the Moon was backward turned and stood between,
  so that on earth no ray of Sunlight shone;

735

e mente, chè la luce si nascose
da sè: però a gl'Ispani ed a gl'Indi
come a' Giudei tale eclissi rispose.   102
Non ha Fiorenza tanti Lapi e Bindi
quante sì fatte favole per anno
in pergamo si gridan quinci e quindi;   105
sì che le pecorelle che non sanno
tornan dal pasco pasciute di vento;
e non le scusa non veder lor danno.   108
Non disse Cristo al suo primo convento:
'Andate e predicate al mondo ciance';
ma diede lor verace fondamento;   111
e quel tanto sonò ne le sue guance,
sì che a pugnar per accender la fede,
de l'Evangelo fero scudi e lance.   114
Ora si va con motti e con iscede
a predicare, e pur che ben si rida,
gonfia il cappuccio, e più non si richiede.   117
Ma tale uccel nel becchetto s'annida,
che se il vulgo il vedesse, vederebbe
la perdonanza di ch'ei si confida: 120
per cui tanta stoltezza in Terra crebbe,
che sanza prova d'alcun testimonio
ad ogni promission si correrebbe.   123
Di questo ingrassa il porco sant'Antonio,
ed altri assai che sono ancor più porci,
pagando di moneta sanza conio.   126
Ma perchè siam digressi assai, ritorci
gli occhi oramai verso la dritta strada,
sì che la via col tempo si raccorci.   129
Questa natura sì oltre s'ingrada
in numero, che mai non fu loquela
nè concetto mortal che tanto vada;   132
e se tu guardi quel che si rivela
per Daniel, vedrai che in sue migliaia
determinato numero si cela.   135
La prima luce che tutta la raia
per tanti modi in essa si recepe
quanti son gli splendori a cui s'appaia;   138

and lies, because the light withdrew its sheen
  spontaneously; hence, as in Jewry, so
  in Spain and India too the eclipse was seen.
Florence of Jims and Sandies cannot show
  such numbers as in pulpits every year
  fables like these are bandied to and fro;
so that the sheep, poor sillies, homeward fare
  from pasture fed on wind; nor merit they
  less blame, that of their loss they are unaware.
Christ to his first assembly did not say:
  "Go, preach to the world vain trifles"; but reveal'd
  the truth and bade them build on that alway.
Ay, and so loudly from their lips it peal'd,
  that of the Gospel, when they went to war
  to light the faith, they made both lance and shield.
The preacher now provides himself with store
  of quips and gibes, and so a laugh be stirr'd,
  the hood puffs out, and he demands no more;
but in its angle nestles such a bird
  that, if the vulgar saw it, they would see
  the value of the pardon thus conferr'd.
Hence comes it that on Earth such fools there be,
  that, without evidence to test it by,
  to every promise they would rush with glee.
Battens on this the pig, your Tantony,
  and others too, pigs of far baser sort,
  paying with coinage never stamped of die.
We have strayed far; the more doth it import
  us now to turn to the straight road again,
  that with the time the way be rendered short.
This nature, mounting upward plane by plane,
  in number tops a height which mortal mind
  and language by no stretch could e'er attain:
and in the thousands thereunto assign'd
  by Daniel, if with care his words be read,
  thou wilt no clear, determinate number find.
The primal light, o'er the whole nature shed,
  impregns it in as many different ways
  as there are splendours wherewithal 'tis wed.

737

onde, però che a l'atto che concepe
seque l'affetto, d'amar la dolcezza
diversamente in essa ferve e tepe.   141
Vedi l'eccelso omai e la larghezza
de l'eterno valor, poscia che tanti
speculi fatti s'ha in che si spezza   144
uno manendo in sè come davanti ».

CANTO 30

Forse seimila miglia di lontano
ci ferve l'ora sesta, e questo mondo
china già l'ombra quasi al letto piano,   3
quando il mezzo del cielo a noi profondo
comincia a farsi tal che alcuna stella
perde il parere infino a questo fondo;   6
e come vien la chiarissima ancella
del Sol più oltre, così 'l ciel si chiude
di vista in vista infino a la più bella.   9
Non altrimenti il triunfo che lude
sempre dintorno al punto che mi vinse,
parendo inchiuso da quel ch'egli inchiude,   12
a poco a poco al mio veder si stinse;
per che tornar con gli occhi a Beatrice
nulla vedere ed amor mi costrinse.   15
Se quanto infino a qui di lei si dice
fosse conchiuso tutto in una loda,
poco sarebbe a fornir questa vice.   18
La bellezza ch'io vidi si trasmoda
non pur di là da noi, ma certo io credo
che solo il suo fattor tutta la goda.   21
Da questo passo vinto mi concedo
più che già mai da punto di suo tema
suprato fosse comico o tragedo;   24
chè, come Sole in viso che più trema,
così lo rimembrar del dolce riso
la mente mia da me medesmo scema.   27

Hence, sith desire for that which draws the gaze
  follows the visual act, diversely bright,
  do love's sweet ardours in it glow and blaze.
Consider now the broadness and the height
  of the eternal Worth, which shines dispers'd
  among so many mirrors yet one light
abideth in itself as at the first.'

CANTO 30

Haply six thousand miles away is shining
  the hot sixth hour, and this world's shadow now
  is well nigh to the level plane declining,
when the mid-heaven, high over us, by slow
  degrees so suffers change, that here and there
  a star fades from our vision on earth below;
and as the Sun's brightest hand-maid draws near,
  so light by light the glittering azure loses
  its jewels, even those that loveliest were:
not otherwise the triumph which carouses
  for ever round the Point of dazzling light,
  which seems enclosed by that which it encloses,
little by little faded from my sight;
  till, seeing it no more, I turned to gaze
  on Beatrice, as well her lover might.
If all thus far related in her praise
  might now in one stupendous paean close,
  'twould serve me here but as a passing phrase.
The beauty I saw, transcending measure, goes
  not only beyond our reach, but I must deem
  only its Maker the full joy of it knows.
Here, I confess, my theme defeats me—theme,
  such as no comic bard, no tragic, e'er
  was baffled by in his sublimest dream;
for, as on feeble eyes the Sun's full glare,
  so to recall her smile's enchanting grace
  lays on my spirit more than it can bear.

Dal primo giorno ch'io vidi il suo viso
  in questa vita, infino a questa vista,
  non è il seguire al mio cantar preciso; 30
ma or convien che mio seguir desista
  più dietro a sua bellezza poetando,
  come a l'ultimo suo ciascun artista. 33
Cotal qual io la lascio a maggior bando
  che quel de la mia tuba, che deduce
  l'ardua sua materia terminando, 36
con atto e voce di spedito duce
  ricominciò: « Noi siamo usciti fuore
  dal maggior corpo al ciel ch'è pura luce: 39
luce intellettual piena d'amore,
  amor di vero ben pien di letizia,
  letizia che trascende ogni dolzore. 42
Qui vederai l'una e l'altra milizia
  di Paradiso, e l'una in quegli aspetti
  che tu vedrai a l'ultima giustizia ». 45
Come subito lampo che dissetti
  li spiriti visivi, sì che priva
  da l'atto l'occhio di più forti obbietti, 48
così mi circumfulse luce viva,
  e lasciommi fasciato di tal velo
  del suo fulgor, che nulla m'appariva. 51
« Sempre l'amor che queta questo cielo
  accoglie in sè con sì fatta salute
  per far disposta a sua fiamma il candelo ». 54
Non fur più tosto dentro a me venute
  queste parole brievi, ch'io compresi
  me sormontar di sopra a mia virtute; 57
e di novella vista mi raccesi,
  tale che nulla luce è tanto mera
  che gli occhi miei non si fosser difesi. 60
E vidi lume in forma di riviera
  fluvido di fulgore, intra due rive
  dipinte di mirabil primavera. 63
Di tal fiumana uscian faville vive,
  e d'ogni parte si mettean nei fiori,
  quasi rubin che oro circumscrive; 66

From the first day that I beheld her face
  in this life, till this vision, my song with power
  unfailing hath pursued her loveliness;
but now, as poet, I must needs give o'er
  pursuit that every artist knows is vain,
  when, having done his best, he can no more.
She—such as I bequeath her to the strain
  of loftier trump than mine, now pressing on
  anigh the goal it long hath toiled to gain—
with act and voice of guide whose task is done,
  resumed: 'We've left the largest body, and move
  now in the heaven composed of light alone:
light of the understanding, full of love;
  love of the true good, full of ecstasy;
  ecstasy sweet all other sweets above.
Here shalt thou look on either soldiery
  of Paradise, and the one host array'd
  as at the final judgment it will be.'
Like to the sudden glare by lightning made,
  which doth the visual spirits so confound
  that from the eye the clearest objects fade,
a living glory compassed me around,
  and left me swathed in such a dazzling sheet
  of its own light, that I saw nought beyond.
'The love that calms this heaven is wont to greet
  after such fashion all it welcomes here,
  thus for its flame the torch to render meet.'
Scarce had this brief assurance reached my ear,
  when I perceived myself with power endued
  surpassing that of any earthly seer;
and with such ardour was their strength renewed,
  that there exists no glory shine it never
  so brightly, which mine eyes had not withstood.
And I saw light which flowed, as flows a river,
  blazing between two banks abloom with spring
  more marvellous than poet dreamed of ever.
Out of that torrent living sparks took wing,
  and settling on the flowers that by it grew
  glittered like rubies in a golden ring.

poi, quasi inebriate da gli odori,
  riprofondavan sè nel miro gurge,
  e s'una intrava un'altra n'uscia fuori.   69
« L'alto disio che mo t'infiamma ed urge
  d'aver notizia di ciò che tu vei,
  tanto mi piace più quanto più turge.   72
Ma di quest'acqua convien che tu bei
  prima che tanta sete in te si sazii ».
  Così mi disse il Sol de gli occhi miei.   75
Anche soggiunse: « Il fiume e li topazii
  ch'entrano ed escon, e il rider de l'erbe
  son di lor vero umbriferi prefazii: 78
non che da sè sian queste cose acerbe,
  ma è difetto da la parte tua,
  che non hai viste ancor tanto superbe ».   81
Non è fantin che sì subito rua
  col volto verso il latte, se si svegli
  molto tardato da l'usanza sua,   84
come fec'io per far migliori spegli
  ancor de gli occhi, chinandomi a l'onda
  che si deriva perchè vi s'immegli.   87
E sì come di lei bevve la gronda
  de le palpebre mie, così mi parve
  di sua lunghezza divenuta tonda.   90
Poi come gente stata sotto larve
  che pare altro che prima, se si sveste
  la sembianza non sua in che disparve,   93
così mi si cambiaro in maggior feste
  li fiori e le faville, sì ch'io vidi
  ambo le corti del Ciel manifeste.   96
O isplendor di Dio, per cui io vidi
  l'alto triunfo del regno verace,
  dammi virtù a dir com'io lo vidi.   99
Lume è là sù che visibile face
  lo creatore a quella creatura
  che solo in lui vedere ha la sua pace;   102
e si distende in circular figura
  in tanto che la sua circumferenza
  sarebbe al Sol troppo larga cintura.   105

Then, as though drunken with the scents they drew,
   they re-endeeped themselves in the mystic gurge;
   and, as one entered, forth another flew.
'The intense desire that now doth burn thee and urge
   for knowledge of what here before thee lies,
   pleases me more the higher its ardours surge.
But, first, drink of this water, for thuswise
   alone canst thou thy raging thirst supply.'
   So spake to me the Day-star of mine eyes.
'The stream, the jewels that thence and thither fly,'
   she added, 'and the smiling herbage near
   are but dim proems of their reality.
Not that these things are in themselves unclear;
   rather, with vision still too weak to soar
   at these great heights, 'tis thou that failest here.'
No infant ever turned his face with more
   of a rush toward the milk, if wakened late
   from slumbering long past his wonted hour,
than I, to make mine eyes as mirrors yet
   more lucid, bent me to that river's bound,
   which pours its flood to aid us mend our state.
And as the eaves that edge mine eyelids found
   and drunk thereof, so seemed it that instead
   of being long it now was changed to round.
Then as a troop of maskers, if they shed
   the semblance not their own, are seen express'd
   in their true likeness, which before was hid,
thus changed, and in more jubilant beauty dress'd,
   the flowers and sparks appeared, so that I saw
   both the high courts of Heaven made manifest.
O splendour of God, by means of which I saw
   the truth triumphant reigning without cease,
   grant me now strength to utter how I saw!
There's light up yonder, and by means of this
   is the Creator to those creatures shown
   who only in seeing him possess their peace.
The light I speak of is diffused in one
   vast circle, of a rondure so immense,
   'twere even for the Sun too loose a zone.

Fassi di raggio tutta sua parvenza
    riflesso al sommo del Mobile Primo,
    che prende quivi vivere e potenza. 108
E come clivo in acqua di suo imo
    si specchia, quasi per vedersi adorno
    quant'è nel verde e nei fioretti opimo, 111
sì, soprastando al lume intorno intorno,
    vidi specchiarsi in più di mille soglie
    quanto di noi là sù fatto ha ritorno. 114
E se l'infimo grado in sè raccoglie
    sì grande lume, quanta è la larghezza
    di questa rosa ne l'estreme foglie! 117
La vista mia ne l'ampio e ne l'altezza
    non si smarriva, ma tutto prendeva
    il quanto e il quale di quella allegrezza. 120
Presso e lontano lì non pon nè leva,
    chè dove Dio sanza mezzo governa
    la legge natural nulla rileva. 123
Nel giallo de la rosa sempiterna,
    che si dilata, ed ingrada, e redole
    odor di lode al Sol che sempre verna, 126
qual è colui che tace e dicer vuole
    mi trasse Beatrice e disse: « Mira
    quanto è il convento de le bianche stole! 129
Vedi nostra città quanto ella gira!
    vedi li nostri scanni sì ripieni
    che poca gente più ci si disira. 132
E in quel gran seggio a che tu gli occhi tieni
    per la corona che già v'è sù posta,
    prima che tu a queste nozze ceni 135
sederà l'alma, che fia giù agosta,
    de l'alto Arrigo, che a drizzar l'Italia
    verrà, in prima ch'ella sia disposta. 138
La cieca cupidigia che v'ammalia
    simili fatti v'ha al fantolino
    che muor per fame e caccia via la balia. 141
E fia prefetto nel foro divino
    allora tal, che palese e coperto
    non anderà con lui per un cammino. 144

'Tis all one beam, that smites upon the sense
  reflected from the summit of the Sphere
  First Moved, which draws its power and motion thence.

And as a slope, rising from some calm mere,
  glasses itself therein, as though to espy
  its wealth of flowers and grass reflected there,

so mirrored in that light, and round it, I
  beheld in countless ranks above it rise
  all that of us have made return on high.

If pent within the lowest tier there lies
  so mighty a radiance, then how vast the space
  that the outmost petals of this rose comprise!

And yet my vision suffered no distress
  at breadth or height, but could in full survey
  the range and quality of that happiness.

There near and far nor adds nor takes away:
  for where, im-mediately, God is king,
  . the natural law, being void, suspends its sway.

To the yellow of the Rose which, blossoming
  for aye, spreads tieréd petals wafting praise
  unto the Sun that makes perpetual spring,

Beatrice drew me, like to one who says
  nothing, yet fain would speak, and 'Look', said she,
  'how vast a white-stoled gathering meets thy gaze!

See the vast compass of our city! See
  our stalls so crowded, that we need but few
  fresh comers to complete our company!

On that great seat, impressed upon thy view
  by the crown poised already o'er its state,
  ere at these nuptials thou art feasting too

shall rest the soul (emperor predestinate)
  of the great Harry, who, before her day
  be ripe, will come to set Italia straight.

Blind greed bewitches you, and 'neath its sway
  ye are like the peevish brat who, though half-dead
  with hunger, yet doth push the nurse away.

And o'er the sacred court will sit as head
  in those days one, that openly and by guile
  will not with him in the same pathway tread:

Ma poco poi sarà da Dio sofferto
  nel santo officio, ch'ei sarà detruso
  là dove Simon Mago è per suo merto,   147
e farà quel d'Alagna entrar più giuso ».

CANTO 31

IN forma dunque di candida rosa
  mi si mostrava la milizia santa
  che nel suo sangue Cristo fece sposa.   3
Ma l'altra che, volando, vede e canta
  la gloria di colui che la innamora
  e la bontà che la fece cotanta,   6
sì come schiera d'api che s'infiora
  una fiata ed una si ritorna
  là dove suo lavoro s'insapora,   9
nel gran fior discendeva, che s'adorna
  di tante foglie, e quindi risaliva
  là dove il su' amor sempre soggiorna.   12
Le facce tutte avean di fiamma viva,
  e l'ali d'oro, e l'altro tanto bianco
  che nulla neve a quel termine arriva.   15
Quando scendean nel fior, di banco in banco
  porgevan de la pace e de l'ardore
  ch'egli acquistavan ventilando il fianco.   18
Nè l'interporsi tra il disopra e il fiore
  di tanta plenitudine volante
  impediva la vista e lo splendore,   21
chè la luce divina è penetrante
  per l'universo secondo ch'è degno,
  sì che nulla le puote essere ostante.   24
Questo sicuro e gaudioso regno,
  frequente in gente antica ed in novella,
  viso ed amore avea tutto ad un segno.   27

whom in the holy office no long while
  will God endure, but there, where for his sin
  is Simon Magus, thrust him, and the vile
man of Alagna make sink deeper in.'

CANTO 31

Before me, then, in fashion as a rose
  of dazzling whiteness lay the soldiery
  of saints whom in his blood Christ made his spouse;
but the other—those that ever as they fly
  behold and chant his glory, who fires their love,
  his goodness which exalted them so high,
like swarm of bees that sometimes from above
  invade the flowers, and sometimes bend their flight
  to where their toil to sweetness they improve,
on the great flower, with leaves so richly dight,
  descending paused, then again upward flew
  to where their love dwells ever in their sight.
With faces all of living flame in hue,
  and wings of gold, their other portions shone
  so white, that never snow attains thereto.
From petal to petal, as they lit thereon,
  they imparted of the peace and the warm love,
  which, beating upward, they themselves had won.
And though, 'twixt flower and that which blazed above,
  the space was thick with wings in myriad flight,
  nought dimmed the splendour or the vision thereof;
because throughout the universe God's light
  so penetrates all parts in due degree,
  that nought avails to screen it from the sight.
This happy realm, from every danger free,
  and thronged with folk of times both near and far,
  looked tow'rd and loved one mark unitedly.

Oh trina luce, che in unica stella
  scintillando a lor vista sì li appaga!
  Guarda qua giuso a la nostra procella!   30
Se i barbari venendo di tal plaga
  che ciascun giorno d'Elice si copra
  rotante col suo figlio ond'ella è vaga,   33
veggendo Roma e l'ardua sua opra
  stupefaciensi, quando Laterano
  a l'altre cose umane andò di sopra;   36
io, che al divino da l'umano,
  a l'eterno dal tempo era venuto,
  e di Fiorenza in popol giusto e sano,   39
di che stupor dovea esser compiuto!
  Certo, tra esso e il gaudio mi facea
  libito non udire e starmi muto.   42
E quasi pellegrin che si ricrea
  nel tempio del suo voto, riguardando,
  e spera già ridir com'ello stea,   45
sì per la viva luce passeggiando
  menava io gli occhi per li gradi,
  mo sù, mo giù, e mo ricirculando.   48
Vedeva visi a carità suadi,
  d'altrui lume fregiati e di suo riso,
  ed atti ornati di tutte onestadi.   51
La forma general del Paradiso
  già tutta mio sguardo avea compresa,
  in nulla parte ancor fermato fiso;   54
e volgeami con voglia riaccesa
  per domandar la mia donna di cose
  di che la mente mia era sospesa.   57
Uno intendeva ed altro mi rispose:
  credea veder Beatrice, e vidi un sene
  vestito con le genti gloriose.   60
Diffuso era per gli occhi e per le gene
  di benigna letizia, in atto pio
  quale a tenero padre si conviene.   63
E « Ov'è ella? » subito diss'io.
  Ond'egli: « A terminar lo tuo disiro
  mosse Beatrice me del loco mio;   66

Oh trinal light which in a single star
   sparkling upon them, so doth pacify!
   Look down on us, storm-beaten as we are!
If strangers, hailing from 'neath such a sky
   as every day by Helicé is spann'd
   revolving with the son she would fain be nigh,
on seeing Rome, so vast, so nobly plann'd,
   were stupefied, what time the stately fane
   of Lateran dwarfed all works of human hand;
in me, to Heaven from the world of men,
   to the eternal from the temporal brought,
   from Florence to a people just and sane,
what stupefaction must the scene have wrought!
   Truly, between sheer gladness and amaze,
   my pleasure was to hear, and utter, nought.
And like a pilgrim who with joy surveys
   the temple of his vow, while in him rise
   dreams of describing it in after days,
so through the living light I let my eyes
   range freely o'er the ranks from place to place,
   now upward, downward now, now circle-wise.
I saw there many a love-persuading face,
   in borrowed light and their own smiles arrayed,
   and gestures decked with every noble grace.
By now my glance had hastily surveyed
   the general form of Paradise entire,
   and on no portion yet had firmly stayed;
and I turned round with new-inflamed desire
   to ask my lady many things that I,
   in keen suspense, was eager to enquire.
But other than I purposed came reply:
   I saw instead of Beatrice an old man,
   like all the rest, apparelled gloriously.
Kindling his glance and o'er his cheeks there ran
   a flush of joy benign, the while on me
   he gazed as only a loving father can.
And instantly my cry was 'Where is she?'
   'I from my place by Beatrice was stirr'd
   to come and end thy longing,' answered he;

e se riguardi sù nel terzo giro
  dal sommo grado, tu la rivedrai
  nel trono che suoi merti le sortiro ».   69
Sanza risponder gli occhi sù levai,
  e vidi lei che si facea corona
  riflettendo da sè gli eterni rai.   72
Da quella region che più sù tuona
  occhio mortale alcun tanto non dista,
  qualunque in mare più giù s'abbandona,   75
quanto lì da Beatrice la mia vista;
  ma nulla mi facea, chè sua effige
  non discendeva a me per mezzo mista.   78
« O donna in cui la mia speranza vige,
  e che soffristi per la mia salute
  in Inferno lasciar le tue vestige,   81
di tante cose quant'io ho vedute,
  dal tuo potere e da la tua bontate
  riconosco la grazia e la virtute.   84
Tu m'hai di servo tratto a libertate
  per tutte quelle vie, per tutti i modi
  che di ciò fare avei la potestate.   87
La tua magnificenza in me custodi,
  sì che l'anima mia, che fatta hai sana,
  piacente a te dal corpo si disnodi ».   90
Così orai; e quella, sì lontana
  come parea, sorrise e riguardommi;
  poi si tornò a l'eterna fontana.   93
E il santo sene: « A ciò che tu assommi
  perfettamente » disse « il tuo cammino,
  a che priego ed amor santo mandommi,   96
vola con gli occhi per questo giardino,
  chè veder lui t'acconcerà lo sguardo
  più al montar per lo raggio divino.   99
E la regina del cielo, ond'io ardo
  tutto d'amor, ne farà ogni grazia,
  però ch'io sono il suo fedel Bernardo ».   102
Qual è colui che forse di Croazia
  viene a veder la Veronica nostra,
  che per l'antica fame non sen sazia,   105

'if thou look upward to the circle third
    from the highest tier, once more she'll meet thy gaze
    on yonder throne, for her deserts prepared.'
He spake: I answered not by word or phrase,
    but looked on high and there beheld her crown'd,
    reflecting from herself the eternal rays.
Not from that heav'n where highest the thunders sound
    is mortal eye so distant, though within
    what sea soever it lie deepest drown'd,
as mine was from where Beatrice was seen
    yet nought it mattered, for her image blest
    came down to me unblurred by aught between.
'O lady in whom my hope is liveliest,
    and who for my salvation didst endure
    in Hell itself to leave thy footprints traced,
of all the things that I have seen 'tis sure
    that from thy power and from thy bounteousness
    alone do they their virtue and grace procure.
Thou hast led me, thou, from slavery to the place
    of freedom, making use, to serve thine aim,
    of all the ways and means thou dost possess.
Preserve in me thy great work still the same,
    that so my spirit, healed by thy dear might,
    may please thee when it quits this mortal frame.'
Thus I; and from that seeming far-off height
    she looked at me and smiled, then turning bent
    her gaze upon the eternal source of light.
And thus the holy elder: 'To the intent
    that thou complete thy course (the end, whereto
    by prayer and holy affection I was sent),
fly with thine eyes this heavenly garden through;
    since thereby to thy gaze, for mounting higher
    through the divine ray, will more power accrue.
And she, with love for whom I am all on fire,
    the queen of heaven, will grant us every grace,
    since I, her faithful Bernard, so desire.'
As is the man who, chance a Croat by race,
    come to see our Veronica, which he
    has hungered for so long, ne'er sates his gaze,

ma dice nel pensier, fin che si mostra:
  'Signor mio Gesù Cristo, Dio verace,
  or fu sì fatta la sembianza vostra?'   108
tal era io mirando la vivace
  carità di colui che in questo mondo,
  contemplando, gustò di quella pace.   111
« Figliuol di grazia, quest'esser giocondo »
  cominciò elli « non ti sarà noto
  tenendo gli occhi pur qua giù al fondo;   114
ma guarda i cerchi infino al più remoto,
  tanto che veggi seder la regina
  cui questo regno è suddito e devoto».   117
Io levai gli occhi, e come da mattina
  la parte oriental de l'orizzonte
  soverchia quella dove il Sol declina,   120
così, quasi di valle andando a monte
  con gli occhi, vidi parte ne lo stremo
  vincer di lume tutta l'altra fronte.   123
E come quivi ove s'aspetta il temo
  che mal guidò Fetonte più s'infiamma,
  e quinci e quindi il lume si fa scemo,   126
così quella pacifica orifiamma
  nel mezzo s'avvivava, e d'ogni parte
  per igual modo allentava la fiamma.   129
Ed a quel mezzo con le penne sparte
  vid'io più di mille angeli festanti,
  ciascun distinto di fulgore e d'arte.   132
Vidi ai lor giochi quivi ed ai lor canti
  ridere una bellezza, che letizia
  era ne gli occhi a tutti gli altri santi.   135
E s'io avessi in dir tanta divizia
  quanta ad immaginar, non ardirei
  lo minimo tentar di sua delizia.   138
Bernardo, come vide gli occhi miei
  nel caldo suo calor fissi ed attenti,
  li suoi con tanto affetto volse a lei,   141
che i miei di rimirar fe' più ardenti.

but while 'tis being shown says inwardly:
  'My Lord, Christ Jesus, very God, is this,
  then, what you looked like in reality?'
e'en such was I, while gazing upon his
  impassioned charity, who here below,
  by contemplation, tasted of that peace.
'Dear son of grace, if on the lowest row,'
  he then began, 'thou fixest still thy gaze,
  what heaven truly is thou'lt never know;
but rather tow'rds the highest circles raise
  thine eyes until thou seest enthroned the queen
  whom all this realm devotedly obeys.'
I raised mine eyes; and as a brighter sheen
  at daybreak gilds the horizon where the Sun
  rises than where his setting orb is seen,
so saw I, with my eyes still climbing on
  as if from vale to mountain, one far height
  by which all else that faced me was outshone.
And as, where soon will heave the pole in sight
  which Phaëthon ill guided, all the sky
  flames, but on either side becomes less bright,
so that pacific oriflamme on high
  at its mid-point burned liveliest, slackening
  its flame in all directions equally.
And, at that mid-point, angels on the wing
  saw I in thousands round it dance and play,
  each one in glory and function differing.
Smiling upon their sports and roundelay
  I saw a Beauty, the vision of whom was bliss
  to all the other saints in that array.
And ev'n did I such wealth of words possess
  as matched my imagining, I should not dare
  to attempt the least of her delightfulness.
Then Bernard, seeing my eyes attentive were
  and fixed on what emblazed him with its blaze,
  his own with such affection bent on her
that he made mine more ardent in their gaze.

CANTO 32

Affetto al suo piacer, quel contemplante
   libero officio di dottore assunse
   e cominciò queste parole sante: 3
« La piaga che Maria richiuse ed unse,
   quella ch'è tanto bella da' suoi piedi
   è colei che l'aperse e che la punse.   6
Ne l'ordine che fanno i terzi sedi
   siede Rachel da sotto di costei
   con Beatrice, sì come tu vedi.   9
Sara e Rebecca, Iudit e colei
   che fu bisava al cantor che per doglia
   del fallo disse *Miserere mei,*   12
puoi tu veder così di soglia in soglia
   giù digradar, com'io che a proprio nome
   vo per la rosa giù di foglia in foglia.   15
E dal settimo grado in giù, sì come
   infino ad esso, succedono Ebree,
   dirimendo del fior tutte le chiome;   18
perchè, secondo lo sguardo che fee
   la fede in Cristo, queste sono il muro
   a che si parton le sacre scalee.   21
Da questa parte onde il fiore è maturo
   di tutte le sue foglie, sono assisi
   quei che credettero in Cristo venturo;   24
da l'altra parte, ove sono intercisi
   di voti i semicircoli, si stanno
   quei che a Cristo venuto ebber li visi.   27
E come quinci il glorioso scanno
   de la Donna del Cielo e gli altri scanni
   di sotto lui cotanta cerna fanno,   30
così di contra quel del gran Giovanni,
   che sempre santo il diserto e il martiro
   sofferse, e poi l'Inferno da du' anni;   33
e sotto lui così cerner sortiro
   Francesco, Benedetto ed Augustino
   e altri fin qua giù di giro in giro.   36

CANTO 32

WHEN he had gazed to his heart's content, that seer
  assumed the instructor's part with ready zeal
  and spake the holy words that follow here:
'The wound which Mary's ointment was to heal,
  she there, so beautiful, at Mary's feet,
  inflicted and then stabbed it deeper still.
Beneath her, where the stalls in circle meet
  to form the third row, sitteth Rachel, placed
  with Beatrice, behold! in the next seat.
Sarah, Rebecca, Judith and the blessed
  great-grand-dame of the bard who with the cry
  Miserere mei to his sin confessed,
from rank to rank descending, even as I
  pass down the rose from leaf to leaf and name
  each one in turn, mayest thou in turn descry.
And downward from the seventh degree, the same
  as upward thence, there follows, parting all
  the locks o' the flower, dame after Hebrew dame;
for 'twixt the holy stairs from stall to stall,
  according as the faith of Christendom
  its aspect took, these form a severing wall.
On this side where the flower is in full bloom
  in all its petals, those are seated, who
  believed in Christ while he was yet to come:
on that, where the half-circles are cut through
  by empty spaces, stationed are all they
  who upon Christ, when come, had fixed their view.
And as our lady's glorious chair this way
  distinction makes, and with the other chairs
  below her serves to part the whole array,
so, that way, the great John's this office shares,
  who, ever saintly, endured the wilderness
  and martydom, then Hell for two whole years:
and 'neath him chosen the same line to trace
  were Francis, Benet and Augustine—these,
  then others, round by round, to the lowest place.

Or mira l'alto proveder divino,
  che l'uno e l'altro aspetto de la Fede
  igualmente empirà questo giardino.   39
E sappi che dal grado in giù che fiede
  a mezzo il tratto le due discrezioni,
  per nullo proprio merito si siede,   42
ma per l'altrui, con certe condizioni;
  chè tutti questi son spiriti assolti
  prima che avesser vere elezioni.   45
Ben te ne puoi accorger per li volti
  ed anche per le voci puerili,
  se tu li guardi bene e se li ascolti.   48
Or dubbi tu, e dubitando sili;
  ma io dissolverò 'l forte legame
  in che ti stringon li pensier sottili.   51
Dentro a l'ampiezza di questo reame
  casual punto non puote aver sito
  se non come tristizia o sete o fame;   54
chè per eterna legge è stabilito
  quantunque vedi, sì che giustamente
  ci si risponde da l'anello al dito.   57
E però questa festinata gente
  a vera vita, non è sine causa
  intra sè qui più e meno eccellente.   60
Lo rege per cui questo regno pausa
  in tanto amore ed in tanto diletto
  che nulla volontà è di più ausa,   63
le menti tutte, col suo lieto aspetto,
  creando, a suo piacer di grazia dota
  diversamente, e qui basti l'effetto.   66
E ciò espresso e chiaro vi si nota
  ne la Scrittura santa, in quei gemelli
  che ne la madre ebber l'ira commota.   69
Però, secondo il color dei capelli,
  di cotal grazia l'altissimo lume
  degnamente convien che s'incappelli.   72
Dunque sanza mercè di lor costume
  locati son per gradi differenti,
  sol differendo nel primiero acume.   75

Now see God's foresight, how profound it is;
    for to this garden shall apportioned be
    both kinds of faith in exact moieties.
And know that downward thence, from that degree
    which cuts midway across the two partitions,
    none sitteth through his own desert made free,
but through another's, under fixed conditions;
    for all of these are spirits assoilzied, ere
    they yet were capable of true volitions.
That they are children do their looks declare,
    an thou observe them well, as doth the sound
    their voices make, an thou but list with care.
Here doubtest thou; but tho' thy doubts have found
    no utterance, I will loose the mighty chain
    in which thy subtle thoughts now hold thee bound.
Within the ample range of this domain
    a casual point can no more easily
    find lodgment, than may hunger, thirst or pain;
for stablished by immutable decree
    is all thou seëst, in suchwise that here
    ring unto finger fits with nicety.
Therefore these hastened comers to this sphere
    of true life are not *sine causa* placed,
    some in a higher, some in a lower tier.
The king through whom this kingdom is at rest
    in love so great and in so great delight,
    that ne'er could will aspire to be more blest,
all minds creating in his own glad sight,
    with grace, at pleasure, variously endows:
    so be it, then, nor dream but God doth right.
And holy Writ expressly and clearly shows
    this truth in the twin boys we read of there,
    'twixt whom, while in their mother, strife arose.
Hence, like as this same grace colours the hair,
    its highest light, proportioned to their worth,
    forms, as is meet, the aureoles they wear.
Wanting, then, merit for their ways on earth,
    they're ranked diversely, only as differing
    in the Prime Insight's love of them ere birth.

Bastavasi nei secoli recenti
  con l'innocenza, per aver salute,
  solamente la fede dei parenti.   78
Poi che le prime etadi fur compiute,
  convenne ai maschi a le innocenti penne
  per circuncidere acquistar virtute;   81
ma poi che il tempo de la grazia venne,
  sanza battesmo perfetto di Cristo
  tale innocenza là giù si·ritenne.   84
Riguarda omai ne la faccia che a Cristo
  più si somiglia, chè la sua chiarezza
  sola ti può disporre a veder Cristo».   87
Io vidi sopra lei tanta allegrezza
  piover, portata ne le menti sante
  create a trasvolar per quell'altezza,   90
che quantunque io avea visto davante
  di tanta ammirazion non mi sospese
  nè mi mostrò di Dio tanto sembiante.   93
E quell'amor che primo lì discese,
  cantando *Ave Maria gratia plena*
  dinanzi a lei le sue ali distese.   96
Rispose a la divina cantilena
  da tutte parti la beata corte,
  sì ch'ogni vista sen fe' più serena.   99
« O santo padre che per me comporte
  l'esser qua giù lasciando il dolce loco
  nel qual tu siedi per eterna sorte,   102
qual è quell'angel che con tanto gioco
  guarda ne gli occhi la nostra regina,
  innamorato sì che par di foco?»   105
Così ricorsi ancora a la dottrina
  di colui che abbelliva di Maria
  come del Sole stella mattutina.   108
Ed egli a me: « Baldezza e leggiadria
  quant'esser puote in angelo ed in alma
  tutta è in lui, e sì volem che sia;   111
perch'egli è quelli che portò la palma
  giuso a Maria, quando il figliuol di Dio
  carcar si volle de la nostra salma.   114

Its parents' faith alone sufficed to bring
   salvation to the child, being innocent,
   in days while yet your world was in its spring.
After those early ages all were spent,
   needs must the males, their guiltless wings to plume,
   acquire the power by circumcision lent.
But after that the time of grace was come,
   lacking the perfect baptism of Christ,
   such innocence had Limbo for its doom.
Now to the face which most resembles Christ
   direct thine eyes, because its spotless light
   alone can make thee fit to look on Christ.'
I saw, rained on her, joy so exquisite,
   borne in the holy spirits framed to soar
   forever to and fro across that height,
that whatsoever I had seen before
   held me not so much wondering, nor display'd
   a semblance which to God such likeness bore.
That love which first had thither downward sped,
   singing 'Hail, Mary, thou with grace endued,'
   hovered before her with his wings outspread.
His song divine the attendant saints renewed
   from all sides, so that every face was fraught
   thereby with more serene beatitude.
'O holy father who disdainest not
   for me to quit the pleasant place, far higher,
   wherein thou sittest by eternal lot,
which is that angel, in yon jubilant choir,
   who with such glee beholds our sovereign's eyes,
   enamoured so, that he seems all on fire?'
Thus once again I turned me to the wise
   instructor who in Mary's loveliness
   glowed like the morning-star in the sunrise.
And he: 'The boldest ardour, comeliest grace,
   that e'er in angel and in spirit lay,
   is found in him; nor would we have it less,
since he it is who did the palm convey
   to Mary, when the Son of God most high
   vouchsafed to assume the burden of our clay.

759

Ma vieni omai con gli occhi sì com'io
  andrò parlando, e nota i gran patrici
  di questo impero giustissimo e pio.   117
Quei due che seggon là sù più felici
  per esser propinquissimi ad Augusta,
  son d'esta rosa quasi due radici: 120
colui che da sinistra le s'aggiusta
  è il padre per lo cui ardito gusto
  l'umana specie tanto amaro gusta;   123
dal destro vedi quel padre vetusto
  di Santa Chiesa a cui Cristo le chiavi
  raccomandò di questo fior venusto.   126
E quei che vide tutti i tempi gravi
  pria che morisse, de la bella sposa
  che s'acquistò con la lancia e coi chiavi,   129
siede lungh'esso, e lungo l'altro posa
  quel duca sotto cui visse di manna
  la gente ingrata, mobile e ritrosa.   132
Di contra a Pietro vedi seder Anna,
  tanto contenta di mirar sua figlia
  che non move occhio, per cantare Osanna.   135
E contro al maggior padre di famiglia
  siede Lucia, che mosse la tua donna
  quando chinavi, a ruinar, le ciglia.   138
Ma perchè il tempo fugge che t'assonna
  qui farem punto, come buon sartore
  che com'egli ha del panno fa la gonna;   141
e drizzeremo gli occhi al primo amore,
  sì che, guardando verso lui, penetri
  quant'è possibil per lo suo fulgore.   144
Veramente, nè tu forse t'arretri
  movendo l'ali tue, credendo oltrarti,
  orando grazia convien che s'impetri: 147
grazia da quella che puote aiutarti;
  e tu mi seguirai con l'affezione
  sì che dal dicer mio lo cor non parti».   150
E cominciò questa santa orazione.

But follow now my words with heedful eye,
   as they the exalted senators disclose
   of this most just and loyal empery.
Yon twain, the chief in bliss, as suits with those
   that sit the nearest to the Imperial Dame,
   are, as it were, two roots unto this rose.
Him to the left doth his high seat proclaim
   to be the father through whose taste, o'erbold,
   mankind still tasteth so much bitter shame.
Upon her right that ancient sire behold
   of Holy Church to whom the two-fold key
   of this fair flower by Christ was given of old.
And he who ere his death was doomed to see
   all the afflictions of the lovely bride
   won by the lance and nails upon the tree,
beside him sits, and on the other's side
   that leader under whom were fed on manna
   the ingrate, fickle nation, hard to guide.
Confronting Peter, look, is seated Anna,
   so rapt in gazing on her daughter's face,
   she turns not from it as she sings Hosanna.
And, fronting the first father of our race,
   sits Lucy, who moved the lady of thy troth,
   when thou, to ruin, wast lowering thy gaze.
But stop we here; and, as good tailor doth,
   (because the time for thine entrancement flies)
   cut we the coat according to our cloth
and to the primal Love direct our eyes,
   that, looking unto him, thou penetrate
   his beams as far as strength within thee lies.
But lest, while thinking to advance, thou yet,
   by beating thy own wings, should'st backward go,
   we needs must pray for grace, and grace may get
from her who hath the power to aid thee so;
   thyself the while in my petition share
   by paying in heart the closest heed thereto.'
And forthwith he began this holy prayer.

CANTO 33

« Vergine madre, figlia del tuo figlio,
    umile ed alta più che creatura,
    termine fisso d'eterno consiglio;   3
tu se' colei che l'umana natura
    nobilitasti sì, che il suo fattore
    non disdegnò di farsi sua fattura.   6
Nel ventre tuo si raccese l'amore
    per lo cui caldo ne l'eterna pace
    così è germinato questo fiore.   9
Qui sei a noi meridiana face
    di caritate, e giuso intra i mortali
    sei di speranza fontana vivace.   12
Donna, sei tanto grande e tanto vali,
    che qual vuol grazia ed a te non ricorre,
    sua disianza vuol volar senz'ali.   15
La tua benignità non pur soccorre
    a chi domanda, ma molte fiate
    liberamente al dimandar precorre.   18
In te misericordia, in te pietate,
    in te magnificenza, in te s'aduna
    quantunque in creatura è di bontate.   21
Or questi, che, da l'infima lacuna
    de l'universo infin qui, ha vedute
    le vite spiritali ad una ad una,   24
supplica a te, per grazia, di virtute
    tanto che possa con gli occhi levarsi
    più alto verso l'ultima salute.   27
E io, che mai per mio veder non arsi
    più ch'io fo per lo suo, tutti miei prieghi
    ti porgo, e priego che non siano scarsi,   30
perchè tu ogni nube gli disleghi
    di sua mortalità coi prieghi tuoi,
    sì che il sommo piacer li si dispieghi.   33
Ancor ti priego, regina, che puoi
    ciò che tu vuoli, che conservi sani,
    dopo tanto veder, gli affetti suoi.   36

CANTO 33

'MAIDEN and mother, daughter of thy son,
    lowly and high, o'er creatures else, display'd,
    chosen of God, ere time had yet begun,
thine's the nobility which so array'd
    man's nature that its Maker thought no shame
    to make himself of that himself had made.
Within thy womb rekindled glowed the flame
    of love that fed the germ from which this flower
    in timeless peace to such perfection came.
Noon-torch of charity to us in our
    world here, thou art a well of hope on earth,
    whence mortal men draw draughts of quickening power.
Lady, so great thou art and such thy worth,
    that whoso longs for grace nor calls on thee,
    bids the wish fly, yet wingless speeds it forth.
Thy loving heart not only grants the plea
    of every suppliant, but ofttimes, ere yet
    'tis uttered, answers prayer spontaneously.
Merciful, mighty in deed, compassionate,
    all virtues that created being can boast,
    in thee, have all in thee, together met.
Behold this man, who from the nethermost
    sink of the whole world up to this high place
    hath seen the realm of spirits, coast by coast,
and now beseeches thee that of thy grace
    strength be vouchsafed unto his eyes yet higher
    to raise him tow'rds the final blessedness.
And I, who for myself was ne'er on fire
    more than for him, to see this vision, pray
    thee instantly—oh, spurn not my desire—
by means of thy own prayers to chase away
    all clouds of his mortality, that so
    he see the perfect joy in full display.
Further I pray thee, sovereign, who canst do
    whate'er thou wilt, after a sight so fair
    keep his affections healthy through and through.

Vinca tua guardia i movimenti umani;
   vedi Beatrice con quanti beati
   per li miei preghi ti chiudon le mani!»   39
Gli occhi da Dio diletti e venerati,
   fissi ne l'orator, ne dimostraro
   quanto i devoti preghi le son grati.   42
Indi a l'eterno lume si drizzaro,
   nel qual non si dee creder che s'invii
   per creatura l'occhio tanto chiaro.   45
E io, che al fine di tutti i disii
   appropinquava, sì com'io dovea
   l'ardor del desiderio in me finii.   48
Bernardo m'accennava, e sorridea,
   perch'io guardassi suso; ma io era
   già per me stesso tal qual ei volea;   51
chè la mia vista, venendo sincera,
   e più e più intrava per lo raggio
   de l'alta luce che da sè è vera.   54
Da quinci innanzi il mio veder fu maggio
   che il parlar nostro, che a tal vista cede;
   e cede la memoria a tanto oltraggio.   57
Qual è colui che somniando vede,
   che dopo il sogno la passione impressa
   rimane, e l'altro a la mente non riede,   60
cotal son io, che quasi tutta cessa
   mia visione, ed ancor mi distilla
   nel core il dolce che nacque da essa: 63
così la neve al Sol si dissigilla;
   così al vento ne le foglie lievi
   si perdea la sentenza di Sibilla.   66
O somma luce che tanto ti levi
   dai concetti mortali, a la mia mente
   ripresta un poco di quel che parevi,   69
e fa la lingua mia tanto possente
   che una favilla sol de la tua gloria
   possa lasciare a la futura gente;   72
chè per tornare alquanto a mia memoria
   e per sonare un poco in questi versi,
   più si conceperà di tua vittoria.   75

Control his human springs with watchful care:
  behold how many saints with Beatrice
  pray thee with claspéd hands to grant my prayer!'
The eyes which God reveres and loves, at this
  gazed on the pleader, and thus proved it right
  how dear to her all true devotion is;
then were directed to the eternal light,
  into whose essence we must deem no eye
  of creature pierces with such keen insight.
And I, who to the end was drawing nigh
  of all desires, the yearning deep instilled
  within me ended, of necessity.
With nod and smiling visage Bernard willed
  that I should upward gaze; but I foreknew
  and had already his behest fulfilled;
because my vision, as it clearer grew
  still more and more kept entering through the ray
  of the high Light, which in itself is true.
Thenceforth my seeing surpassed what we can say
  by means of words, which fail at sight so fair;
  and memory to such excess gives way.
As one who sees in dream, remains aware,
  when the dream's gone, of all it made him feel,
  while all he saw is lost beyond repair;
even such am I; my vision fades, until
  it all but ceases, yet my heart is awed
  by its sweet effluence which pervades me still.
Thus melts the imprinted snow by sunshine thawed;
  thus was the wisdom of the Sibyl, writ
  on frail leaves, to the breezes cast abroad.
O Light supreme, so far above the wit
  of man exalted, let my mind again
  with some pale semblance of thy beams be lit,
and make my tongue so eloquent that when
  it chants thy glory, a future age may find
  at least one spark of it inspire the strain;
for, by returning somewhat to my mind
  and sounding faintly in these verses, thou
  wilt make men to thy victory less blind.

Io credo, per l'acume ch'io soffersi
  del vivo raggio, ch'io sarei smarrito
  se gli occhi miei da lui fossero aversi;   78
e mi ricorda ch'io fui più ardito
  per questo a sostener, tanto ch'io giunsi
  l'aspetto mio col valore infinito.   81
Oh abbondante grazia ond'io presunsi
  ficcar lo viso per la luce eterna
  tanto che la veduta vi consunsi!   84
Nel suo profondo vidi che s'interna
  legato con amore in un volume
  ciò che per l'universo si squaderna: 87
sustanze e accidenti e lor costume
  quasi conflati insieme, per tal modo
  che ciò ch'io dico è un semplice lume.   90
La forma universal di questo nodo
  credo ch'io vidi, per che più di largo
  dicendo questo mi sento ch'io godo.   93
Un punto solo m'è maggior letargo
  che venticinque secoli a l'impresa
  che fe' Nettuno ammirar l'ombra d'Argo.   96
Così la mente mia tutta sospesa
  mirava fissa, immobile ed attenta,
  e sempre di mirar faciesi accesa: 99
a quella luce cotal si diventa
  che volgersi da lei per altro aspetto
  è impossibil che mai si consenta,   102
però che il ben, ch'è del volere obbietto,
  tutto s'accoglie in lei; e fuor di quella
  è diffettivo ciò ch'è lì perfetto.   105
Omai sarà più corta mia favella,
  pur a quel ch'io ricordo, che d'infante
  che bagni ancor la lingua a la mammella.   108
Non perchè più che un semplice sembiante
  fosse nel vivo lume ch'io mirava,
  che tal è sempre qual s'era davante;   111
ma per la vista che s'avvalorava
  in me, guardando, una sola parvenza,
  mutandom'io, a me si travagliava.   114

Bewildered would mine eyes have been, I trow,
  by the keen living ray, whose utmost brunt
  they suffered, had they turned them from it now.
And I remember that on this account
  I endured more boldly, till my look grew one
  with the infinite goodness at its central fount.
Oh abundant grace, whereby thus daring grown
  I fixed my vision through the eternal light
  so far, that sight I wholly spent thereon!
Within its depths I marked how by the might
  of love the leaves, through all creation strowed,
  bound in a single volume, there unite:
substance and accidents with each its mode,
  as 'twere conflated, in such wise that what
  I'm saying gives but a glimmer of how it showed.
The universal form that ties this knot
  I think I saw, because I feel, whene'er
  I speak of it, to ampler joy upcaught.
One moment more bedims what I saw there
  than five and twenty centuries the Quest
  which made Neptune at Argo's shadow stare.
Thus bode my mind, to gazing all-addressed,
  in rapt attention and, the more it tried
  to see, of keener vision was possess'd.
In presence of that light so satisfied
  the mind is, that it never could consent
  to turn therefrom to glance at aught beside;
because the good, on which the will is bent,
  is all there; and, outside it, incomplete
  are things which, in it, find their complement.
Henceforth my tongue, in struggling to repeat
  e'en what remembrance holds, will have less power
  than hath a babe's which still sucks at the teat.
Although there was one aspect, and no more,
  within the living light which met my view—
  for that is always what it was before—
yet as my vision, since it stronger grew
  the more I gazed, kept changing, so it found
  one sole appearance take on changes too.

Ne la profonda e chiara sussistenza
de l'alto lume parvermi tre giri
di tre colori e d'una contenenza;   117
e l'un da l'altro qual iri da iri
parea riflesso, e il terzo parea foco
che quinci e quindi igualmente si spiri.   120
Oh quanto è corto il dire e come fioco
al mio concetto! e questo, a quel ch'io vidi,
è tanto che non basta a dicer *poco*.   123
O luce eterna, che sola in te sidi,
sola t'intendi, e da te intelletta
ed intendente te, ami ed arridi!   126
Quella circulazion che sì concetta
pareva in te come lume riflesso,
da gli occhi miei alquanto circumspetta,   129
dentro da sè, del suo colore stesso,
mi parve pinta de la nostra effige,
per che il mio viso in lei tutto era messo. 132
Qual è il geomètra che tutto s'affige
per misurar lo cerchio, e non ritrova,
pensando, quel principio ond'egli indige, 135
tal era io a quella vista nova:
veder voleva come si convenne
l'imago al cerchio e come vi s'indova.   138
Ma non eran da ciò le proprie penne;
se non che la mia mente fu percossa
da un fulgore in che sua voglia venne.   141
A l'alta fantasia qui mancò possa;
ma già volgeva il mio disire e il velle
sì come rota che igualmente è mossa   144
l'amor che move il Sole e l'altre stelle.

In the sublime light's deep pellucid ground
   did, visibly to me, three circles show,
   of three hues and in one dimension bound;
the first by the second as rainbow by rainbow
   reflected seemed; the third was like a flame
   which equally from either seemed to flow.
How scant is language, all too weak to frame
   my thoughts! And these are such, that, set beside
   my vision, 'faint' is word too weak for them.
O Light that aye sole in thyself dost bide,
   sole understand'st thyself, and being self-known,
   self-knowing, lov'st thyself, self-gratified!
That circle which, begotten thus, was shown
   in thee as light reflected, when I turned
   mine eyes and let them somewhile dwell thereon,
of the same hue with which it inly burned,
   seemed limned in the similitude of Man;
   which made my sight wholly therewith concerned.
As geometrician, trying as best he can
   to square the circle, but without the clue
   he needs to guide him, ends where he began;
so I, before that marvel strange and new,
   wished to discover how the image lay
   within the circle, and how joined thereto—
flight too sublime for my own wings to essay,
   had not a flash of insight countervailed,
   and struck my blindness into sudden day.
To the high fantasy here vigour failed,
   but now, as a wheel's turned that never jars,
   were my desire and will by love impelled,
the Love that moves the Sun and th'other stars.

APPENDIX

The System of Dante's Hell

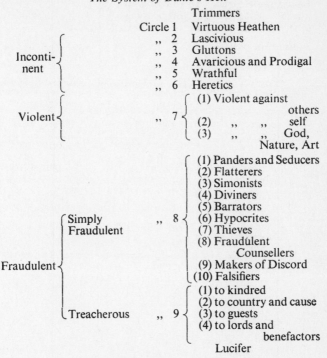

Trimmers

Circle 1   Virtuous Heathen

Incontinent
- ,, 2   Lascivious
- ,, 3   Gluttons
- ,, 4   Avaricious and Prodigal
- ,, 5   Wrathful
- ,, 6   Heretics

Violent   ,, 7
- (1) Violent against others
- (2) ,,   ,,   self
- (3) ,,   ,,   God, Nature, Art

Fraudulent

Simply Fraudulent   ,, 8
- (1) Panders and Seducers
- (2) Flatterers
- (3) Simonists
- (4) Diviners
- (5) Barrators
- (6) Hypocrites
- (7) Thieves
- (8) Fraudulent Counsellers
- (9) Makers of Discord
- (10) Falsifiers

Treacherous   ,, 9
- (1) to kindred
- (2) to country and cause
- (3) to guests
- (4) to lords and benefactors

Lucifer

The System of Dante's Purgatory

The Earthly Paradise (with Lethe and Eunoe)

The Terraces of Purgation
- Excessive Love
  - 7. The Lustful
  - 6. The Gluttonous
  - 5. The Avaricious
- Defective Love
  - 4. The Slothful
- Perverted Love
  - 3. The Wrathful
  - 2. The Envious
  - 1. The Proud

Ante-Purgatory
- 4. Negligent Rulers
- 3. The Unabsolved
- 2. The Lethargic
- 1. The Excommunicated

The sea-shore

The System of Dante's Paradise

The ten heavens

Immaterial Heaven, outside space and time } 10. The Empyrean, the heaven of Light and Love { God, Blessed Virgin, Angels and Saints

Material heavens: nine in number

Supra-planetary heavens

- controlled by Seraphim — 9. Primum mobile or crystalline heaven — { Nine orders of angels in three hierarchies
- controlled by Cherubim — 8. Stellar heaven (of fixed stars) — { Church triumphant. All redeemed souls

Planetary heavens

supra-solar

- controlled by Thrones — 7. Saturn (temperance) — Contemplative spirits or mystics
- controlled by Dominations — 6. Jupiter (justice) — Judging spirits or Rulers
- controlled by Virtues — 5. Mars (courage) — Militant spirits or Warriors

solar

- controlled by Powers — 4. Sun (prudence) — Learnéd spirits or theologians

infra-solar*

- controlled by Principalities — 3. Venus (love, outside wedlock) — Loving spirits who have erred through wantonness
- controlled by Archangels — 2. Mercury (over-active service of others) — Operative spirits who have erred through ambition
- controlled by Angels — 1. Moon (insufficient faithfulness to vows) — Votaries, or spirits who have erred through inconstancy to their vows

* The three infra-solar heavens are within the cone of shadow cast by the Earth, which accounts for the fact that the special virtue of the Saints whom Dante meets in them was in some way defective.

The Virgin Mary excepted, saints who appear in the material heavens are all disembodied. Those in the Empyrean are re-possessed of their bodies, as they will be after the Last Judgment.

772

NOTES

Alternative translations of passages where the Italian admits of more than one meaning, or where there is good manuscript authority for a variant in the text as here printed.

HELL

Canto 1, 104
> Wisdom and Love and Power; and vested in
> habits of coarse cloth shall his kind be found.

reading *feltro* for *Feltro*. The hound, by those who prefer this reading, is thought to be some reforming Pope—not, of course, Benedict XI (Boniface VIII's successor) who was dead when Dante wrote, but, like him, a friar, vowed to poverty, and alluded to here by the dress or habit of his Order.

Until recently, 'Feltro and Feltro' has been taken to refer to Feltro, a castle in the Veneto (cp. *Par.* 9, 52) and Montefeltro in Romagna, between which lay Verona, the lord of which was Can Grande della Scala (cp. *Par.* 17, 70–8), vicar-imperial after 1306 of the Emperor Henry VII, with the implication that he, or this emperor, or some emperor is the hound whom Dante here has in mind.

According to the former interpretation *sapienza*, *amore* and *virtute* are a synonym for the Trinity (cp. *Inf.* 3, 5–6); according to the latter they refer to the moral qualities of the 'hound'.

For a full discussion of this deliberately enigmatic prophecy, cp. Porena, *Commentary on the Inferno*, p. 17 ff.

Canto 1, 116
> shalt see the long-dead spirits in pain, whose quest
> is each by the second death to be destroy'd.

i.e. to be annihilated: taking *gridare* to mean that centuries of intolerable pain cause these spirits to long for their permanent second death; not a temporary one, as, presumably, is that invoked in *Inf.* 13, 118.

But in that case Dante would surely have written 'a' and not as he does 'the' second death. *Gridare* here therefore must mean 'lament with loud cries' the second death which they are suffering: 'second death' being the traditional term for spiritual, as distinct from bodily, death; i.e. the eternal loss of the vision of God (*il ben de l'intelletto,* cp. *Inf.* 3, 18, and *Revelation* 10, 14).

Canto 2, 61
> There's one who's my true friend, not casual
> admirer, on the bare hillside waylaid,

i.e. Dante was the steady friend of Beatrice, not one of those who come and go *secondo la fortuna*, i.e. as their own self-interest happens to dictate. So Casini-Barbi, in their *Commentary*

773

on the Inferno, ad loc. explain the meaning of *ventura* here, by reference to Ovid, *Trist.* 1, 5, 33–4:

> Vix duo tresve mihi de tot superestis amici;
> cetera Fortunae, non mea, turba fuit.

Rocco Montano, however (in his *Storia della poesia di Dante* I, p. 337), thinks Beatrice by *l'amico mio* means that Dante is in love with what she is essentially, 'secundum quod ipsa in se est' not 'secundum id quod accidit' (quoting St. Thomas, *Comm. in Ethicam* VIII): in which case verses 59–64 may be rendered:

> whose fame endures and shall endure unshent
> throughout the world, so long as world there be,
> the friend, not of what's mine by accident,
> but of my essence, on the bare slope waylaid,
> is so let, that by fear he is backward sent;
> and I'm afraid, from things about him said

But this seems to me an unnecessarily far-fetched interpretation. Beatrice speaks here as the Florentine girl, now sainted, who is as deeply in love with Dante as he with her (cp. line 72). There is no need to allegorize her or to suppose that she is addressing Virgil in scholastic terms. To persuade him to grant her plea she stresses her love, which at the same time and for the same reason causes her to suggest that Dante's plight is not so much his own fault as due to bad luck. He deserves Virgil's help. To clinch her appeal she is not ashamed to employ a beautiful woman's last and most powerful means of persuasion when appealing to a man: she weeps (cp. *Purg.* 30, 141). What has all this to do with theology? It is the appeal of one poet to another on behalf of a third. No wonder Virgil consents.

Canto 2, 76

> 'O lady in virtue of whom alone the race
> of man surpasses all contained within

referring *sola per cui* to *donna* not to *virtú*. The praise is extravagant, even if Beatrice here is to be taken as a symbol of theology. Nor, even in that case, is it true. Virgil is merely returning Beatrice's compliment to himself. She is here the Beatrice of the *Vita Nuova,* described there (10, 2) as 'gentilissima','destroyer of all vices and queen of the virtues', i.e. human virtues.

Canto 3, 114

> the bough restores to earth beyond recall

reading *rende* for *vede.* The former has little or no ms. authority: but Momigliano and Porena prefer it, and the latter prints it. The simile is suggested by Virgil, *Aen.* 6, 309–10.

Canto 4, 94

> Thus saw I that fair school, forgathering,
> of masters of the song that's 'loftiest' styled,
> which o'er the rest soars with an eagle's wing.

reading with medieval commentators *di quei signor* instead of *di quel signor*, i.e. Homer (not, as some think, Virgil). The latter is probably what Dante wrote, as *altissimo* (repeated here from line 80) was a technical term for the noble style *par excellence* (cp. *Inf.* 20, 113 *l'alta tragedia*): that namely of epic poetry of which Homer was traditionally the father, cp. *Purg.* 22, 102. (See Parodi, *Bull. Soc. dant.* 23, 12.)

Canto 4, 141
  Livy and moral Seneca; with these
reading *Livio* for *Lino*. The latter is probably correct, as it balances *Orfeo* in the preceding line —a musician followed by a moral philosopher, the first in each case Greek, the second Latin.

Canto 5, 34
  When they arrive before the rush of it, strong
taking *ruina* to refer to the force of the wind, not to the precipitous descent into the circle (as in *Inf.* 12, 4) due to the landslip caused by the earthquake at Christ's crucifixion.

Canto 5, 96
  while the wind here, as now it's doing, doth cease.
taking *ci* to mean *qui*, 'here' not 'us'. 'Here' would mean where the poets are standing, namely out of the wind.

Canto 5, 101
  took *him* with the fair body, from me removed
  after a fashion which still makes me moan.
referring *modo* to *tolta* not to *prese*. This is the traditional interpretation of these lines, and almost necessitated by the rhythm of line 102. On the other hand, by taking *modo* to refer to the exceptional intensity of the love which she inspired and to the irresistible violence of its grip, which was such that, in hell, 'it still hurts me', a formal and logical parallelism is established between the *il modo ancor m'offende* of line 102 and the corresponding *ancor non m'abbandona* of line 105. This is how Buti and other medieval commentators explain the passage, with, among contemporary Italian Dantists, the strong support of Sapegno (cp. his note ad loc. in his *Commentary on the Inferno*).

In my text I have so translated line 102 as to make it possible to refer 'the way' to either 'seized' or 'removed' in the previous line, according as the reader pleases. The style of the Italian is deliberately of the 'sweet new' kind. *Offende* in line 102 and *offense* in line 109 should be translated by the same verb in English.

Canto 5, 107
  to Caina is he by whom our blood was shed
reading *Caina* for *Cain*.

Canto 7, 122
>   made cheerful by the sun torpid were we
>   and did a sluggish smoke within us bear;
>   now in the black ooze torpid shall we be

The usual interpretation is that by *tristi* and *ci attristiam* Dante
is referring to sinners guilty of *accidie* (sloth), the mortal sin
expiated on the fourth cornice of Purgatory (cp. *accidioso fummo*
in line 123). But why in that case should *accidie* be punished
in the same circle of Hell as anger, the sin expiated on the third
cornice of Purgatory?

This question, however, does not arise if, with Porena, we
take *fummo* (smoke) to be a symbol of the blinding effect of
anger, as in *Purg.* 16, 5, and suppose that Dante in this circle
as in the previous one where avarice and prodigality are
punished—the two extremes between which, on Aristotelian
principles, the corresponding virtue, liberality, is the mean (cp.
Purg. 22 49–54)—to be distinguishing here between those
who are righteously angry (like himself, cp. next canto, lines
43–5, and like judge Nino, *Purg.* 8, 82–4) and those who sin
by being too quick or too slow to anger. *Accidioso fummo*
(sluggish anger) characterizes those who are torpid (*tristi*) in
the sense of reacting inadequately or not at all to evils which
should excite their righteous wrath. They are justly submerged
in the Stygian slime. The opposite extreme is illustrated,
generally, by the sinners described in lines 110–14, and in par-
ticular by Argenti in the next canto.

Canto 10, 63
>   whom, it may be, your Guido held in scorn.

referring *cui* to Virgil, not to Beatrice, and *forse* to *cui* not to
mena. But, as thus construed, *forse* is misplaced. It must by
position be referred to *mena*. And why *ebbe* not *ha*, as Guido
is still alive in the flesh (line 111, *infra*)? I take *cui* to refer to
Beatrice, whom, he hopes, but without certainty
(*forse*, cp. *Inf.* 15, 90), to reach by his journey. The translation
in my text follows this, which is Sapegno's, interpretation, which
he claims is the only one that does justice to the grammatical
structure, to the past tense *ebbe* and to the logic of the terzina
as a whole; cp. his note ad loc. For the other view—that *cui*
refers to Virgil—and the arguments in favour of it consult
Porena, *op. cit.*, p. 104 ff. Momigliano rightly criticizes the
verse as being '*certo oscuro e poco felice*'.

Canto 10, 87
>   one hears such speeches in our temple-shrine.

taking *orazion* to mean speeches delivered by the Florentine
Council, which frequently met in one of the city churches.
Or *tempio* here, as Michele Barbi thought, is purely figurative
and means any council chamber.

Canto 11, 48
     and viewing its boons in Nature scornfully:
The above translates this verse as, without any MS. authority, it
was emended by Vandelli, who in the Dantesca printed it
     e spregiando ['n] natura sua bontade;
referring *sua* to God (*la deitade*, line 46) and taking the verse,
as thus emended, to mean despising the *bontà* of God by sinning
against Nature, which proceeds from and conforms to that
bontà; the object of his emendation being to bring this verse into
agreement with *la divina bontade* of line 95 (cp. Vandelli's article
in *Stud. dant*. iv, 54–64). But by emending the MS. reading so as
to refer *sua* to God and not, as it syntactically must, to Nature
(the immediately preceding noun) Vandelli as Chimenz (cp. his
note ad loc.) pointed out, generalizes the sense by failing to
observe the exact correspondence between this verse and verse
50, where *Sodoma* specifically refers to what is here meant by
Nature, namely homosexuals (for whom traditionally Sodom
was famous) and Cahors to what is meant by *bontade*, namely
usurers (for which Cahors was in Dante's day notorious), so as
to distinguish clearly between these two kinds of sinners
against God.

     Sodomites scorn Nature; i.e. their sin is *contra naturam*,
because homosexual intercourse cannot produce fruits (chil-
dren), Nature's (ultimately God's) appointed means for ensuring
as does intercourse between male and female, the procreation
of the race of *animali ch'ella ha più cari* (*Purg*. 29, 138).

     Usurers scorn Nature's *bontade*, which consists 'in her teach-
ing human beings, maternally, their art, the offspring of her own
art (which is in turn the offspring of God's art), their art being
work, and hers to produce—as she providentially does—the
goods necessary to the exigencies of human life and thereby to
give, benignantly, to their work its fruits.' (Chimenz). This
benignity (*bontade*) usurers despise. They prefer to the fruits of
work those of money or the 'breed of barren metal' (Shakespeare,
M. of V. 1, 3, 135).

     Vandelli's emendation of line 48 has been definitely rejected
by Petrocchi in his text of the *Comedy* (which has superseded the
Dantesca) on the ground that it is needless, as also by the most
recent Italian Dantists, so far as I have been able to consult
them.

Canto 13, 15
     They croak laments, perched on the eerie trees.
omitting comma after *alberi* and making *strani* qualify this
noun, not *lamenti*. But the latter is preferable, as the strangeness
of the trees has already been described in detail (lines 4–6),
whereas this *terzina* describes the Harpies and distinguishes them
from birds of normal appearance and voice (cp. Virgil *Aen*. 3,
228, where he refers to the Harpy's voice as *dira*). What Dante

is concerned to express here is the eeriness (1) of the wood and
(2) of what he saw and heard in it. The accent on the 7th
syllable of both lines 14 and 15 should be noted, for 'li musica
con note cupe e spezzate' (Momigliano).

Canto 15, 29
> and '*You* here, Ser Brunetto?' stretching down
> my hand to his face, I said; and my heart ached.

reading *mano* for *mia*. But Dante stoops, in order to bring his
eyes nearer to Brunetto's face, so as to be more certain of his
identity.

Canto 16, 102
> where room for a thousand inmates should be made;

According to Benvenuto da Imola the reference is to the
monastery of San Benedetto dell'Alpe, which owing to its
wealth ought to have had many more monks than it actually
admitted. According to others San Benedetto is the village,
some distance from the waterfall, where a castle was planned,
but never built. But *mille* is clearly antithetical to *una* in the
previous line and must refer to the waterfall which falls sheer,
instead of in numerous broken cascades: cp. Torraca's note
ad loc.

Canto 17, 10
> Its face was a man's face, having clearly got
> skin that was outwardly smooth and soft, but its

taking *giusto*, as Porena does, to mean *uomo dabbene* with
reference to the skin, which was tender and delicate, in contrast
to the hard scaly skin of a serpent (cp. *Inf.* 25, 110–11).

Canto 17, 121
> Then the dismounting frightened me still more,

Scoscio means 'the separating of the thighs' where the legs fork.
To obtain a firm seat a rider, astride, must grip his mount
tightly with his thighs. The word here means either that Dante,
as soon as the fires below him had come into view, fears
separating, or relaxing the pressure of, his thighs on Geryon,
i.e. dismounting when he reaches the end of his descent; or,
that out of fear he already feels his thighs losing their grip
and is therefore in danger of falling off the monster's back.
He therefore tightens (*raccoscio*) his grip. Either meaning
suits the context: I prefer the latter.

Canto 18, 72
> from those eternal circlings we withdrew.

referring *cerchie*, as Buti does, to the two files of sinners going
round the *bolgia* in opposite directions. But, as the two poets
had not yet left them, *cerchie* must refer (1) to the wall of rock

(mentioned in line 3 *supra*) surrounding the whole of Malebolge and (2) to the external wall of the first *bolgia* which they quit to climb the bridge over it leading to the second *bolgia*. There is a variant reading, *esterne* instead of *eterne*; but the meaning of the verse is clear, as it is, reading *eterne*.

Canto 20, 29

> what crime exceedeth his who would subdue
> to his own foresight that of the Godhead?

As thus rendered, this passage is taken to refer to the diviners, and the *qui* of line 28 to the *bolgia* in which they are punished; their crime being that of pretending to know the future and thereby rendering passive (*passion porta a*), i.e. subduing, or trying to subdue, to their own vain pseudo-science, or forcing to agree with it, the omniscient vision of God, which alone is active and eternal and sees the future, like the past, as present.

But, as Porena points out, Dante does not yet know that these sinners are diviners; and even if he had known, it is not true that in foretelling the future a human being is *ipso facto* committing the sin of forcing, i.e. subduing to his own foresight, destinies decreed by God (e.g. inspired prophets and saints see them in God; cp. *Par.* 17, 37–45). In any case that is not the crime for which these sinners are being punished; they are among the fraudulent, who try to deceive their neighbours and do not believe their own predictions.

It is better therefore to take the *qui* of line 28 as referring to Hell in general, and to regard Virgil here as rebuking Dante, his brother poet for showing lack of imaginative insight in pitying any souls in Hell, i.e. the damned as a whole (cp. C. E. Norton's footnote ad loc. in his prose translation of the *Comedy*).

Canto 20, 82

> Passing from there, the unwedded virgin then

or 'the cruel virgin' or 'the maid averse from men' or (according to Benvenuto) 'the wild virago' (cp. Statius, *Theb.* 4, 463 ff., who calls Manto 'innuba' and implies she was cruel). Or *cruda* might mean 'wild' like the country here described, or even 'vigorous' (as in Virgil, *Aen.* 6, 304) with reference to her physical energy (line 55).

Canto 21, 46

> The wretch plunged, and, convolved, bobbed up again;

taking *convolto* to mean 'in a praying posture', head down, back arched, and on his knees, and thus connecting it with line 48. But the word normally meant, in Dante's time, 'entirely covered'—here by the tar (contrasted in line 49 with the Serchio) which showed only so much of the barrator as can be seen in a swimmer, namely his head and shoulders.

Canto 22, 123
>   leapt and thus freed himself from their intent.

taking *proposto* to mean *intenzione*, not *capo*, as in line 94.

Canto 24, 69
>   but he that spoke was angry, or it seemed so.

reading *ira* (lectió facilior), instead of *ire* as read by Pietro di
Dante, who must have been familiar with his father's hand-
writing (which we are told was singularly clear and beautiful,
though none of it survives) and who says that the speaker
'videbatur motus non dicas ad iram, ut multi textus dicunt
falso, sed dicas ad ire id est ad iter'. The speaker was presum-
ably fleeing from a serpent; his voice died away as he ran, and
this rendered his words unintelligible. So Michele Barbi;
Casini and Porena prefer *ira*, Vandelli *ire*.

Canto 26, 127
>   Night was now seeing all the stars that light

taking not Ulysses but Night, personified, to be the subject of
vedea, thus following the medieval commentator Daniello da
Lucca (the first to do this) on the ground that it was more
poetical, quoting as a parallel Petrarch's *sestina* beginning
>   Non ha tanti animali il mar fra l'onde
>   ne lassù sopra 'l cerchio della luna
>   vide mai tante stelle alcuna notte;

itself perhaps recalling Lucan, *Phars.* 1, 526
>   Ignota obscurae viderunt sidera noctes.

But it seems better to suppose, as Scartazzini did, that *la notte*
is here used adverbially (*di notte*) and not to personify it. For
Ulysses in his narrative does not always say *noi* (including his
crew with himself) but speaks in the first person singular in
line 134. 'Besides, the personification of night is not only
required by the sense but would also impoverish—and that not
a little—the poetical content of the passage, if it was the in-
different night, personified, which was seeing the stars (and,
without other indication, sees those of the one pole as much as
it does those of the other) and not the hero.' (Chimenz).

Canto 30, 124
>   The coiner then: 'Thus gapes thy mouth to shoot
>   deceptive words forth, as it's wont to do;

reading *per dir mal* instead of *per tuo mal*. 'Deceptive' in the
sense that Sinon always tells lies and has just told another by
implying that he suffers less and must therefore be less guilty
than Master Adam. But *per tuo mal* 'to thy own detriment or
disadvantage' better explains *chè* in line 126.

Canto 32, 88

    'Now who art thou, whose foot, as thou dost stride
    through Antenora, so kicks others' cheeks
    that, were I alive, 'twere too much?' he replied.
    'Alive am I, and if thou'rt one that seeks
taking *fossi* in line 90 to be first not second person, *troppo fora*
implying that the injury is so outrageous that, if the speaker
were alive on earth, he would retaliate in kind.

Canto 33, 135

    of the shade warbling here behind my own.
The meaning of *verna* here is uncertain. It is usually taken to
be 'passes the winter' (*verno* for *inverno* as in *Purg.* 24, 64).
But it can also, when spelt *sverna* or *sberna* as in *Par.* 28, 118
(where the Dantesca, followed by Petrocchi, prints *sberna* and
the earlier texts *sverna*) mean 'sing as the birds do in spring'
(from medieval Latin *vernare*, formed from Latin *ver*, spring).
Later, in Provençal poetry it came to mean 'sing', simply, with
no reference to bird-song.

Porena's note on *Par.* 28, 118 distinguishes between the
various meanings of the word thus: '*svernare* is, properly, the
singing of the birds in spring (Lat. *vernare*), a verb etymologically
very different from that from which the *sverni* of *Par.* 27, 142
derives. The latter comes from Latin *ex-hibernare* (pass out of
winter), the former from Latin *ex-vernare*, in which the *ex-* is
not negative but intensive.'

Torraca plausibly suggested that *verna* in this verse (*Inf.* 33,
135) means not 'is wintering' but 'is warbling' (as the birds do
in spring) with ironic reference to the souls of the traitors,
described in *Inf.* 32, 36, 'mettendo i denti in nota di cicogna'.
As thus understood, the word here, as Chimenz observed, 'has
the further advantage that the pronoun *mi*, besides being super-
fluous with the other interpretation ('passes the winter') acquires
relevance and a humouristic sense—proprio a me, in questo
luogo, con tanto mio fastidio'.

Canto 34, 79

    his head where first he had his feet and then
or,   his head where first he'd had his feet and then
taking *egli* (as does Benvenuto, who glosses the verse 'vertit
caput ubi primo habebat pedes') to refer to Virgil, the subject
of *volse*, and the verse to mean that having reached (with Dante
on his back) the centre of gravity and of the universe, mentioned
in the previous *terzina*, he (while still in the northern hemisphere)
si capovolse, turned upside down, topsy turvy. With the notable
exception of Moore, all English Dantists and till recently Italian
ones, have understood the verse in this way.

But two higher authorities than Benvenuto, namely Graziolo de' Bambaglioli, the Chancellor of Bologna, in his Latin commentary on the *Inferno*, as also the author of the so-called *Ottimo Commento*, in his Italian (Tuscan) commentary on the *Comedy*, both of them contemporaries of the poet, take *egli* to refer to Lucifer; the former glossing the verse 'Virgilius volvit faciem versus anchas et tibias Luciferi', and the latter 'Virgilio . . . il viso verso l'anche e le gambe di Lucifero (rivolse).' And they must be right for several convincing reasons: (1) *egli*, if it referred to Virgil, would be pleonastic, as he is the subject of both verbs. (2) *ove*, here, as in *Inf.* 2, 84 and elsewhere, means not 'where' but 'to (or towards) where'. (3) *zanca* means neither 'foot' nor the whole 'leg' but 'tibia' the shin-bone or shank, as defined in *Inf.* 19, 23–4 and *ib.* 45 (q.v.) and nowhere else in the poem. (4) This word as Moore incidentally observes (*Studies* II, p. 229) 'is given in the best dictionaries as a colloquial Florentinism', and he compares its use here 'with other contemptuous expressions applied to Lucifer.' It is therefore inconceivable that Dante would have applied it to Virgil. (5) For the same reason it is impossible that he should be asking us to believe that he would have involved Virgil (for whom to run rather than to walk was an action unworthy of his dignity, cp. *Purg.* 3, 11) in the necessity of turning upside down, the grotesque and insulting position reserved exclusively for the simoniac popes and (as seen from the southern hemisphere) Lucifer himself, the first and supreme of sinners; even if in the confined space (*foro*) in which (while still in the northern hemisphere) he found himself, Virgil could have performed this acrobatic feat without throwing Dante (*personaggio*) off his back. Syntactically therefore this verse should be compared to *Inf.* 25, 34, where *egli* (*ei*) is inserted to differentiate the subject of the first verb (in both verses, Virgil) from that of the second, which in that verse is as unquestionably Cacus as it is in this verse Lucifer.

The Italian, thus interpreted, requires us to imagine that Virgil descends Lucifer's huge body (feet first and upright) like a man descending a ladder clamped to a slightly curving perpendicular wall, till he reaches with his feet the centre of gravity; a point actually inside Lucifer's body, but here for Dante's poetic purpose to be taken as on its surface at the level of his navel. At that point, without moving his feet from it, he treats them as the centre of a semicircle of which his body, kept straight, is the radius and his head traces the circumference, as he turns himself round sideways along Lucifer's body. During this action, started on the Earth's North to South diameter, he would have been upright all the time, and would have reached the East to West diameter, on a level with the Earth's equatorial plane, after passing through 90°, where the ice of the Judecca ended, and the rock of the southern hemisphere began. After passing through another 90°, he comes to a halt, being back again on the Earth's North to South diameter, on the same spot at which he started, but now outside Hell in the southern hemisphere. He is directly headed towards Lucifer's shanks (themselves upside down), and he then begins to climb the thigh towards them, and finally detaches first Dante, then himself, from Lucifer's body at the point where the shanks emerge from the *foro* into the free air—'in the little sphere forming the other face of the Judecca.'

In composing his poem 'Dante est un maître dans l'art des correspondances'. (R. Dragonetti, *Dante pélerin de la sainte Face*, p. 25, Ghent, 1968, a massive volume entirely devoted to explaining and illustrating this observation, though he works the idea too hard). The American Dantist, T. G. Bergin (p. 92 of his valuable handbook entitled *Approach to Dante*, London, 1965) is referring to the same 'art' which he called Dante's 'technique of association', when a word is used 'not so much as straw (as it were) in the mystic brick as a kind of conceptual cement to link concepts or to suggest emotional or doctrinal parallels.' Let the reader who takes *zanche* here to refer to Virgil's not Lucifer's shine compare *Inf.* 34, 85–90 with *Inf.* 19, 42–7 and he will see that the two passages exemplify, conspicuously, a correspondence or parallel of this kind; the former being deliberately intended by the poet to recall the latter to our memory—and both should be so translated verbally into English as, with equal conspicuousness, to do the same.

It may be added that there is no part of the *Comedy* where (if we insist on noticing it) its author more noticeably compels what he must have known were the real physical facts to comply with the requirements of his creative imagination than he does in the *paesaggio* of Caina, as he depicts it. But Dante, though aware of the discrepancies between his fiction and scientific fact, expects us to ignore them and helps us to do so by such vivid details in his description of the centre of the Earth that they create the illusion *del vero*. His only serious error here (as Blanc long ago pointed out *Versuch*, p. 304) is due to his ignorance—which he shared with his contemporaries—that at the Earth's centre the force of gravity, far from being at its greatest is nil; so that in fact Virgil could have performed the whole operation, above described, of passing from the north to south terrestrial hemisphere without the smallest *fatica* or *angoscia*. But, even if he had known this, his story, or the moral of it, would have compelled him to ignore the fact; for the point concerned, a crucial one, marks the final moment of Dante's, the pilgrim's, religious conversion and emphasizes its extreme difficulty.

PURGATORY

Canto 1, 115
> The morning breeze had now begun to flee

taking *ora* to mean *aura*, not the 'matin' or last canonical 'hour' of the night (which was also recited at daybreak).

Canto 5, 39
> or clouds in August, as the Sun doth set,

reading with the MSS, *sol calando*. Porena substitutes *solcando* on meteorological grounds—that thunderstorms in Italy during August, the month when they are prevalent, occur late in the afternoon but never, so he says, at sunset. It is certainly difficult to understand why Dante in this line specifies the time of day. His reason for doing so in the previous line is that, though meteors occur all through the night, people after going to bed do not see them.

Canto 6, 111
> and Santafior—how safe it is—then scan!

reading *com' è sicura* (ironically, meaning *ben poco sicura*), and taking the verse to mean that the Emperor is being requested to come to the rescue of the great Ghibelline family of the Aldo-brandeschi, counts of Santafiora (cp. *Purg.* 11, 59 and 67) who are being oppressed by the Guelfs of Siena (*oscura*, here meaning 'afflicted' is preferred by Vandelli and by Petrocchi to *sicura* as being the *lectio difficilior*).

The translation in my text interprets the verse in exactly the opposite sense on the assumption that *come si cura* (literally, 'how it is paying regard to itself') is the correct way of reading *com' è sicura*: so that the verse means 'and thou wilt see how Santafiora is, in their own selfish interest, being misgoverned by the Aldobrandeschi in the absence from Italy of the Emperor, their feudal lord; and his presence is required to exert pressure (*pressura*) on them, so as to remedy the *magagne* (*colpe*, blows, wrongs) which they are inflicting on their wretched subjects, a state of affairs which only the Emperor could rectify by sub-jecting, or threatening, to subject the culprits to his ban'.

Dante is in this and the preceding *terzina* condemning both Guelfs and Ghibellines equally for their internecine family feuds which were destroying Italy. But, with reference to verse 106 it is worth noting that, though the Montecchi were, in fact, a family, 'the leaders at Verona of the faction which may be called Ghibel-line, their Guelfic opponents are always dubbed *Pars Comitum*, party, that is, of the famous Counts of Bonifacio—not a family at all, but one of the two opposed factions in, not Verona, but Cremona, of which the Church party (Guelfs) were called Capellini or Capelletti ("the long-haired") and the Imperialists Barbarasi ("the shavers"). Such nicknames were usual [cp. our Cavaliers and Roundheads]. At Parma, for instance, Ghibellines were called Malafucini ("jerry-built").' (Edward Armstrong, *Italian Studies*, pp. 166–74.) Dante, of course, must have known that the Capulets were not a family, but a nickname for the Guelfs of Cremona; but he would think it no more necessary to say so to the educated public, to which alone his poem was addressed, than we ourselves should to inform a similar public in this country that Whigs and Tories were not family names but nicknames of the two principal political parties at a certain period of English history.

Canto 7, 96
> wounded to have by another her life renewd.

reading *altro* with the Dantesca, instead of *altri*, to avoid its repetition in the next verse, and taking it to refer to the Emperor Henry VII and his invasion of Italy in the summer of 1310 to assert his authority over that country and to receive the imperial crown at Rome. Owing to the opposition of the Guelf League, headed by Florence, and to the Emperor's sudden death in August 1313 at Buonconvento near Siena, the expedition was a complete failure.

But *altro* or *altri*—either, as thus understood—is in flat contradiction to *Purg.* 33, 37–51 (q.v.), where Dante makes Beatrice refer to the same enterprise prophetically (post eventum) with absolute confidence of its complete success. Either, therefore, the poet, in the interval between writing these two passages, must have changed his mind, in which case he would surely have altered the earlier to make it compatible with the later; or *altri* here cannot possibly refer to Henry VII. What Sordello is saying is that Italy, in 1300, as a result of her wounds and the neglect of the then Emperor, Rudolf, to heal them, has died, and that it is consequently too late for anyone to heal her. *Morte* is emphasized by the rhyme and should receive the same emphasis in translation. *Ricrea* is an instance (of which there are many in the poem, e.g. *Inf.* 6, 99, and *Inf.* 16, 54) of the present given the value of the future tense. The reference, as Porena and Sapegno in their commentaries both note is quite indeterminate and, to quote the latter, 'is born of a state of mind of absolute despair and analogous to that which inspires the apostrophe to Italy in the previous canto (lines 76 ff.)'.

Rossi would reconcile this verse with *Purg.* 33, 37–51, by paraphrasing it, 'tal che *solo più tardi* potra risorgere per opra d' altri' (i.e. Henry VII) in which case the whole *terzina* might be translated:

is Rudolf, who was emperor, and could
　　have saved Italia's life, with which she'll be,
　　sole later, by another re-endued.

i.e. by Henry VII. But, though *tardi* could mean 'slowly' (cp. *Inf.*
26, 106) or 'late in the day' and possibly (though I doubt it) 'later',
the context shows, to my mind conclusively, that it must here be
used in the sense of *troppo tardi* not *più tardi*. The *solo* is
bitterly reproachful, implying that but for Rudolf's neglect of
his duty, Italy might have had her health restored much earlier
and enjoyed it much longer (cp. a similar reflection with refer-
ence to Eve *Purg*. 29, 28–30) and, incidentally, Dante could have
returned to Florence from exile.

Canto 9, 4
　　with gems that glittered was her brow array'd,

referring *fronte* to Aurora (to be understood as the lunar, not
the solar, Aurora) and *gemma* to the constellation of the Fishes,
which would at the hour indicated be visible in the East a little
before moonrise.

Dante, however, makes it perfectly clear in the following lines
that the constellation he refers to is the Scorpion, which just
before sunrise is on the western horizon, i.e. on the opposite
side of the sky to Aurora, so that it could not possibly be
described as being on her brow.

The translation in my text therefore follows Porena's interpre-
tation of the line concerned, the meaning of which is made clear
if to *fronte* be given the same sense here as it has in *Par*. 31, 123—
'the sky or region of the heaven opposite to, or facing Aurora'.

It should be added that in the first six lines Dante is describing
the time just before sunrise in Italy. The Aurora is therefore
the solar Aurora, and *concubina* in line 1 means what it does
literally, i.e. bedfellow or wife of Tithonus, not his concubine
(the supposed lunar Aurora) of whom mythology knows nothing.
Not till line 7 does Dante turn to describing what the hour is in
Purgatory; cp. for the same method of stating the time *Purg*.
2, 1–9, by reference to what it was at that moment in both
hemispheres.

Canto 9, 141
　　in tones which through the sweet sound ebbed and flow'd.

reading *al dolce suono*, instead of *a dolce suono* (with Porena).
If *al* be read, the sound must be referred to the gate, as Michele
Barbi argues it does. But how can *dolce* be reconciled with the
rugghiò and *acra* of line 136? What Dante heard was voices
singing the *Te Deum*, after the noise made by the gate had
ceased. For *attento* cp. *Purg*. 17, 79 f.

Canto 10, 30

> where its precipitous face was less upright,

reading *che dritto di*, instead of *che, dritta, di* and understanding
Dante to mean that the cliff, for a short distance upward from
the pathway, was not perpendicular but on a slope; and that it
was on this sloping portion of the cliff-face that the bas-reliefs
had been carved. Otherwise the sinners, bowed knee to chest
under their heavy burden, could not have seen them, just as
they could not see Dante's face, until he stooped to their level.
Porena reads *dritto* (=*drittezza*) and so understands it.

The medieval commentators preferred to read *dritta* and to
interpret the line as meaning that the mountain-side from this
point onward (i.e. inside Purgatory) was no longer climbable,
except by a stairway, as it was too precipitous; and most modern
commentators have followed them.

Canto 10, 120

> how each is self-smitt'n thou canst now descry.

This is the usual meaning attached to this line. It has, however,
been objected to on the ground that, in the position described
in lines 130 ff., these people could not have smitten themselves,
unless, as Benvenuto suggests, what is meant is that it was with
their knees, not with their hands, that they beat their breasts!
It is better therefore to take *si picchia* here as a passive not
reflexive verb.

Canto 10, 126

> which, rid of screens, to justice flies straight on?

taking (with C. S. Singleton, *Dante Studies*, 2, chap. iv) *giustizia*
here to mean 'right order in the soul and right order before
God', the goal (cp. St. Thomas, S.T. I–II, qu. 113, a, 1) which,
in the soul's 'movement towards justice' i.e. 'justification', it
reaches initially, not when it quits the body, but when, after
completion of its purgatorial discipline, all the sins (of which
pride is the root) that have till then screened it from God and
God from it (cp. *Purg.* 2, 123) have been totally expunged
(*senza schermi*), and it becomes qualified to be described not
merely as *farfalla* (disembodied soul) but as *angelica farfalla*,
i.e. *degna di salire al ciel* (*Purg.* 1, 6). To this point Dante, in
the poem, attains when he passes from Virgil's guidance to that
of Beatrice, with whom he ascends to the final Justice at the
end of the *Paradiso*, when for an instant he becomes *deiforme*,
i.e. fully formed and completely justified.

The usual interpretation of this verse takes *giustizia* to be the
equivalent of *giudizio*, the judgment, or judgment-seat of God.
The soul, when at death it quits the body, is *senza schermi*,
without defence, stripped of its trappings (compared to the

gaudy silk spun by the silkworm to form its protective cocoon). Confronted with the divine Judge, it cannot hope to derive any advantage from the showy things—honours, wealth, power, glory, etc. (*schermi*)—which were the source of its pride on earth, but like the angels (*angelica*), bad or good, is damned, or destined to ultimate salvation, according to its actual value, moral and spiritual, in the eyes of God.

Canto 14, 31

for from its starting-point (where teemeth so

taking *pregno* to mean 'rich in, teeming with, waters'. But as the Apennine near Falterona is not particularly *pregno d'acqua*, *pregno* probably means *gonfio* here, to indicate that the mountains, at the part referred to, owing to the lie of the land seem to rise higher than they do on the Casentino side.

Canto 15, 7

And the impact of his beams we now half-faced;

Dante begins the canto by stating quite definitely that in Purgatory (*qui*) it was now 3 p.m., at which hour the sun would be high over the horizon to the N.W., and its beams would therefore be striking his face sideways and not, as he states in this verse, from straight in front of him (*per mezzo il naso*. Cp. *Purg*. 24, 148–9), which could only be the case if he and Virgil were walking, as he says they were (line 9) *già dritti inver lo caso*. The verse, as translated above, gets over this difficulty if *per mezzo il naso* be taken to mean 'half-faced' in the sense of approximately westward.

Canto 15, 73

(1) And souls there, knowing each other, the more they be, taking *s'intendere* to mean 'know or understand one another reciprocally'. '*S'intende*, id est, intelligunt se invicem' is Benvenuto's comment; on the principle stated in *Par*. 28, 109–11— the view of Aquinas (as opposed to that of Duns Scotus who holds that loving precedes and is a higher act than knowing).

(2) And folk up there the closer packed they be, i.e. the more numerous: taking *s'intendere*, as Porena does, to have the same meaning here as in *Purg*. 5, 117, in the sense of *addensare*.

(3) And the more folk up there who enkindled be, reading *s'accende* instead of *s'intende* and linking this line with line 68 *supra* (cp. Blanc, *Versuch*, who notes ad loc. 'Die Leseart *s'incende*, welche Perazzini gefunden und die er durch *incenditur a Deo* erklärt, würde ich allen anderen bei weitem vorziehen, wenn sie auf besseren Autoritäten ruhte'. B. Nardi is of the same opinion).

The rendering in my text takes *s'intendere* (*in*) to be a proven-
çalism meaning *amare*, and *là sù* its grammatical object, *in*
being omitted because implied in the adverb of place.

Canto 19, 84
> discerned by his voice their speaker who was hid;

i.e. because of his position, which was face downwards. This
is Benvenuto's interpretation of this verse and defended by
Michele Barbi, *altro* in that case referring to Pope Adrian V,
and not to the request for information, indirectly expressed,
which Dante detects in the Pope's first words (line 79).

Canto 20, 119–20
> according as the affection spurs us on
> now at greater, now at less, speed to go.

reading, with Vandelli and Petrocchi (followed by most recent
editors) *ad ir* for the MS. *a dir*, on the ground that if the latter
reading is accepted, 'the second part of the terzina would be
only a repetition of what has been said in the first' (Petrocchi).
They attribute, therefore, a metaphorical sense to the whole ex-
pression *ire a maggiore e a minor passo* as thus read, and take it
to mean 'un incedere (ire) nel canto quicker or slower, as in a
singing competition, now in a louder now in a lower voice, as to
each individual his feeling (*affezione*) dictates.' (Giacalone.)

But I prefer to follow Moore in retaining the traditional
reading, *a dir*, as do Porena and Sapegno. 'The operative word
here,' says the latter, 'is *sprona*, emphasized by being in rhyme.
It is better therefore to take *a maggiore e minor passo* as an
adverbial expression strictly united to *sprona* so as to form a
stable nexus with the verb.' Porena paraphrases the terzina: 'The
individual souls recite the examples in a more or less loud voice
according to the more or less warm feeling (*affezione, sentimento*)
with which they accompany the exemplification. The verse 120
has seemed obscure to the interpreters through their not under-
standing that it does not refer to *dire* but to *sprona*. *Spronare a
maggior passo* was a fixed locution for the simple *spronare*, so
that verses 119–20 are the equivalent of "more or less forcibly
spurs us to speak", not of "spurs us to speak more or less loudly
(or quickly)".'

Canto 21, 11
> as we eyed the throng that 'neath us prostrate lay;

referring *guardando* to Virgil and Dante and not to Statius.

Canto 22, 40

> 'O sacred hunger after gold, ah! why
> control'st thou not the greed of mortal men?'

reading *perchè* for *per che*, the meaning being that the 'hunger' is not sinful but virtuous (*sacra*) if it observes, in the Aristotelian sense, the mean between two extremes; namely the avaricious man's excessive and the prodigal's inadequate estimate of the value of gold, entailing the misuse they respectively make of it.

It is extremely unlikely, however, that Dante in a verbal quotation here of Virgil, *Aen*. 3, 57, could have so egregiously blundered as to translate the Latin *sacra* by 'sacred' when it means 'accursed'; nor is there any need to suppose that he did so, if one reads (with Moore) *per che* and understands *reggi* (which Dante substitutes for Virgil's *cogis*) to express Statius's realization—which he owes to Virgil—that the accursed hunger after gold could rule human hearts not only by means of (*per*) avarice, but also of its opposite, the passion for spending.

Canto 25, 41

> virtue informative, like to that flood

This verse is usually thus translated, but wrongly. 'The meaning of *come quello* is not "like that". *Come quello* is a regular Italian idiom signifying "being such that" or "being itself the thing that". It corresponds exactly to the Latin *utpote qui*: cp. *Inf.* 12, 53, where we find this idiom. The *Gran Dizionario* says that *come quello* lays stress upon the thing already spoken of, and quotes this and the above-mentioned passage in illustration' (Warren Vernon: *Readings on the Purg.* 2, p. 338 f.).

Quello here is the semen (*sangue perfetto*, as distinguished from, not compared to, the blood which circulates through and nourishes the male parent's body). The semen, informed by the generative principle (*virtute informativa*) which belongs to the male parent's blood only (the female's being wholly passive) falls, in sexual intercourse, onto the matrix after being redistilled in the male generative organ (testicles) and there mingles with and coagulates the female's blood, thus forming the human embryo. The latter, after four months, during which it acquires first a vegetable then, besides this, an animal soul, develops into the *foetus* which it becomes as soon as the brain has been fully shaped in the womb. At that point God, acting from the outside, informs it with the rational soul (the possible intellect) which survives bodily death, as do all God's immediate creations (cp. *Par.* 7, 67–72). *Feto* (line 68) should not be translated 'embryo' from which Dante distinguishes it. Averroes, for the reason here stated by Dante (lines 64–66), generalized the possible intellect and held that the individual animal soul was informed therewith only while it lived. On death therefore the rational soul ceased, as an individual, to exist—the animal soul having perished with the body; a doctrine which Dante, here following Aquinas, was of course, as a Christian, bound to refute.

Canto 27, 16
> Hands clasped, I stretched them upward, at the same

taking *le man commesse* (commas omitted) to be the object of *protesi*; or,

> I clasped my hands, lent forward over them
>   eyeing the fire, and pictured vividly

reading *in su le man*, with *su* as a preposition.

But it better accords with Dante's attitude as here described, and the state of mind it denotes, to take *in su* as an adverb, *le man commesse* as a separate clause, and the verb *mi protesi* as a reflexive; and so to imagine the poet in the posture in which he is represented in the illustration to this canto by Botticelli, of all the illustrators of the Divine Comedy the most accurate and faithful to the text.

Canto 27, 80
>   and on his staff the shepherd, keen of eye,
>   leans, and so leaning, guards that peaceful spot.

reading *poggiato* for *di posa* (in the sense of *fa dono ad esse del riposo*).

Canto 30, 73
>   'Look hither well! I am verily Beatrice!

reading *guardaci* and *ben son, ben son*, and taking *ci* to mean *qui* (as do Casella and Vandelli), which some commentators take to be its meaning in *Inf.* 5, 96, where however it could also mean 'us' as it can here. I agree with Momigliano in thinking that in this context *ci* in the sense of *qui* gives a prosaic tone to the verse. If taken to mean 'us', it would account for the variant *sem* (plurale majestatis) instead of *son* in some manuscripts and adopted by Moore in the Oxford text. In that case the line may be translated:

>   'Look at us well! We are, We are Beatrice!

Canto 30, 93
>   chime with the notes of the eternal spheres;

understanding by *giri* the nine heavens and by *note* the sound produced by their revolution, the so-called music of the spheres (cp. *Par.* 1, 78). I prefer to follow Porena, who thinks that by *giri* in this context Dante means, not the spheres, but the Intelligences who move them (cp. *Par.* 2, 129) and whose song (*note*) the angels that have descended with Beatrice echo (*notan dietro*).

Canto 32, 51

> that which was of it to it he left tied.

taking *quel di lei* to mean *fatto di lei*, with reference to the legend that the wood of Christ's cross was made out of a branch of the Tree of the knowledge of good and evil, the *temo* (pole of the car) here symbolizing the cross. But as the pole later (line 144) produced three of the seven heads, symbolizing the capital sins, which sprouted from the car, it cannot possibly be intended to symbolize the cross. The words *di lei a lei* simply mean that the Griffin tied the car to the tree by means of one of the tree's own branches.

PARADISE

Canto 1, 50

> and upward re-ascend like falcon fain
> to soar back thither whence he had swooped down,

taking *pellegrin* to mean 'peregrine falcon', as argued by Chimenz (*Giorn. stor. d. lett. ital.* CXXXIII, 180–85), the image being similar to that in *Inf.* 22, 130–2. But the falcon there has missed his prey, and would not soar back, if, as here, he had struck it. And Dante never elsewhere uses *pellegrino* alone to denote the bird, but always refers to it as *falco pellegrino*. Benvenuto, Buti, Vellutello, Lombardi, Landino and all later commentators except Sapegno, explain *tornar* as *tornar a casa* or *alla patria*, and even Sapegno admits that this is the obvious meaning.

Canto 2, 104

> so wide a surface, yet thou there wilt see
> how it must needs with equal splendour glow.
> Now even as that which is potentially
> snow doth, when warm beams strike it, naked lie
> of its late colour and frigidity,
> so thee, left naked in thy mind will I

taking *soggetto* in its scholastic sense 'subjectum' (substance) to mean water, or potentially snow, which when stripped by the sun of its 'accidentals' (whiteness and coldness) thaws, and reverts to water. In the passage as thus understood, the snow symbolizes Dante's intellect, and the whiteness and coldness of the snow the false opinion, and its effect, with which it has hitherto been informed. Beatrice, having stripped Dante's mind of this false opinion, thereby rendering it again 'passible', will now inform it with the truth. Among medieval commentators Benvenuto thus explains the relevance of the simile and he may be right (but see Porena's note ad loc.).

Buti, on the other hand, more simply, takes *soggetto* in its literal sense to signify, in general, anything which 'lies under', and is thereby concealed or obscured by, something else; here, the earth (or 'mountain' as he calls it) which is covered by snow. The earth symbolizes Dante's intellect, the snow the false opinion with which it has been burdened; and the warm beams of the sun (which stands for God) symbolize Beatrice, as the means of divine enlightenment, who will inform his mind, now freed from error, with the truth so clearly that it will shine before him like a star.

Canto 3, 52

> Our feelings, only inflamed and finding rest
> in the Holy Spirit's will, rejoice to be
> formed, and disposed, according to his behest.

This terzina, the meaning of which is highly compressed, can be interpreted differently according to the sense given to *piacere* and *ordine*.

As translated above, *piacere* has been taken to mean *volontà* (cp. lines 85 and 102 *infra*) and *ordine* to mean *comando*: the objection to which is that the spirits in the Moon were not placed there by the will or at the bidding of the Holy Spirit. What Piccarda says that he does is to regulate the degree of their bliss, of which he is the sole source, since their love derives from him as the Third Person of the Trinity (*il primo Amore, Inf.* 3, 6). Why they are in the moon is explained in the following terzina.

As translated in my text *piacere* is taken to mean *godimento* (enjoyment, happiness) and *ordine* to mean 'order' (or 'form') in the sense of (1) the order of the universe which is *deiforme* (cp. *Par.* 1, 103–5), (2) the position of the moon (cp. line 51 *supra*) which is the slowest, hence the lowest, of the spheres, and therefore the farthest from God, and (3) the grade or intensity of bliss enjoyed by the spirits in the moon, which is less than that enjoyed by those in the higher spheres for the reason given in the next canto (lines 37–9): they are the least illumined by God and therefore the least happy.

It should be noted, however, that all the souls whom Dante meets in the nine heavens through which he passes, have their permanent dwelling in the Empyrean where all are equally happy, since each one is happy up to its full capacity. They descend to the various heavens in which he meets them only in order to welcome Dante and instruct him (His story demands this invention, otherwise he would have found the nine heavens empty, and would have had no story to tell). But he sometimes forgets this or ignores it, and speaks as if the particular heaven to which they have temporarily descended—and which is determined in each case by the influence exerted by that heaven on the soul concerned, during its lifetime on earth (in the present case that of the inconstant moon on Piccarda)—was their permanent dwelling place in the hereafter. This is an instance of Dante's theology having to yield to the requirements of his creative imagination, as it did, for example, in the case of the 'trimmer' angels (*Inf.* 3, 37–42) of whom theology knows nothing, and whom Beatrice omits to mention in *Par.* 29, 49–57, because Dante the poet and Dante the theologian are there in accord, and for the former the 'trimmer' angels have consequently ceased to exist, since his story or 'argument' at this point no longer requires their existence (as it did in the former passage), and would, indeed, have been embarrassed by it; for Beatrice's angelology here is strictly Thomistic. Similarly with regard to all souls in Paradise, he forgets here what St. John tells him, *Par.* 25, 127–8; for, with the two exceptions there mentioned, the Empyrean contains, and will contain none of the beatified until after the resurrection of the body. The poem teems with such inconsistencies, and does so inevitably, since 'all religious eschatology is a mass of contradictions' (W. R. Inge: *The Philosophy of Plotinus*, II, 7: Longmans, London, 1923). But when reading the poem and under its spell, we do not notice them: so they do not matter, poetically.

Canto 9, 108

for which the world above sways that below.

taking *torna* to mean 'wheels and governs' and not to be a Tuscan form of *tornia*, 'shapes' (with a lathe, a metaphor from carpentry). *Il mondo di sù* is a synonym for the angelic Intelligences which control the heavens. The meaning of this terzina has been much disputed, as indicated by a variety of readings: *con tanto affetto, al mondo, il modo, al modo.*

Canto 11, 72

she climbed, with Christ, upon the very rood.

reading *salse* for *pianse*. All the best manuscripts read *pianse*, almost all ancient commentators *salse*. But *pianse* (*pati*) accords better with the preposition *con*. Christ did not mount the cross; He was nailed there before it was raised. And Poverty wished to suffer with Christ by sharing His nakedness on the cross. If *salse* be preferred, the line is perhaps better translated:

to be with Christ Himself she climbed the rood.

Canto 12, 115–7

His family, at first right well inclined
to follow where he trod, so much hath wheeled,
that those in front are cast on those behind.

The precise meaning of line 117 has been much disputed. The above translation takes *quel* to refer to the individual members of the saint's *famiglia*. But I agree with Porena in thinking 'che i due *quel* del v. 117 si riferiscono a termine espresso, cioè ai piedi del v. 116.' If *quel* referred to the *frati* 'come si giustifi-

cherebbe il *gitta*?' The translation in my text follows the first
of the two explanations given by M. Barbi (*Problemi* I, 287);
'Instead of thrusting the hinder foot in the direction of the foot
in front as is done by a person going straight ahead, they thrust
the foot in front (swing it round) towards the one behind (i.e. go
backward)'. It would be the same image as the *retrosi passi* of
Purg. 10, 123.

Canto 13, 18

> me counterwise to the other, as round they sped;

i.e. the two concentric circles of saints were revolving *prima* and
poi (counterwise), 'an algebraic expression to indicate two con-
traries, as one says "black and white", "high and low" and the
like' (Porena's note ad loc.). But surely what Dante means is
that the two circles were revolving similarly, but in such a
manner that the saints on the one kept the same position relative
to the saints on the other, which he explains by saying that those
on the outer circle (St. Bonaventura's) necessarily revolved at a
greater speed than those on the inner (St. Thomas's)—as the
Seraphim (symbolizing Love) move faster than the Cherubim
(symbolizing Knowledge), i.e. St. Francis than St. Dominic.
Cp. *Par.* 11, 37–9.

Canto 13, 79

> Yet if the primal Power's clear Vision stand,
> by the warm Love disposed and sealed, thereon,

reading *de la prima Virtù* instead of, with Porena, *e la prima
Virtù* (i.e. the three persons of the Trinity, as in *Inf.* 3, 5–6, but
in the reverse order) which he thinks is clearer, as in fact it is,
than the other reading.

Canto 15, 26

> (if we may trust our greatest poet) when he
> perceived his son in the Elysian glade.
> 'O blood of mine, O grace abundantly
> shed down on thee by God, to whom was e'er
> Heav'n's portal opened twice, as unto thee?'
> The light thus; so I gave it all my care,
> then turned, my lady's face to scrutinise,
> and I was struck with awe both here and there.

It has been much disputed in what language Cacciaguida speaks
to Dante in this and the following cantos. It is obvious (lines
28–30) that he begins by speaking in Latin, and then in terms
which Dante for the reason given in line 39 does not understand.
After this his first intelligible words (lines 47–8) are reported in
thirteenth-century Italian, the *volgare* of Dante's own day,
which he continues to speak to the end of the canto. He then,

we are specifically told in 16, 33, ceases to speak *con questa moderna favella*, though what he says is still reported in this *favella*, and, according to most modern commentators (following the *Ottimo Commento*), changes to archaic Italian, such as was spoken during his own life-time—that is, the language of the troubadours. Others think that he reverted to Latin. Finally, for his last discourse, we are told (17, 34) that he speaks *per chiare parole e con preciso Latin*, where *preciso Latin* must mean Latin, not (as frequently elsewhere) Italian, or it would be a mere repetition of *per chiare parole*. As it is highly unlikely that Dante intends us to understand, for no reason given, that Cacciaguida spoke in three different languages (Latin, modern and archaic Italian) I agree with Porena in thinking that he spoke Latin throughout; though except for the first three verses what he says is, for convenience' sake, reported in Italian, as that, not Latin, is the language in which Dante is writing the *Comedy*. The use of Latin in this context is suggested by the simile immediately preceding it, in which Cacciaguida's reception of his great-great grandson in Paradise is compared to that given by Anchises to his son Aeneas in Elysium (*Aen.* 6, 684 ff.) and, like the quotation in *Purg.* 30, 21, springs from Dante's constant desire to do honour to Virgil. In my text I have therefore, for the same reason as Dante does, left this terzina untranslated.

If in 16, 33 old-fashioned Italian is meant, then *Latin* in 17, 34 must be translated 'language'.

Canto 15, 101
> no gaily-slippered dames, no girdle in hue

reading *donne* for *gonne*. According to Benvenuto and Buti *contigiate* means *calze solate col cuoio stampato intorno al piè*. Most manuscripts read *donne*, but *gonne* fits the context better, and *contigiate* more probably means *ricamate* 'embroidered'.

Canto 16, 96
> the ship will founder and its crew be drown'd,

taking *barca* to refer to the commune of Florence and the total ruin that would befall it (cp. *Purg.* 24, 81) owing to the deadly feud between the Blacks and Whites, headed respectively by the Donati and Cerchi families. But the allusion is more probably to the latter only, who inhabited houses, which had formerly belonged to the Ravignani, near the Porta San Piero (cp. Villani, *Cron.* viii, 39) and were expelled from Florence, Dante with them, in 1302, when Charles of Valois and the Donati had gained control of the city, largely owing to the feeble resistance offered to them by the Cerchi—their *felonia* as Dante calls it; and possibly he calls it *nova* because the Cerchi were not of noble blood, as were the party of the Blacks, but were wealthy upstarts (cp. *Inf.* 16, 73) of low origin, hence called 'rustic' (*selvaggia*, *Inf.* 6, 65) as they came from a small village Acone (cp. line 65 of this canto) in the neighbourhood of Florence. *Barca* is a ship's boat. Had Florence itself been meant here, *nave*, the ship itself, would probably have been the word used.

Canto 18, 123

that temple built with blood and martyrs' throes.

reading *sangue* for *segni* (i.e. miracles, called 'signs' in the Fourth Gospel). But *martiri* would be merely a repetition of *sangue*, so *segni* is preferable.

Canto 20, 76

Such seemed the image, stamp of His signet—His,
    the eternal Pleasure's, at whose will whate'er

The meaning of this terzina and its precise relation to the preceding simile has been much disputed.

As translated above, *tal* refers to line 74; as the lark first sang and then was silent, so the eagle first discoursed and then brought its discourse to an end. The whole phrase *l'imago de l'imprenta de l'eterno piacere* is a designation of the eagle and means 'the image (which was in the shape) of the imprint (justice) imposed upon it (i.e. the spirits composing it whether in reference to their speech or to their silence) by the Eternal Pleasure (i.e. God) in accordance with whose desire (*desio*), or will, all things fulfil their ends'. A few commentators refer *ella* (line 78) not to *cosa* but to *imprenta*, in which case the line should be rendered:

at whose will whate'er
    exists becomes such as the imprint is.

namely, just or righteous.

According to another interpretation of the terzina, which I prefer, *tal* refers to line 75; not, that is, to the lark's song as a whole and to its subsequent silence, but to the last sweetness (*ultima dolcezza*) of its song which satiated it with delight. Only *l'imago* designates the eagle. *De l'imprenta de l'eterno piacere* depends grammatically on *contenta* (line 74) understood in *tal* (=*cosi contenta*), and what Dante is saying is that, as the lark ceased singing because satiated with the sweetness of the last section of its song, so the eagle ceased discoursing because satiated with the exceeding sweetness of the last section of its discourse (lines 67–72), that, namely, referring to Rhipeus. This culminating delight or bliss was the hall-mark on it of the 'eternal joy' (a title of God, cp. *Par.* 18, 16: *il piacere eterno . . . mi contentava*; and *De Vulg. Eloquentia* I, 4, 4: cum . . . ipse Deus totus sit gaudium).

As thus interpreted, this terzina reflects Dante's own joy (and unfeigned surprise, cp. lines 82–4) at receiving this answer to his hitherto persistent doubt—as stated in *Par.* 19, 67–78— concerning the reality of divine justice, with reference to the eternal damnation of good pagans. Not only does God will, but He joys in willing, that an 'anima naturaliter Christiana' like Rhipeus, should (unlike Trajan) before his death actually become (*diventare*) a Christian: such as (*quale*, line 78), though living centuries B.C. (not A.D. like Trajan), and, unlike Trajan, never baptized, yet in virtue of his superlative righteousness (justissimus unus et servantissimus aequi, Virgil, *Aen.* 2, 426–7), he deserved to be counted: and, as Dante now for himself sees, unquestionably by God's grace (lines 121–3 and 29, 64–6) *was* counted, a fact proved by his pre-eminent position here in the heaven of just men made perfect (cp. *Matt.* 25. 31–40).

Canto 20, 80
>   glass to the colour clothing it, to eschew

reading *che 'l veste* instead of *ch' el veste*. But the latter reading, meaning 'which (object of verb) it (*vetro*) clothes (*veste*)' must be right. For Dante, as the context shows, is referring to colour not on but behind white glass and showing through it.

Those who prefer to read *che 'l veste* (glass which the colour clothes) take him to be referring to a stained glass window. But in Dante's day stained glass in windows was pot-metal glass, coloured all through; i.e. the colour was *in* the glass not behind it. Nor can he be referring to ruby glass, which was red glass 'flashed' on white glass by dipping the white in the red at the appropriate temperature, so as to make the red form a thin film on the white—pot-metal red being hardly at all translucent. The metaphor *veste* shows that Dante was not referring to window-glass, but to a white-glass vessel, containing a coloured liquid, such as red or yellow wine, which the glass (cp. French *verre*) covers, as his clothes do a man, and (unlike clothes, being transparent) reveals what it covers.

Canto 23, 131–2
>   stored in those richest coffers which, for sowing,
>   were acres, here below, of fertile plain.

According to all the medieval commentators *bobolce* in line 132 meant 'husbandmen', lit. 'tillers of the soil' (fem. of *bubolco*, from the Latin 'bubulcus' one who ploughs with oxen), and it is thus that I have translated it in my text. But according to Parodi (*Bull. soc. dant.* iii, 144) following Muratori and Tassoni, *bobolce* in this context means an area of fertile ground, as it still does today in north Italian dialects, and as the *ubertà* attributed to it shows that it does here; and it is thus that I have translated it above.

Sapegno very pertinently observes that 'whichever of the two interpretations be preferred (and to choose is not easy) the fact remains that the two metaphors of the *arche* (where the seed is stored) and of the *bobolce* ("sowers" or "land for sowing") are superimposed in the Dantean text with little logical coherence'.

The whole terzina, as is noted by all commentators, has a biblical flavour (cp. the parable of the sower, *Matt.* 13, 3–23 and *Gal.* 6, 8).

Canto 24, 46

> As, while the master states the quodlibet,
>   the bachelor in silence arms his mind
>   not to decide the point but argue it,
> so did I arm myself with every kind
>   of reason, while she spake, for such a querist
>   and such profession ready proofs to find.
> 'Speak: prove thyself a Christian in the clearest
>   terms; what is faith?' Wherefore I raised my brow
>   to who said this, the light there which was fairest;

i.e. to St. Peter (cp. line 19 above).

The simile in the first of these terzine has been differently interpreted according as to whether (1) *fin che* in line 47 be taken to mean 'until' (*fino al momento al cui*) or 'while' (*mentre*): (2) line 48 be referred to *s'arma* or to *propone*, i.e. to the bachelor or to the master; (3) *maestro* be held to correspond, in the other term of comparison, to St. Peter or to Beatrice.

The translation in my text (following P. Rajna in M. Barbi's *Studi danteschi* 2, 78–82. and Barbi himself) takes *fin che* to mean 'until', line 48 to refer to *propone*, i.e. to *maestro* and *maestro* to St. Peter.

The alternative version, printed above (following Porena) takes *fin che* to mean 'while' (with reference to the previous four terzine), line 48 to refer to *s'arma*, and *maestro* to Beatrice.

For the explanation of the academic ceremony or examination, with which the simile deals, of the terms 'questio disputata' (in the arts' faculty) and 'quodlibet' (in the theological school) in the university of Paris in Dante's day, cp. the comprehensive note ad loc. in Casini-Barbi's edition of the *Paradiso*, and Rashdall's *Medieval Universities* (edited by Powicke and Emden) I, pp. 492–4.

Canto 25, 32

> thou knowest that thou as oft its symbol art,
>   as dearer were the three in Jesus' sight.

reading *carezza* for *chiarezza*. The occasions referred to are the raising of Jairus's daughter, the Transfiguration (cp. *Purg.* 32, 73–81) and the Agony in Gethsemane.

Canto 26, 17

> Is Alpha and O of aught, set down with pen
>   taught me by Love, be 't easy or hard to acquire.'

reading *Alfa ed O* instead of *Alfa ed Omega*, and construing

Amore as subject, not object of *legge*, which in any case means 'teaches' here, not 'reads'.

Alfa ed Omega was both written and read aloud *Alfa ed O* by contemporaries of Dante, and some manuscripts have it thus written here.

For the meaning of *o lievemente o forte* cp. Benvenuto's comment ad loc.: 'quasi dicat: omnis lectura facilis vel difficilis', though others take the phrase to mean 'in lower tones or higher'.

Canto 26, 97–9

> Sometimes under its saddlecloth a high-
> spirited war-horse, prancing to make plain
> its ardour, moves what it is covered by;

It has been much disputed what *animale* (Dante's word for any living creature other than plants) he is here referring to. L. Venturi, in his *Le similitudini danteschi*, p. 251 called the simile 'unhappy and not clearly expressed' presumably because the animal is not specified and the exact meaning of *broglia* is doubtful. The animal has been variously supposed to be a kitten, a lamb or a sucking-pig in a sack, a falcon under its hood or a silkworm in its cocoon (cp. *Par.* 8, 52–4). But in any case it is a comparison which by many commentators has been deemed *poco riverente*, when the other term of it is Adam, the paragon of mankind, the mere sight of whom concealed under the dazzling light which completely envelops him, fills Dante the pilgrim with awe when told by Beatrice who he is.

To meet this objection Torraca suggested that the animal intended may well have been a *nobile cavallo*, a war-horse caparisoned for battle; a suggestion elaborated in detail by A. Pézard, the learned French Dantist and medievalist (1953) and warmly supported by G. Giacalone in his commentary on the *Paradiso*, p. 446 (1969), who observes that 'the most interesting contribution of the French critic consists in the fact that the figure of Adam is very greatly ennobled by being compared to a war-horse, caparisoned for battle under its saddle-cloth of glittering chain-mail, rather than to a generic animal in a sack'. I have thus paraphrased, rather than translated it, above. But as A. J. Butler noted (*Par.* 17, 129) in his commentary (pub. 1885) on that *cantica*: 'This is perhaps the most remarkable instance of a characteristic feature of the *Paradiso*; namely the introduction of vulgar and even coarse ("comic") images in the midst of the most elevated ("tragic") passages. Cp. *Par.* 12, 114; 13, 139 and 32, 140, where St. Bernard, in the very highest Heaven, talks of "cutting the coat according to the cloth". It is as if the writer's mind, overwrought by the fervour of his own imagination, sought a certain relief in these trivialities. Hamlet's "Let the galled jade wince" conveys the same idea in a somewhat more dignified image.' It may be added that, if the animal here is a war-horse, the simile is far from exact. For Adam was totally invisible under the light which enveloped him, whereas a horse under its saddle-cloth is still recognizably a horse.

Canto 27, 100
Its parts, the nearest and the loftiest,
reading *vicinissime* instead of the manuscript variants *vicissime* (a non-existent word) and *vivissime* (M. Barbi would like to read *imissime*). But the point here is that no part of the Primum Mobile has a visible body within it, as the lower heavens have; so Dante cannot know at which part of it he entered, whereas all its parts are *vivissime*, which is probably therefore the correct reading.

Canto 27, 136
Thus does the skin turn black, from being white,
at first sight of the fair enchantress, her
whose father brings the day and leaves the night.
The enchantress is Circe, her father the Sun (Solis filia; cp. Virgil, *Aen.* 7, 11 and Milton, *Comus* 50), a 'maga' (or *sirena* cp. *Purg.* 19, 19) at first sight of whose allurements man, as soon as born, becomes corrupted by covetousness and from being rational (*bianco*) becomes a beast (*nera*: cp. *Par.* 22, 93). This is M. Barbi's interpretation, and the one now most generally accepted, of what is perhaps the obscurest terzina in the whole poem (cp. his *Problemi*, etc. I, 2, 92).
Or, with different punctuation and giving a different sense to *così* and *aspetto*, it may be translated:
So quickly does the skin, from being white
at first, grow darkened of the fair daughter
of him who brings the day and leaves the night.
As thus rendered *così* introduces a simile—not, as Barbi thinks, 'an affirmation in figurative language'—and means 'just as', i.e. as quickly as, a baby's skin, which, at first white, is darkened or becomes bronzed the moment it is taken out of doors and exposed to sunlight. The simile merely illustrates how soon, and then how rapidly, a human being's moral degeneration begins and develops. (Cp. Porena's note ad loc.)
Others, notably Parodi, identify *la bella figlia* with Aurora, daughter of Hyperion (the Sun), the sky being the skin of the dawn (cp. *Purg.* 2, 7): and others with Humanity or Mankind of whom the Sun is called father in *Par.* 22, 116.
The translation of the terzina embodied in my text renders the interpretation of it suggested by the distinguished Canadian Dantist, the late Prof. J. E. Shaw of Toronto University, in the article entitled 'And the evening and the morning were one day' (the Vulgate version of Genesis I, 5, not that of the A.V.,

which has 'first day') which he contributed to *Modern Philology*, Vol. XVIII, No. 11, pp. 113–34, March 1921. His argument is too long and closely reasoned to be adequately summarized here, except to note that he connects the meaning of the terzina with St. Augustine's doctrine (*De Civ. Dei*, Lib. XI, capp. vii-ix, xix; cp. also Aquinas S.T. I qu. LXIII, art vi) of (1) the creation of the angels—'Let there be light'; (2) their evening and morning knowledge, i.e. the knowledge of themselves and the knowledge of God respectively, with which, in that order, the Light of the Divine Wisdom (Second Person of the Trinity—'spirans amorem': Aquinas S.T. qu. XLIII, art. V) endowed them at the creation; and (3) the fall of Lucifer and Man. *Lascia sera* (line 138) does not mean 'leaves the evening when he departs', but 'does not take away the evening knowledge', i.e. leaves it still there when he brings the morning knowledge. He adds the latter to the former. Lucifer's fall was due to the fact that, having been granted evening knowledge (knowledge of himself) he did not wait to look for and receive morning knowledge (knowledge of God his creator) as well; cp. *Par.* 19, 46–8. For, had he done so, he would not have lost the former, but retained both. Refusing to accept grace (cp. *Par.* 29, 64–6) he was left with his evening knowledge only, which, unsupported by morning knowledge, instantly became corrupt and darkened into night (*nero*) and corrupted not only him, but also in due time his 'body', mankind.

According to Shaw, therefore, *quei che* etc. is God the Divine Wisdom; *la bella figlia*, the Light of that Wisdom; *il primo aspetto*, the angels; who are at once the first 'appearance' in creation in time of the splendour of that Light, and the first 'view' of it; i.e. both what they are and what they have, with special reference to Lucifer, created the greatest of them (cp. *Purg.* 12, 25); *si fa* (present not past tense) *la pelle bianca nera* refers to the perversion, once and for all (cp. *Par.* 27, 26) of his own knowledge and, consequently, shortly afterward, the *continuous* perversion of the knowledge of the universal body of the wicked, both fallen angels and mankind, of which he is the head. Lucifer fell a few seconds, Adam at the beginning of the seventh hour after being created. (Cp. *Par.* 29, 47–51, and ib. 26, 139–42.)

Shaw anticipated that 'it will be said that this interpretation is not simple. All I can say in reply is that the meaning of this passage no doubt seemed simpler to the author than it does to us; that this interpretation is based not on a few stray sentences by obscure authors, but on whole bodies of doctrine in the writings of Augustine and Gregory, authorities for neglecting whom Dante blames the churchmen of his day (*Epist.* 8, 7), and Aquinas, who is the poet's chief authority; that if the solution had been simple to a modern eye, it would long ago have been stated and universally accepted.'

Its chief merit, in my own opinion, is that, far more than any other of the interpretations that have been suggested, it suits the context and picks up all the main points made by Dante in this canto and the preceding and following canto. In any case I have thought it well worth rescuing from being buried in the pages of a learned periodical.

Canto 28, 91

> To each spark did its circle's blaze pertain;

i.e. each spark (individual angel, a complete species in itself) was as intensely bright as the circle which emitted it, the circles themselves being distinguished from one another by differing degrees of brightness.

Canto 29, 26

> on crystal, glass or amber, all takes fire
> at once, nor stage therein may ye detect,

reading, with Vandelli, *esser tutto*, for which Porena substitutes *esser fratto* (in the sense of 'reflected'), as translated in my text. He denies that it is possible, formally, to force the words *esser tutto* to mean *invadere tutto il corpo*. (See the note in his commentary ad loc.)

Canto 29, 51

> disturbed what is your nourishment's supplier.

reading *alimenti* for *elementi* and taking the former to mean as in modern Italian 'foods' and not, as was common in the *vulgata antica* merely an alternative way of spelling (or pronouncing) *elementi*. If it here means 'foods', by *suggetto* is meant the earth, i.e. the material source of (or 'that which is *sottoposto*', placed under) the means (food) by which you support your life.

If *alimenti* here stands for *elementi*, *suggetto* means either (1) earth, the lowest of the four elements (earth, water, air, fire in that order upwards) or (2) more accurately 'pure matter' which became differentiated into these elements after the fall of the angels (which coincided with the creation of Hell. Cp. *Inf.* 34, 121-6). Pure matter, i.e. potential being, was created instantaneously and simultaneously with the heavens and with the angels (cp. lines 28–36 supra) and is, like them eternal, meaning perennial; for only God is eternal. Before these, nothing was created (*Inf.* 3, 7–8). The element earth was created subsequently and is in fact like the other three elements that were created w n it corruptible (cp. *Par.* 7, 124–38). But the reader, uninterested in these subtleties, can take this verse to be only a way of saying either 'convulsed the earth', the lowest of the four elements; or alternatively, 'convulsed the earth' which is the producer or supplier of what beasts and men require to keep themselves alive, namely food.

The Dantesca prints *alimenti*; so does Petrocchi, but he regards it only as a contemporary way of spelling *elementi*.

Canto 29, 100
and others, that the light withdrew its sheen

reading *ed altri, che* instead of *e mente, chè*.

Canto 32, 1
Absorbed in his delight, the enraptured seer

taking *affetto* to mean 'fixed in contemplation of the object of his pleasure (the Virgin)'. But *affetto* cannot mean *fisso con affetto* (see Porena's note ad loc.), a sense transferred to it here under the influence of *affetto* in line 141 of the previous canto. *Affetto*, according to Buti, is the past participle passive of the Latin verb afficio, adjectival here to *quel contemplante*; and *al suo piacer* means *quanto li piacque*, so that the whole verse means *dopo aver, a piacer suo, goduto del proprio contemplare*, as it is translated in my text. Porena thinks *affetto* (affectus) here means *turbato*, in which case the verse should be translated:

Though it disturbed his rapture, yet that seer

readily (*libero*) began instructing Dante, thus proving his charity (cp. *Par.* 31, 110), for he could not do this, as the sequel shows, while at the same time continuing to contemplate the Virgin.

Canto 32, 70
Therefore, after the colour of the hair
of such grace, each, according to his worth,
must needs the highest light as chaplet wear.

punctuating with a comma placed after *grazia* instead of after *capelli*. But this punctuation, together with the awkward image (the hair of grace) which it involves, is now rejected by the best Italian commentators, though among these Sapegno retains it.

Canto 32, 74
they are graded differently as differing
but in the keenness of their vision at birth

taking *il primiero acume* as referring to the children. In my text I have preferred to take the phrase as a synonym for God, comparable with others of the kind such as *primo amore, prima virtù, prima luce, prima verità*: cp. Gmelin's note ad loc. in his *Dante Die göttliche Komödie*: Kommentar 3, p. 30. Cp. also *Purg.* 16, 85, where it is said of God that he contemplates with love (*vagheggia*) the human soul *primo che sia*, before it exists, except in its Creator's mind.

Canto 33, 89

> as it were fused together, so that what
> I speak of as one simple radiance glowed.

taking *semplice* to mean not *modesto* or *povero*—another asser-
tion like many in this canto, of the poet's inability to express
verbally what he saw—but 'simple' in the sense of 'indivisible'
emphasizing *un*, the organic unity, as seen in God, of the
multifarious individual constituents of the universe.